FLAGSHIP

Also by Mike Carlton

Cruiser: The Life and Loss of HMAS Perth *and her Crew*

First Victory, 1914: HMAS Sydney's *Hunt
for the German Raider* Emden

MIKE CARLTON

FLAGSHIP

THE CRUISER

HMAS AUSTRALIA II

AND THE PACIFIC WAR ON JAPAN

WILLIAM HEINEMANN: AUSTRALIA

A William Heinemann book
Published by Random House Australia Pty Ltd
Level 3, 100 Pacific Highway, North Sydney NSW 2060
www.penguin.com.au

Penguin
Random House
Australia

First published by William Heinemann in 2016
This edition published in 2017

Random House Books is part of the Penguin Random House group of
companies whose addresses can be found at global.penguinrandomhouse.com.

National Library of Australia
Cataloguing-in-Publication Entry

Carlton, Michael, author
Flagship: the cruiser HMAS Australia II and the
Pacific war on Japan/Mike Carlton

ISBN 978 0 85798 778 5 (paperback)

Australia II (Cruiser)
World War, 1939–1945 – Naval operations, Australian
World War, 1939–1945 – Campaigns – Pacific Ocean
Australia – History, Naval

940.545994

Cover design by Luke Causby, Blue Cork
Front cover photograph by Allan Green, courtesy of the State Library of
Victoria; back cover photograph courtesy of RAN Sea Power Centre, Canberra
Maps and diagram of HMAS *Australia II* by James Carlton
Internal design and typesetting by Midland Typesetters, Australia
Printed in Australia by Griffin Press, an accredited ISO AS/NZS 14001:2004
Environmental Management System printer

To all those who served in His Majesty's Australian ships
Australia II, *Canberra I* and *Shropshire*,
with respect and gratitude.

And to my grandson, Jack.

Yours, aye.

CONTENTS

Please note that maps of the Pacific Theatre, Operation Menace, the battles of the Coral Sea, Savo Island and the Surigao Strait, as well as of enemy aircraft hits on HMAS Australia in the Philippines, can be found in the picture section.

Diagram of HMAS *Australia*		ix
Author's note		xi
Notes on the text		xiii

Part 1   **Between the Wars**

CHAPTER 1	So I am to be sunk	3
CHAPTER 2	The way of the Commonwealth is forward	21
CHAPTER 3	The tremendous value of the seas east of Suez	45
CHAPTER 4	Blighted by the withering touch of poverty	66
CHAPTER 5	Hearts of oak are our ships	87
CHAPTER 6	As a result, Australia is also at war	112

Part 2   **Going into Battle**

CHAPTER 7	Put your hand into the hand of God	133
CHAPTER 8	We sighted smoke and hoisted battle ensigns	157
CHAPTER 9	What irresponsible rubbish these Antipodeans talk	181
CHAPTER 10	I therefore decided to engage the enemy	204
CHAPTER 11	I make it quite clear that Australia looks to America	229
CHAPTER 12	To be hanged by the neck till they be dead	252

Part 3   **The Tide Starts to Turn**

CHAPTER 13   Proceed at daylight with your group to
destroy enemy ships   275

CHAPTER 14   Australia cannot escape a blow   300

CHAPTER 15   Each beautiful ship flying a tremendous
white Australian naval ensign   322

CHAPTER 16   For so appears this fleet majestical   346

CHAPTER 17   The unspeakable bloodiness my shocked
eyes took in   369

CHAPTER 18   You have brought to Australia an accession
of naval strength   394

Part 4   **End Game**

CHAPTER 19   We're going into Tiger Country   421

CHAPTER 20   I have been given a splendid opportunity
to die   446

CHAPTER 21   All guns opened fire but he still came on   471

CHAPTER 22   O Lord, thou knowest how busy we
are today   496

CHAPTER 23   Their sacrifice was not in vain   518

CHAPTER 24   The Royal Australian Navy has done
it again   538

Epilogue   557

Who's who   564

Appendix   The legal campaign for the release of
Gordon and Elias   568

Abbreviations   575

Acknowledgements   576

Notes and references   580

Bibliography   603

Index   610

HMAS *Australia*, 1939

Type: 'County' class heavy cruiser

Launched: 17 March 1927

Commissioned: 24 April 1928

Displacement	9072 tons
Length	92.02 metres
Beam	20.83 metres
Draught	6.60 metres
Crew	815

Armament	8 x 8-inch guns
	8 x 4-inch high-angle guns
	2 x 2-pounder octuple pom-poms
	2 x 0.5 inch Vickers quad anti-aircraft guns
	4 x 3-pounder saluting guns
	2 x quad 21-inch torpedo tube sets

Main machinery	8 Admiralty three-drum boilers
	Parsons geared steam turbines on 4 shafts
Horsepower	80,000 shaft horsepower
Speed	31.5 knots (58 km/h)

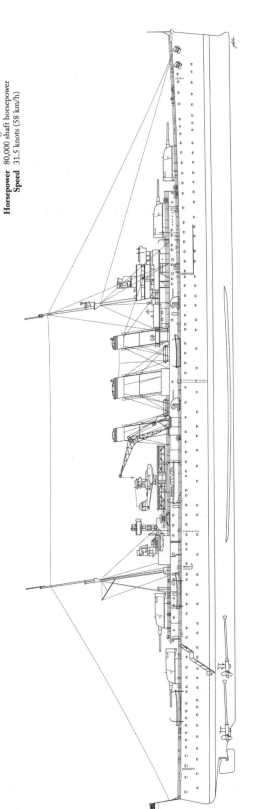

0   5   10   15   20m

AUTHOR'S NOTE

At first I had planned a biography of the heavy cruiser HMAS *Australia II* from her birth on the River Clyde in Scotland in 1928 to her end at the breaker's yard in 1956. Like the men who took her to sea, she lived through the Great Depression and the Second World War, to find a peace of sorts in her final years. Her story was the story of these sailors – and the story of the navy and nation they served in those turbulent decades – and well worth the telling.

But as I dug into the research it soon became obvious that *Australia* could not be separated from her two sister ships in the Royal Australian Navy: first *Canberra* and then *Shropshire*. Their lives and deeds were entwined like strands of cable. Thousands of men sailed in these heavy cruisers over the years, many in all three of them, and I decided it would be futile, if not impossible, to try to pull the cable apart. So while *Australia* leads the squadron in this book, the other two follow closely in line astern.

As always when writing this sort of story, the difficulty lay in deciding what to put in and what to leave out. You cannot interview everybody nor mention everybody, and some naval history buffs might think that one or two famous names have appeared only in passing while lesser figures are afforded more and perhaps undeserved prominence. And while war at sea has its episodes of extraordinary violence, destruction and death, there can also be weeks and even months of tedious plodding around the ocean when nothing happens, which would make dull reading. My only answer in both cases is that I have striven for a balance, to create the truest possible picture of what these ships did and what it was like to sail and fight in them. The story of the one is the story of many.

My second aim was to paint the backdrop before which these ships performed. Although all three were built in Britain, they quickly assumed an Australian character. They were a proud part of the life of the nation, whether showing the flag at a peacetime Melbourne Cup, eking out an existence in the lean and hungry pre-war years, or charging full speed into battle with guns blazing. It seemed important to portray the nation and its people as they were then, not least because I suspect that Australia past is almost a foreign country, barely recognisable, to generations born towards the end of the twentieth century and at the beginning of the twenty-first.

The book is not a comprehensive history of the war against Japan in the Pacific, nor even of the RAN's part in it. Again, I have picked and chosen. How well I have succeeded – or not – will be for you the reader to judge. But it was an honour to write it, and a lot of fun as well.

Clareville, April 2016

NOTES ON THE TEXT

Many place names have changed since the end of the war in 1945. For example, Malaya is now Malaysia. Hollandia in the Netherlands East Indies is on the map today as Jayapura, the capital of the Indonesian province of West Papua. The New Hebrides, once a colony jointly and haphazardly administered by the British and French, and then a great American wartime base, became the Republic of Vanuatu. To avoid confusion I have kept the names that were familiar at the time, with an explanation or an endnote where it might help.

Measurements can also be tricky. In almost every case I have converted to metrics for modern readers, but some figures defy conversion. An 8-inch gun was what they called it then, and it would be plain silly to transform it to a 20.32-centimetre gun. The 8 inches, incidentally, is the diameter of the shell that the gun fired. The bigger the shell the more explosive it carried, the longer its range, and the greater the damage it might cause. Thus a ship with 8-inch guns was a more powerful vessel than one with 6-inch guns or less and – barring bad luck or bad management – would normally win a contest. At the other end of the stick, a battleship with 16-inch or even 18-inch guns could expect to blow an 8-inch gun cruiser out of the water without sustaining a scratch herself. The arrival of air power at sea, though, changed everything.

A few more salty bits: port and starboard. If you are standing on a ship looking forwards over the bow, the port side is on your left hand and starboard is on your right. But it doesn't change if you make an about-turn; port and starboard remain where they were. By night, the port side displays a red light and the starboard side a green one. (A helpful way to remember this: port wine is red.) If you can see both port and starboard lights glowing, it means the ship is coming pretty well straight towards you.

A nautical mile is a distance of exactly 1852 metres, and therefore longer than the statute land mile of 1609.3 metres. One hundred nautical miles is 185.2 kilometres. To keep it simple, I have used kilometres throughout. But I have kept speed at sea in knots, the way it is still described. A knot is not a measurement of distance, although you will sometimes hear landlubbers talk incorrectly of so many knots per hour. It is a measurement of speed: one knot would move you one nautical mile in an hour. Do the sums, and 25 knots is just over 46 kilometres per hour. That speed might seem grindingly slow if you are driving the family car to work, but if you are pushing 10,000 tonnes of heavy cruiser into a storm-tossed, oncoming sea, it's the ride of a lifetime.

The value of money was another difficult area: I have used the calculator on the website of the Reserve Bank of Australia. A basket of goods or services costing A£1000 in 1930 would cost around A$78,700 in 2016. That A£1000 in 1945 would be about $68,400 now.

PART 1

BETWEEN THE WARS

Chapter 1

SO I AM TO BE SUNK

The tugs came for the old ship not long after dawn, the coal smoke from their funnels smudging the pale early light of a promising autumn day. There were four of them – *Heroic*, *Heroine*, *Champion* and *St Olaves* – each a familiar name on Sydney Harbour, tough and stubby little vessels with blunt bows and a workmanlike air.

They went about their business methodically and without ceremony, taking their positions for the tow. Alongside the wharf at the Garden Island Naval Base, the old ship hulked over them, silent and forlorn at this beginning of her last voyage. First the light messenger lines went across, then the heavy manila hawsers, the great ropes that would take the strain. And such a strain it would be. His Majesty's Australian Ship *Australia* had been the flagship and pride of the navy and the saviour of the nation in the First World War. Now she was going to her grave, a sea grave. The tugs were her pallbearers.

It was Saturday 12 April 1924. Crowds had gathered around the harbour foreshores and on the water for the funeral, just as they had thronged 11 years before, when she first arrived. But it had been so very different then – a festival, a carnival. That had also been a Saturday, 4 October 1913. Majestic in her pomp, with ranks of white-uniformed sailors lining her rails, a band playing stirring nautical marches on her quarterdeck, brass gleaming and a rear admiral's red and white flag aloft at her mainmast, *Australia* had led the other six ships of the fledgling Royal Australian Navy (RAN) through the harbour heads for their first grand fleet entry.[1]

Sydney had never seen anything like it. *Australia* was a dreadnought battlecruiser of 18,800 tons, built in the famous Scottish shipyards of John Brown & Co. She was swift and modern, and her eight 12-inch guns made her, beyond any dispute, the most powerful man-o'-war in the southern hemisphere. Friend or foe, there was no ship lying over the horizon to match her. Better still, although most of her officers and senior sailors were Britishers on loan from the Royal Navy (RN), a large part of her crew of some 800 were Australian born, the very flower of a virile young nation trained up for a life at sea.

Not that war was expected. While it was true that the Mother Country and Germany were engaged in a costly naval arms race, each building battleship after battleship, it was also true that King George V and Kaiser Wilhelm II were cousins, grandsons of the late Queen Victoria. Just months before, the Kaiser had sent his yacht *Meteor* to compete at England's renowned Cowes Regatta, with his younger brother, Prince Henry of Prussia, at the helm. Conflict between these interlocked royal families was surely inconceivable.

'Australia welcomes its Fleet not as an instrument of war but as the harbinger of peace,' said the Defence Minister of the day, the New South Wales senator Edward Millen.[2] But should war ever come at some distant time – here White Australia looked nervously north to an emerging Japan – the flagship and her attendant squadron of smaller cruisers and destroyers would be ready to defend the nation's coasts and its maritime trade with the empire to which they so proudly belonged. The cheering had rung from beach to headland and from the flotilla of small craft tossing on the harbour chop to make the new navy welcome. The rest of the country could only read about it enviously as Sydney flung itself into a dizzy week of dinners, balls, receptions, garden parties, ceremonial marches and endless patriotic speeches.

There would be no such celebration this Saturday. A week before Good Friday, Australia was in mourning. For some weeks, there had been notices and advertisements in the newspapers to encourage a proper public respect:

APPEAL FOR FLOWERS
Regarding the sinking of H.M.A.S. *Australia*, people wishing to send flowers for that occasion are asked to leave them before noon on Friday at W. Crane's building, 35 Pitt-street (a few doors from Circular Quay). Flowers sent by train should reach Sydney Station, and be specially addressed 'H.M.A.S. Australia, c/o Rudders, Carriers, Sydney Station.'

Mr. Smith, Director of Education, has expressed regret that, owing to the school holiday, he cannot directly reach the children, but he hopes they will send many flowers.[3]

And so they had. From all over the country, as a reporter for *The Sydney Morning Herald* recounted this very day:

The regard for the old flagship was pathetically evident at the Man-o'War Steps yesterday. On the jetty a great pile of wreaths bore testimony of the sentimental attachment that had developed between the erstwhile protector of Australian shores and the people.

Many of the wreaths bore no cards – a silence more eloquent than the greatest emblazoned scroll. Others bore the simple anonymous words 'Digger,' 'A Loyal Australian,' 'Two Little Aussies,' and others gave only the initials of the sender.

Up till last night over 200 tokens had been received, and they were taken to Garden Island and placed on the deck of the *Australia*. Most of them were artistically decorated with Australian flags and ribbons. At Richmond aerodrome a wreath of cream and pink dahlias, which will be dropped by airmen during the sinking ceremony, was received from 'Three Australian School Children.' It is expected that many wreaths will be received at Richmond station this morning before the departure of aeroplanes at about 11 o'clock.[4]

—

When war did engulf the royal cousins in August 1914, *Australia* was at anchor in Sydney Harbour but armed and ready for the fight.⁵ She put to sea within days, but for those first anxious months she stayed in Pacific waters close to home, searching fruitlessly for the German Navy's *Ostasiengeschwader*, the cruisers of the Kaiser's elite East Asia Squadron. Commanded by an able aristocrat, Vice Admiral Maximilian Graf von Spee, this force had policed Germany's scattered colonial empire in the Western Pacific from its base in China and down to the southern hemisphere, where the red, white and black flag with its imperial eagle flew in New Guinea, Bougainville, Nauru and German Samoa. In the event of war with Britain and her empire, Spee had detailed plans, laid for him in Berlin, to attack Australia's trade at sea and to bombard major port cities on the east coast.⁶

Australia's mighty presence changed all that, shifting the balance of power in the Pacific decisively against Germany. As Spee would write to his wife, 'The Anglo Australian Squadron has as its flagship the *Australia*, which by itself is an adversary so much stronger than our squadron that one would be bound to avoid it.'⁷

And avoid it he did. Within weeks, the *Ostasiengeschwader* headed east towards the coast of South America, leaving behind only the light cruiser *Emden* to circle back west through what were then the Netherlands East Indies and enter the northern Indian Ocean. There she successfully preyed on British merchant shipping, causing havoc for three months until she was destroyed by the cruiser HMAS *Sydney* at the Cocos Islands in November 1914. But Spee and the rest of his squadron had got clean away – not through any fault of the Australians but as the unhappy result of a series of blunders by the Admiralty at Whitehall. As the Australian official historian, Arthur Jose, would write, the admirals in London had kept *Australia* 'like a dog tethered to his kennel'.⁸ She and other ships of the RAN had to content themselves with mopping up the Kaiser's island colonies, a necessary but hardly spectacular business in which they fired not one shot in anger. Spee crushed a largely obsolete British squadron at the Battle of Coronel off the coast of Chile on 1 November, but was himself beaten and broken in early December when he appeared in the South Atlantic off the Falkland Islands and was chased by a force of RN battlecruisers sent after him. The admiral and his two sons were killed.

Britain's First Lord of the Admiralty, the volatile and tenacious young Winston Churchill, had long been pressing for *Australia* to join the RN's Grand Fleet, that vast force of ironclad warships arrayed to contain Germany in the North Sea. Eventually he got his way.

With the *Ostasiengeschwader* no longer to be reckoned with, a few days before Christmas 1914, *Australia* was ordered away around Cape Horn from the Pacific Ocean to the Atlantic,[9] where in early January 1915 she captured and sank one of Spee's supply ships, the *Eleonore Woermann*, near the Falkland Islands. On 17 February, after punching through a ferocious winter gale off Ireland and the Shetlands, she came to anchor at Rosyth, the great British naval base in the Firth of Forth on the east coast of Scotland, near Edinburgh. For the young Australians in her crew, accustomed to the sunshine of their home country and the heat of the tropics, it must have been a chilling, even ominous, arrival: as the anchor chains rumbled through the hawse-pipes, there were ten centimetres of snow on her decks.

Australia was designated the flagship of the RN's 2nd Battle-cruiser Squadron and, from that day on, she was – again in the words of the historian Jose – 'merely one of a number of warships under Admiralty orders, and Australia knew no more of her officially until the war was over'.[10] For all its pretensions to be a navy in its own right, the RAN in these formative years was little more than a branch office of its Britannic parent. In the early decades of Federation, this was unavoidable and in many ways desirable, for it meant that officers and men – and their ships – were trained to the standards and traditions of the most professional navy the world had known. The reverse side of the medal was a lack of independence and a festering discontent at the notion – sometimes real, sometimes imagined – that British-born men were preferred for promotion ahead of the Australians.

Monotony and sickness, hunger, and a longing for home now became *Australia*'s constant companions, riding with the ship's company like the four horsemen of a private apocalypse, for months and years. There were the seemingly endless patrols into the grey wilderness of the North Sea, often in filthy weather and with never a sight of the German foe. Occasionally there might be a gunnery exercise or fleet manoeuvres to relieve the boredom a little, or perhaps a rowing regatta or a boxing tournament between ships in harbour, but that was about it. Between decks, where her ship's company worked, ate and slept, the conditions were cramped and cold, the bulkheads damp with condensation and the air a smelly fug of cigarette smoke, stale food and body odours.

No official figures survive, but it is certain that a number of sailors simply succumbed to the ravages of the Scottish winters and died. It was rumoured that one man had been driven mad. Pneumonia, influenza and tuberculosis were an ever present fear, not helped by a poor diet of RN rations very much meaner than Australian sailors expected in their mess decks. Mail from home arrived in fits and starts at best. One remedy for the tedium was gambling at the dice game of Crown and Anchor, illegal in the navy and therefore played behind closed doors in the mess decks with lookouts on guard. Some men grew rich at it and others lost their pay, increasing the discontent.

This wretched existence wound on for four miserable, seemingly interminable years. Back in Australia, a parent might die or a child fall sick, an unfaithful wife might leave or the family farm might fail. There was nothing a man could do about it, for he would hear the news many weeks or even months later, and no home leave was given. Come hell or high water, he was there on the other side of the world for the duration.

Australia missed the one great clash of naval arms in the North Sea, the Battle of Jutland, when the Grand Fleet encountered

Germany's High Seas Fleet at the end of May 1916. Only weeks before, zigzagging to avoid submarines in a heavy fog, she had collided not once but twice with her sister ship, HMS *New Zealand*. It was not her fault and the damage was not serious, but when the opposing ironclads met off Denmark's Jutland coast in one thunderous day and night of smoke and flame, sinking and death, she was safely in dock in southern England.

Here the fates might have been kind: another sister ship in the 2nd Battlecruiser Squadron, HMS *Indefatigable*, was literally blown to pieces by her German opponent, the battlecruiser *Von Der Tann*, in the opening minutes of the engagement. Of her crew of 1019, only two men from her foretop survived.[11]

The next year, *Australia* collided again, this time with the brand new battlecruiser HMS *Repulse*, and a month after that she fired her guns at what might or might not have been a submarine, with no discernible result. And that was it for her war.

A few of her men did see action. In February 1918, a call went out for volunteers from the fleet to take part in a dangerous venture, a night-time commando-style raid on the port of Zeebrugge in German-occupied Belgium. Eleven Australians were selected, including 22-year-old Leading Seaman Dalmorton Rudd, from the Sydney suburb of Campsie, who was awarded the Distinguished Service Medal for bravery under a storm of enemy fire.

At war's end, they finally got to see the hated Hun. In abject defeat and wracked by mutiny, the High Seas Fleet was ordered across the North Sea to a humiliating internment at Britain's most northerly naval anchorage, the cold and desolate Scapa Flow in the Orkney Islands. *Australia* was in the victorious armada that went to escort the Germans in, and she led the port line with her squadron, the beaten ships trailing in her wake. At anchor in that vast stretch of water, she was posted to guard the new battleship *Hindenburg*.

And so peace at last. But for some reason now lost to history, she stayed on for one last winter Christmas and into the new year. She did not leave for Australia until April 1919, a full five months

after the guns had fallen quiet. Her first touch of home was at
Fremantle on 28 May, where she received an ecstatic welcome.
Yet, as fate would have it, this provoked one of the most wretched
events of her career. Mutiny broke out. As the ship was preparing to leave for Sydney after four days in port, a group of some
80 men gathered on her quarterdeck to ask for the departure to
be delayed for a day so they could repay the hospitality they had
received. Startled, the captain refused their request and the men
dispersed peacefully, though with some grumbling. But below in
the boiler rooms, the stokers went on strike, refusing to shovel
coal, and the ship could not be moved until petty officers were
drafted to replace them.

As mutinies go, it was small beer, saying more about the
unbending insensitivity of naval authority than it did about
the men themselves, but 12 sailors were arrested and charged,
and five were eventually court-martialled when the ship
reached Sydney. One was Dalmorton Rudd, who pleaded guilty
to mutiny without violence and was sentenced to dismissal
from the navy and 18 months' hard labour at Goulburn Jail.
His brother David got dismissal and two years.[12] It was a bitter
homecoming for good and loyal men who had served their
country as best they could.

The years of peace were no more kind to their ship. For all
that she had been the country's deterrent in the hour of need, for
all her dogged if unspectacular service in the North Sea, for all
her renown as the RAN's flagship, the raw truth was that technology had overtaken her. She was fast becoming obsolete. Four
years of war had driven revolutionary advances in the naval arts
and sciences, in the design of ships and their guns. *Australia*'s 31
boilers were coal-fired, served by the backbreaking toil of gangs
of stokers, scores of them armed with shovels, strong men usually
working stripped to the waist, filthy and sweating in the furnace
heat. Coal had powered the world's navies since the end of the age
of sail and the advent of steam, but oil fuel, clean and efficient,
was swiftly replacing it. New and better turbine engines had been
built for greater speed than the now very ordinary 25 knots that

Australia could muster and – the clinching argument – those 12-inch guns that had stunned Sydney with their arrival salute in 1913 were now little more than museum pieces. Shells were no longer being made for them. Britain's newest battlecruiser, HMS *Hood*, launched in 1918, carried eight 15-inch guns and, oil-fuelled, could turn on a best speed of a spanking 31 knots.

Little by little, like an old salt herself, *Australia* fell into quiet retirement. There was a last glow of her glory days when she led the navy's ceremonial welcome to the visiting Prince of Wales at a grand fleet review in Port Phillip Bay in 1920, but her time was drawing to a close.[13] A government and people tired of war and still mourning their dead were in no mood to spend money on naval defence. She lingered for a while with a skeleton crew in the humble role of a gunnery and torpedo training ship at the Flinders Naval Depot in Victoria, but in December 1921 even that came to an end. She was paid off, in the naval phrase, and put into reserve in an isolated corner of Sydney Harbour.

Her death sentence came just a few months later. The President of the United States, Warren Harding, invited the world's major naval powers – the US, Britain, Japan, France and Italy – to a conference in Washington, ostensibly with the aim of preventing yet another international naval arms race that might bring about yet another war. Harding's unspoken purpose, rather more devious, was to ring-fence the rise of Japanese naval power in the Pacific, a source of growing anxiety to both America and Britain, and, indeed, to Australia. For three months, the delegates bargained and argued over warship tonnages and new construction and the like, and on 6 February 1922 they announced a deal. The Five-Power Treaty on the Limitation of Naval Armaments adopted what became known as the 5:5:3 ratio. The United States and Britain would each be allowed to possess battleships to a total displacement of 525,000 tons, with 315,000 tons for Japan. France and Italy accepted a smaller limit of 170,000 tons. Older ships would be scrapped and much new construction halted; some battleship hulls already being constructed in the shipyards could be converted into the new-fangled aircraft carriers. Australia was represented at the talks by the Defence Minister, the West Australian senator George Pearce, but only as a member of the British delegation, and Australia's ships were counted in Britain's totals. HMAS *Australia* was among the 16 'British' capital ships earmarked for destruction.

The Australian Government – a conservative coalition of Nationalists and the newly emerging Country Party – seized the decision with quiet alacrity. The Treasury saw the opportunity for significant cuts to defence spending, and the naval budget of just over £3 million in 1921–22 was slashed to £2.4 million in 1922–23. There was another 20 per cent cut the next year, and a further 11 per cent reduction for 1924–25.

News of *Australia*'s demise was announced in October 1923. The flagship would be scuttled off Sydney Heads next Anzac Day. Controversy flared. Public protest meetings were called in town halls across the country, newspaper editors were deluged with letters, and fiery editorials were written – as often as not invoking the hallowed name of Britain's greatest admiral, Horatio Nelson, and his flagship HMS *Victory*. In *The Sydney Morning Herald*, an anonymous writer waxed lyrical in the Women's Column:

H.M.A.S. AUSTRALIA SPEAKS

So I am to be sunk. The grey iron plates that are my sides and the white wood that is my deck will soon be lying beneath the waves. Mine is not the glorious death in action that came to many of my companions, I have to stand while shots are put into me, unable to volley forth my thunder in return.

No baby hands will hold little objects, cannons and life-buoys, made from my timbers while their fathers tell them how the good ship *Australia* led the convoy that protected them on their way to the Great War. No women will shed tears of thankfulness over these objects, gratitude to me who kept the Huns from descending on our country and treating them as the women of Belgium were treated . . .[14]

The outcry grew louder as the months rolled on. The Prime Minister, Stanley Melbourne Bruce, was bombarded with angry letters. Parsons, politicians and public figures weighed in. 'The expressed intention of the Federal Government to sink the battleship *Australia* aroused indignation in other quarters this morning, following the expression of opinion given yesterday,' reported the *Adelaide News* in high dudgeon.

> Senator J. Newland is still busy upon his task of making a public appeal to save the vessel from destruction through sinking.
>
> 'I am sorry,' said the Ven. Archdeacon Samwell this morning when the subject was mentioned. 'I think it is a great shame when people are satisfied to destroy an emblem of our nationhood. They must be devoid of all imagination and regardless of the fact that future generations will be left unaware of the great work accomplished by the *Australia*. I am opposed strongly to it. If not sunk this ship would not be a nuisance to anybody. The *Australia* to us is really like the old *Victory*.'[15]

Frederick Samwell, the Anglican Archdeacon of Adelaide, who had been an army chaplain during the war, summoned up the big battalions. Returned servicemen's clubs and organisations joined the outcry. The Chief President of the Australian Natives' Association, J. Hood Stevens, proclaimed in a letter to Bruce that the sinking was 'viewed with nation-wide horror' and 'opposed by 90 percent of the people'.[16] A spirited rally called by the Mayor of Newcastle urged that the ship be 'preserved as a national relic and anchored in Botany Bay'.[17]

Not everyone agreed. Beneath the headline 'A FOOLISH STUNT', *The Daily Herald*, a trade union newspaper in South Australia, dripped scorn:

> A lot of sloppy sentimentality is being displayed by a small section of the community regarding the disposal of the huge mass of steel which was once the HMAS *Australia*.
>
> The obsolete vessel has been gathering barnacles in the Sydney Harbor with a lot of useless and costly war tubs for years and now that the time has arrived when the conditions of the Washington Treaty must be observed a feeble attempt is being made to stir up some hollow, shallow kind of feeling against

the sinking of this useless mass of metal . . . the world would be better if all the war weapons and vessels were now at the bottom of the sea.[18]

Despite all the evidence to the contrary, Frank Cotton, a former shearer turned journalist and prominent pacifist, saw a sinister conservative plot to rearm. The sinking of *Australia* would merely clear the way for the government to obtain bigger and more expensive warships, he wrote to *The Australian Worker*, closing with a splendid flourish: 'It seems about time that we had a prime minister in Australia who recognises that he is the representative of a self-governing community and not a liveried lackey of overseas armament trusts and warmongers.'[19]

The liveried lackey and his government remained unmoved. Workmen began dismantling the old ship at Garden Island in the summer of 1924. Oxyacetylene torches cut away at her steel plating and her guns and turrets, the fighting top on her foremast was lifted off, and the floating crane *Titan* plucked the massive boilers and turbines from deep within her. The disembowelling was filmed for posterity, with a much-loved music hall star, Dot Brunton, 'The Diggers' Delight', swooning theatrically over the remains. A syndicate of businessmen paid the government the impressive sum of £3000 for the right to strip the ship and sell whatever they could turn into souvenirs. Brass fittings, timber panelling, wardroom furniture and crockery were snapped up by eager buyers.[20] By April, *Australia* was a wretched, rusting hulk.

—

The sun was fully risen now, in a cloudless sky. A light westerly breeze ruffled the harbour. Promptly at seven o'clock, with the towing lines secured, the waters boiled beneath the stern of the four tugs as they hauled and chivvied their charge away from her Garden Island berth. For this final journey, *Australia* carried just 28 men, all of them chosen from among the officers or sailors who had served in her during her short life. One was Rupert Garsia, now a brass-hatted, three-ringed commander and the captain of the minesweeping sloop HMAS *Marguerite*.

In 1914, Garsia had been a mere retired RN lieutenant planning to take up farming in Tasmania, but when war broke out he had ordered a new uniform and talked his way on board the flagship, where they found him a bunk and gave him a job. He was posted to the cruiser *Sydney* on 1 October 1914 and acquired a certain fame in the navy as the first Australian to board the shattered wreck of the German raider *Emden* after *Sydney* destroyed her at the Cocos Islands in November that year. Today he would be witness to the death of another ship.

Watchers on the foreshores saw the tugs haul *Australia* out of Woolloomooloo Bay towards Fort Denison, the foredeck beneath her bridge smothered in the floral wreaths the public had sent. Then, in a poignant tableau, she wallowed past the naval future she would never know. A rifle-shot away, riding at anchor below Admiralty House on Kirribilli Point, was none other than the mighty *Hood* herself, on a visit to Sydney as the flagship of the RN's Special Service Squadron. Her consort, yet another British battlecruiser, HMS *Repulse*, lay not far away at Athol Bight, beneath the bushy slopes of Bradleys Head. Strung in a line between those two and already raising steam to leave harbour were the squadron's four cruisers: *Delhi, Danae, Dragon* and *Dauntless*.

It was an imposing vision and deliberately so, for the squadron was on a year-long global cruise to fly the White Ensign, to proclaim to the world that, despite the disarmament ordained in Washington, the RN remained a power at sea. Bearing the name of an English seafaring family that had produced no fewer than five admirals over a century and a half, *Hood* was generally acknowledged to be the world's most powerful warship and, with that, was lauded by her legions of admirers as the most elegant, the most graceful, the most magnificent, the pinnacle of the art of naval architecture. It was hard to disagree. Displacing 47,000 tons, she was almost three times the size of *Australia*. Low, long and lean with two tremendous funnels amidships, her decks fore and aft crowned by twin pairs of the most modern gun turrets, her fo'c'sle sweeping forward and upward to the sculpted flare of her bow, she had about her that aura of silent menace that is the birthright of great warships. *Repulse*, although not quite so large or heavily gunned and a couple of years older than *Hood*, was impressive in her own right. The four cruisers were Britain's latest. All of these ships were oil fuelled.

The Special Service Squadron – sporting two admirals, no less, and each of them a knight of the realm – touched at every major Australian port city from Fremantle to Brisbane, welcomed with what must have been an exhausting round of balls, dinners, parties, receptions, golf days, cricket games and football matches.[21] In Sydney, Fleet Week, as the newspapers called it, erupted with merry abandon, turning on everything from a public schools display of marching, drill, dancing and physical culture at the Sydney Cricket Ground to a garden party for 3000 people given by the New South Wales Governor, yet another British admiral, Sir Dudley de Chair. On the Friday night before *Australia*'s execution, there was an admiral's dinner on board *Hood*, and a fireworks display and Venetian carnival on the harbour. The scuttling had been brought forward from the original date of Anzac Day so the squadron could pay tribute.

The Australian light cruiser *Brisbane* was waiting off Middle Head to escort *Australia* to sea, leading the way down the harbour, out past the Sow and Pigs Reef to the Heads and beyond. The Prime Minister and assorted dignitaries followed on board the cruiser *Melbourne* and the destroyer *Anzac*, with small craft bobbing in their wake. Shipping companies – the North Coast Steam Navigation Coy and the Newcastle and Hunter River SS Co. Ltd – had sold tickets to the public for steamer trips to see the sinking, at 3/6 and 5/-, 'refreshments available on board'.

She was through the Heads just after nine o'clock, the tugs heaving mightily as her empty hull dipped and rolled in the sea swell. Watchers on *Brisbane* glimpsed her wreathed in coal smoke from the tugs, moving at almost imperceptible speed, and told each other she seemed reluctant to leave harbour. Minutes later, out from the Heads came the four cruisers of the British squadron, bow waves creaming as they smartly took up station on the plodding *Australia*, two to port and two to starboard. A 21-gun salute rippled out from HMS *Delhi*, returned by *Brisbane*, a recognition of the Australian flag flying from the old ship's jackstaff. Then, with a flick of their tails, the cruisers were off, curving away in line ahead, over the horizon on a course north to Brisbane.

More long hours passed before *Australia* reached the position of her last resting place, some 40 kilometres due east of the coast, in water to a depth of 150 fathoms (275 metres). All was ready. At the very bottom of her hull, the stokers of the skeleton crew opened the Kingston valves to bring the sea flooding in, and a charge of gun cotton was detonated to blow a hole in her bows. Signalman Reg Gottschalk, a young Melbourne man, semaphored a last signal from her decks – 'Everything is open' – and boats took away the men on board. 'Strong men were wet-eyed,' wrote Henry Feakes, the captain of *Brisbane*, a sailor who had learnt his trade on windjammers around Cape Horn. 'Many cursed. It was a tragic blunder.'[22]

A 'special representative' from *The Sydney Morning Herald* on board *Brisbane* reported the last moments in words worth recalling for the flavour of the times:

> Shortly after half-past 2 o'clock, amidst tense silence, a long, sullen roar rose from the *Australia*. Like some sad lament, like a threnody, it rang out across the sea. Smoke poured from the funnel. The old ship, with a list to port, was dying. A gaping hole had been blown in her hull. Ever so gradually she heeled over. The sea seemed reluctant to bring within its embrace this once proud ship, until a hatchway touched the water line. Then the water rushed in, and the end was quick. The *Australia* turned completely over, and plunged stern first into the deep. In 21¾ minutes from the time of the explosion, she had disappeared. There was no whirling suction of water. The sea just swept calmly over her.

Under a perfect Australian sky, on a calm summer sea, and with the ships of the Royal Australian Navy alongside her, the old flagship had been delivered eternally to the waters of

the Pacific. She was no more. The Pacific, in which she drove
Von Spee eastwards to Coronel – and to the Falklands – is her
Valhalla, just as the sea has been the last resting place of so many
great ships.

Australia will probably never again witness such a deeply-
stirring scene as the sinking of the old flagship. Here, on the vast
stage of the Pacific, the scene left the impress of sadness beyond
articulation. It was impressively simple. A great silence swept the
scene, a silence that could be almost felt, as the old ship rolled
gradually over. There were no pompous speeches. There was no
music. There was only a tense silence, and behind it the subdued
emotion that the scene called up, as the ship took her final plunge.
The men at the three-pounders on the *Brisbane* gave a thunderous
Royal salute of 21 guns, an airman cast on to the calm waters, at
the spot where the *Australia* went down, a simple wreath, and the
old ship was left to the companionship of the sea.

It was the simple, yet deeply impressive, passing of a ship
which had filled a great and honoured place in our national life.
The passing away of the great ship, like the passing of great men,
had left upon those who beheld the scene the consciousness of
a sad void. Of the flotsam and jetsam that sunken ships give up
there was practically nothing. The sea just passed placidly over
her as she gracefully dived into the deeps. And, like pilgrims
that had come to bow their heads at the passing of a great figure,
the ships of the Royal Australian Navy turned in stately single
file towards home in the setting sun.[23]

There were more words to be written and spoken. Bruce, the
Prime Minister, paid her a formal farewell:

In her passing she symbolises our contribution to the cause of
peace. We sacrifice her with a regret rendered poignant by the
memory of her great service but tempered with the hope that
the world will see, in the magnitude of our offering, and the
manner in which we make it, a measure of our practical belief in
the principles enunciated at the Washington Conference, which
constitute the only hope of a permanent international peace.[24]

Peace was the hope, the profound longing of the Australian people who had lost so many and so much in a war begun just ten years before. Time and again, the newspaper eulogies for *Australia* clung to the idea like some well-polished talisman, as in this poem from a Queensland writer, Constance Campbell, published in *The Sydney Mail*:

REQUIESCAT
H.M.A.S. AUSTRALIA GREETS THE FLEET.
Stripped of her glory, shorn of pride, the old grey warship lies;
Is this indeed the ship we sent on deeds of high emprise?
Is this old rusted, shapeless hulk our battleship of pride
That kept our name, in days of strife, in honour glorified?
Hark! O'er the harbour waters the roar of the guns is heard,
Then softly, amid the echoes, the gallant ship's last word: —
Sisters! As comrades of the sea I welcome you today.
Who kept that silent watch with me in battle's grim array;
Gladly I give you greeting here, 'ere yet my race is run,
And I go down, to keep secure the sacred peace we won.[25]

Editorials struck an epic note of nation-building:

There would be an element of tragedy in such an end to any ship; but when the ship represents as much, and suggests as much, as the *Australia* does, the tragedy becomes great indeed, for into it is imported a national, almost personal sense of loss as of a well-loved and heroic soul. The *Australia* was well named – she did, in very truth, and in a higher way even than those who named her could have deemed possible, represent this Australian people; and by the dignity and worth and power of her representation, she helped us largely to our nationhood.[26]

Within days, these tides of deep emotion ebbed away in ever-fickle Sydney as the public turned to the next diverting sensation. The Royal Agricultural Society's Easter Show was opening on the following Monday at Moore Park near the Sydney Cricket Ground, and the builders were rushing to get the handsome new members' stand and the Hordern Pavilion finished in time, built

at the eye-watering cost of £90,000. Besides the familiar agricultural exhibits, there were fabulous wonders to be savoured,
all illuminated by electricity for five nights. Dalgetys Ltd were
displaying the Rolls-Royce, the Wolseley, the Hudson, the
Essex Six and the White Truck – and, still more exciting, Wm
Docker Ltd, makers of fine varnishes, paints and enamels, had
much pleasure in extending an invitation to view a 'true-to-type,
working model' of Dr Bradfield's North Shore Bridge, which was
about to be built across the harbour.

'The Fleet is now but a secondary attraction to the Easter
Show,' chortled the *Country Life Stock and Station Journal*,[27]
beneath a cartoon of a Bright Young Thing turning her back on
a uniformed Jack Tar and striding off on the arm of a strapping
stockman.

The sacred peace had 15 years to run.

CHAPTER 2

THE WAY OF THE COMMONWEALTH IS FORWARD

In the late winter of 1918, a few months before the armistice that ended the war, a journalist, author and poet named Edwin Brady, from the drowsy coastal settlement of Mallacoota in eastern Victoria, published a book that gripped the nation.

Australia Unlimited, he called it. For six years, notebook in hand, Brady had explored every corner of the continent – cities and the bush – and interviewed people in every walk of life, from hovels and humpies to the grandest homesteads. Running to 1139 pages of 'Romance, History, Facts and Figures', as the publisher's blurb announced, weighing a hefty five kilograms and studded with quite beautiful black-and-white photographs, it was a symphony of praise to 'this glorious land', as Brady wrote in his introduction. He trumpeted the virtues of rural development – farming and mining – in the deepest purple prose. This passage on southern Queensland is typical:

> You hear it in the lap of tides that make and ebb across those pearling grounds of the deep-dyed Arafura Sea. You hear it when the wind sways those festooned jungles, where the flame trees blaze like torches amid the green.
>
> You hear it through the bronze-green brigalow trees, among the sandalwood, and over the bunya pines.
>
> You hear it down the granite gorges, over the gnarled gums, and out on the hills, where the stampers and rollers are at work

pounding and grinding the glittering metal from its matrices of rock.

You hear it calling from the West, from the rivers of the Gulf, from the Diamantina and the Barcoo, from the farm lands of the Southern Downs, from the sheep lands of the Centre, from the cattle lands of the North, over the salt bush, over the grassy plains, over the forest and scrubs – a wonderful, exultant anthem of boundless potentiality, incalculable riches, undeveloped resources and unlimited opportunities for the profitable investment of Labor, and money and brains . . .

. . . The way of the Commonwealth is forward. Her battalions of the north will march in the forefront of the army of advance, the silken banners of progress waving before them, the golden bugles of prosperity cheering them on.[1]

The reviewers heaped praise. It was 'Australia's greatest book', said Melbourne's *Spectator and Methodist Chronicle*,[2] and no less than King George V himself was graciously pleased to inform his subjects – rather drily – that Brady's work 'both in its content and in the facts regarding its production is of special interest'. That did it. Even at the impressive price of 42/- (42 shillings; $173 in 2016), *Australia Unlimited* walked off the shelves.

Brady had perfectly tapped the national mood, mined its bedrock aspirations. As political and civic worthies endlessly repeated, Australia must welcome its fighting men home to a land fit for heroes. There was no better way for the returned digger to enter this earthly paradise than to take up a block in the bush, where he could build a home, raise his family and farm his bountiful acres to his heart's content. At war's end, the Commonwealth and the states passed laws to make this happen. Soldier Settlement Schemes sprang up. Each and every one of more than 250,000 soldiers and sailors coming home was entitled to apply for a grant of land and for loans to develop it. Tens of thousands of diggers rushed to do it.

The schemes were not as altruistic as their boosters would have it. Governments recognised there would not be enough work for men in the cities, for a variety of reasons. Youngsters who had enlisted at 18 had missed their chance for trade apprenticeships and were skilled only in the now redundant arts of surviving the horrors of trench warfare. Despite all the fulsome public expressions of pride and gratitude, many employers had hired women for jobs that men had once done and were keeping them on at much lower rates of pay.

And the Spanish influenza was sweeping the cities too. This had erupted in Europe in 1918, to become the most lethal pandemic in all history, infecting some 500 million people around the globe and killing as many as 50 million, possibly more. In Australia, strict quarantine precautions kept it at bay at first, but returning soldiers brought it home in early 1919, first to Melbourne and then to the other capitals, where it rapidly spread, despite New South Wales closing its border with Victoria. With regular hospitals overflowing, emergency tent hospitals were thrown up in parks and at racecourses and showgrounds, and for months almost everyone wore gauze face masks when they went out in public. By the end of 1919, when the flu began to disappear, it had killed an estimated 10,000 Australians, many of them hitherto fit young men and women.[3]

There was fear in high places of another and different contagion too: that unemployed men, congregating in the cities, would fall easy prey to socialist and communist agitators spreading the poison of the Bolshevik revolution in Russia.

This dread of social upheaval was real enough. In the winter of 1919, rioting broke out in Melbourne at rumours that the Commonwealth and state governments were planning to stop their contributions to an unemployment relief fund. On Tuesday 15 July, several hundred men and women, many of them ex-soldiers and their wives, some of them with children and carrying babies, marched from the Melbourne Trades Hall towards the state parliament, demanding to see the conservative Premier, Harry Lawson. Police, hurriedly summoned, blocked their way. As the crowd grew angrier – shouting slogans, shaking fists and surging forward – the police first charged on foot with batons, indiscriminately bashing people to the ground, and then charged again on horseback, trampling still more protestors in the panic.

Beaten, the mob dispersed, but the anger seethed and swelled. The next weekend had been set aside for what the government optimistically hoped would be peace celebrations, but it exploded into three frightening days of violent and bloody rioting that shook Melbourne and the nation to the marrow. On the Saturday, waving the naval White Ensign, some 60 or 70 soldiers and sailors, some of them armed and in uniform, marched down St Kilda Road, bawling that they were going to storm the armoury at Victoria Barracks and seize more weapons there. Sentries with rifles aimed held them off for a time, but in the sprawling, brawling melee shots were fired and one returned soldier, 22-year-old James O'Connor of Carlton, was hit. Bleeding from a wound below the heart, he was rushed by two of his mates to the Caulfield Military Hospital, where he died the next morning. Mounted police stormed forward again at the barracks, but this served only to scatter the demonstrators, who fled in different directions to rampage along Swanston, Flinders and Collins streets, forcing drivers and conductors from trams, which they sent crashing into each other. Cars were attacked and seized for joy rides, shop windows were smashed and theatres were invaded. When police tried to take some arrested men into the Town Hall in Swanston Street, they were twice pelted with bottles and rocks.

There was still more upheaval on the Sunday, and by the Monday, 21 July, the mood was uglier still, the crowds now entirely out of control, as the Melbourne *Argus* reported:

AN ANGRY OUTBURST
DENUNCIATION OF POLICE
DEMANDS ON GOVERNMENT
STATE OFFICES STORMED
PREMIER INJURED BY MISSILE

Wild scenes, culminating in the wrecking of some of the State offices and the wounding of the Premier (Mr. Lawson), occurred yesterday afternoon, as the result of a 'deputation' of soldiers to the Premier. The trouble arose from the resentment aroused by the actions of the police on Saturday and Sunday. There can be no doubt that the excesses in which the affair ended were largely due to the action of hoodlums and revolutionists who inflamed the minds of the soldiers and urged them on to violence and destruction.

It was noticeable that when a strong body of police arrived the rioters of this type were the first to disappear, scuttling across the gardens in a twinkling.

In the afternoon the soldiers met at the Athenaeum, and then, dissatisfied with the reply given by the Chief Commissioner of Police (Sir George Steward) to representations made to him, decided to go to his office and to demand to see him in person. Formed in fours, and headed by four men, carrying a Union Jack, a crowd of nearly 3000 men marched to the corner of Russell and Latrobe streets, attracting to itself other elements as it went along. The swaying mass filled Latrobe St from side to side.[4]

Wild-eyed and reckless, some men attacked the Russell Street Police Station with more stones and bottles. Several thousand more stormed up Bourke Street to Spring Street, where they invaded the State Parliament Building, smashing windows and furniture, and trashing offices. Displaying considerable courage, the Premier, Lawson, left his office and attempted to pacify them, but he was felled when someone hurled a wooden inkstand that struck him on the head. Dazed and bleeding, he was dragged back to safety. Rioting continued through the chilly winter's night, and broke out sporadically the next day and again on the Wednesday, when thousands lined St Kilda Road and Swanston Street for James O'Connor's funeral. The young man had served for two years on the Western Front in the 22nd Battalion, which had seen some of the fiercest fighting of the war. He was carried to his grave at the Coburg Cemetery on a gun carriage draped with the Union Jack and smothered with floral wreaths, a squad of uniformed soldiers and sailors marching ahead and 500 men in plain clothes following behind. It may be that this dismal event helped to dissipate the anger, for over the next few days the troubles petered out, leaving the editorial writers to clean up the mess.

'Returned soldiers who disturb the peace must be punished as well as others,' snapped *The Australasian* magazine in an editorial the next Saturday. 'Government is under no obligation to support unemployed people. If it were, the path of every loafer and waster in the community would be made very easy.'[5]

On the soldier settler blocks, life was far from very easy. At first, it had seemed so promising. On the rocky high country of Queensland's granite belt near the town of Stanthorpe, about 225 kilometres south-west of Brisbane, some 700 former diggers moved onto what became known as the Pikedale Soldier Settlement. Poignantly, they gave their hamlets the haunted names of the battles they had fought on the Western Front – Amiens, Bapaume, Bullecourt, Messines, Passchendaele, Pozieres and Fleurbaix – and a humble little timber-planked and tin-roofed Anglican church was named St Denys, in tribute to a patron saint of Paris. In 1920, the Queensland Government completed a railway line to carry their fruit and vegetables to market in Brisbane, opened by no less than the visiting Edward, Prince of Wales, a gala occasion breathlessly reported by the *Brisbane Courier*:

> Trees stood uprooted and upturned in clearings as though there had been an upheaval of nature. It is a way men have of knocking Nature about in order to get on to the soil. Stalwart men were engaged in log-felling, and here and there was a brown bark humpy to catch the curious eye of an Englishman.
>
> Most of the men on the clearings are tent dwellers, while some have their land cleared and rabbit netted already. A collection of very new buildings clustered together announced Amiens itself . . . a splendid and stirring note of patriotism was struck by these sturdy dinkum 'diggers', and by their women folk and children. Two hundred brown and bronzed men stood upright in perfect alignment, and the Prince has never had a more splendid

escort. Ringing cheers echoed through the bush as he emerged from the train.[6]

By all accounts, the Pikedale Settlement succeeded, despite an incessant battle against the scourge of prickly pear, which was spreading across the country like some biblical plague. But other places did not. Far too many of the men lured by the beguiling imagery of *Australia Unlimited* were city born and raised, with no knowledge of farming or any way of acquiring that knowledge beyond fumbling trial and error, and utterly unsuited to the exhausting physical grind of clearing scrub and boulders with only the simple tools they could afford. Others were maimed in body or mind, perhaps with a missing arm or leg, or mentally ravaged by the terror they had endured. Men who had been gassed in the trenches would lie awake at night, writhing and coughing up a black sputum before returning to their toil the next morning. Still worse, all too often the land they were given was barren and worthless, impossible to cultivate. Bank loans weighed them down.

Private Arthur Robinson, of the 13th Battalion, had been wounded at Villers-Bretonneux, the right side of his head blown away when a German bullet penetrated his steel helmet. He was discharged from the army medically unfit in September 1918 but somehow managed to acquire a block at Mullumbimby in the fertile Northern Rivers district of New South Wales, where he tried to grow bananas. But his allotment was on a hard and unforgiving clay ridge. Time and again, his crops failed. Wracked by agonising headaches and the crushing burden of a dream made mockery, he simply walked off the land in 1923, his elderly mother pleading with the state government to write off his debts of £230.

Others fared still worse. Private Bill Brown, born in Belfast, Northern Ireland, in 1878, had fought with the 45th Battalion in France and was also discharged medically unfit to serve in 1918. He and his wife took 4000 acres at Dunedoo in the New South Wales Central West. The property was ravaged by years of drought, and his appeals for help from various authorities were tangled in knots of bureaucratic red tape. In and out of hospitals, in 1924 he took poison and died, in the words of a local Labor state MP, 'a shell-shocked wreck, mentally deficient, who in a fit of madness committed suicide'.[7] He was not the only one.

By June 1924, 23,000 men had gone onto the soldiers' blocks, on 94,192 square kilometres, at a cost to state and federal governments of a staggering £28,465,766.[8] Four years later, by 1928, one-third of them had walked off and returned to the cities. Embittered or humiliated, some broken in body or spirit, they would soon fall prey to the miseries of the Great Depression. They heard no notes from Edwin Brady's golden bugles of prosperity. The land fit for heroes had failed them, and would fail them again.

—

In 1919, uncertain of what to do about the future defence of the nation at sea, the Nationalist government of William Morris Hughes naturally asked the British to send an expert to advise. One duly arrived that June, in the gilded person of Admiral of the Fleet[9] the Viscount Jellicoe of Scapa. John Jellicoe's long and dazzling career at sea had peaked as Commander-in-Chief of the Grand Fleet at Jutland; he had been, in the words of Winston Churchill, 'the only man on either side who could lose the war in an afternoon'. He had not lost the war, but nor had Jutland produced another Trafalgar, the crushing Nelsonian victory that England had expected. Hoisted out of his flagship to become First Sea Lord, the professional head of the RN, he was pushed from that post after some political skulduggery in 1917.

Jellicoe, though, was no fool. Mild of manner and invariably courteous and unflappable, the very epitome of the English officer and gentleman, he conscientiously toured Australia for three months with a small staff in tow,[10] inspecting ports, ships and naval bases, and talking to all the right people. In due course, he produced a weighty *Report on the Naval Mission to the Commonwealth*. Astutely, he identified the protection of trade as the RAN's overarching priority, and Japan as Australia's most likely enemy in any future conflict. Japan had been on the Allied side in the First World War – a Japanese battlecruiser, the *Ibuki*, had been one of the escorts for the convoy carrying the first Anzacs across the Indian Ocean in 1914 – but the post-war rise of militarism there was fomenting an increasing resentment of the English-speaking nations and their interests in the Pacific. Jellicoe rightly put his finger on the White Australia Policy as a particular source of friction and suggested that as long as this existed there would be the danger of a Japanese invasion of Australia. Most prescient of all, he predicted that if Japan went to war, it would be an attack without warning.

To counter this threat – not just to Australia, but to the British Empire, as he saw it – Jellicoe suggested three things. Firstly, the RAN should continue in the closest cooperation with the parent RN, its men and ships to be trained to the highest British standards and sent on frequent exchange duty. Like many a British officer before and since, he detected what he thought was a sloppy Australian approach to discipline, and he devoted an entire chapter of his report to an improving lecture on the subject. 'The Englishman is, on an average, naturally disciplined. He inherits this characteristic, and accustoms himself to it from his earliest days,' he wrote. But Australians were not 'under quite the same parental control as in England'. He fretted that 'one is, in these days, at once brought face to face with the difficulty presented by the prevailing spirit of the times. This spirit is usually roughly described as "Democracy", but to a large extent it means a disinclination to accept any form of restraint, and a desire for unrestricted freedom of life and action.'[11]

The solution was to recruit young men early and train them in the ways of the navy before too many democratic notions entered their heads. If ill-discipline became rife, it was 'hardly necessary to point out the impossibility of maintaining the Royal Australian Navy as an efficient weapon of war'.[12]

Jellicoe's second recommendation was almost panoramic in its ambition. This was unsurprising in an admiral who had commanded 151 warships at Jutland, the biggest British fleet that had ever put to sea or ever would. With the enthusiastic support of the Australian naval officers he consulted, he urged no less than the creation of a Far Eastern Imperial Fleet, a great armada that could meet and beat all-comers in the Pacific or Indian oceans. This is the wish list exactly as printed in his report:

8 Battleships of modern 'Dreadnought' type.
8 Battlecruisers, also of modern type.
30 Light Cruisers.
40 Modern Destroyers.
3 Flotilla Leaders.
2 Depot Ships for Destroyers.
36 Submarines (excluding those stationed in Indian waters).
4 Submarine Parent Ships.
4 Aircraft Carriers.
12 Fleet Minesweepers.
1 Large Seagoing Minelayer.
2 Fleet Repair Ships.[13]

It was truly a nautical vision splendid. Jellicoe estimated that it could be done for some £20 million, with Britain contributing 75 per cent of the cost, Australia 20 per cent and New Zealand 5 per cent.[14] With the benefit of hindsight, it is possible to marvel at how splendidly remote he must have been from the national mood of both Britain and Australia, whose people wanted only peace and disarmament, to beat their swords into ploughshares. Wiser heads recognised that if this proposal were ever to be adopted, it would provoke yet another ruinous naval arms race, with Japan and the United States joining in. But Jellicoe was a sailor, not a politician nor a weathervane for public opinion. He had been asked to provide plans for naval defence, and that he did.

Thirdly, and finally, he suggested that this fleet should be based on the island of Singapore, where the existing dockyard facilities should be expanded to take the largest, most modern ships and placed under the command of 'a flag officer of high rank'. Singapore, he said, was 'the naval key to the Far East'.[15]

His Lordship was politely thanked for his labours and invited to become Governor General of New Zealand, which again he did. With leaden predictability, after a decent interval his report was filed away to gather cobwebs. The recommendations for continued close Australian links with the RN were followed, but that connection would have occurred anyway. The grand imperial fleet in the Pacific never left the paper he had it printed on, all three governments quietly deciding that it was a pipe dream far too expensive in the days of peace and the tight budgets necessary to pay the residual costs of the war. The idea of a great naval base at Singapore was considered in fits and starts, but nothing was done about it until the British Government gave it the green light – a hesitant and feeble green light – in 1923.

Japan and Australia continued to regard each other with outward politeness and inward distrust and suspicion, magnified on the Japanese side, as Jellicoe had foreseen, by resentment of White Australia. While the war had bled the European powers dry, it had left Japan economically and strategically strengthened as a major power in the Pacific. At the Versailles Peace Conference in 1919, over the vigorous opposition of Billy Hughes, Japan had demanded and been given control of Germany's former island colonies in the northern hemisphere of the Western Pacific, a mandate that would be affirmed by the newly formed League of Nations. In turn, Australia had been granted German New Guinea, a realignment of power, territory and influence in the Pacific that brought the two countries virtually face to face across the equator. Hughes was more successful in opposing a Japanese demand for a guarantee of 'the equality of nations and of equal treatment of their nationals' to be inscribed in the League of Nations covenant, fearing that might undermine White Australia. The irritants continued to fester, frequently expressed in the press of both countries.

In Australia, *The Bulletin* magazine, notorious for the line 'Australia for the White Man' splashed across every front cover,[16] railed constantly against the Japanese menace:

> If the Japanese cherish or develop a grievance against Australia or America, or if either of the two gets hold of something which should belong to Japan in the latter's opinion, then Japan will

select a favourable moment and it will fight . . . If Australia happened to be the enemy selected, and if it were required to 'fight on its own', it would not have a dog's chance on the sea in the present condition of the Navy. The RAN is relatively of the same standard of effectiveness as the old subsidised or hired fleet of six years ago and earlier; 'too weak to fight and too slow to run away'.[17]

The Japanese media were no less vigorous. In September 1920, Hughes delivered a keynote speech on defence to the Australian Parliament, a typically belligerent rant in which he vowed that Australia would 'fight to the death' for White Australia. 'I do not believe there are 5 per cent of the Australians who will not readily admit that on this principle there can be no concession,' he rasped. 'On this principle we must be always ready to defend ourselves. We cannot hope to maintain a White Australia policy by mere pious or blatant declarations of our intentions and determination. Behind this there must be some force, and it cannot be anything less than the utmost resources of this nation.'[18]

Tokyo's popular *Yamato Shimbun* newspaper snapped back:

The plea of Mr. Hughes that Australia should be reserved to the whites is another way of saying that no Asiatics should be admitted to Australia. The extension of armaments is designed to enforce it. Therefore, the Australian Premier practically says that Australia should prevent the entry of Asiatics by force of arms. Parochial and audacious!

If Mr. Hughes' speech had been made several years ago we would not have noticed it, but now is the age of the League of Nations. Great Britain and America are primarily responsible for the developments of this international body; yet we now find Australia unfolding the banner of racial discrimination and armament extension.

Is not this restoring international relations to the pre-war chaos? The world has been created no more for whites than for the colored races. If Australia extends her army and navy, and if America constructs gigantic fleets with her enormous riches, all neighboring countries will have to follow suit, and the Pacific, which should be true to its name, will be converted into a ground for warlike competition between Japan, America and Australia.[19]

The vision of Singapore as the empire's impregnable fortress in the Far East would have an almost magical allure for statesmen, admirals and learned defence commentators in the years to come. A catch cry, a slogan, sprang up: Main Fleet to Singapore! The gilded wisdom of the Admiralty in Whitehall, unassailable in the encrusted experience of three centuries, acknowledged that the naval weights had shifted, and radically so. With Germany crushed and no longer to be reckoned with, yet Japan continuing its ascent as a naval power and the United States building a fleet the equal of the RN, the Pacific would be the arena in which British strength would most likely be tested. British policy, once locked in a naval treaty with Japan, began to shift towards an understanding with the United States, which was also anxious about the rising Japanese sun.

On the empire's Pacific rim, the Canadians to the northeast – closest to Japan – tossed up all sorts of excuses for not getting involved, preferring to rely on the Americans to shield them. For them, Singapore was almost a hemisphere away. But Australia and New Zealand seized the concept of Main Fleet to Singapore with fervour. At any threat of war in the Pacific, at the emergence of any menace to Britain's colonies in the Far East, everyone understood that the might of the RN would be despatched south to counter it, with all speed. Main Fleet to Singapore became an article of faith. Britannia, although less mighty than before, still ruled the waves. One or two more thoughtful heads questioned what might happen if that Main Fleet were occupied by a hostile force elsewhere, say in the Atlantic or the Mediterranean, but they were ignored as gloomy pessimists. Singapore proceeded in fits and starts. For a while.

In January 1924, Britain's first Labour government axed any spending there, chiefly as an economy measure but cloaking the decision in the high principle of a gesture towards international peace and disarmament. Very much alarmed, the Australian and New Zealand governments protested vigorously, pointing out that they had set aside the money to pay their share. Not mincing his words, Bruce, the patrician Australian conservative, wrote to his British Labour counterpart, Ramsay MacDonald, that if Singapore were abandoned:

> incalculable harm will be done to the Empire's prestige, the confidence of smaller nations will be shattered, the ambitions of lesser powers will be increased, and deep distrust will be caused throughout the whole Empire . . .
>
> Therefore, on behalf of our Commonwealth, which has on every possible occasion proved its loyalty to the Empire, we urge you even at this late hour to reconsider your decision.[20]

When the Tories returned to power at Westminster at the end of 1924, they announced that work would resume, to great relief Down Under. But by that time, still uncertain of the strength of the British commitment, Bruce's government had bitten the bullet. While still relying on the Mother Country, Australia would look to renew her own defences as well. There would be a five-year development plan to cost just over £36 million, with the lion's share of the money going to the RAN. Orders would be placed for two of the latest cruisers, two large, ocean-going submarines, and five 8000-ton oil tanks to store fuel. The cruisers would be named *Australia* and *Canberra*.

As it always has been with a big-ticket defence purchase, and presumably always will be, controversy snapped and crackled. The Labor Party, reasonably enough, demanded that the cruisers be built in Australia to create much-needed work at the Cockatoo Dockyard in Sydney and Williamstown in Melbourne. Bruce, though, had done his homework, arguing that this would be too expensive, that British shipyards would do the job much more cheaply. To smother the debate, a high-powered committee was set up under the chairmanship of Sir John Monash, the most respected Australian general of the war and an engineer by profession, who duly reported that building a cruiser at Cockatoo would cost £1 million above the best British price. Remarkably, a sensible compromise was reached: to the surprise of the navy and still more the nascent Royal Australian Air Force (RAAF), the money saved by placing contracts in Britain would be spent at home, building a seaplane carrier at Cockatoo.

Australia and *Canberra* would be cruisers of the new County class, designed by Britain's most celebrated naval architect, the resoundingly named Sir Eustace Henry William Tennyson-d'Eyncourt. Five sister ships were also being built for the RN. At 10,000 tons displacement and a main armament of eight 8-inch guns mounted fore and aft in twin turrets, they were the largest cruisers permitted under the Washington Naval Treaty, sometimes known as Treaty cruisers. The design was handsome, even stately, and, to a seaman's trained eye, with a silhouette instantly recognisable as British. The hull, 192 metres long, had an unusually high freeboard, meaning that the ship's sides rose well above the waterline, keeping the long sweep of the upper deck well clear of the sea. There were three tall, distinctive funnels, the centre one being fatter than the other two, and these were made taller still when it was found in early testing that smoke and fumes were choking the men on the bridge. They were raked aft, like the masts – tilted backward, that is – to subtly suggest a ship travelling at speed even when she was at anchor. Eight Admiralty three-drum boilers, oil fired, drove four steam turbines that delivered an impressive 80,000 horsepower to four shafts and their great propellers of solid manganese bronze, producing a top speed of 31 knots, the fastest yet reached by a British cruiser.

The 8-inch guns, known as the BL Mark VIII, could hurl a shell weighing 116 kilograms over a maximum range of 28 kilometres, firing at a rate of five shells per minute in the hands of a well-trained crew. Unusually, the barrels could elevate in their turrets to an angle of 70 degrees, allowing them to fire at attacking aircraft. The anti-aircraft defences initially included four high angle 4-inch guns and four 2-pounder pom-pom guns with their trumpet-shaped barrels, named for the sound they made when firing. There were four 21-inch torpedo tubes mounted amidships on either side, port and starboard, and the design allowed for two cranes that could lower or lift a light seaplane, to be provided later.

By any standard, *Australia* and *Canberra* were fine, seaworthy ships, and comfortable too, for the 680 men who would crew each one in peacetime. Both would be built at Scotland's most famous shipyard, John Brown & Co. Ltd on the Clyde – the firm that had built the first *Australia* – at a cost of £1.9 million each. *Australia* was laid down on 26 August 1925 and *Canberra* in September.

—

William Francis Forbes-Sempill was the scion of one of Scotland's ancient noble families, an aristocrat with ancestors who had fought at the battles of Flodden and Culloden. Known as the Master of Sempill – the title he would carry until he became the 19th Baron Sempill on the death of his father – he had been born and raised in a grim but splendidly turreted castle, Craigievar in Aberdeenshire, speaking Gaelic but educated at Eton. As a young man, he was fascinated with flying, so much so that, instead of indulging in the customary upper-class amusement of an Oxbridge degree, he took up an apprenticeship with Rolls-Royce. A dashing, sociable chap, part Sir Walter Scott, part P. G. Wodehouse, he was famous in early aviation circles for having once arrived for lunch at London's Savoy Hotel by landing a floatplane on the Thames.

At the start of the First World War, Sempill, aged 21, rushed to join the Royal Flying Corps and was commissioned as a second lieutenant, later transferring to the Royal Naval Air Service, the forerunner of the Fleet Air Arm. He ended the war in the newly formed Royal Air Force (RAF) with an expert knowledge of naval aviation, the temporary rank of colonel, and an Air Force Cross for his distinguished service.

He was also a spy for Japan and a traitor to Britain. It is no exaggeration to say that he helped Japan ready itself for the Second World War. Lord Sempill's extraordinary career of betrayal began in 1920, when the Japanese ambassador in London formally asked the British Government if it would help the Imperial Japanese Navy (IJN) create an aviation arm. It was well known that the RN had made great strides in flying aircraft on and off moving ships, in torpedo bombing from the air, and in the design of a purpose-built aircraft carrier. Japan, a good and reliable friend and ally, would very much like to acquire this knowledge and a great deal more, the ambassador explained.

The Admiralty was not keen. Far from it. The admirals had no wish to share advanced British expertise and technology with any other navy, friendly or not, and they flatly refused to assist. The Foreign Office, though, took a different view, believing that British prestige abroad in general and in the Far East in particular would be enhanced by providing this aid. The Board of Trade liked the idea as well, seeing promising opportunities for selling aircraft and weapons to Japan, and the Air Ministry was also keen.

Without Admiralty support, there could not be an official mission of experts and instructors, so the civil service mandarins in Whitehall, employing their legendary genius for compromise and fudge, came up with a neat solution. There would be an *unofficial* mission. And who better to lead it than that splendid fellow Sempill, newly retired from the RAF?

Unemployed and known to be short of a quid, Sempill jumped at the chance and collected a crew of about 30 old service chums, many of them out of work like him. The Sempill Mission, as it became known, arrived in Japan in September 1921 and quickly got on with the job at the Kasumigaura air base on the main island of Honshu. A new runway was laid out. Japanese pilots, eager students all, were taught the skills of carrier take-offs, and landings with an arrestor hook, and the techniques of aerial warfare at sea, including low-level torpedo attacks. Unimpressed by the IJN's instruction manual for pilots, Sempill helpfully wrote a new one. Doing his bit for British exports, he suggested that the Japanese might be interested in acquiring the Gloster Sparrowhawk, a single-seat biplane fighter developed in Britain for carrier flying. Indeed they were. The IJN snapped up 50 aircraft already built in Britain and another 40 in component form to be assembled at the Yokosuka Naval Arsenal.

Sempill was enjoying himself. Ever the life of the party, relishing the roles of Etonian toff and tartan-clad Highland chieftain, he discovered that he liked the Japanese a great deal and that they liked him. One of his keenest disciples was the deputy commander of the Kasumigaura base, Commander Isoroku Yamamoto, who had newly returned from studying at Harvard and spoke excellent English. They got on like the proverbial house on fire, a friendship Yamamoto perhaps recalled when, as a full admiral and Commander-in-Chief of the Japanese fleet 20 years later, he would plan the attack on Pearl Harbor.

Eager to assist still further, Sempill also offered his hosts the plans of HMS *Hermes*, the first ship specifically designed as an aircraft carrier, which was then being built in Britain. With a full-length flight deck and an island bridge structure amidships on the starboard side, *Hermes* was so advanced that she was, in effect, the template for every aircraft carrier since, to the present day. The Japanese gratefully accepted this kind offer too, and were able to put what they had learnt into the design of their first carrier, the *Hosho*, speeding up construction so much that they managed to commission her before *Hermes*.

Job done, Sempill ended his mission in 1923 and left Japan with fond farewells and much regret, carrying with him the Order of the Rising Sun, 3rd Class, and a warm letter from the Prime Minister, Tomosaburo Kato, himself a former naval officer, who wrote in thanks for 'the splendid results, almost epoch making, that have been brought about in the Imperial Japanese Navy'.[21]

At this stage, Sempill had not been spying. His mission to Japan had the sanction of Whitehall, if not the RN. But he kept his contacts with the Japanese, and they with him, and by 1926 he was on the payroll of the Japanese naval attaché in London, Captain Teijiro Toyoda. In the early '20s, analysts at Britain's Government Code and Cypher School had begun to read some Japanese diplomatic codes, and eventually Sempill's name cropped up. Military Intelligence, MI5, discovered that he had been passing defence secrets to the embassy, including information on a top-secret aircraft design, and he was called in for questioning.

Sempill archly denied any wrongdoing and shocked his interrogators by threatening to sue for defamation. The affair wound its way up the food chain as far as the Foreign Secretary, Austen Chamberlain, who ruled that Sempill should not be prosecuted. To do so might reveal that Britain had cracked the codes. Worse, there was that exquisitely English upper-class dilemma, the likelihood of embarrassment. Sempill's father was a leading light in the Conservative Party in the House of Lords and an aide-de-camp to King George V, who must be protected from unpleasant scandal. The Master of Sempill was let go with a stiff warning.

Undeterred, he obtained a job as the European representative for Mitsubishi, which enabled him to continue his spying. His activities in the 1930s are shrouded in mystery and conjecture, for his MI5 file for that decade is inexplicably missing. Publicly, flamboyant as ever, he took part in air races, set flying records, and became president of the Royal Aeronautical Society and the London Chamber of Commerce, in which capacity he visited Australia in 1934. He was feted by Sydney society – 'a slightly built young man of incisive speech and views'[22] – and invited to address federal cabinet. With the cultural cringe well to the fore, he was earnestly questioned by the press. 'The air was the thing of the future, the mainspring and lifeblood of the British empire,' he assured *The Sydney Morning Herald*. But Mascot aerodrome was too far out of town. 'An aerodrome in an important town,' he said, 'should be within five minutes of the heart of the city. Aviation is going to play an important part in our transport, and people don't want to be compelled to drive for miles to the city.'[23]

We will never know if he offered his incisive views on Australia to his Japanese paymasters. But by the late 1930s, he had become a singularly nasty admirer of Fascism and the Nazis.

He was prominent in the Anglo-German Friendship Society and the Right Club, a secretive and subversive circle of such upper-establishment figures as the Dukes of Westminster and Wellington, dedicated to purging the Conservative Party of Jews and to forming a British alliance with Hitler.

MI5 certainly kept a watching brief on Sempill through the '30s and into the '40s, but – and the incompetence here defies belief – on the outbreak of the Second World War, he was given a job at the Department of Air Materiel at the Admiralty, where he had access to the secrets of the most modern military and naval aircraft, and evidently passed them on. In 1941, the intelligence services discovered that he was still on the Japanese embassy payroll, still providing classified information, and after the attack on Pearl Harbor that December he was caught in telephone calls to the Japanese embassy and found with incriminating documents in his office.

Yet again, he was not arrested. Traitor he was, but the Establishment continued to protect its own. Prime Minister Winston Churchill, who had known Sempill's father, was informed of the son's treachery but merely directed that he be posted out of harm's way to a sinecure in northern Scotland. Sempill died in 1965, his treason known only to an inner few until the wartime files were released in 2002. A note provided by the British National Archives concluded, 'On the evidence of these files, Sempill's activities on behalf of the Japanese and his Fascist contacts were motivated less by any desire to help the enemy or to make money than by his own impetuous character, obstinacy, and flawed judgement.'[24]

Another British traitor also spied for Japan in the interwar years. Lieutenant Frederick Rutland had made his name in 1916 as the only naval pilot to take to the air in the Battle of Jutland. Flying from the seaplane tender HMS *Engadine*, he went in search of the German High Seas Fleet and found four light cruisers, which fired on him as he dived out of thick cloud towards them at a height of just 900 feet. It was a gallant effort and more: it was historic, the first ever reconnaissance at sea by a fixed-wing aircraft in battle,[25] a coup applauded by no less than the commander of the battlecruiser fleet at Jutland, Vice Admiral Sir David Beatty. Rutland and his observer were 'to be congratulated on their achievement, which indicates that seaplanes under such circumstances are of distinct value', Beatty wrote.[26]

That exploit won him the Distinguished Service Cross, and he gathered further lustre to his name the day after the battle when he dived overboard from *Engadine* with a bowline around his waist to rescue a wounded sailor. A bar to his Distinguished Service Cross followed in 1917. Feted as a hero, the very model of a modern and progressive young officer, he was known ever after as Rutland of Jutland. Towards the end of the war, he transferred to the RAF. The seaplane he had flown at Jutland, a Short Admiralty Type 184, can be seen to this day at the Fleet Air Arm Museum in Somerset.

The Japanese approached him in 1922 when he was serving as an RAF squadron leader in the carrier HMS *Eagle*, and he accepted money to provide information on British naval aviation. We can speculate that hopes of wealth moved him to do this. Rutland had come from a working-class family – his father was a humble labourer – and had risen to a commission on his talent as a pilot, but as an officer he was expected to keep up appearances from his own pocket, a nagging worry. There would have been the expense of an endless variety of uniforms, formal and informal – frock coats, telescopes, cocked hats – formidable wine bills for hospitality given and received in the mess, and the constant strain of rubbing shoulders with brother officers of 'good family' and independent means, who thought nothing of sending their polo ponies out to Gibraltar or Bombay when they were posted.

MI5 learnt of Rutland's deceit in December that year, again from reading the diplomatic traffic, but for some reason took no action again. He was allowed to resign from the RAF the next summer. At first, he moved to France, and then to Japan itself, where he ostensibly took a job with the shipbuilding arm of Mitsubishi at Yokosuka. In fact, Rutland was on the payroll of the IJN, pouring out everything he knew. MI5 ordered that any mail sent to him in Japan should be opened, warning of codes and invisible inks, and noting in his file that:

> He is an officer who has a unique knowledge of aircraft carriers and deck landings, and his experience, gained as an officer of the RAF will be invaluable to the Japanese; there is not the slightest doubt that he was approached by the Japanese Government solely on this account.
>
> There is also no question that Squadron Leader Rutland is perfectly well aware that in going over to the Japanese Government he is in effect selling to a Foreign Power valuable and secret information which he has acquired solely by reason of his official position.[27]

In 1932, Rutland was approached by another Japanese naval intelligence officer, Lieutenant Commander Shiro Takasu, who recruited him with a down payment of £2000[28] and unlimited funding to set up an espionage ring in the United States. This he did. He was assigned the codename *Shinkawa* – New River – and went to California, where he established a web of dummy companies supposedly involved in security and aviation but in fact operating as cover for running networks of Japanese agents in America. Wealth at last. He lived the life of an expatriate British millionaire in a handsome house in Beverly Hills, entertaining the rich and famous of the US West Coast. Posing as an amateur filmmaker interested in naval affairs, he made frequent trips to the port cities of San Francisco and San Diego to photograph United States Navy (USN) battleships at bases there. He shipped the footage off to Tokyo.

It couldn't last, and it didn't. In early 1941, the FBI arrested a Japanese spy named Itaru Tachibana, yet another navy lieutenant commander, a young man who had been posing as an English-language student and, bizarrely, a brothel keeper in Los Angeles. Fearing he would be unmasked if Tachibana talked, Rutland hurriedly went to the FBI and offered to spy for the United States, but – to his astonishment – he was rejected. The

Americans, though, informed the British, and MI6 – the Secret Service – suggested to Rutland that he return to Britain for his own protection. Thoroughly enmeshed in his web of deceit, he was questioned in London and claimed he had been working for the Americans as a double agent, but was not believed. Unlike Sempill, Rutland the working-class boy had no influential connections, and after Pearl Harbor he was arrested and interned because of his 'hostile associations'.[29] Like Sempill, though, he was never charged with espionage, the powers that be apparently deciding again that the public scandal of a hero turned traitor could not be endured. Rutland committed suicide in 1949.

There were other British naval traitors. In 1927, Colin Mayers, a retired lieutenant commander and submariner, was charged and convicted under the Official Secrets Act for 'retaining in his possession certain plans relating to submarines, contrary to his duty'. The judge in the case said he was satisfied that Mayers had 'no purpose prejudicial to the safety of the state',[30] but that was flim-flam confected for the newspapers. Mayers had been providing the industrious Captain Toyoda with details of experiments in underwater communications technology for the useful sum of £300.

When the activities of these traitors were made known in 2002, some British writers frothed that the IJN could not have attained its standards of excellence before the Second World War, particularly in carrier aviation, without the connivance of these men. That is an unsustainable exaggeration. Japanese scientists and naval officers were not the buck-toothed Asiatic hobbits so often ridiculed by the cartoonists and the Western propaganda of the day; the best of them were at the cutting edge of research and development, blazing trails of their own. From the early 1930s, the IJN began to lead the world in naval aviation, a fact only dimly understood in the western navies, if at all. New, advanced carriers were building in the shipyards, and new aircraft were on the drawing boards or in the air. When the Mitsubishi A6M Rei-sen fighter, the famous Zero, appeared in

1940, it was far and away superior to any British or American warplane. But the rise of Japan in the air at sea had been made immeasurably easier by the treachery of the 19th Baron Sempill and Rutland of Jutland.

CHAPTER 3

THE TREMENDOUS VALUE OF THE SEAS EAST OF SUEZ

The Australians at the launch in Glasgow were pleasantly surprised that the city had turned on fine weather. Almost like a spring day at home, they agreed – glorious, not at all what you'd expect in March in Scotland. There was even a sparkle to the grey–green waters of the Clyde, the river that winds through Glasgow, past the Tail o' the Bank, Greenock and Gourock and out to the Firth of Clyde, beyond the Isle of Arran and into the Irish Sea.

At the famous shipyard of John Brown & Co. at Clyde-bank itself, the hull of the new HMAS *Australia* stood ready in Yard 512, waiting to take to the water. Perhaps intention-ally, perhaps by coincidence, this was the very yard where her battlecruiser predecessor and namesake had been built. The cranes above her were now silent and still. It was Thursday 17 March 1927, and an occasion to be celebrated with due ceremony. The launch was set for high tide at noon.

The cruiser had been under construction for almost two years, since the first steel of her keel had been laid in 1925. Teams of men and boys at Brown's had laboured over her in the smoke and crash and clang of the yard, raising her from the stocks in the way their forebears had wrought so many ships in the decades since the Industrial Revolution had turned Britain into the workshop of the world. Battleships and destroyers, harbour tugs and cargo steamers, and great ocean queens had slid down the slipways. *Hood* and *Repulse* had both been launched here, and also the liner *Lusitania*, so notoriously torpedoed by the Hun off southern Ireland's Old Head of Kinsale in 1915.[1]

They were skilled tradesmen, these Scottish shipbuilders, physically strong and jealously proud of their vocations: shipwrights, platers, plumbers, carpenters, caulkers, moulders, red-leaders, painters, riveters, cloot men.[2] The hours were hard. Summer and winter, rain, shine or snow, they would start as early as 6.30 in the morning, working until five in the evening, when the sirens would sound and they would swarm out of the yard gates and head for the Clydebank pubs. You could tell a man's job by his clothes: a shipwright wore a monkey jacket, invariably with a top button of brass; riveters favoured moleskin, strapped around the knee; foremen were neck-tied, overcoated and bowler-hatted. There was no protective clothing, none at all.

The riveters were the acknowledged kings of the workforce, their skills a miracle. In the days before large-scale electric welding of a ship's hull, the steel plates were held together by hundreds of thousands of rivets – in a big ship, several million. Each one was a peg of iron or steel some eight to ten centimetres long and weighing around 500 grams. The process began with the heater boy, whose first job each morning was to fire up a coke- or charcoal-burning brazier and keep it hot with bellows. He would use long-handled tongs to heat each rivet white hot. That had to be finely judged. Then, with a cry of 'Where's the boy?' he tossed it, sometimes high in the air, to the catch boy, who was the next man in the chain (the term 'boy' was a misnomer). This man scooped it up in a metal bowl or perhaps with a pair of heavy leather gloves and then, with his tongs, thrust it into the holes already punched in the two plates to be joined. The final members of the team, two bashers – always one of them right-handed, the other left – took turns to hammer it home tight. It was an exacting trade that took five years to learn, and was dangerous as well, for many a riveter had lost his balance and fallen from high scaffolding to injury or death on the shipyard floor. The men were paid by the number of rivets they placed per week – so much per hundred – each one of them marked and counted by a chalk boy. Their jobs were virtually hereditary, fathers and uncles handing down their skills.

The launch day of every ship was always a holiday for all who had worked on her, and for their families. It was a display of justifiable pride in a job well done. A crowd of several hundred had gathered to see *Australia* away, womenfolk and children in their best. Over in the next yard, 513, the hull of HMAS *Canberra* was also coming together, some months behind her sister. *Australia* had been painted a pale warship grey, with her upperworks – her superstructure above the upper deck – dull in the highly toxic red lead paint then used to prevent rust. Trained eyes noted the streamlined bulge along each side of the lower hull, extra armour to stop any torpedo penetrating the ship herself. A light breeze lifted the Union Jack hoisted at her bow, John Brown's red-and-white house flag flying at the stump of her mainmast, and the Australian flag at her stern. Promptly at ten o'clock, the big wooden baulks – timber logs that kept her upright – were knocked away; all that held her now was a wrapping of heavy chains. There was a sharp intake of breath from the crowd as she shuddered a little and looked for a minute as if she might head off on her own, but the chains stayed her.

As the morning drew on, the VIPs took their seats on the dais near her bow: the chairman of John Brown's, Lord Aberconway; the RN's Third Sea Lord, Vice Admiral Sir Ernle Chatfield, who had captained the battlecruiser flagship *Lion* at Jutland; and the Australian High Commissioner to London, Sir Joseph Cook, who had been Prime Minister at the outbreak of war in 1914. His wife would do the honours. A reporter filing for Australian newspapers recorded the scene as the cruiser rumbled down the greased slipway and slid into the water, stern first:

> When on the stroke of noon, Dame Mary Cook dashed a bottle of Australian Burgundy against her side as a christening, and pressed a button, which operated the electric rams, the cruiser quivered, and shot off down the slipways, to shrill cheers from

hundreds of school children. It was one of the most perfect
launchings ever seen on the Clyde.

In christening the cruiser, Dame Mary said: 'I name you
Australia. God bless all who helped to build you, those who sail
in you, and those who are interested in you in any way. I pray
that your future may be prosperous.'

The *Australia* was immediately towed by tugs into the
shipyard's dock, where she will be a year before completion.
H.M.A.S. *Canberra* will be launched in two months' time.[3]

The great day was also reported at length in *The Glasgow Herald*.
Dame Mary had been given a bunch of red carnations, and
a diamond brooch in a golden casket as a memento, it noted.
At luncheon, Sir Ernle Chatfield made a stirring speech, his
reassuring words about Main Fleet to Singapore well received
by the Australians:

> The scattered dominions could not have security of trade and
> Empire unless they were supported by the main Fleet, which
> had to be ready to leave at any time for the farthest parts of
> the Empire. That was one reason why so much importance was
> attached to the development of the naval base at Singapore . . .
>
> The fleet could not operate without bases, and now that
> British trade and British men were going East, there had been
> discovered the tremendous value of the seas east of Suez. It was
> imperative that the Grand Fleet must be ready to move wherever
> it was required (applause) . . .[4]

Canberra was launched on 31 May, this time by royalty, George
V's only daughter, Princess Mary. After that, the two ships spent
almost another year fitting out on the Clyde. It was a project
of immense complexity, incorporating kilometres of electric
wiring and plumbing and piping and trunking, much of it insu-
lated with asbestos lagging, the engine rooms and boiler rooms,
the magazines and their electric hoists, masts and rigging and
aerials and wireless gear and steering gear, the ships' boats, the
bridge structure and compass platform, the signal flags and
projectors, the gunnery director above the bridge. From the

mess decks, where men would eat and sleep, from galleys and bathrooms, from anchor chain and capstan to the wardroom carpet and crockery, the furniture for an admiral's cabin and so much more: all would have to come together in due time and place. Then the weapons – above all the weapons, the entire reason for the ship's existence. The big cranes would lower the turrets and their 8-inch guns into position, each turret weighing 187 tons, each gun barrel 17.5 tons. Then would come the 4-inch anti-aircraft guns, the pom-poms, the eight torpedo tubes and the smaller machine guns. Towards the end was the ammunitioning itself, the shells and cordite charges, each shell for the main guns weighing 116 kilograms. And all the time, the painters were hard at work from stem to stern.

Gradually the ships' companies began to form. For *Australia*, a nucleus of officers and key sailors, led by the senior engineer, Commander Trevor Ross, an Australian, had been watching over her from the earliest days, familiarising themselves with the cruiser both on paper and in the flesh as best they could amid the exasperating chaos of the dockyard. Her commanding officer came from the RN, Captain Francis Goolden, who had served at Jutland in Jellicoe's flagship *Iron Duke* and more recently in *Hood*. Most of the senior seaman officers, the men who would sail and fight the ship, were also English, although the gunnery officer, Lieutenant Commander John Collins, was an Australian who had joined the RAN as a boy of 14 in the very first year of the new naval college. Collins had come a long way to this point. And he had a dazzling career ahead, in peace and war. Conscientious and talented, he settled in to learning his new ship.

—

Osborne House looks out over the shore of Corio Bay at North Geelong, at the very western edge of Port Phillip. A colonial squatter, Robert Muirhead, built it in 1858, a striking homestead of grey stone with a colonnaded veranda and some of the light Italianate touches that were all the rage at the time. He named it after Queen Victoria's rather more splendid summer palace on the Isle of Wight.

Today it is an arts centre and museum. In 1913, it was the first home of the newly established Royal Australian Naval College, the RANC, a temporary location while a permanent site was being completed at Jervis Bay in New South Wales. This was a grand experiment. Some people had thought it right and proper to send boys to be trained as naval officers in HMS *Britannia*, the British naval college at Dartmouth in Devon, but the wiser choice prevailed. Australian officers would be brought up for an Australian sea service in an Australian setting. They would be chosen and taught to the same standards, of course, although with two singular exceptions: unlike in Britain, there would be no class distinction, no favouring of birth and blood – talent and ability would count above all – and tuition would be free.

On Thursday 13 February 1913, Osborne House opened to its first entry, its first class or term, as the navy calls it. There were 28 boys aged 13 or 14, from every state in the Commonwealth, chosen from 138 applicants by examination, personal interview and, finally, a draw from a hat. Nervous and excited, these new cadet-midshipmen spent the day meeting their instructors and each other: John Collins and Harry Showers from Victoria . . . Joseph Burnett, Harold Farncomb, Frank Getting and Otto Albert from New South Wales . . . Eric Feldt from Queensland, and more. One of those boys would become a knight of the realm, three would be admirals and two would be killed in action, but for now they were fresh young faces and names to remember.

They went to bed that night in the dormitory still buzzing from the thrill of it all, heard the traditional bugle call of 'Still', and then, with widening eyes, saw the solemn procession for Nine O'Clock Rounds. First came the bugler, and then the master-at-arms bearing a candle-lantern.[5] After them, the first lieutenant in mess undress uniform, and finally the gunner at the rear. These godlike figures paraded through the dormitory in splendid file, uttering not a word, and then vanished as they had come. The bugler sounded 'Lights Out', the call for silence. It was ignored. The chattering and giggling broke out again in the dark, louder by the minute.

But not for long. The master-at-arms burst back through the door, red-faced and bellowing, and within minutes 28 boys were out of their pyjamas and fully dressed, doing the round of the lawn. Five minutes' marching, five minutes' running at the double, repeated for two painful hours, with the laggards whacked on the backside by the stick. The same thing happened again the next night until, as Collins wrote in his memoirs, 'at midnight, sore and weary, we all admitted to ourselves that the Navy had won. Thereafter "Lights Out" meant silence.'[6]

John Augustine Collins was born a Tasmanian on 7 January 1899, the youngest son of an Irish doctor, Michael Collins, who had emigrated to Australia and settled in Deloraine after time at sea as a surgeon with the Royal Mail Steam Packet Company. John never knew his father: Dr Collins died of typhoid seven months before he was born, leaving his wife, Esther, to manage four boys and a daughter as best she could. The family moved to Melbourne, where Esther, the daughter of an Anglican vicar, nonetheless kept her marital promise to raise the children as Catholics and sent the boys to the Christian Brothers' College at St Kilda. John would say later that he had inherited a love of the sea from his father. With its promise of a free, quality education and a respectable, even glamorous career in the new navy, the RANC beckoned to the boy and his mother like a beacon.

The course was tough, to say the least. The syllabus laid out in 1914 was:

Mathematics: Arithmetic, Algebra, Geometry, Trigonometry (Plane and Spherical), Algebraical Geometry, Differential and Integral Calculus.
Physics: Hydrostatics, Mechanics (Theoretical and Applied), Heat, Optics, Electromagnetics (Theoretical and Applied).
Chemistry.
Engineering, with Workshop Practice and Mechanical Drawing.
English: Grammar, Composition, Literature.

French.

German.

History: English, European, British Empire, Australian, Naval.

Geography.

Navigation and Pilotage, with Nautical Astronomy.

Seamanship, with gunnery in the Training Cruiser.

Religious Instruction.

Gymnasium and drill.[7]

Discipline was strict and punishment swiftly applied. For serious offences, you were bent over a vaulting horse in the gymnasium and caned with six of the best. Study was hard grind too, but Collins and his term mates thrived on the outdoor life of a swim or a run before breakfast, and sunny afternoons spent learning boat work, sailing a cutter or rowing a whaler. There was tennis, cricket in summer and rugby in winter, played against private schools from Sydney when the RANC eventually moved to Jervis Bay in 1915, with fiercely fought annual games against the army officer college, Duntroon. Collins, fast and wiry, won his colours as an outside centre for the rugby team, and for athletics. In an era before radio and television, and far from the nearest township, Nowra, the cadets and staff flung themselves into concerts and amateur dramatics. For all of them, life at Jervis Bay was an idyll, passed in a beautiful place extraordinary for its exquisite beaches of snow-white sand and deep-green waters framed by virgin bush.[8] Kangaroos roamed the grass then and still do now, in sight of the Federation college buildings and the clock tower that dominates the parade ground known, inevitably, as the Quarterdeck.

In August 1914, the cadets were called on parade to hear from the college captain, 'His Majesty the King has declared war on Germany.' War! Battle! There were three cheers for the King, and then the first lieutenant read the RN's Articles of War, a litany centuries in the making of conduct to be displayed, orders to be obeyed and crimes to be punished, many of them by death:

Every Officer subject to this Act who shall forbear to pursue the Chase of any Enemy, Pirate, or Rebel, beaten or flying, or shall not relieve and assist a known Friend in View to the utmost of his Power, or who shall improperly forsake his Station, shall, if he has therein acted traitorously, suffer Death; if he has acted from Cowardice, suffer Death or such other Punishment as is herein-after mentioned; if he has acted from Negligence, or through other Default, shall be dismissed from Her Majesty's Service, with Disgrace, or shall suffer such other Punishment as is herein-after mentioned.[9]

A cadet recalled the moment: 'It was all very thrilling and awe-inspiring and little more work was done that day except to talk about when we'd get away – would we be in time for anything? Would we get to the other side? And underlying all, "Death or such other punishment . . ."'[10]

In his final year, 1916, Collins was made a cadet captain, winning first prize for Seamanship and Engineering, and that December, in a passing out parade before the Governor General, he and his term mates wore for the first time the white collar patches of a midshipman. Then they went off to sea and off to that war, tremendously pleased that the fighting had lasted long enough for them to do their bit.

Snotties, they were now, the navy's nickname for midshipmen,[11] and generally recognised to be the lowest form of naval officer life. Early in 1917, each boy was posted to a capital ship of the RN's Grand Fleet in the North Sea, six of them to the old HMAS *Australia* and the rest scattered around. Collins fetched up in HMS *Canada*, a battleship of 25,000 tons and ten 14-inch guns, based in Scapa Flow, where he found, to his youthful bewilderment, that the captain was going mad.

Eccentric captains were not unknown in the RN in and around the Edwardian era; it was almost fashionable. Quite a few of them cultivated their oddities in a faddish sort of way, doing it because, well, they could. But *Canada*'s captain, Adolphus Huddlestone Williamson RN, a birdlike figure known throughout the navy as 'The Quail', had gone over the edge. He was renowned for having offered to fight one of his junior sailors, for giving another a cigar to smoke on watch, and – more notorious still – for once parking himself in a canvas chair atop his polished cabin table and astounding some visiting captains by serenading them with a banjo.

On the bridge one evening, young John was ordered to pop cough lozenges into his captain's gaping mouth at regular intervals. The Quail finally blew it one night at sea when he abruptly ordered a sharp and senseless turn to starboard, alarming the entire squadron and risking a dangerous collision, and then apologised humbly to his admiral in a long and rambling signal. Seizing the moment at last, the ship's executive officer arrested him on the bridge and had him confined to his cabin. For the new Australian arrival, it was a memorable lesson in the perils of leadership.

Collins endured the life of *Canada*'s gunroom, that gloomy compartment below decks in a battleship that was traditionally home for the snotties, under the pestering eye of a sub lieutenant not much older than himself. They never once sighted the German enemy until those beaten ships surrendered at war's end. With the coming of peace, he remained in the navy, returning to Australia and serving in a variety of ships as he rose through the ranks to lieutenant. Marked as a promising junior officer, he was shipped back to Britain in 1922 to spend a year doing a course at HMS *Excellent*, the RN gunnery school on Whale Island in Portsmouth Harbour.

This was a challenge. Whale Island had a fearsome reputation for relentless hard work and iron discipline; the instructors, in addition to knowing all there was to know about guns, were the embodiment of Britannic naval pomp and circumstance, of spit and polish, of parade-ground drill and encrusted ancient ceremony, and everything done at the double. Failure there could be a career stopper.

Far from failing, the young Australian topped the course to win the coveted Commander Egerton Prize, a shining achievement against all-comers. His reward, down the track, was to be

appointed naval liaison officer for the Duke and Duchess of York
when they toured Australia in 1927 to open the new Parliament
House in Canberra.[12] All Australia was en fête for this exultant
celebration of nationhood. A poised and sociable young man,
Collins was well equipped to play the courtier. To rub shoulders
with royalty was glamorous, exotic, fabulous, a giddy whirl of
balls and parades and dinner parties, and a lustrous addition to
an officer's record, although he endured a moment of naked fear
when the horse he was required to ride at the opening ceremony
threatened to bolt with him. He accompanied the couple back to
Britain in the battlecruiser HMS *Renown* – there was a royal deer
hunt in Mauritius, and a spectacular carnival on Grand Harbour
in Malta. 'We lieutenants all adored . . . the Duchess,' Collins
recalled.[13] In December that year, back in the real world, he
was promoted again. Royal duties done, the party over, wearing
the two and a half gold stripes of a lieutenant commander, John
Collins took the train north to join the new *Australia* in the grit
and smoke of Clydebank.

—

A ship is a sailor's home, for months and perhaps years on end.
For all its weapons of war, for all its presence and purpose in the
deployment of power at sea, a warship is also the place where
the sailor eats and sleeps, where he relaxes off watch with his
shipmates, or where in a confined and crowded space he seeks
what privacy he can get to read or write a letter or just dream of
home. Sailors, therefore, care very much about the accommodation on offer. When they join a ship, it's the first thing they seek
out, with a critical eye, as they carry their kitbags below.

Australia and *Canberra* were an eye-opener to the men who
arrived in Britain to form their crews, some 1200 of them. It was
not just that they were new, clean and smelling of fresh paint,
pleasing though that was. The best thing was the size, the room
to move. The mess decks for'ard seemed spacious, almost palatial
compared with the cramped confines of a small destroyer or even
the larger pre-war cruisers in which any of the men had served.

These new ships had been designed to spend long periods at sea, patrolling the trade routes of the globe from the North Atlantic to the tropics. The deckheads – the ceilings, to a land lubber – were high enough so you could walk about without ducking or cracking your head, and with the scuttles open there was fresh air and sunlight to be had, a handsome bonus. Air-conditioning was still several decades away; cooling and ventilation was by air forced through piping and ducts below decks, which would still be hot in a tropical summer.

Another innovation had yet to arrive: cafeteria messing, as it would become known. A ship's captain customarily ate his meals in solitary splendour, in his cabin or perhaps a small adjoining private dining room in a larger ship. This seclusion was both the privilege and price of command. The other officers had their wardroom, which their captain was free to enter but rarely did unless he was invited; how often that happened depended upon how well liked – or otherwise – he might be. The wardroom had a small lounge and bar, and a large table where the officers shared their meals, served by white-jacketed stewards. For the sailors, food was prepared in a central galley and then carried through the ship to be doled out and eaten at long tables in the messes where they slept. It had been that way since the days of Drake and Nelson; the RN, and therefore the RAN, had seen no reason to change it down the centuries since.

Gradually but surely, order emerged from chaos as the ships' organisation took shape. The men were assigned to their messes and their divisions and watches and jobs, some of the names and titles lingering from the days of sail: the captain of the foretop, the mate of the upper deck, the bosun and his mates, the chief gunner's mate, the sailmaker, the shipwright, the chief yeoman of signals. Long practice saw the system slide smoothly into place under the thumb of the executive officers and the routines begin according to that holy of holies, K.R. & A.I., or the book of King's Regulations and Admiralty Instructions. The master-at-arms started to exert discipline: commanders' defaulters at nine in the forenoon watch, where men who'd bent or broken the rules were paraded for a warning or punishment; Evening Rounds with the officer of the watch.

The Paymaster Commander and his assistants laboured over stores and supplies, list upon list. Engineers appeared and went below to their mysterious nether world of main and auxiliary engines, boilers and pipes and ventilators, steering gear and pumps, valves, wheels, cocks, throttles and sprayers. Claude Choules, newly promoted to petty officer as a torpedo gunner's mate, found himself weighing heavy equipment before it was installed. Choules was an Englishman who'd fought as a boy in the battleship HMS *Revenge* at Jutland before transferring to the RAN in 1926. He would serve in the Second World War as well, living to the age of 110, the last surviving combat veteran of the Great War. When he died in 2011, his funeral was attended by cabinet ministers and admirals, and the RAN named a ship after him.[14]

In the bowels of the ships was the crowning glory, a pleasure to be savoured above and beyond all else. No coal. No more would these men arrive in harbour from sea, longing for a rest or a spot of leave for a run ashore, only to hear that dreaded pipe, 'Coal Ship'. No more the aching labour of shouldering big hessian sacks of the stuff, tons upon tons of it, to be manhandled below to the bunkers in any weather, a process that left a ship begrimed in dust from top to bottom, and men exhausted and filthy. And for the stokers, the men who shovelled coal to fire the boilers of the old ships, deliverance had descended.

Stephen Sylvester Valentine Kean was one of the delivered. That was his full name, although his family always knew him as Cyril, and, in a navy that would give you a nickname as soon as look at you, he was inevitably called Mustard. Born in the Sydney working-class suburb of Petersham in 1904, he had left school as soon as he could, at the age of 14, and had knocked around a bit after that. There'd been a job as a warehouse boy in a sports store, and then work with his uncle George, a builder who taught him the painter's trade. His real love was messing about with motorcycles or anything mechanical, but, at the age of 20, he joined the navy as a probationary stoker, second class – about as low down the ladder as you could be.

Stokers were hard men, by trade and by nature. After a bare five months' training at the Flinders Naval Depot at Western Port Bay in Victoria, Mustard Kean's first ship had been the cruiser *Sydney*. To the new recruit, the stokehold of a coal-powered warship underway must have seemed like the very fires of hell. Gangs of men, black and greasy with coal dust and sweat, laboured in heat of 40 degrees and more, near deafened by the roar of the furnaces and the big fans pushing air under pressure to feed the fires. Mustard learnt what it was to shovel coal to a firebox with three doors, two at waist level and one just above your head, bending and heaving, bending and heaving in monotonous, endless rhythm on a lurching deck. And it was not all muscle: there was an art to spreading the bed of coals so the fire would neither choke itself nor burn too fiercely. There'd been a trip to Hobart he'd never forgotten, the worst of the lot, in rough seas that had sent the ship climbing to the top of a wave at one minute and then corkscrewing giddily down to crash into the trough the next, and him shovelling all the while and struggling to keep his feet so as not to be flung against the firebox and burnt.

There were times men were worked so hard their noses bled, or perhaps their ears. And if you got on the wrong side of your petty officer, if the bastard had it in for you, you could find yourself on the shovel without a break for a whole four-hour watch, perhaps with the ship at full speed and the fires voracious. In harbour, there was the grim job of cleaning out, too. The fires would be allowed to burn out; then the men would take turns to clamber into the firebox itself, still hot, to scrape out the residue of unburnt clinker and ash with a heavy rake. They sprayed you with a fire hose then, to keep you from literally cooking in this monstrous oven.

Like most stokers, Mustard got into the odd spot of trouble. At one stage, for sins officially unrecorded but in family legend a disagreement with an officer, he lost his three-year good conduct badge and the extra pay that went with it, and did seven days in the brig, where they made you pick apart a heavy rope hawser with your fingers before you got your evening meal. That must have come close to ending his naval career, for his service record was marked 'D.S.N.L.R.', meaning 'Discharged, services no longer required'. But then someone had scrawled 'not approved' next to that, and he was kept on and after a while promoted one rate, to stoker.

And now here he was on the Clyde, a member of the ship's company of HMAS *Canberra*, in all her fresh-minted glory. The men for *Australia* had arrived three months earlier, in April 1928, sent over as the final crew of HMAS *Melbourne*, taking her to Portsmouth and a British scrap yard. It had been more fun for the *Canberra* boys, who'd been shipped as passengers on a chartered P&O steamer, the *Beltana*. After a hammering in atrocious weather in the Great Australian Bight, in which everyone had been seasick and lining the rails, the rest of the trip had been virtually a pleasure cruise. On Clydebank in July 1928, the height of the Scottish summer, Mustard Kean and his mates in the stokers' mess were looking forward to a new and infinitely easier life. Stokers were being retrained to work on oil-powered ships, where refuelling was a mere matter of connecting pumps and hoses, and heating the boilers was a routine of turning wheels and watching dials.

—

Australia officially became the new flagship of the RAN on 3 May when a newly minted admiral mounted the gangway and ceremonially came aboard amid shrilling pipes, saluting officers and the crew drawn up in rigid ranks. Rear Admiral George Francis Hyde was an Englishman who had come up in the RN the hard way from a slow start. His father had been a bank clerk in Portsmouth, the ancient home of the British fleet, and from his earliest years the young Francis – he used his second name – would have been familiar with the comings and goings of ships and sailors. The life attracted him. With his father unable to afford the cost of tuition at the naval college, he went to sea in the merchant navy in 1894 as a 17-year-old apprentice officer on wool clippers sailing to Sydney via the Cape of Good Hope and back home again around the Horn. He joined the Royal Naval Reserve, and eventually – against high odds – hard work and talent won him the support of influential senior officers and a permanent commission as a lieutenant in the navy proper. In 1910, by then a commander, he was sent on loan to the RAN to command the newly formed destroyer flotilla, an experience he evidently enjoyed, for he decided on a career-defining change. As the *Australian Dictionary of Biography* puts it:

> Already an admirer of Australia, attracted by its bright future, the absence of class prejudice, better prospects of promotion in a young navy, and by higher pay in addition to retirement pay from the R.N., he transferred to the Royal Australian Navy in 1912 in the rank of commander with seniority from 1 January 1911.[15]

In the war, he served first in the old battlecruiser *Australia* and later captained a British cruiser in Irish waters. Hoisting his flag in this, the second *Australia*, Hyde took leadership of the RAN at sea, with the title of Rear Admiral Commanding the Australian Squadron. He would go on to greater things, in time becoming one of Australia's more effective naval administrators and the first RAN officer to reach the rank of full admiral. For now, his task was to ready *Australia* and *Canberra* for sea.

As the two cruisers withdrew from the clutches of the shipyards, they left port for weeks of testing and exercises, to familiarise the crews with their new charges and to ensure that everything was working as it should, from guns and engines to communications. At full-power trials, with all boilers connected and the engine throttles wide open, turbines thundering, the ships dug their sterns deep into the greening seas, 80,000 shaft horsepower sending them knifing through the swell at an exhilarating 31.5 knots, sea mile after sea mile.

The gunnery trials were less successful. In *Australia*, the very first salvo from her 8-inch guns knocked out all the electrical power to the turrets and ammunition hoists, leaving her to retire from the shoot hurt and impotent, much to the chagrin of John Collins. When *Canberra*'s turn came, the same thing happened, with some added comedy: the concussion from A- and B-turrets below the bridge caused chaos on the compass platform, blasting Captain George Massey backward past a startled navigating officer and down a ladder, to land sprawling on the signal deck below in a jumble of flags and halyards.

It was not a good start. And it got worse. During rudder trials, with the ship full speed ahead at some 31 knots, Massey suddenly ordered full astern, followed by hard a'port and then hard a'starboard. *Canberra* shuddered under the enormous force of these contortions. Claude Choules recalled in his memoirs that the whole rudder lifted out of position, causing severe damage to the steering engine and requiring the ship to be dry-docked for more than a week of repairs.[16]

With their faults and failings ironed out, or hopefully so, both ships were at His Majesty's Naval Base, Portsmouth, on 17 July 1928, for a visit from the King himself. In the twenty-first century, when the mystique of royalty has all but evaporated beneath the relentless scrutiny of the mass media, it is difficult to perceive what a momentous occasion this was. In the first decades of the twentieth century, the great mass of Australians, high born and low, were unquestioning subjects of the British crown, and glad to be so. Most never expected to lay eyes on their monarch and never would, beyond the grainy newsreels coming into fashion in the cinemas, where audiences loyally rose from their seats for God Save the King before the feature film flickered to life. But, with a few eccentrics or wicked dissidents aside, they were in thrall to the idea of Majesty, however remote. To see the King in the flesh was extraordinary, a privilege normally reserved only for those rich enough to travel to the home country and with the connections to cadge tickets to the summer garden parties at Buckingham Palace.

Australia was berthed in pride of place, within the shadow of the masts of the hallowed HMS *Victory*, that great, wooden-walled, three-decked ship of the line in which the triumphant Lord Nelson had died at Trafalgar, and which had recently undergone a restoration. *Canberra*, a little further away, was astern of HMS *Nelson*, named for the victor himself and one of two new battleships the RN had been permitted to build under the Washington Treaty. Paint gleamed. Brass shone. The masts were forests of coloured signal flags. The ships' companies were drawn up in rigid ranks. Gunnery petty officers, custodians of proper and pukka, fussed about. Bands played. Royal Guards stamped and crashed to the Present Arms with the regulation smack of hands on rifle magazines.

George V did not disappoint. A stolid figure whose chief occupations were stamp collecting and reining in the extravagance of his imperious wife, Queen Mary, he had nonetheless been trained as a sailor. As a princely midshipman, he had first visited Australia in 1880, later rising to command a light cruiser, HMS *Melampus*, on the North America station. He knew what he was looking at. In the uniform of an Admiral of the Fleet, with its broad gold band and four gold stripes at the sleeve cuffs, he toured both ships, followed by a respectful entourage of Admiral Hyde, the commanding officers, and the Australian High Commissioner to London, Major General Sir Granville Ryrie, a splendidly moustachioed veteran of the Boer and First World wars, twice wounded at Gallipoli.

The King had not seen one of these new County class cruisers before, Australian or otherwise, and, according to the breathless newspaper reports of the day, he rebuked a courtier who had pointed out that he was lingering behind schedule. Duty done, the royal party lunched on board *Nelson*, with Ryrie hot-footing it back to London for a grand ball at Australia House that evening, a lavish affair for 1200 guests including the Australian Olympic team[17] on its way to the Games in Amsterdam, and graced by the Prince of Wales. A select group of Australian officers and seamen had been invited, and they were accorded yet another reception the next morning, with a stirring speech from the High Commissioner himself:

KING IMPRESSED
AUSTRALIAN PHYSIQUE.
Crews of Warships Feted
London, July 18.
'Australia can rely upon you to give short shrift to the Bolshevists who would corrupt the Navy,' Major. Gen. Sir Granville Ryrie (High Commissioner for Australia) told the officers and ratings of HMAS *Australia* and HMAS *Canberra* when they attended a reception in their honour at Australia House today.

'The Soviet emissaries may woo with plausible tales, but I do not fear for your loyalty,' Sir Granville added.

'His Majesty was impressed yesterday with your physique and discipline. The Empire watches you with profound affection, and Australia is preparing a hearty welcome to you.'[18]

Later, on the site where Nelson, Rodney and Hood received the freedom of the city, Sir Charles Batho (Lord Mayor of London) tendered a luncheon to the officers of HMAS *Australia* and HMAS *Canberra*, while the sailors had luncheon in the Crypt. Three former Lord Mayors were present:

Grand Act of Nationhood
Cr. D. G. Collins, in proposing the toast to the Australian Navy, eulogised the Imperialism of the Commonwealth, whose citizens had subscribed on an average £1 each to construct the cruisers. He hoped that they would make enduring history. The construction manifested yet another grand act of nationhood . . .

Rear Admiral G. F. Hyde (Commodore of the RAN) said that the cruisers were visible proofs that Australia had not neglected the teachings of history. The Australian Navy had been developed under the wing of the Royal Navy, and it must continue in that manner for many years.

Lord Lovat (chairman of the Overseas Settlement Committee) occasioned a storm of applause when he paid tribute to the Australians as the finest individual fighters in the world.

Sir Charles Batho said that although they had entertained many potentates, yet no body of guests had given the corporation greater delight, because they were their own kinsfolk.[19]

Australia sailed from Spithead on 3 August, heading for Sydney via Canada, the United States and the Panama Canal. Three days out, proceedings were enlivened by a fierce Atlantic gale, which saw the Chief Buffer,[20] Chief Petty Officer Darby Allen, washed overboard from the fo'c'sle. Allen was an unpopular figure. As Captain Goolden skilfully conned the ship to reach him in the heavy seas, sailors lined the rails calling out 'Let the bastard drown.' To their great disappointment, he was pulled from the water by one of the ship's officers, Lieutenant Commander Harry Howden.

They were given a rousing welcome at Boston, New York and Annapolis, not least because the well-stocked wardroom bar was a magnet for American guests suffering the rigours of Prohibition. There were more calls at Jamaica, Tahiti and Wellington, and in mid-October *Australia* steamed west across the Tasman for the first time. To the fury of the Sydneysiders in her crew, she was diverted to Brisbane, because the Prime Minister, Stanley Bruce, wished to greet her there. The papers reported 'disorderly scenes' as nearly 10,000 sightseers rushed to go aboard, 'sailors on the gangplank using their fists to stop the rush of men who were endangering women and children'.[21] She finally reached Sydney, her home port, on 23 October.

Canberra still had more trials to do and yet another royal visitor to welcome. Mary, the Princess Royal, turned up at Portsmouth on 6 October to see the ship she had launched the year before. By all accounts, she charmed the crew with breezy informality. Mustard Kean was swept up in the magic and ever after would say that Mary was just wonderful, 'the sort of person you could sit in the gutter and have fish and chips with'.[22]

At last, on 4 December, *Canberra* sailed for her new home, south through the Atlantic and around the Cape of Good Hope, and then across the Indian Ocean to make her first Australian landfall at Fremantle, where she arrived on 25 January 1929.

Stopping to show the flag in Albany, Adelaide and Melbourne, she finally secured to the No. 1 Naval Buoy in Sydney's Farm Cove on a perfect summer's day, Saturday 16 February.

That summer of 1928–29 would linger in the memory of many Australians as a time of carefree happiness, when their world was bright with optimism. But dark and frightening years lay ahead.

CHAPTER 4

BLIGHTED BY THE WITHERING TOUCH OF POVERTY

Nobody heard the gunshots in the night. The man and woman had chosen a secluded spot to die under cover of dark, on the Moore Park Golf Course not far from the Sydney Cricket Ground. Their bodies, soaked in blood, were discovered by two golfers playing an early round the next morning. They were lying below a small, grassy hillock known to the locals as Spion Kop, near the fifth tee.

One of the men who found them, a Mr Archibald Brown, who gave his address as Her Majesty's Arcade, Sydney, told the police that initially he had thought they were asleep. 'I did not take any notice of them at first, thinking that they were perhaps just two of the many persons without a home at the present time,' he said. 'They were lying about three feet apart on a slope facing the clubhouse, and I was shocked to find blood on the woman's temple.'[1]

It was Wednesday 3 September 1930. When Detective Sergeant Joe Lynch of Darlinghurst Police arrived on the scene, it was plain enough what had happened. The woman, perhaps in her 40s and neatly though shabbily dressed, was dead from a bullet wound to the head. She was holding a brown handkerchief, wet with dew. The man, in his 50s and also poorly clothed, had an army revolver clutched in his right hand and he too had his brains blown out. There was no sign of a struggle, and when the police prised the gun from his cold fingers they found only two bullets had been fired, with four still left in the chamber.

'A very simple case to solve,' Lynch told the newspapers.[2] It was obviously a murder-suicide. Searching the man's clothing, he turned up just one threepenny piece in a jacket pocket and a Returned Serviceman's Badge numbered 180732 pinned on the lapel, which, in due course, helped identify the two. It was big news, and the Sydney papers set out to find what they could, as *The Evening News* reported that afternoon:

> Behind the tragic discovery of the bodies of a middle-aged couple on the Moore Park golf links this morning is a heart-breaking story of a war romance that, blighted by the withering touch of poverty, ended in a death pact.
>
> The victims, who were married in England during the war, were:
>
> George Bryant, 54, labourer of 117 Palmer St East Sydney, a native of England.
>
> Julia Elizabeth Bryant, 47, of the same address.[3]

Bryant had been a soldier for a fair part of his life. When he enlisted in the Australian Army in 1916, at the age of 40, he gave his occupation as coal lumper, but his service file shows that, born an Englishman, he had previously spent 12 years in the British Army as a private in the 2nd Battalion of the Essex Regiment.

There is no record of how or when or why he emigrated to Australia. The job of coal lumper is exactly what the name suggests, though: the hard and dangerous grind of shovelling coal from a collier or barge into a ship's bunker. It was poorly paid and irregular work where you were never sure of your next job, tougher even than wharf labouring. Bryant gave the army a home address of Prince's Street, Millers Point, now a pleasant park around the south pylon of the Harbour Bridge near the tourist mecca of The Rocks, but then a working-class slum of rat-infested tenements, sailors' brothels and roaming street gangs, where the coal lumpers squatted while they waited to be hired for a day. After passing his medical, he was shipped overseas in the troopship *Argyllshire* and posted to the Australian Imperial Force's (AIF) 22nd Battalion in France, to be wounded by a machine-gun bullet in the leg on the Hindenburg Line in 1917. Convalescing in England, he met a girl named Julia Magrath and fell in love with her. After the war, they were married at a London registry office in June 1919.

In the years after the war back in Australia, the Bryants lived in quiet obscurity until their deaths. The diligent reporter for *The Evening News* dug deeper and pieced together their last weeks and days. The Depression, which had struck in 1929, had thrown George out of work, for there were fewer and fewer ships to be coaled in Sydney Harbour. In the month before he died, there had been a short spell of council relief employment shifting sand at Maroubra, but when that ended – and despite all his best efforts to find work – he and Julia were destitute, no longer able to pay the rent for their one dismal room in Palmer Street, just up the hill from the wharves at Woolloomooloo. From there, it would have been a walk of a little more than half an hour to Moore Park.

Julia's sister, Mrs Augusta Bell, told police, 'the couple were very devoted to each other and had never quarrelled'.[4] Distraught, she was sure they had made a pact to end their lives. Questioned by the *Evening News* reporter, their landlady, Mrs Rhoda Mansell, said the Bryants were quiet and respectable. 'They paid me 16 shillings a week regularly and did not owe me anything,' she said. 'They did not have any money yesterday so far as I know, and for a long time were struggling even to feed themselves.'

The reporter pressed further:

An examination of the room revealed their tragic plight. There was only a small quantity of old clothing in the drawers and wardrobe. Mrs Bryant's handbag was on the dressing table – empty. On a gas ring on the verandah was a small kettle half-filled with water, but there was no food.

The couple left no note, and had locked the door behind them.[5]

In due course, a coroner found that George Bryant had indeed committed suicide, but he could not determine whether George had murdered his wife or she had shot herself first. 'Mrs Bryant had been heard to observe that life was not worth living,' he said.

—

The Wall Street Crash of October 1929 engulfed Australia in a catastrophe that tore at the nation's economic, social and political fabric, and threatened to rip it apart.

Conditions were already ripe for it. Throughout that year, unemployment had been hovering at around 7 per cent, with a wave of sometimes violent strikes and lockouts in essential industries, and Bruce's conservative government in open war with the trade unions. There were ugly riots on the wharves in Adelaide when non-union labour was brought in to break a strike; mounted police charged into the crowd and were stoned in return. Timber workers went out on strike nationwide. Electricians, abattoir workers and coal miners all walked off the job, and at one almost farcical point even racecourse bookmakers refused to field. Stanley Bruce retaliated by announcing that he would abolish the Commonwealth Arbitration Court, which set wages and conditions. This inflamed the unions more, and the temperature kept rising. Eddie Grayndler, the veteran general secretary of the Australian Workers' Union, warned that his men were prepared to fight in the streets and rural camps, 'even against the guns of the military forces'.[6]

The unions and Labour won. In a dizzy whirl of political and parliamentary conspiracy and treachery, much of it fomented by the inevitable Billy Hughes, who was notionally a Bruce ally but betrayed him, the government fell apart and was forced to a snap election on 12 October. It was destroyed, losing half its members, and Bruce himself was flung out of his Melbourne seat of Flinders. The Labor leader, James Scullin, once a grocer in Ballarat and later a newspaper editor and union organiser, became Prime Minister, sworn into office on Tuesday 22 October.

No incoming government has been so accursed, before or since. The Wall Street Crash began two days later, on Thursday 24. Billions were wiped from the New York Stock Exchange that day, and panic raged. On the next Tuesday – Black Tuesday, as it would ever be known – the American market lost US$13 billion by nightfall, the equivalent of US$180 billion today. Australia, already economically fragile, alone and helpless in a hostile world, could only wait for disaster to descend.

As it did. Prices for Australia's chief exports of wool and wheat fell through the floor, taking the economy with them. Foreign investment, mostly British, simply dried up or, worse, panicked and fled. Unemployment soared to 10 per cent in early 1930 and to 30 per cent by 1932. In New South Wales alone, factory output fell almost 10 per cent in 1929–30 and another 30 per cent in 1930–31. Businesses were destroyed. Thousands of men, many of them once the hopeful soldier settlers but now wretched and humiliated, were forced to hump a swag along the bush roads, desperate to work for their keep alone. In the cities, single men and families slept in parks, children went to bed with empty stomachs, wives tried to pawn wedding rings, and soup kitchens sprang up to stem the tide of hunger and misery. There was no universal dole for the unemployed, although state governments provided sustenance relief of food vouchers and handouts – known as the Susso – to the utterly destitute. A children's nursery rhyme put it with acid humour:

> We're on the susso now,
> We can't afford a cow,
> We live in a tent,
> We pay no rent,
> We're on the susso now.[7]

Rich and poor alike were ruined; the Bryants were far from the only people to die in despair. Political parties of all colours devoured themselves or each other in a morass of treachery and incompetence, and extremism took hold at either end of the spectrum. Democracy itself was under threat. A swelling number

of communists plotted and agitated for the working-class revolution to overthrow capitalism; secretive and not so secretive
right-wing vigilante groups sprang up, led by former military
officers, scheming to seize power by armed force if that revolution arrived.

Devoid of ideas, utterly at a loss, in early 1930 the Scullin
government invited the British to send out an expert to advise on
the nation's finances. The Bank of England duly despatched one
of its most exalted figures, Sir Otto Niemeyer, to pull the colonials
into line. Smoothly eloquent, armed with the sublime assurance
of conventional wisdom, he proceeded to advocate exactly the
wrong solution, lecturing his hosts with condescending authority.
Retrenchment! Deflation! Australians were living beyond their
means; cold facts must be faced. 'The practical solution of the
serious problem that the Commonwealth faces is not rendered any
easier by the natural optimism of the Australian,' he told the state
premiers at a conference in Melbourne.[8] There should be belts
tightened everywhere, with government spending on public works
and social services slashed, and wages cut. But above all, Niemeyer
insisted, Australia must not default on its debts to British lenders.
The firebrand New South Wales Premier Jack Lang thundered
that Niemeyer 'had castigated the premiers as though they were
schoolboys ... in one of the most humiliating experiences to
which a self-governing community ever submitted'.[9]

The premiers essentially accepted Niemeyer's deflationary
remedies, a certain recipe for prolonging the agony. In 1931, the
Arbitration Court announced a 10 per cent cut in the basic wage.
Lang, defiant, put forward a radical plan to default on interest
payments to British bond-holders and in March he did just that,
refusing to make a payment of £729,000 due that coming April
Fool's Day. Three weeks later, there was panic in the streets
of Sydney when a run of depositors withdrawing their money
forced the Government Savings Bank of New South Wales to
close its doors.

The economic and political turmoil grew more furious.
Depending upon where you stood, Lang – 'the Big Fella' – was

either the doughty champion of free Australians against the evil
rapacity of capitalism – especially British capitalism – or a dangerous demagogue leading the nation to socialist ruin. As ever, the
truth lay somewhere in the middle, but Lang's defiance plunged
the Labor Party into another of its familiar bouts of tribal
warfare, and the next federal election, in December 1931, saw
the remains of Scullin's hapless government thrown from office.
The new Prime Minister was a Tasmanian, Joseph Aloysius
Lyons, a former Labor state premier and federal treasurer who
had defected from the Australian Labor Party to construct a new
conservative grouping, the United Australia Party. Joe Lyons
would lead the country until his death in April 1939.

In January 1932, the Lang government once again defaulted
on its interest repayments to British lenders; in May, Lang was
dismissed from office by the state governor, Sir Philip Game,
and in June he lost the subsequent election to a conservative
coalition. Between 1929 and 1933, every government, state and
federal, Labor or conservative, had been thrown out of power in
the hope that, somehow, the other lot might do better.

Yet it would be wrong to portray the early '30s as an era of
unmitigated misery for all Australians, for there was the occasional ray of light to pierce the clouds. The 'Boy from Bowral',
Donald Bradman, began to carve his name in the history of
cricket, most notably in the Third Ashes Test at Leeds in July
1930, where he scored a first-innings century before lunch and
another two before stumps to finish on an astounding 334. The
nation rejoiced. That same year, Phar Lap won the Melbourne
Cup; Australia got its first native-born Governor General, the
jurist Sir Isaac Isaacs, appointed over the sulky objections of
George V; and the city of Perth was connected to the rest of the
country by telephone. In 1932, Sydney celebrated as the Harbour
Bridge was finally opened in comic-opera farce, when Captain
Francis de Groot, of the right-wing New Guard, spurred his
horse forward and slashed the ribbon with a sabre before Jack
Lang could lift his scissors. That July, the Australian Broadcasting Commission came into being with its first national radio

broadcast, the opening programs offering a children's session with Bobby Bluegum, 'British Wireless News', a live call of the Randwick races, and a talk on goldfish. In business, a food company run by a former tram driver, Adolphus Herbert Frederick Norman Appleroth, bought time on commercial radio stations to air its exciting new advertising jingle:

I like Aeroplane Jelly
Aeroplane Jelly for me
I like it for dinner, I like it for tea
A little each day is a good recipe . . .

The national mood darkened again when Phar Lap was found dead on a farm in California, where he had gone to race. But, by the end of 1932, there was the first glimmer of hope, perhaps, that the worst of the Depression might be over.

—

The RAN took some heavy body blows as the Depression bore down, strokes that sliced to the bone. In late 1929, the basic pay for an able seaman had been reduced from 7/- (seven shillings) to 5/8 per day,[10] or £1/19/8 per week[11] – well below the civilian basic wage. And worse was to come. In 1930–31, defence spending was slashed by 21 per cent, and then by another 17 per cent in 1931–32.[12] Among the navy's cuts, the naval college at Jervis Bay was closed and shifted to the Flinders depot in Melbourne, with no new cadets recruited for two years.

Under the *Financial Emergency Act 1931*, the pay for officers was reduced by up to 25 per cent. Various allowances were chopped as well, for officers and sailors both. Retrenchments and sackings followed, with hundreds of men thrown out of the service to wrestle with the cold, hard facts of civilian life. By 1933, at rock bottom, there were just 339 officers and 2483 sailors in the RAN.[13]

Some elected to go voluntarily, two of them officers, 380 of them sailors. Mustard Kean was one. He went in June 1930, 'discharged free' in the official phrase, which meant there was no financial penalty for having served only six of the 12 years he had signed up for. He may have regretted the decision, for there was no work, and he was forced to scratch a living shooting rabbits at East Hills on what were then the outskirts of Sydney. Sixpence a pair, he got for them. Sometimes, he would go bush to spend time with relatives on a small property.

Ships went, too. Six of the elderly River Class destroyers, relics of the Great War, were broken up for scrap, and the navy's two submarines, *Otway* and *Oxley*, were handed back as a gift to the RN in 1932, only three years after they had been acquired.[14] Eventually, there were just four ships left at sea: *Australia*, *Canberra*, and the seaplane carrier *Albatross*, with a small S class destroyer, HMAS *Tattoo*, occasionally turning up with a reduced crew to tag along in the rear. It was a navy in name only; in reality barely a squadron and struggling to survive at that. The cuts to the defence budget aroused smouldering inter-service rivalries, with the RAAF in particular indulging in some low-level strafing and bombing:

> The ideal of an Australian Navy has nothing really to recommend itself as a national institution. With the big developments in Naval Disarmament policies it is hardly justified, having regard to the financial position and the marked advantages of employing a British squadron, when the greater and only duty is co-operation with the British Navy. The opportunity is now open to the Australian Nation to develop the Air Force as a national institution of primary importance.[15]

Nice try, but the RAN plodded on. Like two society belles down on their luck, *Australia* and *Canberra* did their best to keep up appearances through the Depression. In the early '30s, the naval year was divided into four cruises, as they were called, timed for the seasons. These were partly exercises in showing the flag to the taxpayers and civic worthies of the port cities, and partly an attempt to keep up some sort of naval efficiency and seagoing competence despite the hot breath of the financial cuts.

After a long and leisurely leave over Christmas, the Summer Cruise officially began in Tasmania. Everyone looked forward to the Pulling Regatta at North West Bay, south of Hobart, an event redolent of the nineteenth-century navy of Queen Victoria and taken very seriously, in which the ships' boats, pulled by the strongest oarsmen, competed for such glittering prizes as the Engine-Room Artificers' Whalers Cup and the Victory Cup for Officers' Gigs. Naturally, the Winter Cruise of a couple of months was spent very agreeably in tropical waters off Queensland, while the Spring Cruise invariably meant an annual visit to the Melbourne Cup in November, replete with coloured flags, sparkling brass, pomp and partying. There were drills and exercises sandwiched in between the partying, but the evidence suggests these schedules were arranged for the enjoyment of senior officers and their admiring guests, who, despite the bitter times, blithely regarded the navy as something of a gentleman's yacht club.

As the Depression deepened, the gulf between officers and men widened along fault lines of social class and status at odds with Australians' rose-coloured view of themselves as a people who, while deeply loyal to the Mother Country, had nonetheless freed themselves of its snobbery and pretensions. This divide was crystallised in the lingering use of the term 'lower deck',[16] a centuries-old and entirely accurate description of the spaces aboard ship where enlisted men lived, ate and slept, but which increasingly carried connotations of inferiority and subordination, them and us. As in the RN, there were Lower Deck Welfare Committees, officially sanctioned, as a channel for the men to air their wants or grievances, but higher authority seemed to honour their complaints and recommendations with lip service only. Officers were generically referred to as the 'Quarterdeck', a far posher place to be. Dress codes reinforced these perceptions. In harbour, the Officer of the Day was still required to turn out and parade up and down in a brass-buttoned, knee-length frock coat with an entirely redundant telescope tucked under his left arm.

Hard times or not, the naval gaiety whirred along ever faster. When Rear Admiral Edward Ratcliffe Garth Russell Evans RN relinquished command of the squadron in 1931 to return to Britain, he and his deliciously exotic Norwegian wife were farewelled in every state of the Commonwealth in a dazzling round of luncheons, dinners, parties, balls and receptions. Florid compliments were showered and even more lavishly returned. Unlike some of his kind before and after, Evans had been a popular figure in Australia and the navy, and deservedly so, for he was a competent and vigorous officer, a likeable man, and never a stuffed shirt.[17] He had been a gallant second-in-command of Robert Falcon Scott's disastrous expedition to the South Pole in 1910–13, and a hero of the RN's famous Dover Patrol in the Great War, when his destroyer, HMS *Broke*, trounced a force of German torpedo boats. Evans of the *Broke*, he was called forever after.

The climax of the farewells for this glamorous pair was an extraordinary party on board *Australia* in Sydney, where the quarterdeck was transformed into an Antarctic wonderland, and sailors hidden above the sparkling scene dropped fake snowflakes on the champagne-swilling guests and a fur-clad midshipman posing on a sled with a pair of huskies. The newspapers went into raptures:

> Not for a long time has there been such a brilliant function as when the Flag Captain and wardroom officers entertained in their honour. The lights of the Aurora Borealis played on snow and ice. In the background was a map of Australia outlined in flowers. Could any other setting have been more original? Mrs. Evans's fair and statuesque beauty was enhanced by a lovely powder blue lace and georgette frock. She carried a bouquet of mauve orchids. A painting by Allcot of the fleet entering Sydney Harbour was presented to them. There was some very lovely frocking, and a galaxy of beautiful girls. Our local peerage turned out in full regalia of diamonds and pearls. The glory of the harbour was flooded in moonlight, and lent enchantment to the sitting-out nooks.[18]

More extraordinary still, this frolic would not have been paid for by the navy but by contributions, voluntary or otherwise, from the pockets of *Australia*'s officers. It suggests a careless insensitivity at a time when the pay cuts for the lower deck were biting hard, and every sailor had family and friends battling for a crust and quite literally wondering where their next meal might come from.

The childish, even stupid behaviour of some officers aggravated the tensions. In his memoirs, Philip Jay, a leading seaman in *Australia*, described petty, bullying orders given by officers who took 'a fiendish delight in thinking up the most grotesque things for the lads to do'. They were pointless, demeaning and insulting. 'Officers' cook to flagship with fried egg' was one such effort: an egg had to be fried in double-quick time and then taken by boat for an inspection by the admiral. Another Jay recalled was 'Ship's Band to play Turkish National anthem'. Perhaps the most bizarre was 'Officers' stewards to Garden Island to bring back ten cats'. Jay recorded that the cats were wild and difficult to catch, and that the stewards returned badly scratched, with torn uniforms.[19] If these officers – some of them brass-hatted commanders and captains – were despised by their men, as quite a few were, they had only themselves to blame.

Sometimes, the lid blew off the pressure cooker. In August 1932, the navy was transfixed by the court martial of Petty Officer Edward Dickerson, a gunnery instructor in *Australia* charged with showing contempt to a superior officer. Dickerson was a man of 30 with 14 years' service behind him, competent, well liked and respected. He had been going through 4-inch gun drills with a group of junior sailors when he was pulled up and corrected on some point by a 17-year-old midshipman, Rendall Collins. Words were exchanged. At the court martial, held on board *Australia*, Collins alleged Dickerson had said to him, 'Fancy a little boy like you teaching me 4-inch gun drill.'

It was no doubt a serious contempt – if it had happened. Dickerson denied it and another petty officer called in his defence said he'd not heard anything like that. Commonsense suggests that Dickerson knew more about the gunnery business than some wet-behind-the-ears snotty – Collins had been a midshipman for not quite three months – but that was not the issue. For the court, it was a matter of upholding authority, however arbitrary and foolish, and of accepting the word of an officer, however junior, against the evidence of a sailor, however experienced. There would have to be an object lesson, a salutary example. Dickerson was found guilty, stripped of two good-conduct badges and disrated back to leading seaman, a humiliating punishment with its loss of the petty officer's brass-buttoned jacket and peaked cap. And a heavy loss of pay as well.

During those turbulent Depression years, senior officers and federal cabinet ministers were haunted by the worry that industrial strife in civilian life might infect the RAN and erupt into outright defiance. In the United Kingdom, there had been the horrible spectre of a serious mutiny in the RN in September 1931, when thousands of British sailors went on strike at Invergordon, on Cromarty Firth in Scotland. Protesting at pay cuts of up to 25 per cent, for four days they simply refused to take the Atlantic Fleet to sea. There was no violence but there was rebellion. In the battleship *Rodney*, a piano was dragged on deck and men gathered around it to sing 'The Red Flag', jeering at officers who tried to disperse them. In *Hood*, the flagship, there were threats of sabotage and desertion. Royal Marines, who could normally have been relied on to put down the troubles, joined the strikes and protests. The Invergordon Mutiny caused panic on the London Stock Exchange and a run on the pound sterling, eventually forcing the government to take the currency off the gold standard. Dozens of sailors were jailed and some 200 dismissed.

The RAN never reached that point, but in the spring of 1932 discontent with pay and conditions burst into the open. In October, *Australia* and *Canberra* went south for the now traditional visit for the Melbourne Cup, berthing at Princes Pier along with the seaplane carrier *Albatross* and the destroyer *Tattoo*. The race was run on Tuesday 1 November, won in sensational style by the chestnut stallion Peter Pan,[20] but the ships had arrived too late for liberty men to get to Flemington to see it, which irritated them. Nonetheless, the squadron stayed on for the customary spell of leave and socialising. A week later, the safety valve blew. On the night of Monday 7 November, a civilian found his way on board at least one of the ships and began distributing printed leaflets calling on the men to rise up. Newspaper reports suggest he was quickly discovered and marched back down the gangway.

But the next evening, Tuesday 8, some 200 sailors from the four ships met on the pier to protest at the cuts to their pay and allowances under the Financial Emergency Act, with some fiery speeches made. That appears to have been all that happened. After about an hour, wiser heads prevailed; leaders of the Lower Deck Welfare Committee apparently counselled the men to stick to the proper channels, and everyone returned on board. But word reached the government in Canberra. Federal cabinet met that evening and swiftly moved to hose things down. Pay for junior sailors would be increased by ten pence per day, the child allowance for family men would be lifted from £9 to £13 a year, and the ration allowance for men on leave would go up from one shilling and fourpence a day to two shillings and threepence.

The gathering on the pier was hushed up, but the Melbourne newspapers got wind of it and reporters in Canberra began putting prickly questions. On the Wednesday 9 November, the Defence Minister, Senator Sir George Pearce, dropped a bombshell in a statement to the Senate, which the newspapers splashed in big, black, three- and four-decked headlines:

SINISTER PLOT TO INCITE MUTINY IN THE NAVY ALLEGED IN SENATE.
False propaganda spread, says Minister
'Organiser boarded ships in Port Melbourne'
Fleet sails: No Trouble.[21]

Pearce was a former Labor politician who had drifted to the political right to become a leading light in Joe Lyons's United Australia Party. He spared no drama. There had been a dastardly and sinister conspiracy to foment trouble, he told the Senate. When the ships had been opened to the public in Melbourne, those behind the plot 'had seized the opportunity to circulate many hundreds of printed pamphlets suggesting that the men of the fleet should organise and join with their comrades ashore to bring about a strike or mutiny'.[22]

Worse, he said, he had received a letter 'which stated in effect that if the government refused to make certain concessions, the men would refuse duty'. On the letter was a picture hinting that armed force might be used. There was a drawing showing bluejackets armed with rifles and bayonets, with a sentence underneath suggesting mutiny.[23] Equally worrying, there had been some threatening but anonymous telephone calls to Vice Admiral Sir George Hyde, the government's senior professional adviser as First Naval Member of the Naval Board, who was told that the fleet would not leave Melbourne.

Pearce's statement predictably caused a sensation, quite eclipsing the news from America that Franklin Delano Roosevelt had been elected President of the United States. Curiously, though, officialdom attempted to play down the meeting on Princes Pier. Pearce claimed it had not happened, and, in a speech at the Lord Mayor's Dinner in the Melbourne Town Hall that evening, Hyde went further, calling it a 'damnable lie'. Pearce had not revealed exactly who or what was behind the conspiracy, leaving that hanging in the air unspoken, but Hyde did. He blamed the troubles on the Red Menace:

> While the ships have been in port during the last few days they have been flooded with seditious literature from the Communist headquarters, to seduce the men from their allegiance, and yesterday a determined attempt was made to prevent the ships going to sea. All I need say is that the ships went to sea this morning as arranged, with the exception of one man out of 2,000.[24]

The ships had indeed sailed, but there was one more alarm for the navy and the government. In Sydney that same morning, the crew of the small depot ship HMAS *Penguin* refused to answer the bugle call to fall in on deck at 8.15. A sub lieutenant found them sitting below in the mess decks and dressed for duty but was told that, unless their grievances were heard, they would not start work until nine o'clock. *Penguin*'s captain, evidently a sensible man, listened to their complaints about pay and allowances and said he would forward them to the Naval Board, promising there would be no retribution. Mollified, the men went back to work forthwith, although the captain himself was later rebuked by his superiors for his leniency.

There the matter might have rested but for a foolish reprisal from the Lyons government. Not content with exposing the dastardly conspiracy and seeing the threat of mutiny snuffed out, the cabinet decided to shoot the messenger. Early in November, before the Princes Pier meeting, the Melbourne edition of *Truth* newspaper, a popular muck-raking scandal sheet, had published a report of the unrest in the RAN under the headline, 'Navy issues strike ultimatum, will refuse duty unless pay cuts are revised.'[25]

Lurid though it was, the story was essentially accurate and undoubtedly a matter of public interest, but it left the government embarrassed, angry and seeking retribution. The Attorney-General, John Latham, a cold and sometimes vindictive King's Counsel, charged *Truth*'s Melbourne printer and publisher, John Payne, with having 'contrary to the Crimes Act . . . knowingly attempted to incite the lower deck ratings of ships of the Royal Australian Navy to commit an act of mutiny'.

Payne pleaded not guilty and with good reason, for he had not even seen the article before it was published, let alone written it. Nor did the story attempt to foment a mutiny – not at all. Pearce and Hyde were called to give evidence at the trial in Victoria's First Civil Court. A table of expensive silk argued back and forth. The judge summed up, fairly enough, and sent the jury of 12 men to consider its verdict. It took them just 18 minutes: not guilty. Exultant, the next edition of *Truth* railed against Latham's 'piffling prosecution' and his vicious attack on the freedom of the press, and demanded Pearce's sacking before 'some irreparable damage should result'.[26]

—

The easing of the Depression towards the end of 1932 brought some relief to the nation and prompted a cautious increase in spending for the navy. Japan's bloody invasion of Manchuria in September the previous year had rung alarm bells in Canberra, and the Lyons government welcomed a British offer for the loan of a flotilla of destroyers to augment the Australian Squadron. The destroyer leader *Stuart* and four V and W class destroyers, *Vampire*, *Vendetta*, *Voyager* and *Waterhen*, arrived in Sydney a few days before Christmas 1933, a welcome present. They were small ships, designed and launched towards the end of the Great War, nearing middle age when they joined the RAN. More importantly for the men who would crew them, they had been built for service in the North Sea and the North Atlantic, not for the tropics, and they could be fiendishly cramped and uncomfortable in summer. For all their faults, they were tough and enduring, and would go on to form the immortal Scrap Iron Flotilla – derided by the Nazis as an Australian 'consignment of junk' – that performed such heroic service in the Mediterranean in the early stages of the Second World War. At about the same time, the government announced that two sloops – ships similar to destroyers but a little smaller and slower – would be built at Cockatoo Island in Sydney, a useful boost for local industry and jobs. They were eventually commissioned as *Yarra* and *Swan*.

In 1934, the government announced a three-year program to expand Australia's defences, much of it centred on the RAN, with the decision to buy a modern new cruiser from Britain. The ship chosen was already building in the Swan Hunter yards at Wallsend-on-Tyne as HMS *Phaeton*, but in 1934 she was bought by the Australian Government and completed as HMAS *Sydney*, the second ship to bear the name. She was a modified Leander Class cruiser, an improvement on an earlier British design, at some 8000 tons a ship smaller than either *Australia* or *Canberra* and carrying eight 6-inch guns instead of their larger 8-inch, but slightly faster at around 32.5 knots. In 1935, John Collins, by now a commander, arrived on the Tyne to become her executive officer, the second-in-command.

New ships meant new people. Recruiting began again, slowly at first, with a target of 700 men to man the vessels. Some sailors who had left the navy during the Depression were invited to rejoin, including Cyril 'Mustard' Kean, who was newly married. He jumped at the chance to get into uniform again and back to sea at his old rate of stoker. Gradually, the RAN began to lift itself from the trough of the early '30s and to approach something like its old strength and energy.

Yet not all was sweetness and light. Sporadic acts of defiance occurred throughout the '30s, some of them actual sabotage. In August 1936, the newspapers were full of reports that firing locks had been removed from two of *Canberra*'s 4-inch anti-aircraft guns on passage from Sydney to Brisbane, with the police called in to investigate.[27] The word around the mess decks was that this had been an individual retaliation by a sailor who held a grudge against an officer, fair or otherwise. In any body of men confined as sailors necessarily are, there would always be the sour and rebellious individual, the bearer of hatreds real or imagined.

And sometimes there would be good, honest men who had been badly handled. In January 1937, just before the beginning of the traditional Summer Cruise, someone in *Australia* threw a cable jack[28] and some other deck equipment overboard, and again there were rumours in the newspapers suggesting the ships might not sail from Sydney. Trouble had been brewing in the squadron for a while over the iron obedience to regulations demanded by the current RN Rear Admiral in Command, Richard Lane-Poole, a severe and much-disliked figure universally known as Plain Fool.

More loathed still was his haughty wife, Sigrid, who regarded herself as an extra admiral and had been known to bark orders at sailors and officers. A delicious story doing the rounds claimed that *Sydney*'s captain had ordered her from his ship – 'There's your barge, madam' – after she had told him the quarterdeck awning was badly set.[29] It was Sigrid's habit to peer through binoculars at ships moored below her husband's official residence,

Tresco, at Elizabeth Bay, and inform him of breaches of uniform and other heinous crimes she spied. Men had been 'crimed' and heavily punished for such minor offences as wearing their caps at the wrong angle or for working stripped to the waist in hot weather – something they had always done.

In mid-February, newspapers around the country published a letter written by an anonymous young sailor in *Australia* to his parents:

> There has been a lot of sabotage going on. First one of the electric leads on a 4-inch gun was cut through. Next night one of the main electric light wires was cut. The following night one of the main telephone lines was cut. Then last night someone threw acid all over a turret superstructure of the fo'c'sle. The acid has eaten holes right through the paint up to the steel. Officers are trying to hush the business up.[30]

Plain Fool and the Defence Minister, Sir Archdale Parkhill, hurriedly issued the usual soothing statements claiming that all was well with morale in the navy, bar a few troublemakers, but this was a lie. Unhappiness festered. The ships did sail to Jervis Bay to begin the cruise, but there was more trouble to come when the men given shore leave were refused permission to use the swimming pool, tennis courts and golf course at the naval college. In fact, with the college still closed, its sporting facilities had been rented out to private interests and the navy had no control over them. But nobody had bothered to explain this to the men, who understood only that they could not get a swim after work on a hot February afternoon.

Anger at that was still seething when the able seaman who had thrown the gear overboard from *Australia* in Sydney was found out and sentenced to 89 days' detention in the notorious Garden Island Naval Prison, a much-feared institution known as 'The Corner'. That night, the falls[31] for one of *Australia*'s boats were cut – a traditional sailors' protest – and the captain was forced to order armed guards stationed around the upper deck, with all the ship's lights burning.

Officers suggested the next day that all would be well if everyone chipped in sixpence to pay for the damaged falls, but the men refused and instead took up a collection for their imprisoned shipmate, whose pay had been automatically stopped. They sent £12/10 to his wife and three young children. Not leaving well enough alone, the ship's commander singled out the sailor who had organised the collection, paraded him publicly on deck and threatened him with a charge of misconduct if he did it again. By now, the atmosphere in the cruiser was poisonous, and the men hit back once more. When *Australia*'s coxswain called for volunteers to man the ship's boats in the traditional pulling regatta scheduled for Hobart the next month, no one came forward. They had to be ordered to do it.

Yet despite these ructions and the headlines they caused, change for the better was quietly on the way for the RAN. For all the upsets and alarms, the great body of the navy's sailors was loyal to the service and the nation, unswayed by agitators and malcontents. The Australian sailor would stand up for his rights and his concepts of fairness, resolutely so and often to the discomfort of his superiors, but he was not interested in breaking the system, only improving it. And in the mid- to late '30s, the first graduates from the naval college were becoming commanders and captains. Australian-born and trained officers, now with 20 years' experience under their belts, were ready to command Australian ships and men, a shift at once both subtle and profound that would alter the character of the service forever.

It would be wrong and grossly unfair to suggest that every British officer or petty officer sent on loan to Australia was a fool or a martinet. Most were not. The RAN could not have grown without them, and they contributed much that was valuable and honourable. But a notable few were failures, and their inability to understand the psychology of the Australians they commanded caused a clash of the cultural gears. RN officers expected automatic respect and obedience, and would normally get it from British seamen. Australian sailors, from a more egalitarian culture, believed officers had to earn respect and would make life difficult for those they felt had failed to do so.

It would be equally wrong to suggest that all Australian officers were shining examples of inspiring leadership. There were duds there too, a leavening of incompetents and bullies. In his memoir, Philip Jay recounted a splendid trick played at the Flinders Naval Depot, where officers would ride the heavy bicycles of the day from place to place. Unpopular officers would find small knots of sailors positioned along their route, throwing textbook salutes as they puffed and pedalled past. There was no choice: the salutes had to be returned, again and again. The pay-off came when an officer saluted, wobbled and crashed from his bike to the ground.

But in the tide of time and the march of events, some fine Australian officers were coming to the fore: men of talent, decency and courage who took their profession seriously, who were ready for command, and whose ships' companies would follow them through hell or high water.

Chapter 5

HEARTS OF OAK ARE OUR SHIPS

Commander Harold Farncomb was out of his bunk and up early as he was each morning, but this day was special, an occasion requiring every scintilla of his legendary attention to detail. *Australia* was berthed at Dalgety's Wharf on the New Farm bend of the Brisbane River, awaiting the arrival of an exalted visitor. His Royal Highness Prince Henry, Duke of Gloucester and the third son of George V, was coming on board to take passage home to England after a triumphant tour of Australia. Farncomb, *Australia*'s executive officer, had the job of preparing the ship for his reception.

It was Monday 10 December 1934. The weather was not promising, with dark clouds over the city threatening a tropical summer storm, but there was nothing to be done about that. Rain or sun, the cruiser was to shine from stem to stern, and it was Farncomb's task, in the naval phrase, to make it so. There was a lot to do. *Australia* had been open to the public a few days before and some 12,000 people had turned up to climb on board, tramping all over the place, grubbying the deck, and smearing the paint and brass work. The ship's company had been hard at it to put things right. This early morning, Farncomb was already on deck, telescope under his arm, when the bugler roused the hands at six o'clock. The captains of the tops sorted their divisions and the divisional officers reported them ready, as the commander gave his orders to the Buffer, the Chief Bosun's Mate, who in turn barked them out so that all might hear. Within minutes, the pale teak of the upper deck was being swabbed, scrubbed and flogged dry within an inch of its life while small knots of sailors here and there touched up grey paint and white rope work, and burnished brass to a golden gleam.

The ceremony of Colours, the hallowed start to a naval day, was at eight o'clock, the changeover from the morning to the forenoon watch. At five minutes to eight, the preparative pennant was hoisted on *Australia*'s foremast, a long yellow flag with a green stripe. Then, on the stroke of eight itself, came the cry, 'Eight o'clock, sir!' and the ritual response from the Officer of the Day: 'Make it so!' All over the ship, above or below decks, the crew stood to attention as the Australian flag was raised at the jack-staff on the bow and the naval White Ensign at the stern, officers saluting. The ship's bell sounded eight times, in strokes of two – ting, ting – and then, with the job done, the bosun's pipe shrilled the traditional call for the 'Carry On'. This day, though, there was an additional touch: a festive string of coloured signal flags broke out from the mastheads to welcome the royal guest. So far, all was well.

Gloucester had been in Australia since early October on a ceremonial visit to mark the centenary of the state of Victoria and to open Melbourne's Shrine of Remembrance. His younger brother George, Duke of Kent, was to have done the honours but that was suddenly cancelled on some pretext or other – possibly because Kent was a notoriously unstable morphine and cocaine addict, not to mention a rampant bisexual whose lovers had included the society beauty and novelist Barbara Cartland[1] and, it was rumoured, Noël Coward. It might not have been wise to unleash him on the colonials. Gloucester took his place at the last minute, apparently reluctantly. The schedule called for him to spend an exhausting 22 days in Victoria, six days in Western Australia and South Australia each, two days in the Australian Capital Territory, five in Tasmania, 13 in New South Wales and nine in Queensland, with the usual frantic round of engagements in the summer heat that would have taxed the endurance of any sane person, English royal duke or not. A pamphlet put out in Adelaide to commemorate the visit distils the loyal fervour of the day:

> South Australia, a member of a great Commonwealth, joins with her sister States in extending to His Royal Highness the Duke of Gloucester a very hearty welcome.
>
> In the cattle country of the north stockmen have turned their horses out to graze, saddles and stock whips have been oiled and hung up.
>
> The station natives have left for their 'walk-about' and so to the hills to tell their tribesmen that the 'White fella boss all go down to see Big King's son.'
>
> In the farm houses scattered throughout the rich agricultural districts, the question of who is to stay home and tend the cows has long been debated; each and all are eager to journey citywards to catch a glimpse of our Royal Visitor. The town dweller watches with critical eye the erection and 'putting together' of the decorations, and readily gives vent to his feelings if any plan may not be in accordance with his idea of a royal and fitting welcome.
>
> The spirit prevails; the bond of affection between the Royal family and the people encircles the whole British Empire; we are proud to offer welcome to HRH the Duke of Gloucester.[2]

Those in the know gossiped to each other that Gloucester was drinking heavily – presumably to dull the endless repetitions of 'God Save the King' and the obsequious drone of speechifying dignitaries battling to outdo each other in fealty to King and Empire – but no hint of scandal leaked out. The only untoward moment came at a ball in a showground shed in Toowoomba, when a local fireman marched up to His Royal Highness and briskly commanded him, 'Put out that cigarette, Your Worship.' Startled, the Duke did as he was told. The local mayor rose in fury. In vain did the fireman protest that the timber building, festooned with paper bunting, was a firetrap and that he was only doing his job, as instructed. Foaming with rage, the mayor ordered the detachment of volunteer firemen from the building and proffered a quivering apology to his guest. It was, he told the newspapers afterwards, 'a monstrous incident, the like of which he had never heard before'. The most brilliant event in the history of the town had been ruined.

The Prince evidently managed to recover from this fright-fulness and, a few days later in Brisbane, he waved off the first flight of airmail from Australia to Britain, carried in *Diana*, a De Havilland biplane of Qantas Empire Airways, call sign VH-UJC, Captain Lester Brain at the controls. All Brisbane turned out – 250,000 people, according to the police:

> A dignified figure in a cavalcade of pomp and pageantry that struck an Imperial note, the Duke, his face browned with Queensland's sunshine, made a truly Royal progress through bannered streets that echoed with the crash of band music and the skirl of bagpipes, and in which cheering thousands formed living colonnades, so densely packed that they seemed a solidi-fied mass, vital and vivid with its pulsating loyalty, pouring forth with mighty voice its affection for the King's son.[3]

Through all the bustle on board *Australia*, her commanding officer, William MacLeod, remained aloof. That was the way the naval system worked, and had for centuries. In the eyes of both the British Admiralty and the Australian Naval Board – and ulti-mately the King himself – Captain MacLeod, a Scottish-born RN officer, would be held responsible for this royal voyage and its success or failure as may be. But it was the job of his execu-tive officer to carry out his orders, to present him with a going concern, a ship and a ship's company of some 700 men that were up to the task, in all respects ready. Farncomb had been appointed to *Australia* in April 1933, MacLeod two months later. After working with him for more than a year, the captain recog-nised that his second-in-command – Australian born and bred, and Australian trained – was a diligent and able officer. Matters were in good hands.

The rest of the forenoon watch passed with agonising slowness, the carefully chosen Royal Guard of sailors rehearsing drill with rifles and bayonets, the band of ship's musicians giving a final polish to their drums and brass. Exactly at noon, the bugle blared again for the entire crew to fall in at divisions, officers and men in fresh white uniforms. On schedule, the Duke's motorcade pulled up on the wharf at 12.30, HRH stepped forward in a white uniform of his own – some sort of Hussar outfit, people thought – and down came the rain. Torrentially so, and for the rest of the afternoon. Doggedly, everyone went through the courtesies: the shrill of bosun's pipes, the Duke bounding up the gangway to be met by Captain MacLeod, the guard crunching to the Present Arms, the Royal Standard broken at the mainmast the moment the royal foot touched the deck. In truth, it was a sodden mess, everyone drenched to the skin and glad to get it done with. Without further ado, *Australia* sailed for New Zealand at 12 minutes past one.

The next day brought perfect sunshine and another attempt at the ducal formalities, this time out in the Tasman Sea. It went off perfectly. The band in its red-and-blue uniforms played 'God Save the King', a royal salute banged out, and the ship's company marched past the Prince on the quarterdeck to 'Waltzing Matilda' and that grand old RN anthem 'Heart of Oak':

> Heart of Oak are our ships,
> Jolly Tars are our men,
> We always are ready: Steady, boys, Steady!
> We'll fight and we'll conquer again and again.[4]

All done, the Duke wrote a note to Captain MacLeod, asking him, 'Please tell the Officers and Ship's Company how pleased I was at their appearance this morning and that I am proud to be their shipmate. Henry.' Perhaps they were proud in return, perhaps not. The journey to Portsmouth – a stately royal progress via Britain's Pacific possessions and through the Panama Canal to the Atlantic – would take three long months.

—

Harold Bruce Farncomb was born in North Sydney in 1899 and raised at what was then the semi-rural outer suburb of Gordon on Sydney's North Shore, where farms and orchards spilt away from the railway line on the ridge. His father was an accountant, comfortably middle class, with a family of three children. Harold was sent to Gordon State Public School, a sandstone colonial pile in the Gothic Revival style, and then briefly to Sydney Boys' High before entering the RANC in that first intake of 1913, the same term as John Collins.

Young Harold got his colours for cricket at the college and in his final year won the Grand Aggregate Prize – top marks – to be promoted midshipman on New Year's Day 1917. His career then took the traditional path as a snotty in the gunroom of a battleship of the RN's Grand Fleet, HMS *Royal Sovereign*. Like his contemporaries from Jervis Bay, though, he saw no action before the end of the war. The post-war years were slow at first, some spent on the Whale Island gunnery course and the like, some at sea in the Australian destroyer *Stalwart*, and back and forth again to the RN, first for a spell as a staff officer in the Mediterranean Fleet, and then in the Atlantic Fleet in the battlecruiser *Repulse*.

He married Jean Nott in 1927 at a Congregational church at Strathfield in Sydney. She went with him to London again, where, as a relatively junior lieutenant commander at the age of 31, he found himself in a class full of captains and above on a year-long course at the Imperial Defence College. This must have been a vote of confidence in his abilities but also, according to a biographer,[5] an economy measure because it was cheaper to send him than a more senior officer. That may or may not be accurate – there was no Australian-born and -trained officer senior to him to send. In 1932, he gained the brass hat of a commander on the last day of June, the same day as John Collins, the two of them equal first of their term to reach the rank.

They were quite different men – Collins sociable and outgoing; Farncomb studious and austere – but their naval careers would run almost in parallel, one occasionally leapfrogging the other with a promotion or an appointment. The many surviving photographs and a few official oil portraits of each man might be instructive. John is often seen smiling or at least relaxed, while Harold invariably appears dour and aloof, as if he had loftier things to do with his time than pose for a lens or a paintbrush. Some in the navy would come to think of Collins as just a little too keen for personal publicity when a sober reticence was the done thing for a naval officer. Others found Farncomb prickly and overbearing, taciturn and difficult to work for; there was a legendary tale of him as the commander in *Australia* seeing his wife standing in a ship's boat and bellowing at her from the quarterdeck to sit down, as if she were some gormless midshipman.

At this stage of their careers, though – 1935 – John Collins had taken one great stride that Harold Farncomb had yet to match. He had commanded a ship, the destroyer HMAS *Anzac*, in 1930. Farncomb's turn would come soon enough.

—

A heavy fog descended on *Australia* on her last night at sea, one of those pea-soupers in the English Channel that could put even the most experienced mariner on edge. Captain MacLeod slowed the ship to a crawl and doubled the lookouts. There was nothing for it: their arrival in Portsmouth would be delayed.

It was 27 March, a Wednesday. The voyage from Brisbane had taken 16 long weeks, with wearisome official calls in New Zealand, Fiji, British Samoa and Kingston, Jamaica. There had been some excitement north of Tahiti in early February, when *Australia* had gone to the aid of a schooner battered by a hurricane, the *Seth Parker*, skippered by a famous American radio personality, Phillips Lord. But the rest of the trip passed quietly, the cruiser gleaming like a new pin, the hands always in spotless uniform.

For all that time, the Prince had to be entertained socially in a manner befitting royalty. Both MacLeod and Farncomb were quietly happy to hand this duty to two of the ship's engineer officers, who unearthed hidden talents for writing and performing amusing ditties, accompanied by a third engineer lieutenant on the wardroom piano. At each port of call, there had to be all the rigmarole of royal honours and courtesies, a business that certainly became more practised but more tedious with it, to be born stoically by them all, including Gloucester himself, who could barely go to breakfast without a guard crunching to attention and a band striking up.

Now, at last, it was over. Gradually, the fog lifted, and the next morning they were able to put on speed again for the approach to Portsmouth. Four destroyers came spanking out from behind the Isle of Wight – *Amazon*, *Ambuscade*, *Sabre* and *Saladin* – to escort them into the Solent, and a flight of flying boats dipped low overhead. Just before one o'clock that afternoon, 28 March 1935, *Australia* secured at the South Railway Jetty, the customary royal landing place in Portsmouth Harbour.

Two more princes came on board to greet their brother: the Prince of Wales and the Duke of York. More ritual, more ceremony. But within an hour or so, they had gone, leaving the ship alone at last. And with that came leave, an exciting prospect for the entire crew, half of whom were newly trained recruits who had never even been to sea until they left Brisbane; now here they were at that storied place many Australians still called the home country. There was an official welcome in the capital of empire, where the ship's company marched through the streets from London Bridge to a luncheon given by the Lord Mayor at Guildhall – officers in the ancient hall itself; sailors separately in the crypt below – and the visiting Australian Attorney-General, Mr Robert Menzies, made a florid speech about freedom and the Anglo-Saxon values. Later, both Captain MacLeod and Commander Farncomb were made officers of the Royal Victorian Order, a princely recognition of services rendered.

Then it was back to work. *Australia* was now under Admiralty orders, to spend 15 months on exchange with the RN – which, in turn, had sent the cruiser HMS *Sussex* to Australia. From her previous existence as flagship of a small squadron Down Under, a big fish in a small pond, she would join Britain's Mediterranean

Fleet, no less, to become part of a mighty array of battleships, an aircraft carrier, cruisers heavy and light, and literally dozens of destroyers, an armada of pomp and power securing the sea road to the empire and the Far East.

—

Australia was at sea in the Atlantic that northern summer of 1935 when decisions were taken in London that would set her, and the world, on a course to war.

In June, Britain and Nazi Germany began talks at the British Foreign Office on the relative size of their navies. On the opening day, the German negotiator, that former champagne salesman and Hitler toady Joachim von Ribbentrop, demanded that Germany should have the right to a fleet 35 per cent the size of the RN. Amply confirming the British perception of Germans as arrogant bullies, he blustered that this figure was not negotiable, it was 'fixed and unalterable', he would accept no less, he would fly home immediately if Britain would not accept it. Startled and offended, the Foreign Secretary, Sir John Simon, withdrew to consider. The next day, the British caved in. As Simon recommended to the cabinet:

> We should accept this offer of Herr Hitler's while it is still open . . . If we now refuse to accept the offer for the purposes of these discussions, Herr Hitler will withdraw the offer and Germany will seek to build to a higher level than 35 per cent . . . Having regard to past history and to Germany's known capacity to become a serious naval rival of this country, we may have cause to regret it if we fail to take this chance . . .[6]

The cabinet agreed. The Anglo-German Naval Agreement was signed on 18 June. Most startling of all, it gave Germany the right to build 45 per cent of the British tonnage of submarines and – in the event of some unspecified crisis – up to 100 per cent. This was extraordinary, almost inexplicable. The Kaiser's U-boats had demonstrated their potential during the Great War, wreaking havoc on British shipping. In 1914, one single boat,

U-9, sank three British cruisers in the North Sea in the space of just an hour, with the loss of 1500 men. In total, with the arrival of unrestricted submarine warfare, they destroyed some 5000 British and Allied ships, of almost 13 million tons. Yet this new treaty would allow Germany to build a new U-boat fleet from scratch, composed of the latest vessels.

Adolf Hitler, informed of Ribbentrop's triumph, proclaimed it the happiest day of his life.[7] He had been German Chancellor only since 1933. By bluff and blackmail, he had now demolished a crucial pillar of the humiliating Versailles Treaty forced on Germany in 1919. It was a diplomatic victory that would whet his appetite for more of the same and lead Western Europe down the disastrous road of appeasement. In fact, Germany had already begun building U-boats before the treaty was signed. Naval construction would still have a lower priority than tanks for the army and aircraft for Hermann Goering's newly reformed *Luftwaffe*, but the shipyards in Bremen and Hamburg, Kiel and Wilhelmshaven began working up to full capacity.

The French were livid, for it meant that Germany could have a navy the size of theirs. They had not been informed of the talks and they argued, quite correctly, that Britain – and still less the Germans – had no right to unilaterally alter Versailles. It might not have helped, either, that the agreement was signed on the exact date that the Duke of Wellington's French and Prussian armies had defeated Napoleon Bonaparte at Waterloo.

But too late. The British cheered themselves with the thought that Germany could not possibly build up to 35 per cent until at least 1942, if then. And anyway, if it came to war, the RN could easily defeat a fleet that size. So they settled back and got on with the Season, that whirl of social and sporting events on the summer calendar: racing at Royal Ascot, blazers and boaters for the regatta at Henley-on-Thames, the newly opened opera at Glyndebourne, and Wimbledon, where the British champion Fred Perry stood every chance of repeating his Men's Singles success of the year before.[8] This year, there would be extra glamour: dazzling celebrations for the Jubilee, George V's 25 years on the throne, to be crowned by a great naval review at Spithead.

The fleet gathered. On 16 July, *Australia* took her place in a pageant of 160 warships strung out in the Solent to the horizon, her crew lining the upper deck and cheering lustily as the King passed down the long grey lines in the royal yacht *Victoria and Albert*. 'The Prince of Wales, Duke of York and Duke of Kent all came aboard to see their brother, the Duke of Gloucester who had come aboard earlier – another great compliment to us,' wrote Midshipman Bill Cook. 'We illuminated ship and at night with flares, rockets, fireworks etc, the Solent was transformed . . . it was all beyond description.'[9]

The next few weeks for the Australians were rather more down to earth, but a landmark nonetheless. In the No. 3 Basin at the Portsmouth Naval Dockyard, workmen fitted *Australia* with an aircraft catapult, a steel contraption mounted behind her rearmost funnel that would launch a small seaplane for reconnaissance work and perhaps the occasional light bombing mission. Both *Australia* and *Canberra* had carried aircraft before this – the British Seagull III, a boxy little wooden biplane flown for the RAN by the RAAF's 101 Fleet Co-operation Flight and which had been used in trailblazing aerial surveys of the Great Barrier Reef. But, without a catapult, the Seagulls had to be lowered to the water by crane, and their light timber hulls and flimsy wings were easily damaged, to the point where the air force became reluctant to let the navy have them.

In 1929, the RAAF asked the British Supermarine company to produce a stronger, tougher aircraft. It came up with the radical new Seagull V, designed by one R. J. Mitchell, who would later create the immortal Spitfire of Battle of Britain fame. The Seagull V, also a biplane, had a hull of light aluminium alloy, an enclosed cockpit for the crew of three, folding wings for shipboard stowage, a retracting undercarriage for use on land, and a 680-horsepower Pegasus radial engine with a rear-facing propeller that pushed it rather than pulled it through the air at around

215 kilometres per hour. The airframe was designed to withstand the shock of a catapult launch.

This was a great leap forward from an entirely Australian initiative. At the Hendon Air Show in 1933, Supermarine's chief test pilot, Joseph 'Mutt' Summers, caused a sensation when he flung the stubby little aircraft around the sky like a fighter, finishing with a soaring loop that astonished even Mitchell. Suddenly, the RN and the RAF were interested – very much so – and the Seagull V went into production. The RAAF ordered 24 of them (the British called them the Walrus), at a cost of £345,000, and the first of these, number A2–1, was assigned to *Australia*, to be delivered at Portsmouth.[10]

On Monday 9 September, the cruiser edged away from the dockyard and anchored out in the Solent. The catapult would have its first test, not with an aircraft but with two loads of timber of about the same weight, 3000 kilograms. The excitement was intense, the hands off watch crowding every vantage point on deck. On the order from the bridge, the catapult's cordite charge was fired with a deafening bang and a cloud of smoke, and the first wooden lump hurtled into the air, satisfactorily clearing the catapult cradle – to rousing cheers – and plunging into the sea. The second followed soon afterwards, with equal success.

A2–1 arrived from the Supermarine factory at nearby Southampton early the next day. She touched down in plumes of spray, taxied alongside, and was quickly hoisted into place on board. With engine roaring, the little aircraft quivered on the catapult until another tremendous explosion rocketed her forward and into the air, where she dipped just a little before she soared skyward in triumph. Over the next couple of days, there were more trial launches, this time with *Australia* underway at sea, and all of them were adjudged a success. On 12 September, the ship sailed, the Seagull proudly aboard, to join the RN's First Cruiser Squadron based in the ancient Egyptian port of Alexandria in the eastern Mediterranean.

—

Enter Il Duce. Obsessed by the glories of Ancient Rome and casting himself as the new Caesar who would restore them, the Italian dictator Benito Mussolini hurled the *Regio Esercito* and the *Regia Aeronautica*, the army and air force of Fascist Italy, into the conquest of an empire in Africa.

At promptly 5 am on Thursday 3 October 1935, the Italians swarmed in their hundreds of thousands into the East African state now known as Ethiopia but then as the Abyssinian Empire. It was brutal, obscene. Employing all the arts and science of modern warfare against a ragged army of tribesmen – many armed only with spears – they ravaged all before them. The figures are elastic, but in the brief duration of this grotesquely unequal war, Italy employed some 100,000 ground troops, 500 fighter and bomber aircraft, and perhaps 800 tanks against an Ethiopian defence that could field just three obsolete French biplane fighters and three creaking tanks of Great War vintage. Leaving nothing to chance, the lavishly gold-braided and fiercely moustachioed Pietro Badoglio, a Marshal of Italy, sought and received permission from Mussolini to use poison gas in bombs and artillery shells against both soldiers and civilians, annihilating entire villages.

The League of Nations, formed to prevent exactly this kind of atrocity, dithered and did nothing. Fixed in its policy of isolationism, the United States wrung its hands and also did nothing. For a fleeting moment, it seemed that Britain might take a stand, and the Mediterranean Fleet was put on alert for a possible attack on the Italian Navy. At Alexandria, *Australia* received secret orders to prepare to join the covering force for an air strike by the carrier HMS *Glorious* at the Italian Navy base at Taranto. But that also came to naught. Britain, too, turned away.[11]

So did France, the other major European democracy. Both wanted Italy's support or at least neutrality in any war against Germany and were not going to let some unpleasantness in a piddling African country stand in the way. As the fighting raged that December, the British Foreign Secretary, Sir Samuel Hoare,

and the French Prime Minister, Pierre Laval, the future Nazi
collaborator, cobbled together a shameless sell-out – the Hoare–
Laval Pact – that essentially offered Italy a free hand to crush
Abyssinia. When the details leaked out, the public outrage in
each country was so hot that the pact was hurriedly abandoned,
but it hardly mattered. Mussolini had won. Strutting his triumph
on the balcony of the Palazzo Venezia in Rome, Il Duce bragged
to the exulting crowds below:

> All knots have been severed by our resplendent sword, and this
> African victory remains intact and pure in the history of our
> Fatherland . . . the people of Italy with their blood have created
> the empire. It will be nourished with their labour and defended
> against anyone with their arms. With these supreme assurances,
> lift on high, legionaries, your standards, your steel and your
> hearts. Salute after fifteen centuries, the reappearance of the
> Empire on the fatal hills of Rome.[12]

With the easing of this now near-forgotten crisis, *Australia*
returned to the daily routine of the cruiser squadron. Christmas was at Alexandria, celebrated in the traditional way with the
officers serving dinner to the hands and a 'Stupendous Pantomime' attended on the first night by the squadron commander,
Rear Admiral Max Horton, a celebrated submarine ace of the
Great War. Horton sat well with the Australians. Over their
months in the Med, he put them through a vigorous round of
drills, trials, shoots and squadron exercises, day and night, almost
to the point of exhaustion at times, but they knew him as a man
who judged a ship by results, not spit and polish.[13]

There was time for recreation. *Australia*'s rugby team
conquered all, beating a team from the battleship *Queen
Elizabeth* 27–0, and another from the battleship *Valiant* 32–0, and
there were some pleasing triumphs in water polo, sailing races
and fleet rowing regattas. They met the Mediterranean in all its
moods: the thunderstorms that would suddenly boil down from
the French Alps; the gritty, choking dust storms out of Africa; or
the limpid days of summer heat when they welcomed the pipe of

'Hands to Bathe' and dived overboard into the Aegean or the Adriatic.

The newly acquired light cruiser *Sydney* joined them on a pilgrimage to Anzac Cove that April, where they were generously welcomed by the Turks. To their solemn surprise, relics of that most bitter affair were still strewn about the Gallipoli battlefields, the sight at Shrapnel Gully recorded in a story by Lieutenant Commander Walter Rands, from Dee Why in Sydney, one of the engineer officers who had kept the Duke of Gloucester amused:

> I looked about me wonderingly. I had wandered away from the stream, and now stood at the foot of a steep slope. This scrub grew on every side, and the slanting sunlight coming through the leaves made all the air seem green. It was intensely still.
>
> A bird flew swiftly through the trees and was gone – silently. Then I looked and saw it . . . a skull and a few poor bones – clean and white and shining in the grass; and close beside the bones a broken bayonet.[14]

This mostly energetic, sometimes idyllic existence came to an end in July. Time to go home. On Monday 13, *Australia* slipped her mooring in Alexandria and, with *Sydney* in company, headed to sea. With her band parading on her quarterdeck, she was cheered by the ships of the fleet as she passed each one. Max Horton sent a gracious signal of farewell:

> I watch with the deepest regret the departure from my squadron of a ship that has proved herself under all conditions such a source of strength, so efficient and well conducted. I wish everyone on board *Australia* good luck and great happiness in a well-earned leave to come, as well as in their future careers.[15]

They passed between the Heads at Sydney on Tuesday 11 August 1936, home after nearly 20 months away.

—

At Sandringham, George V's private estate in Norfolk, the Royal
Physician, Lord Dawson, issued a terse but elegant bulletin for
the newspapers on the evening of 20 January 1936. 'The King's
life is moving peacefully to its close,' it read. Then, just before
midnight, Dawson killed his unconscious sovereign by adminis-
tering shots of morphine and cocaine to ensure – as he frankly
admitted in his diary – that the announcement of the death could
appear in *The Times* rather than 'the less appropriate' evening
newspapers.

Australians were genuinely saddened by the loss. Twelve
months later, on 11 December, as 1936 was drawing less than
peacefully to its close, they were shocked and dismayed by rather
different royal news: the tumultuous abdication of George's son
and heir, Edward VIII, who abandoned kingship to marry the
American divorcee and adventuress Wallis Simpson. As Prince of
Wales, Edward's dalliance with Simpson had made the American
and European gossip columns, but the empire's press proprie-
tors had agreed as one that this awfulness would not stain their
august pages. Eventually, it got out.

In Sydney – 'one of the main focal points of the Empire' –
people gathered at the GPO to hear the announcement of the
abdication. In Melbourne, a small group at the Town Hall burst
into 'God Save the King': 'Men, including the policemen, stood
to attention and hats were removed.'[16] There was uproar in
parliament in Canberra when the Labor loudmouth from East
Sydney, Eddie Ward, shouted – with a depth of scorn matched
only by sheer ignorance – that Edward had been forced from
the throne because 'he would not act the part of a mouthpiece
of British Imperialism'.[17] The next in line, the Duke of York,
who had opened the Australian Parliament in 1928, became
George VI.

These two royal happenings bookended a year in which
the known world for Australians shifted with unnerving force.
Emboldened by his naval agreement with Britain, on 7 March
1936 Adolf Hitler demolished yet another pillar of Versailles by
sending a small force of troops to reoccupy the Rhineland – his

first, tentative step of military aggression. Again it paid off. The British either shrugged or wrung their hands, and the French stamped their feet and shouted a lot, but neither side was willing to risk a new war by moving to reclaim the territory.

Britain was more concerned that month with a new conference of the world's naval powers called in London to limit the growth of navies and the size of their biggest ships. The talks had been under way since December, although there was a rude reverse in January when the Japanese abruptly withdrew in the belief – entirely accurate – that Britain and the United States were intent on keeping them an inferior naval power. Mussolini's Italy also walked out, and Germany, of course, was not present. The Second London Naval Treaty was signed by Britain, France and the United States on 25 March, limiting the size of battleships to 35,000 tons and 14-inch guns, submarines to 2000 tons, and banning unrestricted submarine warfare.

No longer shackled to this or any other agreement, the IJN hurled itself into a frenzy of design and construction, with new battleships, aircraft carriers and destroyers moving from the drawing board to the shipyards at ever increasing speed. The training of fighter and bomber pilots for aircraft carriers went into high gear, and Japanese scientists perfected the development of the oxygen-powered Long Lance torpedo, a weapon which, delivered either from the sea or the air, had a range and speed far and away superior to anything the Americans or British had to offer. The traitor Lord Sempill, still on the payroll of the Japanese embassy in London, continued to betray his country.

Little of this energetic preparation for war was known at the time, but Australia erupted in anger in early 1936 when the newspapers discovered a book by a Japanese naval officer advocating a pre-emptive attack on the empire, including an invasion of Australia. With admirable brevity and candour, this prescient work was called *Japan Must Fight Britain*, and its author, Lieutenant Commander Tota Ishimaru, a reserve officer, laid out a visionary scenario. Attempts to curb Japan's rightful mission of expansion in the Pacific would have to be crushed by force.

Britain, he wrote, 'sees Japan capturing her colonial markets including the Australasian, and naturally she waves an anti-Japanese flag as her possessions are being devoured like mulberry leaves by silkworms'.

He pictured Singapore – 'an insult to the Japanese' – devoid of warships and ripe to be plucked, along with Hong Kong and India. Then would come the invasion of Australia, which, he thought, would require some 30 to 40,000 troops landing in Sydney and Melbourne.

Helpfully precise, Ishimaru foresaw an attack on 9 September 1936 in which a Japanese squadron of three cruisers and an aircraft carrier would appear off Darwin and bombard the town from the air and the sea, sending a 'shudder of fear throughout Australia'. Derby, too, would be bombed. 'Australia's lamentations will be the louder because she unlawfully expelled the Japanese and contemplated greedy enjoyment of a dream of ample clothes and warm food in a land rich in heaven's bounty,' he crowed.[18]

Ishimaru's remarkable crystal ball was headline news for almost a month throughout Australia in even the smallest country newspaper, prompting a barrage of editorials and letters to editors. It had confirmed the worst fears of a nation that saw itself as a citadel of white civilisation menaced by hordes of the Yellow Peril to the north. The shock waves reverberated to Tokyo, where a debate in the Diet solemnly deplored Ishimaru's irresponsible nonsense and the Foreign Minister, Hachiro Arita, smoothly assured an Australian journalist that the author was 'discredited and not taken any notice of in Japan'.[19] The Japanese people wished to live in peace. Laws would be passed to ban these disgraceful scribblings.

By the middle of 1936, great and terrible events piled upon each other, sweeping onwards. On 17 July, a *coup d'état* in Spain by right-wing Catholic and Fascist 'Nationalist' forces against the democratically elected Republican government plunged the country into a savage civil war. Even as it despatched military assistance to the Nationalists, Germany welcomed the world to the Berlin Olympic Games. Hitler, not interested in sports, had shown little enthusiasm for the games at first, but he was convinced by his propaganda chief, Joseph Goebbels, that they would be a showcase for National Socialism. So they were. The signs banning Jews from Berlin were swept away and the city was swathed in red, white and black swastika banners. The opening ceremony on 1 August was a Nazi perversion of the Olympic ideal, an orgy of triumphalist vulgarity where an ecstatic crowd of 100,000 sang the Brownshirt stormtrooper anthem the '*Horst Wessel Lied*', and the Olympic flame – the Germans invented the torch relay for these games – was borne into the *Olympiastadion* by a suitably blond Aryan god. A serene Führer was greeted with the Nazi salute by the German and Austrian athletes, and, shamefully, by the French team as well. An advance guard of the Nazi Condor Legion arrived in Spain the same day.

The civil war raged across the Iberian peninsula, the attention of the world captured by the ferocity of the fighting and the atrocities mounting on both sides, but it was not the only conflict on the planet. In China, the Japanese were cementing their hold on the puppet state they called Manchukuo, where they would act with breathtaking barbarity.

Gratified by the success of the Olympics, Hitler turned his attention again to diplomacy with a skilful wooing of his fellow dictator Benito Mussolini, whose Foreign Minister and son-in-law Count Galeazzo Ciano – Il Ducellino – was duchessed in October at the Führer's alpine retreat at Berchtesgaden. That resulted in an agreement of 'friendship' and mutual interest, the Rome–Berlin Axis. Branching out in another direction, on 25 November Hitler swallowed his racist prejudices and drew Japan into the Anti-Comintern Pact, ostensibly to contain the advance of Communism but secretly to give both countries a free hand in any war with the Soviet Union.

In all, 1936 had been a splendid year for the former Austrian corporal and unemployed postcard painter, one of unalloyed success. He now bestrode Germany unchallenged, and much of the outside world saw him as a statesman – even a genius, some thought – who would keep the peace in Europe. David Lloyd George, the British Prime Minister at the end of the Great War, visited Hitler in Berchtesgaden that autumn, fell for his wily charm, and returned to London blathering about the German 'miracle' and proclaiming in the *Daily Express* that he had met 'a born leader of men . . . A magnetic, dynamic personality with a single-minded purpose, a resolute will and a dauntless heart . . . the George Washington of Germany'.[20]

Thus was the matrix set for the closing years of the dismal '30s, the inexorable descent into the abyss. German and Japanese rearmament rolled ever forward. Japan embarked on the conquest of the rest of a weak and divided China, opening the account with the Rape of Nanking in 1937, in which at least 40,000 and perhaps as many as 300,000 Chinese were massacred. The Nazis, dextrously juggling diplomacy in one hand and the sword in the other, set about their domination of Europe, in the annexation of Austria, the crushing of Czechoslovakia beneath the jackboot, the orgy of anti-Semitic violence and murder of *Kristallnacht* in 1938, and the Pact of Steel agreed by Hitler and Mussolini in 1939.

In a speech to an adoring Reichstag in April 1939, after a torrent of ridicule directed at President Roosevelt, Hitler announced he was abandoning the Anglo-German Naval Agreement. As well he might. The battleships *Bismarck* and *Tirpitz* were rising on the stocks; at over 40,000 tons each, they were well beyond the treaty limit. Most stunning of all was the bottomless duplicity of the Molotov–Ribbentrop Pact agreed between Nazi Germany and the Soviet Union in August 1939, with its secret carve-up of Eastern Europe that allowed Hitler to invade Poland without fear of Russian intervention.

Buffeted by this tumult, Britain and France remained impotent, trapped in the tangled web of appeasement. At the age of 70, the British Prime Minister Neville Chamberlain had never been in an aircraft, but he dutifully found the nerve to fly to meet Hitler three times, at Berchtesgaden, Godesburg and finally at Munich. The Führer toyed with him, cat and mouse.

When this elderly, desiccated, quavering figure with his furled umbrella returned from his travels with a scrap of paper promising 'peace for our time' – Chamberlain's capitulation at Munich and the abandonment of the Czechs – Winston Churchill was prompted to rumble, from the backbench of the House of Commons, 'England has been offered a choice between war and shame. She has chosen shame, and will get war.'

The United States, committed to isolationism and a refusal to become entangled ever again in a European conflict, turned its concerned gaze instead to the rising sun of Japan in East Asia and the Pacific.

—

Australians learnt of these faraway alarms and crises in their newspapers and in the newsreels at the movie theatres, which were increasingly studded with film of marching battalions, rolling tanks and swooping bomber aircraft, both in Europe and in China. Distant though these happenings were, they were ominous developments for a nation that had lost the flower of its young men just 20 years before.

After the coronation of George VI in May 1937, there was an Imperial Conference in London, a gathering of the Prime Ministers of the Empire, where the Australian delegation, led by Joe Lyons, put a list of anxious questions to the British defence chiefs for their professional assessment. These questions all focused on the threat from Japan: what Britain was doing to meet that threat; and what might happen in the event of war with Japan, most especially if Britain found herself simultaneously at war with Germany in Europe. Would it still be Main Fleet to Singapore and, if so, how long would it take to get there? The British Chiefs of Staff offered long and soothing replies:

> the strength of the fleet for the Far East, and the time within which it would reach Singapore, must be variable factors, dependent both upon naval and political considerations. Nevertheless, the basis of our strategy will lie in establishing at Singapore, at the earliest possible moment after the outbreak of hostilities

with Japan, a fleet whose strength, as a minimum, will enable it to act on the defensive and to serve as a strong deterrent against any threats to our interests in the Far East.[21]

And what were the chances of a Japanese invasion of Australia, Lyons wanted to know. Again, the replies were encouraging:

Japan, from the strategical point of view, would be unjustified in committing large military and air forces to such an operation unless the British Fleet had first been defeated and largely destroyed . . .

   With the naval forces of the British Empire at their present strength, and maintained in the future . . . His Majesty's Government in Australia need not regard the danger of invasion as a real one.[22]

Lyons returned home confident of the Mother Country's commitment to the defence of Australia, only to find just weeks later – on 7 July 1937 – that Japan had launched its full-scale invasion of China. In a speech to parliament in August, Lyons laid down the government's belief that the RAN would be first to meet an enemy:

The first line of security against invasion is naval defence, with the army and air force supplementing and cooperating. If the enemy attempts aggression and must be resisted, it is far preferable to fight him away from our shores than when he is seeking to land on our coasts or has actually established himself in our territory . . .[23]

Defence spending was increased, with the lion's share of the money going to the navy. *Australia* was taken out of commission and sent to Sydney's Cockatoo Island for a long refit to modernise her. She was given an additional belt of armour along her sides abreast the engine and boiler rooms to shield them from torpedo attack; and her 4-inch high angle mounts were beefed up with twin guns instead of singles, effectively doubling her anti-aircraft defence, and were relocated on the main deck. Newer light machine guns were added as well, and she was given a bigger bridge structure and a new director tower and main rangefinder for gunnery control. They were big and important improvements but they took time. The work was still being finished when war broke out in 1939.

At the urging of the Naval Board, the government also decided to acquire another two 6-inch light cruisers, sister ships to the new *Sydney*. HMAS *Hobart* arrived in Australia towards the end of 1938, and the third ship, HMAS *Perth*, heard the declaration of war in the Caribbean on the way to her new home. *Perth*'s first captain was Harold Farncomb, who had leapfrogged his term mate John Collins to be the first graduate of the naval college to command a cruiser. Collins would be given command of *Sydney* three months later.

Fear of Japan, though, continued to gnaw at the Australian Government, which sought constant reassurance from Britain. And it was given. On 20 March 1939, the British Prime Minister, Neville Chamberlain, personally cabled to Lyons:

> In the event of war with Germany and Italy, should Japan join in against us it would still be His Majesty's Government's full intention to despatch a fleet to Singapore. If we were fighting against such a combination never envisaged in our earlier plans, the size of that fleet would necessarily be dependent on (a) the moment when Japan entered the war and (b) what losses if any our opponents or ourselves had previously sustained.
>
> It would, however, be our intention to achieve three main objects:
>   (i)   the prevention of any major operation against Australia, New Zealand or India;
>   (ii) to keep open our sea communications;
>   (iii) to prevent the fall of Singapore.[24]

But, by this time, the Admiralty was having its doubts. Very grave doubts. In May 1939 – spring in the northern hemisphere – it sent a top-secret mission for talks with the USN in Washington. It met the most senior Americans – the Chief of Naval Operations, Admiral William Leahy, and his Head of Plans, Rear Admiral

Robert Ghormley – to put to them a most difficult problem and a tentative request.

The Americans were told that if the RN found itself at war with Germany in the Atlantic and the Mediterranean, it might not be possible to send a fleet, or any significant part of one, to the defence of Singapore and the Far East. If that situation arose, the British asked, would the United States be prepared to step into the breach? Would the USN undertake to hold the line in the Western Pacific and Asian waters against any Japanese aggression?

The American reply was polite but non-committal. Of course, if the worst happened, there would have to be cooperation between the two navies – that went without saying. But Leahy refused to commit the United States any further, for two reasons. Although the USN maintained what it called the Asiatic Fleet, based in the Philippines, this was a small force without battleships or aircraft carriers. The great mass of the USN in the Pacific was centred on Hawaii, much further away, where it was placed to defend the continental United States. And second – although the Americans did not say so directly – they saw no reason why American ships should be put on the line and American lives risked in defence of Britain's colonial possessions. The mission went home empty-handed.

In effect, Britain had admitted to the United States that the strategy of Main Fleet to Singapore was now but a hollow shell. The Australian Government was not told this, not told that all the assurances given over all the years had been set at naught.

The Singapore Naval Base, with its giant King George VI Graving Dock, opened with much imperial pageantry on 14 February 1938, before 1000 VIP guests. The Admiralty sent an aircraft carrier, HMS *Eagle*, and a couple of destroyers. The USN turned up with three cruisers, and the French did as well. The BBC broadcast the ceremony around the world, and a handful of Japanese journalists and the Japanese consul general were also invited, presumably to make sure the message of imperial power got back to Tokyo. Australian newspapers reported extensively, with much embroidery about the Gibraltar of the Far East and general agreement that Fortress Singapore was impregnable.

Fine speeches were made. A Civil Lord of the Admiralty, Colonel John Llewellin, offered, 'If this base, by its very strength, should contribute towards peace in the East, we shall not have built the place in vain.'[25]

Not to be outdone, the Governor of the Straits Settlements, His Excellency Sir Thomas Shenton Whitelegge Thomas GCMG, GCStJ, splendidly attired in white tropical uniform and pith helmet, made an equally stirring speech as he declared the great dockyard open. 'The base is not a challenge to war,' he assured his audience and the world. 'It is an insurance against war. It has grown up slowly and surely through the years despite difficulties and setbacks. In the midst of wars and rumours of war it is a symbol of the care which the Mother Country has for the welfare of her people and the protection she will afford them in time of need.'[26]

Sir Shenton would have time to ponder those words. He was still in Singapore in 1942, still stoically dressing for dinner each night in the smoking ruins of Government House, until the Japanese bombed him out of that and into a small flat. Singapore fell four years and one day from the opening of the naval base. Thomas spent the rest of the war in Cell 24 of Changi Prison.

CHAPTER 6

AS A RESULT, AUSTRALIA IS ALSO AT WAR

Jack Langrell was at sea when war broke out. Early on that fateful spring morning of Sunday 3 September 1939, he left his parents' home in the Sydney suburb of Chatswood for the city, and then caught the 7.15 am ferry from Circular Quay to the naval base at Garden Island. His ship, the light cruiser HMAS *Hobart*, was raising steam preparing to sail, and at 9.15 am she cast off, heading down harbour and out into the Tasman, turning south in company with the destroyer *Voyager*.

Everyone knew war was very likely, probably inevitable, although the delusions of Neville Chamberlain and his ilk had continued to the last gasp. In Australia, Prime Minister Joe Lyons had died that April to be succeeded – after some political backstabbing – by Robert Gordon Menzies. As late as Thursday 31 August, Chamberlain was still hoping that Germany might back away from yet another grab for territory, cabling Menzies 'something, at any rate, has been achieved by inducing Hitler to agree to negotiations with Poland and the possibility some neutral meeting place for the negotiations is in mind though this may well be difficult'.[1] The next day, Friday 1 September, literally hours before the *Wehrmacht* stormed across the Polish border, the Australian High Commissioner in London, Stanley Bruce, offered Menzies his view 'that Hitler realises the dangers of the position he has got into and is seeking a way out'.[2]

The delusions were dashed. On the Saturday morning, and in special editions through the weekend, Australia's newspapers were full of the horrors of the German attack on Poland and the bombing of Warsaw; of Hitler's violent, hate-filled rant to the Reichstag; of the ultimatum Britain had sent to Berlin; of the evacuation of children from London. People were glued to radio stations for the latest news, tense and grimly expectant. A society gossip columnist in *The Sydney Morning Herald* noted:

> Crowds in the city last night heard the war news with an air of courage, in restaurants, hotels, and night spots. There were diners clamouring for accommodation at all eating places, and the majority of them scanned papers gravely during their meals.
>
> At the Carl Thomas Club, a wireless set was placed on the band stand. Whenever a news bulletin came on, the band stopped playing, and the patrons listened to the news. One could have heard a pin drop. At 9.30 p.m., all the patrons stood up and sang 'God Save the King'.[3]

By sunset on Sunday 3 September, *Hobart* was nearing Gabo Island just south of the Victorian border, where she and *Voyager* were to patrol the shipping route to and from Bass Strait. Jack Langrell had nothing much to do that evening. A young man just a few weeks short of his 18th birthday, he was a canteen assistant in the ship. At 9.15 pm, *Hobart*'s loudspeakers crackled into life for a radio broadcast from the Prime Minister, Robert Menzies. It was the news they had expected:

> Fellow Australians, it is my melancholy duty to inform you officially that, in consequence of the persistence by Germany in her invasion of Poland, Great Britain has declared war upon her, and that, as a result, Australia is also at war . . .
>
> In the bitter months that have come, calmness, resoluteness, confidence and hard work will be required as never before. This war will involve not only soldiers and sailors and airmen, but supplies, foodstuffs, money. Our staying power, and particularly the staying power of the Mother Country, will be best assisted by keeping our production going; by continuing our avocations

and our business as freely as we can; by maintaining employment and with it our strength. I know that, in spite of the emotions we are all feeling, you will show that Australia is ready to see it through. May God in his mercy and compassion grant that the world may soon be delivered from this agony.[4]

There was a sombre silence through the ship. When war was declared in 1914, there had been cheering in the navy's mess decks and wardrooms from men eager to have a crack at the Kaiser, but this time it was different. Almost every Australian family had been hurt in some way by the last war – a relative or friend or neighbour dead or wounded, or perhaps maimed for life – and there was no enthusiasm for another fight with the Germans or anyone else, however important it might be.

Wartime reality struck almost immediately, with the pipe 'Darken Ship'. Every light on deck was doused and every scuttle closed so that no gleam or flicker could be seen – a precaution against submarine attack, however remote that might be. This would become a familiar part of the routine of war at sea and for good reason: even the brief flare of a match lighting a cigarette or a pipe on deck could be seen for a long distance on a clear night. *Hobart* steamed on, a dark shape in a dark world.

—

Young Jack had salt in his veins. His father, Jack senior, had been navy too, signing on as a young Ordinary Seaman in 1911, the year the RAN got its royal title. He became a sailmaker, one of the last to follow that fading trade, and he served in the old battlecruiser *Australia* during the Great War, first off New Guinea and then in the North Sea. After that, he had stayed on in the service, rising to the rate of chief petty officer sailmaker and finding himself a most agreeable posting to the RANC at Jervis Bay, where, on 15 September 1921, young Jack was born.

It was a good place to grow up. Jack's father was an Irishman, born in County Wicklow, and – unusual in a sailor – a skilled horseman as well. He drove a sulky. Occasionally, he would go bush with the local Indigenous people, rounding up wild horses and breaking them in for the college officers and their wives, who valued his services and helpfully ensured that his posting there kept being extended. Young Jack came to know two worlds: the carefree, sunlit existence of a lively boy in coastal Australia, and the naval routine of the college, with its bugle calls and ceremonies and marching cadets, the occasional grey warship in the bay.

Eventually, the posting ended and the family moved to Chatswood. When Jack senior left the navy proper in 1932, he stayed on in the naval dockyard police, a job available to senior petty officers with a good record, which allowed them to keep working in familiar surroundings before they took their deferred-pay pension. And Jack junior found a position as a trainee at McIlrath's, the state-wide grocery chain, which had a shop at Chatswood and where he learnt the arts of carving hams and slicing cheeses and packing eggs in the days before everything was pre-packaged.

In 1938, Jack senior happened to bump into a former shipmate, Vic Zammit, who had run the canteen in the old *Australia*. Vic was still in the same line of business and was looking for a young bloke to take with him to commission the new cruiser *Hobart* in Britain. The Langrells jumped at the chance and, almost before he knew it, young Jack, fresh faced and bright eyed, was on his way to the United Kingdom in the seaplane carrier HMAS *Albatross*, which was being given back to Britain in part payment for the new cruiser.

Naval canteen staff were a sort of hybrid sub-species in those days, half-civilian and half-navy. Like the RN, the RAN contracted out the management of its ships' canteens to a civilian manager, who would go aboard with two or three assistants and run the show under the watchful eye of the senior supply officer. The canteen was nothing to do with preparing or eating meals. Depending on the size of the ship, it was generally a little shop somewhere around the mess deck where the crew could get those extras and comforts the navy didn't provide: cigarettes, razor blades, toothpaste, writing paper and stamps and envelopes, a tin of jam or maybe baked beans – 'yippee beans' – or soft drinks – 'goffers' – and sometimes even ice cream. The men would generally buy on credit and fix up on payday. For reasons lost in time but almost certainly something to do with the RN's centuries in the Mediterranean, the canteen managers were often Maltese, like Vic Zammit, and they tended to keep it in the family, so it was unusual to see a young Irish-Australian like Jack in with them.

And he loved it. You wore a sailor's uniform and you were subject to naval discipline, but there was none of the rigmarole of falling in for divisions, or swabbing decks, or cleaning guns or boilers, or standing a watch in a hot and greasy engine room, or on a cold and rainy bridge or signal deck. In the way of things, you got to know everyone on the ship, pretty much from the captain down to the lowest Ordinary Seaman. The canteen staff knew all the gossip and were always a reliable source for a buzz, as the navy called a rumour.

Jack and his shipmates joined the new cruiser at the Devonport Naval Base at Plymouth in England's West Country, a cradle and a nursery for British seafarers since Elizabethan times, the dockyard itself invariably known to navy men as Guzz or Guzzle,[5] just as Portsmouth was always called Pompey. It was on Plymouth Hoe[6] that Sir Francis Drake had supposedly finished his game of bowls before setting out to deal with the Spanish Armada in 1588. Now, exactly 350 years later, there was rather more urgency. *Hobart* had spent two years in the RN as HMS *Apollo* before Australia bought her. With the Munich crisis building, she was hurriedly rushed into commission at Guzz and renamed on 28 September 1938, just two days before Neville Chamberlain's return to Britain with his scrap of paper. When the alarm subsided, she did her working-up trials and was back in Australia by the end of the year. Jack stayed with *Hobart* for another year, until Vic Zammit transferred to *Australia* just a month after the start of the war and again took the young bloke with him, on 6 October.

If *Hobart* was big – and in Australian terms she was – then *Australia* was bigger still, an eye-opener for the newly joined canteen assistant. That day, he took his belongings for'ard, to mess in the fo'c'sle with the ship's cooks. It was the beginning of an extraordinary odyssey.

—

Both afloat and ashore, war threw the navy into a frenzy of activity. Navy Office, the RAN's headquarters, was in Melbourne, manned by a small staff, both naval and civilian, who burnt the midnight oil on the thousand and one tasks, great and small, that confronted them. Ships at sea, or about to put to sea, knew what their orders were in the event of war, and that machinery slipped smoothly into gear. But the process still had to be overseen by Navy Office. Men of the naval reserve had to be called to duty and fed and accommodated. Ships in repair or reserve were hurriedly readied and rearmed, and suitable merchant ships were requisitioned, smaller ones to be minesweepers or harbour defence vessels, larger ones to be equipped with guns and the crews to man them as armed merchant cruisers. The passenger liners *Manoora*, *Moreton Bay*, *Kanimbla* and *Westralia*, familiar peacetime sights in Australian ports, became HMA ships with naval commanding officers and crews, all within weeks. And new ships would have to be built, destroyers and corvettes. A gunnery school was swiftly set up at Rushcutters Bay in Sydney, and the Flinders Naval Base in Victoria began to prepare for a tide of new recruits. In the longer term, it was likely that Australia would want to send an Anzac force to Europe, as it had in 1914, and a convoy would have to be formed for that, with a naval escort.

The tasks mounted but, in essence, the navy was as ready for war as it could have been, as indeed it should have been. It had mobilised for Munich in 1938, a useful test, and the lessons learnt served well enough in 1939. In an ideal world, there would have been more ships and more men at the very start, but the penny-pinching years of peace had put paid to that. Still, as it happened, the RAN was reasonably equipped for the task ahead, which was essentially the protection of trade in Australian waters and, where at all possible, the provision of ships and men to assist the Mother Country in the northern hemisphere.

And all the available ships *were* at sea, or very nearly. *Australia* was at Cockatoo Island in Sydney, in the final weeks of that refit begun after her return from the Mediterranean. *Canberra*, wearing the flag of the acting squadron commander, had returned from New Guinea waters and was patrolling off Sydney. *Hobart* and *Voyager*, as we have seen, were watching Bass Strait from the east. The destroyer *Vendetta* was off Port Stephens on the New South Wales Central Coast, with her sister ship *Vampire* cruising near Cape Otway in southern Victoria to cover the western end of Bass Strait and the sea road to Port Phillip. Of the other two light cruisers, *Perth* stayed in the Caribbean under Admiralty control to intercept any German merchant vessels trying to make a run across the Atlantic for home, and *Sydney* was in the west at Fremantle. The two little Australian-built sloops *Yarra* and *Swan* were on anti-submarine patrol off Sydney, and in the harbour itself the old cruiser *Adelaide* and the two destroyers *Stuart* and *Waterhen* had been hurriedly brought out of reserve to be stored, crewed and ammunitioned. All in all, it was not a bad performance.

This despite the fact that the RAN's senior leadership was not in position. The most senior of them all, Admiral Sir Ragnar Colvin, was on leave at home in Britain. An RN officer of wide experience and ability, and with considerable political skills as well, Colvin, the Chief of the Naval Staff, was also First Naval Member of the Naval Board, meaning that he was the Australian Government's paramount professional adviser in the way that Britain's First Sea Lord served the Board of Admiralty in London. Early in 1939, Colvin had suggested that Australia should buy or borrow a battleship from Britain as a deterrent to Japanese aggression, but he was fobbed off – once again – by the First Sea Lord, Admiral Sir Roger Backhouse, with the usual assurances:

> there has never been doubt that a force of Capital Ships would have to be sent to East in event of war with Japan. What is uncertain is strength of this force as this would necessarily depend on

situation in Europe. In any case I feel sure that force sent would be sufficient to safeguard communications in Bay of Bengal and Indian Ocean, and act as a strong deterrent to any Japanese expedition against Australia.[7]

Colvin hastened back to Melbourne as soon as war happened, but for those first few crucial days he was missing. More difficult still, the RN flag officer nominally in command of the squadron at sea, Rear Admiral Wilfred Custance, was stricken with cancer, had resigned his post, and would indeed die just a few weeks later on his way back to the United Kingdom. The machinery had to whirr along without these two, which it did, but it meant that some crucial strategic decisions were delayed.

In 1914, Australia had placed its navy under the command and control of the Admiralty. In this war, it would happen again, but with one significant reservation. On 30 August 1939, in a cable to the Secretary for the Dominions in Whitehall, the government made clear that it wanted to be consulted first:

IMMEDIATE SECRET

In the present international situation the Commonwealth Government desire to place the ships of the R.A.N. and their personnel at the disposal of the United Kingdom Government, but find it necessary to stipulate that no ships (other than HMAS *Perth*) should be taken from Australian waters without prior concurrence of Commonwealth Government.[8]

The British accepted gladly, and a week later, with the war under way, the Dominions Secretary, Anthony Eden, sent a long cable outlining the assistance Britain would like from Australia. It was virtually a shopping list for men and materiel. Eden urged Australia to 'exert her full national effort including preparation of her forces with a view to the despatch of an expeditionary force',[9] and suggested everything from whole air force squadrons to electricians, scientists and yachtsmen who could be trained as naval officers.

The first blows had already been struck in the war at sea. Within hours of the British declaration of war, a German submarine, *U-30*, torpedoed and sank the liner *Athenia* off Ireland, with the loss of 122 lives. It was the opening shot in what would become the Battle of the Atlantic, as the Admiralty well recognised. Eden asked Australia for as many trained naval personnel as could be spared and, significantly, for the provision of a second cruiser and the RAN's five destroyers 'for service other than on the Australian station'.[10]

It was the request for the ships that loomed large, always with the spectre of Japan hovering in the background. Japan was neutral for the moment, but that could change overnight. To send the ships the British had asked for would mean stripping away a significant part of Australia's sea defences at home. Eden had suggested in his cable that:

> So long as Japan remains neutral it is considered that Australian waters may be regarded as unlikely to suffer submarine attack ... the most likely danger to be guarded against on Australian Station under present circumstances is that of attack on shipping by armed raiders. It is considered that two cruisers and HMAS *Australia* (when ready) should prove adequate for this purpose.[11]

After long debate, and at Colvin's prompting, the government agreed. Eventually, the cruiser *Sydney* and the five destroyers would be sent to serve in the Mediterranean, where, with Italy also still standing on the sidelines, the war was – if not dormant – at least relatively quiet.

———

In that same clamorous month of September 1939, Navy Office took another decision that would, quite literally, alter the course of the war. Its execution would save many lives, perhaps tens of thousands of them. It would be an extraordinary Australian contribution to victory, but one still only rarely recognised to this day.

Two men put it together, friends from that first intake at the naval college in 1913. Rupert Basil Michel Long had been a cadet captain, a midshipman in the old battlecruiser *Australia*, and he had done the long course at the Royal Navy Torpedo School, HMS *Vernon*. But it was staff work that attracted his agile mind, and gradually he turned to the black arts of naval intelligence. Not being in the business of dashing about in cruisers or destroyers, his promotion was slow. He made lieutenant commander in 1928 and was still in that rank at the outbreak of war when most of his peers were commanders or captains. But he held the post of Director of Naval Intelligence and he set to wartime work with creative energy. Rupert Long was convinced, beyond any doubt, that Japan and Australia would eventually be at war, and he was determined to be ready for it.

He invited to his office another lieutenant commander, Eric Augustas Feldt, a Queenslander who'd been on the navy Retired List and then the Emergency List to be called back to service if needs be. Feldt had also graduated from the college in January 1917, also with the usual spell in a Grand Fleet battleship and time as a lieutenant in the cruiser *Melbourne*, but by 1922 he had decided there was little future in the navy. With that post-war purge of officers and men, he quit and went seeking adventure up in the islands, shouldering the white man's burden as a patrol officer in New Guinea. He was good at it. He loved the outdoor life of the colonial administrator and travelled everywhere, building an intimate knowledge of the territory and its peoples. He knew everybody who was anybody – his fellow administration officials, the planters, the miners, the missionaries, the soldiers of fortune, and many of the indigenous chiefs – and he moved steadily up the official ranks until, in 1939, he was based at Wau as New Guinea's Chief Mining Warden.

Feldt was just the man Long needed, although they made an odd couple. Long was tubby, urbane, quick-brained, a chain smoker, and well connected in Australian society. His nickname was 'Cocky'. Feldt once described himself as 'that oddity of inheritance, a dark Swede, thin, bull-necked and with thinning hair, vehement and forthright . . . [who] never yet called a man a stupid bastard unless he failed to adopt my views within five minutes of my expressing them'.[12] But the two got on well, and

there was a job to do. For many years, there had been a handful
of coastwatchers dotted here and there on Australia's northern
shores, and one or two in the islands – cattlemen and fishermen
and the like who would occasionally report the odd unusual
happening, generally by sending a telegram from a local post
office. But the organisation was almost comatose, which would
not do in war. Would Eric like to kick it into life?

Feldt accepted. Cocky Long put his friend back on the books
as a lieutenant commander from 8 September. Feldt spent a busy
fortnight in Melbourne getting his plans together, including
a hunt for suitable radio sets that could be used for reporting,
and then he flew to Port Moresby, where he arrived on the 21st.
His contacts stood him in good stead and so did his knowledge.
With almost crystal-ball foresight, he went first to Rabaul on
the north-eastern island of New Britain 'to commence work
on the outer perimeter, which was obviously the most urgent
part', as he would write later.[13] It was an arduous journey, even
for the experienced New Guinea hand:

> My travels took me all around the areas by ship, motor boat and
> canoe, boot, bicycle and aeroplane, so that I saw nearly every-
> body, and nearly everybody saw me. I already knew more than
> half of those I met, and all were helpful. In the Solomons, the
> Acting Resident Commissioner (Mr Johnson) placed an auxil-
> iary vessel at my disposal and in it I traversed most of the group,
> being defeated only by a raging south-easter which kept me
> from Vanikoro and drove me back with the port bulwarks stove
> in by the seas.[14]

The teleradio Feldt chose was an Australian invention, a product
of the days when Australia was a world leader in wireless technology. Amalgamated Wireless (Australasia) Ltd, an offshoot of the
Marconi company, half-owned by Australians and better known
as AWA, had designed the teleradio specifically for communications in the bush and the islands. The first was in use in New
Guinea in 1935, and by 1938 there were about 100 of them scattered around with the planters and settlers, the men who would

be the first recruits to the coastwatching network. As he took on more volunteers, Feldt would provide them with radios and instructions on how to work them, along with a simple code they called 'Playfair'.

The radios were known as the AWA 3BZ, a contraption of three large steel boxes of knobs and dials – transmitter, receiver and batteries – which could send either voice or Morse code; up to 1000 kilometres for Morse in good atmospheric conditions. The drawback was their size and weight. With a loudspeaker and a petrol generator for recharging the battery, plus cables and aerials, they weighed some 150 kilograms and had to be carried, often through steamy jungle terrain, by a team of strong men; for that reason alone, the coastwatchers were reliant on the loyalty of the local people, or the 'native boys', as they called them in the language of the day.

By the time the Japanese war broke out, there were more than 700 coastwatchers in place on the Australian mainland and the string of islands to the north, with Feldt running the network as Staff Officer (Intelligence) Port Moresby. Whimsically, he christened the operation 'Ferdinand', after *The Story of Ferdinand*, a children's book about a bull that would rather sit and smell the flowers than enter a bullfight. He drummed into his people that their job was to wait, observe and report, not to engage in skirmishes with the Japanese.

Leaving Feldt to run Ferdinand, Long busied himself with another vital aspect of his job: setting up a signals intelligence network with specialist cryptographers working to crack Japanese codes. He achieved extraordinary success there too. As naval officers, neither he nor Eric Feldt ever saw the enemy through binoculars from a spray-drenched bridge; they never heard a shot fired in anger. But their contribution was beyond measure. And the work of their coastwatchers would be intertwined, like strands of stout cable, with the destiny of *Australia* and *Canberra*.

—

On 1 September 1939, the RAN had exactly 5440 officers and men on its books. The call-up of the reserves would swell that figure to more than 10,000, literally within weeks, and over the coming Australian summer thousands more would join. Some were fresh out of school, kids who had never been to sea before. Others were young midshipmen, newly graduated from the college. And quite a few were old navy, who had known the days of coal-fired ships, had retired, and were now back in uniform for the service of their country.

If Jack Langrell had salt in his veins, then Harold Eastick was tar and oak, canvas and gunpowder. Two of his great-great-grandfathers fought in 74-gun battleships of Nelson's fleet at Trafalgar: Spencer Lone Eastick as an able seaman in HMS *Achille*, and John Eastick as a private of marines in the fabled HMS *Bellerephon*.[15] A great-grandfather, a sailing captain, had died at sea in the Baltic, and the forebear who carried the family name to Australia, his grandfather Charles Ambrose Eastick, had served in ships of the RN during the Crimean War and the American Civil War.

Harold Lone Eastick was one of six children, born in the Adelaide suburb of Hyde Park on 29 September 1908. His brother Thomas, eight years older, would break the navy line of things to become a decorated army brigadier in the Second World War and a knight of the realm, but Harold was content with a life at sea. He joined up in 1926 at the age of 17, and after training at Flinders he was posted to ships here and there until 1932. Then, as an able seaman, he bought his way out of the RAN by forfeiting deferred pay of £36 – a considerable sum – and on condition that he joined the reserve. Like so many men in his position, he found it cold on the outside during the Depression and he was back in the navy again just a year later, signing on for another five years in 1933. Once more he left, and once more he came back, on the day Hitler invaded Poland, this time as a married man, a qualified plumber and petty officer. Against all the rules, Harold would very quietly keep a diary while he was at sea in *Australia*, a record of all he had seen and endured.

That 1 September was a red-letter day for another young man, Mac Gregory. At the age of 17, newly minted from the naval college with 11 of his peers, he got to wear the white patches of a midshipman. He was in *Canberra* then, but a week later – a slender, handsome young man – he was posted to the gunroom of *Australia*.

Mackenzie Jesse Gregory also had a naval background, although of a very different colour to Harold Eastick's heritage. His father, Jesse Gregory, was an officers' steward, a chief petty officer, and still in the RAN when Mac graduated. Jesse must have been good at it, because he had spent a lot of his naval career serving chiefs of the Naval Staff in their private homes, more or less as a uniformed butler, and at the outbreak of war he was looking after none other than Sir Ragnar Colvin.

Mac had grown up around admirals, living in the servants' quarters of their houses in Melbourne's Toorak or St Kilda Road, and he regarded himself as a working-class boy. Even with his father in the navy, he knew the hard times of the Depression, retaining forever the memory of his mother stuffing her shoes with old newspaper to block up the holes. It was a brave decision for a lad of such humble background to become a naval officer, but at the age of 13 young Mac filled out the forms, passed a medical exam, and took himself to Victoria Barracks to be interviewed by a gilded panel of admirals and captains. Evidently, he answered their questions to their satisfaction, for he entered the college at Flinders in 1936, survived the bullying initiation rituals administered by the senior cadets and graduated – with immense pride – as the only Australian midshipman ever to be the son of a serving sailor.

His war began less than happily, though. On that very Sunday night of Menzies' declaration, the new Midshipman Gregory was in charge of one of *Canberra*'s boats, running the libertymen back to the ship from the Man o'War Steps in Sydney Harbour. To his bottomless embarrassment, he gave the order 'astern' instead of 'ahead'; the boat crashed into the sea wall, tipping the bow man into the water and provoking sniggers and chortles from the families gathered there to farewell their men.

By accident perhaps, although more likely by design, the navy never posted Mac and Jesse together, thus saving them the embarrassment of the father having to salute the son. Mac would spend most of his war at sea, a participant in – and eventual survivor of – the great Pacific battles.

Seasoned and senior men were ready too, officers who had trained all their lives for war. As *Australia* was finishing her refit in Sydney, Commander John Malet Armstrong was appointed her executive officer, to shoulder the 1001 tasks of getting the ship and crew ready for sea. Before that, he had been the executive officer at the Naval College, where he himself had graduated in 1917, a chief cadet captain with colours for rugby and swimming, and known to his term mates as Jock or, sometimes, Jamie. His sailors, though, called him 'Black Jack', most probably in tribute to his dark, almost piratical features.

Born in 1900, the son of a prominent doctor in Sydney's Eastern Suburbs, tall and wiry with a craggy face – a nose broken on the rugby field, topped by bushy black eyebrows – Armstrong had Scottish blood. In 1927, he commanded the naval guard at the opening of the new Parliament House in Canberra, a landmark in a career that had taken him on the usual rounds – a spell in the old *Australia*; a cruiser on the China Station; a Whale Island gunnery course; command of a destroyer; executive officer of another cruiser, HMS *Shropshire*, during the Spanish Civil War – and now his new posting to the newly refitting and replenishing *Australia II*. His captain, Ross Stewart, was RN, the man who had brought the new cruiser *Hobart* out from Britain. The two would make a formidable pair.

—

Crace is a shiny new dormitory suburb of Canberra, well to the north of the parliamentary circle, a little off the Barton highway out beyond Lyneham and Braddon. A decade ago, it was grassy paddocks. Its developers have spruiked 'the flair and functionality of the modern building designs; the sustainable planning ... the buzz of the urban centre; the parks and open spaces; and so much more.'[16]

They named the place for Edward Kendall Crace, an Englishman who had survived a shipwreck off the coast of Brazil to arrive in Australia in 1865. It's not known what brought him out. His father, John Gregory Crace, was a celebrated interior designer who had worked on the new Houses of Parliament at Westminster and on Windsor Castle, but Edward had chosen to go farming in the colonies. He bought two grazing properties in what would become the outer suburbs of Canberra, Ginninderra and then Gungahlin, one of which had on it a small but elegant Georgian homestead of two-storeyed rendered brick. He and his wife, Kate, a daughter of the prosperous colonial entrepreneur Henry Mort, commissioned a handsome mansion extension in grey stone, with driveways, gardens and parks reminiscent of an English country estate.[17] They bought a third property, Charnwood, ran some 25,000 merino sheep and a herd of Devon cattle, and lived there with their family of seven girls and two boys in an ideal Australian bush setting of grassland, lakes and creeks against the backdrop of the far Brindabella Ranges.

The second boy, John Gregory Crace, known as Jack, was just five when his father died. In September 1892, Edward Crace and his coachman, George Kemp, drowned when their sulky became snagged in the swollen Ginninderra Creek and the horse panicked, tossing the two men into the water. 'A catastrophe', as the *Goulburn Herald* called it.[18] With the help of her father, Kate stayed on the land, heavily mortgaged though it was, and managed to send Jack for a year to the King's School at Parramatta, outside Sydney. There, at the age of 13, he decided he wanted a naval career. In the spring of 1899, still clad in widow's black, Kate hosted a grand ball and supper at Gungahlin to speed her boy on his way to England, a glittering event respectfully covered by *The Queanbeyan Age*:

The ball room was most tastefully decorated, the entire walls were covered with flags of the British nation, and a plentiful supply of greenery gave it a very gay appearance. The members of Mrs Crace's family participated in the dancing during the greater part of the night, which added much to the harmony of the evening. Between the dances some good singing was given, among which 'Sons of the Sea,' the 'Soldiers of the Queen,' and a hunting song given by Mr Circuitt met with great applause. The supper, which was held as usual on the large verandah, was a most elaborate affair . . . The toast was enthusiastically received with musical honors. Master Jack Crace responded in a neat address, thanking them for the manner in which they had drunk his health and trusted that upon his return he should have the pleasure of again meeting those kind friends and old familiar faces.[19]

Sponsored by an uncle, Jack enrolled at Foster's Academy at Stubbington in Hampshire, near the Solent, a salty preparatory school where – uniformed in an Eton jacket with waistcoat, black-and-grey striped trousers and a boater in summer, bowler hat in winter – young chaps of good family swotted to pass the rigorous entrance exams for the naval college HMS *Britannia*.[20] He gained entry there in 1902, in one of the places set aside for colonial cadets in that spartan naval nursery:

At night hammocks were slung above our chests and in these we slept. Our bathing arrangements were also rather primitive and consisted of large tanks containing cold salt water about two feet deep some way from our hammocks. In winter the run to and from the bath and the plunge into icy water was not enjoyable but doubtless helped to harden us up. In winter, too, the ships were very draughty as the squareports (or windows) were so thick with paint that they could not shut properly and the decks were always wet and very slippery.[21]

He graduated in the middle of his class of 77, joining his first ship, the cruiser HMS *Good Hope*, as a midshipman in 1903, where he served for three years. Diligent and likeable, Jack attracted the attention of his superiors, earned quick promotion and, in 1908, was sent back to his home country for an 18-month stint in the protected cruiser HMS *Powerful*, flagship of the Australia squadron based in Sydney. Sensibly, the navy was happy for him to water his Australian roots, and on Australia Day, 26 January 1913, by now a lieutenant and a torpedo specialist, he joined the battlecruiser *Australia* and was with her when she led the grand fleet entry into Sydney of October that year. He stayed with her in the Pacific and then through the dreary North Sea years until 1917, with a spell ashore towards the end of the war and then a posting to the brand new *Hood* in 1918.

Jack Crace's career through the '20s and '30s was solid if unspectacular, a growing reputation as an innovator and author of professional essays and manuals sparing him from the several cost-cutting axes that wrecked the lives and hopes of so many of his contemporaries. In 1920, he married Carola Baird, the daughter of a Glasgow lawyer. In 1924, he was back in Australian waters yet again as the commander in the cruiser *Danae*, part of that Special Service Squadron that had saluted the rusting, flower-strewn *Australia I* at her dismal end off Sydney – a sight he must have viewed with some clenching emotion. He climbed the promotion ladder – destroyer captain in the Atlantic Fleet, cruiser captain on the East Indies Station – and, as war drew closer in 1939, he was commanding a desk at the Admiralty in Whitehall as naval assistant to the Second Sea Lord, bored by the routine of sorting out officers' postings. That August, he was promoted to rear admiral – flag rank at last – and sent on leave while the powers that be considered his future.

The next act played out as one of those timeless vignettes of British naval life. For centuries, the King's sea officers, junior and senior, had settled in the county of Hampshire in estates large and small, the size of their house and holding depending on their luck with prize money or the lack of it, but invariably within a day's posting distance by horse or coach from both Pompey and the Admiralty in Whitehall. There they would hopefully await their next ship, their next promotion, their next squadron or even fleet. Jack Crace had acquired the comfortable, six-bedroom Hawkley House outside the sleepy Hampshire village of Liss near the Old London Road on the woodland slopes of the South Downs, and it was there, on a sunny Saturday 16 September 1939, that he came in from the garden to take a telephone call from the Admiralty. It was short notice, unfortunately, but would he accept the post of Rear Admiral Commanding the Australian Squadron?

A week later, Crace was on board the Orient Line's *Orontes*, sailing as a passenger to Melbourne, leaving Carola to manage the house and their three sons – the inevitable lot of navy wives. The eldest boy, Allan, was in the RN as a midshipman, with Christopher, 14, and Nicholas, 11, still at school. It was a wrench to leave them behind in wartime Britain, but this was both a call to duty and the opportunity of a lifetime. Crace would have an active command at sea, the most ardent desire of any admiral worth his salt, and one in which, he thought, he would have a measure of independence beyond the oversight of the Admiralty. Personally, he was returning to the land of his birth, for which he still held a warm regard. For all his time spent away, Crace emphatically regarded himself as an Australian, and never hesitated to say so. His mother had died in 1926 and the Gungahlin properties were no longer in the family, but his sisters were still living in Australia and he looked forward to seeing them again.

The *Orontes* arrived in Melbourne on the evening of Sunday 29 October. On the Monday, Crace plunged into business, first meeting his immediate superior, Sir Ragnar Colvin – another Foster's Academy alumnus – and then lunching at Government House, where he met the Governor General, Lord Gowrie. And from there to Sydney, where, on Wednesday 1 November, he took command of the squadron. At 9.30 that morning, to the high shrill of the bosun's call and the crash and stamp of marching and rifle drill, the blare of bugles and the beat of drums, his rear admiral's flag of the red cross of St George with two red balls in the left quarters was hoisted to the mainmast of *Canberra*. The next day, he put to sea, to see what his flagship and her men were made of. The war was two months old.

PART 2

GOING INTO BATTLE

CHAPTER 7

PUT YOUR HAND
INTO THE
HAND OF GOD

Ten days before the *Wehrmacht* smashed into Poland, the pocket battleship *Admiral Graf Spee* slipped her moorings at Wilhelmshaven under cover of darkness and nosed out into the North Sea, where she turned to starboard and headed north. It was the evening of Monday 21 August 1939. Keeping northward for the next few days, Kapitän zur See Hans Langsdorff nursed his ship along just outside Norwegian territorial waters, making sure to avoid any other vessels that might report her presence, and then turned west in a great arc towards Iceland. From there, he headed south in the Atlantic to take up his preliminary war station. He met his supply ship, the tanker *Altmark*, south-west of the Canary Islands on 1 September, to replenish and await orders.

Graf Spee had been specifically designed and armed for her task: *Kreuzerkrieg*, or cruiser warfare, the role of the lone sea wolf seeking out and destroying enemy merchant shipping. Technically, she was a heavy cruiser, although in fact she was much more. It was the British who coined the term 'pocket battleship' when she visited Spithead for the Coronation Review in 1937, an imposing sight at nearly 15,000 tons – well outside the cruiser treaty limit of 10,000 tons – and armed with two triple turrets of 11-inch guns, one fore, one aft. She was far more powerful than any cruiser of the RN. In a radical innovation, she and her sister ships, *Deutschland* and *Admiral Scheer*, were powered by diesel engines, eight of them coupled to two shafts to give a top speed of some 28 knots. This was not particularly fast, and the engines were not always as reliable as the designers had hoped, but for a commerce raider relying on stealth and concealment they could apply power instantly – no need to raise steam – and they produced very little smoke to be spotted on a far horizon. *Deutschland* had also sailed for the Atlantic, three days after *Graf Spee*.

Langsdorff cooled his heels for a fortnight, ever more impatient, aware that Germany and Britain were at war but forbidden to act until the order came from the *Seekriegsleitung*, the naval high command in Berlin. Hitler was still hoping that Britain and France might negotiate yet another capitulation after his successful seizure of Poland. On 26 September, the *Seekriegsleitung* finally let Langsdorf off the leash, and *Graf Spee* headed for the shipping lanes off the easternmost point of Brazil. Just after noon on 30 September, she made her first kill: the 5000-ton British steamer *Clement*.

Before she was taken and sunk, the *Clement* managed to get off the distress signal RRR, Allied code for 'I am being attacked by a raider'. Later that afternoon, Langsdorff, a chivalrous man, sent an uncoded signal to a Brazilian radio station requesting the rescue of the men he had turned loose in the *Clement*'s lifeboats – using, as a ruse, the call sign of his sister ship *Admiral Scheer*. It was the first indication to the Admiralty in London that a pocket battleship was on the loose in the South Atlantic. Every available ship, British and French, was ordered into the hunt.

For the next month, Langsdorff played cat and mouse, doubling back on his tracks, turning up where he was least expected, sinking four more ships, always a jump ahead of his pursuers. At the end of October, he rounded the Cape of Good Hope into the Indian Ocean, where, on 15 November, he sank the small tanker *Africa Shell* south of Madagascar.

This radically changed the game for Australia: a German in the Indian Ocean. It aroused solemn memories of 1914, when the cruiser *Emden* of the Kaiser's navy had caused three months of havoc there until she was run down and destroyed by HMAS *Sydney I* at the Cocos Islands in November that year. *Emden* had been caught just 80 kilometres away from the great convoy carrying 20,000 men of the 1st AIF to the Middle East. Now that nightmare returned. At this very moment, the 2nd AIF was forming to go to the aid of the Mother Country, an Anzac force with a New Zealand contingent, all to be convoyed across that same Indian Ocean route towards Suez with another raider, probably the powerful *Admiral Scheer*, on the prowl.

In addition to the British and French ships in the search, the Australian cruiser *Hobart* and the five destroyers *Stuart*, *Vampire, Vendetta, Voyager and Waterhen* were positioned at points in the Indian Ocean where a raider might appear. But there was also the possibility that the *Scheer* – or whichever ship it was – might even range into the Pacific, so *Australia* and *Canberra* were held in readiness in Australian waters. In fact, Langsdorff did exactly the opposite. Returning to the Atlantic in early December, he sank in quick succession the Blue Star liner *Doric Star* – which also got off an RRR signal – and the Shaw Savill steamer *Tairoa*, both of which had sailed from Australia carrying passengers and cargo to Britain.

This brought about his undoing, in the first true naval battle and significant British victory of the war. Putting two and two together, Commodore Henry Harwood of the RN's South America Cruiser Squadron guessed the German would very likely head for rich pickings off the River Plate, where Argentina meets Uruguay. He was right. On 13 December, *Graf Spee* was boldly harried to her destruction there by Harwood's ships *Exeter* and *Ajax* and the New Zealand cruiser HMNZS *Achilles*. Rather than finish the battle, and on Hitler's direct order, Langsdorff scuttled *Graf Spee* in the River Plate estuary. Days later, on 19 December, in a Buenos Aires hotel, he wrote a note that began, 'I can now only prove by my death that the fighting services of the Third Reich are ready to die for the honour of the flag . . .' Wrapped in his ship's battle ensign, he shot himself.

The Battle of the River Plate was hailed in Australia with joy and relief, a ray of light in the dark days of the seemingly unstoppable German onslaught in Europe and the rising toll of sinkings by U-boats in the North Atlantic. The newspapers had a field day, with the Melbourne *Argus* so excited that, under the headline 'HOW WE CHASED THE GRAF SPEE OFF THE HIGH SEAS', it ran a page of theatrically fanciful 'artist's impressions' of the affray that bore little or no relation to what had actually happened.[1] Winston Churchill, politically resurrected and back at the Admiralty as First Lord, would write that the victory 'lightened the dreary and oppressive winter through which we were passing'.[2]

But the Admiralty and the Australian Naval Board in Melbourne remained very much alive to the danger of another German raider appearing in either the Indian or Pacific Oceans to menace the maritime trade of Australasia. As the British High Commissioner in Canberra, Sir Geoffrey Whiskard, wrote in a letter to Menzies in late October:

> While Germany remains the only enemy, U-boat activity in Australian waters is considered by the United Kingdom authorities to be most unlikely, and the greatest threat to Australian shipping from submarine attack is expected to be in home waters and in the Atlantic. The only form of attack on shipping in Australian waters which the United Kingdom authorities consider probable is by an enemy surface raider.[3]

So it might be one of the other pocket battleships or, more likely, a wolf in disguise, posing as an Allied or neutral merchant vessel. U-boats did not have the range to travel so far south; they confined themselves to the Atlantic, where there were more than enough targets available. And apart from the merchant sinkings – at a rate of about ten per week – *U-29* had sent the elderly aircraft carrier *Courageous* and 519 of her crew to the bottom in Britain's Western Approaches on 17 September. And more. In a daring raid at Scapa Flow on 14 October, *U-47* – captained by a future U-boat ace, Günther Prien – sank the old battleship *Royal Oak* with the loss of 833 lives, including an admiral and more than 100 boys under 18. Distant though they were, these tragedies struck home in Australia – and in the navy in particular. They were grim evidence that the *Kriegs-marine*'s submarine arm was a potent force and a threat to Britain's very existence.

So planning went on for the Anzac convoy with much negotiation over the strength of the escort it would need to shield it from surface attack. Churchill emphasised to the First Sea Lord, Sir Dudley Pound, 'The transportation of the Australasian divisions is an historic episode in Imperial history. An accident would be a disaster.'[4]

The British offered the battleship *Ramillies*, an old stager of Great War vintage, obsolete and ponderously slow at around 21 knots top speed, but with eight 15-inch guns that should be enough to see off any German attacker. There was some British pressure for *Australia* and *Canberra* to join the escort across the Indian Ocean as far as Ceylon, but the government resisted it, concerned that this would strip Australian coastal waters of adequate protection. Two of the three 6-inch cruisers were already overseas – *Hobart* based on Singapore and *Perth* still in the Caribbean – and in mid-November, at Britain's urgent plea, the five destroyers had been sent to the Mediterranean, on the promise that they would be returned if Japan were to enter the war. *Australia* and *Canberra* would accompany the convoy only from Sydney to Fremantle, no further.

—

These first months of the war were dog days, long and monotonous. Both cruisers were now almost constantly at sea, patrolling here and there in waters close to home, occasionally exercising alone, occasionally with each other or with aircraft of the RAAF. Sometimes, there would be a practice gunnery or torpedo shoot, and the irritating wild goose chase after a report of a 'suspicious vessel', but little else happened. For most of the time, it was boredom mounted on tedium mounted on fatigue, a far cry from those leisurely pre-war days of the regatta in Hobart or the Spring Cruise to Melbourne for the Cup.

And it was arduous. The big cruisers were more spacious than the old destroyers, certainly, but they had not been built for tropical or even warm summer conditions, and their ventilation below decks was primitive. Each night at sunset, the pipe to darken ship turned them into a closed steel box, hot and airless, where sleep was difficult. The air below decks was a sour cocktail of engine-room vapours, of stale cooking, of human body odours. The food, which sailors called 'scran', was plentiful enough but plain with it, in an era when the Australian diet – cuisine is hardly the word – did not reach much beyond the Sunday roast and three veg. Often, what you got depended how long the ship had been at sea, for refrigeration space was limited, and perishable stores of fresh milk ('cow juice'), fruit, vegetables and eggs ('bum nuts') could run down quickly. On a good day, breakfast might be a boiled or fried egg, followed by sausages or bacon and toast, sometimes with 'red lead', which was the sailors' name for canned tomatoes, and plentiful cups of tea. In winter, porridge might appear as well, a glutinous starch the old hands called 'burgoo'. The midday meal – oddly known as dinner for the sailors, lunch for the officers – could be a salad or that roast, depending on the weather and the whim of the supply officers and the cooks, and it was much the same again in the evening. Sometimes, the galley might turn out bully-beef sandwiches or Tiddy Oggies, old navy slang for Cornish pasties, which were always a favourite, or a duff, which was a steamed pudding, served with a gluggy custard. Once in a blue moon, a tin of Golden Syrup might appear. In the evening, especially if it was cold on deck, the favourite drink was cocoa, brewed villainously thick and always called 'kai'. The men were not allowed alcohol at sea but officers were – a privilege that some abused. Midshipman Edgar Blau, a Queenslander in *Canberra*'s gunroom, scorned this in his memoirs:

> That officers were allowed to drink at sea while the lower deck was dry seemed plain crazy to me. Many a middle watch have

I spent cruising the Indian Ocean where the officer of the watch arrived pissed to the gills and settled himself in the wind flare of the bridge and slept off his excess whilst I, a midshipman of 18, was left in charge of the 1,100 lives on board. That plus the fact that this went unpunished, whilst an able seaman who failed to salute an officer was likely to get seven days jankers[5] which, although not as bad as a flogging, was still very painful and debilitating in the tropics. (Frog-marching with a rifle held above the head during an hour of the dog-watches.)[6]

You pretty much made your own entertainment. A concert from the ship's band was always popular, and individual bandsmen would sometimes knock up a sing-song in the mess decks. A board game known as Uckers, similar to Ludo, was a perennial pastime, and so was gambling on the popular but illegal dice game of Crown and Anchor – which would get you jankers if you were caught, and the money confiscated. Boxing on the quarterdeck was a crowd-pleasing sport in fine weather on a calm sea, and a few enthusiasts might go for a jog or do physical jerks in the mornings if they were off watch. Beyond that, you could find a quiet corner in which to read and reread letters from home and write the replies, or just sunbake beside a turret on the fo'c'sle.

That first wartime Christmas saw both *Australia* and *Canberra* back in Sydney, with locals and some others given a week's leave to go home. If you had a run ashore and a few hours on your hands, there were always the Woolloomooloo pubs, or the picture shows, where the all-star offering was *The Wizard of Oz*, with Judy Garland 'In Technicolor! Holiday happiness for all; bring the kiddies'. Even at the cinema, it was hard to escape the war. There was *Thunder Afloat* starring Wallace Beery – 'see how the German U-boat menace is fought' – or *The Lion Has Wings*, 'Alexander Korda's dramatic romance of the RAF with Merle Oberon and Ralph Richardson'.

Failing that, you could gather around the wireless, for something like this offering for listeners in Brisbane:

HERE'S FUN!!
A REAL CHRISTMAS PANTOMIME
4BK – 7.45 TO-NIGHT – 4AK
'CINDERELLA'
60 minutes of gay Xmas entertainment! In a brand new, sparkling merry-making show. Humphrey Bishop's All Star Cast, supported by 30 voices and a band of 12.

Followed at 9 o'clock by another rollicking 30 minutes of music and merriment – 'THE 4BK MINSTREL SHOW'

Then Look At This Array of
XMAS DAY FEATURES!
A RADIO FEAST FIT FOR A KING
*8.30 a.m. – 'Skeeter's' Xmas Party.
*10.15 a.m. – Greetings from Dad and Dave and others
 relayed from Snake Gully.
*11 a.m. – Brilliant Presentation of Charles Dickens'
 immortal 'Christmas Carol.'
*12.30 pm. – Special Xmas Dinner Revue.
*5.30 pm – Xmas Carol Singers.[7]

For all the contrived gaiety, there was, though, a national sense of foreboding, of worse to come, voiced in the Christmas messages of both the Prime Minister, Robert Menzies, and the Leader of the Opposition, John Curtin. Menzies strove for some optimism:

Christmas Day will find Australia this year with her sailors, soldiers, and airmen ready to fight, and with vast plans in train for the gathering of munitions and supplies of war.

These activities seem far removed from the ideal of peace which we associate with Christmas, but the contrast is perhaps not so stark as we might imagine. Peace and goodwill cannot be won easily in this world of ours. We must earn them by sacrifice.

If out of the disaster of war there comes the defeat of the forces which have made peace and goodwill a mockery for so many, our people, and the people of other nations, will not have suffered in vain.[8]

Curtin was more pessimistic, writing in the *Westralian Worker*, the Labor paper he had once edited:

> We are now on the threshold of 1940. What it will produce is not known. All the portents are black with doubt and uncertainty. The terrors of war indicate that misery, suffering and death await many of our people and of the peoples of the world.
>
> Time, the reaper, has gathered another year. Death, the Grim Reaper, stalks hand in hand with the prosecution of war – a war not of our making and beyond our power to avert . . .
>
> I look to 1940 with one dominating hope. That hope is that peace will come again during the ensuing 12 months; that reason and human brotherhood will replace force and aggression. A just peace for an unhappy world is a New Year's Gift the peoples of the world desire and need.[9]

Remarkably, it was the King, George VI, whose words would resonate for posterity. Anxious for the future of the Empire and their place in it, Australians found him reassuring, even inspiring. We know now with what difficulty this shy, tongue-tied man rehearsed his speech and read it, but he did his kingly duty. George, a genuine veteran, had been at Jutland as a turret officer in the battleship *Collingwood*. Uniformed as an Admiral of the Fleet, he broadcast from his study at Sandringham live to the Empire on Christmas Day, concluding with lines from a poem suggested to him by his elder daughter, Princess Elizabeth:

> I said to the man who stood at the Gate of the Year,
> 'Give me a light that I may tread safely into the unknown.'
> And he replied, 'Go out into the darkness, and put your hand into the Hand of God.
> That shall be to you better than light, and safer than a known way.'[10]

———

As the gate opened on that new year, *Australia* and *Canberra* were engaged on the important but essentially humdrum task of escorting the convoys carrying the 2nd AIF to the Middle

East. The first of these, codenamed US.1, sailed from Sydney on Wednesday 10 January 1940, cheered out of the harbour by friends and relatives of the soldiers on board, despite the supposed secrecy of the date and timing. The two cruisers shepherded the convoy to Fremantle and left it there, as agreed.

The second convoy was split into two elements, fast and slow, codenamed US.2 and US.3, and scheduled to leave in April and May. By this time, there was concern that Italy might be about to enter the war on the German side, and both London and Canberra considered the possibility of routing them not through Suez but by the Cape of Good Hope, and not to the Middle East but to Britain. On 30 April, Anthony Eden, the Dominions Secretary, generously cabled Canberra and Wellington that:

> Owing to fact that better training facilities exist in the United Kingdom than in other possible destinations, and that equipment must be supplied from this country, it is suggested that the best course would be that these contingents should be diverted to the United Kingdom. It would of course give us incomparable pleasure to welcome the Australian and New Zealand troops here.[11]

As it happened, US.2 sailed from Fremantle on 22 April and continued on through the Red Sea to Suez. Both the Admiralty and the Naval Board now agreed that the enemy threat in Australian waters was low enough to permit *Australia* and *Canberra* to accompany the fast US.3 convoy as far as Colombo in Ceylon, in company with the light cruiser *Leander*. In late April, Sydneysiders living around the harbour were startled to see the great bulk of the Cunard ocean liner *Queen Mary* glide to anchor off Taronga Zoo, no longer in her peacetime colours of black hull and white upperworks with the famous three red-and-black funnels but now painted a drab troopship grey. Almost as impressive, the brand-new liner *Mauretania* arrived as well, to be joined by another five ships whose names resounded like a roll call of Britain's merchant service: *Empress of Britain*, *Empress of Canada*, *Empress of Japan*, *Andes* and *Aquitania*.

US.3 sailed on 5 May. Ten days later, on 15 May, almost midway between Fremantle and Colombo, great and grave events in Europe caused the convoy to be rerouted to the Cape. *Canberra* returned to Fremantle, her place taken by an RN sister ship, HMS *Shropshire*. *Australia* continued on as part of the escort, sailing into Cape Town's Table Bay on 26 May.

As the Nazis grew ever more naked in their thirst for power and conquest, they devised ever more grotesque fig leaves to cover themselves. Before dawn on Tuesday 9 April 1940, the German ambassador to Denmark called upon the Danish Foreign Minister to inform him that German troops were moving in to Danish territory to save the country from a British and French invasion. The Danes would do well to accept the Führer's protection, he said; otherwise, unfortunately, the *Luftwaffe* would have to bomb Copenhagen. Utterly outnumbered and outgunned, Denmark capitulated within a few hours.

Shielded by its mountains and fjords, Norway proved a harder target. Hitler needed Norwegian coastal waters for shipping his supplies of iron ore, which was mined in northern Sweden and sent through the Norwegian port of Narvik, and the country could also provide useful U-boat bases and airfields for the *Luftwaffe*. The attack on Norway – Operation *Weserübung* – began on the same day as the subjugation of Denmark, with an invasion by sea and air, and the declaration of a Nazi puppet government by the man whose name would become synonymous with treachery, Vidkun Quisling.

With British and French help, the brave Norwegians fought back for a month until they, too, succumbed to overwhelming force. The struggle was notable for its extraordinary encounters between the British and German navies, known as the two battles of Narvik. In the first, on 10 April, a flotilla of five British destroyers charged through pre-dawn showers of driving snow into Ofotfjord, the waterway leading to Narvik, where, in a storm of gunfire and torpedo attacks, they sank two German destroyers and 11 merchant ships, for the loss of two of their own. The flotilla commander, Captain Bernard Warburton-Lee, was posthumously awarded the war's first Victoria Cross.

In the second battle, from just after midday on 13 April, nine destroyers and the battleship *Warspite*, a veteran of Jutland, re-entered Ofotfjord to finish off the remaining German ships. *Warspite* opened the play in splendid style by launching her Swordfish aircraft, which found and sank *U-64* and then flew on to observe the rest of the engagement. The snow-clad hills of the fjord echoed to the thunder of the battleship's 15-inch guns, with the British destroyers dashing here and there through the shell splashes and the smoke and flames of burning German ships. In addition to the U-boat, eight German destroyers were lost that afternoon, with only minor damage to two British ships. The battle over, *Warspite*'s captain, Victor Crutchley, a Victoria Cross winner from the First World War, reputedly turned to his admiral on the bridge, removed the pipe from his mouth and said, 'Just like shelling peas, sir.' Crutchley will return to this story later.

But for all the dash and enterprise afloat, the battle for Norway was lost on land. The Norwegians fought on bravely for a month, but the 38,000 British and French soldiers sent to their aid had to be evacuated by the navy in retreat and confusion, along with King Haakon VII. Norway fell on 10 June. And the Germans somewhat evened the score with the RN when the aircraft carrier *Glorious* and two accompanying destroyers were sunk in the Norwegian Sea by the battleships *Scharnhorst* and *Gneisenau*, with the loss of 1519 men. Hurriedly planned, haphazard and chaotically executed – much of it directed by Winston Churchill – Britain's attempt to save Norway from the Nazis was a fiasco. Yet this would be eclipsed by a still greater catastrophe.

—

Few dates in history resonate with such consequence as Friday 10 May 1940. It was a mild spring morning across Western Europe, the chestnut, oak and birch trees well into leaf. Shortly before dawn, Adolf Hitler's armoured train *Amerika* rolled into the German village of Euskirchen, some 50 kilometres from the Dutch and Belgian borders. A waiting motorcade took the Führer and his entourage to the *Felsennest*, a headquarters bunker carved into a rocky hilltop, from where they would command the invasion of Western Europe.

As dawn broke, 2500 aircraft of the *Luftwaffe* began to bomb airfields in Holland, Belgium, France and Luxembourg. Airborne troops, 16,000 of them, parachuted into Rotterdam and The Hague, and more captured Belgian bridges and the border fortress of Eben-Emael. By 7 am, the Dutch and Belgian Governments had appealed to Britain and France for help, even as the German onslaught continued by air and land. And Britain itself was rocked by a political crisis. After days of uproar in the House of Commons, much of it brought about by the debacle in Norway, the discredited Neville Chamberlain was forced to resign. By the evening, Winston Churchill was Prime Minister.

On the next Monday, 13 May, Churchill rallied Britain – and the Empire – in the House of Commons:

> I have nothing to offer but blood, toil, tears and sweat. We have before us an ordeal of the most grievous kind. We have before us many, many long months of struggle and of suffering. You ask, what is our policy? I can say: it is to wage war, by sea, land and air, with all our might and with all the strength that God can give us; to wage war against a monstrous tyranny, never surpassed in the dark, lamentable catalogue of human crime. That is our policy. You ask, what is our aim? I can answer in one word: It is victory, victory at all costs, victory in spite of all terror, victory, however long and hard the road may be; for without victory, there is no survival. Let that be realised; no survival for the British Empire, no survival for all that the British Empire has stood for . . .[12]

Some 300,000 troops of Generaloberst Fedor von Bock's Army Group 'B' were now wheeling through Belgium, closing in on France from the north. On the very evening of Churchill's speech, Generaloberst Gerd von Rundstedt's Army Group 'A' streamed west through the supposedly impenetrable Ardennes Forest and crossed the River Meuse at Sedan, to devastate the

French Second and Ninth Armies and rampage across France towards the Channel Coast. The *Blitzkrieg* poured ever onwards, the *Luftwaffe* bombing and strafing, the army and Waffen-SS divisions swallowing villages and cities at breathtaking speed. Holland surrendered in just five days, on 15 May. By the third week of May, the Germans had reached the Channel, tumbling the French and British Armies before them, virtually cutting them in half.

At home, the British scored a victory of immeasurable importance on 22 May, when the cipher experts at the top-secret Government Code and Cypher School at Bletchley Park found they could read the *Luftwaffe*'s Enigma code. But not this nor any power on earth could halt the German onslaught.

Britain had sent more than 300,000 men to France in the British Expeditionary Force, the BEF, including ten infantry divisions. They fought bravely and well, even managing a spirited counter-attack at Arras in northern France, but they could not contain the German tide. On 23 May, fate intervened on their side. Concerned that his armoured divisions were getting too far ahead of his infantry and that his supply lines were overstretched, von Rundstedt ordered his tanks to halt for 36 hours to allow the foot soldiers to catch up. The order was approved by Hitler: Goering had promised him that the *Luftwaffe* could finish the job.

This gave the British a breathing space, a respite desperately needed. They had gained some of that most precious commodity in war: time. The next day, 24 May, around 1000 British soldiers were evacuated from the port of Boulogne. On 25 May, the BEF commander, General Lord Gort, recognised that the only possible course left was the evacuation of all his forces. Independently, Winston Churchill reached that same conclusion the same day. The French Government was mired in the fear of defeat, virtually catatonic. The French High Command had collapsed in recrimination and despair; the French armies had been everywhere routed. All that could be done was to save as many British soldiers as possible from death or captivity, and as many French as could be rescued as well. Von Rundstedt's gift of time had allowed the BEF to fall back on the small Channel port of Dunkirk in northern France, just ten kilometres south of the Belgian border. It would have to leave from there. Or not leave at all.

—

In London, the Admiralty had been planning for just such a disastrous event. Every available naval vessel, big and small, would be rounded up and sent to France to carry the army home. The headquarters for this vast enterprise would be Dover Castle, ancient redoubt of kings since the Plantagenet Henry II, the largest castle in England, a fortress with a commanding view of the Channel. A warren of tunnels and barracks had been dug beneath its walls in Napoleonic times, and these would serve again in this war against a new European despot.

The operation was given the codename Dynamo, taken from what had once been the castle's electrical dynamo room, which would now be the nerve centre. There, Vice Admiral Bertram Ramsay – known as the Vice Admiral, Dover – was ready and waiting to act. From an old Highland Scots family, Ramsay had a justly deserved reputation as a brilliant naval staff officer of forthright integrity,[13] and Churchill had wisely brought him out of an early retirement to employ his talents. At the hour of need, he had his plans and his ships and his men in place.

On 26 May, a Sunday, Churchill, now master of all he surveyed, took himself to a special service of prayer at Westminster Abbey, where, he wrote later, 'I could feel the pent-up, passionate emotion, and also the fear of the congregation, not of death or wounds or material loss, but of defeat and the final ruin of Britain.'[14]

At the Admiralty, there was a less spiritual event, a morning meeting to fine-tune ways of finding and manning small craft – yachts, private motorboats, pleasure steamers – that might help the navy. As the situation in France worsened through the day and the reports came in, the Admiralty acted. In the words of the RN staff appreciation, written after the war:

> under the pressure of the acute military situation, the Admiralty
> informed the Vice Admiral, Dover, that it was imperative for
> *"Dynamo"* to be implemented with the greatest vigour, with a
> view to lifting up to 45,000 of the BEF within two days, at the
> end of which it was probable that evacuation would be termi-
> nated by enemy action.[15]

Ramsay and his staff waited, poised for the signal to go. At
6.57 pm, the teleprinter at his headquarters clattered out the
historic signal: 'Operation Dynamo is to commence.' In small
numbers at first, but steadily building in strength and urgency,
Ramsay's motley fleet of cruisers, destroyers, minesweepers,
tugs, corvettes, trawlers and an ever-growing flotilla of those
privately owned small craft sailed for the Dunkirk beaches.
Perhaps, with luck, they might bring off the 45,000.

—

The order from the Admiralty reached Commander Emile
Dechaineux at Newcastle upon Tyne in northern England on
Tuesday 28 May. It was terse, explicit. Dechaineux was to report
to the Vice Admiral, Dover with all despatch. He understood
immediately what it meant. 'I guessed it would be as spare
commanding officer of a destroyer, as the Captains of destroyers
were cracking up like ninepins under the severe strain,' he wrote
to his wife, Mary, back in Tasmania.[16] Duty called. He packed a
bag and his regulation gas mask, and, at 10.30 that evening, he
caught a train south to London.

Emile Dechaineux's forebears were Belgian. His grandpar-
ents, François and Josephine Dechaineux, had emigrated to
Australia from the French-speaking city of Liège in 1884, hoping
to make their way in the New World by working an orange
orchard and a gold mine they had purchased sight unseen. Their
hopes were dashed: they had been swindled. The orchard was
a swamp and the mine had been salted. Bankrupt, they settled
instead in Sydney, where their teenage son Lucien studied art,

first at the Sydney Technical College and then under the tutelage of the pre-eminent art teacher of the colony, Julian Ashton. Lucien married a Tasmanian, Ella Briant, and moved first to Launceston in 1895, and then to Hobart, where, for 33 years, he built a life and a career as a painter, sculptor and teacher admired throughout the island. Much of his public work can still be seen, most notably the stained-glass war-memorial window he created for Hobart's Holy Trinity Church.

Ella gave birth to their first child, Emile Frank Verlaine Dechaineux, in 1902. His parents sent him to The Friends' School in Hobart until 1916, when he was accepted for the RANC at Jervis Bay, graduating as a midshipman in 1920. Tall and lanky, popular with his term mates, he won the nickname 'Dishy'. Navy life suited him well and he suited it. He qualified as a torpedo specialist and a naval air observer, and in 1935, as a lieutenant commander, he became squadron torpedo officer in *Canberra*. That was followed by a spell at the RN Staff College, where he was marked out for greater things, and when the war broke out he was a commander and working in London at the Admiralty's Tactical and Minesweeping divisions. In April 1940, he was offered every naval officer's dream, command of a brand-new destroyer, which is how he came to be in Newcastle. He was preparing to commission HMS *Eglinton*, a Hunt class destroyer fitting out in the Swan Hunter yard on the Tyne, when the Admiralty ordered him south.

After a long, jolting night and a pre-dawn change of trains in the London blackout, Dechaineux arrived at Dover at 10 am the next day, Wednesday 29 May. The weather was fine, the sea calm. The faint grey line that was the coast of France lay dimly on the horizon with a broad smudge of smoke above it, and the thump of distant gunfire was borne in on the breeze. The port was full of ships big and small, some berthed and resting, others coming or going. The Australian snatched a hasty breakfast and then climbed the hill to the castle, where he found Ramsay's headquarters deep in those famous white chalk cliffs. There he was asked to hold himself in readiness. He cooled his heels for an hour until at noon he was told to take command of HMS *Vivacious*, lying alongside in the port below.

Vivacious was anything but. Picking his way along the docks, he found an old V and W class destroyer commissioned in 1917, her shabby grey paint streaked with rust, a ship that looked to be exhausted, on her last legs. And so was her crew, as Dechaineux had suspected:

> The captain was a nervous wreck and his ship's company in a worked-up state. They had been bombed a bit during the last few days. The old captain was landed and I asked for a night's rest for his ship's company. At 0530 the following morning we sailed for a beach about eight miles to the east of Dunkirk.[17]

Wartime or not, this was an extraordinary predicament for Dechaineux to confront. For all his experience, this was his first ever command at sea, in peace or war. *Vivacious* was a sister ship to four of the five Australian destroyers, but he had never served in any of them, not even as a midshipman, let alone as a watch-keeper. And his specialty was torpedoes, not navigation. Normally, a commanding officer might take weeks to get to know his new ship; now he was required immediately to take to sea a strange old crock manned by a crew whose strengths and competence – even whose names – were unknown to him but who were clearly at the ragged edge of their endurance.

But there was nothing for it. Undaunted, he set to. Ramsay's staff had printed charts of the Channel that laid down three separate routes to and from France, a measure chiefly to avoid ships crashing into each other all over the place, but it meant that accurate navigation was crucial; not least because the northern-most route skirted the notorious Goodwin Sands, a graveyard of ships for centuries. That morning, 30 May, *Vivacious* was assigned the southern course, Route Z, a trip of about 60 kilometres with a dogleg to port at a naval buoy laid off Calais and then a run – or a crawl – up the French coast. With her new captain alert on an unfamiliar compass platform, and her crew closed up at action stations, the old destroyer butted out into the Channel.

As she made the turn at the Calais buoy, they could see Dunkirk town aflame ahead on the starboard bow, an inferno topped by billowing clouds of viscous, stinking black smoke from burning oil tanks. 'I did not believe so much smoke could come from one town,' Dechaineux told his wife. Picking their way gingerly past sunken wrecks still protruding from the shallow waters, they stopped about one and a half kilometres off the Bray-Dunes beach to the east of Dunkirk – as close as they could get in the shoaling waters – and went to work.

There were literally thousands of soldiers waiting there, a crawling, trudging mass of khaki, and with *Vivacious* having only one serviceable boat, the evacuation was agonisingly slow. Smaller civilian craft helped bring men out: some of them exhausted, some bleeding and bandaged, some wide-eyed and staring like zombies, others doing their bold best to put on a cocky, cheerful front as they struggled up the boarding nets slung over the destroyer's side and crowded together on deck. Every so often, the *Luftwaffe* would appear, dropping a bomb here and there but hitting nothing except a few of the wrecks. That afternoon, though, the tempo lifted:

> At about 4pm we saw a most thrilling dog fight. About 20 Messerschmitts and 15 Heinkels came over. We shot down at least one Heinkel. Then nine Spitfires appeared. The sky seemed full with planes. One or two further Heinkels were shot down by Spitfires, of which two came down, but the pilots had bailed out. One pilot drifted away towards the enemy lines, the other came down in the sea and was rescued. The Heinkel we shot down was an enormous one, which took fire in mid-air. He circled around for about two minutes, a blazing mass, and then dived into the sea.[18]

On that day, *Vivacious* rescued 1023 men, even as the carnage grew ever more bloody, more savage. The next day, 31 May, more than a score of ships were sunk or damaged, most by *Luftwaffe* bombing. It was *Vivacious*'s turn that day, too. A concealed enemy gun battery opened up on them from the shore near Bray-Dunes, sending up shell splashes of muddy brown water far too close for comfort. Dechaineux turned his stern to the line of fire, presenting the smallest possible target, and the 4-inch guns of the aft X- and Y-turrets hammered back, but the German gunnery was good. The ship was hit twice, causing not much damage, but three soldiers and three sailors were killed, and more were wounded. *Vivacious* shifted seawards out of range, but a small piece of shrapnel ripped a hole in the seat of Dechaineux's trousers and another tiny fragment cut him above one eye. He would joke afterwards that he was glad he had been heading west, not east, in which case the personal damage might have been far less amusing.

Ashore in his castle, the Vice Admiral, Dover was despatching ever more ships to the fray, with the Dutch and the French joining in. The Dutch contribution was especially welcome: 50 *schuyts* – or skoots, as the British called them – flat-bottomed coastal craft ideal for getting into the shallows off the beaches. The navy plugged grimly on, although, after days of stark terror, a few of the civilian and merchant sailors threw in the towel. It was true that one or two crews of the bigger transports had to be sent back out at gunpoint. The Channel itself had become a modern River Styx, the boundary between Earth and Hades, a violent tableau of fire and smoke, of diving aircraft, of bombs and bullets, of weaving and sometimes burning and sinking ships, of beaten men struggling for life itself. But each time, each day, more and more soldiers were brought off. *Vivacious* kept at it, back and forth across this grim, grey stretch of water, her men snatching a scratch meal or grasping a fragment of sleep whenever they could still their jangling nerves.

Saturday 1 June 1940 was another perfect day, fine and sunny. Late on the Friday, a light surf had whipped up, hindering the rescue from the sands, but – to everyone's enormous relief – that had abated overnight. *Vivacious* was returning again to her assigned beach at daybreak when another destroyer swooped up abeam and a rear admiral on the bridge bellowed to Dechaineux that he was to go alongside the mole at Dunkirk to take off troops there.

On a curve of the coast, Dunkirk's little port – destroyed and useless by now – faced more or less due north. It was reached through a narrow, dredged channel flanked by two jetties – or moles – east and west, built of latticed timber. The west mole was a wreck. The east mole, still standing and packed with soldiers, was accessible from the sea – only just – through a gap about 150 metres wide. When Dechaineux arrived there, he found another five destroyers milling about and waiting to go in before him, which left him no choice but to join the queue, hovering back and forth between half-sunken wrecks and the traffic jam, always at the risk of collision.

The *Luftwaffe* found them at exactly 6 am. A bridge lookout reported a big, four-engined Junkers roaring out of the blue, straight towards them. *Vivacious* fired back with everything she had, which was precious little. Ships of the First World War had not been designed or armed to fight aircraft. 'As our guns were very old and would not go above 30 degrees, our protection or offensive gunpower was extremely small. I wished I had my *Eglinton* here; she would have made those enemy bombers sit up,' Dechaineux told Mary.[19]

The Junkers levelled out at about 1000 feet, Dechaineux estimated, so close that they could see the black crosses on its fuselage and the swastika on its tail. It released what appeared to be four 250-pound (113-kilogram) bombs. They missed, but only just, showering columns of dirty water over the ship as the aircraft thundered away unharmed. Seizing the moment and a gap in the queue, Dechaineux thrust *Vivacious* in through the entrance to the mole, only to have another bomber come at him. That missed, too, as he inched the ship ahead.

This manouevre was fraught with difficulty and danger. Almost like threading a needle, he had to insert *Vivacious* between two wrecks, one of which was a trawler that had taken a direct hit and whose shattered, blackened superstructure still protruded above the water a stone's throw away to starboard. It was 6.30 am. Somehow, he pulled it off, and the destroyer nudged her bow into the little quay, to be rushed by the waiting men. In just 15 minutes, according to the post-war Admiralty report, exactly 475 soldiers scrambled aboard onto the fo'c'sle. That was all they could take. Dechaineux rang for slow astern and eased back out again into the Channel, heading once more for Dover.

Dunkirk was that curiously English phenomenon: a wartime muddle of error and folly rescued and made great by relentless determination and extraordinary feats of courage, a disaster turned triumph. The early estimate that 45,000 might be plucked from the beaches proved to have been wildly pessimistic, again in that subdued English way. When Bertram Ramsay finally shut down Operation Dynamo on the afternoon of Tuesday 4 June, the truly astounding total of 338,226 men – British and French – had been carried to safety, in the face of everything the Germans had thrown at them. An army had been saved. Its guns and its transport lay wrecked and rusting on the beaches and on the blasted roads that led to them, but the great majority of its men were alive to fight another day.

The cost, though, had been devastating. Not everyone was saved – far from it. Some units of the BEF had been cut off and never reached the Dunkirk beaches. More than 68,000 soldiers were left behind dead, wounded or captured since the BEF's arrival in France at the start of the war, with 34,000 prisoners taken in and around Dunkirk itself. Of nearly 900 British and Allied vessels that took part, 200 were sunk, most of them small craft of one sort or another, but including the sombre total of six RN and three French destroyers. The RAF – often unfairly accused of being absent from the skies over the beaches – in fact lost 145 aircraft, including 42 precious Spitfire fighters.

That afternoon, 4 June, Churchill rose in the Commons to deliver a speech that lasted for just over half an hour. The rescue at Dunkirk had produced, if not euphoria in Britain and the Empire, at least wave of joyful relief at a task successfully accomplished. Brilliantly, Churchill began by capping that joy. 'We must be very careful not to assign to this deliverance the attributes of a victory,' he cautioned. 'Wars are not won by evacuations.'

It was a sombre message that struck the perfect note, laying a foundation for a defiance that would echo for eternity:

> Even though large tracts of Europe and many old and famous States have fallen or may fall into the grip of the Gestapo and all the odious apparatus of Nazi rule, we shall not flag or fail.
>
> We shall go on to the end. We shall fight in France, we shall fight on the seas and oceans, we shall fight with growing confidence and growing strength in the air, we shall defend our island, whatever the cost may be.
>
> We shall fight on the beaches, we shall fight on the landing grounds, we shall fight in the fields and in the streets, we shall fight in the hills; we shall never surrender, and even if, which I do not for a moment believe, this island or a large part of it were subjugated and starving, then our Empire beyond the seas, armed and guarded by the British Fleet, would carry on the struggle, until, in God's good time, the New World, with all its power and might, steps forth to the rescue and the liberation of the old.[20]

Beaten and broken, the French sued for peace. On 22 June, France and Germany signed an armistice at a clearing in the Forest of Compiègne some 60 kilometres north of Paris. Hitler chose the site himself: it was the exact spot where Germany's humiliation in the armistice of 1918 had been played out. France was divided in two: occupied by Germany in the north and administered in the south by a government of Nazi collaborators under the aged Great War hero Marshal Philippe Pétain, set up in the spa town of Vichy in the Auvergne. On 23 June, Hitler made a gloating visit to Paris to see the sights, and on his return to Berlin he was greeted by cheering crowds in the hundreds of thousands and driven through flower-filled streets from the railway station to the Chancellery. He was now at the zenith of his power, with an additional reason for celebration: his fellow dictator Benito Mussolini had declared war on Britain and France on 10 June.

The Vice Admiral, Dover was awarded the accolade of Knight Commander of the Most Honourable Order of the Bath by a grateful George VI. In 1944, by then a full admiral, Sir Bertram rose to still greater heights in the planning of the D-Day invasion of Normandy as the Naval Commander-in-Chief of the Allied Naval Expeditionary Force. But in an ending of almost Shakespearean tragedy, he did not live to see the fruits of the victory he had done so much to bring about. He was killed on 2 January 1945, in a plane crash outside Paris.

HMS *Vivacious* kept her tall and laconic Australian captain for another couple of weeks after Dynamo. His appointment to her in those dark days at Dover was so brief and sudden that it does not even appear on his RAN service record. The RN record shows he handed over command on 19 June and returned to Newcastle to take up with HMS *Eglinton* again. The next year, 1941, he was awarded the Distinguished Service Cross after a bruising tussle in *Eglinton* with German motor torpedo boats – E-boats – in the Channel.

Emile Dechaineux was one of the first Australian sailors to experience the perils and terrors of the Second World War at sea, not least in the novelty of attack from the air. At Dunkirk, training, discipline and sheer courage carried him through an ordeal he could not have begun to imagine as a fresh-faced boy at Jervis Bay and the likes of which had yet to be encountered by his contemporaries. These strengths would sustain him through greater trials and hazards to come.

CHAPTER 8

WE SIGHTED SMOKE AND HOISTED BATTLE ENSIGNS

The first sign that something unusual was happening came when *Australia* moved to the Simon's Town Naval Base to the south of Cape Town. Workmen arrived on board and began to wrap the hull in kilometres of cable, which was explained as degaussing gear to protect the ship against magnetic mines.[1] Putting two and two together, the wise heads in the crew realised that the Germans had sown magnetic mines in the sea approaches to Britain and figured that's where they were heading.

They were right. In May 1940, with no apparent threat from the enemy in Australian waters, the Australian Government had offered *Australia* and *Canberra* to the Admiralty, a contribution accepted with alacrity. *Australia* would head for the northern hemisphere; *Canberra* would stay in southern waters east or west of Cape Town. So it was that, on 25 June, *Australia* sailed from Simon's Town into the Atlantic to escort a small convoy of three ships north to Freetown, a British naval base at the colony of Sierra Leone on the westernmost bulge of Africa. They left the Cape with some regret, for the local hospitality had been lavish, as the captain, Ross Stewart, noted in his Report of Proceedings. Like many an RN officer before him, Stewart fretted about the discipline of the Australians under his command. There had been 66 leave-breaking offences and two outright desertions in just 17 days at Simon's Town, although, he added with some relief, 'the low incidence of venereal disease is most gratifying'.

From there on, things began to get serious. Britain stood in dire peril. France lay conquered, with Germany triumphant and Hitler quite possibly planning an invasion across the Channel. The fall of France and the entry of Italy into the war had profoundly upset the balance of power at sea, chiefly in the Mediterranean but in the eastern Atlantic as well. Mussolini's navy, the *Regia Marina*, was of unknown quality but relatively modern and well equipped. With six battleships, 19 cruisers, 59 destroyers and 116 submarines, it was, on paper, a formidable force far stronger than the RN's Mediterranean Fleet. It would also have the support of the *Regia Aeronautica*, operating from Italian land bases.

As for the French fleet, its future was the stuff of British nightmares. The *Marine Nationale* numbered nine battleships, including the modern and powerful *Richelieu* and her near-complete sister ship *Jean Bart*, with an imposing array of cruisers and destroyers; many of these ships were scattered around the Mediterranean and France's colonial possessions in Africa. If they were to come under German control, Winston Churchill feared the worst:

> The addition of the French Navy to the German and Italian Fleets, with the menace of Japan measureless on the horizon, confronted Great Britain with mortal dangers ... At all costs, at all risks, in one way or another, we must make sure that the Navy of France did not fall into the wrong hands, and then perhaps bring us and others to ruin.[2]

The French Commander-in-Chief, Amiral de la Flotte François Darlan, had promised Churchill that he would never allow the Germans to seize his ships, but Darlan was a devious and notorious Anglophobe,[3] and not to be trusted. In the first week of July, Britain acted. It was, said Churchill, 'a hateful decision, the most unnatural and painful in which I have ever been concerned'.[4]

At Portsmouth and Plymouth, before dawn on 3 July, British troops seized control of French ships berthed there and interned their crews. That same day, the Admiralty gave the order for Operation Catapult. In the Mediterranean, the RN's newly formed Force H of HMS *Hood*, the battleships *Resolution* and *Valiant*, and the carrier *Ark Royal*, with two cruisers and 11 destroyers, appeared off Mers El Kébir, the French naval base in Algeria. Inside that harbour lay four French battleships, including the flagship *Dunkerque*, and a flotilla of destroyers.

What followed was a tragedy that both nations would prefer to forget. The British commander, Vice Admiral James Somerville, was ordered to give four options to his French opposite number, Amiral Marcel-Bruno Gensoul, which he did. They were to:

1) Join the British fleet and continue to fight the Germans.
2) Be escorted to the West Indies or to a British port.
3) Have the ships disarmed at Oran under the supervision of the British.
4) Scuttle the ships where they were harboured.

After a day of ever more tense and painful negotiation produced no result, and under sharp prodding from London, Somerville opened fire shortly before 6 pm. He did so with heavy heart and personal revulsion, but his orders were direct from Churchill and explicit beyond doubt or disagreement. Confined in harbour, the French ships were sitting ducks. Within minutes, the battleship *Bretagne* blew up, with the loss of 977 men, and the carnage continued unabated, a cauldron of smoke and flame in the July heat. The *Dunkerque* and *Provence* were also damaged, along with a destroyer.

In the confusion, the battleship *Strasbourg* and a handful of destroyers managed to escape, and reached the French Mediterranean port of Toulon. Three days later, on 6 July, aircraft from *Ark Royal* raided Mers El Kébir again, putting *Dunkerque* out of action for a year. In all, 1297 French sailors were killed. 'We all feel thoroughly dirty and ashamed that the first time we should have been in action was an affair like this,' Somerville wrote later to his wife, adding that it was 'the biggest political blunder of modern times and I imagine will rouse the world against us'.[5] The French saw it differently. Seventy years later, Leon le Roux, a sailor from *Bretagne*, recalled an unforgivable betrayal: 'It was murder. A crime. Yes, a real crime.'[6]

Further east in the Mediterranean, at the British base at Alexandria in Egypt, the French commander there was persuaded to disarm his ships, including the old battleship *Lorraine*. There remained one last nut to crack: the battleship *Richelieu* in port at Dakar, on the West African Atlantic coast (at what is modern-day Senegal). Dakar was the capital of *l'Afrique occidentale française*, a federation of France's eight West African possessions, a harbour and city in its own right as important to colonial France as Hanoi or Beirut.

—

Australia arrived at Freetown on 3 July – the same day that Force H was attacking Mers El Kébir – to find the harbour crammed with British ships of all shapes and sizes, civilian and naval, including the old aircraft carrier HMS *Hermes*. Some of the ship's company were allowed a quick run ashore, but Freetown was a steamy, ramshackle colonial outpost with no excitement to offer, and there was no great disappointment when they were ordered to sail again that night, in company with *Hermes*.

Two days later, both ships were off Dakar, patrolling up and down with the cruiser *Dorsetshire*, a sister ship to *Australia*, and a small sloop, HMS *Milford*. *Hermes*'s captain, Richard Onslow, with a promotion to acting rear admiral, was ordered to give the French captain in *Richelieu* the Admiralty ultimatum, which he did. Again, there was no response. After sunset, Onslow ordered *Milford* to tow a fast motorboat into Dakar under cover of darkness, where its crew – faces suitably blackened for the night – would drop depth charges beneath *Richelieu*'s stern.

It was a comedy of errors. The motorboat kept breaking down. The depth charges were released but the water was too shallow and they failed to explode. The next morning, *Hermes* sent in six torpedo bombers, which scored one minor hit, damaging one of the battleship's propeller shafts and giving her a slight list.

And that was largely that. *Australia* took no part in this desultory action until that afternoon, when a lone French aircraft appeared overhead and dropped a stick of bombs into the sea some distance away, hitting nothing. Everyone opened fire, including *Australia*'s anti-aircraft guns, with Harold Eastick recording in his diary:

> Engaged enemy aircraft believed to be Dago, but owing to it being well out of range for accurate spotting, our AA people were unable to get to it. But they sure had a good go. About a dozen rounds were fired and everyone was quite downhearted because he wouldn't come down lower.[7]

Onslow had no more appetite for attacking the former French ally than did Somerville, and there was relief all round when the Admiralty called a halt. The next morning, *Australia* was heading north again, ordered to catch up with a convoy on its way to Britain. However minor, Dakar had been a baptism of fire, the first taste of warlike activity. As offensive as it was, Operation Catapult achieved one important purpose beyond disabling the French Navy. As Churchill had intended, it served notice to the world, friend and foe, that Britain was deadly serious in its waging of war and its determination to retain command of the sea against all odds.

The rest of the trip was uneventful, a pleasant interlude while the war raged elsewhere. *Australia* parted company with the convoy off the Mull of Kintyre in the early evening of 16 July, the sun setting slowly through clouds on her port quarter as she passed the lovely Scottish foothills framing the Firth of Clyde. Shortly before ten o'clock, she was through the anti-submarine boom between Dunoon and the pleasing symmetry of the eighteenth-century Cloch Point Lighthouse to starboard. Minutes later, she was coming on the bearing at the Tail o' the Bank, the naval anchorage off Greenock, her fo'c'sle hands ready for the familiar routine of anchoring. Stop engines.

Slow astern. Let go. Then, in the gently purpling night, the final command: finished with engines. *Australia* was back at rest in the river where she had been born.

There was a welcome waiting, not least from the Admiralty – both First Lord and First Sea Lord – who signalled:

> we offer you a warm welcome upon your arrival in British waters ... we are very glad of your assistance and grateful to your government for letting you come. We wish you all good luck and an early opportunity of engaging the enemy.[8]

On a less exalted plane, the pubs of Sauchiehall Street in Glasgow did their hospitable best as well, prompting another bout of prim disapproval from Captain Stewart, in his Report of Proceedings for the month:

> There were 40 cases of leave breaking at Greenock and nine cases of drunkenness ... There are in the ship's company a number of ratings with insufficient strength of mind to resist filling themselves up with liquor after a long period without it, particularly if they are without the restraining influence of a home or their fear of having their leave to their home port stopped.[9]

After three days, it was back to work. They left the Clyde late on 19 July and the next afternoon dropped anchor at Scapa Flow, to join the 1st Cruiser Squadron of the RN's Home Fleet. No fewer than five battleships, two aircraft carriers and countless cruisers and destroyers lay scattered about the anchorage – an encouraging sight.

—

Australia was the first ship of the RAN to reach British waters in the war, but she was far from the first to see action. The five destroyers had been with the RN's Mediterranean Fleet since the beginning of 1940, and in May that Australian contribution was strengthened by the arrival of the light cruiser *Sydney*, under the command of John Collins. Within weeks, they were at war with the Italians, *Sydney* as a member of the 7th Cruiser Squadron.

On 28 June, she was involved in the very first action with Italian ships, a messy affair that became known as the Battle of the Espero Convoy. In fading evening light south-west of Crete, the squadron jumped three Italian destroyers, two of which took to their heels behind a smokescreen, leaving their flagship, *Espero*, hit and dead in the water. *Sydney* was ordered to sink her, which she did by 6-inch gunfire. Then, in the dark, and at great risk of submarine attack, Collins ordered two boats to be lowered and scrambling nets rigged to pick up survivors. In about an hour, they rescued 47 men before being ordered to rejoin the squadron, leaving behind a cutter with oars, sails and provisions to be found by those they could no longer see in the black of night but whose haunting cries for help they could still hear.

This was a time of dark foreboding in the war at sea, with British survival hanging by a thread. The U-boats now had the use of the French Atlantic ports of Brest, Lorient and La Rochelle, in what their crews would call *die Glückliche Zeit*, the Happy Time. In the month of June alone, they sank 285,000 tonnes of Allied shipping without losing a boat – a record for the war so far. And there was always the danger, too, that one or more of the *Kriegsmarine*'s battleships or heavy cruisers might break out into the Atlantic to wreak havoc. The Germans had not yet entered the Mediterranean in any numbers, but the British and Italians there were testing each other like boxers in the opening round.

On 9 July, *Sydney* and the destroyers *Stuart*, *Vampire* and *Voyager* were with the fleet at the Battle of Calabria, Britain's first full-scale engagement with an enemy battle line in the Med for more than a century. On a calm, sunlit afternoon in the Ionian Sea east of the toe of Italy, the squadron came under heavy fire from two Italian battleships, *Giulio Cesare* and *Conte di Cavour*, and their attendant cruisers. *Sydney* had some of her signal halyards shot away, but that was all. They were rescued in the nick of time when the British battleships turned up over the horizon, led by *Warspite*, which eventually put the Italians to flight in what turned out to be an inconclusive scrap. Not a ship was sunk, but there was damage on both sides, with the cruiser *Gloucester* taking a direct hit on her bridge, killing her captain and 17 men.

Sydney's great moment came just over a week later in the Aegean Sea off Cape Spada on the island of Crete, a dashing encounter that made Collins's reputation as a fighting captain. It was Friday 19 July, a bright morning that promised another beautiful Mediterranean day. As dawn broke, there were two Allied forces working to the north of Crete: *Sydney* and a destroyer, HMS *Havock*, were on their way from Alexandria to patrol off Piraeus, the port of Athens. To the south of them, zigzagging in line abreast on a westerly course, four more destroyers, led by HMS *Hyperion*, were on an anti-submarine patrol slightly northwest of the island. They were aware of each other, but were well out of sight.

At 7.20 am – on *Hyperion*'s bridge, the agreeable smell of frying bacon was wafting up the voice pipes – two Italian cruisers emerged from the western haze some 16 kilometres ahead. Breakfast abandoned, alarm bells ringing, their crews racing to action stations, the four destroyers wheeled hard to starboard and raced north-east to join *Sydney*. After a few minutes of indecision, the Italians gave chase, confident of an easy kill. They were both light cruisers – *Giovanni delle Bande Nere* and *Bartolomeo Colleoni* – each mounting eight 6-inch guns and capable of an impressive 40 knots, more than enough to run down the slower and far more lightly armed destroyers in a stern chase.

It was here that Collins's skill and years of training paid off. If he had been strictly following the orders he had been given in Alexandria, he should have been several hundred kilometres to the north of the destroyers, much closer to the Gulf of Athens. But the evening before, intuition had warned him that *Hyperion* and her companions might well strike trouble the next morning: they were in dangerous waters and, in those days before radar, dawn was the most risky, the most unpredictable moment at sea. Enemy ships, enemy aircraft, a prowling submarine: you never knew what might turn up in the sunrise. So that night, Collins, loosely interpreting his orders, had kept just 60 kilometres away on a parallel course to the destroyers, able to go to their support if needed.

As needed he was. *Sydney* heard *Hyperion*'s enemy report at 7.30, and she and *Havock* immediately turned south to close the destroyers, working up to full speed. Collins kept wireless silence so as not to alert the enemy to his presence, but with *Hyperion* continuing to send her course and speed and the enemy position, he knew exactly where he had to go.

'From the plot it was obvious that we could not get into action till about 8.30, so opportunity was taken to pipe hands to breakfast. Everyone feels better after breakfast. All stations reported closed up again at 8.20, just before we sighted smoke and hoisted battle ensigns,' he wrote.[10]

Sydney opened fire from her two for'ard turrets at 8.29, at a range of about 18 kilometres. The Italians were taken utterly by surprise, startled out of their wits as the dirty brown shell splashes erupted off their port beam. Expecting Collins to have been much further north, the destroyers were equally surprised, but rather more pleased. So battle was joined: *Sydney* closing at full speed, signal flags and battle ensigns bar taut, white foam boiling at her forefoot, stern buried deep, orange flashes bursting from her two for'ard turrets, the air thickening with smoke. The two enemy cruisers returned a ragged fire and curved away to make a run for the south-west. *Sydney* and the five destroyers went after them in hard pursuit, almost in line abreast now.

With their superior speed, the Italians looked as if they might make good their escape until, at 9.23, *Colleoni* took a shell from *Sydney* that jammed her rudder, and then another in her boilers that stopped her dead. She was on fire and down by the bow, her main armament out of action. *Bande Nere* appeared to hesitate for a moment as if to go to her consort's aid, and then turned and fled. Ordering three of the destroyers to finish off *Colleoni* with torpedoes, Collins and the other two continued to chase the fleeing Italian, scoring some minor hits, but after an hour their faster quarry was clearly beyond reach. The Battle of Cape Spada was over.

The Allied ships rescued 555 of *Colleoni*'s ship's company; 121 had been killed, and her captain would die of his wounds. *Bande Nere* made it safely to Benghazi in Libya. The *Regia Aeronautica* launched some high-level bombing raids that just missed *Sydney* and caused some minor damage to *Havock* as they returned to Alexandria. Paint scorched and blistered on her gun barrels and a big Australian flag at her foremast, *Sydney* was cheered to the echo when she entered harbour, not least by the other Australians there. *Stuart*, the battered old destroyer leader, hoisted a flag signal 'Whacko Sydney' – a naval round of applause from her captain and Collins's naval-college term mate Hec Waller.

It was a victory much needed in those anxious days of 1940, a rousing demonstration of the offensive spirit, a fillip to morale for the Allies, and a depressing fiasco for the Italians, who should have given a much better account of themselves. Mussolini was reportedly 'far from happy' with the lacklustre Italian perfor-mance.[11] *Sydney* had taken only one hit, a shell that bored a picturesque but trivial hole in her for'ard funnel. A day after the battle, George VI made Collins a Companion of the Order of the Bath, a traditional honour for a victorious captain at sea.

And Australia was ecstatic. The news was splashed across all the newspapers, with general agreement that *Sydney* had followed handsomely in the wake of her predecessor, the coal-burning *Sydney I*, which had hunted the German raider *Emden* to destruc-tion in the Indian Ocean in 1914.

'Once again the Australian Navy has shown the splendid fighting quality and efficiency of the last war. *Sydney* out fought and destroyed the famous *Emden* and now her younger sister writes another page of naval history that will thrill the civilized world,' said the Melbourne *Herald*.[12]

In the public eye, the ship radiated an aura of competence and success, generating hope for better days to come.

—

As the northern summer of 1940 became autumn and then winter, *Australia* encountered incidents and episodes that lingered in the collective memory of her ship's company – some for the violence and fear they unleashed, some because they were a job well done, some simply because they were out of the ordinary run of things.

In late July, the ship got her first coat of dazzle camouflage, the crew wielding pots and brushes to break up her uniform light-grey paint with swoops and darts of charcoal shapes. In addition, the pale teak decks – uncomfortably visible from the air at night – were turned a dark grey. For a couple of days that month, they put to sea with the Home Fleet battlecruisers *Renown* and *Repulse*, searching off the coast of Norway for the enemy battleship *Gneisenau*, which was making a run back from Trondheim to Kiel, but they drew a blank.

In August, *Australia* and her sister ship HMS *Norfolk* punched their way through a spell of filthy weather to reach Bear Island, a barren speck of rock in the icy Barents Sea at a latitude of 74 degrees north, about halfway between Greenland and the northernmost tip of Russia. Again, it was a search for the enemy, this time a German fishing fleet thought to be operating there, but again there was no result, not a trawler to be seen. It was the miserable conditions on that trip that stayed in the mind: first a savage sea that sent the ship pitching and rolling to a sometimes alarming degree, with torrents of icy water sluicing down broken air vents into the chaos of the fo'c'sle mess decks; then a bitter cold that penetrated even the heaviest jumpers, duffel coats and seaboots of the watch on deck.

There was little to do ashore at Scapa. The wretched place had a 'wet' canteen (as in it sold alcohol) and a cinema at Lyness on the island of Hoy, a joyless barn where they issued you with tickets for two pints of flat English beer. Young Jack Langrell, not a drinker, preferred to stretch his legs with a long walk on the bare, almost treeless island of Flotta. Or there was Kirkwall, the capital of the Orkneys, which offered a twelfth-century cathedral, such antiquity a source of wonder to Australians. One day in August, a few of the men ventured a swim over the ship's side, but not for long. 'Was it cold or was it?' Harold Eastick wrote in his diary.

Their far northern purgatory came to an end in September, when they were ordered back to the Clyde again. On the evening of 2 September, anchored off Greenock, Stewart received a long and detailed signal from the Admiralty, orders that would enmesh *Australia* in a bold attempt to place a little-known French army *général de brigade* and junior cabinet minister, Charles de Gaulle, in power in France's colonies in West Africa. Four days later, on 6 September, with two small French Luciole biplane aircraft secured on her catapult deck and a handful of French air force officers and men aboard to crew them, the ship sailed once more for the British base at Freetown. Operation Menace had begun.

De Gaulle had arrived in Britain after the fall of France in June, setting up a headquarters in London to rally his compatriots against the German conquerors and their Vichy collaborators. In an electrifying broadcast on the BBC, he sounded the call to arms:

> *Mais le dernier mot est-il dit? L'espérance doit-elle disparaître? La défaite est-elle définitive? Non! Croyez-moi, moi qui vous parle en connaissance de cause et vous dis que rien n'est perdu pour la France. Les mêmes moyens qui nous ont vaincus peuvent faire venir un jour la victoire.*
>
> *Car la France n'est pas seule! Elle n'est pas seule! Elle n'est pas seule!* [13]

> But has the last word been said? Must hope disappear? Is defeat final? No! Believe me, I who am speaking to you with full knowledge of the facts, and who tell you that nothing is lost for France. The same means that overcame us can bring us victory one day.
>
> For France is not alone! She is not alone! She is not alone!

That August, a Vichy court martial pronounced de Gaulle guilty of treason – *in absentia* – and sentenced him to death. The British found him haughty, prickly, aggressive, extraordinarily difficult to deal with, but Churchill, impetuous as ever, persuaded the War Cabinet that it would be a stirring political and military coup if he could raise the tricolour of Free France in Dakar. Operation Menace would have a strong British naval squadron of two battleships, an aircraft carrier, and the usual attendant force of cruisers and destroyers to get him there and, if necessary, to deal with Vichy opposition. There would be British Royal Marines and Free French *fusiliers marins* if – as a last resort – an armed landing was needed.[14] But the breezy hope was that de Gaulle would be welcomed with open arms as the saviour of French honour and, indeed, of France herself. And there was an additional attraction. The gold reserves of the Banque de France had been sent to Dakar at the start of the war.

Things did not start well. British intelligence picked up some worrying security lapses in London, when Free French officers were seen and heard drinking a noisy toast – à Dakar! – at a West End restaurant, and de Gaulle himself, visiting Simpson's, the gentlemen's outfitters in Piccadilly, announced that he wished to buy tropical kit for West Africa. There was more trouble when French crews of the transport ships mutinied over unpaid wages and refused to sail from Liverpool until they were provided with champagne and pâté de foie gras.[15]

After unloading the French airmen and their machines in Freetown, *Australia* was ordered back north again to relieve another 8-inch cruiser, HMS *Cumberland*, which had been patrolling off Dakar to keep watch on three French light cruisers bottled up in harbour there. *Cumberland* had hardly left when the three appeared – *Gloire*, *Montcalm* and *Georges Leygues* – heading south from Dakar on the opposite course to *Australia*. It was around nine in the morning on 19 September. Captain Stewart signalled to *Cumberland* to rejoin him, and the game of cat and mouse began: the French ships continuing doggedly south-east at some 15 knots in line ahead; the Allied cruisers shadowing them on the beam, zigzagging through intermittent rain squalls.

At nightfall, the game abruptly changed. The French suddenly doubled back to the north and picked up speed. That afternoon, the Admiralty had ordered Stewart to prevent the three cruisers returning to Dakar; now it seemed likely they were heading back there. *Australia* and *Cumberland* turned to follow, working up to 30 knots as the chase began, but the French had a slightly better turn of speed and, in the dark, through heavy tropical rain, they drew ahead and disappeared. Stewart decided to make directly for Dakar to somehow head them off, *Australia* pounding along at her best 31 knots.

Just after eight in the evening, a nightmare vision loomed out of the murk, described by one of *Australia*'s turret officers, Lieutenant Guy Ashley-Brown, of Kew in Melbourne:

> *Australia* was steaming at full speed through a thick rain squall when suddenly, on passing out of the rain into brilliant moonlight, there, on our starboard bow and heading straight for us amidships at high speed, was the *Gloire*, only a cable or two away. Collision appeared inevitable and only the smart handling of the ship by Captain Stewart averted what would have been a major disaster.[16]

Stewart flashed his searchlight, summed up the situation in seconds flat and ordered *Australia*'s helm hard over. The two ships swept past each other at a stone's throw, *Australia* then turning to tail her quarry again. And there was more drama to come on this tense and testing night. Not long after this, *Gloire* broke down. Shortly after ten o'clock, she was wallowing in a rising swell at around four knots, *Australia* circling suspiciously around her with guns trained, Stewart trying to work out what on earth was happening. Eventually, he signalled to her, in more than passable French, that she must not go to Dakar but to Casablanca. He had orders to use force to compel her if necessary but he sincerely hoped not to, he said.

Gloire had apparently had enough. She switched on all her navigation lights – 'like Woolworths on a Friday night', wrote Harold Eastick – and, gradually picking up speed as she repaired her engines, she headed north again. Warned by the Admiralty that there might well be Vichy submarines in the area, Stewart signalled *Gloire*'s captain, Jean Paul Broussignac, that he would immediately sink him if he was attacked by one. *Gloire* acknowledged and, after some more polite exchanges, Broussignac offered his parole that he would head to Casablanca.

The two stayed together until the morning of 21 September, when Stewart sent a gracious farewell signal, again in French – *Je vous remercie pour votre courtoisie dans une situation difficile* – and headed south again to rejoin the squadron. Broussignac kept his word, but *Cumberland* was not so fortunate in her chase. The other two French cruisers eluded her and made it back to Dakar.

At dawn on 23 September, the grand enterprise to install *le général* got under way. There were three groups in this expeditionary force: the first two of transports carrying some 7000 French and British troops, with de Gaulle himself – tall and imperious in khaki drill and pith helmet – on board a Dutch passenger liner, the *Westernland*. The third was the naval group of the battleships *Barham* and *Resolution*, the aircraft carrier *Ark Royal*, five light and heavy cruisers including *Australia*, and no fewer than 11 destroyers – a display of sea power deliberately contrived to impress and intimidate the Vichy governor and his adherents ashore in Dakar as they gazed upon it.

Which was where things started to come unstuck. The French could not gaze upon it. They couldn't even see it. Confounding all the weather forecasts, there was low cloud and a heavy sea fog. This misfortune eventually forced the fleet uncomfortably close inshore, within easy range of the gun batteries at Dakar and the battleship *Richelieu*, which, although still berthed and immobile, was able to fire her main armament.

Australia was at action stations. Here, at last, was the hour they had trained for, that moment of test, the reason for all those gunnery exercises, the justification for all those long and fruitless patrols in weather fair and foul, the purpose of all the discomfort and the discipline, the monotonous food and the boredom and the homesickness. Throughout the ship, there was a burden of anticipation, a knotting of the stomach, and that peculiar, sombre quiet that comes over men alone with their thoughts as they are about to go into battle.

'It was my first time under real action conditions as it was for most of the ship's company,' wrote the commander, John 'Jamie' Armstrong, in a letter home to his parents in Sydney. 'The worst part was immediately before action, especially in the early morning – a little something in the tummy I find has a good effect in dispelling that exceedingly empty feeling!!'[17]

'Battle flags were hoisted,' wrote the young midshipman Mac Gregory. 'The Australian Ensign at the fore, a large White Ensign at the main, and our usual Ensign at the gaff. I recall the huge surge of pride I felt observing our Commonwealth Ensign flying at the foremast for the first time in this war.'[18]

The opening move began at 6 am. *Ark Royal* flew off Sword-fish aircraft to drop propaganda leaflets over the town and also launched the two Free French aircraft and airmen Australia had carried to Freetown. They landed at the Dakar air base with de Gaulle's message of liberation but, to their startled distress, they were arrested and imprisoned. *Ark Royal*'s aircraft were fired on from the ground.

This was not a good start, and the troubles mounted. De Gaulle then sent in an emissary by launch, a Carmelite friar turned naval captain named Thierry d'Argenlieu, flying the *tricolore* with the Free French Cross of Lorraine and a white flag of truce. He was fired on and badly wounded, and by ten o'clock there was gunfire rumbling from the shore batteries, the shell splashes landing in the midst of the fleet. The Allies shot back and the Vichy submarine *Persée* was detected, depth charged and sunk. At 11 o'clock, *Barham* and *Resolution* bombarded *Richelieu* for 20 minutes but, in the murky visibility, scored not a hit. Over the next hour, two British destroyers were lightly damaged and *Cumberland* was more seriously punished, forcing the expedition commander, Vice Admiral John Cunningham, to withdraw seawards out of range. *Australia* herself came under fire. In the bowels of the ship at the high angle transmitting station, Mac Gregory could hear fragments of the shells 'striking the ship's side, well below the waterline', which he described as 'very, very scary indeed!'.[19]

Australia was sent in to chase two Vichy destroyers back to port, which she did without mishap, and then, as the fog came in again, the shooting stopped and everyone settled down to an action-stations lunch of bully-beef stew.

Play resumed that afternoon. At four o'clock, with visibility only a little better, aircraft from *Ark Royal* spotted a French destroyer coming out from behind Gorée Island, a rocky outcrop at the entrance to Dakar, and Cunningham ordered *Australia* in to stop her, with the destroyers *Fury* and *Greyhound*.

With the ship moving at an easy 20 knots, the captain and his officers and the bridge lookouts peered through their binoculars, seeking their quarry on a grey sea that blended seamlessly into a grey sky. As ever in the tropics, Ross Stewart was clad in white shirt, baggy khaki shorts and a splendid if battered tropical helmet – beneath which he puffed incessantly on a foul-smelling pipe. He would select the target through one of the two Evershed Bearing Indicators on the bridge, port or starboard. They were basically a pair of binoculars linked to a calculating mechanism. High above him, the director control tower would get the information from the Evershed and train around to that target, then transmit the bearing down to the gun turrets and to the transmitting station – the TS – deep below decks. In the TS, officers and sailors manning a device known as the Admiralty fire control table – in effect, a primitive analogue computer – would calculate the complex mathematics and geometry of bearing, range, elevation, the speed of both hunter and target, and 'aim off', which pointed each gun turret slightly differently. The result of that calculation would go to the turrets. Then, with the guns aimed and loaded, the gun-ready lamps would light up back in the TS and firing gongs would ring in the director control tower. Shoot! The director layer would press his triggers to fire the guns electrically. The control officer, spotting officer and rate officer in the tower would observe the fall of shot – over, short or straddling (meaning landing close around the target) – and send through any corrections to the TS, and the whole intricate process would begin again.[20]

In the turrets fore and aft, the guns were loaded with a mix of semi-armour-piercing and high-explosive shells, although the shell hoist to X-turret jammed immovably, consigning its furious occupants to the role of impotent spectators. At 4.24 pm, an indistinct shape was seen moving against the low line of land on a bearing of Green 10, and the thrilling cry went up: Alarm Starboard!

Within minutes, they identified a destroyer of the *Fantasque* class, a new and handsome ship of nearly 3000 tonnes, five 5.4-inch guns, a top speed of 40 knots and a crew of around 220, almost a small cruiser. Stewart increased speed to 25 knots and turned to port to open his A-arcs, which meant bringing all his guns to bear, trained out to starboard. At 4.27 pm, he gave the order to open fire, three guns at a time, one per turret, at a range of just under 4000 metres. The gun-ready lamps glowed red. The firing gongs ting-tinged. Simultaneously, thunderously, the muzzles belched flame and smoke. *Australia* shuddered beneath the shock. At that distance, it was almost point blank. Stewart's Report of Proceedings tells the grim tale:

> Salvo 1 was short. Salvo 2 right. Salvo 3 dismasted the enemy. Salvo 4 was over with one hit (fire started forward.) Salvo 5, hits. After Salvo 8 at 1630 fire was checked, as the enemy was on fire fore and aft and I wished to avoid loss of life if possible.[21]

It had taken three minutes. Destruction. The Vichy destroyer managed to return only two shots, and the men in *Australia*'s director control tower thought they saw the tracks of a couple of torpedoes pass harmlessly by, but no more. From his vantage point in one of *Australia*'s turrets, Harold Eastick, a compassionate man, watched the carnage first-hand:

> Salvos hitting her everywhere ... she immediately burst into flames from her bridge and right aft, and it was a terrible sight watching the poor devils rushing right forward on the fo'c'sle to get out of the way, as she was one mass of flames.[22]

Jack Langrell had slipped away from his action station in the sick bay flat, up a ladder and out onto the 4-inch gun deck, where he had a grandstand view of the stricken enemy. 'She was a roman candle in no time,' he recalled. When the firing ceased, some of the younger sailors on the upper deck began cheering as if they were at a football game, but they were swiftly cut short by an icy command from the bridge. It was the Jimmy – the first lieutenant – Lieutenant Commander Jack Donovan. 'Stop that down there,' he snapped. 'You don't know what those men are going through.' Silence fell.[23]

Other men were more reflective, disturbed by what they had done. 'Our first blood, but it tasted rather like murder to me,' Armstrong wrote to his father. 'I think we behaved with credit . . . we were lucky, and there was no occasion for anyone to perform any of those deeds of gallantry that go into the story books.'

Stewart sent *Greyhound* to rescue any survivors, but she was fired on from the battery on Gorée and forced to withdraw. The destroyer slowly drifted ashore, still burning, her upperworks charred and shattered, 81 of her crew dead and 71 wounded. Later, the Australians learnt her name: *L'Audacieux*. They could not know it at the time, but she encapsulated the tragedy of beaten France, the melancholy fortunes of war. On the Allied side, she had fought off German air attacks, taken part in the hunt for *Graf Spee* and sailed in the Dunkirk rescue. It was her allegiance to Vichy that brought on her destruction by her former allies.

A little later that afternoon, just after five o'clock, Cunningham and de Gaulle made yet another effort, sending several boatloads of the *fusiliers marins* to make a landing on the beach at Rufisque, east of the Dakar township. They were met with a storm of machine-gun fire and de Gaulle quickly withdrew them, to avoid the catastrophe of Frenchmen shedding each other's blood, he said.

This first day had been a debacle for the Allies. With the fleet standing out to sea that night, messages flashed to and from London, with Churchill sending one of his stirring calls for action: 'Having begun we must go on to the end. Stop at nothing.'[24]

De Gaulle, despondent, wanted to call an end to the operation but was persuaded by Admiral Cunningham that they should try again the next day. Late in the evening, he radioed another appeal for Dakar to receive him but was rebuffed by the Vichy governor, Pierre Boisson, who signalled from *Richelieu* after midnight:

> *La France m'a confié Dakar, je défendrai Dakar jusqu'au bout.*
> France gave me Dakar, I will defend Dakar to the end.[25]

The next day, 24 September, brought slightly better weather but no better luck. Debacle became fiasco. As the fleet approached the shore, the two land batteries opened up once more and the two British battleships began exchanging fire with *Richelieu*, again with neither side hitting the other. Aircraft from *Ark Royal* made several bombing runs on *Richelieu* and met heavy anti-aircraft fire. Three were shot down. In a confusing melee that morning, hindered by poor visibility and a smoke-screen laid by a Vichy destroyer, *Australia* exchanged ineffective fire with what appeared to be two cruisers and was eventually ordered to withdraw. Vichy aircraft attempted to bomb her as she did, but it was a high-level attack and nothing landed too close. As the morning wore on, one of *Richelieu*'s lighter guns managed to score a hit on *Barham*, causing some minor damage below the bridge, and the Vichy submarine *Ajax* was sunk by two destroyers.

By this point, it should have occurred to even the most optimistic strategist that de Gaulle would not be welcomed in Dakar then or at any time in the near future, but he continued to broadcast appeals to the population. They fell on deaf ears, because the civilians had fled. That afternoon, *Barham* was hit four times again by small-calibre shells, still with little serious damage. With that, the fleet moved out to sea again for yet another confused and uncertain night.

The third day, Wednesday 25 September, dawned brilliantly sunny and clear at last, and once again Cunningham doggedly resumed the action. But if day one had been a debacle and day two a fiasco, this day was a disaster. Moving into position to bombard the battery on Gorée, *Resolution* was torpedoed by a Vichy submarine. The hit flooded her port boiler room, brought on a 12-degree list and sent her limping away at ten knots behind a destroyer smokescreen. Shortly after eight o'clock, *Australia* and one of her RN sister ships, HMS *Devonshire*, were sent in to attack two cruisers in the bay – presumably *Montcalm* and *Georges Leygues* – with *Australia* catapulting her little Walrus into the air to observe the fall of shot. This time, the range was some 25,000 metres, in good visibility, although a Vichy destroyer began to make smoke to conceal the bigger ships. The Walrus reported several straddles, and Stewart was confident he had gained a hit when a pillar of flame and smoke shot into the air and one of the cruisers stopped firing.

Then *Australia* was hit. At 9.12 am, doing 25 knots and with the wheel hard over to bring her around to a southerly course, she was struck in quick succession by two 6-inch shells. They both landed aft, but caused only minor damage. One crunched into both the Admiral's and wardroom galleys and tore up the decking in the wardroom flat; the other pierced the armour on the ship's side about three metres above the waterline, putting the port distiller out of action. But with the crew at action stations, there was no one nearby and no one was injured. *Australia* pulled out of the scrap at 9.17, and exactly three minutes later, at 9.20, Vice Admiral Cunningham called the whole thing off, ordering a general withdrawal of the fleet. It was over. His decision was accepted by Churchill in London that afternoon. Operation Menace had been a dismal, humiliating failure.

For *Australia*, though, the mixed emotions of relief and elation at sustaining only trivial damage from those two shell hits was soon to vanish. As she departed from her encounter with the cruisers, her Walrus was still in the air, returning from the spotting mission. One of the bridge lookouts reported an aircraft plunging into the sea well astern of *Barham*, with two of the crew bailing out, but it was quite some distance away and indistinct, the parachutes little more than white flecks in the sky. There was no sign of a third chute. Only later – too late – did they learn that it was their Walrus that had gone, attacked and shot down by three Vichy Curtiss Hawk fighters. If only they'd known, they would most certainly have raced to join the search for survivors, but no luck. It was a cruel finish. Captain Stewart had to report to the Naval Board – 'with deep regret' – that *Australia* had lost the first of her ship's company killed in this war. They were all young men, all from the suburbs of Sydney: the pilot, Flight Lieutenant George Clarke RAAF; the observer, Lieutenant Commander Francis Fogarty RAN; and the telegraphist/air gunner, Petty Officer Colin Bunnett RAN. Their bodies were never found.

—

Dakar was reported in Australian newspapers for the failure it was, with much shaking of editorial fists at Nazi wickedness and Vichy perfidy. Launceston's *Examiner* captured the mood:

> The news of the abandonment of the Dakar expedition conducted by General de Gaulle and supported by the British Navy comes as a shock. Many conflicting statements as to the nature and intention of this venture had given the world a rather confused picture of the situation at Dakar, an important strategic point on the west coast of Africa. But one thing of which nearly everybody felt quite certain was that, no matter what the cost, Dakar would be wrested from the control of the Nazi-dominated Vichy Government. There was complete confidence that, if only for reasons of prestige, Britain would not be associated with another withdrawal of her forces, as from Norway, France and British Somaliland.[26]

Australia's presence at Dakar was not reported for another month, and only then after letters from crew members to their families at home reached the newspapers. On 25 November 1940, the Minister for the Navy, Billy Hughes, confirmed that

Australia had taken part, but refused to comment on 'rumours' that she had sunk a Vichy destroyer. In fact, a first-class diplomatic row was brewing. Behind the scenes, the Menzies government was furious it had not been informed about Operation Menace, either before it began or after it failed. Menzies himself fired off a scorching cable to Bruce, the High Commissioner in London, which he was to present to Churchill in person:

> 29 September 1940,
> MOST SECRET FOR THE PRIME MINISTER HIMSELF
> We are very disturbed in regard to the Dakar incident which has had unfortunate effect in Australia. First, as to matter of substance: It is difficult to understand why attempt was made unless overwhelming chances of success. To make what appears at this distance to be a half-hearted attack is to incur a damaging loss of prestige. Second, as to matter of procedure: It is absolutely wrong that the Australian Government should know practically nothing of details of engagement and nothing at all of decision to abandon it until after newspaper publication. I have refrained from any public criticism but privately can tell you that absence of real official information from Great Britain has frequently proved humiliating . . .[27]

Churchill snapped back on 2 October, in a long and caustic telegram rejecting Menzies' objections:

> With regard to your criticisms, if it is to be laid down that no attempt is to be made which has not 'overwhelming chances of success' you will find that a complete defensive would be imposed upon us . . . I cannot accept the reproach of making 'a half-hearted attack'. I hoped that you had not sustained the impression from these last five months of struggle which has excited the admiration of the whole world that we were 'a half-hearted Government' or that I am half-hearted in the endeavours it is my duty to make . . .[28]

Bruce was also given a Churchillian dressing-down in person at 10 Downing Street, which he reported back to Canberra.

Tempers simmered, until a few days later a second cable from
Menzies sought to pour oil on these troubled waters, and
Churchill offered a soothing reply. But this first wartime spat
between Dominion and Mother Country was a straw in the
wind, a vexing sign of things to come. The Admiralty had been
entirely within its rights to include *Australia* in the expedition for Menace; the ship had been placed at its disposal by the
Australian Government. But diplomacy, or even common politeness, should have suggested to someone in London that Australia
had the right to know what was going on when one of its ships
was involved. Churchill himself paid elaborate lip service to the
notion of Australia as an independent nation but, as the war
years ahead would reveal, he saw himself very much in the role
of the stern but paternal headmaster dealing with a troublesome
colonial pupil.

That said, and in fairness, his irritation at being lectured from
faraway Canberra should be seen in the context of what else was
on his plate at the time. The RAF had defeated the *Luftwaffe* in
the Battle of Britain by mid-September, but only on a wing and
a prayer, and Hitler had switched his attention to the night-time
bombing Blitz that was raining death and destruction on London
and other British cities. The Battle of the Atlantic was growing
in ferocity, and the war in the Western Desert and North Africa
had begun with the Italian invasion of Egypt.

Most ominous of all, perhaps, was the tightening of the Axis
alliance. Putting aside his fantasies of Aryan racial supremacy,
Hitler was willing to deal with the Japanese if they could make
life difficult for the Allies. In Berlin on 27 September 1940,
Germany, Italy and Japan signed what became known as the
Tripartite Pact, recognising their right to establish 'a new order
in Europe' and 'Greater East Asia'. Japan continued its thrust
to the south that month, sending its armies to invade French
Indo-China, where they seized control of the cities of Hanoi
and Saigon, and – more ominously – the French naval base on
the Vietnamese coast at Cam Ranh Bay, with its commanding
position on the South China Sea.

CHAPTER 9

WHAT IRRESPONSIBLE RUBBISH THESE ANTIPODEANS TALK

Australia was back on the Clyde by late October, after a side excursion to Gibraltar, where she endured some largely futile bombing raids from Vichy French aircraft carrying out reprisals for Dakar. There was mail from home waiting at Greenock – 83 bags and parcels of it, recorded a jubilant Harold Eastick – but it wasn't long before they were at sea again.

On the afternoon of Monday 28 October 1940, Captain Stewart was ordered to raise steam 'with all despatch' and join the hunt for a German commerce raider thought to be at loose north-west of Scotland. That turned out to be a false alarm, but the next morning, at seven o'clock, *Australia* received a signal that a Sunderland aircraft from the RAF's Coastal Command had been forced to ditch in the Atlantic and was radioing for help. From the position given, Stewart and his navigator, Commander John Rayment, reckoned that the plane was about ten kilometres away, and they turned to go to the rescue.

The day was filthy and it grew worse, with a southerly gale mounting in strength by the minute. In fact, it was the weather that had brought the Sunderland down, about 300 kilometres north-west of Cape Wrath, on the northernmost tip of the Scottish mainland. From the RAF's 204 Squadron, it had taken off from its base at the small west coast port of Oban on the 28th, on what should have been a routine flight to meet a convoy and escort it into harbour. But that evening, it flew into a violent electrical storm and was struck by lightning, which put its radio out of action and wrecked the compass. Suddenly, it was flying blind.

Sunderlands were the workhorse aircraft of Coastal Command, built for long-range reconnaissance patrols far out of sight of land. Officially known as the Short S.25 Sunderland, they were adapted for the military from a commercial airliner designed before the war for Britain's Imperial Airways and also flown by Qantas Empire Airways on the Kangaroo Route between Sydney and London. They were a genuine flying boat, which meant that the hull itself could land and rest on water, the wings supported by a small float on either side. And they were big, too, one of the largest aircraft of the war years, 26 metres long with a wingspan of 34 metres. Powered by four Bristol Pegasus engines, each of 1010 horsepower, the Sunderland could reach a top speed of 340 kilometres per hour and, with long-range fuel tanks, could stay in the air for up to 14 hours. They were well armed with bombs and depth charges, making them successful U-boat killers,[1] and they bristled with machine guns in nose and tail turrets and on each side. There was a crew of 13, with the fat-bellied fuselage divided into two decks. The upper deck contained the cockpit for two pilots – or the bridge, as they called it, as if in a ship – and stations for the flight engineer, navigator and wireless operator. The lower deck had a bomb bay, a wardroom, a galley and a toilet, and bunks for men resting off-duty.

But now Sunderland P9620 was lost. The captain, Flight Lieutenant Sidney Gibbs, a Canadian in the RAF, was an experienced pilot with more than 600 operational hours under his belt and a Distinguished Flying Cross, which he had won only weeks before for a successful attack on German Heinkel flying boats in a Norwegian fjord, but he now had no idea where he was and no way of finding out. The compass was useless. In the black and storm-lashed night, the navigator could not take a star sight to at least estimate their position. Below them lay a heaving sea dimly glimpsed by its breaking white caps. Working frantically, the wireless operator managed to get his set partly functioning again, enough to transmit messages but not to receive them. Gibbs could only keep flying in the faint hope that luck might bring him in sight of land before his fuel ran out.

Luck was not with him. The Sunderland droned on through the night until the next morning, when, in a grey dawn, with the fuel gauges flickering near empty, Gibbs's only chance was to put her down in the ocean. It must have been terrifying. A gale blowing at around 100 kilometres per hour was lashing the Atlantic into long waves some nine metres high. Gibbs dropped three flame-floats to try to find out the wind direction on the surface, but they did not burn, and he had to guess it instead from a parachute flare they fired. With the crew braced in the crash position, he worked the controls: mixture, propeller pitch and flaps, throttling back to the slowest possible air speed and easing down towards the water. There could be only one attempt, no second try. If a wingtip or even a float were to strike the sea, the aircraft might well cartwheel to its destruction.

Gibbs did it perfectly. The Sunderland touched down with a bone-jarring thump in the trough between two waves. The oncoming crest lifted up the boat and took all speed off it, so that it came to a halt with both wingtip floats intact. And it stayed afloat, tossed mercilessly by the ocean and with everyone violently seasick but still alive.

Ashore, RAF wireless stations had managed to get a bearing on the plane by radar – or radio direction-finding, as it was known then – and it was this position that was given to *Australia*: 60°10' north, 10° west. Stewart brought the cruiser up to 26 knots, as fast as he dared go with a heavy following sea that sent her surfing and pitching down the face of the waves and burying her bows deep before she rose, groaning, on the next one. She was rolling heavily too, and with the barometer still dropping there could only be worse to come. And come it did. The gale grew stronger, the ship tossing and driving more deeply still. The fo'c'sle mess decks and storerooms were a wreck, awash with water sluicing back and forward, with toolboxes and gear from the blacksmiths' shop adrift and smashing against the ship's sides and bulkheads, and Jack Langrell's canteen in ruins.

On the bridge, Stewart and Rayment reckoned at about nine o'clock that they had reached the position they'd been given, but with visibility in the murk down to barely three kilometres there was no sign of the Sunderland in the peaks or troughs. It was likely, they thought, that the plane had drifted to leeward, so they wallowed in that direction for some 20 kilometres, but still without luck. The next thing to do was to zigzag back again, and by this time *Australia* was taking such a pounding that she was down to 11 knots.

Then came a breakthrough. As this bitter morning wore on, they began to hear wireless transmissions from the Sunderland, faint and difficult to read, but enough to give hope that at least some of the airmen were still alive, afloat, and not too far away. In fact, by some miracle, the plane's wireless operator had managed to dismantle and rebuild his set, and could now receive signals from his shore base as well as send them. At 2.15 that afternoon, still searching, still slowly zigzagging, *Australia* suddenly picked up a clear transmission from the Sunderland, which allowed them to fix a direction, and five minutes later they heard a signal: 'Hurry. Cracking up.'

Stewart knew then that he was near. He ordered the engine room to make clouds of smoke from the cruiser's funnels and swept a searchlight across the sea in the direction he expected to find his quarry, and at 2.35 pm he was rewarded. Lifted by a wave, the Sunderland suddenly appeared about three kilometres off *Australia*'s port bow, still upright. Someone fired a couple of distress flares into the gloom and an Aldis signal lamp flashed out a single word in Morse code: 'Hurry.'

Then a new disaster. At that very moment, a big wave caught the plane head-on and flipped it over on its back. After floating for nearly eight hours in that surging, storm-tossed sea, the Sunderland had finally given up and almost gone. But not quite. On *Australia*'s bridge, they could see two small figures clinging to the aircraft's upturned keel and more men in lifejackets struggling in the water. The problem now was how to get them on board.

Stewart brought *Australia* around to windward, taking as much way off the ship as he could so as to drift slowly down on the airmen. With remarkable seamanship, he placed the cruiser so the men were abreast of *Australia*'s bridge, which towered above them one minute and then rolled below them the next. There were scrambling nets and ladders over the starboard side, but it quickly became appallingly clear that the survivors, weighed down by their heavy and sodden flying gear, were exhausted and utterly unable to help themselves. There was only one thing for it. It would be impossible to lower boats in this sea; men would have to go over the side to help.

The commander, Jamie Armstrong, said he would go himself, and he called for volunteers, strong swimmers to join him. Twelve men stepped forward. The bosun's mates swiftly fashioned them lifelines, one end of the rope secured to the ship and the other with a bowline knotted around their chests and shoulders, and they scrambled down the nets. This was an extraordinary feat in itself: when the ship rolled to port, they were slammed against the side; when it came back again to starboard, they were swinging in midair or plunged beneath the surface, possibly to be scraped against the razor-sharp crust of barnacles on the hull below the waterline. Jumping from the nets into the water was still more perilous, not just because of the roiling sea and the biting chill but for the chance that a wave larger than the rest might send *Australia* quite literally crashing down upon them.

Kicking and struggling, half-drowned themselves, Armstrong and his volunteers dragged nine of the airmen to safety at the nets, where other men hauled them on deck. Four, though, could not be reached. They drifted slowly forward along the ship's side. Mac Gregory was with a team of sailors in the bows trying to throw them lines to catch, again and again, but the wind kept blowing the ropes back on board. One of the airmen was actually hit by the ship's anchor as the cruiser plunged upon him, and he disappeared without trace. The others were slowly washed away.

'As soon as possible I got under way again in an attempt to locate the remainder,' Stewart wrote in his report. 'I saw two or three bodies to windward and my only hope to get them inboard was to get the ship in a position to drift down on them. This necessitated running up to windward and then sighting the bodies in time to take the way off the ship and drift down. I continued up and down across the sea for over two hours, unfortunately without success, and finally abandoned the search when darkness fell.'[2]

The ship's company was deeply affected by this tragedy. 'I can still visualise the joy on the faces of those we rescued, and remember the anger and sadness we all experienced at having to leave the remaining four airmen to face a certain death,' wrote Mac Gregory years later.[3]

'God I shudder as I think of them waving us goodbye,' said Harold Eastick.[4]

Sidney Gibbs and eight of his crew had survived against all the odds, a triumph of man's capacity for endurance. Ross Stewart's consummate ship-handling and the sheer courage of Armstrong's rescue team had been extraordinary, beyond all praise. That night, a cruel sea, as if cheated of its prey, turned on them with a vengeance, forcing *Australia* to wallow back to harbour in the teeth of the storm at a bare ten knots. She dropped anchor at Greenock again at 9 am on the last day of October.[5] One of her torpedomen, Able Seaman Ray Nicholls, from Bondi, wrote a sailor's poem to mark the affair:

> Now this isn't a tale of glory
> Of battle against England's foe
> It's the tale of a work of mercy
> And that's the greatest work we know.
> But we've shown once more that the 'Aussie'
> Has fought against odds and won
> And our reward lies in the thought:
> 'That's another job well done.'[6]

—

The closing months of 1940 saw the war at sea reach a new ferocity in both the Atlantic and the Mediterranean, with wins and losses on both sides. The struggle to get convoys of food and supplies to Britain grew more violent as the U-boat chief, Karl Dönitz, refined his *Rudeltaktik*, the technique of hunting in wolf packs. In just five hideous days from 16 to 20 October, two convoys crossing the Atlantic from Canada had 32 ships sunk – a loss of 150,000 gross tonnes – many of them to the wiles of U-boat commanders who would gain fame as 'aces': Günther Prien, Otto Kretschmer, Engelbert Endrass and Joachim Schepke. The next month, on 5 November, the armed merchant cruiser HMS *Jervis Bay* – the sole escort for another convoy from Canada – was lost in a gallant but hopelessly one-sided battle with the pocket battleship *Admiral Scheer*. *Jervis Bay*'s captain, Fogarty Fegen, who had commanded the RANC in the '20s, was awarded a posthumous Victoria Cross.

But the fight was not all going the way of the Axis navies. In the Mediterranean, the RAN had continued to play its part, with *Stuart* of the Scrap Iron Flotilla hunting the Italian submarine *Gondar* to destruction near Alexandria on 29 September. Mussolini's *Regia Marina* was on the back foot in the waters he had boastfully named *Mare Nostrum*, Our Sea. That 11 December, in one of the most brilliant offensive strokes of the war, 20 Swordfish torpedo bombers from the brand-new carrier HMS *Illustrious* raided the naval base at Taranto in southern Italy, laying waste to the Italian battle fleet. For the loss of just two men and two of these lumbering, obsolescent aircraft, the RN sank one battleship, *Conte di Cavour*, and severely damaged two more, which had to be run aground. It was the first ever attack on a fleet in harbour made solely from the air, and a crushing victory that sapped Italian morale and swung the balance of power in the Mediterranean towards the Allies.

This was noticed on the other side of the world in Tokyo, and a Japanese naval attaché in Berlin, Lieutenant Commander Naito Takeshi, flew to Taranto to study the operation in detail. Valuable lessons that he learnt in the use of torpedoes in shallow water were put to good use at Pearl Harbor a year later.

For *Australia*, though, it was time for a rest and a long-overdue refit. The ship and her crew were taken in by the warm-hearted city of Liverpool, that great port on England's north-west coast from which, surely, many of their forebears would have sailed for the New World. On 21 November, nudged along by two tugs, the cruiser cautiously felt her way into the Brocklebank Graving Dock at Bootle on the mouth of the River Mersey. There, she was propped up by great baulks of timber as the water was pumped from the dock and her hull was exposed. There was a lot of work to do. *Australia* had steamed some 53,000 miles – 85,000 kilometres – since leaving Sydney. Her engines and shafts were showing signs of wear, with broken turbine blades needing to be replaced, and her hull was foul with marine growth. Worse, the bombing and shelling at Dakar had sprung leaks in her forepeak, flooding some minor compartments and damaging her oil fuel tanks, which would have to be repaired, along with the port condenser in her stern, also wrecked at Dakar.

More interesting, though, *Australia* would be fitted with radio direction-finding, the first ship of the RAN in the long queue to get hold of this new and mysterious British invention. An aerial that looked like a tangle of bent coathangers sprouted below her bridge, a primitive affair known as Type 286, which could detect objects up to 60 degrees off the bow, meaning that the ship had to be turned to read anything else.

Better still, the crew got long leave, in three watches of ten days each. The Royal Over-Seas League had arranged hospitality for these visiting Australian sailors in British homes, and the welcome was more than generous, not least because food rationing was already in force on everything from eggs and bacon to tea and sugar. It must have been a struggle for the hosts, but it didn't seem to matter.

Harold Eastick was taken up by a Mr and Mrs Davies, who met him at the Birkenhead railway station on the other side of the river and drove him to stay at their cottage in the pleasant little village of Oxton. After the arduous hours at sea and the stresses of war, it was a haven, a blessed release into quiet domestic comfort, and Harold's diary is suffused with gratitude: 'Arrived home for dinner at 1300. Spent a nice afternoon in front of the fire and played darts in the evening . . .'[7] Petrol rationing notwithstanding, Mr Davies and another friend, Mr Little, took him for drives into the countryside to the city of Chester and as far as the seaside town of Rhyl on the Welsh coast, where, he recorded happily, they had tea at the Cafe Royal.

Jack Langrell went further afield. Curious to explore his Irish roots, he took a ferry across to Belfast, but was warned not to go south into the neutral Republic in case he was interned as a combatant.

But even in harbour, the war was never far away, thanks to the *Luftwaffe*. For all the time *Australia* was there, Liverpool was heavily bombed, almost every night. The air-raid sirens would sound at about 7.30 pm – you could almost set your watch by it – and not long afterwards there would be the hostile throb, throb, throb of aircraft engines high in the black above. The search-lights played back and forth, there were the eerie white lights of falling parachute flares, and the night was rent by the thump of anti-aircraft fire, the whistle of falling bombs, and then the crump and roar as they exploded.

The devastation was searing, horrifying. On 29 November, just after midnight, an air-raid shelter beneath a school on Merseyside took a direct hit from a parachute mine, burying some 300 people alive and setting the wreckage ablaze. Rescuers toiled for two days to retrieve the living and the dead, eventually deciding that no more could be done. As they were about to fill the crater with lime and seal it, the hand of a 12-year-old girl was seen moving limply in the rubble and she was freed, the very last. It was a similar, appalling story everywhere you went in the city, around almost every corner: whole buildings and blocks of homes collapsed into blackened, skeletal ruins.

Surprisingly, *Australia* went almost unscathed. She had no way of fighting back because, in dry dock, the cordite charges for her 8-inch guns had been removed and there was no power to arm, direct and fire her 4-inch anti-aircraft weapons. By December, with work on her hull completed, the dock was partially flooded to about a metre below her normal waterline, which allowed her to run her own electric power and water for her fire mains. But she was a sitting duck, immovable and undefended at the height of the most ferocious onslaught of all, the atrocity that became known as Liverpool's Christmas Blitz.

The first of these raids was on the night of Friday 20 December. The city copped a packet, as the saying went. A timber yard just half a kilometre away from *Australia*'s dock went up in soaring flames, providing an aiming point for successive waves of attackers. Bombs fell on dockyard buildings and warehouses all around the ship, fore and aft, port and starboard. It probably did not help that the brand-new battleship HMS *Prince of Wales* was still fitting out at the Cammell Laird yard just across the river, a sure and certain target for the *Luftwaffe*, and far too close to *Australia* for comfort.

Disaster was a hair's breadth away: later that night, a large bomb thundered down between the ship and the dock, through a gap only a couple of metres wide abreast of B-turret. By extraordinary good luck, it did not explode. If it had, *Australia* would have been blown apart, her back broken. When the water was pumped from the dock the next morning, the disposal experts found a new type of aerial torpedo, of about three tonnes, which had left a crater two metres deep in the dock floor.

On the next night, a Saturday, the timber yard was still burning and still a beacon to the returning bombers. This time, incendiaries plummeted down around *Australia*, six of them falling on board, although they were quickly extinguished. Another bomb of about 500 kilograms fell off the port quarter and hit the dock wall, showering the ship with rubble, blowing one of the ship's doctors, Surgeon Lieutenant Malcolm Stening, off his feet and breaking square glass ports in the captain's cabin. 'Another unpleasant night was spent by all,' Ross Stewart wrote in his Report of Proceedings.

The Australians cheerfully did what they could to return Liverpool's hospitality. Fire-fighting parties went ashore to help out each night, and on the Sunday a demolition team brought down a dangerous concrete wall by the unusual method of detonating two depth charges beneath it.

'The ship's company remained calm and the various damage control parties went about their tasks efficiently and cheerfully. The ship's organisation was adequate to cope with any emergency that occurred,' Stewart informed the Naval Board. 'It is regretted that both the ship's cats deserted the ship sometime on Friday night and have not been seen since. Another regrettable occurrence was the total destruction of the ship's company Christmas dinner ducklings, which were incinerated when the contractors' premises were burnt out.'[8]

Harold Eastick did rather better that Christmas Day. He woke late at the Davies' house to find they had wrapped a present for him: a cigarette case engraved with his initials and the inscription 'Birkenhead, Xmas 1940'. That was the last day of his leave, so they gave him a farewell party in the evening and drove him back to the ship the next day, Boxing Day. 'I felt quite downhearted when we reached the ship and I had to say goodbye to them, as they couldn't have done any more for me than my own parents,' he confided to his diary.[9]

And so back to the war. On 27 December, all hands turned out to paint the ship a new dark grey, the same as the RN Home Fleet, and by New Year's Eve they were back at Greenock again, with heavy snow on the Scottish hills and a thick coating of frost on the weather decks. But not for long. Leaving the dock at Liverpool, *Australia* had scraped over some big submerged object, very likely debris from the air raids, setting up a severe vibration on the port outer shaft. Divers sent down at Greenock found the propeller had been badly bent. There was nothing for it but to return to the Mersey for a replacement, where they stayed for just over a week in freezing weather, with the ship coated in ice and snow, and the temperature, on one miserable, foggy day, dropping to 20 degrees Fahrenheit, or minus seven Celsius.

Relief, though, was on the way. On 10 January 1941, they sailed again to join the escort for a large convoy bound for South

Africa and the Indian Ocean. At last – at long last – it was the
end of *Australia*'s long sojourn in the grey and cold of the North
Atlantic. On the last day of January, they crossed the equator,
with the hands off watch sunbaking on deck and everyone hoping
that soon they might see their homeland again.

—

The Melbourne Cup of 1940 was run in cold weather and
showers of rain, but a crowd of 90,000 turned out for that first
Tuesday in November. The gardens were as magnificent as ever,
and fashions for the ladies were gay and sparkling, leavened by
a gallant dash of gentlemen in uniform, as the newspapers dutifully reported. To everyone's astonishment and the bookmakers'
delight, the race was won by Old Rowley, a 100/1 outsider who
spreadeagled the favourites and bolted home: 'one of the great
romances of the turf', said the Melbourne *Argus* approvingly.[10]

The war itself was far beyond the horizon, the Australian
people barely touched by it. Thousands of young men were away
from home either training for the services or already overseas,
but very few had seen combat and fewer still had been killed or
wounded. The first casualty lists did not appear in the newspapers
until January 1941. Life went on almost as normal. Petrol was
lightly rationed, but food and clothing were still freely available,
unlike in Britain, where shortages and hardships were beginning
to bite. By the end of the year, some 20,000 British civilians had
been killed in the Blitz, but while Australians were genuinely
sympathetic to their plight and admiring of their fortitude, this
epic tragedy had afflicted few of them personally.

In some quarters, there was a fear that the people were living
in a fool's paradise, heedless of the perils. Newly returned home
from London, the scientist Ian Clunies Ross, who was also a
prominent political commentator, sounded the alarm in a speech
to the Sydney Legacy Club a few days after the Cup:

> Australians on the whole are distantly complacent about the war.
> They congratulate themselves on having a record crowd at the
> Melbourne Cup race; they resist petrol rationing, the control

of civilian spending – anything, in fact, that interferes with the ordinary life of the community. They are, moreover, too interested in political faction fights and industrial disputes and strikes to realise that their country is in danger.[11]

Thoroughly alarmed, on 9 November *The Sydney Morning Herald* mounted its high horse to lead the charge, with a thin-lipped editorial the next day that railed against 'the mood of careless abandon that flaunted itself at Flemington':

> After fourteen months of war, during which we have seen one country after another overwhelmed and held down by brute force, and Britain placed in the most appalling peril, many people in this country still go about their affairs as though they had observed all these disasters from a distant planet. When it is announced that the investments on totalisator betting at the Melbourne Cup meeting were a record and more than £8,000 above those of last year, it seems hard to believe that the war news on the same page of the newspaper can really be true . . .
>
> The war must have the first call upon the energies of Australians in every walk of life. Our Empire is in danger; our future is at stake. Lethargy and indifference must be swept away, and our strength as a nation bent single-mindedly to the task of waging the struggle for freedom.

Petrol rationing had been a big issue at the federal election held the previous September, with the automobile and transport industries and the various state motoring bodies railing against it in naked self-interest. The Menzies government, a shaky coalition of his United Australia Party and the Country Party, scraped back into office. Menzies himself, not a personally popular figure, had campaigned on the slogan 'Back the Government that's Backing Churchill', and the advertising posters had featured Churchill's picture, not his own. It was barely enough. With a majority of one after providing the Speaker, he would have to rely on the support of independent MPs to govern. Labor had surged, chiefly with a swing in New South Wales, with the Sydney lawyer H. V. 'Bert' Evatt resigning as a judge of the

High Court to run for and win the seat of Barton, and the party stalwart Ben Chifley returning to the seat of Macquarie he had lost in 1931.

Governing on a knife edge and all too uncomfortably aware of rivals in his own party sharpening their knives to plunge between his shoulder blades, Menzies invited the Opposition Leader, John Curtin, to bring Labor into a national, all-party government. Curtin and the caucus considered the idea but rejected it, correctly assessing that Menzies was on borrowed time and would inevitably fall sooner rather than later. Instead, Labor offered to join what it called an Advisory War Council, which, it said, 'should be representative of all parties and empowered to investigate, advise and assist the government in its war efforts'.

It was a sensible proposal in the national interest, which Menzies recognised and accepted. There would be four government ministers named to it, including the Prime Minister, plus four opposition frontbenchers, including Curtin. It would not have the power to govern – that remained with the cabinet – but it would oversee the conduct of the war both at home and abroad, in a constructive spirit. Curtin promised that Labor would 'not take political advantage, as an Opposition, of its numerical strength to embarrass the Government in its war efforts'.[12] The Council held its first meeting in Melbourne on 29 October 1940.

That same month, senior army, navy and air force brass from Britain, Australia and New Zealand spent ten days at a secret conference called in Singapore to assess the threat of Japanese aggression and the defence of the Far East. The Australians were Captain Joseph Burnett, the Assistant Chief of the Naval Staff; Air Commodore Bill Bostock, Deputy Chief of the Air Staff; and Major General John Northcott, Deputy Chief of the General Staff. They went home dismayed at the flimsy, almost derisory forces available to meet any Japanese advance upon the Empire. The conference estimated that the RAF should have 582 aircraft stationed in the Far East, from Malaya to Hong Kong, but found in fact there were only 88. Of those, just 48 were modern, Blenheims and Hudsons; the rest were obsolete. On the ground, it was thought that 26 infantry battalions, five artillery regiments and three light tank companies would do the job; the reality was just 17 infantry battalions (six British, ten Indian and one Malay), one artillery regiment and no tanks at all. As for the navy – it was still the chimera of Main Fleet to Singapore.

Burnett reported back that the war effort in Singapore appeared half-hearted, with the booming market for rubber and tin of far more importance to the locals. 'The security of Singapore is of vital concern to us, and it is most disquieting to find a state of affairs there far removed from what was expected at the Empire's main naval base in the Far East,' he told his chief, Sir Ragnar Colvin.[13]

The Cabinet and the War Council were equally perturbed. They agreed that Menzies should fly to London to press the case for reinforcing the Far East, hopefully by stationing 'three or four capital ships at Singapore as a deterrent to Japanese action'.[14] The government fired off a cable to London saying it was:

> gravely concerned at the most serious position revealed in regard to the defence of Malaya and Singapore . . . we would urge immediate action to remedy deficiencies in Army and Air Forces both in numbers and equipment, which is all important, in view of inadequacy of Naval Forces.[15]

And it offered to send an army brigade, weapons, ammunition and equipment to beef up the ground forces.

Churchill replied two days before Christmas in his customary soothing style, elegantly explaining why nothing could or would be done:

> The danger of Japan going to war with [the] British Empire is in my opinion definitely less than it was in June after the collapse of France . . . We must try to bear our Eastern anxieties patiently and doggedly . . . The only way in which a naval squadron could be found for Singapore would be by ruining the Mediterranean situation. This, I am sure, you would not wish us to do unless or

until the Japanese danger becomes far more menacing than at present . . .[16]

Menzies flew to London in late January 1941. At home, the government, the Advisory War Council and the service chiefs continued to worry about the Japanese menace, but to little avail. All through the summer, there were more meetings and conferences and reports on Far Eastern Defence, not one of them achieving a thing. In February, the British Commander-in-Chief in the Far East, Air Chief Marshal Sir Robert Brooke-Popham, visited Australia and smoothly assured the cabinet that Hong Kong could hold out for at least four months and that Singapore could defend itself for six months and possibly nine until capital ships could arrive. This might or might not have been reassuring. Brooke-Popham, described by one of his contemporaries as 'damned near gaga',[17] was a Boer War veteran, a blimp who habitually fell asleep at meetings and was chiefly known for his determined rearguard fight against enclosed aircraft cockpits.

In Westminster and Whitehall, Menzies found Churchill and the British preoccupied with the war in the northern hemisphere and little interested in Singapore and the Far East. In February, with the High Commissioner Bruce and Sir Frederick Shedden, head of the Australian Defence Department, he met two grandees of the Foreign Office, Richard 'Rab' Butler and the permanent head, Sir Alexander Cadogan, hoping to convince them of the gravity of the Japanese threat. The Australians came away disappointed. 'Butler and Cadogan fail to prove that they know more than we do,' Menzies noted in his diary.[18]

Cadogan, a mandarin of Olympian hauteur, dismissive of mere colonials, was not impressed either. 'Had a meeting at 3.30 with R.A.B., Menzies, Bruce and Shedden – mainly about Far East. What irresponsible rubbish these Antipodeans talk,' he sniffed to his journal.[19]

The long march to disaster went on, the blind leading the blind.

—

With the war now more than a year old and no end in sight, the RAN had girded its loins with an energy unimaginable even five years before. The leisurely yacht-club days of regattas, sporting gunnery exercises and the Spring Cruise to Melbourne for the Cup were a distant memory. The federal budget for 1940–41 doubled expenditure on the navy from £11,000,000 to £22,000,000.[20] Recruiting was at capacity, the Flinders Naval Depot echoing to the tramp of newly issued boots and the bellow of drill petty officers. Groups of Volunteer Reserve officers and sailors were training in anti-submarine warfare at a new school set up at Rushcutters Bay in Sydney, many of them to be sent off to the RN for the Battle of the Atlantic.

Suitable merchant ships were requisitioned, equipped with 6-inch guns bolted to their decks, and pressed into service as armed merchant cruisers to guard convoys and deal with commerce raiders in Australian waters. Five brand-new N class destroyers were being acquired from Britain – HMAS *Napier*, *Nepal*, *Nestor*, *Nizam* and *Norman* – and, more important still, a local shipbuilding program was under way on an unprecedented scale.

In February 1940, Sydney's Cockatoo Dockyard laid the keel of HMAS *Bathurst*, the first of 56 corvettes that would become the RAN's workhorses throughout the war. A unique Australian design, eventually built in different shipyards around the country, they were chunky vessels of some 950 tonnes (full load), just 58 metres long, grindingly slow with a best speed of just 15.5 knots, and, as everyone said, notorious for their ability to roll on wet grass. Oddly, their armament varied, apparently depending on what was available at the time. Some ships had a light 12-pounder gun on the fo'c'sle; others a more punchy 4-inch, with a sprinkling of Oerlikon 20-millimetre cannon, Vickers .303 machine guns and the occasional Bofors anti-aircraft gun. All of them carried Asdic and depth charges for convoy and anti-submarine work, and quite a few were equipped with tackle for minesweeping and paravanes – floating contraptions that looked a bit like a torpedo with wings and fins, which towed a wire cable to deflect mines, port and starboard, away from a ship's hull. Crucially, they were rough and tough, relatively simple to sail and maintain, and their crews – around 85 officers and men in each ship – were often reservists or 'hostilities only' recruits, with none of the naval spit and polish of the big cruisers. They were also stiflingly hot in summer and chillingly cold in winter, with the sailors jammed in damp and stuffy mess decks barely bigger than large cupboards, where the hatches and scuttles had to be closed in anything more than a moderate sea. Cooking and washing facilities were primitive, and laundries non-existent.

The corvettes produced the RAN's best and worst. In December 1942, Ordinary Seaman Edward 'Teddy' Sheean, an 18-year-old from Tasmania, displayed extraordinary bravery in HMAS *Armidale*, shooting down a Japanese bomber and still firing his Oerlikon gun at more attacking aircraft as the sinking ship carried him down to his death in the Timor Sea. Less commendably, at Townsville in 1943, after suffering months of bullying mistreatment, junior sailors in HMAS *Pirie* mutinied against their captain, a cowardly lout of a lieutenant commander named Charles Mills, who had infamously thrown himself face down on the deck beneath a Japanese air attack and left the coxswain to con the ship. It was a peaceful affair, really only a sit-down strike by men who had been pushed to the limit, but ten of them were sent to jail – a gross injustice. Very quietly, Mills was later relieved of his command.[21] Fortunately, he was the exception, not the rule. In the Australian tradition, the men who sailed the Bathurst-class corvettes cursed them for the bastard ships they were but, for the great part, served them with a perverse pride in all the world's oceans.

—

In 1936, at the age of 12, David Hamer came to a striking conclusion. A thoughtful, intelligent boy, he had pondered the news of Mussolini's invasion of Abyssinia and Hitler's march into the Rhineland. He decided that war was inevitable and – rather hopefully – that he would be drawn into it. The question was how best to go about this.

Stories of the horrors of the trenches in the Great War steered him away from the army. 'Most off-putting,' he recalled,[22] and the air force looked no better. The popular 'Biggles' books of the British author W. E. Johns, the stirring but wildly improbable tales of a fictional RAF hero, did not appeal either; everyone but Biggles himself and a handful of his friends got killed. To the dismay of his parents, young David announced that he wished to join the navy. As an officer, naturally.

David's father was a successful Melbourne solicitor. The Hamer family had a comfortable home on a tree-lined street in Toorak, a short stroll from the Yarra River. Born in 1923, David sailed through childhood blissfully untouched by the Depression, the family cared for by a cook, maids, a live-in gardener who tended the neatly clipped lawns and the tennis court, and a nanny who presided over the nursery. Summer holidays with his parents, two elder brothers and a sister were at the family beach house at Mount Eliza, with visits to friends at Portsea. School for the boys was at Geelong Grammar.[23]

Both parents stormed down to Geelong to talk their youngest child out of his naval ambitions, but eventually they allowed him to sit for the RANC exam, on the assumption that, with 700 candidates for just 17 places, he did not have a chance. They were wrong. He passed it, and the medical, and the face-to-face grilling by a bench of captains.

In late January 1937, he and his 16 term mates – all aged 13 – arrived at the college, still at HMAS *Cerberus* in Victoria, with an outfit of brand-new uniforms. They got their first beating that day – with a gym shoe on the backside – for the crime of failing to salute when they crossed a white line that marked out the quarterdeck, a sin they had no idea they had committed. There was a second beating when they saluted incorrectly, the army way with the palm facing outward rather than the navy version with the hand held horizontal.

A quarter of a century had encrusted the college with the worst aspects of the British public school system. The younger boys were expected to fag for the older cadets and were mercilessly bullied and beaten by the cadet captains, or prefects, for failures real or imagined. The college officers, who had endured exactly the same regime themselves, turned a blind eye, on the presumption that this was how real men were made. David estimated that he was beaten an average of four times a week in his first year, for such outrages as imperfectly polished boots or a cap not worn straight. 'The amount of organised, systematic bullying was outrageous,' he recalled in his memoirs. 'This was quite serious, for the leadership processes, based on bullying, that we learned at college were frequently most inappropriate for Australian sailors.'24

There were redeeming moments, plenty of them. He enjoyed the sport – playing cricket, tennis, hockey and also rugby, which, as a Victorian, he resented at first but later came to like and do well at. He breezed through the naval and academic subjects, excelling both in the classroom and at the outdoor skills of swimming, boatwork, signalling and rifle-shooting. The outbreak of war thrilled them all, and in their fourth and final year, 1940, they avidly followed the news in the papers and on BBC short-wave radio. There was an exciting purpose to their lives and their profession, King and Country to be fought for.

For all its grievous faults, the RANC did fulfil its intended purpose of producing competent young seagoing officers. And this 1937 entry was a stellar bunch of talent. Two would go on to flag rank: Guy Griffiths, from the New South Wales Hunter Valley, and Jim Willis, from Mount Gambier in South Australia, who, as a vice admiral, was the last Chief of the Naval Staff to be awarded a knighthood. Three would be killed and three badly wounded in the war they so much looked forward to.

David Hamer topped his term – the Grand Aggregate Prize, as it was known – with first prizes in English, history, navigation and mathematics, and an award of four months' seniority, an important step for promotion. His family and his girlfriend, Barbara McPherson, turned up for the formal passing out parade in late December and the glamorous ball that followed that night, and the next day he found out his seagoing future. Cadets with names A–G would be sent to England, to become midshipmen in the elderly RN battlecruiser *Repulse*. The rest, H–Z, would join the gunroom in HMAS *Canberra*. In January 1941, 17-year-old Midshipman Hamer took his first ever trip to Sydney, on the spanking new *Spirit of Progress* interstate express; first class with a sleeper, he noted excitedly. *Canberra* was alongside at Garden Island.

—

Other men and boys were joining the RAN with rather less style and dash than the young gentlemen of the naval college. Some did because their fathers had done it before them; others because it seemed like a life of travel and adventure, or a better option than foot-slogging and humping a rifle in the army.

And there were those who saw it as a patriotic duty. Russell Keats signed up within weeks of war breaking out, at the age of 18. His full name was Horace Russell Keats, after his father, but everyone used the second name to avoid confusion. Horace senior was a classical musician, a composer and pianist employed by the ABC in Sydney and a prominent figure in Australian cultural life, described by his contemporaries as 'modest, amiable and gentle'.[25] Born in Britain, he had run away to sea himself at the age of 16, playing piano on passenger ships before finding his way to Australia in 1915. In the 1920s, he had been the first conductor of the Radio 2FC orchestra, the infant beginnings of today's Sydney Symphony Orchestra. His wife and Russell's mother, Janet le Brun Brown, was a pianist and soprano who performed under the professional name of Barbara Russell. Their first child had books and music woven into the fabric of his life from the day he was born in 1921, and their home in Mosman, on the northern shores of Sydney Harbour, was a gathering place for singers, musicians, actors and writers. One of Horace's triumphs had been to set to music some of the works of Christopher Brennan, the most dazzling Australian poet of the early twentieth century.

A quiet, slight, bespectacled boy, Russell was educated at the academically selective Sydney Technical High School on its old site in inner-city Paddington. But his true love was to study at the Conservatorium of Music at the former Government House stables in the Botanic Gardens, where he practised the flute and organ and worked on the occasional composition himself, hoping to please his parents.

Surprisingly, Horace and Janet tried to steer their son away from a musical career. More surprising still, Russell joined the army militia, training as a signaller at a depot in Brookvale, on Sydney's Northern Beaches. When the war came, he pleaded with his parents for permission to enlist in the regular army:

> I am writing mainly to ask you to lift your ban upon me in listing [*sic*] for the twenty thousand forces. Will not commit myself finally until I hear from you, which I would like to do as soon as possible, as I should give a decision tomorrow but have put it off for two or three days.[26]

Eventually, he prevailed, and Horace signed the enlistment papers for him, although not for the army but for the navy. Russell walked through the gates at Flinders on 1 December 1939. The navy had picked him to become a supply assistant, a lowly, largely clerical job to do with provisioning a ship under the eyes of its paymaster officers. But he had to be trained as a sailor as well, and the hard-case petty officers at the depot put him through the usual recruit drills of seamanship, rifle, and square-bashing. It cannot have been easy for the cultured, sensitive young man that he was, but he bore it without complaint and even with a certain mental toughness. Once, he was beaten up by a gang of sailors for boldly standing up for a young midshipman; it was not the last beating he would get.

Supply assistants and navy stewards wore a different uniform to the bell-bottoms, jumper and striped collar of regular sailors. Square rig, it was called, with a peaked cap and double-breasted jacket in winter, similar to a petty officer's uniform, one sleeve badged with a red letter 'S'. Clad in this new finery, Russell Keats set foot on the deck of his first ship, HMAS *Canberra*, in Sydney on Christmas Day 1940.

Most of the crew were on leave, to return by midnight on 27 December. Before dawn the next day the ship slipped quietly from the No. 1 Naval Buoy at Farm Cove, to escort a troop convoy through the Great Australian Bight and on into the Indian Ocean to Ceylon.

The war still seemed far away, a European affair. But the enemy was closer than they knew.

CHAPTER 10

I THEREFORE DECIDED TO ENGAGE THE ENEMY

Exciting news swept the nation in the summer of 1941, exhilarating tales of a grand feat of Australian arms in North Africa. The army had been in action for the first time, and triumphantly so. The 6th Division, under the command of a militia officer, Major General Iven Mackay, routed the Italians at Bardia, a harbour town on the coast of Libya some 24 kilometres inside the border with Egypt.

Before dawn on 3 January, Mackay launched his 16th Infantry Brigade against Bardia's fortress defences of concrete bunkers, deep anti-tank ditches and vast tangles of barbed wire. It was so cold that the men, wrapped in heavy woollen greatcoats, were given a tot of rum before they went in. Mussolini had ordered the Italian commander, the heavily bearded Lieutenant General Annibale Bergonzoli – known to his men as *Barba Elettrica*, Electric Whiskers – to hold Bardia to the last, but to no avail. The Australians cut the town in two, then encircled it, and in three days it was all over. Some 40,000 Italians surrendered with their weapons and stores, although not Electric Whiskers himself, who fled westward on foot to another fortified port, Tobruk. The Division of 16,000 lost just 130 killed and 326 wounded.

The Australian newspapers were ecstatic, drumming up comparisons with the Anzacs of the 1st AIF and reporting gleefully on the spoils:

How sumptuously the Italian officers must have fared at Bardia, in contrast to the men of the ranks, has been revealed by discoveries made in the dug-outs and messes found there after the victory on January 5. In one dug-out I saw a tiled bathroom, fitted up with built-in bath, with a hot water shower, and tiled floor. On a mirrored washstand stood half-emptied bottles of eau-de-cologne, jars of powder, and toilet requisites. In the officers' mess a huge lacquered sideboard filled one side of the room. A polished table, with upholstered chairs to match, ran down the centre of the room. The most moveable furnishings, such as decanters and glasses, had already been removed by souvenir hunters.

In contrast to the extravagant living of the officers, I passed, on the way from Bardia to Fort Capuzzo, a straggling line of prisoners, stretching for two miles and in some places 10 men wide, dragging their feet. In spite of the fact that they had been well watered and fed by the British and Australian units after the battle, several of the men had laid down by the roadside and died.[1]

The Australians rolled westward along the coast, and by 7 January they had joined the tanks of the British 7th Armoured Brigade on the outskirts of Tobruk. For the next fortnight, they patrolled and probed the defences by night, disarming booby traps and land mines, seeking the weak spots. On Tuesday 21 January, in another dawn attack, the 16th and 17th Brigades broke through again, supported by a naval bombardment that included the Scrap Iron destroyers *Stuart*, *Vampire* and *Voyager*. It was another rout. By nightfall, the Australians held half of Tobruk, and the Italian commander surrendered the rest the next morning. Another 25,000 dispirited prisoners were taken, with a great haul of tanks, guns and vehicles, for the cost of just 49 Australian lives.

And still the Italians continued to reel from this combined British and Australian advance, with town and harbour falling like ninepins – Derna, Beda Fomm, Benghazi – until, by the second week of February, it was all over. In two months, the

Italian 10th Army had been shattered, the Allies taking 130,000 prisoners (including Electric Whiskers, captured by the Australians at Benghazi), 400 tanks and 1290 guns.

Yet in this stunning success lay the seeds of disaster. Instead of pressing further west to take the last Italian stronghold in the great city of Tripoli, which they could easily have done, the British commanders paused to regroup. It was a decision that military historians have argued about ever since. Mussolini, humiliated, turned to Hitler for help, and the Führer responded. On 12 February, one of his most forceful *Panzer* generals from the invasion of France, Erwin Rommel, arrived in Tripoli to command Operation *Sonnenblume*, the despatch of the *Afrikakorps* to the Western Desert.

—

Closer to home, the news at sea was less cheering. In late 1940, German surface raiders had begun to roam both the Pacific and Indian Oceans, laying mines in shipping lanes and sinking the occasional steamer. *Orion*, a former cargo vessel with the Hamburg-Amerika Line, and disguised as a neutral freighter, had rounded Cape Horn into the South Pacific in June 1940 and laid mines in the Hauraki Gulf off Auckland. Armed with six concealed 6-inch guns taken from the old battleship *Schleswig-Holstein*, and six torpedo tubes, she wandered the Pacific and Southern Oceans for several months, releasing more mines and using a small Arado float plane she carried to search for her prey, sinking ten ships.

In October, she teamed up with another raider, *Komet*, and they ranged up and down New Zealand's east coast, where they sank a small coaster and the 17,000-tonne ocean liner *Rangitane*. In December, disguised as Japanese freighters, they headed north to disrupt the phosphate trade from the island of Nauru, sinking five ships there in quick succession: a heavy blow to the Allied war effort, for the phosphates were vital for fertiliser production. That done, unhindered, they vanished into the empty Pacific for a few weeks, but on 27 December *Komet* returned to Nauru and spent a leisurely hour bombarding oil tanks, boats, stores and wharf installations.

Yet another raider, more aggressive still, raised havoc in both the Indian and Pacific oceans. In August, the converted freighter *Pinguin*, also equipped with 6-inch guns, torpedo tubes, mines and two search aircraft, entered the Indian Ocean from around the Cape of Good Hope, sinking four ships and capturing two, including the Norwegian tanker *Storstad*, which she kept with her. *Pinguin*'s captain, Fregattenkapitän Ernst-Felix Krüder, then headed east in a long loop around southern Australia to the Pacific, where he boldly cruised up and down to lay mines along the New South Wales coast between Port Stephens and Sydney, at times so close inshore that he could see local navigation lights and the lighthouse on Barrenjoey Head north of Sydney. That done, he sped south to release more mines off Hobart. *Storstad* dropped still more off Cape Otway and *Pinguin* more again in the Spencer Gulf, west of Adelaide's Gulf St Vincent. By November, they were back in the Indian Ocean again, where a fourth German raider, *Atlantis*, was also causing mayhem, sinking nine ships and capturing three in the second half of the year.

The navy had no answer to these raiders. There were too few ships to cover the vast expanse of three different oceans. Not every victim managed to radio the raider distress signal – QQQ – and their position, and those that did were generally days and sometimes a week from the nearest British or Australian warship that could come to their aid or pursue the attacker. When coastal minefields were discovered – often the hard way, by a ship striking one – the Naval Board would despatch whatever minesweepers could be rounded up to deal with them, but invariably the bird had flown. The disruption was immense – exactly as the Germans intended. When the freighter *City of Rayville* struck one of *Storstad*'s mines off Cape Otway in November – to become the first American ship sunk in the war – Bass Strait had to be closed for nearly a fortnight.

From time to time, *Canberra* took part in these long and fruitless pursuits in the Indian Ocean, but not under orders from Melbourne. She was based at Colombo in Ceylon, under the command of the RN's Commander-in-Chief, East Indies, Vice Admiral Ralph Leatham. Ceylon was an 'eye-opener' of a place, according to David Hamer, who 'had never seen a naturally dark-coloured person in the flesh'.[2] But the ship spent little time in port there, passing the weeks and months trudging back and forth, here and there, on the important but tedious work of convoy, for more Australian troops were constantly being sent to the Middle East and the Mediterranean. It had been good for a while, exciting even, to be in company with some of the world's great ocean liners – *Queen Mary*, *Aquitania*, and so on – but the novelty quickly began to pall.

Harold Farncomb had taken command of *Canberra* in June 1940, the first ever Australian-born RAN officer to be given one of the heavy cruisers. Just six years before, he had been *Australia*'s executive officer on that royal voyage with the Duke of Gloucester; now, he had moved into the captain's quarters of her sister ship. It was a signal honour, an important milestone in his career, a step ahead of John Collins and the rest of his college term, a vote of confidence in his considerable abilities.

Farncomb had been at sea when war broke out, as captain of the newly acquired light cruiser *Perth*, bringing her to Australia from Britain for the first time. On the voyage home, he was angered and embarrassed by a minor mutiny during a visit to New York, when some of the ship's company staged a sit-down strike on the fo'c'sle over the uniforms they had been ordered to wear ashore. The incident had been deftly and sensibly handled by his gunnery officer, the able and well-liked Lieutenant Commander Warwick Bracegirdle, but it had made the newspapers in America – not a good look for the navy. More successfully, Farncomb had skilfully taken *Perth* through a severe Caribbean hurricane that had genuinely terrified the younger, greener members of his crew, and at one tense moment he had prepared to take on the German pocket battleship *Deutschland*, thought to be in the area.

That last affair earned him a nickname that would travel with him through the rest of his career: 'Fearless Frank'. He had let it be known on *Perth*'s bridge that if he encountered the considerably more powerful *Deutschland*, he would go for her at full speed, guns blazing, and ram her if necessary – not at all a prospect that appealed to his crew. As it happened, the German was nowhere nearby, but the nickname stuck, usually spoken with a tinge of sarcasm.

Fearless Frank was a more than competent captain, undoubtedly one of the RAN's best and brightest, but he had a forbidding manner that did not sit well with his officers and men. One of his midshipmen in *Canberra*, Gavin Campbell, a young paymaster from Victoria, never forgot a bruising encounter he had with him. In the Indian Ocean one day, Campbell was abruptly summoned to Farncomb's sea cabin and accused of failing to salute when the captain passed him on the 4-inch gun deck. The young man protested that he had not been there, that Farncomb must have mistaken him for someone else, but the captain would have none of it. He accused him of lying and announced, with some venom, that his insubordination would be formally and officially recorded in the ship's log. Campbell would later spend three years as a prisoner of war of the Japanese, after the loss of HMAS *Perth* in 1942, but this bruising clash with Farncomb gave him nightmares for the rest of his life.[3]

By and large, *Canberra*'s midshipmen were a cheerful, knockabout bunch – as snotties usually were – taking the rough with the smooth. All of them had very much enjoyed the lecture on venereal disease they had been given by the ship's Surgeon Commander, Charlie Downward, when they joined: a brisk talk in which they were told to 'take sensible precautions'.

Midshipman Edgar Blau, from Warwick in Queensland, had entered the RANC in 1939 at the age of 17, with a handful of others his age – special or mature entry cadets, as they were called, to be rushed through a year's officer training before being sent off to war. He too would write later about the 'sadistic bullying' he encountered, although – as a Queenslander – he got his own back on the rugby field with 'killer tackles . . . it was a lovely feeling to sink one's shoulder into the unprotected belly of a sadist . . .'4

Blau stood out from his peers, for he spoke with a slight German accent. He was born in Vienna, and his English mother had brought him out to Australia at the age of 13 when his Austrian father died of a sudden heart attack – a decision that probably saved their lives. The Blau family was Jewish. After the war, Edgar would find that his uncles and aunts had all been murdered in the Holocaust. In *Canberra*, his first ship, he had an amused contempt for authority and the strange life he was leading:

> When not on watch we continued our training, marching up and down the quarter deck or stewing away in gun turrets, listening to chief gunners' mates expounding on such subjects as what colour armour piercing shells were and how anti-personnel shells were constructed, and how many people they could kill within a given radius. Cheerful stuff. What little sleep we got was obtained in the midshipmen's flat, 3 decks down in hammocks, and as we were at sea with all watertight doors closed, the only ventilation we got was when one of the midshipmen farted.5

After an embarrassing bout of seasickness off the New South Wales coast, David Hamer found his sea legs and took his turn as Midshipman of the Watch, learning the ropes on the bridge from whoever was Officer of the Watch and from an even more godlike figure, the Principal Control Officer, who was responsible for directing the fighting of the ship:

> Some of them let you do the zig-zag, which involved changing course at prescribed times, giving the correct orders and bringing the ship up on the new course before handing over to the Quartermaster, who was in the bowels of the ship on the end of a voice pipe . . . some were untrusting bastards, others were very helpful. But three things you always had to do. You were a not-very-glorified messenger boy; you had to see that the routine administrative orders were given at the correct time, and you had to wake all the officers for their night watches. You also had

to distribute the kai – the hot, sweet cocoa which was provided every hour during the night watches.[6]

For much of the time, boredom was a constant companion. That and the heat, which was fierce and unrelenting at the equator, so much so that Farncomb bent the rules and permitted his sailors – although not his officers – to work in shorts, stripped to the waist. 'There can be no doubt of the use of Tropical Dress without shirts as a deterrent to Prickly Heat,' he told the Naval Board.[7] With the war more than a year old, *Canberra* had yet even to glimpse the enemy, let alone fire a shot in anger. Dull routine gripped them, day after day at sea: dawn and evening action stations, the changes of the watch as regular as clockwork, the monotonous food, the ever distant horizons. Midshipmen had a bar in the gunroom where they ate, but it was never open at sea and only rarely at lunchtime in harbour, with the young gentlemen permitted to spend only ten shillings a month on alcohol if they were under 18, or 15 shillings if they were over. Officers were allowed a wine bill, as it was called, up to £5.

Neither *Canberra* nor *Australia* had a laundry – another strange British defect, like the antiquated messing. Sailors washed their uniforms in a bucket of water on the deck, hot if they could get it, sloshing the clothes up and down with what they called a pogo stick – something like a plunger with holes at one end to stir the suds. The result was hung out to dry wherever you could find a space, and you ironed your own. Officers, though, would usually pay a sailor to do their washing – dhobying was the navy slang for it.

The food was more of a problem. Sometimes, it was downright unhealthy, especially if they had been at sea for some time and the supplies of fresh meat, fruit and vegetables had run low. Tinned bully beef and powdered eggs could make you impotent or drive men mad, they would say, only half-joking. Astounding as it might sound, there were even reported cases of that old sailors' malady scurvy – almost 200 years after the RN had discovered the anti-scorbutic properties of lime juice. As the official history would later report:

In 1941, Surgeon Commander C. A. Downward in *Canberra*, which had been in a tropical zone for some time during which it was impossible to obtain adequate quantities of fresh fruit, vegetables or eggs, noted that numbers of men had become debilitated and weak. Although still on duty, these men were victualled with those in the sick bay, for whom the cooking was done by sick-berth attendants who had received special instruction in the preparation of nutritious and appetising food.

This treatment proved satisfactory for those losing strength and weight, and cast some light on the dietetic aspect of tropical fatigue.[8]

For all that, there were consolations for men who had the sensitivity to appreciate them. Far from the gunroom and still further from the wardroom, the flautist turned supply assistant Russell Keats could find beauty and cause for reflection upon the world he saw around him on watch at sea, writing home to his father, mother and baby brother Brennan in Mosman:

> I look out from where I sit on the bridge and see an eternity of heavy, divinely deep blues sparkling as a never-ending sea of diamonds. The sky is pale and has a reflective appearance . . . most peaceful . . .
>
> We have recently been to yet another part of God's Own Country and all appeared perfect. Yet the oceans are littered with battlewagons spitting fire and the lands are split asunder by man-made volcanoes hurling thunder, hell and destruction. Queer, isn't it, that the pride and glory of creation should be so childishly destructive. I fear me, 'ere this century closes, the result may be suicidal for nations . . .[9]

Gently brought up in an artistic household, Russell recoiled from the blokey crudity of the mess decks, the swearing, the blasphemy, the endless sailor talk about sex and drunken runs ashore. 'Such a pack of barbarians I never knew lived,' he complained in one letter home. But he was not particularly prudish. He wrote to a girlfriend named Joy in Perth – 'my angel', he called her – and another letter has a hilarious account of a visit to a brothel, presumably when *Canberra* called at Port Louis in Mauritius, for he conducted the negotiations in his schoolboy French. He was just helping out some shipmates, he hastened to reassure his parents, not speaking on his own account. 'Remember, your son has not done anything you would greatly disapprove of,' he added.

Russell's solace was his music. He had a collection of 78 rpm records, and he once persuaded the powers that be to let him play a Mendelssohn violin concerto over the ship's PA system. He struck up a friendship with a couple of the midshipmen and *Canberra*'s bandmaster, Harry Blaskett, a man in his late 40s who had been an army trumpeter at Gallipoli in 1915 and had signed up for the navy in this war. They formed a ship's choir together. Disaster struck, though, and murder was on his mind when a new supply assistant who had just joined threw out all Russell's sheet music, including some of his own precious compositions, thinking it was mere scribbling. The loss nearly broke his heart and spirit, but not quite. Russell Keats would always be a square peg in the navy's round hole, but he had signed up to serve his country as a matter of duty, and he did his best to perform it. He held his uniform 'in the highest honour', he told his mother and father.

—

After the pocket battleship *Admiral Scheer* sank the armed merchant cruiser *Jervis Bay* in November 1940, she lingered in the mid-Atlantic for another couple of months, taking and sinking four more British ships and eluding her pursuers. In January of the new year, she headed south and east, passing well below the Cape to enter the Indian Ocean on February and refuel from a supply ship east of Madagascar. Her captain, Theodor Krancke, then sailed her further north towards the Seychelles, where, in quick succession, he captured a British tanker and sank three more merchantmen. The last two managed to get off distress signals, on 21 and 22 February. The British cruiser HMS

Glasgow was nearby, and she picked up the raider messages and launched her reconnaissance aircraft. The plane actually spotted *Scheer* on the afternoon of the 22nd, but then lost her in heavy cloud, never to find her again.

In Colombo, Admiral Leatham deployed the carrier *Hermes* and five widely separated cruisers, including *Canberra* and *Australia*, to join *Glasgow* in the search for the German, but with no luck. Krancke had no intention of lingering, to meet the same fate as Hans Langsdorff and *Graf Spee*. He doubled back into the Atlantic, heading for home. On 1 April, after successfully avoiding the British blockade, he reached Kiel. *Scheer* had sunk 17 British and Allied vessels, making her the most successful German naval raider of the war.[10]

Yet commerce raiders continued to be a threat in the Indian Ocean, and the search for them went on. *Australia* finally made it home from her long spell in distant waters, touching first at Albany and arriving in Sydney at last on 23 March 1941, but *Canberra* continued the thankless drudgery of convoy and patrol. In early March, in baking heat off the Seychelles, she joined the light cruiser HMS *Leander*, a ship largely manned by New Zealanders,[11] on a new search for enemy vessels. Just a few days before, on 27 February, *Leander* had met and sunk an Italian raider, *Ramb I*, after a short, sharp battle west of the Maldives. The two cruisers separated at dawn on the morning of 4 March. That afternoon, *Canberra* struck gold.

She was cruising alone to the south-east of the Seychelles at an easy 17.5 knots, in a calm sea, the weather sunny and clear with a little light cloud, when her masthead lookout reported smoke on the starboard bow and, shortly after that, two masts and a funnel. Captain Farncomb ordered action stations, increased speed to 25 knots and headed towards the sighting. The men ran to their positions, the gun crews cursing as they struggled into their cumbersome anti-flash gear in the heat. The familiar reports began to come in from around the ship:

'A-turret closed up.'

'After damage control party closed up.'

'Quartermaster on the wheel, sir.'

There was a new tension to the routine this time, a feeling that – at last – the long and fruitless weeks of searching might produce a result. *Canberra*'s aircraft was already in the air on a reconnaissance flight, and within minutes her observer, Lieutenant Claud Malleson, an RN officer, radioed that he could see not one but 'two unknown types of ships'. That instantly aroused suspicions – what would two ships be doing together? – and then, within minutes, Malleson upped the ante by reporting that they were an enemy raider and a tanker.

Canberra was now pounding through the sea, guns loaded and ready, the direct control tower high above the bridge and the 8-inch turrets training on the targets. The two ships apparently saw the aircraft at the moment it spotted them, just before five o'clock, and they took fright and quickly separated, the tanker turning south and the other one, the likely raider, fleeing in the opposite direction. On *Canberra*'s compass platform, the excitement was intense. Farncomb told the Yeoman of Signals to order the two to stop and then reverse course, but they took no notice and kept going.

Time to start shooting. Deep below decks in the transmitting station, David Hamer was on the range plot, the analogue computer cranking out its calculations of bearing, course and speed to be fed to the guns. Hunter and hunted were now about 20,000 metres apart. Farncomb ordered his gunnery officer, Lieutenant Commander Donald Hole, to put a salvo across the bows of the ship heading north. The shells thundered away from the two forward turrets and splashed into the sea well ahead, sending up great gouts of dirty water, but still the ship kept going. As Farncomb later reported:

I therefore decided to engage the enemy and opened fire at 1706, at about 21,100 yards [19,300 metres]. At this stage I was still under the impression that the enemy was an armed raider, as reported by the aircraft, and though she did not immediately reply to my fire, I considered that this was due to the fact that we were outside his maximum range. I also thought it possible that he would withhold his fire in the hope that HMAS *Canberra* would close and present a favourable torpedo target. HMAS *Canberra* was therefore manoeuvred to keep the range over 19,000 yards [17,000 metres].[12]

In fact, there was no raider. The ship he was shooting at was the *Coburg*, an unarmed freighter of some 7400 tonnes, deployed from Germany to the Indian Ocean specifically to replenish raiders, which she had been doing for several months. The other was the *Ketty Brøvig*, a small Norwegian tanker that had been captured by the raider *Atlantis* west of the Seychelles the previous month and kept as a supply vessel with a German prize crew on board. But Farncomb had no way of knowing any of this, and his decision to stay his distance was a sensible precaution, allowing him to keep up the attack with his big guns while remaining well out of range of a surprise enemy torpedo.

But there was one flaw in this tactic: *Canberra*'s shooting was atrocious. She had no radar of any sort, let alone for gunnery control. Ranging, aiming and spotting – the lot – were done visually. Her two forward turrets kept hammering away but scored not a hit, although after ten minutes they thought they had when a fire blossomed out just behind the *Coburg*'s bridge. They were wrong. The Germans had begun to scuttle their ship, opening the sea cocks in her bottom and blowing her innards apart with small explosive charges. And much the same was happening with the *Ketty Brøvig*. Malleson, circling above in the Seagull aircraft, saw a small explosion on her deck. Hoping to slow her down, he dropped four small bombs nearby, two of them landing in the tanker's wake, which did bring her to a halt, but it was obvious that she was already down by the stern and beginning to founder. And some of her crew had started to lower a couple of boats.

Claud Vivian Stanhope Malleson, 28 years old, son of Major General Sir Wilfrid Malleson of the Indian Army and Budleigh Salterton in Devon, was a vivid character, something of an eccentric in the English tradition, known to the rest of the wardroom as 'Mad' Malleson. On secondment to the RAN, he had achieved a certain fame in the ship for his habit of reclining in the bath for long periods, smoking his pipe and reading a book, although young David Hamer was wary of him. 'He was a peculiar bloke ... it was unpleasant as Midshipman of the Watch to have to wake him, for his cabin gave off the strongest pong of *musk* I have ever experienced,' he wrote.[13]

Musky or not, Malleson then did an extraordinary thing, entirely off his own bat. He told the Seagull's pilot, an RAAF flight lieutenant from Melbourne, Peter Lavarack, to put the plane down next to the tanker, and announced that he was going to take a look. To the astonishment of Lavarack and the third crewman, Ernie Hutchison, a leading telegraphist from Adelaide, Malleson stripped to his underpants, told Hutchison to cover him with the plane's antiquated Lewis machine gun, jumped from the fuselage and struck out the 20 metres to the tanker's stern. 'I regret that the sensible course of using the rubber dinghy did not occur to me,' he wrote later. 'And for my own peace of mind I did not see the several sharks that were cruising around until I was safely back in the aircraft.'[14]

Somehow, he scrambled on board, wandered around the abandoned bridge to see if there were any documents worth taking and then returned to the aircraft, where he signalled to *Canberra* that the *Ketty Brøvig* might be saved if a boarding party was sent to her. At around this time, just after half past six, with the sun beginning to set, *Leander* reappeared and Farncomb asked her to deal with the *Coburg* while he went to the tanker. A salvage party was rustled up, including young David Hamer, summoned from the transmitting station and excited beyond measure to be chosen. Hastily snatching up his ceremonial midshipman's dirk – a slender sword about half a metre long – he tumbled into the ship's cutter, where he found a dozen sailors armed with .303 rifles and the Boarding Officer, a lieutenant, carrying a revolver. As he wrote in his memoirs:

> We came alongside the tanker and there we lay, with 20 feet of steel ship's side above us, rolling slowly in the Indian Ocean swell. I remember thinking 'We don't seem to be very well organised for this, what do we do now?'

Fortunately the Germans were nice enough to lower us a rope ladder so we could board and capture them. My problem was that as we approached the tanker I had drawn my dirk (remember that I was only 17 and this was my first action), and it didn't seem appropriate to sheathe it again. But a rope ladder needs two hands, so where do you put your dirk? Anyway, I followed the Boarding Officer over the side of the German ship with my dirk between my teeth, looking like a sixteenth century pirate. I must say the Germans didn't seem very frightened.[15]

Malleson had been rather too optimistic. A quick inspection showed the *Ketty Brøvig* was heavily flooded, with scalding water surging through the engine spaces and the decks above, the hull sinking lower by the minute. There was nothing to do but take off the few of her people still there and send them back to *Canberra*. The Germans were imprisoned in the cell flat in the cruiser's fo'c'sle, where they were eventually questioned – without much result – by Edgar Blau. The Norwegians and Chinese of her original crew were freed, much to their delight. The captain ordered Lieutenant Commander Hole to put a few shells from the 4-inch guns into the tanker to hasten her end, and down she went. *Leander* could not save the *Coburg* either, and she, too, plunged to the bottom in a roar of steam and a great swirl of water.

All the while, a running commentary on the action had been broadcast over *Canberra*'s loudspeakers for the men below decks – it 'held the ratings' interest more than a broadcast description of a Test Match with Bradman batting against Larwood', according to Otto Francis McMahon, the engineer commander.[16] Russell Keats found it nerve-racking:

We would hear shell after shell leave us with a mighty crash and waited. Waited! The suspense was terrific. Was she going to hit us? What would we do if one lobbed in the store? Wonder if any of our pals would collect one? Wonder if they carry torpedoes . . . passing around personal addresses and instructions should anyone be killed . . .[17]

But as the drama sputtered to its end and night fell, a sense of dull anticlimax began to spread through the wardroom and the messes. The gunnery had been truly dreadful, and everyone knew it. They had fired exactly 215 of their 8-inch shells at the enemy but not one had hit or even done any apparent damage through a near miss. Midshipman Alan Parker, from the same class as David Hamer, wrote in his journal that 'only nine straddles were reported',[18] but that seems optimistic, to say the least. It was an abysmal effort, made worse, if anything, by the embarrassing fact that the *Coburg* had been such an easy target: virtually dead in the water after the first few minutes and not shooting back. The Germans had sunk themselves, all too swiftly and efficiently. 'Makes you wonder what would happen if we actually met the *Scheer*,' they told each other.

Farncomb was clearly upset. Alone at dinner in his cabin that night, when his steward, Fred Goodeve, passed some remark about the action, he snapped back, 'Bloody bad gunnery, Goodeve.'[19] The debacle cannot have helped Farncomb's already spiky relationship with Donald Hole, the unfortunate 'Guns', a languid figure who sported a monocle and had once famously arrived on watch trailing a cloud of gentleman's eau de cologne. 'Get off the bridge, Hole, and come back when you smell like a man,' Farncomb had barked at him. The story had gone around the ship at lightning speed, earning Hole the nickname 'Gertie'.

Farncomb glossed over the failure in his Report of Proceedings, calling it 'an excellent rehearsal for the real thing, with the added advantage that the enemy was unable to profit by our errors'.[20] But this wanton expenditure of ammunition did not go unnoticed at the Naval Board in Melbourne, where Farncomb's term mate from the RANC, Captain Joe Burnett, was reportedly scathing of the waste.

The next day brought a new and chilling alarm. On a routine search patrol that afternoon, the Seagull dipped out of some cloud cover and spotted a large, single-funnelled warship on the horizon. Malleson decided it was the *Admiral Scheer*, and

Hutchison, the telegraphist, broke radio silence to report to *Canberra* that they had seen a pocket battleship, giving course and position.

Again, the cruiser went to action stations, increasing speed and making for the enemy. Farncomb signalled Admiral Leatham in Colombo and *Leander*, somewhere nearby, that he would shadow the enemy until nightfall and then mount a torpedo attack. It was a pregnant moment. *Scheer*, with her 11-inch guns, could stand off well out of *Canberra*'s range and pound her to pieces. *Canberra*'s only advantage was in speed, perhaps an extra five knots, with luck, which would allow her to make a run for it. But not if Fearless Frank was going in for the attack.

On the compass platform, at the lookout stations, on the signal deck and high in the director control tower, every pair of binoculars was trained to the horizon. Edgar Blau, on the bridge as the navigator's midshipman, saw his life pass before his eyes and told himself that 18 was too young to die. Gradually, a pair of masts, then a funnel, then a smudge of superstructure emerged. The captain ordered the challenge to be sent, the secret signal that should bring about the correct coded reply if the ship were friendly. But even as the big signal projector was clattering out the Morse letters, someone in the director tower shouted, 'Christ, it's the *Leander*!' And so it was. Mad Malleson had got it wrong. *Leander* flashed back the proper response and the emergency subsided like a pricked balloon. 'What a relief, and off to the bathroom to wash underwear,' wrote Blau. In fact, the *Scheer* was thousands of kilometres away, already back in the South Atlantic and sailing for home.

—

For most of the rest of 1941, the war at sea was waged largely in the northern hemisphere, in the Atlantic and the Mediterranean, a battle of mounting intensity that brought victory and defeat to both sides in almost equal measure. In March, the RN scored a welcome success against the U-boats, with Dönitz losing three of his much-vaunted aces: Günther Prien, sunk in *U-47*; Joachim

Schepke, an ardent Nazi, crushed on his bridge when *U-100* was rammed and sunk by the destroyer *Vanoc*; and Otto Kretschmer, captured after being forced by the destroyer *Walker* to scuttle *U-99* in the same battle.

That same month, in Mussolini's *Mare Nostrum*, the British Mediterranean Fleet put the Italians to flight at a helter-skelter battle fought off Cape Matapan, the southernmost tip of mainland Greece. It would be the last fleet action ever fought by the RN – battleships against battleships. The RAN played a dashing part, with the cruiser *Perth* under fire from the Italians' heavy guns, and the feisty *Stuart*, with Hec Waller in command, charging about in the midst of a confused night action in a gunnery and torpedo scrap with cruisers and destroyers, at least one of which *Stuart* helped to sink. Matapan put paid forever to the *Regia Marina*'s dream of dominance in the Mediterranean.

In early May, the British also notched up a triumph that literally changed the conduct of the war and brought victory at sea closer to the Allies. On 9 May, after a short, sharp battle with a convoy escort to the east of Greenland, *U-110* was abandoned by its captain and crew who, believing their boat was sinking, surrendered to the destroyer *Bulldog*. It wasn't; the U-boat stayed afloat. A party from the destroyer went aboard and captured codebooks and, more valuable still, one of the top-secret Enigma ciphering machines at the heart of the *Kriegsmarine*'s communications. It was a stroke of extraordinary good fortune kept so secret that even President Roosevelt was not told of it for another year.

But May would also bring a British defeat at sea so shocking, so melancholy, that it was barely credible when the news came through. Breaking out into the Atlantic through the fogbound Denmark Strait between Iceland and Greenland, the battleship *Bismarck* sank the pride of the RN and the world's most famous capital ship, the battlecruiser *Hood*. 'One of our most cherished naval possessions,' wrote Winston Churchill. 'Her loss was a bitter grief.'[21] The lightly armoured and obsolescent *Hood* had blown up in virtually the first exchange of fire, leaving only three survivors from the 1421 people on board. It was a dismal end for this magnificent ship, that great, grey colossus that had excited so much admiration on her Australian visit in 1924.

At Churchill's insistent command, every British warship that could be mustered pursued *Bismarck* for three days in what would become a legendary chase of vengeance and destruction. On 27 May, reduced to an inferno of white-hot steel, she sank some 500 kilometres off the French port of Brest. One of *Bismarck*'s pursuers, the battleship *Rodney*, was navigated by an Australian on exchange duty, Lieutenant Commander Galfrey Gatacre, who was mentioned in despatches and awarded the Distinguished Service Cross for his 'accurate navigation and judicious selection of courses' during the action.

May, too, saw terrible Allied reverses in the Mediterranean. Mussolini's humiliating failures on land and sea had forced a reluctant, exasperated Hitler to pick up the pieces. General Erwin Rommel and his *Afrikakorps* began their rampage across the North African Western Desert, sending the British Army tumbling back east towards Egypt and mounting siege on the port of Tobruk, held by the Australian Army's 9th Division – the famous Rats of Tobruk – and resupplied from the sea by the Scrap Iron Flotilla in the daring and dangerous operation the sailors christened the Tobruk Ferry.

In another of his grand strategic follies, Churchill mounted an ill-planned invasion to push the Germans out of Greece, largely employing the Australian Army's 6th Division and the New Zealand 2nd Division, with the British 1st Armoured Brigade. The Allies were outnumbered and badly equipped – the Australians, fresh from North Africa, shivered in the searing cold of snowy mountain passes – in what became first a rout and then a disastrous retreat to the island of Crete. That in turn became a catastrophe. Crete was another heavy Allied defeat. Towards the end of May, after almost a month of savage combat with the Germans, some of it literally hand to hand, thousands of troops waited on the south coast to be rescued by sea: beaten men, exhausted and hungry, many wounded.

The evacuation struggled on, with a devastating toll of five cruisers and eight destroyers of the Mediterranean Fleet sunk by the *Luftwaffe* and the *Regia Aeronautica*, and three battleships, a carrier, six cruisers and seven destroyers damaged. Urged by his staff to call off the rescue, the Commander-in-Chief, Admiral Sir Andrew Cunningham, defiantly declared that he would not abandon the army. 'It takes the navy three years to build a new ship. It will take three hundred years to build a new tradition,' he told them.[22] On 30 May, on the way back from Crete to Alexandria, HMAS *Perth* was struck by a stray bomb that penetrated a boiler room, killing four of her sailors and nine soldiers. Despite the navy's gallantry, some 12,000 Allied troops, including 3000 Australians, had to be left on Crete to become prisoners of war.

As Rommel tightened his noose of steel around Tobruk, the little ships of the Scrap Iron Flotilla found themselves in ever more dangerous waters, under relentless air attack of increasing ferocity, sometimes from high altitude, at other times from the nerve-racking Stuka dive bombers that would plummet towards them with engines screaming and sirens howling. Eventually, inevitably, one was lost. *Waterhen* – 'The Chook', as everyone called her – was bracketed by dive bombers off the little Egyptian port of Sollum on the evening of 29 June. The bombs missed, but they were close enough to hole her badly and she slumped to a wallowing halt, although no one was killed and the only injury was said to have been to a sailor hit by a falling can of bully beef. Another destroyer, HMS *Defender*, took off her crew and tried to tow her back to Alexandria, but in the early hours of the next morning she rolled over and sank. The Chook was the first ship of the RAN to be lost to enemy action in the war.

Adolf Hitler very publicly gloated over the fiasco of Greece and Crete. 'Thus did Mr Churchill commit one of the greatest strategic blunders of this war,' he sneered in a speech to the Reichstag, to thunderous applause. Swollen with hubris, lusting for conquest, convinced of his own genius, the Führer then proceeded to make a blunder that dwarfed any of Churchill's, undoubtedly the most catastrophic miscalculation of modern warfare. He invaded the Soviet Union.

On 22 June, the *Wehrmacht* launched Operation Barbarossa, some 4,000,000 German troops smashing into Russia across a front of nearly 3000 kilometres, the greatest invasion in history. The Red Army, hamstrung by the murderous incompetence of Joseph Stalin, fell back in retreat.

—

If there had been complacency about the war in Australia at the beginning of 1941, it was long gone by the winter. The casualty lists in the newspapers were growing longer, and a furious controversy erupted over the sending of the 6th Division to be cut to pieces in Greece and Crete. On 19 June, the Minister for the Army, Percy Spender, told parliament in Canberra that 5951 Australian troops were 'not accounted for', adding the pious hope that most were 'probably alive and well as prisoners of war'.[23] By July, even with press censorship in place, the scale of the disaster and the incompetence that brought it about were all too apparent. The Labor frontbencher Jack Beasley – a member of the Advisory War Council, known to friend and foe alike as 'Stabber Jack' – charged in parliament that the Menzies United Australia Party government had been 'grossly misled' by Churchill and the British.

'It is a hard thing to say – but it must be said that the information conveyed to our Ministers was based on false grounds and, in fact, our soldiers were sent into a struggle in which, from the beginning, it was obvious that they never had a chance. It was most unsatisfactory, and a stain upon the standard which Australians nobly carried in the last war, and in this, that will never be forgotten.'[24]

Beasley's attack, and others like it, hit hard at a government already tottering and about to fall apart. Menzies' trip to Britain had been roundly criticised as a failure, not least within his own party, where disloyal colleagues were openly scheming against him. He floundered on for a few more weeks, publicly unperturbed, privately sick at heart. He again asked Labor to join a government of national unity, astonishing everybody by announcing that he would be prepared to see John Curtin become Prime Minister and would serve under him. That overture also failed. The knives were sharpened again. On 29 August, Menzies resigned as Prime Minister and, with the brawling United Australia Party unable to settle on a man of its own, his place was taken by the Country Party leader, Arthur Fadden, a jovial Queenslander. Fadden lasted just six weeks until the crossbench independents keeping the government in power in the House of Representatives decided they could stomach the chaos no longer and brought him down. Labor took office. John Curtin was sworn in on 7 October 1941 as Prime Minister and Minister for Defence Co-ordination.

—

Crowned with the laurels of victory in the Mediterranean, John Collins had brought the light cruiser *Sydney* back home in February 1941 to a rapturous welcome. Tens of thousands turned out to cheer the ship's company on a march through the streets of her namesake city, and her captain was feted as a naval hero. In August, Collins left the ship and was posted to Singapore on the staff of the RN Commander-in-Chief, Admiral Sir Geoffrey Layton.

Sydney's new captain was Joe Burnett, who left his job as Assistant Chief of the Naval Staff ashore in Melbourne to take command on 14 May, when the ship was at Fremantle. Burnett had not shot ahead so fast as his college term mates Collins and Farncomb, perhaps because – unlike them – he was not an aggressively ambitious man. He was no less able, though, competent without being showy, with high marks in his gunnery and staff college courses. His previous spell at sea, before the war, had been as executive officer of the RN battleship HMS *Royal Oak*, where he had been well respected. An outstanding rugby centre (he had played for a winning RN team), a genial companion with a sense of fun and the ridiculous, a devout Anglican, a much-loved husband and father of two boys, he was well liked by officers and sailors. Collins would write of him:

> Joe Burnett was one of our finest officers. An outstanding sport with a good brain – an unusual combination. With these qualifications and ... a happy and cheerful disposition, it is not surprising that he was one of the most popular of our year.[25]

Sydney was his first command, in peace or war. He learnt to handle the ship on convoy duties in the Pacific and Indian Oceans, without any sight of the enemy. On 11 November 1941 – Armistice Day – he sailed from Fremantle to escort the troopship *Zealandia* to the Sunda Strait in the Dutch East Indies, handed her over to a British cruiser six days later, and then turned for home. *Sydney* was due back in Fremantle on the afternoon of 20 November, but there was no great concern when she did not appear on time. That sort of delay happened often enough in wartime. It was not until 23 November that the Naval Board signalled Burnett to report his position. And signalled again and again, ever more urgently. There was no reply.

The loss of *Sydney* and her entire ship's company was – and remains – Australia's greatest naval disaster. The enormity of the tragedy has provided fuel for conspiracy theories ever since, each more fanciful than the one before it, all without a scrap of truth and convincingly disproven, most recently by a Commonwealth Commission of Inquiry that brought down a searching, voluminous report in 2009. The facts it found are incontestable.

On the afternoon of Wednesday 19 November, at around 4 pm, *Sydney* was steaming south some 200 kilometres off the coast of Western Australia, west of Shark Bay, when her lookouts sighted a merchant vessel. Burnett turned towards her and signalled the challenge, but got only slow, fumbling replies: a not uncommon occurrence with civilian ships. At five o'clock, with *Sydney* drawing ever closer, the ship broadcast a distress message, claiming to be a Dutch vessel, the *Straat Malakka*, and threatened by an unidentified warship. It was a clever ruse, and it worked. Rashly, Burnett drew closer still, until, by 5.15 pm, he was only 1.5 kilometres off the stranger's starboard beam, on a parallel course, with his guns trained.

At 5.30, the mystery ship suddenly rattled down her Dutch ensign, hauled up the Nazi swastika and opened fire. *Sydney* had been snared by the German raider *Kormoran*, a converted freighter armed with six well-concealed 15-centimetre (5.9-inch) guns, a secondary armament of anti-tank and anti-aircraft guns, and no fewer than six torpedo tubes: four of them hidden on deck, two angled aft below the waterline. Her captain, Fregattenkapitän Theodor Detmers, was an experienced naval officer who had once visited Australia, in the cruiser *Köln* in 1933.

Kormoran's gunnery was superb, at almost point-blank range. Her very first shot almost certainly destroyed *Sydney*'s bridge, quite probably killing Burnett and everyone there. *Sydney* opened fire with her 6-inch guns nearly simultaneously, but her first salvo scored not a hit. The duel then raged for about an hour, with *Kormoran* pouring in a withering fire that gradually pounded the cruiser into a blazing, drifting wreck. One German torpedo blasted into *Sydney*'s hull below A- and B-turrets.

Almost miraculously, *Sydney* managed to land some blows on her assailant, shells from X-turret wrecking *Kormoran*'s engine room and bringing her to a halt. She also kept up a ragged fire from her 4-inch armament, and fired a torpedo that missed. Her heroes of that battle will be forever anonymous, but there must have been many. By 6.30 pm, though, it was over. The Germans watched as the cruiser, burning fiercely and clearly out of control, limped slowly away to the south-east. There were flickerings of light from her over the horizon in the night, but they too disappeared around 11 pm. Detmers ordered the damaged *Kormoran* to be scuttled, and the surviving crew took to the boats, 318 of them to become prisoners of war in Australia.

We can never know why Burnett brought his ship so close. It was incautious at best, reckless at worst. It is also fair to wonder whether any of his senior officers, several of them Mediterranean veterans, had tried to dissuade him. Perhaps he recalled his criticism of Harold Farncomb's long-range and ineffectual shelling of the *Coburg* and was determined to do better. Whatever his reason, it killed him and it cost the lives of 645 men, many of them teenagers or in their early 20s.

The entire nation was stricken, the grief profound and indelible. John Curtin, in office for not yet two months, wept when he was told the news. The great metropolitan newspapers were drenched with the tragedy, but the sorrow of family loss was captured more intimately, perhaps, in the country papers, such as *The Dungog Chronicle and Durham and Gloucester Advertiser* in New South Wales:

> LOCAL BOY
>
> Word was received from the Naval authorities on Wednesday by Mr. and Mrs. George Wilson, of Abelard Street, that their son, Cliff, was missing. They knew that he was on the *Sydney* in the wireless telegraphic unit. He had several years' experience in wireless with Mr. Geoff Pettett, of Dungog. Cliff's age is 23 years, and he is a fine, quiet young man. It is to be hoped that better news will be received of him following the search by sea and air that is now proceeding.[26]

The pain of the *Sydney* disaster was still raw when there was more to lament at sea. The sloop *Parramatta* was lost off Bardia on the Tobruk Ferry Run on 27 November 1941, torpedoed and sunk by *U-559*, with 138 men dead and only 24 survivors.

And the year had more bad news in store.

CHAPTER 11

I MAKE IT QUITE CLEAR THAT AUSTRALIA LOOKS TO AMERICA

Tenno Heika Banzai! Long live the Emperor! In five tumultuous months, the Empire of Japan inflicted upon the English-speaking peoples the most devastating defeat in their history.

From the bombing of Pearl Harbor on 7 December 1941 to the surrender of the last American troops on the island of Corregidor in the Philippines on 6 May 1942, the Japanese ran rampant and apparently unstoppable over South-East Asia, and the Pacific and Indian Oceans. For all its evil intent, and sown with the seeds of an ultimate Japanese catastrophe though it was, this great thrust across land and sea was a miracle of planning, of logistics, of naval and military execution.

In fact, the first act of invasion was at Kota Bharu on the north-east coast of Malaya, where more than 5000 troops stormed ashore to begin a relentless advance on Singapore to the south. The attack on Pearl Harbor by carrier-borne aircraft began about 70 minutes later. When it was over, the US Pacific Fleet had been cut to pieces, with 18 ships sunk or damaged, including four great battleships sitting on the bottom, and 2403 men killed. The British traitor William Francis Forbes-Sempill, the man who had sold Japan the secrets of carrier aviation, had done his work well.

Across the Pacific in the Philippines, the American command in Manila received the telegram 'AIR RAID PEARL HARBOR. THIS IS NO DRILL' at 3 am, only minutes after the first strike. In a display of incompetence inexplicable even to this day, the morning in Manila drifted by in confusion and inertia, with almost nothing done to prepare for a Japanese attack. The air commander, Major General Lewis H. Brereton, agitated for pre-emptive air strikes against Japanese bases on Formosa (modern Taiwan), but for several hours the Commander-in-Chief, General Douglas MacArthur, refused even to see him. Brereton's B-17 Flying Fortress bombers were still lined up in neat rows at Clark Field north-west of Manila when the Japanese Naval Air Force arrived overhead at 12.40 pm and blasted all 96 of them to ruins. 'On the ground! On the ground!' exclaimed a furious President Roosevelt when he was told the news at the White House.

Incompetence was not the sole preserve of the Americans. Winston Churchill had responded to the rising Japanese menace by despatching two capital ships to Singapore, the battleship *Prince of Wales* and the elderly battlecruiser *Repulse*, which arrived at the island naval base with a fanfare of carefully contrived publicity on 2 December. A modern aircraft carrier that was to have accompanied them, HMS *Indomitable*, ran aground in the Caribbean. And that was that. The RN was stretched to near breaking point. Fighting the U-boat war in the Atlantic, running the desperate and dangerous supply convoys to Russia, and still enmeshed in the Mediterranean, it could do no more for the Far East. So much for all those years of the grand design, the great promise, the solemn intent of Main Fleet to Singapore. It had been worthless, empty rhetoric.

A week later, on 10 December, *Repulse* and *Prince of Wales* lay on the bottom of the South China Sea off Malaya's east coast: sunk by land-based Japanese aircraft, but victims as much as anything of the folly of their commander, Admiral Sir Tom Phillips, who had come straight from a staff job at the Admiralty, had never been under air attack, but believed that a battleship would always beat a bomber. Five Australian midshipmen from the college entry of 1937 were aboard *Repulse*: John Austin, Bob Davies, Bruce Dowling, Guy Griffiths and Peter Gyllies, all still in their teens. Four of them survived the sinking, to be rescued by accompanying destroyers. Guy Griffiths managed to squeeze out of a scuttle on the starboard side, grateful that he had kept his shoes on to clamber over the sharp, encrusted growth below the waterline. More dramatically, Peter Gyllies executed a perfect swallow dive from the air defence position atop the ship's mainmast. Bob Davies, though, ignored the order to abandon ship and kept fighting, his last moments described by a writer in *The Naval Review*:

> It was a glorious day with the bluest of blue seas. The port side of the ship, usually about twenty feet above the water, was just awash, and the starboard side correspondingly higher. Forward, the boatswain was chucking wooden planks over the side, and aft of me an Australian midshipman was still madly firing his Oerlikon gun at an aircraft and blaspheming anyone who dared to foul the sight. The group of men with me, some blinking in the unaccustomed sunshine, showed no sign of fear; in fact, considering that they were still grappling with death, one might have described their attitude as jocular.
>
> I looked over the starboard, or high, side and saw we were still doing a good 16 knots . . .[1]

Davies, a slender, fair-haired boy from Greenwich in suburban Sydney, had turned 18 just three weeks before. He was still shooting when the sea closed over him.[2]

A day later, on 11 December, Hitler sealed his doom by declaring war on the United States, even as his armies on the Eastern Front were turning to retreat in the face of the Russian winter, where temperatures had plunged below −10°C.

But in Australia that summer, each week seemed to bring a new and ominous hammer blow. British, Australian and Indian troops were forced back down the Malayan Peninsula even as the grandees in Singapore continued to radiate gritty optimism, as reported by the Perth *Daily News*:

POPHAM ON MALAYA
SINGAPORE, Tuesday.

Decrying defeatist talk about the situation in Malaya, British
Commander-in-Chief Sir Robert Brooke-Popham said yesterday that, though we had lost a large part of North Malaya it was
only for a time.

'If we had had more equipment, things might have gone
differently,' he said. 'The Japanese introduced a new method of
operation, moving lightly-equipped and wearing singlets and
sandshoes so as to appear like civilians.

'Moreover, they are able to live on the country, which our
troops are unable to do.'[3]

On 22 December, Winston Churchill cabled one of his stirring
exhortations to the Governor of Hong Kong, Sir Mark Young.
There must be 'no thought of surrender', he told him. 'Every part
of the island must be fought, and the enemy resisted with the
utmost stubbornness ... there must be vigorous fighting in
the nner defences and, if the need be, from house to house . . .'[4]

Hong Kong surrendered three days later, on Christmas Day,
the first British possession to fall to the Japanese, with 11,000
British troops taken prisoner. Churchill heard the news in wintry
Washington, where he was meeting Roosevelt and the senior
military chieftains of both countries for what became known as
the Arcadia Conference. The two sides agreed on a strategy to
'beat Germany first', a remarkable concession from the Americans, given the Japanese onslaught in the Pacific, and a Combined
Chiefs of Staff Committee was set up in Washington to run the
joint war effort. Australia was not consulted – much to the chagrin
of the government in Canberra, when it found out – but the
British and Americans agreed to set up another joint command
in the Pacific: ABDA, standing for the Americans, British, Dutch
and Australians, led by a British General, Sir Archibald Wavell.
This would hold what was known as the Malay Barrier above
Australia, from Malaya in the north-west to the eastern end of
the Netherlands East Indies.

By now, Prime Minister John Curtin had no illusions about the capacity of Britain to come to Australia's defence. He remained loyal to King and Empire, and proudly so, but he had the acuity to see that Australia must rely on America for its security. On 27 December, the Melbourne *Herald* published Curtin's New Year's message, which turned the nation's gaze to a powerful friend across the Pacific. He laid down a cornerstone of Australian foreign policy that endures to this day:

> we refuse to accept the dictum that the Pacific struggle must be treated as a subordinate segment of the general conflict. By that it is not meant that any one of the other theatres of war is of less importance than the Pacific, but that Australia asks for a concerted plan evoking the greatest strength at the Democracies' disposal, determined upon hurling Japan back.
>
> The Australian Government, therefore, regards the Pacific struggle as primarily one in which the United States and Australia must have the fullest say in the direction of the democracies' fighting plan.
>
> Without any inhibitions of any kind, I make it quite clear that Australia looks to America, free of any pangs as to our traditional links or kinship with the United Kingdom.
>
> We know the problems that the United Kingdom faces. We know the constant threat of invasion. We know the dangers of dispersal of strength, but we know too, that Australia can go and Britain can still hold on.
>
> We are, therefore, determined that Australia shall not go, and we shall exert all our energies towards the shaping of a plan, with the United States as its keystone, which will give to our country some confidence of being able to hold out until the tide of battle swings against the enemy . . .'[5]

The conservatives were outraged. Menzies called the article 'a great blunder', and his former Army Minister, Percy Spender, blustered that it was 'deplorable . . . an egregious blunder'.[6] Billy Hughes, now leading the United Australia Party, thought it 'loose and ill-considered'.[7] Churchill – who never fully grasped the idea that Australia was no longer a colonial possession – took personal affront, cabling from Washington to his deputy, Clement Attlee, 'I hope there will be no pandering to this,' and asserting later in his memoirs that the words had been 'flaunted around the world by our enemies'.[8]

Yet Curtin had merely reflected reality, a truth that became ever more apparent in the opening months of 1942. The Japanese took Rabaul, the capital of Australian Mandated New Guinea, on 23 January, overwhelming a small Australian garrison – Lark Force – and massacring 160 prisoners. Rabaul would become a pivotal naval and air base for the Japanese in the Pacific.

The burning ruins of Fortress Singapore fell on 15 February in scenes of carnage and horror, the Japanese taking more than 130,000 civilian and military prisoners of war. The Australian Army commander in Malaya, Major General Gordon Bennett, deserted his command and scuttled home, leaving some 15,000 soldiers of the 8th Division to go into captivity. Many of these men would die on the Burma–Siam Railway. At the same time, Churchill attempted to bully Curtin into diverting a convoy carrying the Australian 7th Division home from the Middle East, hoping to send the Australians to stem the Japanese advance in Burma. It was a strategic folly that would have seen yet another Australian Army division chewed to pieces, but, after a fiery exchange of cables, Curtin forced a petulant Churchill to back down.

But still the tide rolled on. Darwin was bombed for the first time on 19 February, with 243 people killed and eight ships sunk in the harbour. Half the population stampeded south in panic, including servicemen who deserted from the local RAAF base, in what became known as 'The Adelaide River Stakes'. The Japanese, meanwhile, were turning their attention to the rich prize of the Netherlands East Indies, where the dysfunctional ABDA command was preparing a forlorn last stand. An Allied force of cruisers and destroyers was all but wiped out in the Battle of the Java Sea on 27 February, and the early hours of 1 March saw another grievous Australian loss: the light cruiser *Perth* succumbed to an overwhelming Japanese squadron in the Battle of the Sunda Strait, 353 of her crew dying with her, including her captain, Hec Waller. Of the 328 men who survived the sinking, only 214 would make it home after the war. The American heavy cruiser USS *Houston* went down in the same battle half an hour later, with the loss of nearly 700 sailors.

At Batavia in Java, with the grimly absurd title of Commodore Commanding China Force, John Collins was battling to find transport for the flood of frightened refugees fleeing Singapore. He himself escaped the Japanese advance by the skin of his teeth, leaving for Australia on 2 March on an overcrowded corvette, HMAS *Burnie*. Others were not so lucky. Two days later, escorting a small convoy to Australia, the sloop *Yarra* made a defiant, fatal stand against a force of Japanese cruisers in the Timor Sea. Her gallant captain, Lieutenant Commander Robert 'Oscar' Rankin, was among the 138 dead.

And all to no avail. The ABDA command collapsed in chaos, with the Dutch colonial administration surrendering the Netherlands East Indies three days later, on 7 March. For another month, the beleaguered American and Filipino armies fought on in the Philippines, a battle of increasing horror centred on the Bataan Peninsula, which separates Manila Bay from the South China Sea. Sick and nearly starving, some 76,000 men finally surrendered there on 9 April, to be forced into the atrocities of the Bataan Death March to imprisonment, in which at least 10,000 died or were murdered. On the last redoubt, the island fortress of Corregidor at the mouth of Manila Bay, 13,000 survivors put down their arms on 6 May.

Thrusting into the Indian Ocean with a powerful fleet of carriers and battleships, the victor of Pearl Harbor, Vice Admiral Chuichi Nagumo, put to flight the elderly remnants of what the British euphemistically called the Far Eastern Fleet, based on Ceylon. In early April, in quick order, Nagumo's aircraft bombed the bases at Colombo and Trincomalee. They sank first the cruisers *Cornwall* and *Dorsetshire* – sister ships of *Australia* – and then the old carrier HMS *Hermes* off the island, finally turning their attention to her escort, the destroyer HMAS *Vampire*, veteran of the Tobruk Ferry Runs. The plucky little *Vampire* fought back, shooting down at least one attacker, but a direct hit in her boiler room broke her back, and eight of her men, including her captain, Commander Bill Moran, were killed or died of wounds. The Far Eastern Fleet retreated out of Japanese reach, to the East African port of Kilindini, near Mombasa in Kenya. Courageous it had been, in its highest traditions, but – to all intents and purposes – the RN had faded away as a fighting force in the Far East. And the RAN had begun to take heavy punishment.

Australians looking north could see the red-and-white rising sun of Japan flying above them, menacing and omnipotent, from Burma in the west to the Philippines in the east. Their darkest fears were coming true.

—

The little town of Terowie in South Australia is a ghost of its past, almost empty. Squatting just off the Barrier Highway on the plains 225 kilometres north of Adelaide and just over 100 kilometres east of Port Pirie, its main street is lined with the handsome colonial pubs and banks of its heyday, when Terowie was a bustling railway terminus where the narrow-gauge tracks from Alice Springs and Broken Hill met the broad-gauge line to the south. Most of those buildings are closed and shuttered now, and the railway-station platforms are abandoned and crumbling.

Terowie, though, had its moment in history. On Friday 20 March 1942, a small train from the north pulled into the station and from it stepped none other than General Douglas MacArthur, clad in a plain khaki uniform without medal ribbons or badges of rank, but wearing the gold-braided cap he had designed for himself as a Field Marshal of the Philippines. It had been a long and arduous journey, with still more to come, and, at the age of 62, his face showed the fatigue of it.

Roosevelt himself had directly ordered MacArthur to leave the Philippines and go to Australia. With his wife, Jean, their four-year-old son, Arthur, and their Cantonese amah, Ah Cheu, MacArthur slipped away from Corregidor in a USN PT (patrol torpedo) boat on the night of 11 March, beating through buffeting seas to the southern island of Mindanao. There, after a flurry of arguments and mishaps, two B-17 bombers arrived to fly him, his family and a small staff to Darwin. It was a gruelling, ten-hour flight in the dark and cold – MacArthur himself perched in the radio operator's seat, the child shivering in the amah's arms – and when they arrived early on the morning of 17 March, they found the town in the middle of a Japanese air raid. So the B-17s flew on to another air field at Batchelor, about 100 kilometres to the south.

As strange as it may seem, neither the Australian Government nor the military had the faintest idea that the great man was coming. Curtin was telephoned that morning by the senior American officer in Australia, Lieutenant General George Brett, who read him a prepared statement:

> The President of the United States has directed that I present his compliments to you and inform you that General Douglas MacArthur, United States Army, has today arrived in Australia from the Philippine Islands. In accordance with his directions General MacArthur has now assumed command of all United States Army Forces here.
>
> Should it be in accord with your wishes and those of the Australian people, the President suggests that it would be highly acceptable to him and pleasing to the American people for the Australian Government to nominate General MacArthur as the Supreme Commander of all Allied Forces in the South-West Pacific. Such nomination should be submitted simultaneously to London and Washington . . .'[9]

Unsurprisingly, a startled but ecstatic Prime Minister and War Cabinet agreed. This was momentous news, a triumphant vindication of Curtin's vision in his New Year message. The nomination went off that afternoon while the government lunged into a frenzy of preparations to welcome the new ally.

Meanwhile, at Batchelor, after a breakfast of tea and canned fruit, the party boarded two rather more comfortable DC-3 aircraft of Australian National Airways that had been hurriedly chartered to take them to Alice Springs. But there, Jean had had enough, and she flatly refused to fly any further. So a small private train was hurriedly put together for the leg to Terowie, where they would change for Adelaide.

Despite the official secrecy, the newspapers had got wind of the journey, and some reporters and photographers were waiting. They were not disappointed. The history of warfare is studded with generals hungry for fame, but few have ever courted it so eagerly and skilfully as MacArthur. The reporter for the Adelaide *Advertiser* was swept away:

> This remarkable soldier looked an impressive figure as he walked easily out of the train. Much to his surprise, and that of those who hoped his arrival at Terowie would be a profound secret, there was a burst of cheering and cries of 'Welcome to Australia' from people partly hidden by a line of railway carriages.
>
> Turning swiftly, General MacArthur strode towards an opening and saluted the Terowie people and passengers on a nearby train. His flashing smile was a tonic for those around, and there was another round of cheers and cries of 'Good-bye and good luck' when he joined his wife and son, who had been watching admiringly from a few yards off the world's most famous and dashing general.[10]

Modestly assuring the newsmen that it was his policy to limit himself 'to the briefest publicity', MacArthur then delivered to them the lines that would echo around the world and attach to him forever:

> The President of the United States ordered me to break through the Japanese lines and proceed from Corregidor to Australia for the purpose, as I understand it, of organising an American offensive against Japan, the primary purpose of which is the relief of the Philippines.
>
> I came through and I shall return.[11]

Roosevelt had specified no such thing. MacArthur's keenness to return might well have been sharpened by a gift of US$500,000 paid to him just weeks before by an old friend, the President of the Philippines, Manuel Quezon, a fact not revealed publicly until 1979, well after his death.[12] But both the United States and Australia needed a champion and a saviour at this dark hour, and, although Roosevelt had private misgivings about his dithering in Manila and his thirst for the spotlight, MacArthur was the best on offer.

A day later, he was accorded a rapturous welcome by crowds lining the streets in Melbourne. 'I shall keep the soldier faith,' he proclaimed to another pack of adoring journalists. On 26 March, he was driven to Canberra to attend a session of parliament, and to meet John Curtin and the War Cabinet. That night, there was a banquet at Parliament House, where he soared to new heights of oratory: 'My presence here is tangible evidence of our unity. I have come as a soldier in a great crusade of personal liberty, as opposed to perpetual slavery. My faith in our ultimate victory is invincible . . .'[13]

It was the start of one of the more unlikely partnerships of history. Curtin, the self-educated socialist orator, atheist and reformed alcoholic, and MacArthur, the deeply religious West Point military patrician with strong roots in the Republican Party, hit it off from their first meeting, as the American would note later in his memoirs:

> We promptly came to a sense of mutual trust, co-operation and regard that we never once breached by thought, word or deed. He was the kind of man the Australians called 'fair dinkum'. As I rose to leave, I put my arm around his strong shoulder: 'Mr Prime Minister,' I said, 'we two, you and I, will see this thing through together. We can do it and we will do it. You take care of the rear and I will handle the front.'[14]

Curtin told MacArthur that day of the agreement that he would be the Supreme Commander, with the additional good news that he had been awarded the United States' highest decoration, the Medal of Honor.

MacArthur and his 'Bataan Gang', as his closest aides became known, then turned to the fight ahead. The task would be daunting, monumental. On the train trip south, MacArthur had enquired about the American troops available to him in Australia. The answer, as he would say later, gave him 'the greatest shock of the whole damn war'. There were only about 25,000 men, many of them clerks, drivers and cooks, with no tanks, little artillery and only a handful of combat aircraft. 'God have mercy on us,' he said.[15]

Back in Melbourne, he settled with his family into a suite at the Menzies Hotel in Bourke Street, where a grand piano had been installed at his request. Each day, the Supreme Commander drove the few blocks to his headquarters at 401 Collins Street in a black Cadillac with a licence plate bearing the four stars of his rank and the number USA-1. One of the Bataan Gang had thoughtfully carried the plate all the way from Corregidor.

—

Jack Crace had not been having a good war. The Rear Admiral Commanding the Australian Squadron did not have a squadron to command. Almost from the first, his ships had been scattered far and wide, deployed out of his reach by the Naval Board in Melbourne and under the control of the Admiralty in London, leaving him to spend the first two years of the war in mounting frustration, much of it ashore in Sydney, gripped by a sense of futility.

Dutifully, he put to sea whenever he could in whatever ship was available to him, but there was not much for a flag officer to do on the humdrum business of convoy in Australian or New Zealand waters. He came to believe – with good reason – that the Naval Board was taking decisions out of his hands, and more and more he found himself diverted to a dreary round of conferences and cocktail parties. By the spring of 1941, after an exchange of ever more acrimonious phone calls and letters with Melbourne, he was fed up and ready to resign. In Sydney on 12 October, a Sunday, Crace met the new Chief of the Naval Staff, Vice

Admiral Sir Guy Royle, another RN officer, who had succeeded the ailing Ragnar Colvin, and told him he intended to quit the next morning. It was a fiery encounter, Royle telling Crace that he could not leave his post in wartime and that, if he tried to, his letter of resignation would be torn up.

Japan changed all that. Suddenly, Jack Crace had a war on his hands. The Naval Board began calling its far-flung ships back to home waters for the defence of Australia, and the new American ally – slowly at first, but with increasing speed and urgency – began to regroup in the South-West Pacific. On 19 December 1941, Crace was at sea again, his flag hoisted in *Canberra* and with *Perth* and the New Zealand cruiser *Achilles* in company under his command, a squadron worthy of the name at last. Off New Caledonia that day, they met what became known as the *Pensacola* convoy, the first great shipment of American men and equipment to Australia.

This was a rich argosy: seven troop transports escorted by the heavy cruiser USS *Pensacola*, carrying more than 5000 US Army and US Army Air Force personnel, the ships' holds laden with field guns, ammunition and motor vehicles, and 60 bomber and fighter aircraft packed in crates. The convoy had been destined for the Philippines, but with the situation there growing ever more dire, President Roosevelt himself ordered that it be diverted to Australia, first via Fiji and then on to Brisbane.

In the early hours of Monday 22 December, the convoy spotted the loom of the Cape Moreton lighthouse and by midday it was safely at anchor in Moreton Bay. Wartime secrecy and censorship had held, and not a word of the arrival appeared in the newspapers, but news of American ships in the bay and the Brisbane River spread like a bushfire, and by the time the troops marched ashore beneath a blazing Queensland sun the next day – in those glamorous khaki uniforms, those curiously big steel helmets, the slender Garand M1 rifles at the slope – there was a wildly cheering crowd to see them parade through the streets of Brisbane to one of the transit camps at the Ascot racecourse. They were hardly crack troops – most of them were National Guardsmen – but no matter. The Yanks had come!

Crace and *Canberra*, with *Perth* and *Achilles*, returned to Sydney on 24 December 1941, where they found that *Australia* had arrived three days before. The crews were weary, looking forward to snatching a little leave over Christmas. *Australia* had barely rested for a minute these past six months, it seemed. Traversing the length and breadth of the Indian Ocean, she had been from baking Aden at the mouth of the Red Sea to the bleak and barren Kerguelen Islands at almost 50 degrees south, where it was thought enemy raiders might have been repairing and replenishing. Snowy blizzards buffeted the ship there, but all they found was a sealing vessel with the bottom blown out of her and an uneaten meal on the mess deck table, with three graves on a nearby beach: one of those melancholy mysteries of the sea.

Christmas Eve or not, there was no time to waste, not a moment to lose. That very day, Crace transferred his flag to *Australia*, taking Harold Farncomb with him from *Canberra* to be his flag captain. At last, the *Aussie* had her first Australian-born commanding officer, a graduate of the RANC. Jamie 'Black Jack' Armstrong remained in the ship as her commander, the executive officer.

Four days later, on 28 December, the four cruisers sailed north, escorting convoy ZK.5 carrying 4250 fresh Australian troops and 10,000 tonnes of equipment and supplies for Port Moresby. They spent New Year's Eve at sea.

—

On the other side of the world, the locus of Allied power and command had crossed the Atlantic from London to Washington. Winston Churchill never for a moment loosened his grip on the conduct of the war, but the sheer mass and energy of the American commitment – military, political and economic – gave primacy to President Roosevelt and his newly established Joint Chiefs of Staff. Together, Churchill and Roosevelt and their service chiefs carved up the battlefield. Where this most closely touched Australia was in the eventual dividing up of the Pacific into two great commands. The South-West Pacific Area, under MacArthur and therefore a US Army responsibility, would include Australia, New Guinea, most of the Netherlands East Indies and the Philippines. The rest of the Pacific theatre – to be known as the Pacific Ocean Area, from New Zealand in the south to California in the east and Japan in the north – would belong to the USN, led from Hawaii by Admiral Chester W. Nimitz, who had been hurriedly sent there to take command after Pearl Harbor.

Nimitz and MacArthur were chalk and cheese, fire and stone. Hungry for glory and adulation, a bully who picked favourites, MacArthur saw the admiral as a rival for power. Nimitz was a mild-mannered and amiable Texan of German heritage, well liked by his subordinates, 57 years old, a man in command of every aspect of his profession and a leader by example, with a backbone of steel and a strategic vision that would make him the foremost admiral of the war, of any side. He would have to provide the ships for MacArthur's planned campaign of island hopping to the north, but he would not be stampeded into meeting the general's often extravagant demands.

As the chain of command lengthened, Jack Crace found himself serving two masters. He was still responsible to the Naval Board in Melbourne, but he was now under the operational orders of MacArthur's naval commander in Melbourne, Vice Admiral Herbert F. Leary, USN. This could well have made life difficult for him, but it actually turned out to be more workable, less complex rather than more. Crace's cruisers were now to be known as Anzac Force. *Canberra* went in for a long-overdue refit at Cockatoo Island in early January 1942, with her place taken in early February by an American heavy cruiser, the USS *Chicago*, which thrilled Sydney when she eventually turned up in the harbour with her sailors manning the rails in those famous white 'Dixie Cup' caps,[16] and the Stars and Stripes flying at her stern.

Chicago was marginally smaller than *Australia*, by a few metres in length and a few tonnes' displacement, but she carried nine 8-inch guns in turrets of three, and no fewer than four scout aircraft. Like most American cruisers, though, she had no torpedo tubes, but she could turn on a top speed of almost 33 knots. Her commanding officer, Howard D. Bode,[17] was a man marked for higher things, for he had been captain of the battleship *Oklahoma* when she was sunk on Battleship Row at Pearl Harbor with the loss of 429 of her crew. He had been ashore that morning, which probably saved his life, but it would be fair to say that many of *Chicago*'s ship's company wished he had gone down with her. A short and stocky figure with curiously long hair that he let grow below his collar – seen as highly eccentric in a USN captain – Bode was a rude and truculent tyrant, notoriously ready to publicly insult his officers, most of whom were frightened of him and called him 'Captain Bligh' behind his back. To his credit, though, Bode made an effort to be agreeable to Crace and submitted happily enough to his command.

Anzac Force officially came into being at Suva in Fiji on 12 February 1942, the two heavy cruisers supported by two Royal New Zealand Navy light cruisers, *Achilles* and *Leander* – 6-inch gun ships similar to the sole surviving Australian light cruiser, HMAS *Hobart* – with the addition of two fast, 36-knot American destroyers, *Perkins* and *Lamson*. Crace at last had a command fit for a rear admiral. Now, with the blessing of his superiors, he had to put it to good use.

—

The quickening tempo of the war drew more and more men to the RAN, and women too. The classrooms and drill fields at the Flinders Naval Base were at full stretch, turning out young sailors and midshipmen to crew the new ships coming into service and to replace the hundreds of men who had already been killed. And over hidebound opposition, women were taking on jobs traditionally the preserve of men.

The wall had been breached in 1941, when 14 women were employed at HMAS *Harman*, the navy's main communications base outside Canberra, 12 of them as telegraphists and two as stewards. Federal cabinet had agreed to it with foot-dragging reluctance, with the then Navy Minister, Billy Hughes, insisting that there be no publicity and that women should be paid only two-thirds of a man's wage. Curtin's new Labor government was no more friendly to working women in uniform, the trade unions fearing that they might well be the thin end of a civilian wedge into men's work, but in the end there was no choice. There were jobs to be done in all three services, and not just in the traditional women's realm of nursing. The Women's Royal Australian Naval Service of 580 personnel – 280 telegraphists and 300 on other duties from clerking to driving – would come into being on 24 July 1942.

Many young men found themselves moved around, suddenly posted here and there on some mysterious whim of the shore-bound pen-pushers who controlled their lives from afar. Mackenzie Gregory, the young sub lieutenant who had taken part in the fiasco at Dakar and the Sunderland rescue on board *Australia* off Scotland, had spent the last nine months of 1941 in Britain doing gunnery and torpedo courses. On Boxing Day that year, now a qualified junior watch-keeper and back home, he joined *Canberra* in Sydney.

Guy Griffiths and Peter Gyllies, who had survived the sinking of *Repulse* off Malaya, found themselves inexplicably stuck on board the ancient R class battleship HMS *Revenge* in the western Indian Ocean, where they were joined by their RANC classmate David Hamer and four other reluctant Australian midshipmen. 'A most frightening ship,' Hamer recalled in his memoirs.[18] 'The sailors were midgets, mostly from Liverpool' and the captain 'should have been running a girls' school, not commanding a battleship'. Almost entirely unmodernised since 1916, *Revenge* could barely make 16 knots, often in circles when her steering gear broke down; the gunnery-control system was antiquated and there was a perpetual shortage of fresh water on board. She was a part of that Eastern Fleet that had retreated from Ceylon to East Africa, which meant she spent most of her time swinging off a buoy, going nowhere.

This was probably for the best. Hamer recorded that, after the traditional RN 'Up Spirits!' issue of rum at midday, everyone was 'half-drunk and somnolent for several hours . . . with a dull miasma of rum rising to the sky'.[19] The young snotties were relieved when, after a few months of crushing boredom, they were shipped off to training courses in Britain, the single gold stripe of a sub lieutenant beckoning them on.

Still younger men were putting on an officer's uniform for the first time, boys from every part of the country. Dick Bourke's family had farmed wool and wheat near Northam in Western Australia since 1853, on a place called Loughmore Farm, named for the village his forebears had left in Ireland. A grass fire destroyed a crop and then the 1930s Depression ruined his parents, a bitter harvest. The bank foreclosed on the property and they moved to Perth, his father, Patrick 'Paddy' Bourke, finding what work he could as a shearer or on the wharves at Fremantle, his mother, Doris, returning to the teaching job she had trained for.

Times grew tougher. Paddy died of cancer in 1934 when young Dick was ten, leaving him and his younger brother to be schooled on the charity of the Christian Brothers at their college on St Georges Terrace. Doris had ambitions for her sons, but never in farming. Dick would join the navy, she decided, and great were the celebrations when he sat for and passed the RANC exams, to enter the college in 1938 at the age of 14.

Bruce Loxton was also a 1938 cadet, but from a very different background. His father, Dr Edward Hamilton Loxton, had served as an army medical officer in the First World War on the Somme and at Ypres and Passchendaele, where he had treated victims of mustard gas. Returning to Sydney after the war, Dr Loxton built a substantial medical practice in his equally substantial home at Enmore, became an elder of St Stephen's Presbyterian Church in Macquarie Street, and sent young Bruce first to Newington College and then, for his secondary schooling, to the Scots College in the Eastern Suburbs.

Like Dick Hamer, Bruce Loxton knew the middle-class comforts of nannies and housekeepers, with summer weekends and holidays spent mucking around on Sydney Harbour or canoeing on the lagoon at Wamberal, north of Sydney. But he took well to the spartan, sometimes bullying rigours of the RANC, as did Dick Bourke, who gained six sporting colours: for cricket, rugby, tennis, swimming, hockey and rowing. The Catholic farmer's boy from Western Australia and the Presbyterian doctor's son from Sydney must have had something in common, for they shared one of the RANC's glittering rewards in their graduation year, the Otto Albert Prize for Seamanship.

Bruce Loxton had another inspiration. He was in love. Home in Sydney on leave, he had met Dahlis Robertson at a dance in the Eastern Suburbs, and the two of them – still teenagers – had fallen head over heels. He had been just 15, manly and dashing in his cadet uniform with its white lanyard and rows of gleaming brass buttons. Dahlis, a vivacious, artistic girl, was a flower of the high-society Playfair family and still a student at Ascham, the exclusive girls' school at Edgecliff. She was captivated. They began writing to each other, sweet teenage letters bubbling with innocent longing, signed 'Brucie' and 'Bubsie'.

In December 1941, these two new midshipmen were sent to their first ships, the telegrams from the Naval Board directing them, in the time-honoured phrase, 'to repair to your duty'. Bruce was posted to *Canberra* two days after Pearl Harbor. Dick Bourke joined *Australia* that Christmas Eve.

—

The Americans and the Australians had precious little time to get to know each other, but it had to be done. There was a lot to learn. Ships and men of the RAN worked easily with the British because their training, their customs, their practices and procedures were identical. The USN frequently had other ways of doing things, sometimes with small differences of language or technical terms that were overcome easily enough. But in other ways, especially in communications, signalling and codes, and in such complex areas as squadron and fleet evolutions, there was a yawning gap. Foreign sayings, strange orders, peculiar happenings. With the Americans in the majority and in command, the Australians had to adapt to their ways, and very quickly.

To their enormous credit, they did. Signalmen and tele-graphists from both navies exchanged ships, working alongside each other on flag decks and in wireless rooms – 'radio shacks', the Yanks liked to call them – to cut through confusion or misun-derstanding. The exchanges worked because there was a genuine desire on both sides for them to do so, although the Americans found the messing and laundry arrangements on Australian ships to be surprisingly primitive. Not so the other way around. In Suva, Harold Eastick was invited on board *Chicago* for a visit. 'She certainly is a ship and a half,' he told his diary. 'Spotless and well kept. Had supper on her cafeteria-style and fit for a king.'[20] Ships of the USN had laundries for their officers and sailors (often operated by African-Americans or Filipinos) and central dining spaces – cafeterias – where you queued to be served by the cooks and ate at tables. Some even had air-conditioning. The RAN was still washing its clothes in buckets and messing in a way largely unchanged since the Napoleonic Wars.

Crace and Anzac Force were based on Noumea, in French New Caledonia, which – by some skilful Australian diplomacy – had been persuaded away from its allegiance to the Vichy Govern-ment to align with the Allies. In February and March, they began to work with the Americans at sea, in the tentative opening moves to take the war to the Japanese. On 16 February, they rendez-voused between Noumea and Suva with the USN's Task Force 11, led by the carrier *Lexington*, a sight as grand and awe-inspir-ing as anything most of the Australians had ever seen, the great flat-top escorted by no fewer than four cruisers and ten modern destroyers. The *Lady Lex*, as everyone called her, had been away from Pearl Harbor on 7 December – as had the other two Pacific Fleet carriers, *Saratoga* and *Enterprise*, an extraordinary stroke of luck that had spared all three to fight another day.

At 33,000 tonnes and 270 metres long, with seeming acres of flight deck, and her smokestacks encased in a mighty island along her starboard side, *Lexington* towered above the smaller ships of her flock, stately and imposing. More remarkable still, she was almost as fast as a destroyer, capable of 33 knots. Jack Crace visited her that day, piped aboard with all due courtesy, to meet the Task Force 11 commander, Vice Admiral Wilson Brown, and to coordinate offensive operations against the Japanese in the waters and islands of New Guinea.

It was an unhappy encounter. Hoping to be given a position in the front row for an attack on the Japanese base at Rabaul, Crace found instead that Brown wanted his squadron well in the rear, guarding a fleet oil tanker. It was a gnawing disappointment to an admiral who had hungered for action for so long, but he had no choice. In the words of the official US naval history, 'Admiral Crace, after protesting that he was out there to "shoot Japs" and not to "chaperone a blooming oiler", accepted the assignment and did it well.'[21]

As it happened, Brown had to abort this raid on Rabaul after the *Lexington* task force was discovered by a Japanese air-reconnaissance patrol and attacked on 20 February. But it was a turning point, a landmark in naval history, for it produced the first ever encounter between carrier-based aircraft in the war. Better still, it was a victory for the Americans, for the Japanese had underestimated their enemy, inexplicably failing to send in fighter cover with their two waves of bombers. The American F4F-3 Wildcats clawed them out of the sky, shooting down at least 16, they claimed, although that may have been an exaggeration, as these estimates usually were. Only two American aircraft were lost, with just one pilot killed – Ensign J. Woodrow Wilson – but there was a scary close shave for the *Lady Lex* herself when a crippled Mitsubishi G4M 'Betty' bomber (code-named Betty by the Allies), still airborne on only one wing and one engine, attempted to crash into her. *Lexington*'s captain, Frederick 'Ted' Sherman, wrenched his ship hard to starboard. For a few breathtaking seconds, the bomber flew low and alongside, trailing smoke, before cartwheeling into the sea off the port bow.

Far from this action, *Australia* sustained her own airborne loss. Returning from an anti-submarine patrol on the Suva–Noumea line on 19 February, the ship's Walrus aircraft made a hard landing and smashed headlong into *Australia*'s port quarter just above the waterline, breaking up and catching fire. Captain Farncomb got two whalers away to the rescue, but a motor launch from *Chicago* reached the wreckage first. They saved the observer and the air gunner but they could not find the pilot, Flying Officer Edward James Rowan RAAF, a 20-year-old from Ashford, near central Adelaide.

Prodded by Nimitz in Hawaii, the cautious Wilson Brown was urged to make another attempt on Rabaul in early March. Brown asked for and got two carriers this time: *Lexington*'s Task Force 11 was joined by *Yorktown* and her Task Force 17, flying the flag of Rear Admiral Frank Jack Fletcher. Again, to Crace's mounting chagrin, the Anzac group was assigned a subsidiary role. His force was augmented by two more American cruisers, *Astoria* and *Louisville*, and four destroyers, but the job was to patrol as a back-up to the south-east of New Guinea, beyond a radius at least 900 kilometres from Rabaul. Again, Crace went on board *Lexington* to protest and again he was rebuffed, rather more crisply this time. 'It actually means we shall do nothing at all,' Crace wrote in his diary.[22]

He needn't have worried, because Brown missed Rabaul yet again. On the way there, coming up from the south, he learnt from intelligence reports that the Japanese had made two landings on the New Guinea eastern coast at Lae and Salamaua, on the Bismarck Sea. The landings were reported by an Australian coastwatcher, Leigh Vial, a young assistant district officer who had struggled into the hills with two New Guineans to set up an observation post for his teleradio just days before. Vial's calm, methodical reports over the coming months would win him the nickname 'Golden Voice'. The Japanese searched for him but never found him.[23]

Brown hastily changed his plans to abandon the attack on Rabaul and strike the enemy at Lae and Salamaua instead. On

10 March, from the Gulf of Papua south of Port Moresby, he launched aircraft from both carriers, 104 of them, to bomb and strafe whatever enemy shipping they could find at the landings. It was a bold stroke, for the planes had to fly high over the peaks of the poorly mapped Owen Stanley Ranges, but they made it through a mountain pass some 7500 feet high, unopposed, and had what the US official historian called 'a field day' over their targets.

Still relatively inexperienced, the American pilots made wildly extravagant claims about transports, cruisers and destroyers sunk, when in fact only three ships were destroyed, and none of them of any particular value. But it was enough at the time for President Roosevelt to cable Churchill that the raid on Lae and Salamaua was 'the most cheering thing that had happened in the Pacific so far'.[24]

The Australian newspapers reported the affair as a smashing Allied victory, but in truth it was but a small, flickering ray of light through the heavy clouds of war that hung over Australia's northern approaches. Rabaul remained untouched, to grow in strength as the Japanese pivot in the South Pacific. There was still the fear that invasion was imminent, threatening Port Moresby first and then Australia itself.

Far from the action against Lae and Salamaua, Jack Crace and *Australia* suffered yet another disappointment that month when the ship's replacement Walrus aircraft made a heavy landing and, badly damaged, put itself out of action.

And there was worse to come, a dark and dismal affair so horrifying that, for decades afterwards, those who were there could not bring themselves to speak of it.

CHAPTER 12

TO BE HANGED
BY THE NECK TILL
THEY BE DEAD

T he knife blade flashed up and down, again and again, in a
frenzy of cutting and stabbing, a vicious attack in the night.
When it had done its work, Stoker John Joseph Riley, a teenager
from Bellerive in Tasmania, lay face down on *Australia*'s upper
deck on the port side just below the bridge, his life's blood
draining into a crimson pool on the teak planking. The crime
horrified the entire crew, officers and men alike, leaving many
distressed and fearful and ashamed for their ship's reputation. In
time, it would plunge both Australia and Britain into years of a
difficult and protracted constitutional dilemma that would reach
all the way to King George VI. There would be a public outcry
in the press and parliament.

It was Thursday 12 March 1942. The day had ended badly,
with a worrying search for some missing American aircraft.
Australia and Anzac Force were in the position assigned to them
by Wilson Brown, steaming in a lightly ruffled sea and oppressive heat some 200 kilometres south-east of the Louisiades, the
small chain of island atolls scattered where the Coral Sea meets
the Solomon Sea off the tail of Papua New Guinea.

That afternoon, the two new cruisers in the squadron, the
USS *Louisville* and *Astoria*, had launched four of their Curtiss
floatplanes on reconnaissance flights and they had all failed to
return. With radio silence in force, nothing was heard of them,

not a sound. As the sun began to set over the port quarter, there was not much Jack Crace could do except head north-west in the direction they had taken, the cruisers and destroyers making smoke to act as a beacon.[1]

The night came down quickly, with *Australia*'s deck log noting sunset at 6.21 pm and the last rays of tropical twilight disappearing not quite an hour later, plunging the world into a velvet black. There was no moon to be seen, no stars. Moonrise was not due until after midnight. *Australia* was a blackened shape herself, gliding along at an easy 17 knots, darkened down, no chink of light showing on deck beyond the faint glow of the binnacle on the compass platform. The admiral and Captain Farncomb were in their separate cabins. The Principal Control Officer, Lieutenant Commander Jack Donovan, had the ship and was looking forward to handing over to his relief at 8 pm, the end of the last two-hour dog watch.

This is the time many sailors savour, even in war. The work of the day is done. The evening meal has been eaten, for better or worse. A calm descends. The ship continues on its familiar routine, with the chance for men off watch to relax: officers in the wardroom or aft on the quarterdeck; men in the messes for'ard, where there is light to play the interminable navy board game of Uckers,[2] or perhaps to reread a cherished letter and write a reply. Others enjoy the cooler air on deck, a particular pleasure for those who work in the heat and the roar of the boiler rooms and engine spaces.

So it was on this night. Some of the hands were chatting in scattered groups on the fo'c'sle by A-turret or on B-deck below the bridge, or leaning over the guard rail idly watching the white of the bow wave foaming past. A few were preparing to go on watch, or to snatch a few hours' kip if they had the later middle watch from midnight.

At 7.40 pm, Able Seaman Jim Ormonde, the bugler of the watch on the forebridge, checked the time in the lobby behind the compass platform and then went to the ship's PA system. He switched on the microphone and blew the call for 'Night Defence

Stations', followed ten minutes later by two blasts of what were called 'the Gs', which was the signal to get on with it, to execute the order. The notes echoed throughout the ship.

Just below the bridge on B-deck,[3] Ken Holt, a 21-year-old Acting Leading Stoker, had been sitting on a big paravane, part of the minesweeping gear stowed there, talking with a few mates. Hearing the 'G', he went to the winch on the port side of the deck where he had slung his hammock for the night and began to slip out of his work overalls and into his shorts, getting ready to turn in. As he did, he heard a voice cry out. At first, he took no notice and continued undressing.

That cry was also heard high above. Up on the bridge, Acting Leading Signalman John Hagan had been reading a signal flashed by lamp from *Astoria*. He noted the time. As he finished, he heard a voice shout, 'Leave me alone!' Looking down through the dark, he saw three indistinct figures struggling by the Carley float, a large life raft secured directly below him on the main deck.[4] The man in the centre was being lowered to the deck by the other two, like a sack of potatoes. One of the standing figures began swinging his right arm in what Hagan thought might be a rain of punches. There were more cries.

Ken Holt heard them too and, alarmed, he also bent over to look towards the Carley float just a couple of metres below him. He saw much the same: a man writhing on the deck, held at the armpits and legs by two men standing above him. It looked to Holt as if the two were trying to throw the third man overboard.

Another man on the compass platform, Charlie Nicholls, the ship's Signal Boatswain and therefore a senior and experienced warrant officer, heard a loud laugh or perhaps a scream. Probably some of the hands skylarking below, he thought. He walked to the port side of the bridge and called out, 'Stop making that noise down there!'

There was a brief silence. Then the screaming started again, more loudly. And continually. To Lieutenant Commander Donovan, it sounded like a pig being killed. 'I have heard pigs being killed many times, and that is what it reminded me of,' he would testify later.⁵ He sent the Signals Yeoman, a Scot named Foster McKenzie, down to find out what was going on. The screams brought other men running along the deck, perhaps a dozen of them. Some had also heard the cry of 'Leave me alone!'. What they found was so appalling – breathtaking – that for some moments they simply stood there, gazing in horror.

The man on the deck was lying face down, his feet hanging over the side through the guard rail. He was covered in blood, his overalls smeared with it, with more spreading on the deck itself. Fred Rogers, a leading telegraphist, turned the scream-ing man's head over, saw still more blood on his bare chest, and then pushed his way back through the knot of stunned sailors to get help. Someone else had already raised the alarm. Two sick-berth attendants were on their way with a stretcher. Other sailors noticed another two men mingling with them, also apparently splashed with blood, although it was hard to tell in the crush and the gloom. Rogers helped bundle the prone figure onto the stretcher, which was carried below to the sick bay at about eight o'clock.

On the bridge, there was concern and some confusion, not helped by men coming and going for the change of the watch. McKenzie returned and reported that he had seen a sailor covered with blood. Still unsure of what had happened, Lieu-tenant Commander Donovan sent for the master-at-arms, Regulating Petty Officer Alf Brown, who, as the ship's official policeman, was the man to deal with this sort of thing. Brown was still on his way when there was a disturbance at the bridge ladder: two sailors appeared there and asked a midshipman to point out the Officer of the Watch. They wanted to speak to him urgently – an unusual occurrence, to say the least. They gave their names as Leading Stoker Gordon and Stoker Elias.

Even in the dark, Donovan could see – to his astonishment – that both were smeared with blood, their white tropical shorts splashed with it. Gordon spoke first and then Elias, the two of them interrupting each other, their voices tumbling together in haste. They had been talking on deck with a shipmate, Stoker

Riley, they said. Riley had left them to go on watch and they had
walked away aft. They, too, had heard cries for help and, running
back, they saw Riley slumped on the deck with two dark figures
hurrying away into the gloom. They bent to help him, they
claimed, and then – as Elias told it – he found a knife protruding
from Riley's stomach. He pulled it out, but then dropped it. Both
men urged Donovan to send someone to look for it. It might be
important, Elias said.

By this time, the master-at-arms had arrived. Donovan told
him to take the two below; he would see them in his cabin. Alf
Brown hustled them down the ladder to the brightly lit passage
lined by the officers' cabins. A richly tattooed Englishman,
like all his trade Brown had encountered and dealt with the
creative variety of naval sins and misdemeanours and was no
longer surprised by any of them, but in his 17 years in uniform
there had been nothing like this. Both men were bare-chested.
Gordon had heavy streaks and blotches of blood from his neck
to his legs, daubs of it already drying on his shorts. Elias was
not so badly smeared but was bloodied on both arms and above
one ankle, which appeared to have been gashed.

Shocked but purposeful, Brown left them with two other
petty officers and went with the senior engineer officer, Lieutenant Commander Ron Phillips, to look for the knife at the scene
of the crime. Phillips had a torch with him, which revealed the
large patch of blood on the deck by the Carley float, a pair of
shoes and a crumpled singlet, but no sign of a knife. *Australia*
steamed on through the night, a squadron flagship now bearing
a heavy private burden, her ship's company alarmed and, as the
word spread, unable to sleep.

In the sick bay, Surgeon Lieutenant Malcolm Stening set to
work. It was a few minutes after eight o'clock. From a prominent
Sydney medical family, a graduate of Sydney University now aged
30, Stening had joined the Reserve in 1937 and had done a spell
of naval surgery at Haslar, the RN hospital at Portsmouth. Called
to full-time duty with the war, he had joined *Australia* as one of
her three doctors in November 1940.[6] He recognised Riley as a

former patient and, as he began to treat what were obvious stab wounds and many of them, he asked what had happened.

Weak from shock and loss of blood, drifting in and out of consciousness, Riley mumbled a reply: 'I've been stabbed.'

'Who stabbed you?' Stening asked, still swabbing at the blood and cuts.

'Leading Stoker Gordon.'

'Why did he stab you?'

'Because I found out that he was a poofter.'[7]

—

John Joseph Riley was just 19 years old. He had joined the navy before the outbreak of war in June 1939, giving his religion as Presbyterian and his parents as next of kin. Small and slender, standing just 162 centimetres tall, brown haired and blue eyed, a good-looking kid with a fresh complexion, he had been in *Australia*, his first and only ship, since June 1941. Jack Langrell, the jovial canteen assistant who knew everyone, remembered him as 'a real cheeky little feller and a bit of a pug'.[8]

Albert Ronald Gordon, now 23, was born at Portsmouth in Britain, just a few blocks away from the great naval dockyard, on 26 October 1918. There is no record of him emigrating to Australia, but by the time he entered the RAN on his 18th birthday in 1936 he was an orphan. Dark haired and slightly built, he was about the same size and height as Riley. He gave as his next of kin his only known relative, his elder brother, Francis Gordon, who had enlisted in the RAN as an Ordinary Seaman in 1930 and had been recommended for an officer's commission in 1936, training as a naval air observer. Lieutenant Francis Gordon died while serving with the RN Fleet Air Arm's 817 Squadron in the aircraft carrier HMS *Victorious*. His Albacore aircraft was lost in filthy weather during an abortive hunt for the pocket battleship *Admiral Scheer* and the heavy cruiser *Prinz Eugen* off Norway on 23 February 1942, not quite three weeks before his brother's troubles began. Albert Gordon did not yet know it, but he was now alone in the world.

Edward Joseph Elias, also 23, was Australian born, in the working-class Sydney suburb of Newtown, on 19 September 1918. He too had joined the RAN on his 18th birthday in 1936, the son of a widowed mother, signing up for the required 12 years. Black haired, with a sallow complexion, he was another small figure, the same build as the other two. Elias had risen to the rate of Leading Stoker – a rank equivalent to an army corporal – but he had been busted back to stoker and stripped of a good-conduct badge in October 1941 after overstaying a run ashore by four hours, a second offence. He had been with the ship since just after the outbreak of war, sharing a mess with the other two. Jack Langrell knew Gordon and Elias as well. 'They were both nice, lovely men,' he recalled. 'They always looked immaculate. They were nice people.'[9]

Many of their shipmates believed the three were homosexual, with perhaps a handful of others. That was the gossip, the buzz. In a ship of war, men eat, sleep, bathe, work and relax in conditions far more crowded and confined than any civilian jail ashore. People often know or at least suspect each other's secrets, however guarded they might be. After a while, in a testosterone-charged milieu where sex is a constant topic of conversation, a gay man tends to stand out. The system works because, for the most part, sailors have the good sense not to intrude on each other's private lives, however those lives might be led. In the eyes of the lower deck, the three unforgivable naval sins were thievery, bludging or dobbing on your mates, and personal uncleanliness. But acts of homosexual sex were illegal at this time, both in the navy and in civilian life ashore, and men caught at it and convicted faced a jail sentence, which was not uncommon. On land, the police actually trawled to entrap the guilty.

The navy, though, exhibited a tolerance born of centuries of experience. In the 1940s, it was a century and more since naval life had been the caricature of rum, sodomy and the lash expressed by Winston Churchill,[10] but homosexuality was inevitable with young and not so young men at sea away from the presence of women for months on end. In most ships – particularly those as

big as *Australia* – there were plenty of isolated rooms and compartments where men could meet undisturbed for furtive sex. And it
was always a small minority. The powers that be recognised this
unfortunate truth. As long as there was no disclosure or discovery, the navy mostly turned a pragmatic, Nelsonian blind eye
to these abominable crimes, as they were called, although it was
very different if there was a formal complaint, and especially so if
an older man had pulled rank to bully or lure a younger man into
coercive sex. In the eighteenth and early nineteenth centuries,
a few captains and lieutenants in the RN had been hanged for
the rape of young boys.

But now here it was in *Australia*, a scandal in the fleet flagship,
and shockingly out in the open. In all the history of the RAN,
there had never been anything like it. As the gossip flew at lightning speed around the messes and the wardroom, the common
opinion grew that Riley, Gordon and Elias had been in a three-
way homosexual affair but had somehow quarrelled. One theory
was that Riley had been trying to blackmail his former lovers
in retaliation, threatening to report them. This was the line of
questioning taken up by the commander, 'Black Jack' Armstrong,
who – as *Australia*'s executive officer – would have to run what
was in effect a police investigation and sort out the affair for a
report to the captain.

At nine o'clock that evening, just over an hour after the crime,
Armstrong formally questioned Gordon and then Elias, in the
presence of Alf Brown, the master-at-arms, and another petty
officer. They were cautioned in the usual way – told that they
could remain silent although anything they did say might be
used in evidence – but they stuck to the story they had babbled
to Donovan on the compass platform: they had been talking to
Riley; he left them and walked out of sight; they heard cries and
went to see what was happening; they found Riley slumped on
the deck, with two other men they could not identify fleeing
into the dark; Elias had pulled a knife from Riley's back but had
dropped it as he and Gordon tried to help the victim; they did
not know what had happened to the knife.

That, anyway, was the official version of the interrogation, as it was recorded and typed up in the notes of interview. It seems likely the questioning was far more tough. Armstrong had also been in the ship since the outbreak of war, but he had just been posted away, to leave within weeks. This was one of his last tasks as the commander, and – beyond any doubt – the most unwelcome, the most distasteful of his career. On the day he left, 22 March 1942, he typed a private note that survives in the archives, signed by him and – although this is not clear – presumably addressed to Farncomb, his commanding officer:

> . . . It became apparent after the attack on Riley and his remarks to the surgeons that the motive and the basis of the crime would probably turn out to be found in certain alleged practices of unnatural vice which had been going on in the ship unknown to authority. This was all hearsay, but the people mentioned and concerned were Leading Stoker Gordon and Stoker Elias; Stokers R____ and W____; Leading Stoker M____ and Stoker Riley.[11]
>
> Riley had heard of the association between Gordon and Elias and/or others was trying to blackmail them/him.
>
> The attached statements were taken in an endeavour to get a line on the business. They were taken privately by me under *a certain amount of third degree conditions.*[12]

On the day after the attack, late in the afternoon, Armstrong questioned Riley himself in the sick bay, in the watchful presence of the ship's three surgeons. Aroused from his coma, the young sailor was still in a lot of pain, heavily sedated and bleary after a great deal of stitching and several blood transfusions. Malcolm Stening had counted 14 stab wounds, four of them deep and traumatic, the worst of them penetrating the young man's stomach, small intestine and liver, and grazing a lung. None of them could have been self-inflicted, a physical impossibility. The knife had been plunged long and deep into Riley's back, with savagery. But he managed to speak, and the junior doctor, Surgeon Lieutenant Nicholas Larkins, kept notes:

Commander: Who attacked you?

Riley: (No answer)

The Surgeon Commander repeated the question: Who attacked you?

Riley: Leading Stoker Gordon and Stoker Elias.

Commander: I want you to think carefully, as these two have been arrested.

Riley: They did it.

Commander: Can you tell me exactly what happened?

Riley: We were standing up on deck talking and the 'G' went for the First Watch. I turned to walk away and copped it in the back.

Commander: Had you been quarrelling?

Riley: No sir.

Commander: Did you accuse them of being bugger-boys?

Riley: Yes.

Commander: Are you certain of this?

Riley: Yes.

Dr. Larkins: Had you ever seen them at it?

Riley: No, but I have certain proof.

Commander: Did you try and get money from them at any time?

Riley: No.

Commander: Was there anyone else there at the time?[13]

That was as far as it got. Exhausted, Riley mumbled something unintelligible and lapsed back into a coma from which he never awoke. The doctors could do nothing more for him. He died that night, Black Friday the 13th. *Australia* now had a murder to deal with.

It was a sombre, even frightened ship's company that went about its business that evening, on watch or in the messes. Two men had been arrested, but perhaps a killer was still at large. 'I don't think I will sleep on deck tonight,' wrote Harold Eastick in his diary. 'The whole of the ship's company badly shaken by this, and my own thoughts and nerves are on edge.'[14]

John Riley was buried at sea the next day. Gordon and Elias were formally charged with his murder and held in the cells in the fo'c'sle as the ship headed back to Noumea.

—

The court martial began on Wednesday 15 April 1942, on board *Australia* at anchor in Noumea Harbour. A panel of five officers would sit in judgement, three of them from the New Zealand cruiser *Leander*, including her RN commanding officer, Captain Robert Bevan, as President of the Court. His executive officer, Commander Stephen Roskill, sat with him,[15] alongside yet another RN officer, Lieutenant Commander Francis Mansell. There were two from *Australia* herself: Lieutenant Commander John Rayment, the ship's long-serving navigator; and Lieutenant Commander John Bath. None of these men was a lawyer, but to guide them through the legal maze they had Paymaster Commander Patrick Perry, who was Admiral Crace's secretary, advising them as the Deputy Judge Advocate.

The decision to hold a court martial had been taken at Navy Office in Melbourne, for several reasons. In peacetime, the navy would most likely have sent a murder trial off to one of the state Supreme Courts for judge and jury to deal with, but in the spring of 1942 that was impossible. A Japanese advance towards Australia was expected at any time. The fleet flagship was in the front line and could not be called home and put out of action while witnesses from her ship's company were kept hanging around for however long a civil trial might take. And secrecy, too, was important. A murder trial involving the navy, reported by the newspapers in lurid detail, would alarm Australians at home and be a gift for enemy propaganda, it was thought. And the enemy would know *Australia* was out of the fight. With strict censorship of the crew's letters home, a court martial at distant Noumea could be kept conveniently quiet.

The prosecutor would be Fearless Frank himself. Captain Farncomb had no legal qualifications either, but in the few weeks before the trial he immersed himself in what law books could be found and put together the case he would bring against Gordon and Elias. Appointing counsel for the defence – the Prisoners' Friend, as the navy called it – was a far thornier problem. In theory, the job could have been done by another of *Australia*'s officers but – to their credit – both Navy Office and Crace determined that, in all fairness, the two should have a professional lawyer to represent them.

A hurried search produced Paymaster Lieutenant Trevor Rapke, a 33-year-old officer serving ashore in Darwin but who, before the war, had been a successful criminal barrister in Melbourne. He was a good choice, willing to do it, and he was ordered to get to Noumea. That turned out to be easier said than done: Rapke had to fly to Adelaide, take a train to Sydney, and then find a steamer bound for New Caledonia.

As custom dictated for a court martial, the Australian flag was flown at the ship's mainmast and everyone wore formal white uniform, officers with medals and swords, all sweating in the heat. Seated in two chairs, Gordon and Elias pleaded not guilty, and the trial got under way. Although there had been no murder weapon found and the evidence against the accused was entirely circumstantial, Farncomb's task as prosecutor would be relatively simple. Gordon and Elias had been at the scene of the crime, smeared with blood, seen by a dozen or more witnesses. Farncomb merely had to prove, to the court's satisfaction beyond reasonable doubt, that they – and only they – were the killers.

Rapke's job was far more difficult, but he went at it with dogged skill, determined to pick holes in the prosecution case. He knew he would have to be very careful how he did it, for, as a naval officer, he was almost everything the others were not, a mere Paymaster Lieutenant outranked by all of them. Worse, the epaulettes on his shoulders carried the distinctive wavy gold stripes of the RANVR, the Volunteer Reserve, a sure sign that he was a civilian temporarily in uniform and therefore a vastly inferior species to Farncomb and the other gilded career professionals who confronted him across the room. He would have to be deferential even as he tried to tear Farncomb's case to shreds in front of the captain's brother officers. He would emphasise the circumstantial nature of the evidence: that none of the prosecution witnesses could say under oath they had positively recognised either Gordon or Elias as the dark figures who had struck the blows. And he would hint, as much as he dared, that they had been improperly coached in their evidence by Black Jack Armstrong, which was not too far from the truth.

But the truly astounding feature of the trial was this: homosexuality was never mentioned. Not by the prosecution nor by the defence. No one dared speak its name. If the motive for the attack had been as Riley claimed or as the gossipers believed, it was ignored for the entire four days of the hearing. There was no discussion of motive at all, of why Riley had been killed. No reason or explanation for the murder was ever raised.

In part, there was a sound legal reason. Although Riley had told the doctors and Armstrong – not once but twice – that Gordon and Elias had stabbed him because he'd threatened to expose them as homosexuals, the law at the time deemed that to be mere hearsay. It was inadmissible as evidence. The words of a dead man – a confession, an accusation or anything else – could only be put before a court *if that man had known that he was dying when he spoke*. Or, in the legal phrase, if he had 'a well settled expectation of death'.[16] And Riley did not know that. The surgeons had not told him he was dying. By the time they realised he was, it was too late. He was in a coma, never to recover.

But there was another reason as well, and that was the reputation of the ship and the RAN itself. It was unspoken and unacknowledged, this reason, but it was surely there. The mores of the times held homosexuality to be a sin, a crime, a disgusting perversion. It carried a deep stigma. Evidence of it brought into the open would leave an indelible stain on everyone and everything it touched. Farncomb felt he did not need to bring up the subject to make his case for the prosecution, and it was obviously not in the interests of Rapke, the Prisoners' Friend, to cast his clients in that light. And Commander Armstrong's investigation had turned up other names in the ship as well; who knew where that might lead? Best for all concerned, therefore, to keep it quiet. And so it was. The blind eye was turned again.

The parade of prosecution witnesses began, led by Alf Brown, all of them sticking to their stories of what they had heard or seen. In cross-examination, Rapke picked what holes he could, although there were precious few. But by the second day, he had endured enough of this circumstantial evidence and, in a bold address to the court, he attempted to have the case thrown out.

'There is no prima facie case made out by the prosecution,' he said. 'A judge, sitting with a jury, would direct the jury that it would be dangerous to convict on the evidence before the court and would therefore direct the jury to acquit . . .

'My submission goes further. I suggest that the evidence in this case would not warrant a conviction for shoplifting . . . I submit that this court here and now should acquit the prisoners of murder.'

Farncomb responded with elaborate courtesy, remarking caustically that he could not hope to compete with Rapke's eloquence, but accusing him of misrepresenting the evidence.

Unsurprisingly, the court took Farncomb's side and the case continued. More witnesses were called. When the prosecution case ended, both Gordon and Elias set aside their right to remain silent and chose to give evidence – Gordon to begin, Elias next. They were questioned for long hours by Rapke and then by Farncomb. The transcript shows that they remained calm and held to their story to the end.

On the third day, 17 April, Farncomb summed up his case. For a non-lawyer, it was a bravura performance, reasoned and logical, rising at times to eloquence. Only once did he go too far, which was to cross that invisible but vital line that should have separated prosecutor from commanding officer. It was a bad mistake. Farncomb told the bench of his brother naval officers that he, personally, believed the two to be guilty. 'I entered this court holding certain views, and at the end and towards the close of this long hearing I have found no reason to modify those views in any major point,' he said. 'I can therefore assure the court that what I propose to say will in fact carry my own conviction.'

Rapke jumped to his feet with an objection, accusing Farncomb of expressing personal views that he was not entitled to give but that might influence the court. It was a valid point, entirely fair and proper, but it cut no ice. Farncomb continued at length and ended by arguing that the entire evidence 'points directly to the two accused . . . there is no reasonable doubt of their guilt'.[17]

The Prisoners' Friend took his turn on the next and last day, 18 April. Privately, Rapke was still furious with Farncomb, but publicly he poured oil on troubled waters, offering that 'the role of the prosecutor in this case has been filled with dignity and restraint'. He spoke for two long hours, filleting the prosecution case, casting as much doubt as he could on the testimony of the witnesses, and praising the honesty and candour of his clients, who, he said, could have chosen to remain silent. 'This court must come to the conclusion that the prosecutor has failed to prove his case beyond reasonable doubt,' he argued. 'Therefore either the verdict of not proven or a verdict of not guilty . . . should be recorded by the court.'

Shortly after 11 am, the bench of officers trooped out of the room to consider a verdict. They returned at 3.30 that afternoon, with the only and obvious answer: guilty as charged. Rapke had done his best and more, but it had not been enough.

On his advice, Gordon and Elias elected not to bring character witnesses to speak for them. After a little more legal flummery, the Court President, Captain Bevan, handed down the prescribed sentence for murder, the death penalty.

'The court having found the charge against the accused proved, adjudges them, the said Acting Leading Stoker (Temporary) Albert Ronald Gordon, Official Number 20871, Royal Australian Navy, and Stoker Edward Joseph Elias, Official Number 20975, Royal Australian Navy, of His Majesty's Australian Ship *Australia*, to be hanged by the neck till they be dead on board such one of His Majesty's Australian Ships and at such time as the board of Administration of the Naval Forces shall direct.'[18]

—

Rapke was devastated by the result, so much so that he abandoned the customary legal and naval courtesies and gave Farncomb the cold shoulder, leaving the room without speaking to him – a risky career move.[19] But with the court martial over, the guilty verdict secured and sentence handed down, the tensions eased in the flagship. Everyone breathed more easily. The next day, *Australia* slipped and sailed for Sydney for repairs to a worn shaft. The wardroom buzz now had it that Fearless Frank, the unbending disciplinarian, was itching to hang the two murderers from the mainmast at sea, at the first chance he got. When he did not, the gossips then had it that only Crace had restrained him.

In fact, there were other wheels grinding away. There was no legal avenue of appeal from a court-martial verdict, no superior court that could review the evidence or the conviction as there could be after a civil trial, but Rapke had not given up. As the flagship headed home, he worked away at a letter to Farncomb forcefully setting out his objections to the way in which the court martial had been conducted. It filled just one page, pointed and direct. Most notably, it touched indirectly on the homosexuality issue and suggested, very subtly, that the court might have been biased:

> Certain inadmissible evidence, particularly the statements of the deceased rating implicating the accused, and suggesting a strong motive for the crime, were rigorously excluded from the trial, but on joining *Australia* I found that the nature of this evidence was common knowledge in the ship. Two members of the court were officers in *Australia*.[20]

Those two were Bath and Rayment, who certainly would have known of the homosexual gossip. It would be hard to believe they had not discussed it with the officers from *Leander* sharing the bench with them. Rapke finished with a flourish, arguing that 'the conviction was wrong in law and in fact', that the court 'had misdirected itself', and that 'evidence of identification was insufficient in law'. Farncomb got the letter on 20 April. But he was working away at one of his own, dated that same day and addressed to Jack Crace.

It was a remarkable document. As prosecutor, he had steamed full speed ahead to secure the convictions of Gordon and Elias.

As their commanding officer, he now threw his engines into reverse, with an appeal for clemency from 'Higher Authority'. Whatever the wardroom and the mess-deck chatter might say, Farncomb had no appetite for a hanging, far from it. Nor did Crace. It was 'almost certain that the men will not be executed', the admiral noted hopefully in his diary.[21]

Farncomb gave an eloquent and strikingly compassionate account of the strain of wartime life at sea. Full knowing that what he wrote for Crace would eventually be read ashore at Navy Office in Melbourne, he underscored the oppressive heat and humidity of the tropics, of the long and arduous working hours, especially for men tending the boilers and engines. He wrote of the 'monotonous and uncomfortable conditions with little opportunity for relaxation', and the scarcity of leave ashore even in a 'civilised' port. And he, too, hinted at the homosexual aspects of the murder:

> The softening influence of the opposite sex is accordingly absent and there is practically no contact with anyone outside the service. Finally, the circumstance of the war, in which life seems to be held so cheap, is an especially evil influence.
>
> I am certain that the effect of 2½ years of these conditions in wartime is such as to produce an abnormal, unnatural and perhaps perverse state of mind in some men so that they acquire a peculiar outlook which warps the reason and the judgement.
>
> The special circumstances in which this murder took place seem to indicate clearly that the two men convicted of the crime possess most abnormal minds, and that therefore they were not in full possession of their faculties at the time. Both these men have been in the ship since the outbreak of war and have been continuously subjected to the influences I have referred to.[22]

He concluded by reminding the admiral of the youth of both men, that Gordon was an orphan, and that Elias 'had no father to control him for 21 years. He is his widowed mother's only child.'[23]

The letter speaks highly for Farncomb. He could well have rested on the laurels of a successful prosecution, putting it out of his mind to return to the business of his ship and leaving two insignificant young sailors to their fate. He did not. His plea for mercy was a testament to his humanity and decency, and to a profound understanding of the men in his charge – attributes that few of his contemporaries would have allowed him. Essentially an aloof and private man, by now well accustomed to the lonely burden of command in war, he kept these admirable qualities well hidden. History has not been much kinder to him either, but he deserves better. For all his flaws, Harold Farncomb had demonstrated that he was a fine commanding officer who cared for the least of his crew. The coming months and years would put him to that test again, sterner still.

On the trip back to Sydney, he summoned Rapke to his cabin. The young lawyer lieutenant feared a verbal savaging or worse and was astonished to be offered a position as Farncomb's secretary. Apparently mollified by the captain's appeal for clemency, Rapke took the job and the two became lifelong friends.[24]

—

When *Australia* arrived in Sydney, on 22 April 1942, Gordon and Elias were marched away and taken straight to Long Bay Jail to await their hanging. The ship itself went into dock for the necessary repairs. And the legal wheels began to pick up a little speed. Three days later, the Naval Board passed the case on to the federal Attorney-General, Dr H. V. 'Bert' Evatt. Two days after that, on 27 April, lawyers acting for the two men went to the High Court of Australia for a writ of habeas corpus, a complex legal device that would stop the execution in its tracks, at least for the time being.

This was the first time the newspapers and their readers got a whiff of the murder, if only briefly. The names of Riley, Gordon and Elias were reported, but there were no details of the killing, which was described as having taken place only 'in an Australian warship at sea'. But a tremendous legal tangle was beginning to grow and tighten to a near impenetrable knot.

In 1939, the Menzies conservative government had placed every warship of the RAN under the control of the British Admiralty. This meant that the court martial in *Australia* had been held not under Australian law but a cobwebbed British law, the *Naval Discipline Act 1866 (Imperial)*, which specified the death sentence for murder.

The relevant Australian law did not. The *Commonwealth Defence Act 1903–1941*, Section 98, was crystal clear:

> No member of the Defence Force shall be sentenced to death by any Court Martial except for mutiny, desertion to the enemy, or traitorously delivering up to the enemy any garrison, fortress, post, guard, or ship, vessel, or boat, or aircraft, or traitorous correspondence with the enemy.

The High Court would have to decide which law applied: the British or the Australian. It would have to rule on whether the court martial had been properly and legally established, and whether the death penalty could be exacted. The thing was further complicated when the lawyers discovered, as lawyers will, that there were two more bits and pieces to fiddle with: *The Imperial Naval Discipline (Dominion Naval Forces) Act 1911* and *The Naval Defence Act 1910–1934*.

A full bench of the High Court began to hear the matter on 4 May and handed down its judgment on 9 July. Everything had been perfectly legal, it found. The British law applied, not the Australian. The court martial had been properly constituted and the sentence of death was valid. Gordon and Elias would hang.

At which point, the federal Labor government became involved. Labor policy abhorred capital punishment in either civil or military cases and had no wish to see it happen here. Nor did the navy want its first ever hanging. The Navy Minister, Norman Makin, called for the documents and on 16 July publicly promised there would be no further action until there had been a full government enquiry. And public disquiet was growing at the idea of British law disposing of Australian lives. Some people recalled the Breaker Morant controversy of the Boer War, in which the Australian lieutenants Harry Morant and Peter Handcock had been convicted of murder by a British Army court martial and shot by firing squad in 1902.

Gordon had no one to speak for him, but Elias's widowed mother was a resourceful woman and a devout Catholic, and she and her friends began to prod the bishops of the church and others into action. Doc Evatt, both as Attorney-General and Minister for External Affairs, began to talk to the British Government to seek ways of having the death sentence commuted. Trevor Rapke, although still Farncomb's secretary, kept up a personal interest in the case and would offer his services from time to time, the Prisoners' Friend to the end. Public controversy swelled.

From this point, the story moves beyond the scope of this book. For the rest of the war and for some years afterwards, a legal and constitutional crisis ebbed and flowed, with Gordon and Elias at its core. It was an imbroglio that eventually became a legal landmark – almost forgotten today, but one that profoundly affected the course of Australia's standing as an independent nation.

Interested readers will find a summary in the appendix. For the moment, it is enough to report that the two did not hang. In September 1950, Albert Ronald Gordon and Edward Joseph Elias were released on parole from the Emu Plains Prison Farm in outer western Sydney. They disappeared into oblivion. Their shipmates and the navy itself tried to forget. The official history of the RAN in the Second World War contains not a word.

PART 3

THE TIDE STARTS
TO TURN

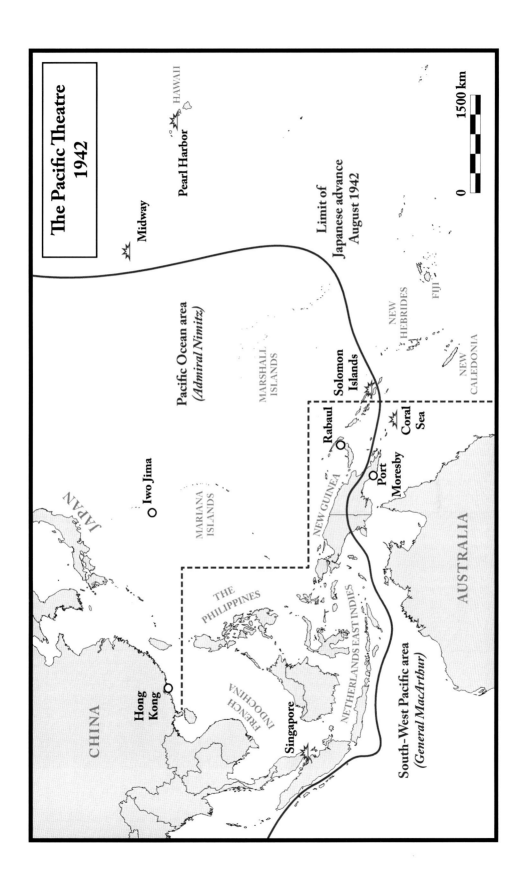

The Pacific Theatre 1942

CHINA

JAPAN

Iwo Jima

Midway

Pearl Harbor

HAWAII

Pacific Ocean area
(Admiral Nimitz)

MARSHALL
ISLANDS

MARIANA
ISLANDS

THE
PHILIPPINES

Hong Kong

FRENCH
INDOCHINA

Singapore

NETHERLANDS EAST INDIES

NEW GUINEA

Rabaul

Port
Moresby

Coral
Sea

Solomon
Islands

Limit of
Japanese advance
August 1942

NEW
HEBRIDES

FIJI

NEW
CALEDONIA

South-West Pacific area
(General MacArthur)

AUSTRALIA

0   1500 km

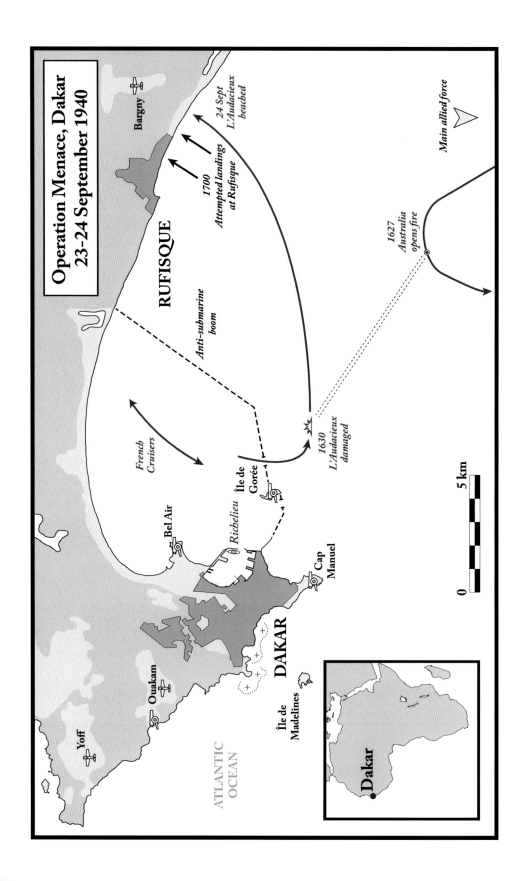

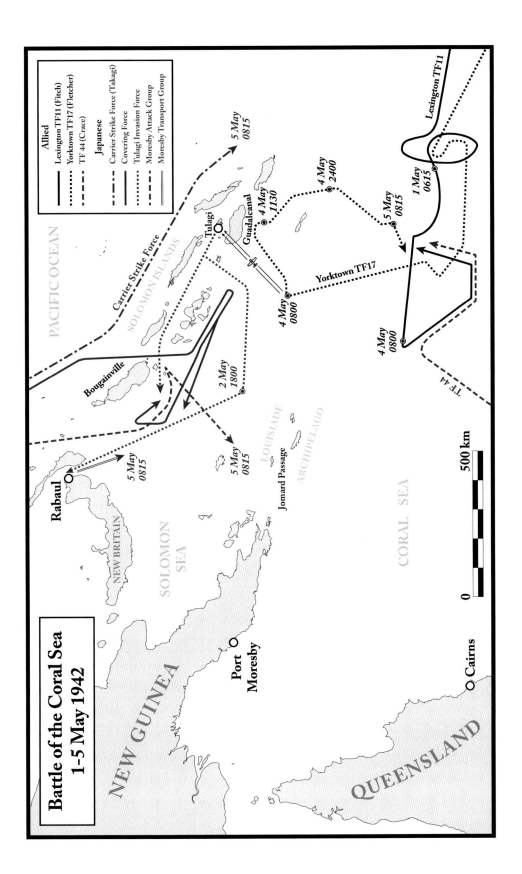

Battle of the Coral Sea
1–5 May 1942

Allied
Lexington TF11 (Fitch)
Yorktown TF17 (Fletcher)
TF 44 (Crace)

Japanese
Carrier Strike Force (Takagi)
Covering Force
Tulagi Invasion Force
Moresby Attack Group
Moresby Transport Group

PACIFIC OCEAN

Carrier Strike Force

SOLOMON ISLANDS

Bougainville

Tulagi

Guadalcanal

4 May 1130

4 May 2400

5 May 0815

5 May 0815

1 May 0615

Lexington TF11

Yorktown TF17

4 May 0800

4 May 0800

TF 44

2 May 1800

5 May 0815

5 May 0815

Rabaul

NEW BRITAIN

SOLOMON SEA

LOUISIADE ARCHIPELAGO

Jomard Passage

CORAL SEA

NEW GUINEA

Port Moresby

QUEENSLAND

Cairns

0   500 km

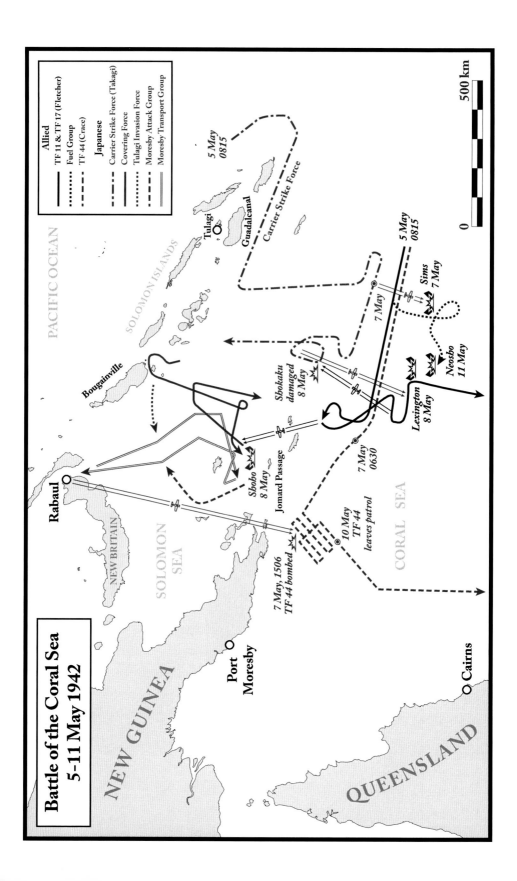

Battle of the Coral Sea
5–11 May 1942

Allied
TF 11 & TF 17 (Fletcher)
Fuel Group
TF 44 (Crace)

Japanese
Carrier Strike Force (Takagi)
Covering Force
Tulagi Invasion Force
Moresby Attack Group
Moresby Transport Group

500 km

PACIFIC OCEAN

SOLOMON ISLANDS

Tulagi

Guadalcanal

5 May
0815

Carrier Strike Force

Bougainville

Shokaku
damaged
8 May

5 May
0815

Sims
7 May

7 May

Neosho
11 May

Lexington
8 May

7 May
0630

Shoho
8 May

Jomard Passage

Rabaul

NEW BRITAIN

SOLOMON
SEA

10 May
TF 44
leaves patrol

CORAL SEA

7 May, 1506
TF 44 bombed

Port
Moresby

NEW GUINEA

Cairns

QUEENSLAND

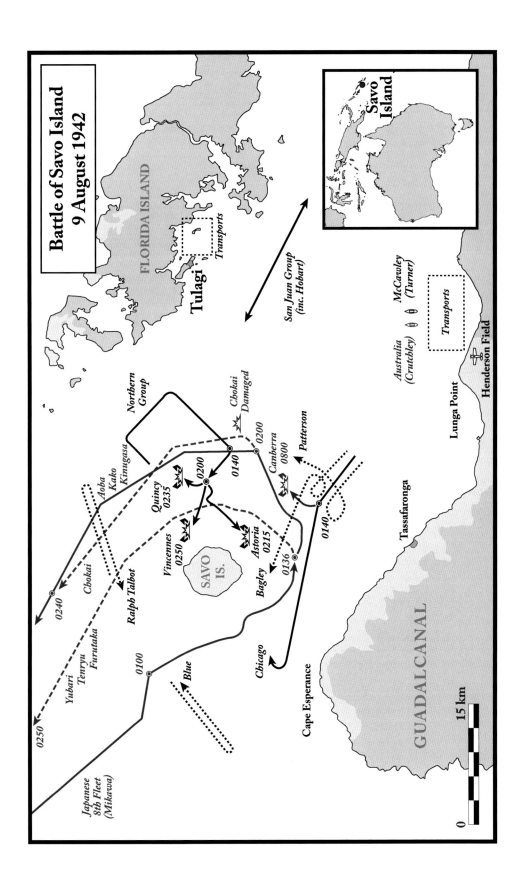

Battle of Savo Island
9 August 1942

Savo Island

FLORIDA ISLAND

Tulagi

Transports

San Juan Group
(inc. Hobart)

Australia
(Crutchley)

McCawley
(Turner)

Transports

Lunga Point

Henderson Field

Northern
Group

Aoba
Kako
Kinugasa

Chokai
Damaged

0200

0140

Canberra
0800

Patterson

0200

Quincy
0235

Vincennes
0250

Chokai

Astoria
0215

SAVO
IS.

Bagley

0136

0140

Chicago

0240

Ralph Talbot

Yubari
Tenryu
Furutaka

0100

Blue

Cape Esperance

Tassafaronga

GUADALCANAL

0250

Japanese
8th Fleet
(Mikawa)

15 km

0

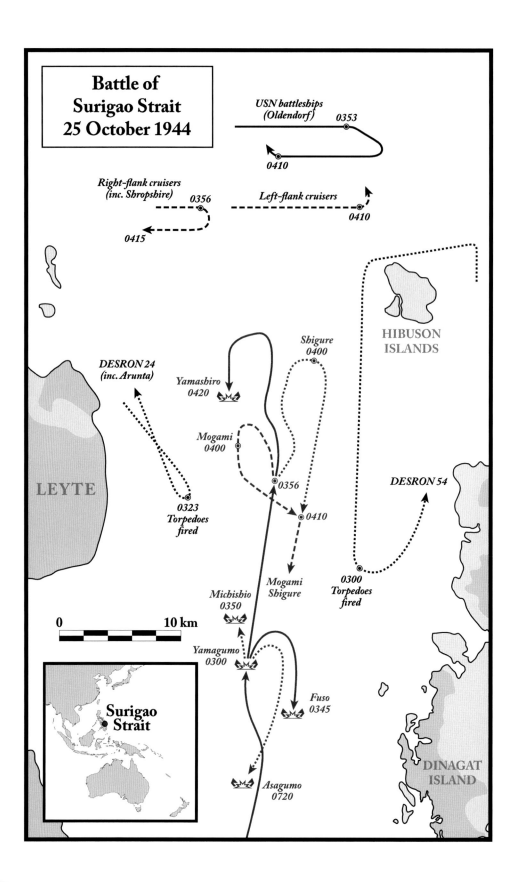

**Battle of
Surigao Strait
25 October 1944**

USN battleships
(Oldendorf)
0353

0410

Right-flank cruisers
(inc. Shropshire)
0356

Left-flank cruisers
0410

0415

HIBUSON
ISLANDS

Shigure
0400

DESRON 24
(inc. Arunta)

Yamashiro
0420

Mogami
0400

0356

DESRON 54

LEYTE

0323
Torpedoes
fired

0410

Mogami
Shigure

0300
Torpedoes
fired

Michishio
0350

0   10 km

Yamagumo
0300

Fuso
0345

Surigao
Strait

Asagumo
0720

DINAGAT
ISLAND

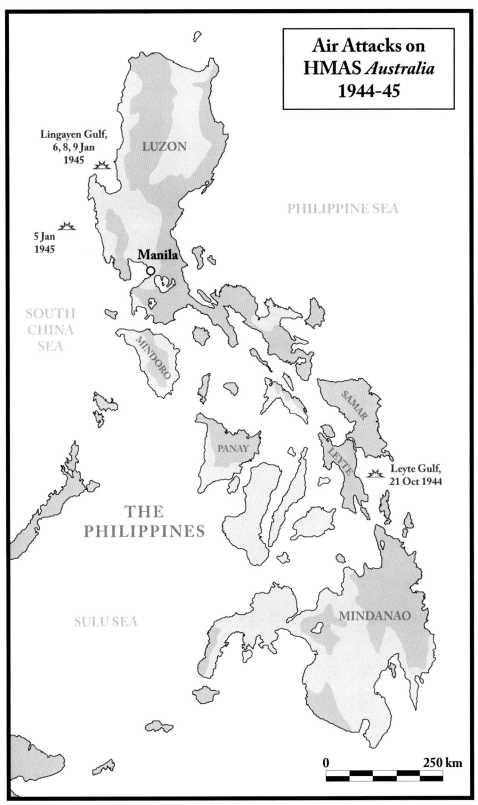

**Air Attacks on
HMAS *Australia*
1944-45**

Lingayen Gulf,
6, 8, 9 Jan
1945

LUZON

PHILIPPINE SEA

5 Jan
1945

Manila

SOUTH
CHINA
SEA

MINDORO

SAMAR

PANAY

LEYTE

Leyte Gulf,
21 Oct 1944

THE
PHILIPPINES

SULU SEA

MINDANAO

0   250 km

Enemy aircraft hits on *Australia* in the Philippines

Launch of HMAS *Australia* in Scotland, 1927 (*Royal Australian Navy*)

King George V inspects *Australia*, 1928 (*Royal Australian Navy*)

Australia, Sydney Harbour (with radar aerials) (*Royal Australian Navy*)

Australia's 8-inch guns (X and Y turrets, aft) (*Royal Australian Navy*)

Australia in wartime camouflage (Seagull aircraft on catapult) (*Royal Australian Navy*)

Canberra, with *Australia* astern (*Australian War Memorial 044097*)

HMAS *Canberra*, 1942 (*Australian War Memorial 016664*)

Canberra with Seagull on catapult (*Australian War Memorial PO2550_023*)

Captain John Collins
(*Australian War Memorial 002447*)

Frank Getting, as a Lieutenant
Commander (*Australian War
Memorial P09023.001*)

Harold Farncomb, as a
Commodore 1st Class
(*Australian War Memorial 112187*)

Jack Langrell (*private collection*)

Petty Officer Harold Eastick
(*private collection*)

Lieutenant Mackenzie Gregory
(*private collection*)

Captain John 'Jamie' Armstrong
(*Royal Australian Navy*)

Rear Admiral John Crace and Prime
Minister Robert Menzies, 1940
(*Australian War Memorial 000790*)

Captain Emile Dechaineux
(*Australian War Memorial 106692*)

Lieutenant David Hamer
(*Royal Australian Navy*)

Russell Keats
(*Australian War Memorial P11328.001*)

General Douglas MacArthur
and Prime Minister John Curtin
(*Australian War Memorial 052512*)

Admiral Chester Nimitz (*US Navy*)

The cruiser USS *Chicago*
(*US Navy*)

Vice Admiral Frank Jack Fletcher (*US Navy*)

Admiral Isoroku Yamamoto, the victor of Pearl Harbor (*US Navy*)

Midshipman Bruce Loxton
(*private collection*)

Rear Admiral Victor
Crutchley VC (*Australian
War Memorial 305286*)

The Thurlow brothers, Jim and Tom (*private collection*)

Vice Admiral Gunichi
Mikawa, the victor of Savo
(*US Navy*)

Rear Admiral Kelly Turner USN and US Marine Major General Alexander Vandegrift
(*private collection*)

Lieutenant Commander Warwick Bracegirdle (*front left*) and Petty Officer Arthur Cooper (*front right*)
(*private collection*)

USS *Bagley*, the destroyer that torpedoed *Canberra* (*US Navy*)

HMAS *Shropshire* (*Australian War Memorial 301309*)

Shropshire's ship's company (*Australian War Memorial 305317*)

Kamikaze pilots before
take-off

Kamikaze aircraft heading for the battleship USS *Missouri*
(*Australian War Memorial 306769*)

General MacArthur returns to the Philippines at Leyte (*US Navy*)

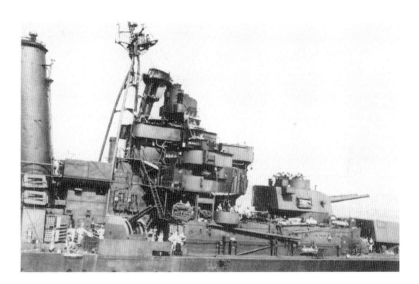

Damage to *Australia* after the Battle of Leyte Gulf (*Royal Australian Navy*)

An American destroyer aids the damaged *Australia* at Lingayen (*Royal Australian Navy*)

The Japanese surrender on USS *Missouri* (*US Navy*)

Australia's ship's company, 1945 (*Royal Australian Navy*)

CHAPTER 13

PROCEED AT DAYLIGHT WITH YOUR GROUP TO DESTROY ENEMY SHIPS

The clear blue waters of the Coral Sea form Australia's north-eastern sea frontier. The western waves beat onto the Great Barrier Reef and the Queensland coast. To the north lies the tail of the Bird of Paradise island of Papua New Guinea and the beautiful volcanic island chain of the Louisiades, named for Louis XV of France. Eastward, the sea is bounded by the long run of the Solomon Islands, the New Hebrides – modern-day Vanuatu – and then, further south, New Caledonia. For much of the year, the Coral Sea is calm and tranquil, until the tropical-cyclone season comes storming in over the hotter months from November to April.

In early 1942, still on the march, Japan resolved to take command of this great sweep of sea and its island borders. The original plan had been to invade Australia itself, an ambition favoured by the IJN but eventually, after much haggling, rejected by the Imperial Army General Staff: there were not enough troops to do it. China had been overrun but by no means subdued, there was still heavy fighting in the Philippines, and great numbers of men were needed to garrison the empire Japan had already conquered since Pearl Harbor. An invasion of Australia would need another 250,000 fighting troops, and the logistics to support them. In a rare display of hard-headed prag-matism, the army decided that Australia's vast open spaces were

beyond reach. The Chief of the Army General Staff, General
Hajime Sugiyama, put it in writing to his naval counterpart,
Admiral Osami Nagano, on 16 February:

> It is thought that Australia will be the main base for mounting
> the US and British counter-attack against Japan, so strategies to
> crush this counter-offensive are essential. However, these strat-
> egies, which will not aim to deal with the entire continent, will
> probably develop from operations in one part of Australia into a
> war of attrition spread over many areas.
>
> There are grave fears that the operation will gradually expand
> uncontrollably and slide into a total multi-front war. Conse-
> quently, because measures to control all of Australia should not
> be adopted, *it is felt necessary to refrain from invasion operations in
> any part of Australia* [the italics are the author's].
>
> However, it is essential to blockade the transport of troops
> and matériel to Australia in order to smash the enemy counter-
> offensive. To this end, the operations to occupy Fiji, Samoa, and
> New Caledonia in the Pacific are felt to be of great importance.[1]

The compromise would be to secure the southern and eastern
perimeter of the *Dai-to-a Kyoeiken*, the Greater East Asia
Co-Prosperity Sphere, by seizing control of the Pacific Ocean.
The IJN would draw the USN into a climactic battle of annihi-
lation, a victory that would force the weakened and demoralised
Americans to sue for peace. Australia would be 'freed from the
shackles of Britain and the United States'[2] to become a vassal
state paying tribute to Tokyo.

In his newly commissioned flagship, the battleship *Yamato*,
the architect of Pearl Harbor began to plan his new campaign.
Admiral Isoroku Yamamoto, Commander-in-Chief of the IJN's
Combined Fleet, and one of the few Japanese leaders with any
understanding of the United States, had reckoned he would have
roughly a year, to mid-1943, before America's industrial and
economic might became unbeatable. 'If I am told to fight regard-
less of consequence, I shall run wild considerably for the first
six months or a year,' he had told the Prime Minister, Prince

Konoye, in 1940. 'But I have utterly no confidence for the second and third years . . .'[3]

Time was now running out. But in early 1942, the IJN was at the zenith of its pomp and power, proclaimed in the massive steel form of *Yamato* herself, the greatest battleship of all. At 72,000 tonnes full load, she and her nearly completed sister ship *Musashi* were almost half as big again as the new design of Iowa-class battleships still being built in the United States. The two battleships' 18-inch guns, nine in each ship, were the biggest naval guns ever mounted. The Japanese were confident that more victories at sea lay in store.

After much tortured negotiation with his rivals in the Naval General Staff ashore, Yamamoto devised a two-part strategy. The primary plan, Operation MI, would be to lure the US Pacific Fleet to its destruction near the coral atoll of Midway, which, as its name suggests, lies about halfway between Asia and the Americas, some 2000 kilometres north-west of Hawaii. The secondary plan – but carried out first – would be Operation MO, the invasion of Port Moresby in New Guinea and the occupation of the Solomon Islands, to enforce a virtual blockade of eastern Australia. This grandiose scheme was given sudden impetus by a grave and unforeseen event in April 1942: the Americans bombed Tokyo, in what became known as the Doolittle Raid.

On 18 April, a flight of 16 US Army Air Force B-25B Mitchell bombers lumbered from the flight deck of the carrier USS *Hornet* in the far western Pacific, led by Lieutenant Colonel James 'Jimmy' Doolittle, a renowned pioneering aviator of the pre-war years. It was a bold gamble. The steam catapult had not been invented, nor the long, angled flight deck. Aircraft so big and slow had never taken off from a carrier before, and nor had any of the pilots, including Doolittle himself. And they could not land back on, so, after bombing their targets in Japan, those that survived (and they had no fighter escort) would have to fly on to airfields in China.

The raid was of no account in military terms, for no valuable targets were destroyed, but as a propaganda coup it was a brilliant success that sent American morale soaring. The Japanese were stunned. Bombs had landed near the Imperial Palace in Tokyo, no less, a direct threat to the sacred person of the Sun God himself and a humiliating loss of face for the generals and admirals sworn to defend him. Revenge would have to be exacted.[4]

Yamamoto issued his orders. Operation MO would be launched in early May, from the new and expanding Japanese base at Rabaul on New Britain, under the command of the chief of the IJN's Fourth Fleet, Vice Admiral Shigeyoshi Inoue. In typical IJN style, never content with a simple plan when an elaborate one would do, Yamamoto and Inoue put together a complex, five-part attack.

The Tulagi Invasion Group, consisting of a troop transport, a seaplane carrier and an escort of destroyers and minesweepers, would swoop on the Solomons to capture the small island of Tulagi and set up a base there.

The Moresby Transport Group, a landing force of 11 troop transports carrying some 5500 soldiers, would leave Rabaul, loop around through the Jomard Passage in the Louisiades and then turn north-west to take Moresby itself on 10 May.

The Moresby Attack Group, consisting of a light cruiser and six destroyers, would escort the transports.

As a covering force for the two Moresby Groups, the light carrier *Shoho*, four heavy cruisers, a destroyer and a tanker would patrol the northern Coral Sea.

A Carrier Strike Force of the fleet carriers *Shokaku* and *Zuikaku*, with two heavy cruisers, six destroyers and a tanker, commanded by the experienced and newly promoted Vice Admiral Takeo Takagi, would move down the eastern side of the Solomon chain. From there, it would pass into the Coral Sea south of Guadalcanal to provide air cover and to deal with any Allied naval force there.

In addition to all of this, a fleet of six submarines would patrol for reconnaissance and destroy whatever it could find, and there would be land-based air support from the navy's 25th Air Flotilla, operating out of airfields at Rabaul and on the northern coast of Papua New Guinea at Lae and Buna.

Yamamoto and his subordinate admirals – dozens of them, it seemed – had little intelligence of what Allied forces might confront them in the Coral Sea, although they suspected that an American carrier and perhaps a British battleship might be there. This would not stop Operation MO. In the opening days of May, these various Japanese groups, forces and squadrons were at sea, exactly as planned.

An early element of the plan, calling for the aircraft of the Carrier Strike Force to attack the Allied air bases at Townsville and Cooktown in North Queensland, was abandoned on 30 April. Tulagi would be taken on 3 May, and Port Moresby, as planned, on 10 May. With the Solomons and New Guinea secured, Australia would lie naked and defenceless.

There was only one flaw in this otherwise seamless progression: the Allies knew they were coming.

—

Beyond the toll of men and ships, Pearl Harbor had been a disaster for American intelligence. Coded Japanese diplomatic cables that should have warned of the coming attack had lain untouched in pigeonholes in Hawaii and Washington while the USN and the US Army waged an intelligence and bureaucratic turf war with each other.[5] Pearl Harbor was the wake-up call. The navy redoubled its efforts to crack the main Japanese naval communications code, known as JN-25, and by early 1942 it was making strides. Almost by coincidence, the Americans found that British and Australian code breakers had been working in the same direction, and, after overcoming initial reluctance and suspicion on both sides, the work was pooled, almost doubling the results. In this, they were assisted by Japanese hubris and arrogance, the IJN being convinced that the Japanese language was beyond the understanding of Westerners and that its codes were impenetrable.

This was a great mistake. On 28 March, the Americans decoded a Japanese signal stating, 'The objective of MO will be first to restrict the enemy fleet movements and will be accomplished by means of attacks on the North Coast of Australia.'[6]

By 17 April, Douglas MacArthur's Combined Operational Intelligence Centre – an American–British–Australian command based in Coventry Street, South Melbourne – was able to piece together much of the Japanese plan with considerable accuracy, including the order of battle and the names and numbers of ships and their ultimate destination: Port Moresby. This, and more, was passed to CinCPac, the Commander-in-Chief Pacific, Admiral Nimitz, at his headquarters in Hawaii, who moved swiftly to make his own plans. Officially, the Coral Sea was MacArthur's territory, but it was CinCPac who would have to provide the ships to do the job.

Unlike his enemy, Nimitz kept it simple, although perhaps this was partly because he had fewer cards to play. His most able and pugnacious commander, Vice Admiral Bill 'Bull' Halsey, and his Task Force 16 – the carriers *Hornet* and *Enterprise* – were away to the north, still returning to Hawaii from the Doolittle Raid. Halsey would be ordered south as soon as he refuelled at Pearl, but for the moment there were only three other groups to rely on.

The first of these, Task Force 17, was centred on the carrier *Yorktown* and a strong escort of cruisers and destroyers, commanded by Rear Admiral Frank Jack Fletcher.

Then there was Task Force 11, composed of the *Lexington* and another escort force, commanded by Rear Admiral Aubrey Fitch, who had succeeded the cautious Wilson Brown a week before.

And Task Force 44 was the new name for the Anzac Force. Still under the command of Jack Crace, it included the cruisers *Australia*, *Hobart* and *Chicago*, and would eventually be bolstered by a handful of American destroyers.

These three forces would have to do. Fletcher would be in overall command, although he was junior to Crace. The Australian had no experience with carriers and, anyway, the Americans were providing most of the muscle – a fait accompli that Crace graciously accepted. Nimitz himself had private doubts about Fletcher's aggressive qualities, but there was nothing he could do about that now. He ordered Fletcher and Task Force 17 to link up with Fitch's Task Force 11 in the eastern Coral Sea, some 500 kilometres south of the Solomons, on 1 May, which they did, in heavy seas and driving rain. Crace and Task Force 44 would join them on 5 May. Nimitz's order was admirably simple: the ships were to 'operate in the Coral Sea according to circumstances'.[7]

Frank Jack Fletcher was what the USN called a 'black shoe' admiral, meaning a seaman of the old school who did things by the book. He had not qualified as a pilot, which bothered some of the rising breed of 'brown shoe' officers with their khaki uniforms, leather bomber jackets and gold aviator's wings, who held that carrier admirals and captains should have learnt to fly first. After all, Bull Halsey had done just that at the age of 52.[8] But Fletcher was the nephew of an admiral and, as a lieutenant, he had won the Medal of Honor at the Battle of Veracruz, an armed scuffle with Mexico in 1914. Now 57, he was described by one of Nimitz's staff officers as 'a big, nice, wonderful guy who didn't know his butt from third base'.[9] Others were more charitable. Fletcher could also be determined, as the coming weeks and months would show.

—

So, as April turned to May, the stage was set and the players were taking their positions for a clash in the Coral Sea. When the curtain opened, they would seek battle over four days, groping to find each other on the surface and in the air. As it happened, it would be the first sea fight in all history in which the opposing ships never laid eyes on each other. Instead, they sent their aircraft into combat.

The weather, so critical in early carrier warfare, favoured first one side and then the other. At times the battle would be a grim comedy of errors, accidents and missed chances; at other moments a confrontation where fatal blows were given and received. As in so many battles at sea, luck played its part, both good and bad, and he who made the fewest mistakes would emerge the winner. For all the confusion and uncertainty, it would change the course of the war in the Pacific.

The Japanese made the first strike. Early on 2 May, a New Zealand-born coastwatcher concealed on Ysabel Island in the Solomons, Donald Kennedy, radioed that he had seen Japanese ships he thought might be heading south-east for Tulagi. He was right. That same day, the Japanese bombed Tulagi Harbour, where there was a small RAAF base for Catalina reconnaissance aircraft. Duly warned, two groups of RAAF and Australian Army men quickly destroyed what they could and, led by their commanding officer, Flying Officer Reg Peagam, a former accountant from Perth, they made a risky escape on a small island trading vessel, reaching Port Vila in the New Hebrides a fortnight later.

The Tulagi Invasion Force swept ashore unopposed the next day, 3 May, and set about its assigned task of building a seaplane base. Well to the south in the Coral Sea, Admiral Fletcher learnt of the landing late that afternoon from another of Kennedy's reports, and, as the sun set, he took his Task Force 17 – *Yorktown*, four heavy cruisers and six destroyers – north at 27 knots. Admiral Fitch with *Lexington* and Task Force 11 remained behind to complete refuelling from a fleet tanker. By dawn the next morning, 4 May, Fletcher was within striking distance of Tulagi, about 240 kilometres to the south-west of the Solomons group and his target. Under overcast skies, from morning until mid-afternoon, *Yorktown* launched three waves of aircraft: 12 Douglas TBD Devastator torpedo bombers and 28 SBD Dauntless dive bombers.

They were beaten by both the weather and inexperience. Low clouds drifted across the Tulagi Harbour, and the dive bomber pilots found that their windscreens and bombsights fogged up when they plunged from cool higher altitudes to warmer, humid air closer to sea level. Most of the bombs and torpedoes missed their targets. But the crews returned to *Yorktown* with extravagant claims of cruisers, destroyers and freighters sunk. That afternoon, satisfied with what everyone agreed was a good day's work, Fletcher sent a destroyer to pick up two pilots who had come down on a beach, and then in the evening took Task Force 17 back to the south-east to reunite with Fitch and Task Force 11.

In fact, only one small Japanese destroyer had been torpedoed, and that was run ashore before it capsized. A couple of smaller, minor craft were sunk or damaged. All the air raid on Tulagi had achieved was to alert the Japanese that at least one American carrier was in the area – something they had expected but not definitely known. Now, they were warned; the intelligence gap was closing. To his chagrin, Admiral Inoue at Rabaul had no carrier force close enough to Fletcher to respond to the Tulagi raid, but at last he had some idea of the opposition he faced and where it might be. Vice Admiral Takagi's Carrier Strike Force, *Shokaku* and *Zuikaku*, had been steaming to the east of the Solomons chain, heading south-east. He now swung to the west and into the Coral Sea.

—

'Hands to stations for leaving harbour. Special sea duty men close up. Close all scuttles and X and Y doors.'

Crackling over *Australia*'s loudspeakers – and in the nearby *Hobart* as well – the familiar pipe meant different things to different men. For a few, it sparked the keen anticipation of going to sea, the bargain they had made when they joined the navy. For others, it was more of the bloody same, here we go again and God help us. For the married men with families in Sydney, there was always the pang of parting. Many felt the chill of apprehension at the thought of once again going in harm's way, although that was not something you shared with your shipmates.

The two cruisers slipped and sailed from Sydney on the morning of Friday 1 May, heading north. *Canberra* should have been with them as a part of the squadron, but she was still undergoing her long refit and was not ready in time. On Sunday 3 May, the two refuelled at Hervey Bay, north of Brisbane, and that evening set off north-east into the Coral Sea accompanied by a Great War – vintage American destroyer, the four-funnelled USS *Whipple*. The *Chicago* and a modern destroyer, the USS *Perkins*, were sailing from Noumea to meet up and come under

Crace's command, no longer to be known as Anzac Force. Now, they were Task Force 44.

As it is with ships and sailors, there was a buzz that something might be up this time, although what that might be was anyone's guess. A bit of gossip in the wardroom overheard by a steward; a chance remark on the bridge; even a discreet hint from a friendly officer: a ship's company was experienced at putting clues and fragments together and coming up with what was often a remarkably accurate guess as to what lay in store.

The admiral and his flag captain knew rather more. Jack Crace and Harold Farncomb had been warned that the enemy was stirring in Rabaul and was expected to penetrate the Coral Sea in the first week of May. They had been ordered to join Fletcher south of the Solomons, Crace hoping that this time it might mean something more than hanging about in the background escorting an oiler while the real action happened elsewhere. And time at sea again would help wash away the distasteful memory of the murder and the court martial.

Monday 4 May dawned fine and sunny, a beautiful tropical day with a slight morning haze that added to the drama of meeting up at sea. *Australia* had just stood down from dawn action stations when Fitch's Task Force 11 loomed over the horizon, dominated by the imposing bulk of the *Lexington* – the *Lady Lex* – ploughing her stately way through a calm sea, with two cruisers, six destroyers and an oiler, the *Neosho*, in company. It was exactly eight o'clock and some 500 kilometres due south of the Solomons. The navigator, John Rayment, had got *Australia* to the rendezvous on time, to the minute. On the upper decks of the two Australian cruisers, men stared in open admiration at this display of American might.

It became still more impressive the next day, 5 May, when Fletcher and Task Force 17 returned from the strike on Tulagi. The ships steamed slowly westward together, a veritable armada, all within visual signalling distance in perfect Pacific weather, Fletcher refuelling his force from the *Neosho*. Shortly after dawn the next day, with that American addiction to labels and acronyms, Fletcher reorganised everything again. From 6 May, the three task forces – the two carrier groups and Crace's cruisers – would now become one integrated unit under his command, all to be known as Task Force 17.

Seen through the lens of history, this was a seminal moment in the history of the RAN. For all its life, the Australian Navy had operated as a virtual arm of the Royal Navy, interchangeable in ships and men, in traditions and practices. The fall of Singapore and the disappearance of the British from the Pacific altered all that, irrevocably. The centre of gravity had shifted. In joining Task Force 17, *Australia* and *Hobart* were to be assimilated into the USN as closely as foreign ships could ever be. No longer were they under the wartime control of a distant Admiralty in Whitehall; the new chain of command ran to Douglas MacArthur's naval chief in Melbourne, Vice Admiral Herbert Leary USN, who had been designated Commander, South-West Pacific Force, or COMSOUWESPAC.

The Australian Naval Board would remain in charge of discipline and personnel, logistics and supply, but that was it. Here, in practice – in Australian sailors, guns and steel – was the pivot towards the United States that John Curtin had proclaimed in his New Year's message in December 1941.

The weather roughened on 6 May, the seas pitching up and making refuelling difficult. All the while, Fletcher was receiving intelligence on Japanese movements, some of it from Nimitz in Hawaii, some from MacArthur's command in Melbourne, derived both from radio intercepts and long-range surveillance patrols by Australian and American land-based aircraft. It was fragmentary and at times confusing, but by the afternoon it was apparent that a Japanese invasion force was heading from Rabaul towards Port Moresby, probably passing through the Jomard Passage some time in the next two days. Fletcher turned Task Force 17 to the north-west to intercept it, at the same time sending the oiler *Neosho* and a destroyer, the *Sims*, to the next refuelling point in the opposite direction, further south.

At this time, he had no idea of the whereabouts of the carriers of Takagi's Strike Force, with their cruisers and destroyers.

And Takagi had no idea where Fletcher was. In fact, in one of the series of mistakes and mischances that afflicted this affair, in the late afternoon of 6 May they were a mere 110 kilometres apart. Takagi was actually refuelling virtually due north of Fletcher but, incredibly, he did not have reconnaissance aircraft in the air. If he had, they could hardly have missed Task Force 17 steaming along in broad daylight. Fletcher did have air patrols out, but the fickle weather had turned against them: a cold front to the north concealed the Japanese beneath a layer of heavy cloud. Overnight, Fletcher and Takagi moved further apart, although both steamed broadly in a north-westerly direction towards New Guinea. The battle would have to wait another day.

—

Fletcher and his staff spent a restless night pondering their next move. They had intelligence reports from MacArthur's head-quarters in Melbourne: American B-17 bombers flying from Townsville had seen what was most likely the Moresby Invasion Force and a Japanese carrier, to the south-east of New Guinea. They had attacked, but unsuccessfully.

At last, there was something solid to go on. Before dawn the next day, Thursday 7 May, Fletcher issued his orders, with two objectives: stop the invasion and get the carrier. He would have to divide his force – never a palatable option and in this case one pregnant with hazard, but he saw no choice. Shortly after 5.30 am, a signal projector on the darkened *Yorktown* blinkered out an order to Crace: 'Proceed at daylight with your group to destroy enemy ships reported passing through Jomard Passage and threatening Moresby. Conserve fuel. Fuel destroyers from cruisers. Retire to Townsville when necessary to fuel.'

It was the order Crace had been waiting for – hoping for – and yet it was a double-edged sword. He had been given an offen-sive role and an independent command, a great and welcome leap forward from shepherding an oiler in the rear; a chance to kill Japs, as he had said. Yet he would be taking his ships away without air cover, away from the umbrella protection of the American carriers, exposing himself to enemy air attack. At that stage, he may well have thought of the fate that had befallen *Prince of Wales* and *Repulse* off Malaya just five months before. And fuel, too, would be a nagging worry. But it had to be done, and he went to it with a will.

As the sun rose, his own orders went out, gathering what would now be designated Task Group 17.3: the two heavy cruisers, *Australia* and *Chicago*; the light cruiser *Hobart*; and three American destroyers assigned to him, *Farragut*, *Perkins* and *Walke*. The USN was famously reluctant to place its ships under foreign command, but Crace now had four of them obedient to his orders. This was a vote of confidence, and the respect was mutual. One of his American destroyer captains, Commander Francis McInerney, would later write that Crace was a 'gallant gentleman who accepted the United States ships into his command with warmth, affection, and admiration for their efficiency'.[10]

Picking up speed, they headed north-west, working up to a cautiously economical 25 knots. Fletcher himself turned due north and despatched a reconnaissance patrol ahead, believing the main Japanese carrier force might lie in that direction. The torpedo and dive bombers on *Saratoga* and *Lexington* were armed and waiting on deck, their crews on edge in the ready rooms.

The enemy was stirring too. Well to the east of Fletcher by now, Vice Admiral Takagi roused himself from his lethargy of the previous day and sent search aircraft ranging to the south. Each side was feeling, groping, probing for the other. Takagi's aircraft scored first, although not by much. At 7.45 am, a scout from *Shokaku* radioed that it had found one American carrier, one cruiser and three destroyers. It was electrifying. Convinced that he had the hard core of the American enemy within his grasp and ripe for destruction, Takagi launched everything he had from *Shokaku* and *Zuikaku*. No fewer than 78 aircraft – a mix of dive bombers and torpedo bombers, with 18 Zero fighters for cover – formed up and headed for the sighting.

By 9.15 am, they were on the scene, but after a confused search came sour disappointment. All they found was the oiler *Neosho* with its escorting destroyer the *Sims*. The reconnaissance report had been wrong, and badly so. Dismayed, Takagi recalled his torpedo bombers and ordered the dive bombers to sink the two.

At around midday, *Sims* was hit by at least three bombs, breaking her in half and causing a massive explosion that sank her quickly. Only 14 of her crew of 192 survived. The *Neosho* managed to shoot down three of the attackers, with her captain, John Phillips, trying desperately to manoeuvre his unwieldy tanker as the dive bombers swooped upon him, but at least five bombs struck home. And one of the aircraft, hit by gunfire, crashed headlong into his stern, starting a raging fire. *Neosho* was left listing badly, burning fiercely and drifting without power, in a steadily rising sea. Some of her crew panicked, including four officers, who took to the life rafts; most of them died at sea over the next few days. Those who remained on board were rescued by an American destroyer four days later.

———

Meanwhile that same morning, Fletcher also thought he had struck the jackpot. At 8.15 am, Lieutenant John L. Nielsen, patrolling in an SBD Dauntless dive bomber from *Yorktown*, reported two enemy carriers and four heavy cruisers some 400 kilometres north-west of Task Force 17. Elated, Fletcher picked up speed to close the range, and by 10.30 no fewer than 93 of his fighters, torpedo bombers and dive bombers were in the air and heading for the target.

So began another comedy of errors. The SBD's sighting report was also wrong. When Nielsen landed back on *Yorktown*, they discovered he had coded it incorrectly: he had seen only two cruisers and four destroyers. Ordered up to the flag plot to explain himself, Nielsen found the admiral enraged that his aircraft were away on a wild goose chase, leaving him defence-less. 'Young man, do you know what you have done?' he bawled. 'You have just cost the United States two carriers!'[11] Fletcher was about to recall the aircraft when fortune turned his way again. Port Moresby radioed that US Army B-17s had seen a carrier, ten transports, and 16 warships just south of Nielsen's sighting.

This was the enemy covering force, the 11,000-tonne light carrier *Shoho*, surrounded by four heavy cruisers and a destroyer, placed to the south-east of New Guinea as a shield for the Port Moresby Invasion Force. Directed to the sighting position, *Lexington*'s Air Group attacked first, in clear blue skies, setting the Japanese carrier's flight deck and hangars on fire with four 250-kilogram bombs and putting five torpedoes into her hull. Most of the *Shoho*'s aircraft were below decks, being prepared for a strike, but eight fighters were above in a Combat Air Patrol, and they shot down three of the SBD Dauntless dive bombers, for the loss of five of their own.

At eleven o'clock, with the enemy carrier now dead in the water and burning fiercely, the aircraft from *Yorktown* lined up for their turn. Half an hour later, *Shoho* had sunk, the first Japanese carrier to be lost in the war, taking with her more than 600 men. The Americans should have turned their attention to the cruisers too, but they did not. These were early days in carrier warfare and the elation of destroying the *Shoho* was too much. *Lexington*'s dive bomber squadron commander, Lieutenant Commander Bob Dixon, sent a signal to his ship that eventually echoed around the world: 'Scratch one flat-top.' It became one of the legends of the Pacific War, a tremendous fillip to morale at home in the States, and 'flat-top' entered the USN lexicon as slang for a carrier.

The American aircraft returned to their ships before two in the afternoon and were hurriedly readied for another launch.

At Rabaul, shocked beyond measure at this loss, Admiral Inoue ordered the remains of the *Shoho* group to retreat north, and the Moresby Invasion Force to temporarily reverse course as well. Operation MO was beginning to falter.

—

After leaving Fletcher and Task Force 17 that morning of 7 May, Jack Crace and the cruisers and destroyers of Task Group 17.3

altered course to west by north, both blessed and cursed by the beauty of a splendid tropical day of perfect visibility. Each hour brought them closer to the risk of attack from enemy aircraft based in Rabaul or perhaps in northern New Guinea. The admiral and John Rayment, the navigator, estimated that this more westerly course would put them some 65 kilometres off the Jomard Passage at about two o'clock, where the Moresby Invasion Force was expected to emerge. But as the morning wore on, Crace's worries grew.

Frank Jack Fletcher had not communicated with him again, not once. On *Australia*'s bridge, they could tell that great events were taking place, but not what or where they were, nor how they might have turned out. They could hear the often garbled chatter of the *Yorktown* and *Lexington* pilots in the air, and at one stage they picked up a fuzzy signal that seemed to suggest that the tanker *Neosho* was being bombed, but beyond that there was nothing of any use to go on. Fletcher seemed to have forgotten all about them.

By ten o'clock, Crace had air intelligence reports from Australia of a substantial enemy force some 200 kilometres to the north and east of him, perhaps including a carrier and an unknown number of cruisers and transports. This was dire news, suggesting an imminent air attack. He formed his group into a defensive diamond, with *Hobart* eight cables (about 1500 metres) on his port quarter, *Chicago* the same distance to starboard, and the three destroyers in a screen ahead – a formation that could throw up a concentrated barrage of anti-aircraft fire, the ships protecting each other.

He was unaware that the Japanese had already found him. An enemy seaplane had discovered Task Group 17.3 at about eight that morning and had shadowed them unseen from a long distance astern, reporting back to Rabaul. Another seaplane picked them up again shortly after midday, and a third about an hour after that. The Japanese, believing the trap was closing, launched an attack force of 12 Mitsubishi G4M torpedo 'Betty' bombers and 19 Mitsubishi G3M high-level bombers (codenamed Nell by the

Allies) from the newly formed 25th Air Flotilla at Rabaul. They would be met on the way and escorted by a flight of 11 Zero fighters from Lae.

Chicago spotted them first. At about two o'clock, her CXAM radar, an early and relatively primitive model, picked up a flock of strange aircraft rapidly approaching from astern, but well off to port and flying fast, low and level. *Australia* flashed a challenge, and when there was only a garbled reply *Chicago, Hobart* and the destroyers opened fire. There was mild confusion in the cruisers at this time, with some lookouts identifying these mystery intruders as American Dauntless dive bombers, or perhaps even B-17s. In fact, they were the 11 Zeros from Lae. Apparently low on fuel, they chose not to make a strafing attack on the ships with machine-gun or cannon fire and disappeared into the distance, untouched.

There was more confusion a few minutes later when a Dauntless SBD actually did turn up. Alone and hopelessly lost on the way home from the *Shoho* raid, the pilot circled low overhead and, rather plaintively, asked for directions back to the *Yorktown*. As nobody had the faintest idea – there had still been no contact from Fletcher – the orphan was given a course to Port Moresby.

Jack Langrell was enjoying himself. The flagship had been closed up at action stations for most of the morning, but around lunchtime Captain Farncomb allowed non-essential personnel – those not at the guns, and so on – to relax and stretch their legs, so long as they did not stray too far from their posts.

Jack had been below with a medical party in the recreation room on the main mess deck, so he took the opportunity to snatch a little fresh air and climbed a ladder up for'ard, through a hatch and out onto the fo'c'sle in the sun. Another young kid from the canteen, Stan Cureton, went with him. The two stood there near the port guard rail, in their action-stations battledress with the white flash hoods. It was an impressive sight arrayed before them: *Hobart* forging through a calm sea out on the port quarter, with the wakes of the destroyers *Walke* and *Perkins* spreading away up ahead. Jack saw the 11 Zeros shoot past, black specks in the distance, and, thrilled and incurably curious, he decided to stick around, leaning back on the barbette that supported A-turret. Thirty minutes later, he was frightened out of his life. Literally out of the blue, from almost directly ahead, the 12 Betty torpedo bombers roared in for the attack, barely above sea level.

Task Group 17.3 was ready for them. Crace gave the order for his charges to act independently, but the six ships were already putting up a storm of gunfire. *Chicago* hit one of the Bettys, which appeared to be dropping a flare as some sort of marker. *Perkins* got another, which exploded in a ball of orange flame and plunged into the sea some distance ahead. The rest released their torpedoes, two each, from a height of perhaps ten metres and a distance of around 1500 metres.

This was a hesitant attack, poorly executed: a frontal approach minimised the danger from anti-aircraft fire, but it also created the narrowest possible target for the attacker, the ships bow-on rather than presenting the entire length of their sides. And the relatively long range and the clear day played into the hands of the defenders. In the calm and sunlit seas, the torpedo tracks were visible from a long way off, a greenish-white line bubbling through blue water. On *Australia*'s bridge, the lookouts spotted three coming straight for them.

This would be the acid test for Harold Farncomb, a measure of his worth far above and beyond all the formal deference to his rank, the gold braid and the saluting. At this moment, the safety of his ship and the lives of her sailors were in his hands, and his alone. He would have to comb the tracks, as they called it, to thread the big cruiser between the missiles speeding her way at 42 knots and each carrying a warhead containing 500 kilograms of high explosives. A misjudged distance, a late helm order, a turn in the wrong direction could bring disaster. All of his naval training since the age of 13 had brought him to this point, and he met the occasion magnificently. Gazing from the compass platform at the sea ahead, fixed on the torpedo tracks, Fearless

Frank handled the big cruiser with consummate skill in a succession of rapid-fire helm and engine orders:

Port 35 . . .
Full ahead starboard, half-ahead port . . .
Midships . . .
Full ahead all . . .
Starboard 20 . . .

Below decks at the main steering position, the quartermaster wrestled with the wheel, eyes riveted on the compass, sweat pouring from him. He, too, could bring disaster with a slow reaction, an uncertain move, a turn of the wheel too far. Further below still, stokers worked the throttles to speed or slow the great turbines at the jangled commands of the telegraph, men deafened by the roar of the racing fans, their greasy boots sliding on the vibrating deck plates as the ship heeled beneath them:

All sprayers!
More air . . .
Watch your steam . . .

On the bridge and high in the director tower, everyone stared down at the water rushing by them, frozen to the spot, fascinated and appalled. Two torpedoes passed down the ship's starboard side, mere metres from the thin steel of her hull. The other sped by to port. Crace wrote later:

How those torpedoes were avoided beats me, and I could have laid very long odds that two on the starboard side must hit. They can only have missed by a matter of feet. Farncomb handled the ship extremely well and it was entirely due to him and a great deal of luck that *Australia* was not hit.[12]

Jack Langrell, still on deck and huddled for protection behind A-turret, saw the first Betty get shot down. He had tried to go below again, back to his action station, but found the hatch he had climbed through closed and locked from beneath. He was stuck there, out in the open. The noise of the anti-aircraft fire – the deep thump of the 4-inch high angle guns, the chatter and rattle of the 5-inch machine guns – was deafening, indescribable, almost physical in the buffeting shock to the eardrums. After the bombers released their torpedoes, they flew on over the ships, well below mast height, to strafe the upper decks. It took quite some moments for the men on *Australia*'s bridge to realise that the strange zips and pings they could hear were machine-gun bullets spraying around them. It was too late for them to take cover, but, somehow, no one was hit. One of the bombers blasted straight past Jack from fore to aft just 50 metres away at eye level, two 14-cylinder Mitsubishi radial engines howling at their peak of 1500 horsepower, a sound and image burnt on his memory:

> It came past me on the port side, a big torpedo bomber; a nice-looking plane. Brown, with the big red ball on the side, level with the upper deck. He was gone in seconds. I was only a kid of 20 . . .[13]

Not long afterwards, another Betty cartwheeled into the sea astern of *Australia*. The 25th Air Flotilla had paid heavily, losing at least five aircraft shot down for no tangible result; two more are thought to have crashed on the return home. Two of *Chicago*'s sailors were killed by stray bullets, and six Australians – three on the flagship, and three on *Hobart* – had minor flesh wounds. That was the toll so far. Task Group 17.3 steamed on. But the torpedo bombers had hardly been dealt with before the next attack came upon them. The high-level Nells appeared out of the sun astern in close formation, armed with 250-kilogram bombs. Jack Langrell was still out there:

> There was an Oerlikon gun up on B-deck, near where I was. I heard this sailor there sing out 'Aircraft!' and when I looked up, coming over the mast of the ship were these 19 high-level bombers. Now, when you see 19 in a group, they look like 59. They were about 19,000 feet up, and I saw one of the bombs coming down. I saw it pass through a cloud and I said to myself, 'These are big ones,' so I ducked and put my head down. Looking out to the port side, I saw the first bomb hit the water not far

away from the ship, about 20 metres away. Then I closed my
eyes. I didn't want to see any more.

This attack was far better directed than the first. Clearly, the
Nells had singled out the distinctive, three-funnelled shape of
Australia, the central ship and the biggest, and, therefore, most
likely the flagship. Jack the admiral had the same frightening
vision as Jack the canteen boy:

> I saw the bombs drop and again Farncomb did the right thing
> and put the wheel hard a' starboard. The ship had just started to
> swing and list when down whistled the bombs all around us, and
> all on the Compass Platform crouched down . . . I think most
> fell on the port bow and starboard quarter, so that we should
> have bought it good and hearty if the wheel hadn't come over
> when it did . . .[14]

At action stations, most of *Australia*'s crew were below decks,
working deep down in the engine and boiler rooms, at the magazines and shell hoists, in the transmitting station, which controlled
the guns, in the sick bay, as a skeleton staff in the galley, or waiting
throughout the ship in medical and damage control parties. For
these men, the high-level bombing was by far the worst, the most
terrifying ordeal of all. They knew little or nothing of what was
happening above them: each new shock might be the fatal last.
They could only wait and perhaps pray, and then get on with
the job. All that stood between them and disaster were the thin
steel plates of the hull, riveted together. If those plates were penetrated by a torpedo or wrenched apart by a mine or a bomb, they
might die instantly in the explosion or in the oncoming rush of
the sea, the hull their tomb. If not, and they were not then killed
in a crushed compartment or slowly drowned in rising water, the
only hope of survival would be a desperate, crowded struggle up
narrow ladders and hatches in the pitch dark of a listing, sinking
ship. These risks they knew and sometimes joked about, but they
were very real and never far from the front of the mind.

At his station at the high angle control position, three decks
down, almost at the bottom of the ship, Midshipman Dick

Bourke, the farmer's son from Western Australia, was having his first taste of enemy action, facing the possibility of death at the age of 17. He busied himself at the fire control table for the ship's 4-inch guns. That deep in the ship, you could hear the bombs burst in the water close by with a tremendous, ringing clang, like the very hammers of the Devil on the anvil of Hell itself. Shock waves caused the plates of the hull to flex and vibrate, and here and there some rivets popped with a sharp crack, sending in a fast stream of water under pressure. Shrapnel from the blasts struck the ship's sides as if she were being flayed by some massive steel chain. *Australia* shuddered each time her own guns fired, and to add to it all there was the sudden, lurching heel of the deck below your feet as the cruiser turned and weaved to dodge the attack.

For the onlookers, it was different again. They thought the flagship was gone. The high-level bombing was so accurate, so well delivered that *Australia* quite literally disappeared behind a curtain of filthy brown water that towered high above her masts. On *Hobart* and *Chicago*, still on the port and starboard quarters, they feared they would not see her again. It was said later that *Chicago*'s captain, Howard Bode, had come to attention on his bridge and saluted in farewell.

But *Australia* did not die. Miracle of miracles, she was not even hit. The awful columns of water came crashing back down upon her, quite literally forcing the men on the bridge and at the open guns to their knees beneath the weight, but she steamed on through it all and out into the sunlight again. The admiral and the captain staggered to their feet on the compass platform, drenched to the bone, white uniforms dishevelled and stained with the brown and black filth of the explosives. All the bridge personnel were in place, unharmed. The Nells had gone. The Japanese attack had failed, utterly.

Yet there was still one more trial to come. The Yanks bombed them. Hardly had the enemy left when three more aircraft appeared, higher than the Japanese had been, and shaped up for an attack. Just five bombs whistled down towards the destroyer *Farragut* out to starboard, which went to flank speed[15] and heeled hard to port. *Australia* opened fire with her big 8-inch guns and the other ships began firing too but scored no hits, and the bombs splashed into the water about 200 metres off the destroyer's starboard quarter. The Australians thought the aircraft were B-26s, the Martin Marauder, but *Farragut*'s crew, who knew better what they were looking at, correctly identified them as four-engined B-17 Flying Fortresses. It was found later that they'd come from the US Army Air Force's 435th Bombardment Squadron, flying out of Townsville. Crace was understandably furious. 'Fortunately, their bombing, in comparison with that of the Japanese formation a few moments earlier, was disgraceful,' he wrote in his diary.

The admiral now had to decide what to do next. It was possible that the Japanese could return at any time, so he radioed Fletcher at 3.26 pm that he could not proceed on his mission without air support. 'Consider fighters to be essential if my object is to be attained,' he sent. He got no reply. Fletcher's silence had moved beyond mere discourtesy to negligence. It was not that he had been keeping radio silence to conceal his location from the Japanese; he had been in sporadic contact with both Hawaii and Melbourne. It appeared the American admiral had despatched Task Group 17.3 and then put it out of his mind, as if it was of no further consequence. As sunset approached, Crace had to make his own moves.

'I had received no information from the Commander, Task Force 17, regarding his position, his intentions, or what had been achieved during the day,' he noted towards evening.[16]

He was also worried about conserving fuel, so he decided to retire slowly to the south-east for the night and then move west again, minimising the risk of another air attack but still being in a position the next day to intercept an enemy force heading for Port Moresby.

He could have no idea of the furore he had provoked in Rabaul. The Japanese pilots had returned from their raid on Task Group 17.3 with wildly absurd accounts of success, claiming to have sunk an American California-class battleship, to have badly damaged a British Queen Elizabeth-class battleship, and to have left a cruiser burning. This nonsense helped save Crace. Elated by this supposed triumph, Admiral Inoue saw no point in a follow-up raid. But *Australia* and her companions spent a restless night wondering what the morrow might bring.

Further to the south and east, the weather that had smiled on the Coral Sea that morning began to turn in the afternoon, with heavy cloud concealing *Lexington*, *Yorktown* and the rest of Task Force 17. It also closed in over Vice Admiral Takeo Takagi's Carrier Strike Force of *Shokaku* and *Zuikaku*, which was some 350 kilometres to the east of Fletcher. Each side had only a rough idea of where the other might be, with Takagi guessing, correctly, that Fletcher was within reach somewhere to his west. Despite the lowering weather, at 4.15 he launched 12 Type 99 dive bombers – the single-engined Val, as the Allies called them – and 15 Type 97 torpedo bombers – designated Kate – in that direction.

With the heavy cloud as far as the eye could see and the onset of night, the Americans had prudently decided not to launch a strike of their own, but Fletcher had Combat Air Patrols of Wildcat fighters in the air to protect his two carriers. The Japanese blundered straight into them, birds to the slaughter. The Wildcats shot down seven of the Vals and one Kate for the loss of only three of their own (one of which radioed that it had lost its way in the murk, and was never seen again). Shattered, the Japanese formation withdrew, jettisoned its bombs and torpedoes, and prepared to head for home in the dark. That too was a shambles, another example of grim farce. By now utterly confused, several Japanese pilots mistook the *Lexington* for one of their own carriers and attempted to land on her, only to be frightened off by anti-aircraft fire from the accompanying destroyers.

It was the close of a miserable day for Operation MO. The Japanese had crippled the tanker *Neosho* and sunk the destroyer *Sims*, but against that they had lost a carrier, the *Shoho*, and a lot of aircraft and pilots. They thought they had also scored a striking triumph over Crace's force, but that was a delusion. They had not dealt with the American carrier force, and they'd had to stop the Moresby invasion in its tracks, at least temporarily. That night, Inoue postponed the landings for two days, until 12 May. Far away to the north in the mighty *Yamato*, Admiral Yamamoto read the reports of his subordinate admirals and, ever the pessimist, feared the worst:

> The dream of a great victory is gone. The battle belongs to the enemy. It was impossible, as feared. When the expected enemy raid came, we could not even mobilise the slightest united strength. In the end, we cannot even blame inadequate reconnaissance seaplanes. I am all the more concerned.[17]

The night of 7 May saw the Allies with the upper hand. But the battle was not yet over.

CHAPTER 14

AUSTRALIA CANNOT ESCAPE A BLOW

Well before dawn the next morning, Friday 8 May 1942, the carriers readied for the battle: the great *Lexington* and the smaller *Yorktown*, named for famous victories of the American Revolution; *Shokaku*, meaning 'Soaring Crane', and *Zuikaku*, 'Auspicious Crane', sister-ship veterans of Pearl Harbor. Their attendant cruisers and destroyers steamed with them, on guard.

There were (and still are) few more dangerous workplaces than a carrier's flight and hangar decks. It is a furiously busy airport condensed into a small, moving space. Aircraft are being lifted from the hangar deck below, or struck down again. On the upper deck, others are being towed into position, or are coming and going in waves, and those landing back on have to be quickly parked somewhere out of the way – an added problem before the invention of the modern angled flight deck. Fuel lines, bombs, torpedoes, and machine-gun ammunition lie here, there and everywhere, in apparent chaos to an untrained eye. Engines may start up at any time, which, in 1942, meant spinning propellers that could slice an unwary man to mincemeat. The noise, too, is deafening. Only intensive training, teamwork and constant vigilance keep disaster at bay.

Carrier evolutions in 1942 were rudimentary but confined by unalterable rules. No matter in which direction the target or objective might lie, the ship itself had to turn into the wind to fly off or recover its aircraft. Carrier admirals and captains were constricted by the range of their aircraft, too; in the early war years, this meant being no more than 500 kilometres from the target. Aircraft navigation was largely by compass and rule of thumb: if you flew out north-west, or 315 degrees, you flew back on a reciprocal course, south-east at 135 degrees, hopefully taking into account variations in wind speed and drift, which you had to judge from the waves below. Pilots were given what was called a Point Option, which was where their carrier expected to be on their return some hours later. American carriers also had a radio homing device, known as the YE-ZB system, which transmitted Morse code signals that a pilot could latch on to and follow, but it was far from foolproof. These were pioneering days, and many aircraft and crews were lost on the way home.

The Japanese moved first. At 6.15 am, shortly before sunrise, from a position about 200 kilometres east of the Louisiades, seven Kate torpedo bombers launched and headed out to search to the south, where they were fairly sure the Americans would be. Twenty minutes later, *Lexington* turned south-east into the wind to despatch her first aircraft, a Combat Air Patrol of four Grumman F4F Wildcat fighters that would stay above to protect her, and 18 SBD scout planes to find the enemy. Task Force 17 was some 300 kilometres south-east of the Louisiades, beyond the reach of Japanese aircraft from Rabaul. Overnight, the weather had changed again: the Americans were now in clear sunlight with perfect visibility and the Japanese were concealed by low cloud and occasional squalls.

They found each other at almost the same moment. At 8.20 am, Lieutenant (junior grade) Joe Smith, in a *Lexington* SBD, spotted the Japanese carriers through a gap in the storm clouds. Two minutes later, Petty Officer Ist Class Kenzo Kanno, the observer in one of the three-man Kates, glimpsed the Americans. Task Force 17 and the Carrier Strike Force were 360 kilometres apart, the Japanese to the north-east.

Each side raced to get into the air. Between 9 and 9.30 am, *Lexington* and *Yorktown* launched 75 attack aircraft: 15 fighters,

39 dive bombers and 21 torpedo bombers. The Japanese, after their losses of the previous evening, sent off 69 aircraft: 18 fighters, 33 dive bombers and 18 torpedo planes. Frank Jack Fletcher then handed over tactical command to his junior admiral, Aubrey Fitch, who had more carrier experience. In his turn, the Japanese commander, Takeo Takagi, gave way to his carrier expert, Rear Admiral Chuichi Hara, a man with almost the build of a sumo wrestler and known to his friends as 'King Kong'. With their planes in the air, the carriers and their escorts changed course to draw closer to the enemy, the Americans steaming north-east at 25 knots in clear daylight, the Japanese due south at 30 knots, still helpfully hidden by heavy cloud.

Battle was joined at three minutes before 11 am, the Americans drawing first blood. *Yorktown*'s Combat Air Patrol could not find *Zuikaku* in the cloud and a rain squall, but a gap revealed *Shokaku* twisting and turning below. The dive bombers went in. Two 450-kilogram bombs scored direct hits for'ard on *Shokaku*'s flight deck, starting a fierce fire. Then came the torpedo bombers, low and level, but they all missed. The air was thick with anti-aircraft fire from the Japanese cruisers and rent with the scream and roar of the fighter planes soaring and diving in dogfights. The Zeros of the Japanese Combat Air Patrol shot down two dive bombers and lost two of their own as well. This account by one of *Yorktown*'s SBD dive bomber pilots, Ensign John H. Jorgenson, is sharp with the cut and thrust of battle in the air:

> We dived and released below 2,000 feet. I saw the skipper's bomb hit flush on the carrier's deck amidships near the Island. While closing my diving flaps as I pulled out the plane was hit by anti-aircraft fire.
>
> It lurched and started into a left spin. After recovery I saw a shell hole through my left aileron and wing. Fabric quickly ripped off and the wiring and tubing protruded. As I gained a climbing attitude three fighters jumped my tail. Their bullets peppered the plane, especially the wings and front end of the fuselage.
>
> Some passed in over my right shoulder and tore the rear of my telescopic sight away. Others hit the back of the seat and more

came into the cockpit, wrecking most of my instruments. One bullet passed through the oxygen tube lying on my forearm, causing the tube to smoke. Three bullets hit or grazed my right leg, and I got some shrapnel or powder burn in feet and toes.

The plane flew very hard, the left wing being heavy. I flew through clouds and saw my radioman shoot down one fighter. Three more attacked from ahead and above. One came in head-on and I fired into him until he veered off smoking.

After this attack my engine began to lose power, missing on one or two cylinders. So I joined a group of SBDs and followed them home. Arriving, I tried to lower my wheels with my flaps down. But when I did this the plane dropped off quickly. I then notified the carrier I was going to land in the water. I went into the sea near a destroyer, hit the water at 12.48 and was picked up at 12.52.[1]

Lexington's aircraft arrived on the scene at 11.30. Half of them found nothing below the cloud cover and had to return low on fuel, but the rest managed to land another 450-kilogram bomb on the crippled *Shokaku*, enough to tear up her flight deck and make it impossible for her to launch or recover her planes. This time, they found *Zuikaku* as well but did not hit her, and none of *Lexington*'s torpedo bombers achieved a thing either. In fact, all the torpedo bombers failed dismally, possibly because American torpedoes at that stage of the war were scandalously riddled with defects and often refused to run or explode.

The Zeros, a faster, more manoeuvrable aircraft, also destroyed three American Wildcat fighters. With his ship now useless and still burning, and with 223 of his men dead or injured, *Shokaku*'s captain was given permission to withdraw from the battle, and he sped off to the north-east with a small destroyer escort. *Zuikaku*, with Admiral Hara on board, remained unharmed. She would now have to recover *Shokaku*'s returning aircraft as well as her own.

Task Force 17 had been at General Quarters since sunrise. Admiral Fletcher paced his flag bridge in an old First World War tin helmet, listening to the chatter of his pilots as they attacked the enemy to the north. He and the small staff with him knew their turn would come at any minute, and so it did. As *Lexington*'s Action Narrative put it:

> The weather in our vicinity was clear, unlimited visibility and ceiling, few clouds, no rain squalls, wind about 15 knots, from southeast. Radar reported at 1100 many enemy aircraft approaching from northward, distance about 75 miles [120 kilometres]. First enemy planes were sighted from the ship at 1113. They were torpedo planes. They were at about 6–7000 feet altitude and split and came in from both bows. Ship's speed had been built up to 25 knots at 1100 when the attack was expected and was immediately increased to 30 knots when the hostile aircraft were sighted.[2]

The two American carriers were steaming some 3000 metres apart, surrounded by a protective steel screen of cruisers and destroyers. Both got their reserve Wildcats off the decks to intercept the oncoming Japanese and then began an irregular zigzag at flank speed, using full rudder. The Val torpedo bombers went for them first, 14 aiming for *Lexington* and four for *Yorktown*, flying on through a storm of fire from both carriers and their escorts. *Yorktown*'s captain, Elliott Buckmaster, counted six torpedoes coming at him; handling the big carrier like a nimble destroyer, he evaded them all. The bigger and more ponderous *Lexington* was not so fortunate. The Vals caught her in a pincer movement from port and starboard, in the same way that *Repulse* and *Prince of Wales* had been attacked off Malaya, an onslaught almost impossible for a ship to evade. Her captain, Frederick 'Ted' Sherman, gave it all he could, but it was not enough:

> I manoeuvred with full rudder both ways as I considered best to avoid torpedoes. Some from starboard crossed ahead; two others ran parallel to the ship, one on each side; some from port ran ahead; two ran under without hitting. At 1120, first torpedo hit ship and exploded just forward of port forward gun gallery; at 1121, one hit a little further aft about opposite the bridge.[3]

That first torpedo ruptured some aviation fuel tanks on the port side, sending gasoline vapours wafting through nearby compartments, but the ship was only slightly slowed. Again, there were furious aerial dogfights and gun battles. Three Japanese torpedo planes were shot down, and four American torpedo bombers were lost.

Next came the Japanese dive bombers, plummeting from out of the sun, which made them hard to detect until they were virtually overhead. The Kates from *Shokaku* swooped on *Lexington*, scoring several near misses and three hits, one of which penetrated four decks. The carrier had now begun to list to port and four fires were burning, but she was still making 25 knots and eventually able to recover her aircraft. Again, *Yorktown* was luckier. One bomb drilled a small hole on the flight deck and travelled three decks down before it exploded, killing or wounding 66 men, and there were a dozen near misses, two of them on the starboard quarter that literally lifted her stern and screws clear out of the water. But she also steamed on.

By 11.40 am, the first carrier battle in history had ended, with the surviving aircraft beginning to return to their ships. Some Japanese and Americans met each other on the journey home and duelled again, with more death and destruction. In all, the Americans lost 33 aircraft and the Japanese 43 – some in combat and others in what were called operational losses, meaning that they had become lost, or perhaps crashed on landing, or were just too badly damaged to repair. Each side exaggerated its successes. The Japanese believed they had sunk *Lexington* and damaged *Yorktown* so badly that she must sink, along with a battleship and a cruiser. In turn, the Americans thought they had sent *Shokaku* to the bottom. As the afternoon began, each side started to assess the damage, count the dead and bind up the wounds. Neither commanding admiral, not Frank Jack Fletcher nor Takeo Takagi, had the will or the resources for a second round. Task Force 17 headed south-west, and the Japanese retreated north towards the Solomons.

———

Jack Crace and the Australians and Americans of Task Group 17.3 knew none of this. They too had spent a restless night wondering what the morning might bring. The dawn of 8 May found them poised about 350 kilometres to the south-east of Port Moresby, in a position to block an invasion force or whatever else might emerge from the Jomard Passage, but still shrouded in the fog of war, without any word from Fletcher far away to the south. If the American was not willing to signal him by radio, Crace hoped that he might send an aircraft or perhaps even a destroyer with a message, but there was nothing. All he could do was to stick to his original orders.

Yet his mere presence was having the desired effect. Japanese search planes had tried and failed to find him through the previous night, but in the morning he was discovered. Another reconnaissance aircraft spotted the Task Group at about 10.30 am, reporting back to Rabaul that it had sighted an enemy battleship, two cruisers and four destroyers. *Australia* was presumably the battleship. This well and truly put the wind up Admiral Inoue, who had no ships within reach capable of dealing with such a force. A battleship alone could make mincemeat of his troopships. Inoue renewed his order to the invasion force not to enter the Jomard Passage and kept it milling around well to the north-east. He pondered another air strike from Rabaul, like the one that had failed in its attack on Task Group 17.3 the previous day, but again the weather and the fortunes of war intervened. A massive tropical downpour kept his bomber squadrons grounded.

But Crace's problems were by no means over. As the carrier battle was joined, he could snatch fragments of news from the radio talk of the American pilots but nothing that gave him any clue as to Fletcher's whereabouts or intentions. As he wrote later:

> The carriers' aircraft could be heard conversing with their parent ships; but as was the case yesterday, their reports were entirely valueless to me. Late in the forenoon it seemed from reports on Fighter Direction Wave that our carriers were not only attacking the enemy but they themselves were being attacked from the air. The situation was far from clear but it was learned from intercepted aircraft reports that an enemy carrier in an unknown position had received two hits from torpedoes and two from 1,000-lb bombs.

This was apparently the second carrier to have been damaged while two others were now thought to be in the area.[4]

His second problem was fuel. The destroyers in particular were getting low, as was *Hobart*, and he had no means of replenishing them. That afternoon, he reluctantly decided that *Hobart* would have to go back to Brisbane, and she left with the destroyer *Walke*, which had engine trouble. *Australia*, *Chicago* and the two remaining destroyers would plug on, still hoping for something – anything – from Fletcher.

Again, fortune turned, to smile on the Allies. Still wary of Crace and shocked by the Japanese losses in the carrier battle, Admiral Inoue blinked. At 2.30 that afternoon, he ordered the invasion force to return to Rabaul, postponing the invasion of Port Moresby for almost a month, until 3 July. *Zuikaku* and her escorts were also recalled to Rabaul, and the badly wounded *Shokaku* was sent limping back home to Japan.

Operation MO had failed. It was the first check to Japanese conquest in the Pacific. They did not know it yet – nobody did – but Frank Jack Fletcher and John Crace had won the Battle of the Coral Sea.

—

By this autumn of 1942, the war was placing enormous strains upon Australian life. Raw figures tell part of the story. When the Pacific War broke out, there were 431,300 men in the three services and 3600 women. Over a year, by March 1943, those figures swelled to 825,500 men in uniform, and an astonishing 40,260 women. Offices, shops, factories and farms were being stripped of their male workers, distorting the economy and society itself in new and unexpected ways. Single women often enjoyed the liberating opportunity to work in new jobs, but many wives were ground down by the burdens of managing homes and families with their husbands away (and often earning less money).

Rationing was coming in for food and clothing, a constant irritant made worse by tangles of bureaucratic red tape and bossiness. The rationing of tea was typical. On 30 March 1942, households had to declare how much tea they had in the kitchen and how many people there were over the age of nine. Then they registered with a grocer, who would dole out a supply of two ounces (about 56 grams) of tea a fortnight for ten-year-olds and above. Records would be kept. Inspectors would check. Severe penalties would apply.

In the week of the Coral Sea Battle, there was a rush to buy clothing after the federal government foolishly gave advance warning that it would be rationed from the next Monday, 11 May. A nationwide stampede to the shops that Saturday upset the newspapers, including the Western Australian *Sunday Times*:

> A lot of goods that would be normally in the shop counters today are now in the homes of hundreds of purchasers, and, therefore, stocks are already substantially depleted.
>
> The workers, of whom the Government is supposed to be the particular guardian, of course suffered the most because, not having the spare cash nor the spare time, many of them could not attend today for a last opportunity of buying unrationed goods.[5]

The Brisbane *Worker* was more scathing still:

> War economy has some queer by-products, the queerest of all being the self-important official persons who, 'dressed in a little brief authority,' strut about issuing fantastic orders and regulations by which common working people are expected to be bound.[6]

And on top of that, the Yanks were here, with thousands more flooding in. They were genuinely welcomed as saviours and comrades in arms, but their mere presence caused huge upheaval. In January 1942, there were 4600 US Army and Air Force personnel in Australia; by June, there were 88,569, all of them to be accommodated, fed and entertained by whatever Australia could provide.[7] They camped on racecourses and took over the best hotels for headquarters and officer's messes.

The trouble with the Yanks was that they had money to splash around, and splash it they did. An Australian Army private made

£9.15s a month; his American equivalent got about £17, and the gap grew wider up the ranks. A major in the Australian Army was paid £44.15s a month, while a US Army major got £106.[8] Flush with cash, glamorous and exotic in their smartly cut uniforms, they looked and sounded like Hollywood. They had Coca-Cola, chewing gum, Hershey Bars and nylon stockings to give away; they had Glenn Miller, the Andrews Sisters and Betty Grable, and they danced the jitterbug. Well mannered with their 'ma'ams' and 'yessirs', they found young women flocking to be with them. Publicans would often serve them first, and taxi-drivers bypassed the locals to pick them up, correctly anticipating a lavish tip.

Unsurprisingly, resentments and jealousies grew in the deep divide between two cultures. The sight of an Australian girl hanging off a uniformed American could provoke a drunken brawl in a flash. A US Army Publication, 'Instructions for American Servicemen in Australia, 1942', explained to wide-eyed GIs from Maine and Texas, Georgia and Idaho:

> Being simple, direct and tough, especially if he comes from 'Outback,' the Digger is often confused and nonplussed by the 'manners' of Americans in mixed company . . . The commonest swear words are 'bastard', (pronounced 'barstud,') 'bugger' and 'bloody,' and Australians have a genius for using the latter nearly every other word . . . Of course the best thing any Australian can say about you is that you are a bloody fine barstud.

Apart from the rush to buy shirts and woollens that Coral Sea weekend, much of the nation was looking forward to the start of the Aussie Rules football season. The hot tickets at the pictures were 'the screen's supreme adventure hit', Zane Grey's *Western Union* in Technicolor with Robert Young, Randolph Scott and Virginia Gilmore or, if you preferred a guaranteed tear-jerker, Vivien Leigh and Robert Taylor in *Waterloo Bridge*.

In Canberra, the leaves on the poplars and the liquidambars had begun to turn and fall in the cool, and the wood fires were burning. Parliament sat that Friday 8 May, and rumours of a great naval battle had begun to circulate in King's Hall and to percolate through the offices and lobbies of both government and opposition.

Question Time in the House of Representatives began at 10.30 am, with a couple of pot-boilers about the sugar crop and the like, until the young Melbourne conservative MP for Fawkner, Harold Holt, rose from the green leather benches to the left of the speaker and put the rumours directly to the Prime Minister. Had there been 'an impressive victory in the Pacific area?' he asked. John Curtin gave him a polite, noncommittal brush-off, but then apparently received new information:

> No announcement will be made by the Australian Operational Command for reasons which I need not disclose. However, the following announcement has been made from Washington regarding the naval engagement – very excellent news has been received. A naval engagement between United States of America and Japanese forces on 4 May resulted in the following damage to the enemy:—One light cruiser, two destroyers, four gun-boats and one supply vessel were sunk. One 9,000-ton aircraft tender, one light cruiser and one cargo vessel were damaged. Six enemy aircraft were destroyed. This highly successful action took place in the vicinity of the Solomon Islands. It was accomplished with the loss of only three aircraft.[9]

This was the American attack on Tulagi, complete with the absurdly optimistic accounts of damage done by the American pilots. Even as Curtin spoke, the carrier battle was under way far to the north-east, and that afternoon, as the House prepared to adjourn for the weekend, he electrified parliament with stirring news. John Curtin did not have the mellifluous, patrician tones of a Menzies. He spoke with an Australian accent that today sounds curiously old-fashioned, but he could hold an audience in the palm of his hand, and he did so that day:

> I have received a communiqué from the Commander-in-Chief of the Allied Forces in the South-West Pacific Area stating that a great naval battle is proceeding in the South-West Pacific zone.

This battle arises from the operations which began on the 4th May and to which I referred in the House this morning.

The events that are taking place to-day are of crucial importance to the whole conduct of the war in this theatre. I have no information as to how the engagement is developing, but I should like the nation to be assured that there will be, on the part of our forces and of the American forces, that devotion to duty which is characteristic of the naval and air forces of the United States of America, Great Britain and the Commonwealth.

I should add that at this moment nobody can tell what the result of the engagement may be. If it should go advantageously, we shall have cause for great gratitude and our position will then be somewhat clearer. But if we should not have the advantages from this battle for which we hope, all that confronts us is a sterner ordeal and a greater and graver responsibility.

This battle will not decide the war; it will determine the immediate tactics which will be pursued by the Allied forces and by the common enemy. I ask the people of Australia, having regard to the grave consequences implicit in this engagement, to make a sober and realistic estimate of their duty to the nation.[10]

Parliament was not then broadcast on radio.[11] The journalists of the press gallery raced to their telephones to catch the late edition of the afternoon newspapers or to file their stories for the next morning, but Curtin decided that the news was so momentous that he would convey it directly and rally the people. That evening, he spoke to the nation on the ABC:

I tell you bluntly that the whole world may very well shake within the next few weeks under the blows that full-scale warfare will strike. Australia cannot escape a blow. Happenings of great magnitude are at hand. The European campaign has been uncovered from its blanket of snow. Vichy France is in open collaboration with the Axis. The Middle East theatre has many possibilities. Britain, embattled and alert, still apprehends invasion. The shipping war is but temporarily lulled. Japan thrusts at a gateway to India. The grim fighters of Corregidor have been subdued.

Australian and American fighting men daily give their lives in defending Australian territory. We face vital, perilous weeks, fraught with exceedingly important happenings for Australia. Invasion is a menace capable hourly of becoming an actuality.[12]

Curtin's words in parliament and his radio broadcast were splashed across all the newspapers the next day, with the added excitement of a communiqué from MacArthur's headquarters trumpeting the supposed Japanese losses of an aircraft carrier, a heavy cruiser, a light cruiser, two destroyers, four gunboats and a supply ship, and damage to another aircraft carrier – which it was thought would be lost – and a seaplane tender, two cruisers and a cargo vessel. 'Allied losses were light,' it said blandly.

This was fiction, whether deliberate or not. Either way, it was the first encouraging war news Australians had received since Pearl Harbor, a fillip to morale in a nation that desperately needed one. The heavy Allied toll in the Battle of the Coral Sea was kept from them, and, for that matter, from the American people as well.

—

As the guns fell silent and the enemies steamed apart on that afternoon of 8 May, fate made another play. Aboard *Lexington*, damage control parties had at last been getting the upper hand over several fires burning below decks, and, by shifting oil fuel about, her list had been corrected and she was making a good 25 knots, heading south. Then, just before one o'clock, a massive explosion ripped through her. At first, they thought it might have been an unexploded bomb detonating, but eventually it was found that the gasoline fumes released by the first torpedo hit had gone up, killing 25 men. New fires began to burn out of control, new explosions tore at her from time to time, and, as her electrics and communication systems gradually succumbed, Captain Sherman was reduced to steering by his engines. He requested destroyers to come alongside to pump water from their fire hoses, but it was all in vain. The *Lady Lex* was dying. Sherman's action report is worth quoting at length:

At 1707 Admiral Fitch directed me to abandon ship. I issued the orders and orderly disembarkation began. Boats from accompanying ships came alongside and assisted. Preference was given to lowering wounded and injured into the boats. Most of the men went hand over hand down lines over the side and into the water on life rafts. Most of the men were off by 1800.

Admiral Fitch and myself were the last to leave the bridge. He disembarked forward where practically all had gone and I made a final inspection aft. I found a number of men aft on the starboard side and in the port after gun gallery where there seemed to be some difficulty; men in the water were having trouble getting away from the ship due to drift. I directed those men still on board to shift to the starboard side aft where getting away was easier. I made a final inspection and went aft where my executive officer, Commander Seligman, reported to me all men were off the ship.

At this time a tremendous explosion about the vicinity of the elevator shook the ship and we had to duck to avoid falling debris. I directed Commander Seligman to disembark. I saw him in the water swimming toward an approaching motor whale boat. Having assured myself there was no other living person on the ship, I went down a line hand over hand and dropped off into the water, to be picked up by a motor whale boat of the USS *Minneapolis*. This boat took me to the USS *Minneapolis* where I reported to Admiral Fitch.

The picture of the burning and doomed ship was a magnificent but sad sight. The ship and crew had performed gloriously and it seemed too bad that she had to perish in her hour of victory. But she went to a glorious end, more fitting than the usual fate of the eventual scrap heap or succumbing to the perils of the sea. She went down in battle, after a glorious victory for our forces in which the *Lexington* and her air group played so conspicuous a part.

The *Phelps* was directed by the Task Force Commander to sink the *Lexington* by torpedoes. Five torpedoes were fired, at least three hit, and she finally went under on an even keel. As she went under, a tremendous explosion occurred which rocked ships for miles around. It was the end of the *Lexington*.[13]

Two hundred and sixteen of her crew of 2951 had died, either in the air or in the fires and explosions, but not a man was killed in the evacuation – a remarkable feat of seamanship and courage. Her loss to the USN and the Allied cause was tremendous, though. Admiral Nimitz in Hawaii was left with just three carriers to counter the next Japanese move: *Enterprise*, *Hornet* and the damaged *Yorktown*, which was still heading home. When *Yorktown* arrived at Pearl, the dockyard estimated she would take two weeks to repair and make ready for sea again. Displaying the iron resolve beneath that mild exterior, Nimitz ordered that it be done in two days, and it was.

The destruction of *Lexington* tilted the crude arithmetic of the battle towards the Japanese, whose losses in men and ships were smaller. That gave them a tactical victory of sorts, but it did not alter the strategic score. It remained a fact that the Japanese hopes of taking Port Moresby from the sea had been thwarted, and forever. A few weeks later, the idea was abandoned entirely and it was decided instead that the army would advance on Moresby overland, on a trail over the impossibly rugged Owen Stanley Ranges through the small village of Kokoda.

—

Frank Jack Fletcher had still not contacted Jack Crace. Nor had anyone else. Late on 9 May 1942, more than a day after the battle, *Australia* and Task Group 17.3 were still ploughing back and forth in a position to intercept a Japanese force coming west around the tail of New Guinea, but, beyond that, Crace had no idea what was expected of him nor what might have happened to Fletcher. At seven that evening, he put together what scraps of information he had and decided:

> it seemed probable that *Yorktown* and *Lexington* at this time were badly in need of replacement aircraft, bombs, and torpedoes, while the destroyers of this group were probably in need

of fuel. Again I had received no intimation of Commander Task Force 17's position or intentions but I considered it probable that he had, by now, retired. It seemed equally probable, from the absence of reports of vessels in the Louisiades area, that the enemy's advance had now definitely been checked.[14]

Fletcher's silence, beginning as discourtesy, had escalated by now to a culpable failure of command. He had sent six Allied ships and several thousand men in harm's way without air cover – a high risk, but certainly one worth taking. Yet he had no apparent interest in their welfare nor in the outcome of their mission, which, after all, had been the entire point of the exercise: forestalling the attack on Port Moresby. For all he knew or apparently cared, Task Group 17.3 could have gone to the bottom. It is no excuse to say that he was maintaining radio silence or that he was preoccupied with the carrier air battle. Once the Japanese had found *Lexington* and *Yorktown*, there was no point in a communications blackout, and Fletcher had given tactical command of the battle to Fitch, leaving himself free to deal with the wider picture. During the conflict, and still more so a day after it, as he was withdrawing, there was plenty of time and every reason for him to get in touch with Crace. He did not.

With his fuel situation edging towards critical, Crace gave himself until 1 am on 10 May to maintain his blockade. Then, with no further information, he turned south-west for home and by noon the next day he was in the shelter of Cid Harbour in Queensland's Whitsunday Islands, where an oiler was waiting.

Then, at last, he heard from Fletcher, a signal that read, 'Sorry to leave you in precarious situation and congratulate you on your victory over bombers. Thank you for your unselfish and efficient co-operation.' It was not much, but it was something. Now able to relax from the tensions and dangers of operations at sea, Crace was more preoccupied with doing something about the bombing attack on his task force by the American B-17s. The more he thought of it, the more his anger grew. Determined to expose the fiasco, he fired off crisp letters to both the RAN Chief of the Naval Staff, Admiral Sir Guy Royle, and MacArthur's naval chief, Vice Admiral Herbert Leary, both of them in Melbourne. To Royle, he wrote:

> Can nothing be done to train observers in the recognition of their own and enemy ships? Is the present inefficiency to be accepted and condoned? After all, Australia hasn't got many ships and they are all very distinctive, and the Japs should be easy enough to recognise . . .
>
> It is distressing to feel that we have to contend with the American air menace in addition to the Japanese, and it is perhaps fortunate that the former are less efficient than the latter!!!! Joking apart, I would suggest that immediate steps be taken to institute regular and intensive training in the recognition of ships by all flying personnel of whatever nationality.[15]

Crace also complained about being kept in the dark about Fletcher's movements, although he did not especially blame Fletcher himself. He was more concerned about the lack of information getting to him from the Central War Room in Melbourne, which he icily described as 'a rather indifferent post office'.

Leary sent back a soothing reply expressing sympathy and promising to take up the bombing matter with MacArthur's air force commander, Lieutenant General George Brett, which he did. And there both admirals hit a brick wall. At that time, and for a good while later, the South-West Pacific Command was a snake pit of feuds and rivalries, much of it a turf war between the USN and the US Army Air Force, with American generals and admirals barely on speaking terms. Within the army, soldiers and aviators fought each other as well. Brett himself was a mediocre bureaucrat with a vastly inflated opinion of his own abilities, who, before MacArthur's arrival, had spent much time and energy parading in Melbourne's gentlemen's clubs and the drawing rooms of Toorak, duchessing Australian politicians in the hope of getting the supreme command himself.[16] MacArthur despised him and very pointedly snubbed him when they first met in Melbourne.

Brett solved this new problem dumped in his lap by pretending it had never happened. He denied point blank that his aircraft had bombed Task Group 17.3. This was not easy to do. There was actually photographic proof of it available; one of the B-17 crews had taken pictures of the attack, which clearly showed they had bombed Allied ships. There was also the report from the USS *Farragut*, which had taken the brunt of the attack.

Brett ignored both. And when Leary pressed it with him, he snapped back that he would not discuss the matter further. Case closed. Worse, Brett apparently took no steps to improve the ship-recognition skills of his air crews, both American and Australian – a failure that would have disastrous consequences down the track. A few months later, MacArthur had him sacked, for unrelated reasons, and he was shuffled off to an inconsequential command somewhere in the Caribbean. But the damage had been done.

—

With the battle over, Task Group 17.3 reverted to being Task Force 44. Pleasingly, Nimitz despatched new ships to join it, beefing up the permanent American presence in Australian waters. In Brisbane, Crace welcomed to his command the cruiser *Salt Lake City* and the destroyers *Bagley*, *Flusser*, *Helm*, *Henley* and *Mugford*.

But the admiral's time in Australia was drawing to its end. He had been wanting to go for a while, largely for personal reasons. His wife, Carola, was homesick. Her life in Sydney had been moving from rented flat to rented flat in the Eastern Suburbs, a not uncommon existence for a naval wife but never enjoyable, and even less so when her family home was a spacious cottage and garden in the green and pleasant fields of Hampshire. And she was missing the family. Their two elder sons were still back in Britain, the oldest boy, Allan, a midshipman in the navy and the second, Christopher, at Eton. Their third boy, Nicholas, barely a teenager, was in Australia but also away at boarding school, Geelong Grammar. Carola had been taken up by Sydney society and she had involved herself in charitable war work, but the novelty had evidently begun to wear off. She had talked about going home by herself.

Professionally and personally, Crace was tired. The post of Rear Admiral Commanding the Australian Squadron had not been the glittering prize he had hoped for. For more than two years, he had performed an exacting job diligently and well, but it had often meant dreary weeks at sea not doing very much, with little leave or leisure. As a flag officer, he had plenty of subordinates who respected him and even liked him, but no friend or confidant of equal rank with whom to unwind. He had wearied, too, of the constant tug of war with Navy Office in Melbourne, which he felt – with reason – had often gone over his head or behind his back. Coral Sea had certainly been a fillip. He could forever after say he had commanded a squadron in battle, and successfully so. But he increasingly looked forward to definite news of his replacement arriving from Britain, and towards the end of May he got it. Rear Admiral Victor Crutchley was on his way.

—

'A bloody war or a sickly season!

'A willing foe and sea room!

'Wives and sweethearts – may they never meet!'

The toasts at a formal wardroom mess dinner, a different one prescribed for each day of the week, are as old as the navy itself, an echo of the time when ardent young officers sought glory in the thunder of cannon and the headlong rush with sword and cutlass to board a dismasted enemy.

Australia's officers farewelled their admiral with just such a dinner, alongside the Hamilton Wharf in the Brisbane River. They did it in proper style, decked out in black tie and gold-buttoned white mess jackets with epaulettes and decorations, a common enough occasion in peace time. This was the only one they held during the war, a unique tribute. The wardroom rang with the cries of Mr Vice – the vice president of the mess, who runs the show in strict accordance with ancient ritual. No officer may leave the table without permission, least of all to visit the head. The loyal toast – His Majesty the King! – is drunk with everyone remaining seated, a custom said to date from Stuart times, when Charles II stood for the toast in one of his ships o'the line and smacked the royal skull on a low deckhead beam. With much hilarity, Mr Vice hands out fines and punishments for crimes and misdemeanours real or imagined, the more colourful the better. The port decanter is always passed from right to left. The old tradition was that officers never clinked their glasses in a toast, for the sound would remind the Devil of the tolling of a ship's bell for a burial at sea and encourage him to seize new victims for a watery grave. (This could be rectified by a quick second clink, which would so confuse the Devil that he would take a soldier instead.)

Another old tradition was the well-lubricated romp of wardroom games after dinner, when distinctions of rank were abandoned in a sprawling, brawling free-for-all that sent the furniture flying. *Australia*'s officers went for it with gusto, a frolic best described by Surgeon Lieutenant Malcolm Stening, who was there:

> The unlikely interlude of playing 'Is That You, Moriarty?' by the Admiral ('Hellfire Jack' Crace) and the Captain ('Fearless Frank' Farncomb) lying prone on the deck blindfolded and striving to lunge at each other with truncheons of rolled-up newspaper at the call of 'Is that you, Moriarty?' to provide direction is not easily forgotten.
>
> In 'High Cockalorum,' the participant runs the length of the wardroom to gather speed to vault over a platform of crouched backs of others aligned head first against the bulkhead. Crace, in his turn on leaping, missed the platform of his colleagues' backs and fell to the deck breaking his arm. Fortunately all that was needed in treatment was the positioning of the fractured humerus in a cuff and collar sling which he wore on leaving the ship on the following forenoon. Not really a war wound at the Battle of the Coral Sea nor deserving of a Purple Heart decoration.[17]

Sadder and wiser, perhaps, Rear Admiral John Crace hauled down his flag on Saturday 13 June, to be piped over the side for one last time and never again to command at sea. After leave back in Britain and a promotion to vice admiral, he was put in charge of one of the great naval dockyards, Chatham, in Kent, where he saw out the war. His replacement, Victor Crutchley, would have a new title: Commander, Task Force 44. He hoisted his flag in *Hobart* the same day.

—

Rear Admiral Victor Alexander Charles Crutchley VC DSC RN was a minor blue blood whose maternal grandfather had been Charles FitzRoy, 3rd Baron Southampton. The FitzRoys could trace that bloodline back to one Henry FitzRoy, First Duke of Grafton, a bastard son of Charles II by his mistress, the beautiful but bed-hopping and bad-tempered Barbara Villiers, Countess of Castlemaine. The line included a slew of admirals, generals and members of parliament. Victor's mother, Frederica, had been a maid of honour to Queen Victoria, who had graciously consented to be the boy's godmother.

With a noble profile and a piercing gaze, a head of wavy ginger hair and a neatly trimmed beard rumoured to conceal an old war wound, Crutchley had a sea-dog air that would have been entirely at home on an Elizabethan quarterdeck with Drake or Raleigh. His record in the navy was illustrious. As a junior lieutenant, he had been at Jutland in 1916 in the battleship *Centurion*, where his zeal and efficiency brought him to the notice of his superiors. In 1918, he took part in the first Zeebrugge Raid, a bold navy commando-style attempt in the dead of night to close the Belgian port of Zeebrugge to German U-boats by sinking block ships in the entrance canal. The raid was one of those fiery, gallant skirmishes where much blood was shed – more than 200 British sailors died – for very little result. Two block ships were indeed sunk, but the Germans managed to get around them two days later. It was, however, ballyhooed into a British propaganda triumph. Eleven Victoria Crosses were awarded, and Crutchley himself had dashed about enough to win a Distinguished Service Cross and a place on a similar night-time raid on the harbour at Ostend a few weeks later.

That was an even wilder melee. Crutchley took over the ancient cruiser *Vindictive* when her captain was killed in a storm of gunfire, and, steering with the engines, he rammed her into place to block the pier. After searching for survivors with a torch – German bullets zipping around him – he then escaped in a motor launch, *ML 254*, a feat described in the citation for the Victoria Cross he was awarded:

> Lieut. Crutchley took command of *M.L. 254* when the commanding officer sank exhausted from his wounds, the second in command having been killed. The vessel was full of wounded and very seriously damaged by shell fire, the fore part being flooded. With indomitable energy and by dint of baling with buckets and shifting weight aft, Lieut. Crutchley and the unwounded kept her afloat, but the leaks could not be kept under, and she was in a sinking condition, with her forecastle nearly awash when picked up by HMS *Warwick*. The bearing of this very gallant officer and fine seaman throughout these operations off the Belgian coast was altogether admirable and an inspiring example to all thrown in contact with him.[18]

Between the wars, Crutchley VC led the conventional life of the independently wealthy naval officer with connections, passing a leisurely couple of years in a cruiser on the New Zealand station and playing polo in Malta with the likes of the Duke of York and Lord Louis Mountbatten. The new war found him in command of the battleship *Warspite*, where he took her storming into that fjord in Narvik in 1940 to wreak havoc on a flotilla of German destroyers. After that, he was promoted to Commodore but put ashore to run the naval barracks at Devonport in Plymouth, an important but sedentary job he detested. His posting to Australia was a godsend, another chance for action at the relatively youthful age of 49. Like his predecessor, he went to it with a will.

CHAPTER 15

EACH BEAUTIFUL SHIP FLYING A TREMENDOUS WHITE AUSTRALIAN NAVAL ENSIGN

The rain and southerly gales of the day had died away, but the evening of Sunday 31 May 1942 in Sydney was cloudy and unusually cold – no night to be outdoors, an unpleasant herald for the start of winter.

Things were rather more agreeable indoors at Tresco, a handsome stone and slate Italianate colonial mansion with magnificent views down the harbour from the shores of Elizabeth Bay, where a cheerful fire burnt in the drawing room and the dining table was set with fine china and the best silver. Tresco was the official residence of the Flag Officer in Charge, Sydney, Gerard Muirhead-Gould, an RN officer newly promoted to the rank of acting rear admiral and who, on this night, was giving a dinner party for friends and colleagues, among them the captain of *Chicago*, Howard Bode. Muirhead-Gould had been the British naval attaché in Berlin for three years before the war and an informant for Winston Churchill during his lean years out of office. He had once chatted privately with Hitler at a banquet in Berlin and would forever after tell of them discussing a Gary Cooper film the Führer had enjoyed, *The Lives of a Bengal Lancer*.[1]

The evening began with that favourite wardroom tipple, pink gin, but history does not record the food, perhaps for good reason.

A month before, Mrs Grace Muirhead-Gould, a woman at the dreadnought end of the spectrum of admirals' wives, had clashed with her chef, Petty Officer Cook Spencer Selsby, who chased her from his kitchen bellowing and brandishing a carving knife. This gross act of mutiny with violence was hushed up and Selsby was hurriedly packed off for a pier-head jump[2] to the officers' galley in *Australia*, where, as Malcolm Stening gleefully reported, 'we had PO Cook Tregidgo, an expert with soups, but otherwise his presentation of tinned food was uninteresting. With the advent of PO Cook Selsby, the meals became more imaginative.'[3]

Dinner was interrupted shortly after 10 pm by some confused messages about an unidentified object in the harbour that might, perhaps, be a submarine. Muirhead-Gould was doubtful, even dismissive, but at 10.27 pm he put out an order requiring warships in the harbour to take anti-submarine precautions, and he repeated that order a little more firmly at 10.36. A minute later, there was a thumping explosion out towards the Heads. Then, at 10.53, *Chicago*, moored within sight of Tresco, opened fire with her pom-pom guns and a 5-inch. To add to the din, just after 11 pm there were six more explosions: the unmistakeable whooping sound of depth charges detonating. Sydney was under attack from three Japanese midget submarines.

Very few people come out of this affair with any credit. On the Allied side, complacency ruled. The Japanese had actually made two daring reconnaissance flights over Sydney Harbour before the attack, with Yokosuka E14Y seaplanes (codenamed 'Glen' by the Allies) launched from giant I class submarines over the horizon off the New South Wales coast.[4] The last flight had been just before dawn on 29 May, with the Glen wheeling slowly back and forth over the fully lit harbour – its navigation lights switched on – while its crew of two checked out the targets below. At one stage, it had flown as low as 160 feet (50 metres), within a stone's throw of *Chicago*, where the watch spotted it but did nothing. It was also seen several times by navy and army observers on the ground and tracked for some distance, but everyone blithely assumed it must be American. The Glen returned to its mother submarine and reported that the harbour bristled with valuable prey, including an American battleship.

This was more exaggeration by an inexperienced aircrew, but there were still plenty of targets to attack, big and small. Newly out of her refit, *Canberra* was swinging off the No. 1 Naval Buoy at the entrance to Farm Cove, a pistol shot from where the Opera House now stands. *Chicago* was on the No. 2 buoy to the east of the Garden Island Naval Base. The old light cruiser *Adelaide* was alongside Garden Island itself, the big armed merchant cruisers *Kanimbla* and *Westralia* were moored off the North Shore below Neutral Bay and Taronga Zoo, and a scattering of destroyers, corvettes, minesweepers and two submarines, one Dutch and one Free French, lay here and there. *Australia* and *Hobart* were still in Brisbane.

On the night of the attack itself, confusion piled upon error, with an added dash of still more complacency. The first midget sub to enter the harbour, *M-14*, managed to back herself into a boom net near the entrance off Watsons Bay and lay stuck there, only partly submerged, where she was seen at about 8.15 pm by one Jimmy Cargill, a nightwatchman in a rowing boat. He had trouble convincing anybody that he had found a submarine. It was almost ten o'clock before navy channel patrol boats were sent to investigate. One of them, *Lolita*, dropped two depth charges but they failed to explode. Trapped immovably, *M-14*'s crew destroyed themselves and their craft with scuttling charges at 10.37, the first explosion to disturb the admiral's dinner.

After this, Muirhead-Gould suspected that something rather unpleasant was happening, but he kept the harbour lights burning and ordered that the ferries should keep running because, as he later put it in his report, 'the more boats that were moving about at high speed the better chance of keeping the submarines down till daylight'. It was a foolish decision. The harbour lights stayed lit until well after eleven o'clock. At Garden Island, where work was going around the clock to build a great new dry dock, the lights there were ablaze until much later, a gift for a submariner peering through a periscope.

The second midget, *M-24*, followed a Manly ferry into the harbour and was eventually spotted by a searchlight operator on *Chicago*. This was when she opened fire, but with no luck. *M-24* vanished again. The third submarine, *M-21*, arrived at about this time and was seen on the surface by a patrol vessel, HMAS *Yandra*, which at first tried to ram the boat and struck her a glancing blow, and then dropped the six depth charges that finally convinced Muirhead-Gould to leave the table. Barely damaged, *M-21* waited on the bottom for things to calm down and then apparently headed out to sea again.

By this time, most of Sydney was thoroughly awake and thoroughly alarmed. Lights were going on in homes all over the foreshore suburbs and beyond. Patrol boats criss-crossed the harbour waters. Signals, messages and phone calls were pouring in to the Port War Signal Station at South Head and to naval head-quarters, jamming the system. Sailors on leave ashore began to hurry back to their ships, among them young Russell Keats, the quiet musician from *Canberra* who was staying at his parents' home in Mosman with a shipmate. Russell had recognised *Chicago*'s guns when they opened fire and decided they had better return. His father, Horace, walked them to a tram stop and farewelled them.

For all the uproar, two of the most senior naval officers in Sydney still had their doubts. The official report states that Howard Bode hurried from the admiral's party at 10.20, saying he would take *Chicago* to sea with one of the American destroy-ers. But, for reasons never explained, he didn't make it back to the ship until an hour later, even though the cruiser was but five minutes by boat from Tresco. When he finally appeared, he berated his officers in his customary abusive style, accusing them of being drunk and incompetent and of firing at shadows, and then retreated to his cabin.

Muirhead-Gould finally sallied forth in his admiral's barge at around 11.30 and reached the boom net across the harbour mouth at midnight, where he boarded the channel patrol boat *Lolita* to ask what on earth was happening. This was a poor decision too. He should have sent a staff officer. An admiral's place was at his headquarters, in command at the centre of things, rather than wandering around the harbour in the dark and out of touch. *Lolita*'s crew would say later that he had been by turns belligerent, sarcastic and sceptical, demanding to know what they thought they had been playing at. He left half an hour later, still apparently unconvinced that a submarine had been seen.

In his superbly detailed account of the affair, the historian Peter Grose leaves the very clear impression that both Bode and Muirhead-Gould were – if not drunk – at least well affected by alcohol.[5]

The furious activity on the harbour continued. *Chicago*, *Canberra* and other ships as well were all trying to raise steam to put to sea as soon as possible, where they would not be sitting ducks. But on Garden Island, the floodlights on the graving dock building site were still ablaze, outlining *Chicago* in perfect silhouette for the commander of *M-24*, Sub Lieutenant Katsuhisa Ban, at periscope depth off Bradleys Head below Taronga Zoo.

Ban fired his first torpedo at 12.29 am and a second about a minute later. They both missed *Chicago*, the second one eventually running harmlessly ashore and failing to explode. The first passed beneath the Dutch submarine *K9* and the harbour ferry *Kuttabul*, which was tied up alongside Garden Island as a floating barracks for sailors. It hit the Garden Island sea wall and exploded, flinging the wooden *Kuttabul* into the air like a toy. Her back broken, the little ferry slid straight to the harbour floor with 21 sailors killed, 19 of them Australian and two British. With extraordinary courage, some of the survivors and other men who rushed to the scene dived into the black and wintry waters to rescue the wounded. As *The Sydney Morning Herald* reported:

> The explosion of the torpedo which sank the old ferry boat was heard by people a mile away. Although muffled, the explosion was sufficiently violent to shake thousands of houses and blocks of flats along the water-front.
>
> Picture-frames fell from mantelpieces. Ornaments toppled from bookshelves, and crockery rattled in the kitchens.

Hundreds of people thought there was an air raid, and hurriedly dressed, but their fears were allayed when no further explosions of the same violence occurred.

There was much speculation as to whether the reverberation was caused by an earthquake. Most people, however, contented their minds with the thought that heavy blasting was in progress. Few guessed the real explanation.[6]

It was not until 1.10 that morning that Muirhead-Gould finally put out a general signal explaining – at least partly – what had happened: 'Enemy submarine is present in the harbour and *Kuttabul* has been torpedoed.'[7]

The rest of the story can be told simply. The harbour erupted in a fury of activity. Searchlights stabbed the waters. Gunfire thumped and rattled, with the glow of tracer bullets streaking here and there, and flares from Verey pistols lighting the sky. Harbour defence vessels searched and found nothing. Amid all the uproar, *M-24* slipped out through the Heads and disappeared to history – until 2006, when a group of amateur scuba divers discovered her lying upright on the sea bed some five kilometres off Bungan Head on Sydney's Northern Beaches, at a depth of about 55 metres. She is now a protected war grave.

Chicago got to sea at around three in the morning and reported sighting a periscope passing her on the way back in. Howard Bode, at last, was convinced that enemy submarines had been at work. The periscope belonged to *M-21*, which was boldly returning for another attack she never got to make. Her torpedoes had jammed in their tubes and, after being depth charged herself, she sank to the bottom of Taylors Bay to the east of the zoo. Her commander, Lieutenant Keiu Matsuo, shot his companion, Petty Officer Masao Tsuzuku, in the back of the head and then killed himself. When divers eventually found them, the sub's propellers were still turning.

Canberra, too, had been raising steam to go to sea, and she managed to use her engines to swing on her buoy and point her head to make the smallest possible silhouette against the shore lights. At around 4.40 am, she signalled she had seen the bubbles of a torpedo track going past her, but this seems to have been a spectre of someone's imagination. She eventually sailed later that morning to join Task Force 44 in Brisbane, as planned. Horace Keats watched from Mosman as she carried his son Russell down the harbour and away. He would never see the boy again.

Censorship was clamped down. The Monday-afternoon newspapers were not permitted to report a word, and the morning papers of Tuesday 2 June were given a carefully constructed official version of events, including this bland communiqué from MacArthur's headquarters:

> In an attempted submarine raid on Sydney three enemy midget submarines are believed to have been destroyed, one by gunfire, two by depth charges.
>
> The enemy's attack was completely unsuccessful. Damage was confined to one small harbour vessel of no military value.[8]

It was a cold epitaph for the *Kuttabul* and the 21 killed aboard her. Three weeks later, Muirhead-Gould filed his official report, a document that carefully played down his blunders and emphasised those of others. In truth, luck alone had prevented a great naval disaster, the fortunes of war favouring the undeserving defenders and playing hard against the enemy.

There was a postscript a week later, just after midnight on Monday 8 June, when two of the I class submarines shelled Sydney's Eastern Suburbs and Newcastle Harbour, causing minor damage to bricks and mortar. No one was killed. As in the midget-submarine attack, Japan had scored a propaganda victory but little else.

—

As Sydney sighed with relief and returned to its normal wartime self that first week of June, huge forces were massing far to the north. Great events were playing a tremendous crescendo that would conclude in arguably the most decisive and crushing victory in the long history of war at sea.

The Battle of Midway, fought from 4 June to 7 June, was an American naval triumph that ensured the eventual destruction of the Empire of Japan. The fine and fascinating details of the battle are beyond the scope of this book, for no Australian ship was there, but an outline is important, for this American success at Midway led to other conflicts that drew Australians in. It left the IJN down, and very much so. But not out.

As we saw in Chapter 13, Admiral Yamamoto, the IJN Commander-in-Chief, believed his best hope lay in bringing the United States Pacific Fleet to a climactic defeat from which it could never recover. This would be centred on the coral atoll of Midway, lying in the northern hemisphere equidistant from Asia and the United States, where there was a small American garrison with an airfield for bomber squadrons and an advanced submarine base. For Yamamoto, Port Moresby and the Coral Sea Battle – Operation MO – had been a secondary affair, almost a distraction. Operation MI, the clash at Midway, would be the main event. The island would be attacked. The Americans would rush to defend it and be lured into a lethal trap.

The Americans struck the first blow, silently and unseen. Able to decrypt a great deal if not all of the Japanese naval code JN-25, they were aware by mid-May 1942 that a big offensive was in the planning. The question was where. The Japanese messages they were getting at Nimitz's headquarters in Hawaii constantly referred to an objective designated 'AF'. Some intelligence officers began to suspect it might actually mean Midway. To confirm it, they devised a simple but stunning trick.

The American commander on Midway was instructed – by a secure undersea telephone cable – to radio a signal in plain English reporting that the island's fresh water supplies were dangerously low. He did. A day later, the listening Americans heard the Japanese report that AF was short of water. Chester Nimitz now knew where his battle would be, and he made his moves to outwit Yamamoto and turn the trap upon him.[9]

As ever, the Japanese plan was highly complex. A significant force would feint towards the Aleutian Islands south-west of

Alaska – Operation AO – to lure the Americans there. The main Japanese force would then crush Midway and wait for the enemy to rush south again and into the trap.

Nimitz did not fall for it. But even with the intelligence he had, he was still taking a daring gamble. There were but three aircraft carriers available to him: the hastily repaired *Yorktown* in Task Force 17, with Frank Jack Fletcher still in command, and *Enterprise* and *Hornet* from Task Force 16, which – with Bull Halsey ill in hospital – was led by Rear Admiral Raymond A. Spruance. Nimitz had no battleships, none at all, and much smaller numbers of cruisers and destroyers than the Japanese could range against him. Yamamoto, on the other hand, could throw in four large fleet carriers and five lighter carriers, with, if he chose, up to 11 battleships. It was an American David against a Japanese Goliath.

David prevailed. Another American intelligence coup delivered the Japanese starting date, 3 June, and Nimitz was able to get his forces into position. The Japanese could not read the American naval codes and had no useful idea of the strength arrayed against them, let alone that an ambush awaited.

After some preliminary skirmishing, battle was joined on Thursday 4 June. Land-based bombers from Midway attacked the Japanese first, followed up by the dive bombers and torpedo bombers of the two American carrier task forces, flying in wave after wave. The enemy hit back fiercely, but by mid-morning the Americans held the upper hand, the Japanese reeling beneath the onslaught. Luck again played its fickle part, alighting on the shoulders of Lieutenant Commander Wade McClusky, *Enterprise*'s air group commander. Low on fuel and with no target in sight, McClusky on a hunch decided to follow a Japanese destroyer steaming north at full speed. This led him and his squadron of SBD Dauntless dive bombers to the Japanese carriers, which they caught with aircraft, fuel lines and munitions strewn across their decks, vulnerable and helpless. They burnt like torches.

There had never been a sea battle like this. Coral Sea was a prelude but this was the tumultuous symphony itself, a violent clash of ships and aircraft on an epic scale. When it was over, the carriers *Akagi*, *Soryu*, *Kaga* and *Hiryu* lay at the bottom of the Pacific along with a cruiser and several destroyers, and 3057 Japanese sailors and airmen were dead. The Americans had lost just one carrier. Bombed and torpedoed from the air on the first day of the fight, and then torpedoed again by a submarine the next day, the veteran *Yorktown* finally rolled over to port, turned upside down and then sank, stern first, early on the morning of 7 June, 'with all battle flags flying', as Captain Buckmaster reported to Nimitz. A destroyer was also sunk, and 307 American sailors and airmen died.

Frank Jack Fletcher had been in overall command at Midway, and the victory was his to claim, but it was generally acknowledged that the brilliant tactical performance of his junior, Ray Spruance, had sealed the triumph beyond doubt. And once again, the Japanese had faltered, curiously unwilling to deliver the killer blow. With hindsight, it is inexplicable that Yamamoto did not deploy his battleships. The appearance of even one, the leviathan *Yamato*, would almost certainly have tipped the battle his way, enabling him to go on to take Hawaii at will and leaving him master of the Pacific. But he failed. Just six months after Pearl Harbor, the seemingly invincible IJN had been dealt a grinding defeat. It would take time, but the empire was doomed.

—

The Thurlow brothers were inseparable. Jim was the elder, born in 1921. Young Tom came along in 1923. With their younger sister Dorothy, they grew up first in the Melbourne suburb of Brunswick and then at Belmont in Geelong, a tight-knit, loving family.

Life was hard, fraught with the disappointments and humiliations that ground away at the poor and needy. Their mother, Margaret, was a miner's daughter. Their father, Tom senior, had fought in the trenches of France with the New Zealand Army's Canterbury Regiment in the First World War before emigrating to Melbourne, where he owned and drove a taxi for a while. The Depression broke him and he counted himself lucky to find a job he had once sworn he would never do: working as a dunny man, carting and emptying the household toilet pans for the Geelong Waterworks and Sewerage Trust. Much later, Tom junior would recall:

> In the lean times, Mum used to clean houses, do washing and ironing etc, to help Dad keep food on the table. I have seen my Mum and Dad cry at Christmas because they couldn't buy us presents. Good years we would get an orange and a pair of canvas tennis shoes. Some charities were good to the unemployed and on occasions we benefitted.[10]

Yet life in Geelong had its pleasures for active kids. Far better than the streets of Brunswick, there was space to run and swim, or to go chasing rabbits, collecting birds' eggs, or fishing. They loved nothing better than mucking around on the Barwon River. Young Tom saved his pennies and bought himself a single-shot .22 rifle for the princely sum of 30 shillings, which got him and his dog Roy seriously into the rabbit business and paid for itself many times over. Like most boys of the time, they were good with their hands, at making something from nothing. A clapped-out pram provided the wheels for a billy cart, a contraption held together by nails they nicked from fences. Both boys had chores to do, feeding the chooks and chopping wood for the kitchen stove and the open fireplaces that warmed their small cottage in the winter. School was first the Belmont Primary School, a few blocks away from the Barwon, and then Geelong Junior Technical School, where both boys did well at their studies and Tom topped his class one year on the promise of getting a bicycle.

Holidays were the best. For years, the Thurlows would visit Myrtlevale Farm in the exquisitely lovely hills and dales of the Pennyroyal Valley on the Barwon Downs, staying for the raspberry season, when they earned their keep and 7/6 a week for picking the fruit. On Saturdays, it would be off to Lorne on the Great Ocean Road, to splash sixpence of their wages on ice cream and forbidden cigarettes.

The boys' father had dreams of his two sons going to university, a goal well within their academic reach. Instead, they left school at the age of 15, with first Jim and then Tom getting jobs at Henderson's Federal Spring Works in North Melbourne, boarding with friends while they studied by night at Melbourne Tech. Tom did fitting and turning, and Jim was a welder. At weekends, they would pedal their bicycles on the long road home to Geelong, until Jim bought himself a battered old Indian Scout motorbike for next to nothing.

The war ended all this. One of the neighbours at Bailey Street in Belmont was a bloke named Fred Cusworth, who had been in the RAN in the 1920s, a knockabout able seaman in some of the old cruisers. Fred had made a name as a navy boxing champion, and he would occasionally take the boys shooting, spinning enthralling yarns of a life at sea. It seemed the natural thing to follow that up, and on Tuesday 21 May 1940 they enlisted with consecutive service numbers. Jim was 24364 and Tom, a year and a half younger, was 24365. Together, they went through their basic training at Flinders; together, they were spotted as bright lads with a future; together, they were rated as Ordinary Signalmen on 1 June 1941.

The next month, again on the same day, they were posted to the armed merchant cruiser HMAS *Manoora*, in which they served until that November. Still inseparable, they joined *Canberra* on Sunday 23 November 1941. Funnily enough, Fred Cusworth re-enlisted for the war and turned up in *Canberra* himself, shipmate instead of neighbour. There are photos of the Thurlow boys at the time: two bright-eyed, handsome men on the edge of adulthood, both with their caps cocked askew, both smiling for the camera, Tom standing slightly taller than Jim. Together.

—

For the last weeks of June and the first weeks of July, the new commander of Task Force 44, Victor Crutchley, put his ships through their paces off Queensland in the Coral Sea. He had to get to know them, they had to get to know him, and there was no time to waste, for the admiral had no experience working with Australians or Americans, nor of conditions in the Pacific. And

Task Force 44 had grown bigger, too. There were now the three Australian cruisers: *Australia*, which Crutchley chose for his flag; plus *Canberra*, fresh from her refit; and the ever reliable *Hobart*. The American contingent had been beefed up as well, with the two heavy cruisers *Chicago* and *Salt Lake City* – known for her ungainly silhouette as Old Swayback, or sometimes the Swayback Maru – and three destroyers, *Patterson*, *Ralph Talbot* and *Jarvis*. It was a useful force but it had to be bonded into a team, and quickly.

And *Canberra* had a new captain, in his first true cruiser command. Frank Edmund Getting, born in the Sydney beach suburb of Manly, had been in that first entry to the RANC, a contemporary of Collins, Farncomb, Waller and Burnett. Muscular and nuggetty, he had won his colours for rugby and rowing at the college, and later in his career he attained some renown as a man who knew his way around a boxing ring. Professionally, he had made a mark by becoming the first RAN officer to qualify as a submarine commander and to actually captain one, HMAS *Oxley*, which he took over as a lieutenant in 1928. That cannot have been a happy time. *Oxley* and her sister boat *Otway*, which were never particularly reliable, cost a fortune to maintain, and with the Depression they were handed back to the British with more than a sigh of relief.[11]

Frank Getting remained on the surface after that, in a conventional if unspectacular career. At the outbreak of war with Germany, he had actually been *Canberra*'s executive officer, so he certainly knew his way around the ship. After that, there had been a spell as captain of the armed merchant cruiser *Kanimbla*, and then just over a year ashore in Melbourne as Deputy Chief of the Naval Staff. He took command of *Canberra* in Brisbane on 17 June, his fourth wedding anniversary.

Getting, too, had to settle in. And while many of his officers and senior petty officers had been in the ship for a while, some of them from well before the war, there was new blood as well. A lot of youngsters in the ship's company were fresh from training at Flinders and had never been to sea. Others, such as the young midshipman from Sydney Bruce Loxton, were also finding their way. Mac Gregory, who had been a snotty in *Australia* at the start of the war, had returned from training in Britain and was now a fully fledged sub lieutenant and watch-keeper. But a long period in refit takes the edge off a ship, and *Canberra* and her crew had to be fully worked up to combat readiness in a hurry.

For what seemed like endless hours of endless days, in heavy heat, the men found themselves jumping to some sudden new order from the bridge: to fend off an imaginary air attack, to fight an imaginary fire on the quarterdeck, to deal with an imaginary explosion in a boiler room. *Canberra* now had radar, too, a Type 271 set for surface work, and an A290 air warning system, complete with a technical expert to get the system running: David Medley, a bright young physicist with a masters degree from Sydney University, who had been hurriedly commissioned as an RANVR sub lieutenant. Medley was one of the few people in Australia at that time who knew how radar worked and what it could do, but he was treated in the wardroom as a harmless boffin who was clueless about naval warfare, and he was largely ignored. After the war, he would write to Mac Gregory:

> I have never forgotten the short time I served on *Canberra* and have been haunted throughout the years about what I could or should have done to make the more senior officers aware of the capabilities of the radar equipment on board . . . I constantly remind myself that in those days an RANVR sub lieutenant, wet behind the ears, was regarded as the lowest form of animal life and not to be taken seriously. I doubt that Capt Getting even knew that I existed. He certainly never exhibited the slightest interest in the radar installations.[12]

Nobody had even thought to install any form of communication between the radar office and the bridge, not by telephone nor by voice pipe. Medley was allowed to fiddle away in his own little world, an unsung prophet.

Russell Keats, working the middle watch – midnight to 4 am – in the plot, which kept track of the ship's movements, was feeling the strain, as he wrote to his parents:

The Plotting Staff, of late, amongst its many other responsibilities and attributes, has now been turned into a squad of walking
chronometers. Every few minutes, according to the ship's
zig-zag, we have to yell to the bridge the time and alteration
of course to be made. Would drive you crazy. Every half dozen
words I write I have to glance at the clock to check how the
time's going. Lord only knows what will be piled on our heads
next. In some ways I'm very happy on this ship, but in others
I'd give ten years of my life to get off it.[13]

Far above and beyond the heads of young Russell and his shipmates, yet another act in the drama of their lives was being
written for them. Though stunned by their defeat at Midway,
the Japanese had by no means given up the aggressive drive to
consolidate the perimeters of their empire in the South-West
Pacific. Aware of the growing threat posed by MacArthur's
build-up in Australia, they resolved to strengthen their position
in New Guinea and the Solomon Islands, and, eventually, to
reach as far as the New Hebrides, the Fiji Islands and Samoa.
Rabaul would be expanded as a pivotal air and naval base, with
a chain of lesser airfields in New Guinea, and Port Moresby
remained to be taken. Another major airfield would be built in
the Solomons, where they still held Tulagi. With the IJN still
bleeding from the loss of four carriers, the admirals in Tokyo
were at angry loggerheads with the army about how best to
achieve all this, but they patched together an agreement to seize
the tail of New Guinea.

On 21 July, two transports and an escort of destroyers landed
some 2000 troops between the little settlements of Buna and
Gona on the upper coast of the tail. Then they thrust into the
foothills of the Owen Stanley Ranges, and by 29 July – after a
scrambling Australian defence that was as brave as it was futile –
they had taken Kokoda itself, some 400 metres above sea level.

There would also be a new Japanese commander at Rabaul.
Vice Admiral Inoue, who had faltered at Coral Sea, was relieved
of his command there and ordered back to Japan to take charge of
the naval academy. His place was taken by Vice Admiral Gunichi

Mikawa, a veteran of both Pearl Harbor and Midway, who was now given command of the IJN's 8th Fleet, made up of the fast and powerful heavy cruiser *Chokai* and an impressive force of six other heavy and light cruisers, and four destroyers. On 30 July, the fleet dropped anchor in Simpson Harbour beneath Rabaul's smoking twin volcanoes, where, as his Chief of Staff, Captain Toshikazu Ohmae, recorded, 'Vice Admiral Mikawa moved ashore that same day, and his flag was raised above a ramshackle building near the Second Air Group billets. The modest, indeed humble, quarters lacked even toilet facilities, but Admiral Mikawa was not discouraged . . .'[14]

The admiral had two main challenges. The first was to crush the Australians in New Guinea by pushing the army up along the Kokoda Track and over the Owen Stanleys to Port Moresby, and by resurrecting the plan for an invasion by sea. Milne Bay in the south-east would also have to be taken. Mikawa's second headache was to get on with building an airfield on the island of Guadalcanal in the Solomons, a task made increasingly difficult by regular Allied bombing. Undaunted, he set to.

The Americans were stirring too, urged and driven to action by one of the more controversial figures of the war, the brilliant but deeply flawed Admiral Ernest J. King, who combined in one volatile, abrasive person the posts of USN Commander-in-Chief and Chief of Naval Operations. King was an extraordinary figure. One of his daughters reputedly said that he was the most even-tempered man she knew: always in a rage. President Roosevelt once quipped that he shaved every morning with a blowtorch. All of Washington knew him as a hard-driving, even merciless boss, a heavy drinker and an enthusiastic party-goer.

King was also notoriously anti-British, supposedly the result of some unpleasant but unspecified encounters with the RN in the First World War and a loathing he nursed ever after, one that cost his country untold thousands of lives and untold hundreds of millions of dollars. When the United States entered the war in 1941, the British advised him to organise commercial shipping along the American East Coast into convoys for protection against U-boats, but King, believing he knew better, refused to listen. The *Kriegsmarine* seized the opportunity with relish; packs of U-boats ranged along the Atlantic seaboard sinking lone ships at will. Over the first seven months of 1942, they destroyed some three million tonnes of shipping, for the loss of only 22 U-boats, until King finally relented and set up a convoy system.

His Pacific strategy was rather better directed. While remaining obedient to the agreement between Roosevelt and Churchill that Germany should be beaten first, King and the rest of the USN had Pearl Harbor to avenge, and they meant to do so. From Australia, Douglas MacArthur kept putting up plans and schemes for a Pacific offensive under his command, but King successfully convinced the Joint Chiefs of Staff in Washington that it would have to be a navy operation at the overall direction of Nimitz in Hawaii. Now was the time to build on the successes of Coral Sea and Midway, to catch the enemy off guard and grasp the initiative.

Thus was Operation Watchtower born. On 2 July, the Joint Chiefs issued a directive that would shape the course of the war in the South Pacific for the next year and a half. The primary objective of Watchtower would be to seize Guadalcanal from the Japanese as a springboard for retaking the rest of the Solomons and New Guinea and, eventually, Rabaul. A newly appointed Commander South Pacific Force, Vice Admiral Robert L. Ghormley – one link down the chain from Nimitz – would have overall charge from the rapidly expanding American base at Noumea in New Caledonia.

Three days later, 5 July, the urgency escalated several notches: American air reconnaissance had discovered the Japanese airfield being built on the northern coast of Guadalcanal, on a promontory known as Lunga Point, across the strait from Tulagi. This was confirmed by detailed reports from coastwatchers hidden in the jungle, chief among them a Scottish-born former district officer named Martin Clemens, who was a key part of the network set up before the war. Deciding there was not a moment to lose, King pushed Watchtower forward, ordering it to begin on Saturday 1 August. Ghormley was dismayed. He and MacArthur – who would have to provide the air support – both protested that this was rushing things, that much more time was needed to get their ducks in a row, but King was obdurate. The date was set in concrete.

This would have to be an amphibious operation, with the navy carrying US Marines to storm ashore on Guadalcanal and Tulagi. It was a bold concept but fraught with uncertainties. Joint operations involving both naval and land forces were – and are – infinitely complex, posing special problems of command and control. Each service involved has to be aware of the capacities and limitations of the other. Admirals have to understand what generals require and can perform, and vice versa. The Japanese had managed it successfully in Malaya, the Philippines and the Netherlands East Indies, but the Allies had yet to try it in this war. There had been theorising and peacetime exercises, but the United States had not mounted an amphibious operation since the Spanish–American War of 1898. Now, they were about to attempt it on a grand scale. The forces began to gather: tens of thousands of men; 48 combat ships; some 670 aircraft, both land and carrier based; and 28 transports, supply vessels, oilers and the like.

The Allied Expeditionary Force was centred on the aircraft carriers *Saratoga*, *Enterprise* and *Wasp*, with the handsome new battleship *North Carolina* (known in the navy as The Show Boat) and a protective screen of six cruisers and 16 destroyers. It was led by Frank Jack Fletcher, who had been promoted to Vice Admiral after Midway. Fletcher would have tactical command in the battle space, answering up the chain to Ghormley in Noumea.

The amphibious force of transports would carry the troops and supplies for the landings, commanded by Rear Admiral Richmond Kelly Turner, who was subordinate to Fletcher. Kelly Turner (as he was known) would be backed up by the cruisers and destroyers of Task Force 44, with Rear Admiral Crutchley flying his flag in *Australia*. To confuse things, Task Force 44 was now redesignated Task Group 62.6. Crutchley would be second-in-command to Turner.

The 1st Division of the United States Marine Corps would actually do the landings, hitting the beaches under fire. In mid-July, the division was scattered here and there across the Pacific, around 19,000 men under the command of the newly appointed Major General Alexander Archer Vandegrift. Some were already in Samoa and New Caledonia; most were in transports heading for New Zealand. Vandegrift would have to bring them together and weld them into one.

Air support would come from bomber groups scattered around New Caledonia, Fiji and Samoa, commanded by Rear Admiral John S. McCain Snr,[15] and from airfields under MacArthur's overall command in Australia and New Guinea.

On paper – and in the reality of men, guns and steel – this was a mighty armada. But there were deep-cut flaws in Watchtower, some of which were chillingly obvious to the senior commanders in the beginning, and others that would be revealed over time.

General Vandegrift – Archer to his friends – was a son of rural Charlottesville at the foot of Virginia's Blue Ridge Mountains, and a man admired for his Southern courtesy and sunny optimism. He had been schooled in the military tradition by a grandfather who had fought for the Confederacy, had been wounded in the legendary Pickett's Charge at Gettysburg, and who prayed each night to 'the God of Abraham, Isaac, Jacob, Robert E. Lee and Stonewall Jackson'.[16]

Vandegrift had expected to have six months to knock his division into shape in New Zealand. He was stunned when a terse and harried Ghormley told him he would hit the Solomons in five weeks. Most of his Marines were kids fresh out of boot camp, and the ships that had carried him to New Zealand were not combat loaded, meaning that he might well arrive under fire on a hostile shore and find himself unpacking typewriters, tents and mosquito nets when he urgently needed guns, ammunition and medical supplies. More critical still – as Vandegrift admitted in his memoirs – he did not then know even where Guadalcanal was, and he had no idea of the terrain he would have to fight on, of the weather he could expect, nor the strength and dispositions of the enemy he would confront. Every ounce of his renowned optimism would be required.

He set his intelligence officers to compile as much information as they could – and there again the coastwatchers were invaluable – but the reloading of his transports would be harder. First, there were not enough ships to carry everything he needed; a lot would have to be left behind. Second, unaware of any urgency and to the amazed dismay of the Americans, the waterside workers in Wellington plodded along at a peacetime pace, taking long tea breaks, lunch breaks and smokos. Vandegrift eventually got his Marines unloading and repacking the ships themselves, which caused a major diplomatic and industrial crisis in Wellington, but he had no choice.

After intense haggling up through Nimitz to Washington and back, Admiral Ghormley managed to get the invasion date postponed a week to 7 August, but beyond that Admiral King would not move. It was not much, but it was something. It would give the amphibious force and the Marines themselves a chance for a dress rehearsal to be held on the small Fijian Island of Koro, roughly halfway between New Zealand and the Solomons.

Victor Crutchley sailed *Australia* and the rest of his force from Brisbane on 14 July, the Australian ships newly stripped of their impressive but futile camouflage patterns and painted an overall dark grey like the American ships. The weather on the way to Wellington was filthy, and *Australia* sprang a leak in the fo'c'sle that required pumps to keep the water down, but they made New Zealand without any other mishap and joined Kelly Turner's invasion force, an awe-inspiring sight. It was still more inspiring on 26 July when this force rendezvoused mid-ocean south-west of Fiji with Fletcher's carrier covering force, ships stretching as far as the eye could see and beyond. Two days later, the entire fleet was in the midst of the Fiji Islands for refuelling and rehearsals, operating under the most strict radio silence.

At this point, the deep divisions within Watchtower began to emerge. Disturbed by the headlong rush to pull the invasion together, Vandegrift's Marines and some of the navy people were already making wry jokes about 'Operation Shoestring'. It was about to get worse. That afternoon, Fletcher summoned his senior commanders (but not Crutchley) to a conference in his spacious stateroom on board *Saratoga*, where he delivered some news that shocked them to the core: he had no faith that Watchtower would work. In Vandegrift's words:

> Fletcher received us in the wardroom. I had never met him. He was a distinguished-looking man but seemed nervous and tired, probably the result of the recent battles of Coral Sea and Midway. To my surprise he appeared to lack knowledge of or interest in the forthcoming operation. He quickly let us know he did not think it would succeed. To his arbitrary objections, expressed forcefully, we replied as best we could, but obviously failed to make any impression.[17]

The unravelling had begun, and seriously so. This vital conference should have been held by Vice Admiral Ghormley, the overall operational commander of Watchtower. But he had already expressed his doubts and now, virtually washing his hands of the whole thing, he had elected to stay nearly 1600 kilometres away in Noumea, sending only a junior rear admiral to represent him. Fletcher's similar lack of confidence, and his lack of interest and detailed knowledge, was another blow.

Then it got worse again. Fletcher asked Kelly Turner how long it would take to land the Marines, with their equipment. When Turner answered that he would need at least five days, Fletcher stunned the meeting by saying that he planned to leave after two days; he would not subject his carriers to the risk of Japanese air attack for any longer.

Accounts of this conference vary. Fletcher's few post-war supporters claim that it was calm and reasoned. Others say it erupted in acrimony, which seems more likely. Kelly Turner – nicknamed 'Terrible' Turner for his fiery Irish temper and a reputation for know-all arrogance – protested angrily that he could not get his job done in two days and virtually accused Fletcher of planning to cut and run, leaving him nakedly exposed to Japanese bombers. Turner's Chief of Staff, Captain Tom Peyton, recalled the conference as 'one long, bitter argument ... I was amazed and disturbed by the way these two admirals talked to each other. I had never heard anything like it.'[18]

Vandegrift, too, was furious:

> My Dutch blood was beginning to boil, but I forced myself to remain calm while explaining to Fletcher that the days of 'landing a small force and leaving' were over. This operation was supposed to take and hold Guadalcanal and Tulagi. To accomplish this I commanded a heavily reinforced division which I was to land on enemy-held territory, which meant a fight. I could hardly expect to land this massive force without air cover – even the five days mentioned by Turner involved a tremendous risk.[19]

Pressed hard, Fletcher agreed to stay on for three days instead of two and then closed the conference. That was it. The normally mild-mannered Vandegrift left in a temper, by his own admission. One report has it that Turner turned on Fletcher after the meeting and snarled at him, 'You son of a bitch, if you do that you are yellow.'[20] Vandegrift's Chief of Staff, Marine Lieutenant Colonel Merrill 'Bill' Twining, summed it up best:

> The stage was rapidly being set up with all the props needed for a first-class disaster ... His [Fletcher's] somewhat brutal conduct of the *Saratoga* conference was totally incorrect from every point of view, and that damage was compounded by Ghormley's flagrant evasion of his plain duty to be present at and conduct the *Saratoga* conference in person.[21]

For the next few days, the forces threw themselves into rehearsals, with varying success. The Marines scrambled down cargo nets into the boats and headed for the Fijian beaches, only to find that hidden coral reefs blocked their way and they could not land. But it did give both Turner and Vandegrift the chance to shake out some of the rust and wrinkles. The skies above were black with Fletcher's aircraft, and Crutchley's cruisers and destroyers turned on a virtuoso performance in dummy runs at shore bombardment. Bill Twining (who much later would command the 1st Marine Division in Korea) wrote:

> I will never forget the Australian cruiser squadron, *Australia*, *Canberra*, and *Hobart*. They made the last firing run of the day, each beautiful ship flying a tremendous white Australian naval ensign from the mainmast, flags at least four times the size of our largest. These firing ships were accompanied by their single spotter plane, an ancient Walrus biplane, a relic of World War I.[22] The old string-bag strutted proudly along at its top speed of about eighty knots. The ships' gunnery was excellent. I wondered if they would fly the big ensigns again on D day; they didn't, but the Walrus came close to being a victim of friendly fire.[23]

Another, very much more amiable conference was held in *Australia* on the morning of 29 July, with Turner and Vandegrift outlining their plans for the landing and the role expected of the cruisers and destroyers. Crutchley was cautiously reluctant to be Turner's number two, writing to him:

> I am very honoured to hear that you are contemplating nomi-nating me as Second-in-Command of what amounts to a very considerable United States Expeditionary Force. I must say that I doubt the propriety or wisdom of this suggestion. It is mainly a U.S. Force and you have another U.S. Flag Officer on the scene. I have not yet been able to ascertain his seniority, we are both too junior to appear in our respective Navy lists . . . I feel that as long as there is a U.S. Flag Officer present, he should be in charge.[24]

Turner insisted, and Crutchley succumbed. He would be in command of a protective screen, to shepherd the troop trans-ports and cargo ships to their assigned positions, to keep enemy heads down as much as possible by bombarding the beaches, and to see the empty ships safely out of harm's way when their jobs were done. He would have to take into account the possibility of attack by air, by a surface force, or by submarine. It was a heavy responsibility and a daunting one to discharge, not least because Crutchley had never had the opportunity to meet or assess most of the American cruiser or destroyer captains under his command, to seek their comments and suggestions, or to give them his orders in person. He had never been placed in charge of such a large Australian–American force before; it is no criticism of him to say that he was finding his way in a novel and challenging arena.

The capacities of his ships were another question: most had radar, but of varying quality. Some of the Americans had the relatively new TBS system, which stood for 'talk between ships', a short-range-radio set-up that allowed captains and officers of the watch to chat to other nearby ships in plain language, as if they were on a telephone. But none of the Australians had TBS and nor did the USS *Chicago*, so their communications would have to be done the old way, by light or radioed Morse. These were added, unavoidable layers of complexity. But Crutchley laid his plans and prepared his dispositions in considerable detail, for both day and night action, and had them approved by Turner and distributed to the vessels under his command.

The fleet sailed from Fiji again on 31 July, steaming slowly north-west towards the Solomons beneath heavy cumulus cloud and through a sea haze that, pleasingly, lessened the chance of being observed by any wandering Japanese reconnaissance patrols. By the late afternoon of Thursday 6 August – and undiscovered by the enemy – ships and men were in their positions for their great enterprise to begin, the war's first Allied counter-offensive against Japan.

CHAPTER 16

FOR SO APPEARS THIS FLEET MAJESTICAL

The Solomon Islands lie to the east of New Guinea and some 2000 kilometres to the north-east of Brisbane, on an axis that runs north-west to south-east. Guadalcanal, the principal island, is in the south-east, and almost entirely covered in dense tropical rainforest, a near impenetrable jungle that climbs the high mountain peaks of the interior.

To the north of Guadalcanal there is Florida Island, some 45 kilometres across a strait that history now knows as Ironbottom Sound, an epitaph for the ships that lie there in a graveyard on the sea floor. Tulagi, a very much smaller island only five kilometres long and a kilometre wide, is tucked in close below the southern shore of Florida.

The Allied invasion force of August 1942 made its approach from the west, passing the towering but extinct volcanic cone of Savo Island, which stands in the middle of the entrance to the sound like a stopper released from a bottle. Kelly Turner had divided his ships for a two-pronged attack. Group Yoke would swing around to the north of Savo and then haul east to hit Tulagi and another still smaller island nearby, Tanambogo. Yoke would be escorted by *Canberra* and *Chicago* and another cruiser, the USS *San Juan*, backed up by six destroyers and five minesweepers.

Passing to the south of Savo to descend on Guadalcanal, the larger Group X-Ray was led by *Australia*, with *Hobart* and the American cruisers *Astoria*, *Quincy* and *Vincennes*, and nine destroyers. Turner and Vandegrift were in the amphibious-force flagship, the 9000-tonne attack transport USS *McCawley*, which was with Group X-Ray.

Fletcher's carrier force would not enter the confined waters of the sound but would prowl in the open sea some 40 kilometres to the west of Guadalcanal, which would place its fighters and bombers within 70–90 kilometres of the landing zones. At around sunset, Turner put out a stirring call to arms:

PUBLISH TO ALL HANDS:
On August seventh, this Force will recapture Tulagi and Guadalcanal Islands, which are now in the hands of the enemy.

In this first step forward toward clearing the Japanese out of conquered territory, we have strong support from the Pacific Fleet, and from the air, surface and submarine forces in the South Pacific and Australia.

It is significant of victory that we see here shoulder to shoulder, the U.S. Navy, Marines and Army, and the Australian and New Zealand Air, Naval and Army Services.

I have confidence that all elements of this armada will, in skill and courage, show themselves fit comrades of those brave men who already have dealt the enemy mighty blows for our great cause.
God bless you all.

R. K. Turner, Rear Admiral, U.S. Navy, Commanding[1]

So the scene was set.

—

In *Australia*, men were sleeping at their posts in the first degree of readiness, bodies curled up on a hard, unyielding deck, sprawled on a locker, or slumped in the seats of a gun house. For those on watch on the upper decks, it was a night of brilliant beauty lit by the infinite stars and a thin crescent moon, with a pervading calm broken only by the low rumble of the engines and the occasional hiss of the bow wave breaking in a calm sea. A light breeze was blowing, cool after the heat of the day.

In *Canberra*, the scene was similar, although perhaps with an added chill of uncertain, sleepless anticipation for – unlike the men of *Australia* – most of her ship's company had never seen action. Midshipman Bruce Loxton, 18 years old, had written tenderly and passionately to his girlfriend Dahlis at home in Sydney:

> Did I tell you how much I miss you? No? Well it's about time I did, I think. Every time that I have left you so far the desire to see you has got worse . . . I'd give anything just for the pleasure of seeing you, of being with you and hearing you talk. I want to take you places, to Prince's, to the pictures. I'd like to go for a walk, in fact anything so long as you were involved . . . Which all goes to show how much I am in love with you. Which again shows how conceited I am . . .[2]

In the transport *McCawley*, General Vandegrift was finishing a letter to his wife, Mildred, before turning in:

> Tomorrow morning at dawn we land in the first major offensive of this war. Our plans have been made and God grant that our judgement has been sound. We have rehearsed the plans. The officers and men are keen and ready to go. Way before you read this you will have heard of it. Whatever happens, you'll know that I did my best. Let us hope that best will be enough . . .[3]

Australia altered course to starboard just after midnight to take herself and Group X-Ray towards Lunga Point, about one-third of the way along the north shore of Guadalcanal, where the Japanese airfield was located and the Marines would go ashore. At exactly 2.45 am on this Friday 7 August, the bugle blared for action stations, bringing the sleepers to their feet and to their posts, fumbling for their helmets and Mae Wests and eagerly draining the mugs of steaming-hot cocoa laid on by the cooks. At his station on the bridge, Charlie Nicholls, *Australia*'s Signal Boatswain, saw poetry in the heavens:

> The Cross blares in the zenith, and presently Jupiter and Venus come wheeling up in the eastern sky in an effort to overtake

Orion and the Keys of Heaven which have proceeded them. They see the beginning of our operation but rapidly lose interest in earthly affairs when the mighty orb of day comforts us with his appearance, and presently embarrasses us with his fiery rays.[4]

In his jungle retreat high on Guadalcanal, the coastwatcher Martin Clemens had gone to sleep that night unable to eat and in a mood of deep depression. For months, he had been broadcasting what he could see of the Japanese; just two days before, he had radioed that they had finished building their airfield and that it was ready for use. His food and supplies were running low, his radio batteries were dying, and he was barefooted, for his shoes had disintegrated. After the perils he had faced, the risks he had taken, the hardships he had endured, he felt lost and abandoned, close to breaking down in tears:

> All I could taste was the bitterness of defeat. We were cut off. I would never see home again. I couldn't stand it. Turning face down on my bed roll, I lay there, listening to the water roaring down the river till my ears hurt.[5]

Clemens was awoken shortly after 6 am by the crump of distant explosions. One of the locals told him the Japanese Navy had arrived, which sent his mood sinking still further, but turning on his radio and fiddling urgently with the dial he picked up the chatter of American voices: 'Orange Base ... Red Base ...' He knew it could only be carrier pilots going in for the attack. Running to a vantage point overlooking the sound, he counted more than 50 ships, two of which he recognised as Australian cruisers. His spirits soared; his heart sang. Being a Cambridge-educated man, he turned to Shakespeare's *Henry V* on the eve of Harfleur:

> Oh, do but think
> You stand upon the rivage and behold
> A city on th' inconstant billows dancing,
> For so appears this fleet majestical . . .[6]

Clemens had heard the cruiser USS *Quincy* opening the bombardment, her nine 8-inch guns belching orange flame as she poured a tremendous fire on Lunga Point, the smoke from the high explosive shells billowing in the air. To the north across the sound off Tulagi, *San Juan* and two destroyers were repeating the performance. The fleet majestical was doing its stuff.

From that moment, the action erupted in an orchestrated crescendo of sound and fury, exactly as the admirals and generals had planned. The cruisers got away their scout aircraft at around 6.15 am, *Australia*'s Walrus catapulting into the air for an anti-submarine patrol. Dawn was just breaking over the scrubby, palm-covered coastline and the dark-green jungle ridges above. At 6.23, *Australia* fired three salvoes of her own 8-inch guns into Lunga Point, while the transports took their positions some ten kilometres offshore and anchored in an arc before the landing zones. The Walrus was nearly blown out of the sky when it lumbered past the *McCawley* at masthead height. 'Shoot down that plane!' Turner bellowed from his flag bridge. Luckily, the talker on the phones – the sailor who passed his messages – recognised it as friendly and did not repeat the order.

Fletcher had turned his three carriers into the 18-knot south-east wind well before sunrise, with a total of 93 aircraft – fighters and bombers – warming up on the flight decks and readying to launch. The plans called for simultaneous attacks on Guadalcanal and Tulagi at dawn, and the planes began to roar aloft, their exhausts spitting eerie blue flames in the early light. On the decks of *Canberra*, they heard them coming before they saw them: 'Suddenly every man on deck straightened, listening. A deep purring hum was approaching from the open sea. The hum grew to a terrifying roar as giant bombers came rushing through the sky,' recalled Torpedoman A. B. Fox.

Our own, thank heaven! Wave upon wave of bombers from American aircraft-carriers well out at sea. The sky now was vibrating thunder as these metallic waves roared overhead – straight to Tulagi. Away across at Guadalcanal similar waves must be roaring over *Australia* and *Hobart* and the American squadron there . . . quietly we stared at the terrifying monsters of modern warfare sweeping on Tulagi.

Crunch! ... Crunch! ... Crunch! ... Crunch! ... Smoke and flame and flying debris rose from the shores of Tulagi. The fight was on.[7]

The Japanese were taken entirely by surprise. The American bombers destroyed 13 enemy seaplanes in the water at Tulagi. There was no opposition in the air whatsoever, and almost nothing in the way of anti-aircraft fire from the ground. Shortly before 7 am, the landing craft were lowered from the transports and the Marines began to load into them, thousands of men clambering down cargo nets with packs and rifles over their shoulders. Each boat was carefully numbered, and they formed up into waves to head to the beaches, butting through a gentle surf to crunch onto the coral sands.

Again, there was no opposition. Any Japanese defenders appeared to have fled. For the watching Australians, it was exciting, exhilarating, enthralling. They cheered as the Yanks went by, and got the thumbs-up in return. For a while there, it was almost anti-climactic. At 7 am, *Australia*'s cooks, busy as ever, served up a breakfast of bread and butter and fishcakes, washed down with coffee. To some of the younger men, it seemed almost like a picnic.

This was a little premature. The Guadalcanal landings had been unopposed because the Japanese there were largely construction workers for the airfield, not combat troops. They simply fled, leaving half-eaten breakfasts and vast quantities of construction equipment, tractors and bulldozers untouched. On Tulagi and Tanambogo, though, there were seasoned infantry soldiers, and they began to compose themselves and regroup, to begin a bloody fight to the death. Concealed in foxholes, trenches and caves, they fought with suicidal ferocity, new men taking the place of the dying or the dead until they were all killed.

—

Emperor Hirohito, the Sun God himself, was holidaying for the summer at the elegant Tamozawa Imperial Villa in the Nikko hills north of Tokyo when news came through of the American attack on the Solomons. He decided to return to the capital but was persuaded not to by the Chief of the Naval Staff, Admiral Osami Nagano, who crawled face down into the Imperial presence in the approved grovelling manner, uttering soothing assurances. 'It is nothing worthy of Your Majesty's attention,' he explained. Hirohito stayed where he was.[8]

At Rabaul, Vice Admiral Gunichi Mikawa took a rather different view. He was awoken at 4.30 am by a staff officer with the first signal sent from Guadalcanal: 'Tulagi being heavily bombarded by air and sea.'[9] More reports kept coming in, each of them more disturbing than the last, and it became very quickly apparent to Mikawa and his staff that this was not merely a hit-and-run raid but a full-on invasion. They began to pull together a response.

Aircraft of the 25th Air Flotilla were already being prepared on Rabaul's runways for a raid on Milne Bay in New Guinea. These were hastily retargeted. At 9.30, a wing of 27 Mitsubishi G4M Betty long-range bombers with an escort of 17 Zero fighters was in the air and heading south-east to Guadalcanal, a flight of slightly more than 1000 kilometres, or about three hours. At the same time, Mikawa put together a small naval landing force of some 400 men in the troopship *Meiyo Maru*, and submarines in the Coral Sea and the Solomon Sea were ordered to concentrate on Guadalcanal at all possible speed.

An Allied air raid by a handful of American B-17 bombers interrupted things in the mid-morning but did no damage. Mikawa got back to work. The cruisers and destroyers of his 8th Fleet were scattered around nearby islands, but not widely, and after his flagship, the heavy cruiser *Chokai*, collected him in Rabaul Harbour and his red-and-white flag was hoisted, they rendez-voused in St George's Channel that afternoon, in fine weather.

This was a truly formidable array of eight ships, painted in the IJN's dark and sombre navy grey. At around 16,000 tonnes full load – built in defiance of the pre-war naval treaty limitations – *Chokai* was a superior Japanese version of the German pocket battleships, although very much faster, with a top speed of 35.5 knots. She mounted ten 20-centimetre or 8-inch guns and six tubes for the Type 93 torpedo, the famous Long Lance, which was far and away the best torpedo of the war. Remarkably, she carried two catapults amidships between her funnels, and three reconnaissance seaplanes.

The rest of the squadron – Cruiser Division Six, or CRUDIV6 – included another four heavy cruisers, almost as powerful; two light cruisers; and one large destroyer. Heading east around the island of Bougainville, they detected an American submarine, the ancient *S-38* of First World War vintage, which they simply outran, and then set a course south-east down the passage through the Solomons that would eventually be known as the Slot.[10] With the squadron travelling at 25 knots, Guadalcanal would be in sight within 24 hours.

Not long out of Rabaul, Mikawa's bombers and fighters passed in clear skies over Bougainville's southern coast. In one of the great intelligence coups of the campaign, if not the Pacific War itself, they were observed by a vigilant Australian coastwatcher, Paul Mason. Sydney born, Mason had been a plantation manager on Bougainville before the war, 'regarded as an ill-kempt, unlettered eccentric, most genial but gauche and shy, with the taint . . . of having mixed-race relations, and distinguished only by navigational and ingenious mechanical skills, particularly with wireless'.[11] He was also short-sighted and suffered from malaria. But Eric Feldt, the brains behind the coastwatchers' Operation Ferdinand, had recognised his talents and recruited him. Mason had stayed on at the relatively advanced age of 41, bravely dodging Japanese search patrols, always at risk of betrayal by villagers selling him to the enemy.

This morning, high in a jungled mountain camp, he first heard the thrum of engines and then saw the planes above him. Turning on his teleradio, he broadcast, in plain English, a simple message of enormous import: 'Twenty four torpedo bombers headed yours.' The count was wrong, but it was enough – far more than enough. Picked up in Port Moresby and Townsville and broadcast then by Pearl Harbor, Mason's warning was read by the entire Allied force. The Japanese were still 500 kilometres away and could be expected, therefore, shortly after one in the afternoon. The invasion force and the carrier force could prepare to meet them at their leisure, which is exactly what they did. In *Canberra*, they heard one of the more unusual pipes of the war: 'D'you hear there. The force will be attacked by enemy aircraft at about 1300. Hands to dinner.' Lunch was that eternal naval favourite Tiddy Oggy, known to civilians as a Cornish pasty, washed down with mugs of tea.

The Japanese were 15 minutes late. A hot welcome awaited them. The landings and unloading had been suspended, and all the warships were ready. Fighters from the carriers intercepted them first, and the bombers that survived that had to fly through a storm of anti-aircraft fire, the skies thick with the black, mushroom puffs of exploding shells. They made a medium-level pattern-bombing attack on the X-Ray transports, hit nothing and fled, for the loss of seven bombers destroyed, five probables, and two Zero fighters. But the Americans were bloodied too, losing nine of the carriers' F4F Wildcats to the superior Zeros.

A second Japanese attack by nine dive bombers, at around three o'clock, was a little more successful. They landed one small bomb on the destroyer USS *Mugford*, killing 21 men, but it cost five of their own.

And that was it for the first day. A glorious sunset brought in the tropical night, and the men in the ships went to whatever rest they could find. On land, there was still no fighting on Guadalcanal but close combat had flared at Tulagi and Tanambogo, where the Japanese were hitting back. Rather more worrying for both Admiral Turner and General Vandegrift, the air attacks had seriously disrupted the landing of supplies, which was now well behind schedule.

—

The Fall River air base at Milne Bay on the tail of New Guinea was 'a mongrel of a place; slush and mud, mosquitoes and malaria', according to Sergeant Eric Geddes of the RAAF. Base is too grand a word, perhaps. Hurriedly thrown together by the

Australians and Americans in June 1942, Fall River was a runway of steel mesh laid down over a stinking jungle quagmire, with the RAAF air and ground crews sleeping and eating in leaky tents or locally built huts of palm fronds. Wretched though it was, it played a pivotal part in the Pacific War.

Geddes was a young man from Parkes in country New South Wales, tall and lanky, one of those boys who had always wanted to fly. In 1942, he was 24 and a wireless operator and air gunner with the RAAF's 32 Squadron, flying fat-bellied, twin-engined Lockheed Hudsons on light bombing and reconnaissance missions. At 6.30 am on Saturday 8 August, the second day of the Guadalcanal invasion, his Hudson A16-218 squelched and shuddered off the Fall River runway, slowly picking up height as it headed on a patrol north-east towards Bougainville, a flight of some 1400 kilometres there and back.

There were four men on board, all sergeants in their 20s and not very long out of advanced training school. Bill Stutt, the pilot, was from Melbourne, Wilbur Courtis was the navigator, and John Bell was the other radio operator/gunner with Geddes. They had been briefed in the Ops Room – another thatched hut – where they were assigned a patrol area, told to look out for enemy submarines and surface craft, and given the recognition signal of the day, the letter K. They were told not a thing about Operation Watchtower; they had no idea of it whatsoever.

These were long flights of up to eight hours at the Hudson's cruising speed of some 180 knots, mostly boredom piled upon monotony, with only cans of preserved peaches and some jaw-breaking chunks of something the crews called dog biscuits supplied for nourishment. This mission, though, would be different. Mid-morning, coming down out of high cloud some 50 kilometres east of Bougainville, they saw below them a line of eight dark-grey ships, heading south-east. Stutt thought at first they might be friendly and flew lower for a closer look; Geddes flashed the challenge with an Aldis lamp, expecting to get the letter K blinked back in return. Instead, there were some confused flashes, which – they realised to their startled surprise – were anti-aircraft fire. Worse still, they saw two float planes on the water, which they took to be Zeros, readying to take off. Time to get the hell out. Stutt threw open the throttles and headed 'back towards a nice healthy cloud'[12] over Bougainville, where he and the other three discussed what they had seen and debated how to describe it.

At exactly 10.26 am, Eric Geddes broke radio silence to tap out a signal to Fall River in uncoded Morse, which read: 'Sighted Japanese Force. Three cruisers, three destroyers, two seaplane tenders or gunboats, Latitude 0459-S, Longitude 156–07E, Course 120 degrees, speed 15 knots.'

There was no reply, no acknowledgement. Geddes tried to send it again, several times, but still could not get through. There was no way of telling whether Fall River had heard him. Realising the importance of what they had discovered, Stutt abandoned the rest of the patrol and headed back to Milne Bay to report in person. On the way, they sighted two Japanese submarines on the surface, which they bombed, but by 12.42 they were touching down. A Jeep bounced across the runway to pick them up and hurry them off to a debriefing. After a short delay, Fall River then sent the Geddes message on to Port Moresby, confident that it would go straight to MacArthur's headquarters in Australia. About half an hour later, another Hudson, piloted by Flying Officer Mervyn Willman, also reported seeing eight Japanese warships in much the same area as the earlier sighting. This, too, was passed on.

At which point, the system collapsed. Both messages disappeared. They lay untouched somewhere on the communications chain between Port Moresby, Townsville and Brisbane, ignored for hours. Nothing happened. The two Hudsons had both sighted Gunichi Mikawa's cruiser force heading south-east in the direction of Guadalcanal, discoveries that could have and should have driven Operation Watchtower to a triumphant conclusion. Had Admirals Fletcher and Turner been informed immediately, there was still enough of the afternoon left to mount a daylight carrier air strike that would almost certainly have stopped Mikawa in his tracks. But Brisbane did not discover the signal until 6.20 pm, almost eight hours after Eric Geddes had first tried to send it to Fall River. Fletcher and Turner did not get it until 6.45 pm, when the tropical night had already closed in and an air strike was no longer an option.

After the war, blame for this failure was heaped on Bill Stutt and the crew of Hudson A16-218. Somehow, a snide rumour spread, a falsehood claiming they had not tried to radio the sighting back to their base and had foolishly kept patrolling for hours. When they finally returned to Fall River, so the rumour went, they had gone off to have a lazy afternoon tea before reporting to the debriefing office. This was written as fact by the US naval historian, Samuel Eliot Morison, in his official account of Guadalcanal and repeated – often colourfully embroidered – by other American and Australian writers thereafter.

Eric Geddes, deeply wounded by this stain on his reputation and the dishonour done to his aircrew mates, sought justice for the rest of his life. In 1984, there was a breakthrough. A search of the records in Tokyo produced the deck and signal logs of *Chokai*, Mikawa's flagship, and there it was in black and white: an exact copy in every word and numeral of Geddes's signal. It had been received in *Chokai*'s radio room at exactly the time Geddes had tapped it out, a bottomless irony. Further research found the radio at Fall River had been knocked out by a violent electrical storm as Geddes had been transmitting, and a check of the base operations books put paid to the notion of the relaxed afternoon tea. Finally, in 2008, Geddes himself, the last survivor, wrote a personal letter to President Barack Obama, setting out his case.

At last – at long, long last – he got the result he had hoped for. In 2014, the USN's History and Heritage Command wrote to him accepting his version of events, admitting the flaws in Morison's account and agreeing to correct the record. 'Thank you for your faithful service to your country and to the Allied cause in World War II,' it began.[13] Eric Geddes, a proud and cheerful man, showed me this letter in July 2014 when I interviewed him at his Sydney home for this book. 'Now I can die happy,' he said, with a grin.

—

A heady combination of luck, boldness and good judgement now played a hand for the Japanese admiral. Realising he had been sighted by the Hudsons, Mikawa changed his plans. As his Chief of Staff, Toshikazu Ohmae, put it:

> These contacts naturally caused us to assume that our intentions had been perceived by the enemy and that more search planes would appear, increasing the imminent possibility of an attack. An early approach to Guadalcanal became increasingly dis-advantageous. The decision was made, accordingly, to decrease our speed of advance and delay our assault until 1.30am.[14]

A battle after midnight: this was an extraordinary risk to take. A daylight encounter in the confined and poorly charted waters of the Solomons would be difficult enough. To go charging in at night raised the hazards to a very much higher plane, not least because the Japanese did not have radar. It would be like a knife-fight in a darkened dockyard, shadowy shapes suddenly looming from nowhere in the glare of a searchlight or a star-shell burst, the perils of collision at speed, the difficulty of telling friend from foe. Reports from Japanese aircraft had given Mikawa at least a rough idea of the enemy forces he might encounter – although no one had discovered the whereabouts of Fletcher's carriers – but he could only guess where or how or in what strength they might be deployed after sunset.

Yet there were a couple of advantages too. American carrier aircraft would not fly at night, leaving him free from air attack. And, more importantly, the IJN had been rigorously trained to fight night battles, long practice burnishing its skills to a level unmatched by any of the Allied navies. Mikawa issued his battle instructions:

> In the approach, the cruiser force will pass south of Savo Island and will torpedo the main enemy force in the Guadalcanal anchorage; after which it will head towards the Tulagi anchor-age to shell and torpedo the enemy. The cruiser force will then withdraw north of Savo Island. Each commanding officer will operate independently as regards gun and torpedo firings.[15]

The Japanese admiral and his staff officers were confident they had more than a fighting chance.

—

Day two of the landings did not go as well as the admirals and generals had hoped. Some of the more optimistic assessments were falling apart. Around 11,000 Marines had been landed on Guadalcanal, largely unopposed, but the fighting on Tulagi and nearby Tanambogo had grown ever more bloody, with heavy casualties on both sides.

Shortly after ten that morning, another Australian coast-watcher on Bougainville, Jack Read, radioed that he had seen 26 enemy bombers and 15 Zero fighters heading towards Guadalcanal. For some reason, the timings were bungled on board Fletcher's carriers, and when the Japanese swooped in low over Florida Island, there were only three Wildcats in the air to meet them. The two invasion squadrons had already weighed and were moving, which made them much less of a target, and the Japanese torpedo bombers – skimming low over the water – flew into a fiery cauldron of high explosive anti-aircraft shells and bullets. Both *Australia* and *Canberra* got their main armament, the 8-inch guns, into action, as Bruce Loxton recorded in his midshipman's journal:

> *Canberra* opened fire as they came down close to the water. They passed down our port side out of range of the Oerlikons but the port 4-inch had an excellent target. We fired an 8-inch barrage but the results were not seen. Two bombers sheered out of line and headed towards our bow. We turned away, at the same time opening fire with Oerlikons. We succeeded in bringing down one if not both of them.[16]

Australia had a closer shave, recorded by an officer from Kew in Melbourne, Lieutenant Guy Ashley-Brown:

> One of the torpedo bombers coming in at about 50 feet was continuously hit by Oerlikon fire on her approach and was blazing as she flew straight at the forward Oerlikon battery and bridge of

Australia. It looked as though it was to be a kamikaze do. She lifted just in time and skimmed over our heads on the top of the turret – we certainly felt the heat of the blaze as we ducked. We could even see inside the plane and the contorted faces of the crew as they fought their machine guns and tried to cope with the flames in the plane. She crashed into the water a hundred yards away. Another plane came in quickly from our starboard quarter to drop her torpedo just as the destroyer *Jarvis* was coming up past us on the starboard side. *Jarvis* unfortunately took the torpedo that was intended for us – *Australia* was indeed a lucky ship.[17]

Apparently unnerved, most of the Japanese dropped their torpedoes too early. They scored just one hit, on the destroyer USS *Jarvis*, which was sent listing and limping from the battlefield. One plane crashed into the transport *George F. Elliott*, setting her on fire; she had to be grounded in shoal water near Florida Island and abandoned. Seventeen Japanese aircraft were lost, either shot down or crashing on their return to Rabaul, figures that allowed a handsome victory to the defenders. The destroyer USS *Bagley* came across a downed Japanese bomber still floating, with the pilot standing on one wing and the radioman slumped in his seat. The Americans threw rescue lines but the pilot ignored them. He pulled a pistol, shot his mate, and then blew his own brains out.[18]

But, once again, the unloading of supplies to the beachheads had been disrupted and it was now getting worryingly behind schedule. An enormous amount of gear was still sitting in transport ships when it should have been ashore, and the problem was getting worse, not better. Boats were circling in a traffic jam off the beaches waiting for their chance to land, and on Guadalcanal Marines 'whose equipment had not been landed, lounged around the beach in undisciplined idleness, shooting down cocoanuts or going swimming. There was no apparent reason why these men could not have rendered valuable assistance in unloading the boats.'[19] And the loading problems in Wellington had not been fully solved, either. Some Marines found themselves unloading soggy cartons of cheese.

That evening, the invasion plans began to fall apart still further. The heaviest blow came not from the enemy but from within, at the top. Frank Jack Fletcher decided to cut and run. From his flagship *Saratoga*, at 6.07 pm, he sent this signal to the nominal commander of Operation Watchtower, Admiral Ghormley, in his flagship 1500 kilometres away in Noumea: 'Total fighter strength reduced from 99 to 78. In view of the large number of enemy torpedo planes and bombers in this area, I recommend the immediate withdrawal of my carriers. Request tankers sent forward immediately as fuel running low.'

Fletcher was already well to the south-east of Guadalcanal, some 200 kilometres distant from the landing beaches. Without waiting for a reply from Ghormley, either yes or no, he simply turned his three carriers around, along with the *North Carolina* and his cruiser and destroyer escort, and headed off the battle-field at a leisurely 15 knots. Ghormley's belated approval of his retreat did not arrive until shortly before midnight. The invasion force was now left without air cover.

With the long vision of hindsight, the unfortunate conclusion must be that Fletcher lost his nerve. He had already fought a long war as the most senior American admiral in command at sea in the Pacific since Pearl Harbor, including the battles of Coral Sea and Midway, which had claimed two carriers, *Lexington* and *Yorktown*. To borrow from Winston Churchill, he was the only man who could have lost the Pacific War in an afternoon. The strain must have been immense, and the prospect of losing a third or even fourth carrier can only have weighed heavily upon him.

Throughout that afternoon of 8 August, he had become increasingly worried about being attacked by submarines and ever more obsessed with the idea that there must be a Japanese carrier somewhere to the north of him. He came to that conclusion, logically enough perhaps, because the Japanese air raids had been conducted by naval aircraft capable of carrier operations: therefore, there must be a carrier. It did not occur to him that these planes might have been land based, as they were. In fact, there was no Japanese carrier in the southern hemisphere at the time. The claim that the fuel for his ships was running low simply does not hold water. Post-war inspection of his figures found that he had fuel aplenty. His aircraft losses had been heavy, it is true, but not ruinously so. He had more aircraft left in these three carriers, *Saratoga*, *Wasp* and *Enterprise*, than he had been able to field at Midway.

In Fletcher's defence, it can be said that he had been ordered by Nimitz not to risk his carriers against a superior force without every prospect of success. But that argument hardly applied here. In Ghormley's defence, there is nothing to be said. He was dilatory and incompetent, inexcusably remote from the operation he was supposedly commanding; the surprise is that it took another two months for Nimitz to fire him and replace him with Bull Halsey.

Kelly Turner was stricken when he learnt of Fletcher's departure. Later, he would call it 'desertion', and would say that he had been left 'bare ass', which was true enough.[20] Vandegrift in his memoirs called it 'running away',[21] virtually an accusation of cowardice. At the Fiji conference, Fletcher had grudgingly promised to remain in the area for three days. Now, he was leaving 12 hours earlier. Turner, equally nervous of more air attacks, felt his hand had been forced, that he had no choice but to leave with his transports as well. There is a valid comparison to be made with the Mediterranean war in May 1941, when the RN's Andrew Cunningham risked his all and sustained terrible losses in the operation to rescue the Commonwealth troops defeated on Crete. Cunningham was staunch, principled, unswerving in his determination to support and succour the men in khaki ashore, come hell or high water. Fletcher was not.

The demands of command can be unceasing, unremitting. Hardly had this blow of Fletcher's departure landed when Kelly Turner had to face his next decision. The report from Bill Stutt's RAAF Hudson of the Japanese squadron heading south-east had finally arrived on his flag bridge: 'Three cruisers, three destroyers, two seaplane tenders or gunboats . . .'

This was a puzzle. The word gunboats made no sense to a naval officer. Gunboats were small craft, lightly armed, generally employed in coastal waters or rivers; they would never accompany a cruiser force at sea, least of all one bent on seeking battle. So that part of the report could be discounted. Seaplane tenders was also curious. These were not combat vessels either. They were a floating air base, capable of transporting seaplanes and of fuelling and servicing them, but not to be sent into action. Turner and his staff, and Victor Crutchley too, decided that the Japanese were not heading their way but were planning to establish a seaplane base in the northern Solomons, some distance away. That would have to be dealt with in time, but it posed no immediate threat and was not urgent.

It was no fault of Stutt and his crew that they got this so badly wrong. Identifying ships from the air was difficult for even the most experienced pilots and observers, especially if you were catching only a glimpse through scattered cloud or sea haze. The crew of A16-218 was not experienced. Not long out of training, they had received only sketchy instruction in picking one type of ship from another, friend or foe. Their error can be traced directly up the line to MacArthur's air commander, the egregious Lieutenant General George H. Brett, who had refused to order better ship-recognition practices after that friendly-fire attack by B-17s on Crace's squadron at the Coral Sea in May. Coincidentally, MacArthur had finally got rid of him just days before the landings on Guadalcanal, but the shadow of his stupidity lived on, to disastrous effect.

Turner was let down again in the air, too. He had asked Admiral McCain to run extra reconnaissance aircraft over the Slot that day, flights that would have revealed Mikawa heading towards him. For some reason, McCain did not, and, worse, he failed to inform Turner, who was left to assume that the coast was clear.

So night fell. After two days of air attack, of the strain of being closed up at action stations from dawn till dusk, everyone was tired and hoping for at least a few hours of undisturbed sleep.

It seemed, perhaps, that they might get it. In *Australia*, Crutchley ordered his screening force of cruisers and destroyers to take up their night positions to block any enemy approach from the north-west.

Seawards, the first line of defence would be two destroyers equipped with radar, the USS *Blue* and the USS *Ralph Talbot*, assigned to patrol on two lines to the north and west of Savo Island to give early warning.

Blocking the southern route past Savo towards Guadalcanal were the three heavy cruisers *Australia*, *Canberra* and *Chicago*, with two destroyers, the USS *Bagley* and the USS *Patterson*.

The northern route around Savo towards Tulagi was guarded by another three cruisers, *Vincennes*, *Quincy* and *Astoria*, with the destroyers *Helm* and *Wilson*.

Other cruisers and destroyers, including *San Juan* and *Hobart*, stood closer in to the transports and the landing beaches.

This was a sensible, practical division of Crutchley's force. The three cruisers of the southern group had all worked together in Task Force 44 for some months and were familiar with each other's methods. As strange as it may seem, Crutchley had never laid eyes on the three American cruisers of the northern force and still less had he met their commanding officers, but he assumed, correctly, that it would be best if they were kept together as well, under the tactical command of the captain of *Astoria*, Frederick Riefkohl. In an emergency, either group would be available to go to the assistance of the other.

The fine skies of the day had gone with the sunset, replaced by that oppressive tropical evening heaviness of sultry heat, a clouded moon, and the eerie crackle of lightning. An occasional squall brought a curtain of rain, suddenly reducing visibility to 100 metres or so. In each ship, men snatched what sleep they could. In theory, they were all at the second degree of readiness, which required half the men to be at their action stations, but individual captains had taken it on themselves to relax this by allowing groups of men away from the guns for meals and to snatch a nap – a practice not officially approved but quite common after long and arduous days. In *Canberra*, only half the armament and damage control crews were closed up, and the guns were not loaded.

Just after 8.30 pm, Crutchley got a signal from Turner asking him to attend a conference aboard *McCawley*, which was lying off the Guadalcanal landing beach at Lunga Point. General Vandegrift was summoned too. For Crutchley, it would mean a trip of some 33 kilometres, which by day he might have done in his admiral's barge. By night, it made more sense to go in his flagship rather than floundering around in a boat in the dark looking for *McCawley* in the crowded anchorage, so he set off in *Australia*, ordering Howard Bode of *Chicago* to take command in his absence. Bode considered taking *Australia*'s place at the head of the southern patrol line but decided it would only cause a disturbance, so he ordered his officer of the deck to remain in the rear of *Canberra* and then went to his cabin to get some sleep. Crutchley did not tell Riefkohl in the northern group that he was departing but assumed, reasonably enough, that he would have heard the signals.

They had trouble finding Vandegrift and he had trouble finding *McCawley*, so he was late for the conference. When Vandegrift turned up at around 11.30 pm, tired himself, he was shocked by the fatigue that hung heavily on the two admirals. They looked ready to pass out, he thought.[22] Turner ordered coffee and explained first that he expected no Japanese attack that night and, second, that Fletcher had left him no choice: without air cover from the carriers, he would have to withdraw in the morning, taking with him all the unloaded equipment and supplies. Vandegrift was dismayed but recognised there was nothing he could do about it. His men would be left ashore on their own, abandoned.

This was a night of fateful decisions, and Crutchley made another one. After he farewelled Turner, he gave Vandegrift a lift to a minesweeper, and it was well past 1 am of that Sunday 9 August before he returned to *Australia*. There seemed little point in causing yet another disturbance by taking *Australia* back to the patrol line with only a few hours left until the dawn. He decided instead to remain near the transports. More rain squalls blotted out his world, the inky blackness relieved only by the ruby glow of the *George F. Elliott* still burning over by Florida Island.

While the three men were meeting, there was something of a disturbance above the ships patrolling around Savo. First the sound of engines, and then the glimpse of an aircraft. *Ralph Talbot*, the northern radar picket destroyer, noticed it first and radioed a caution: 'Warning, warning, plane over Savo headed east.' *Blue*, the other picket, picked up another aircraft flying low in the same direction, and so did *Quincy* and *Vincennes*, whose captain assumed the planes were friendly because they were displaying navigation lights. It was exactly as it had been with the Japanese reconnaissance flights over Sydney Harbour: nobody did a thing. Inertia weighed heavily, almost as if each ship was reluctant to make the first move and risk looking foolish.

And so it was that two of Admiral Gunichi Mikawa's reconnaissance seaplanes flew unmolested over the Allied force arrayed beneath them, watching and counting for something like an hour. It had been a risk catapulting them from the cruisers at night, for the pilots had never done it before, but the gamble paid off. They reported three enemy cruisers patrolling to the south of Savo Island. The Japanese admiral now had a very fair idea of what he was up against, an intelligence pearl of infinite price.

Nightfall lifted a weight from Mikawa. He did not know that Fletcher's carriers had already turned tail, but the onset of night removed the threat of air attack that had gnawed at him all day. Every ship was ordered to throw overboard anything on deck that would burn fiercely – aircraft fuel – and they each hoisted a long white banner at their signal yards to distinguish friend from enemy. As the sun set, crimson as the Japanese flag itself, Mikawa signalled a Nelsonian exhortation: 'In the finest tradition of the Imperial Navy we shall engage the enemy in night battle. Every man is expected to do his best.'[23]

He then formed the squadron into line astern, with his flagship *Chokai* at the head, followed by the heavy cruisers *Aoba*,

Kako, *Kinugasa* and *Furutaka*; then the two light cruisers *Tenryu* and *Yubari*, and bringing up the rear the destroyer *Yunagi*, all spanking along at 28 knots. Saturday had turned to Sunday. At about 12.40 am, the volcanic cone of Savo Island loomed on the port bow, exactly as expected. As planned, they would enter through the southern channel, heading first for Guadalcanal.

Then came a shock, with a cry from a lookout: 'Ship approaching, 30 degrees starboard.' Every set of binoculars on the bridge turned to see it, a destroyer about ten kilometres away and moving from right to left across *Chokai*'s bows.

In a split second, Mikawa had to decide whether to attack or evade. He chose the latter, signalling the squadron to come left and to slow back to 22 knots, which would lessen the telltale white plumes of their bow waves and wakes. Guns trained, they held their breath for what seemed like an eternity, but it became clear the enemy had not seen them. A minute later, the stranger turned sharply to starboard and retraced her course, disappearing into the night. The USS *Blue* had failed the first test.

Hardly had that moment passed when a new danger appeared, this time to port. Another destroyer. Mikawa came around 20 degrees to starboard, and they noticed that this new intruder had her stern exposed and was moving away, also evidently blind to them. The USS *Ralph Talbot* had failed the second test.

It is incredible that both these ships missed an entire Japanese squadron steaming between them. They were equipped with radar, they had lookouts posted, and they had been specifically tasked with keeping watch for an approaching enemy. But miss they did. Radar, still in its infancy, had let them down, its signals very likely distorted by the high mass of the Savo volcano. The Japanese surged past them and onwards, working up to 30 knots now, an almost reckless speed for ships heading into action in confined waters by night. Captain Ohmae watched from the flag bridge:

> I stood beside Admiral Mikawa. Before me was a chart on which were plotted the locations of enemy ships. We peered into the darkness. The voice of a lookout shattered the tense silence: 'Cruiser, seven degrees to port!'

The shape that appeared in that direction seemed small; it could only be a destroyer. It was still a long way off.

'Three cruisers, nine degrees to starboard, moving to the right!'

And then a parachute flare from one of our planes brought reality to the scene. There they were, three cruisers! Range, 8,000 metres.

The *Chokai*'s skipper, Captain Mikio Hayakawa, was ready. His powerful voice boomed throughout the bridge, 'Torpedoes fire to starboard – Fire!'[24]

Victor Crutchley, Kelly Turner and Archer Vandegrift had just finished their meeting in the *McCawley*.

CHAPTER 17

THE UNSPEAKABLE BLOODINESS MY SHOCKED EYES TOOK IN

At midnight, Sub Lieutenant Mac Gregory took over as *Canberra*'s officer of the watch. All was peaceful, the night still moonless, with drifting curtains of rain shrouding Savo Island. There was the occasional rumble of distant thunder. Captain Getting was on the compass platform with the Principal Control Officer, Lieutenant Commander Ewan Wight. The navigator, Lieutenant Commander Jack Mesley, turned the ship to starboard for the next leg of her patrol.

Course 130 degrees, speed 12 knots. Gregory glanced aft to see *Chicago* following suit three cables astern,[1] and the two destroyers, *Patterson* and *Bagley*, keeping station on either side. With the turn made, the captain and the navigator left to get some rest. Captain Getting slumped fully clothed in a chair in his sea cabin, a deck below the bridge. The ships would head almost due southeast for an hour, until 1 am, when they would turn again and retrace their steps, course 310 degrees, near enough to northwest. It was simple, routine. In the plot behind the bridge, young Russell Keats was keeping a dutiful eye on the clock, allowing plenty of time to warn Gregory for the next set of helm orders.

Then the furies arose. At 1.43 am, there was a distant boom almost due north, sounding rather like a torpedo exploding, and a lookout reported a ship ahead. A flare burst above them, fired by one of the loitering Japanese seaplanes, perfectly placed, throwing a ghastly white light on *Canberra* and the sea around. At that same moment, *Patterson*, off to port, gave the alarm: 'Warning, warning. Strange ships entering harbour.' This was done first on the TBS, which *Canberra* did not have and could not hear, and was then repeated to her on a blinker tube.[2] Almost simultaneously, Wight sighted the wakes of three ships silver-bright against the black bulk of Savo, moving from port to starboard. He sounded action stations, the dreaded and hated alarm screeching through the ship, and he gave the order to ready the 8-inch guns. 'Alarm Starboard, Green 20, Load, Load, Load!'

Tired men hauled themselves to their feet from the depths of sleep and ran to the turrets, the torpedo tubes, the shell handling rooms, the engine spaces, the sick bay, the flats where the damage control parties would wait in groups. Bruce Loxton, who had been dozing in the charthouse, clattered up two ladders onto the bridge to his action station, at the port enemy bearing indicator. The engine-room telegraphs jangled for full speed ahead. Frank Getting burst back onto the bridge, along with the gunnery officer, the monocled Lieutenant Commander Donald 'Gertie' Hole, and the torpedo officer, Lieutenant Commander John Plunkett-Cole. Hole ran to the starboard enemy bearing indicator, where he could direct the main armament, searching for a target for his guns.

As he did so, Gregory and Wight saw the bubbling tracks of torpedoes racing down the starboard side. These were the first fired from *Chokai*. They missed, and shot past into the darkness astern. Mesley the navigator arrived on the compass platform to take the con and saw two more torpedoes passing ahead, crossing from port. *Canberra*, wheeling hard over under starboard helm, avoided them by metres. Then, still more torpedoes, on either side this time. Mesley bellowed into a voice pipe down to the lower steering position, calling first for Midships and then Port 35 to check the ship's swing. He got it right. *Canberra* groaned and lurched back over, and once again the torpedoes sped harmlessly past. Mac Gregory, relieved of the watch, clambered to his station in the fore control, above the bridge.

In the space of minutes, *Canberra* dodged 19 torpedoes in all – a remarkable combination of good luck and good seamanship – but, even as the ship straightened, a shell from the first enemy salvo smashed into her. Russell Keats, the quiet young musician, was among the first to die. That shell slammed straight into the plotting office, where he was sitting. It was wrecked, a shambles, every man in it killed, the remains of their bodies never found. The melancholy consolation must be that Keats could never have known what hit him.

Canberra was now under the guns of at least four of the Japanese cruisers as they swept past in one menacing line. In the black of night, at speed, their shooting was extraordinary, devastating in its accuracy. They poured full broadsides into her port side, shell after shell after shell, but *Canberra* had yet to fire a shot. Twisting and turning like a hunted animal, she could not fix her guns steady on an enemy ship. Increasingly desperate to pick a target, Donald Hole scrambled across from the starboard side of the bridge and pushed Bruce Loxton aside from the port enemy bearing indicator. 'Get out of the way, Snotty, let me have a look,' he snapped. He bent to the eye-pieces. This saved the midshipman's life:

> I stepped back and, almost as I did so, there was an explosion close to my left. Thrown back against the magnetic compass binnacle, I ended up on the deck. A telephone buzzed and I reached it with difficulty, but no one was on the other end. I let it fall and lay back against the binnacle. Although I knew nothing of my injuries at the time, I had been literally peppered with pieces of metal. While losing a great deal of blood, I was extremely fortunate that nothing vital had been hit.[3]

That shell brought more death. Hole lay on the deck, killed outright. Captain Getting was sprawled by the pelorus within arm's reach of Loxton, mortally wounded but still able to speak. Others on the bridge were dead or dying as well, the deck slowly soaking with their blood. And still the Japanese kept up their fire. Up on the air defence platform above the bridge, Leading

Seaman Bill Devine had a terrifying view of the storm of steel raining down upon them:

> . . . *Canberra* rocked and trembled under bursting shells. We crouched against steel wherever we could as those screaming salvoes smashed into our 4-inch gun position and deep into the vitals of the ship. Those exploding shells made night brilliant under a storm of beautiful, terrifying coloured dazzling sparks. Flames shot up from *Canberra*. In the frightening roar of them the upper decks appeared like a scene in Hades as the ship writhed under the explosions.[4]

All this happened in less than two minutes, a cascade of infinite horrors compressed into fragments of time. Shells kept crashing into the port side, some landing on the upper decks, some penetrating her hull. More fires broke out on deck. The Walrus aircraft was in flames on the catapult, and drums of aviation fuel erupted nearby. The fires began to spread, setting off some of the 4-inch ammunition.

In the midst of this fury of death and destruction came perhaps the most devastating hit of all: *Canberra* was torpedoed by the destroyer *Bagley*. Friendly fire. At least one torpedo from the *Bagley* struck amidships on her starboard side, penetrating a boiler room and exploding with catastrophic force. It was the killer blow.

The destroyer had been out to starboard when the battle began, caught by surprise like everyone else, startled into action. Her captain, Lieutenant Commander George A. Sinclair, raced to the bridge and seems to have panicked. Sinclair was an engineer with very little deck experience as a seaman officer, and *Bagley* was his first command, a job that was apparently beyond him. It was known throughout the ship that when things got difficult he would hand over to his executive officer, Lieutenant Commander Thomas Chambers.

That happened this turbulent night. When he reached the bridge, Sinclair shouted for full speed and ordered an emergency turn to port, which took him away from the enemy but put him directly on a collision course with *Canberra*. Sizing up the impending disaster, Chambers seized command – by some accounts after threatening Sinclair with his pistol – and continued the turn, which kept the *Bagley* going in a full circle. In the alarm and chaos, with the circle almost complete, the destroyer loosed off four torpedoes from her port tubes. One sped straight towards *Canberra*, a distance of some 2000 metres. It struck at about 1.47 am.

The explosion in *Canberra*'s bowels almost certainly caused a boiler flashback – a massive loss of pressure and an explosion of gas and unburnt fuel – that must have killed every man there. Steam pressure expired on all eight boilers. The engines stopped, lapsing into a shocking silence. Dynamos failed too, plunging the engine rooms and every space below decks into blackness until the emergency battery lighting came fitfully on. There was no power left, nothing. On the bridge, Lieutenant Commander Mesley noticed the ship beginning to slow and to take a list to starboard. The Chief Quartermaster called up the voice pipe from below that the wheel was useless. There was no way to train the gun turrets, which were locked solid out to port. Neither the guns nor the torpedo tubes could fire, and the fire hoses trickled and stopped. *Canberra* began to die, and more of her men with her.

The ship's doctors and sick-berth attendants were battling to deal with the wounded, in scenes of appalling carnage. Another shell smashed into the flat outside the sick bay, a jagged shard of shrapnel tearing away half the chest of Stoker Ray Boys, a kid of 18 from St Peters in Adelaide. When the flash and the smoke cleared, his mate George Yeates, 20 years old and another South Australian, from Glenelg, shouted that he could see a bloodied arm lying on the deck. It was his own. The ship's butcher, who was in one of the first-aid parties, whipped out a ligature and tied it around the stump, saving the boy's life. The Surgeon Commander, Charlie Downward, was called to the bridge to attend to the captain, but Getting protested that he was okay and waved him away, telling him to look after other men first. Downward stepped over Bruce Loxton, thinking he was dead, until the youngster called out to him. The doctor gave him a shot of morphine and called for a stretcher to take him below.

The numbing noise, the violent concussion, the sheer physical shock of combat upon the body and the senses can disrupt the mind and brain. Realising there was no point staying in the fore control, Mac Gregory went down to help dump ammunition and see what he could do for the wounded. When he was below decks, the ship gave another shudder and took on a sharper list, which sent him scrambling back up again. Suddenly, he remembered his cap, which he had left behind. It was special, with a much prized, gold-embroidered officers' cap badge he had bought at Gieves, the naval outfitters in London. Wartime badges were stamped out of cheap, thin metal. He clambered up again to retrieve this treasure, to find only a shell hole where he had left it.

As suddenly as it began, the shooting stopped. All told, it had lasted for barely three minutes. As Mikawa had planned, his force was now sweeping anticlockwise around Savo Island, heading for the northern patrol of the three American cruisers. He would wreak more havoc there.

Canberra was left a burning hulk.

—

Of the ships with *Canberra* in the southern group, the *Bagley* simply disappeared after firing her torpedoes and took no further part in the battle, although she would later help with rescue efforts. The other destroyer, the USS *Patterson*, performed very much better. It was *Patterson* that had given the initial warning, and her captain, Commander Frank Walker, reacted swiftly and effectively. He fired star shells to illuminate the dim shapes over by Savo, and in the light they shed he swung hard to starboard to close the range and opened fire with his main armament of 5-inch guns. He also shouted for a torpedo attack, but – to his later chagrin – that order was lost in the noise of his guns opening fire. *Patterson* scored some minor hits on one of the Japanese light cruisers but was pummelled in return, with a hit on a gun turret that killed ten men and injured eight others. She had tried.

Chicago, astern of *Canberra*, was caught unawares as well. Howard Bode had also been asleep when the shooting started. Called to his bridge by the General Quarters alarm, he saw *Canberra* make her sudden turn to starboard and gave the order to follow, until he saw the telltale phosphorescence of torpedo trails heading towards his port side. He shifted the helm hard over to port, but one torpedo clipped his bow and took out a chunk of the forefoot. Damage control parties shored up the nearby bulkheads and the ship could still make a safe 25 knots. The gunners fired star shells but for some reason they all failed to light and the guns were unable to acquire a target. The enemy did, though. One shell struck the foot of *Chicago*'s mainmast, killing two sailors and injuring 13, including her executive officer.

At this point, Captain Bode – the much-feared martinet and bully – apparently lost his head. Nothing else adequately explains his conduct, unless, perhaps, it was cowardice. One of his 5-inch guns managed to get off a shot or two at the Japanese cruiser *Yubari* when she was briefly lit by a searchlight, but that was all. As inconceivable as it seems, Bode turned away from the battle and continued steaming seawards, west by nor-west, away from the sound and fury, away from the transports he was there to protect, away from Mikawa's cruisers, which were heading east and then turning north. All hell was breaking loose astern but he chose to ignore it and kept going.

Worse, he failed to raise the alarm. Bode had been explicitly left in tactical command by Admiral Crutchley when he went to the conference with Turner, but it never occurred to him to do anything about it. He did not rise to his duties, his responsibilities. He did not signal Crutchley or Turner that the southern force was under attack and that *Canberra* appeared to have been brought to a burning standstill. More culpable still, he did nothing to warn the northern force – *Quincy*, *Astoria* and *Vincennes* – that a battle was raging and heading their way. Mute and inglorious, Bode simply vanished into the night for at least another 40 minutes, a failure that would have tragic consequences. Samuel Eliot Morison, the US naval historian, refers to his conduct as 'stupidity', but that seems insufficient.[5]

Barely scratched, elated at their success so far, Mikawa's cruisers ploughed on exactly according to plan. Rain squalls were coming in more heavily now, helpfully concealing him as he curved away from the flaming remains of *Canberra*, but also serving to split his force as he ordered a turn to the east nor'east. This division was unintentional, an accident, but in fact it served him well, for it set up the jaws of a lethal trap for the *Vincennes* group. *Chokai* led one column on the right, followed by *Aoba*, *Kako* and *Kinugasa*. *Furutaka* swung more sharply northward and formed another column of the two light cruisers *Tenryu* and *Yubari* to the left. The destroyer *Yunagi* played no further part.

The northern group was not patrolling a straight-line course like the southern group but following the sides of a box, each leg of it eight kilometres long, led by *Vincennes* at an easy ten knots. *Quincy* was second in line, with *Astoria* in the rear, and the destroyers *Helm* and *Wilson* out to port and starboard. The distance between the southern and northern groups at the furthest leg of their patrols could be as much 20 kilometres, which meant they were out of visual touch in the dark and, on this fateful night, frequently separated by sheets of tropical rain. The ships of the northern group had been aware of some sort of activity to the south ever since they caught *Patterson*'s warning of strange ships broadcast over the TBS. They heard the occasional thump of gunfire, saw the flares and star shells, and assumed – as one – that it did not involve them. Perhaps a Japanese submarine had tried to sneak through and was being dealt with; perhaps it was a night bombardment of the Guadalcanal beaches.

Suddenly, they were caught in the blinding white glare of searchlights. It was about 1.50 am. Seconds later, *Chokai* opened up with her main battery on *Astoria*, the last and nearest in the American line. These opening shots missed. Acting without orders but with some instinctive commonsense, a junior sailor on *Astoria*'s bridge sounded the General Alarm. The gunnery officer was already on watch, and he gave the order to open fire. Rushing to his bridge, Captain William Greenman was aghast, thinking his ship was shooting at a friend, not at an enemy. He shouted the order to ceasefire and the guns fell silent. Only as more salvoes rained down around him did he realise *Astoria* was under enemy attack, but by then it was too late.

Soon enough, the Japanese got the range and their shells began to land with ever increasing destruction, causing fires that rapidly flared out of control. The two forward turrets were knocked out, men began to die on the bridge and the upper deck, and *Astoria* slowed to a limping seven knots. She lurched out of the line. At least one of her shells, though, hit home, putting one of *Chokai*'s turrets out of action.

The *Quincy* was next. Caught in a crossfire between the two Japanese columns, she too was quickly reduced to a floating funeral pyre, ablaze from stem to stern and sinking by the bow. One of her salvoes hit *Chokai*'s chartroom just metres from where Mikawa was standing, but the admiral was not hurt. With *Quincy*'s captain, Samuel Moore, dead on his bridge, the gunnery officer gave the order to abandon ship, and she heeled over and went to the bottom at about 2.30 am.

Vincennes, first in the column, was the last to be engaged. The slaughter continued. The Japanese were bemused to see her guns still trained fore and aft, as if she were in harbour. Compounding this tragedy of errors, her captain, Fred Riefkohl, also thought the searchlights playing on his ship were from friend, not foe, and he actually radioed for them to be turned off. *Vincennes* was struck by at least three torpedoes, which silenced her engines, and she was smashed about by at least 74 shell hits. Riefkohl ordered the crew to abandon ship at 2.16 am, and *Vincennes* sank just before 3 am. *Astoria* lingered on, fighting for her life, but later that morning, in broad daylight, she too rolled over and went under.

Gunichi Mikawa had won a stunning victory. Savo Island was, and remains, the USN's worst ever defeat at sea. Three American cruisers were sunk, and another damaged, for the loss of 992 lives and the wounding of thousands more. The Japanese had escaped with barely a scratch and just 58 men killed (although one of the cruisers, *Kako*, was torpedoed by an American submarine on her

way home the next day, with the death of another 74 men). More
than satisfied with his night's work – in fact, less than an hour's
work – Mikawa gathered his force about him, formed them
once again into an orderly line with *Chokai* at the head, and set a
course to the north-west and his base at Rabaul.

Curiously, that was probably his only mistake of the battle.
He could have – he should have – turned back east again and gone
on to destroy the invasion force off Tulagi and Guadalcanal,
his original objective. With only a thin line of cruisers left
between them and the enemy – *Australia*, *Hobart* and *San Juan*,
plus a handful of destroyers – Turner's transports were virtually defenceless. Mikawa could easily have picked them off, and
then settled down to a leisurely bombardment of the Marines
ashore, rendering Operation Watchtower a complete instead of
a partial disaster for the Allies. But, as they had done at Pearl
Harbor and Coral Sea, the Japanese failed to land that final,
lethal blow.

Mikawa's excuses were many and various. He was low on
torpedoes; he feared air attack by carriers the next day, or perhaps
by submarines. It seems more likely that, having scored this
substantial triumph, he had decided quite understandably not to
push his luck. In that sense, his mission had failed. He had not
stopped the American invasion of Guadalcanal in its tracks, and
this fact would be waved around and ballyhooed by the Allied
command in the weeks and months to come.

But the price paid by the Allies was crushing. And the
night was not yet done. As Mikawa's cruisers headed home,
Canberra was still afloat.

—

With no power and no fire hoses, chains of men doggedly fought
the flames with buckets of seawater hauled on board. A heavy
shower of rain helped them for a while but added to the ordeal
for the wounded, who were being laid out in the open on the
fo'c'sle. The doctors did their best to treat them by torchlight, as
Surgeon Lieutenant Ken Morris later wrote to a friend: 'There

was some pretty grim stuff also – trunks without limbs, heads without bodies etc – one poor devil with his belly split open saying as everyone passed "Don't tread on me guts."[6]

Canberra's executive officer, Commander John Walsh, had been at his station in the after control when the battle began, sustaining a head wound that afflicted his eyesight, but he went to the bridge and took command when he heard that Frank Getting was no longer capable. The list to starboard gradually increased to about 15 degrees, and the fires on the 4-inch gun deck began to set off ammunition stored there, adding still more lethal hazards to this tableau of horrors. The Engineer Commander Otto McMahon, went to the bridge to report that all power was lost, with no hope of regaining it. Stoker Jack Rozynski, a 19-year-old from Randwick in Sydney, had been knocked unconscious by a shell exploding below decks and woke with a mouth full of blood and broken teeth, in time to hear the order to go up into the night:

> My mind had been somewhat prepared for the terrible sights which I imagined I might see, but never in a thousand years could it have been prepared for the unspeakable bloodiness my shocked eyes took in. Why, there was a cobber of mine – only a couple of hours ago we had been laughing and joking together – and as I stared down at him the hot sea wind ruffled his curly brown hair and the blood-stained overalls he wore.
>
> I forced myself away to where heroes in tattered clothes were dumping red hot boxes of cordite and gun cotton into the sea. I will not, I could not describe some of the scenes about me – of maimed and broken bodies – some piteously calling for Mothers or water; some in the still stiff pose that could only be death . . .
>
> I see the red glare of the burning plane outline gaping shell boxes and twisted gun barrels, all that is left of the 4-inch gun deck. I see the yellow glare creeping along blood spattered walls and still huddled forms. I smell the choking black smoke pouring from the ventilators from the inferno below; I see men hurrying to and fro with pitifully inadequate buckets of sea water and sand; the epic of the medical officers working under the weak

glow of torchlight, trying to bring peace and quiet to men in
gore soaked overalls. I see, too, the Ensign fluttering proudly,
defiantly, above the death and destruction below.[7]

At about 3.30 am, the destroyer *Patterson* returned out of the dark,
to be welcomed like some ministering angel. After waiting for
more 4-inch ammunition to explode, Commander Walker skilfully nudged his ship along *Canberra*'s port side, the two hulls
grinding together. The Americans sent over portable pumps and
hoses to fight the fires and began to take the Australian wounded
on board, some of them carried down on planks, others handed
over on stretchers, including Captain Getting and Bruce Loxton.
The boy who had lost his arm, George Yeates, still groggy from
the morphine, was lowered strapped to a mess table. Two of the
doctors, Charlie Downward and Ken Morris, went over too,
for *Patterson* had her own dead and wounded to be dealt with as
well. It was slow, agonising work for an hour until, abruptly, the
destroyer's captain shouted that he had to leave – there was a radar
contact off to port, possibly hostile. 'We'll be back,' he bellowed.

Patterson surged forward, snapping the lines and dropping the
planks that had connected her to *Canberra*. She turned on her
searchlights and was immediately fired upon by the intruder. On
this night of nights, folly was heaped upon error. The mystery
ship was the *Chicago*. With the battle well and truly over,
Howard Bode had returned for one final display of rank incompetence. The shooting subsided after each ship recognised the
other and, with no damage done, *Patterson* eventually returned
to the rescue with the destroyer *Blue*, which also joined in.
Patterson, though, had bad news: Admiral Turner had directed
that if *Canberra* could not make steam and get moving again by
6.30 am, about an hour away, she would have to be sunk. Sick at
heart, Commander Walsh gave the order to leave.

Men made their farewells in their own way. Able Seaman
Stephen St George, one of the ship's bolder and more colourful
characters, dived over into the sea to clear some of the entangled
rafts that were getting in the way of the rescue. He swam down
the starboard side and there, abreast of the boiler rooms, he

could see the top of the gaping black hole made by the torpedo from the *Bagley* . . . 'big enough to drive a loco through on our starboard side amidships', he recalled after the war.[8] Then he scrambled aboard the *Blue*, where he found *Canberra*'s Chief Bosun's Mate – the Buffer – Bob Bevern, standing on deck in tears. Bevern was old navy, tar and rope, a *Tingira* boy who had joined up in 1925 at the age of 16. He had been in the cruiser as a leading seaman in the early '30s and on this posting as a petty officer since 1937. Together, they stared across at their stricken home, still smoking and now listing further. 'We could save her, we could tow her out,' Bevern croaked.

For others, there was a more intimate agony of grief, for the dead would have to be left behind with no last rite, no funeral, no burial at sea. The Thurlow brothers, the inseparable pair of signalmen from Geelong, were torn apart at last. In that bloody dawn, Tom Thurlow, the younger lad, still only 19, searched for Jim and found him at his action station on what remained of the flag deck. He was dead. His shattered body lay splayed amid the wreck and ruin of blackened, twisted steel where one of the first shells had hit, a life ended in its 21st year.

There was but one more act of brotherly love for Tom to perform. He pulled a handful of signal flags from a nearby locker and tenderly spread them over Jim as a shroud. That would have to do. He said his goodbyes and left the ship, a boy no more.

———

Trying to snatch some sleep in *Australia* after his midnight meeting with Kelly Turner and Archer Vandegrift, Victor Crutchley became aware of the battle in small, disjointed increments. The flagship was out of visual touch, too far to the east off Guadalcanal to see the action, but flares were most certainly sighted from *Australia*'s bridge, followed by soaring arcs of tracer shells and then by the sounds of heavy gunfire in what could only be a major engagement.

Yet Crutchley stayed where he was, patrolling as protection for the transports. It is extraordinary that he did not speed to rejoin his command, but, as he explained in a memorandum later in the war, 'I felt confident that our five 8-inch cruisers and four destroyers then on patrol immediately inside Savo Island could effectively deal with any force likely to have been available to send against us.'[9]

By any standards, this was curiously incurious, and, as it turned out, it was a calamitous misjudgement. It is true that neither Bode in *Chicago* nor anyone else thought to tell him that battle had been joined, and Getting in *Canberra* never had the chance to, but that is hardly an excuse. With the sound of guns in the distance, Crutchley should have gone to investigate on his own account, but at 2.26 am – with the battle already been and gone – he contented himself with a signal asking his screening groups if they were in action. As the official RAN history puts it: '*Chicago* replied "Were, but not now," and *San Juan* said "No." The action appeared to be with a surface force between Florida and Savo Islands.'

Through the remainder of the night, scraps of information reached Crutchley, but at 5.47 am he was still much in the dark when he signalled to the escort forces: 'Situation obscure. Be prepared to give battle at dawn in vicinity transport groups.'[10]

Dawn brought him only the icy reality that his force had been destroyed. It was another transparently beautiful day, mocking the catastrophe of the night. Some of the American destroyers were off to the north rescuing the survivors of *Vincennes* and *Quincy* struggling in the water, with others trying to help the *Astoria* stay afloat while taking off her wounded. And *Canberra* awaited her execution.

Obedient to Turner's order, Crutchley instructed the destroyer USS *Selfridge* to sink her, but she would not go willingly. *Selfridge* fired exactly 263 5-inch shells and four torpedoes into her but still she floated, a Scots-built vessel defiant to the last. Eventually, another destroyer, USS *Ellet*, torpedoed her at point-blank range. She could resist no longer. Destiny claimed her. His Majesty's Australian Ship *Canberra* rolled over to starboard and – never to see another forenoon watch – sank by the bow at exactly 8 am.

Mercifully, the ship's company did not see her end. The rescuing destroyers had steamed out of sight to the east before she went down, and the men, including the wounded, were being transferred to the transports for the withdrawal to Noumea. Three more died before they could be lifted from the destroyers. The transport USS *Barnett* was equipped with every possible medical service, including operating theatres of hospital standard, but this was not enough to save Frank Getting. He succumbed to his wounds and was buried at sea at the age of 43, the third of the navy's cruiser captains and the third of the first-year entry at the RANC to die in this war.

As he regrouped, Kelly Turner had to postpone the departure he had planned that morning. The invasion force was infinitely fortunate that the Japanese made no follow-up air attack, for the invaders would have been almost entirely defenceless and torn to shreds. But, before sunset, both Group X-Ray and Group Yoke had formed up with the remnants of their naval escorts, including *Australia* and *Hobart*, and were making their way south-east from this most bitter defeat, leaving the Marines alone on Tulagi and Guadalcanal. Forever after, the United States Marine Corps would look on this, sourly, as 'the great Navy bug-out'. There would be months of savage fighting ahead.

—

A week later, a telegram from the Navy Office in Melbourne arrived at the Loxton family home in Sydney, at 19 Edgeware Road, Enmore. Its message was chillingly succinct:

REGRET TO INFORM YOU THAT YOUR SON MIDN BRUCE H LOXTON RAN HAS BEEN SERIOUSLY WOUNDED AS A RESULT OF ENEMY ACTION. MINISTER FOR NAVY AND THE NAVAL BOARD DESIRE TO EXPRESS TO YOU THEIR SINCERE SYMPATHY. FURTHER INFORMATION WILL BE FORWARDED WHEN RECEIVED.[11]

Fit and resilient, the young man had survived and was recovering from his wounds in a hospital at HMNZS *Philomel*, the New Zealand naval base in Auckland. From there, he wrote to his girlfriend Dahlis, in a hand rather more shaky than his customary neat script:

> The main thing is that I am alive, got all my legs etc, and love you as much as ever . . . I must be one of the luckiest men alive, I think. I got or had bits of Nip scrap iron in all parts, the main bits being in the head, jaw, face, tummy, back, legs, arms, wrists and ankles. And every one of those multiple pieces missed anything that matters and I'll be able to enjoy Princes as much as ever. (I hope the thought didn't cause you too much anticipated agony.)
>
> By the way, please excuse my writing but I've got lots of little pieces of scrap iron in my right wrist and it's a little stiff, but will be OK soon . . .[12]

The arithmetic of Savo was appalling. Of her crew of 819, *Canberra* had lost 84 men killed outright or later to die from their injuries. Another 109 men were wounded to one degree or another but would recover. The American toll was higher: 992 men dead. When Admiral King in Washington got the signal reporting the defeat, he was so shocked that he believed some mistake had been made and demanded that it be decoded again.

Australians were not told of this tragedy until Thursday 20 August, when it was jointly announced to the newspapers by John Curtin and Douglas MacArthur. Curtin said:

> I have received a message praising the gallantry of the ship's company of the *Canberra* in this action. The battle record of the ship bearing the name of the national capital will add another illustrious page to the imperishable record of the Australian forces in this war . . .[13]

There were long lists of the dead, the wounded and the unharmed. The release of the news seems to have been carefully timed to coincide with the arrival home of the uninjured survivors on the same day, who were photographed grinning cheerfully, thumbs up, many of them in whatever clothing they had been able to scrape together:

Wearing his naval epaulettes on the shoulder of the US Army uniform in which he came ashore, Lieutenant Victor Smith DSO, RAN, said that his experiences during the shelling of HMAS *Canberra* had been just as 'unpleasant' as when he was rescued after the sinking of HMS *Ark Royal*.

Lieutenant Smith said the crew had tried in every way to save the ship until it was realised she was beyond saving. The men did 'a magnificent job all through' said Lieutenant Smith.[14]

Vic Smith, a young man from suburban Chatswood in Sydney and the observer for *Canberra*'s Walrus, was having an interesting war. He had already been shot down twice and rescued twice while flying RN Swordfish aircraft in the Mediterranean, and he had indeed been in the carrier *Ark Royal* when she was torpedoed by a U-boat near Gibraltar in November 1941.[15] Other survivors were also interviewed and gave straightforward accounts of their ordeal, often with high praise for the doctors.

In general, Australians were relieved that the casualty list had not been higher, but the loss was still sharply felt. The literary lioness Dame Mary Gilmore wrote a poem for the *Women's Weekly*:

The sea-bird breasting out upon the main
Was not more lovely on the void than she.
The waters kissed her in her going,
Lisping at her prow, and whispering at her side.
Australia loved her as they who manned her
Mess and ward, and were her living soul
But home she was to them.
They walked her decks
And slept against her heart.
Now homeless look they at the sky,
And homeless at the sea
Empty their eager hearts now she has gone
Their days are orphaned.
How lone for them the deep.[16]

Out of the blue, the Loxton family got another telegram on Monday 14 September:

YOUR SON IS EXPECTED AT SYDNEY TUESDAY 15 SEPTEMBER STOP IF YOU DESIRE TO MEET HIM PLEASE BE AT MAN O WAR STEPS AT 8AM. ADMIRAL GARDEN ISLAND.[17]

The sweetness of the homecoming was soured by that very same Admiral Garden Island, none other than Gerard Muirhead-Gould, the man who had so botched the handling of the Japanese midget-submarine attack in Sydney Harbour. Lining up some of *Canberra*'s survivors for an official welcome, he told them – with an obtuse and offensive lack of tact – that 'we should feel ashamed that our ship had been sunk by gunfire without firing a shot in return'.[18]

This low blow struck Bruce Loxton to the core, and it would remain with him for the rest of his life, with fruitful results. Muirhead-Gould was instructed to hold an official enquiry into the loss of *Canberra*, which he duly did over a hurried three days in late August. In short, his reports – he wrote two of them – concluded that the ship had not been in a proper state of readiness on the night of the battle, that there should have been less reliance on radar and more lookouts on duty, and – controversially – that it was unlikely *Canberra* had been torpedoed. Her list to starboard had most probably been caused by shells that had struck her on the port side passing through her hull and exiting to starboard. Muirhead-Gould recommended that another Board of Inquiry should be held to 'consider the reason why such a well armed and highly trained ship should have been put out of action by 24 shells from a destroyer or medium cruiser'.[19]

That last suggestion touched off a new furore, although a necessarily discreet one within naval circles, away from the public eye. The enquiry had taken evidence from very few eyewitnesses. Many of them were scattered around the country and were simply unavailable. The conclusion that *Canberra* had not been torpedoed was based largely on the personal testimony of the engineer commander, Otto McMahon, who said he had noticed nothing like a torpedo explosion at any time.

Others disagreed, including the commander, John Walsh, and Rear Admiral Crutchley himself, who wrote to Muirhead-Gould to dispute the finding. Both were convinced the ship had been struck by at least one torpedo, although neither man – nor anybody else at the time – suggested that it had come from the *Bagley*. Able Seaman St George, who had seen the torpedo hole while swimming around the ship, and other seamen and officers who had noticed a torpedo explosion, were simply not consulted. And, with the perspective of time, the notion that 24 shell hits to *port* could have caused a list to *starboard* seems perverse and improbable, to say the least. It implies that the shells had been so powerfully penetrating that some, at least, went clean through the hull, creating exit holes enough to flood her. Yet when the destroyer *Selfridge* had fired more than 200 rounds in an attempt to sink her – under controlled conditions in which each shell hit – it simply did not work. A torpedo did the job.

This controversy faded in time. A second and more detailed enquiry was never held. There was a war to get on with. In later years, long after the war, the dispute would bubble to the surface again when a sailor published his memoirs or books began to be written about the battle.

Then, in 1994, Bruce Loxton produced a book that nailed the matter once and for all. Loxton stayed on in the navy and built a distinguished career, rising to command ships and to reach the rank of Commodore. He also gained experience as an intelligence officer, and studied professionally in the United States. Burdened by a sense of injustice done not to himself but to the entire ship's company, and inspired to find the truth for history, he began a detailed forensic examination of the entire Battle of Savo in general and of *Canberra*'s role in particular. He interviewed and wrote to anybody and everybody who might shed new light; he spent months poring over documents and reports, official and unofficial; he drew maps and charts; he brought all his accumulated naval training and professional judgement to bear. It was a judicious effort, fair and balanced, propelled not by malice but by a search for answers.

The book was called, with heavy irony, *The Shame of Savo*. Written in clinical detail, its inescapable conclusion was that

Canberra had indeed been torpedoed and that only the *Bagley* could have done it. The evidence it presents is overwhelming, irrefutable – although it was disputed to the end by *Bagley* veterans, who – understandably – maintained the innocence of their ship.

Only one piece of proof evaded Bruce Loxton: *Canberra* lies on the floor of Ironbottom Sound on her starboard side. No one will ever see the torpedo hole that must be there.

———

The American enquiry into Savo was far more searching than Muirhead-Gould's haphazard effort, although it naturally concentrated rather more on the performance of the USN ships and men involved. Dissatisfied with the early reports he had been given, King fired up a searching investigation in December, asking one of his predecessors as Chief of Naval Operations, the scholarly Admiral Arthur J. Hepburn, to go through the battle from every angle.

Hepburn travelled the Pacific, rounding up all and sundry to seek the explanations for this most devastating American defeat. He talked to Admirals Nimitz, Ghormley, Fletcher and Turner. He flew to Melbourne, where, with some diplomatic finesse, he interviewed Crutchley in *Australia*; he was feted in Canberra with an audience with the Governor General and an invitation to a meeting of the War Cabinet. Back in the States, he spent long hours questioning Riefkohl of the *Vincennes* and Bode of the *Chicago*, and some of their surviving officers.

His report, delivered in 1943, was kept secret until long after the war. It was a masterpiece of tact and diplomacy, accurately uncovering the chain of error and failure that had led to the disaster but delicately declining to apportion fault or blame to the principal players.

'In my opinion, the primary cause of defeat must be ascribed generally to the complete surprise achieved by the enemy,' Hepburn wrote. He pinpointed the failings of aerial reconnaissance; of too great a reliance on the embryonic technology

of radar; of ships' commanding officers and crew being inexperienced, weary and unready for action; of communications
breakdowns that ensured the left hand never discovered what the
right hand was up to. Yet he ascribed no blame to Ghormley for
his remote, hands-off command, nor to Fletcher for his precip-
itate withdrawal of the carriers. Turner and Crutchley escaped
any censure for their deployment of the radar picket destroyers
and the two cruiser groups, and, on reading the report, King
went further and gave them a green light:

> I deem it appropriate and necessary to record my approval of
> the decisions and conduct of Rear Admiral R. K. Turner USN
> and Rear Admiral V. Crutchley RN. In my judgement, these
> two officers were in no way inefficient, much less at fault, in
> executing their parts of the operation. Both found themselves
> in awkward positions and both did their best with the means at
> their disposal.[20]

Two men were criticised. Captain Riefkohl of the *Vincennes* was
described as 'far from impressive', and in short order he found
himself assigned to the US embassy in Mexico, never to go to
sea again. The heaviest blow landed on Howard Bode. 'There is
only one instance in the circumstances immediately attendant
upon the Savo Island battle in which censure is definitely indicated,' Hepburn wrote. 'That was in the action, or inaction of
the Commanding Officer of the *Chicago*.'

Bode was plucked from his ship and sent off to command the
15th Naval District in the Panama Canal Zone, a job so demeaning to a once high-flying officer who had captained a battleship
and a cruiser that he can have been in no doubt that his career
was finished. Deeply depressed – quite possibly clinically so –
he wrote to Hepburn, 'I have decided that the only honorable
course is to atone for my errors of judgement in the only way I
can.' On the morning of 19 April 1943, he was found lying on the
floor of his bathroom with a Colt .45 revolver in his hand and a
bullet in his head. He died in hospital the next day.

Crutchley would always maintain that his cruisers and destroyers had fulfilled their primary purpose of keeping the enemy away from the transports and the Marines ashore, and there is some validity to that. But the price paid was out of all proportion. And, in a letter to Hepburn, he regretted that *Australia* had not been there in the line of battle, with a backhander for Frank Getting:

> *Australia* has, during this war, seen much service, including service in the British Home Fleet and she successfully engaged in surface [*sic*] against the French naval forces at Dakar – the bridge officers in the *Australia* are experienced. I know that they were informed by their captain of the object of the movements of the Group and that they were constantly alert. I am confident that *Australia* would have been quickly into action and that she would have given a good account of herself. Whereas *Canberra* leading the line by order of *Chicago* . . . was a recently commissioned ship commanded by a captain who had been there less than two months.[21]

The overarching truth is that inexperience was to blame for the Savo disaster, inexperience from the top down. Admiral King's rush to launch Operation Watchtower was understandable in its urgency but culpable in its failure to allow adequate time for proper planning and execution. Most of his junior admirals echoed that inexperience in different ways: Ghormley's pessimistic reluctance to exercise command; McCain's neglect to provide air support; Fletcher's shameful decision to depart with his carriers before the job was done. All these faults contributed to the tragedy.

After a decent interval, Ghormley was relieved of his command, to be replaced by the vigorous Bull Halsey. Fletcher brought the Japanese to action once more at the Battle of the Eastern Solomons on 24 and 25 August – yet another carrier encounter in which the opposing ships never saw each other. Crutchley was there in *Australia*, with *Hobart*. It was a narrow

American victory, forestalling a Japanese attempt to retake Guadalcanal. The carrier USS *Enterprise* was struck by three bombs but survived, and the Japanese carrier *Ryujo* was sunk – which, with the loss of some 70 aircraft, was enough to send Admiral Yamamoto's Combined Fleet retreating from the fray. Fletcher, though, incurred the wrath of Admiral King for not pursuing the Japanese as they withdrew, and this may have been the last straw for him. Deemed to lack aggression, he too was sent ashore, in November 1942.

A graveyard of ships and men, Savo became also a graveyard of reputations.

—

Far from the South Pacific, the northern summer of 1942 saw the Allies and the Axis locked in a titanic struggle of ever increasing ferocity, with nation states and hundreds of millions of their citizens convulsed by violence. The swastika now flew from the fjords of Norway to the sands of North Africa, from the Brittany coast of France to the wheat fields of Ukraine.

In the month of June, the mass gassing of Jews had begun at Auschwitz; in the Libyan desert, Erwin Rommel's *Afrikakorps* captured the besieged port of Tobruk and rolled eastward to El Alamein in Egypt. In July, Hitler ordered a summer thrust towards Stalingrad that would climax in the most bloody battles of the war and a massive German defeat. August saw General Bernard Montgomery take command of the British 8th Army to counter Rommel.

In the war at sea, July brought a humiliating debacle for the RN in the destruction of Convoy PQ-17, an argosy of 35 merchant ships loaded with war supplies voyaging east across the Arctic Ocean from Iceland to Archangel in Russia. Harried mercilessly by the *Kriegsmarine* and the *Luftwaffe* through the long summer daylight hours, PQ-17 fell to pieces when the Admiralty in London withdrew its naval escort and ordered the convoy to scatter, in one of the worst tactical blunders of the war. Ship after ship was sunk. Of the 35, only 11 reached their destination. Winston Churchill called it 'one of the most melancholy naval episodes in the whole of the war',[22] an understatement if ever there was one.

In the Mediterranean in August, a convoy sent to relieve Malta, known as Operation Pedestal, was also mauled by the enemy, at a loss of nine merchant ships sunk plus the aircraft carrier *Eagle* and two cruisers. Pedestal, though, ended in triumph, with the bombed, battered and barely floating tanker *Ohio* limping under tow into Grand Harbour at Valletta with a cargo of desperately needed fuel.

Throughout these tumultuous events, Churchill maintained a punishing pace. In mid-August, he flew to Moscow for an arduous negotiation with a suspicious and demanding Joseph Stalin, and then on to Teheran and Cairo to shore up his armies against the Germans and Italians. Remarkably, he held distant Australia in his thoughts, and from the Egyptian capital on 23 August he dictated this note:

> *Prime Minister to First Lord and First Sea Lord.* Australia have lost their 8-inch cruiser *Canberra*. It might have lasting effect on Australian sentiment if we gave freely and outright to Royal Australian Navy one of our similar ships. Please give your most sympathetic consideration to the project and be ready to tell me about it when I return. Meanwhile I am not mentioning it to anyone.[23]

With the RN reeling from its recent losses, it is unlikely that their Lordships greeted this suggestion with any enthusiasm, but they agreed to it nonetheless. On 9 September, Churchill told the House of Commons that the cruiser HMS *Shropshire* would be given to Australia as a gesture of kinship and empire solidarity. Perhaps it was a Churchillian olive branch extended after the row with John Curtin earlier in the year. If so, it was a big one and much appreciated. From Canberra, Curtin replied that this British generosity would be met with 'the warmest feelings'.

And so it was. Australians were delighted. While they had turned to America for their defence, they still held the Empire close. *Shropshire* was virtually a sister ship to *Australia* and *Canberra*. She would have a tradition to uphold.

CHAPTER 18

YOU HAVE BROUGHT TO AUSTRALIA AN ACCESSION OF NAVAL STRENGTH

None of the sailors and very few of the officers had ever known such comfort. They crossed the Pacific from Sydney to San Francisco in the transport USS *Mount Vernon*, a ship that before the war had been the luxury American transatlantic liner *Washington* and which, even in its wartime conversion, boasted accommodation pleasingly superior to the cramped and crowded mess decks of a warship.

In the States, things got better again. A long train of Pullman carriages and a gleaming locomotive was waiting to carry them from California to New York. There was snow as they climbed the Rockies and for six days they rolled across America like millionaires, 250 of them, their meals served in restaurant cars and their beds made up each night by white-jacketed attendants. Flouting all the rules, *Shropshire*'s prospective new gunnery officer, the amiable Lieutenant Commander Warwick 'Braces' Bracegirdle, had somehow arranged for copious supplies of beer to be loaded on board, and for bars to be open at whistle-stops – a popular gesture. One of the sleeping-car porters taught them how to shoot craps. The Americans they met were warm and hospitable, entranced by their Australian accents. In New York City, they marvelled at the Empire State Building, Grand Central Station, Radio City Music Hall. For a while, the war seemed far away.

It came back with a thump in Britain. *Shropshire* was shored up in dry dock at Chatham, the great naval base at the mouth of the Medway in Kent, and to a seaman there can be few sights more forlorn than a ship empty and silent, hull exposed, stripped of her vitals, decks strewn with tools, spares and rubbish, swarming with dockyard workers. It was the early spring of 1943, grey and bleak in a nation pinched by austerity. Trucked to the Chatham barracks, this advance guard of the new ship's company bedded down for the first few weeks in an old and dirty billiard room. By nights, the air-raid sirens would sound for a scramble to the shelters. Their meals were paltry, cold and tasteless, and dished out in a shed several hundred metres away.

The good news was that the British were doing their ship proud. Far more than a boiler clean and a lick of paint, *Shropshire* was getting a thorough refit from stem to stern, with new diesel generators and new anti-aircraft weapons that would see her bristling with 20-millimetre Oerlikon guns and the quick-firing, eight-barrelled pom-poms the Americans called the 'Chicago Piano'. The catapult was removed: the latest, most up-to-date radar being installed had ended the need for reconnaissance aircraft, which had often been more trouble than they were worth, not least as a fire risk. Most miraculous of all, there would be cafeteria messing, the first ever for the RAN. Bracegirdle, who had seen it in American ships, came up with the idea on the trip across the United States; he put it to the powers that be, and they agreed to have it installed. The days of carting half-cold food along passageways from a distant galley would soon be over – a giant leap forward.

Shropshire was a step up from *Australia* and *Canberra* in more ways than this. Though technically a County class cruiser like them, commissioned in September 1929 she came from what was known as the London sub-class, meaning that she had been tweaked and upgraded from the original design in various subtle ways. To an untrained eye, she might have looked the same – greyhound-lean and three-funnelled – but her hull was nearly a metre longer and she had no anti-torpedo bulges on her sides, which gave her almost an extra knot in speed. The funnels were slightly shorter, too, and the bridge structure had been moved aft a little to lessen the effect of the blast from the 8-inch guns of B-turret when they were fired abaft the beam. In 1943, she was the most modern and powerful ship in the RAN.

Her only problem was the name, which aroused a ruckus up to the level of Labor's War Cabinet and beyond, to Buckingham Palace. Some people thought it odd, to say the least, for an Australian warship to bear the name of a remote English county, and they agitated for her to become the new HMAS *Canberra*. Traditionalists protested that it was always bad luck to rename a warship. Others wanted to keep *Shropshire* in recognition of British generosity, and the controversy rattled around Canberra, Navy Office in Melbourne, and the newspapers for months. In the beginning, John Curtin and most of his ministers favoured the change to *Canberra*, and they advised the King to agree. In September, George VI gave it the royal rubber stamp:

> I feel sure the people of Australia will wish the name of their capital city should continue to be borne by one of their warships, and I shall therefore be pleased for HMS *Shropshire* to be renamed HMAS *Canberra* as soon as the transfer to the Royal Australian Navy has been effected.

Then the government discovered that the Americans were going to call one of their ships *Canberra*. That complicated things; it would be confusing to have two of the same name running around the Pacific. Perhaps they could be asked not to? No, they couldn't; it turned out that President Roosevelt himself had made the decision. The cruiser *Pittsburgh*, still being built, would become the new USS *Canberra* in tribute to the Australian loss at Savo. It would hardly do to knock the President back.

The controversy bubbled along. An Englishwoman, writing from the Shropshire market town of Shrewsbury, made an impassioned plea to the Minister for the Navy, Norman Makin:

> Don't think we grudge you our ship, but it has hurt us badly that her honoured name has been taken from her . . . there is enough

sadness in the world without unnecessary hurting. I don't think
out there you have realised what our ship has meant to us all
these years or you wouldn't have changed her name.

Yours truly

Miss Dolly Robinson,

Daughter of the late Col. F. W. Robinson, King's Shropshire
Light Infantry[1]

Dolly got her way. The Curtin cabinet caved in, and in February
1943 the King did an about face; the name *Shropshire* would stay.[2]
At Chatham, more drafts of men were arriving to make up the
numbers, many of them survivors from *Canberra* who had decided
to stick it out and go to sea once again. One of them was Tom
Thurlow. After the death of his brother, Tom had been given
survivor's leave by the navy and then three months as a signalman
at the Point Lonsdale Lighthouse at the mouth of Port Phillip Bay,
where he thought deeply about his future and decided to stay on.

Others came from far and wide. Guy Griffiths, the midshipman sunk in *Repulse* off Malaya, turned up as a newly promoted
sub lieutenant, fresh from a spell in an RN destroyer in the English
Channel. Edgar Blau, a snotty in *Canberra* for the *Ketty Brøvig*
incident in 1941, was now a fully fledged lieutenant who had done
the hard lying, as they called it, in another destroyer on the miserable Arctic convoys to Russia. The irrepressible Braces Bracegirdle,
mates with everyone who was anyone, had managed to hand-pick
his senior gunnery sailors from here, there and everywhere, not
least among them his Chief Gunner's Mate, Chief Petty Officer
Arthur Cooper, a salty Western Australian who'd been in the navy
since 1926.

Bracegirdle was naval royalty himself, a son of the mag-
nificently named Rear Admiral Sir Leighton Bracegirdle, a
Hornblowerish figure who had served at the Boxer Rebellion and
Gallipoli and been private secretary to four Governors General.
Much loved and respected by his men, Braces was renowned
for having quietly and sensibly defused a sit-down strike over
uniforms in the cruiser *Perth* and for being blown into Piraeus
Harbour when the *Luftwaffe* bombed Athens in 1941.

Shropshire's new captain would be John Collins. Since the headlong retreat from Java, he had been whiling away the time as a Commodore and Naval Officer-in-Charge, Western Australia. The offer of another cruiser command meant dropping a rank back to captain again, but he seized the opportunity for an additional spell at sea. After a dash to America by air and an Atlantic crossing on the liner *Queen Elizabeth*, he turned up at Chatham on 7 April 1943. His arrival was not entirely welcome. One of his first acts was to cancel the issue of a daily tot of rum to the ship's company, a 300-year-old tradition in the RN but never adopted in the RAN. With some paperwork push and shove, *Shropshire* was hastily switched from HMS to HMAS, and the rum ration stopped. Some of the men never forgave him.

For the next couple of months, they worked to get the ship ready for sea, scraping rust and chipping paint, stowing stores, complaining about the English drizzle, and dodging irritably around the dockyard workers and engineers performing mysterious functions above and below decks. Chatham had been building ships since the time of the first Elizabeth, not least among them Nelson's flagship *Victory* and *The Fighting Temeraire*, the mighty wooden battleship immortalised in the great Turner painting. A cruiser was neither here nor there. All in good time, *Shropshire* returned to life, floating out of the dry dock and into No. 3 basin, where the dynamos began to hum again and power and lighting returned: the pleasingly familiar sights and sounds of a ship breathing. The watches were set and that eagerly awaited cafeteria messing got into its stride, the miracle reported with wide-eyed wonder in the RAN annual:

> Each man collects an aluminium tray which is recessed into a number of 'plates,' so that he can, on the one dish, be served with meat, vegetables, sweet, bread and so on, as he passes along a series of hot plates. Having collected his issue, he goes to his mess and has his meal, then takes the tray, knife, fork, spoon and cup to an appointed spot where they are collected and washed ready for the next meal. This latest edition of 'cooks to the galley' appears to have found favour.[3]

The cafeteria would come to be known as Otto's Grotto, in honour of the man in charge, Chief Petty Officer Otto Smith.

Many of the men were sent on courses in gunnery and the like, including Collins himself, who had some catching up to do in radar and in fighter direction, the control of aircraft at sea. The war was always present, in the moan of air-raid sirens at night or the thunder of bombers overhead on their way to Occupied France and Germany, and in a sad incident that brought *Shropshire* her first casualty. Skylarking with a few mates, Able Seaman John Stanbury, from Essendon in Melbourne and a *Canberra* survivor, jumped a wall to retrieve his cap and was blown to pieces when he touched off an unexploded German land mine. He had just turned 20.

It was not all work. There was time to relax, time to take the train up to London to see the fabled sights of the capital of Empire, battered though many of them were by the Blitz. The coming of spring brought the delights of the Kentish country-side to one of the Sin Bosuns, Chaplain Bill Hunkin:

> My most vivid recollections are the green fields with their butter-cups and daisies and the pink and white may; the thatched roofs of the little villages through which we passed in our walks and the little village churches with their atmosphere of a picturesque past; the village pubs which I came to realise were an institution just as much a part of England as anything else in the village.[4]

Hunkin may or may not have hoisted a pint of ale in one of the institutions – he was a Methodist – but the ship's officers found themselves welcomed at the Hook and Hatchet, a quaint little country pub of mellow old brick and whitewashed timber that was a pleasant morning's walk from the dockyard. Others were invited for tennis on the beautifully manicured court of the Commander-in-Chief, the Nore, Admiral Sir George D'Oyly Lyon, an amiable figure who had captained England in the first ever rugby Test against Australia in 1909.[5] It was an English idyll before their return to the horrors of war.

After some unspecified scrape with the naval shore patrol in Chatham, Tom Thurlow and a mate took their weekend leave

further afield, one day taking a train up to Oxford to wander
around the colleges. They had lunch at the YMCA and got
chatting to one of the volunteers working there, who gave her
name as Harriet Simons and asked where they were staying for
the night. They didn't know, so she invited them home, a more
than generous offer when British families were struggling along
on food rationing, but Harriet had two sons in the navy herself.

That evening, when the two Australians knocked on the
door of the little cottage at Shelley Road in suburban Cowley, it
was opened by the most beautiful girl Tom had ever seen. Her
name was Audrey. 'Don't tell me, I know, Mum sent you,' she
said. A petite, brown-eyed brunette with the exquisite complexion of the English rose, Audrey Simons had been a bookbinder
in peacetime, but with the coming of war she had taken a job
welding jerry cans, and would work later as an inspector in an
aircraft factory. Tom fell head over heels. She did too. After that,
he got away to Oxford whenever he could; they went out for tea
and sometimes to the pictures, and, when *Shropshire* sailed from
Chatham, they promised to write to each other.

That day came on Saturday 26 June, when the cruiser farewelled Kent for the last time and Collins took them down the
Medway into the English Channel off Sheerness for those
101 tests and trials to make sure a ship is ready for sea. In July,
they were with the Home Fleet in Scapa Flow, turned inside
out and back again by an exhausting fortnight of exercises to
whip them into fighting efficiency. There seemed to be barely
a moment they were not raising the anchor by hand, refuelling
a destroyer, towing a cruiser, firing at towed aircraft targets,
mounting an 8-inch bombardment, spotting by searchlight,
dodging torpedo bombers or fighting imaginary fires.

The engineers discovered a problem that had dogged
Shropshire for years: the starboard outer shaft running so rough
that the ship usually limped along on just three engines. Suspect-
ing – with good reason – that the Admiralty had happily passed
on a lemon it was glad to be rid of, they took the shaft to pieces,
found the wrong thrust block pads had been installed and put

in the correct ones. In Collins's words, she 'ran like a sewing machine for the rest of her life'.[6]

On 12 August at Scapa, George VI came on board for a royal visit of inspection, in the uniform of an Admiral of the Fleet. It had been a good idea to keep the name *Shropshire*, he told Collins, and what splendid physiques the men had, although he thought perhaps their jumpers were not quite regulation, the collars being a bit low cut. This horror surmounted, Collins dined with the King that night in the battleship *Duke of York*, and the next morning *Shropshire* weighed and turned her heads towards Australia and her new home. She escorted a convoy bound for Gibraltar without incident, rounded the Cape of Good Hope, crossed the Indian Ocean and touched at Fremantle on 24 September, where the Western Australians were given leave. A week later, on 2 October, she eased alongside the cruiser wharf at Garden Island in Sydney, to be welcomed by the Governor General, Lord Gowrie. Captain Collins was handed a letter from the Prime Minister:

> . . . You have brought to Australia an accession of naval strength which is especially welcome at this time when the tide having turned, we and our allies are now pressing the offensive against the enemy in the Pacific as well as in other seas.[7]

The tide had indeed turned. But there were nearly two more years of war to come.

———

John Curtin had every reason for confidence and optimism. The year 1942, which had begun so badly, had ended well for Australia and Australians, perhaps better than anyone had expected. In the Middle East in October and November, the Australian Army's 9th Division had played a pivotal role with Montgomery's British 8th Army in the victory over Rommel at El Alamein, the last great imperial battle.

Closer to home, and more resounding still, the army had crushed a Japanese attempt to take Milne Bay in September, the

first defeat on land for Japan. By November, the ragged heroes
of Kokoda had driven the enemy back to the sea in New Guinea,
a triumph cemented with the victories at Buna and Gona by
January 1943.

Throughout the Pacific, the rising sun of Nippon had reached
its zenith and was beginning to set. At Guadalcanal, the Japanese
had thrown everything into the attempt to prise the Americans
off the island and out of the Solomons, running what came to
be known as the nightly 'Tokyo Express' of IJN destroyers,
and later submarines, down the Slot to resupply their troops
ashore. The Americans, reinvigorated by the energetic Bull
Halsey, bested them in a series of ferocious battles, a desperate
struggle of attrition. Six months of fighting on land, much of it
unmatched in savagery, ended in yet another Japanese defeat and
final withdrawal.

Guadalcanal had been won, though at tremendous cost. For
the Japanese, of some 38,000 who fought there, around 28,000
were killed, or died of disease. The US Marines lost more than
4000 dead.[8] Years after the war, Halsey paid generous tribute
to the matchless contribution of the Australian coastwatchers
hidden in their lonely jungle camps. 'I could get down on my
knees every night and thank God for Commander Eric Feldt,'
he told guests at a Coral Sea commemorative dinner in Brisbane
in 1954.[9]

In March 1943, the Battle of the Bismarck Sea saw American
and RAAF aircraft virtually obliterate a Japanese attempt to
reinforce Lae with troops from Rabaul. In two days, eight transports and five destroyers were sunk from the air, with some
3000 troops killed. American PT boats sent in to finish the job
machine-gunned Japanese survivors in the water, claiming –
in words later echoed by Morison, the official historian – that
'it had to be done'.

Just weeks later, United States intelligence learnt of Admiral
Yamamoto's schedule for a flying visit from Rabaul to Bougainville, and on the morning of Sunday 18 April his aircraft and its
escort were jumped by a flight of 16 P-38 Lightning fighters from

Guadalcanal. The admiral's body was found in the wreckage in the Bougainville jungle the next day with one bullet wound in the head and another in the chest, a blow so shattering to Japanese morale that a month was spent inventing heroic details of his death and discovery. It was not until 21 May that the high command in Tokyo announced that Yamamoto had been found sitting upright in his seat, head bowed as if lost in thought, still clutching his Samurai sword in white-gloved hands.

The string of victories was not achieved without cost and strain in the alliance. At his Australian headquarters in Brisbane, Douglas MacArthur had begun to display swelling signs of the rampant egotism that would eventually lead to his downfall in another war under another President. Under pressure to produce swift and dramatic results, he had come to the conclusion that the Australians in New Guinea were not up to the job of delivering him the victories he craved.

'The Australians have proven themselves unable to match the enemy in jungle fighting,' he cabled his chief in Washington, General George Marshall. 'Aggressive leadership is lacking.'[10] MacArthur conceived this fanciful notion from a distance, never bothering to place his valuable person anywhere near the sight nor sound of gunfire. 'Dugout' Doug was living up to the name his troops had cynically given him in the Philippines. The relationship between him and the Australian commander, General Thomas Blamey, was mutually distrustful, not least, perhaps, because both men were vigorous self-promoters who recognised it in each other. In fairness, MacArthur also fought furious battles with his own countrymen, especially Admirals Nimitz in Hawaii and King in Washington, who, he believed – with no small degree of paranoia – were out to do him down. Lower down the totem pole, he could be ruthless with generals and even colonels he felt had failed him.

Inevitably, these tensions between and among the Allies worked their way downwards. By June 1943, there were 200,000 American troops in Australia, most of them based in Queensland. Jealousies and resentments festered. The occasional loud-talking, big-noting

Yank would run hard into a cocky, resentful and often drunken Aussie. Insults would erupt, fists and sometimes knives would fly. Towards the end of 1942, there was a spate of ugly brawls between American and Australian troops in Brisbane and Townsville, culminating in the notorious Battle of Brisbane, which saw violent riots on the nights of 26 and 27 November, and one Australian shot dead in a struggle for a gun held by a US Military Policeman. Censorship kept a tight lid on the news, the Brisbane *Courier-Mail* reporting only that 'servicemen' had rioted, without mentioning any nationalities. Eventually, the troubles died away, or at least simmered quietly below the surface. At the sharp end where the fighting was done, by land or sea, there was far more often than not a genuine mutual respect for each other's capacities, which matured over time into a strong sense of comradeship. There, the alliance was solid and burgeoning.

Curtin had more cause for confidence, too. In Australia's interests, he had stood firm against Churchill and won. At great personal and political cost, he had convinced the Labor Party and the nation that young men must be conscripted for the fight, that members of the Citizen Military Forces should be liable for service outside Australia, in New Guinea and the islands of the South-West Pacific Area. It was one of the most courageous decisions he ever took. As a young Labor firebrand, he had vociferously opposed conscription for the First World War, being briefly imprisoned for refusing to take a medical exam. With the weight of the prime ministership on him in this war, he came to the conclusion there was no alternative, not least because American conscripts had begun arriving for the defence of Australia. It was the right decision, but it brought him anguish when some of his oldest Labor friends accused him of betraying his principles and the party's policy.

Vindication came at the federal election held on 21 August 1943. Labor returned to power with thumping majorities in both the House of Representatives and the Senate, in a record swing away from the conservative parties unmatched to this day. In the lower house, Labor won 49 seats against just 19 for the coalition of the Country Party and the United Australia Party, a resounding vote of confidence in the government's handling of the war. The Senate vote was equally emphatic. Curtin had been handed the prime ministership by the Governor General after the conservative collapse in 1941. He had now won the people's mandate to govern, more than convincingly.

There was another step forward as well. Women were elected to parliament for the first time. Dame Enid Lyons, widow of the former Prime Minister Joe Lyons, entered the House of Representatives for the (now abolished) Tasmanian seat of Darwin, and schoolteacher Dorothy Tangney won a Western Australian Senate seat for Labor. The times were changing.

Both publicly and privately, Curtin and MacArthur continued to have full confidence in each other. This most unlikely partnership held firm through all the ups and downs of war. Each man recognised that he needed the other and, in the beginning, responded to that need sensibly and properly. Later, MacArthur would play upon this closeness to keep Australian troops mopping up pockets of the enemy in sometimes futile actions in the rear while the Americans surged gloriously forward, but that was not yet.

Curtin's other achievement – although it was not his alone – had been to unite the Australian people in the war effort. The early speeches of his prime ministership bristled with exhortations to put shoulders to the wheel and noses to the grindstone, coupled with the fear that Australians did not realise the peril they were in. By 1943, that changed. The existence of that peril was beyond doubt, and, although it was generally believed by then that Australia was safe from invasion, there was a national determination to strain every sinew and muscle in rolling back the Japanese Empire.

At home, people complained or made jokes about rationing and the often erratic and eccentric dictates of the various bureaucratic nabobs in charge of supplies and manpower. The Minister for War Organisation, a dour but able Scot named John Dedman, was regularly lampooned by the cartoonists as the

Minister for Austerity, the wicked figure who, in the words of
his official biography, had 'deprived men of their waistcoats and
shirt tails [hence the nickname "Lumbago Jack"], brides of pink
icing on their wedding cakes [white was the mandatory colour]
and children of Father Christmas [restrictions on seasonal advertising in 1942]'.[11]

Yet Australians also chipped in generously for the war loans
the government announced every so often. 'Money you save
and lend for war increases available manpower,' they were told.
'When you refuse to buy anything unless you really need it, you
help conserve manpower for urgent war work – manpower which
would otherwise be dissipated in non-essential industries. When
you lend what you save to Australia you make a further direct
contribution to Australia's war effort. So keep on buying War
Savings Certificates . . .'[12]

There was another, darker imperative. It was not forgotten that
tens of thousands of young men were prisoners of the Japanese,
with the first reports of atrocities in Thailand and Burma beginning to filter through via the Swiss Red Cross. Their families
lived in both dread and hope, listening anxiously to the radio
for the news of prisoners' names infrequently released by the
Japanese.

Radio came into its own during the war as a source of information and entertainment, on both the ABC and commercial
networks. Families gathered around the wireless each night in
the lounge room to hear the news and enjoy the quiz and variety
programs. There was an earnest determination to be gay in
the old sense of the word, with a high premium on humour. A
soaring radio star of the time was the American-born Bob Dyer,
the son of the traditionally dirt-poor Tennessee share cropper,
who had found his way to Australia before the war and made it
onto the Tivoli Music Hall circuit as a harmonica and ukulele
player with a jokey line in hillbilly patter. Radio made him.
Married to a blonde Tivoli showgirl, Thelma McLean – whom
everyone called Dolly – he was nightly listening with *The Last of
the Hillbillies* and *Bob Dyer's Variety Show*, which promised you:

Crazy comedy . . . hit tunes . . . red hot rhythm . . . everything that makes a terrific show. Produced and directed by Bob Dyer himself – the man who keeps Australia laughing – and supported by leading stage and radio personalities. Presented by the makers of Persil and Guardian Family Health Soap.[13]

For young people, the jitterbug was the hot craze, a hectic dance imported by the Americans and described by one of its many disapproving critics as 'gyrations, contortions, convulsions, crawlings, jumpings, tossings, tumblings, wrigglings, assaults and batteries'. But the *Army News* reported happily that:

Jitterbug, jazz and jive flourish. Dances for American and Australian servicemen on leave in the south are nearly as popular escapist fare as screen entertainment.

Now that the nip of winter is in the air more devotees than ever are crowding the floors. Boys from New York, Chicago, Ypsilanti, and points west, to whom 'jumpin' jive,' and those 'killer-diller' rhythms of off-the-note music are a 'honey,' find something of their old home town atmosphere in Australian dance halls.

Every night, including Sunday, clarinets are tilted towards the ceiling, pouring out a flowing rhythm. Saxophones and 'bull' fiddles come in with their throaty tones, and then the whole band goes off into a sort of jungle chant that sets American feet beating time. That's how the dancers like it. They twist and twirl and shake their hips, as the music gets in the groove . . .[14]

Young men rushed to fit themselves out with zoot suits, again copied from the Americans, an outfit of a knee-length jacket and trousers baggy at the knees and tight at the ankles. But woe betide you if you attracted the vengeful attention of John Dedman's fun police, as *The Sydney Morning Herald* sternly reported in an article of September 1943, which so delightfully illuminates the spirit of the times that it is worth repeating in full:

ZOOT SUITER'S NEW JOB. Tailor May Be Prosecuted
Sydney's first 'zoot-suiter,' George Paulos Kiouzcois, 16, a youth

of Greek descent, has been found a job in heavy industry by the man-power authorities.

The tailor who made the suit will probably be prosecuted for alleged infringement of the clothing restrictions and the 'zoot suit' is being held by the authorities to be used as evidence if a prosecution is launched.

Kiouzcois had been a constant attendant at dance halls, and his appearance in a 'zoot suit' aroused the interest of many, including the Deputy Director of War Organisation of Industry, Mr. Ifould.

When the authorities got in touch with the youth, he was instructed to report at 10 a.m. on Wednesday. He arrived at noon, explaining that he danced every night and was so tired that he never arose before 10 a.m.

After Mr. Ifould had questioned him about the origin of the suit Kiouzcois was questioned by man-power officers. The youth said that he did casual waiting in restaurants. He was found a more stable occupation in heavy industry at Waterloo, and he started work at 2 p.m.

Mr. Ifould said yesterday that he was recommending the prosecution of the tailor who had made the suit which, he said, was wasteful of material. He understood that orders had been placed with certain other tailors for similar suits, and he warned them that they would be prosecuted if they infringed the regulations.

'I have received several letters about this "zoot suit,"' Mr. Ifould added, 'and I want to assure the public that such flouting of the restrictions on clothing styles will not be permitted.'[15]

Women had it just as tough. In August 1943, when a rumour spread like a bushfire that nylon stockings imported from America would suddenly become available in the shops, it had to be officially denied:

NYLON STOCKINGS NOT FOR AUSTRALIA.
SYDNEY. An announcement that thousands of pairs of Nylon stockings would be sold throughout Australia within the next

few days was officially denied today by the Director of the Division of Import Procurement (Mr. Moore).

'Even the most Spartan-like Australian woman no doubt will have experienced an anticipatory glow of satisfaction at the announcement, but it is a pity that it has no foundation in fact,' said Mr. Moore.

'There are two important reasons why the statement has no foundation. Firstly, no requisition or demand has been made by the Australian Government for Nylon stockings, and secondly, the U.S. Government has taken steps to ensure that Nylon is used for war purposes in preference to its use in the manufacture of stockings.'

Nylon stockings look like silk but are really a by-product of coal tar.[16]

The war was changing Australian society in profound and unexpected ways, not always recognised at the time. The fall of Singapore had weakened the ties of empire, and new bonds to the United States were being woven.

—

If Australia was now safe from invasion, it was certainly not immune from individual attacks at sea. In early 1943, Japanese submarines ranged along the east coast at will, hunting and sinking merchant vessels in lightly defended convoys as far south as the Victorian border and north to Rockhampton and beyond. The account was opened in January by the submarine *I-21*, which had been one of the mother boats in the midget raid on Sydney Harbour and which now began to lay a trail of destruction in the Western Pacific. On 17 January, *I-21* torpedoed and sank a small freighter of the Union Steam Ship Company, the SS *Kalingo*, 180 kilometres east of Sydney on her way to New Zealand – a success that she followed up, almost unhindered, with four more sinkings in the span of a fortnight. In the coming months, other Japanese submarines joined the fray, leaving both the navy and the RAAF struggling to respond, for it was the attacker that always had the overwhelming advantage of stealth and surprise.

The newly commissioned submarine *I-177* sailed from the Japanese base at Truk on 10 April 1943, under the command of an experienced captain, Lieutenant Commander Hajime Nakagawa, whose orders were to sink what he could find off the Australian east coast. His first kill was the 8724-tonne British freighter *Limerick*, which he sent to the bottom off Cape Byron in the far north of New South Wales a few minutes after 1 am on 26 April, with the loss of two lives. Nakagawa successfully evaded a search by the corvette HMAS *Colac* but then spent nearly three weeks more wandering in Queensland waters without a target in his periscope.

His luck changed in the very early hours of Friday 14 May. With *I-177* patrolling on the surface 80 kilometres east north-east of Brisbane, Nakagawa was called to the bridge in fine weather with good visibility and a calm sea, to see a brightly lit ship steaming northward, on her own, and well within reach. He submerged to periscope depth, lined up his target and, just after 4 am, fired a single torpedo at point-blank range. He could not miss and he did not. The torpedo hit the hospital ship *Centaur* in a fuel tank on her port side, which exploded in flames. It was catastrophic. *Centaur* sank within three minutes.

There can be no doubt that Nakagawa knew he was attacking a hospital ship, a war crime under the Geneva Convention. Like all hospital ships, *Centaur* was painted white with a broad green stripe down each side of her hull, those stripes broken by three unmistakeably large red crosses. The number 47, her registration with the International Red Cross as a hospital ship, was clearly visible on her bows. She was brightly lit specifically so those markings could be easily seen and identified, and, moreover, it was a clear, moonlit night. A warship, or a merchant vessel travelling alone, would have been showing no lights at all. Lieutenant Commander Nakagawa had deliberately committed an act of mass murder.

There were 332 souls on board, including 12 women army nurses and 192 medical personnel of the army's 2/12th Field Ambulance, all of them heading to the war in New Guinea. They were non-combatants. Almost all were asleep and died quickly, killed by the explosion and the fire, or by drowning. Only one of the nurses survived, Lieutenant Ellen Savage, a 30-year-old from Quirindi in New South Wales:

> Merle Morton and myself were awakened by two terrific explosions and practically thrown out of bed . . . I registered mentally that it was a torpedo explosion . . . In that instant the ship was in flames . . . we ran into Colonel Manson, our commanding officer, in full dress even to his cap and 'Mae West' life-jacket, who kindly said 'That's right girlies, jump for it now.'
>
> The first words I spoke was to say 'Will I have time to go back for my great-coat?' as we were only in our pyjamas. He said 'No' and with that climbed the deck and jumped and I followed . . . the ship was commencing to go down. It all happened in three minutes.[17]

Savage was dragged under by the suction of the sinking ship, down and down, battered and tossed by debris, breaking some ribs and her nose and perforating her eardrums, until suddenly she was shot to the surface in the middle of an oil slick. Despite these injuries, she clambered onto a raft with a handful of other survivors, alternately singing and praying to keep up everyone's spirits until they were rescued 36 hours later. There were only 64 of them, plucked from the water by the American destroyer *Mugford*.

Nakagawa's atrocity outraged Australia and the world, although his name was not known at the time and the government in Tokyo blandly denied all knowledge of it, and continued to do so long after the war. Curtin called it 'an entirely inexcusable act, undertaken in violation of the convention to which Japan is a party and of all the principles of common humanity', and MacArthur said it was an example of Japanese 'limitless savagery'. This crime became a symbol of all that was evil in the Japanese war machine and a weapon of Allied propaganda, with the Australian Government printing a widely circulated colour poster depicting the sinking with the legend 'Avenge

The Centaur'.[18] It aroused in the Australian people a fiery urge
for retribution.

—

By the middle of 1943, the RAN had grown to a size and strength
unimaginable before the war. From a slow and uncertain start,
local shipbuilding had begun to hit its stride, and a steady stream
of the workhorse corvettes and destroyers had begun to run down
the slipways. At the end of June, the navy could count a remarkable 83 ships on its combat strength, including three cruisers,
ten destroyers, three sloops and 48 corvettes, plus various motor
launches, and landing and supply craft. The two new Tribal-class
destroyers commissioned in 1942, *Arunta* and *Warramunga*, were
a special pride: spanking new, up-to-the-minute ships boasting
six 4.7-inch guns and a handsome 36 knots, built at Cockatoo
Island in Sydney. *Warramunga*'s commissioning captain was Emile
Dechaineux, back from his destroyer exploits with the RN for his
first command of an Australian ship in Australian waters.

This expansion meant a rush of new people too, all of whom
had to be trained to man these new ships. If you were a young
bloke who had ever skippered a yacht and held a sextant outside
Sydney Heads or Port Phillip Bay, you were almost guaranteed
a sub lieutenant's single wavy stripe or better in the Volunteer
Reserve. Some of these officers, hastily signed on, rose to great
heights. Lieutenant Commander Stanley Darling, a former ABC
radio announcer from Hobart who had been rushed through the
reserve officer training course at Sydney's Rushcutters Bay, was
awarded the Distinguished Service Cross and two bars for sinking
three U-boats while in command of the frigate HMS *Loch Killin*
in the North Atlantic. Others were less successful, verging on the
downright dangerous and incompetent, regulars as well as reserves.
In 1941, the crew of the destroyer HMAS *Nestor* refused to put to
sea because the officers, including the captain – a commander and
an RANC graduate – were perpetually drunk.

Sometimes, this helter-skelter expansion grew beyond
anyone's ability to control it. At Navy Office in Melbourne, and

for just about everybody else as well, even the most simple logistics tasks could be an unending nightmare. At the beginning of 1943, a navy detachment helping to build a new base ashore at Oro Bay on the north-eastern coast of New Guinea found itself grinding along in something close to abject poverty. An officer who arrived to inspect them, Captain Rupert Garsia, was shocked to see that they were living:

> on the charity of a United States Army military mess. They have neither knife, spoon, fork, mug or plate. They have nothing . . . the position is one that will bring the naval service into disrepute with the United States Army, the Australian Army and also the United States Navy if they witness it.[19]

The commanding officer there, Commander Charles Webb, reported:

> The place itself, especially around the waterfront, is pretty awful. A dark hut is our dining room and a rough table and old cases make up the furniture, and the food consists of bully beef, tinned sausages, tinned vegetables etc etc, never hot and practically the same for every meal, and washed down with a mixture that is either tea or coffee or both. Outside each tent we have a hole boarded and bagged for officers to hop into in case of need . . .[20]

This was hardly an isolated happening, and the food at sea was often little better, especially if a ship had been out for weeks in waters far from home. The contrast with the well fed and supplied Yanks could be galling and at times embarrassing, like finding yourself the shabby country bumpkin at a society wedding, but, to their credit, the Americans rarely rubbed it in, as they might well have. And the Australians did have one ace to play: alcohol in ready supply. The USN was dry and had been since 1914. It was a rare Australian wardroom that couldn't somehow lay its hands on a carton of beer or a bottle of scotch for a spot of bartering, and some dizzy deals were done. Legend had it – and likely close enough to the truth – that Warwick Bracegirdle once traded a case of scotch for half a dozen American Bofors anti-aircraft guns and the ammunition to go with them, all delivered and installed on *Shropshire* in an afternoon.

One American practice caught on happily as well. In late 1942, Navy Office decreed that officers could and should wear khaki shirts and shorts, with khaki cap covers, instead of the starchy white uniforms that were impossible to keep crisp and clean for more than half an hour at work. If they weren't as smartly cut as the American khakis, they were at least comfortable and practical, although the stuffier traditionalists snorted at this lapse of standards; the RN stuck with white to the end. By 1943, sailors were permitted to wear khaki too, another welcome leap forward in the tropics, where the usual working gear was just a pair of shorts, boots, a cap and a suntan. In theory, men were supposed to keep their shirts on, but it was a rule impossible to enforce, and few officers were silly enough to try. There were bigger things to worry about than that.

—

The new year of 1943 began quietly for *Australia*. The Americans did yet another of those reorganisations and renumberings they seemed to enjoy, so that the Naval Forces South-West Pacific magically became the USN's Seventh Fleet. That in turn had the numbers filtering downwards, so Victor Crutchley's Australian Task Force 44 was rebranded Task Force 74. In February, *Australia* had yet another refit at Garden Island to upgrade her radar, and by March she was back at sea again, caught up in the monotonous routine of patrols and exercises, and the occasional convoy along the east coast without even the slightest hint of enemy activity. The ship spent so much time at anchor off Palm Island that the crew began to call themselves Curtin's Koalas – not allowed outside the Barrier Reef. It was a respite, though, a tropical idyll for many. Lieutenant John Stokes, from Henley Beach in South Australia, an RANVR intelligence officer on Crutchley's staff, recalled it fondly:

> Most sailors rarely see their own ship except when alongside a wharf, but many and many a time the men of *Australia* saw her

lying at anchor silhouetted at sunset, as they returned from leave ashore. Very many perhaps remember her most vividly in the setting of Palm Island, with the drone of Wilbur, the wonderful Duck, overhead, as it returned from Townsville with mail and steak, and then alighted with a roar.

Good days they were, when afternoons could be spent playing football or swimming and men picnicked with billies on the beach; when there were coconuts to eat and villages and mountains to explore. Friends were made with the inhabitants. There were even white women to speak to. The aboriginal children came to recognize each person and in the evenings under the palm trees they sometimes danced. There were also afternoons sailing and fishing, there was frequent visiting between ships when Americans and Australians made many enduring friendships. There was fishing from the side of the ship (an occupation which usually produced much more laughter than fish). And there was oystering: oysters three inches across with shells twice that width, oysters in unlimited profusion and a high premium on chipping hammers with which to prise them up. A happy, lazy time, yet it was one of intense boredom, broken only once by a memorable trip to the New Hebrides – memorable not for action but for games of softball at Espiritu Santo and for the hospitality of American ships and a never completed boat-pulling regatta in Havannah Harbour.[21]

In fact, the Pacific War itself was in stasis, a curious period of inactivity in which each side, bloodied but unbeaten, regrouped to decide what to do next. The Japanese and the Americans continued to grapple with each other in the waters of the Solomons north of Guadalcanal, each side losing ships and men without any decisive result, but there was no great clash of arms on the scale of Coral Sea or Midway.

In January, the American President and the British Prime Minister met again, this time at Casablanca in Morocco (Stalin was invited, but replied that he was too preoccupied with the Battle for Stalingrad). They proclaimed, at Roosevelt's inspiration, that their overarching war aim was the unconditional surrender of the Axis powers. Much of the emphasis was on the war in Europe and the Mediterranean, with the Pacific tacked on as an afterthought. Later, from Washington, the Joint Chiefs asked MacArthur and Nimitz to put up their plans for 1943, letting it be known that they were not expecting much to happen until the middle of the year, when new ships would be available.

Refusing to sit back twiddling his thumbs, MacArthur had other ideas, which he put together in a plan codenamed Elkton. Broadly, he wanted to take Rabaul in a major offensive. Elkton went through a series of changes as it was batted back and forth around the Pacific and up to Washington, principally because the navy believed the army and MacArthur were biting off more than they could chew. The rivalry between the two services was fiery and at times viciously personal. In February 1943, MacArthur haughtily refused to supply Bull Halsey with bombers he needed for Guadalcanal. The Bull wrote a private letter to Nimitz complaining about the insult and snapped, 'I refuse to get into controversy with him or any other self-advertising Son of a Bitch.'[22]

But the two had to work together, like it or not, and it was Halsey who broke the ice, offering to fly to Brisbane to meet MacArthur in April. In short, the son of a bitch charmed the pants off him. The general greeted the feisty little admiral with the warmest of handshakes, put him up at a suite at Lennon's, Brisbane's best hotel, and engaged him in long private talks in his spartan office in the AMP building, beneath portraits of Washington and Lincoln.

'Five minutes after I reported I felt as if we were lifelong friends,' Halsey recalled later. MacArthur responded in kind, saying, 'I liked him from the moment we met,' and that he found Halsey 'blunt, outspoken, dynamic'.[23] The war effort was on an even keel again, at least for the time being, although MacArthur would remain perpetually suspicious that the USN was conspiring to dim the light of his triumphs.

—

Australia's next brush with the enemy came in the winter of 1943. It was Tuesday 20 July, on another of those lovely tropical evenings of fine, clear weather with perfect visibility and a moderate sea. The newly named Task Force 74 was steaming some 320 kilometres west of the New Hebrides, on a course almost due east for the island of Espiritu Santo with *Australia* in the lead, *Hobart* following 600 metres behind her, and three American destroyers, *O'Bannon*, *Radford* and *Nicholas*, forming an anti-submarine screen. With the last rays of the setting sun astern to the west, the customary orders had been given to darken ship, and the force was zigzagging at a comfortable 23 knots, an added anti-submarine precaution.

It was not enough. Patrolling on the surface, Lieutenant Commander Meiji Tagami in command of the submarine *I-11* saw the ships outlined in perfect silhouette against the afterglow, at a range of around 16 kilometres, and he conned his boat for an attack. Tagami was a recognised ace, one of the IJN's most successful submarine captains. He fired two of his Type 95 21-inch torpedoes, one for each cruiser, each with a warhead carrying 400 kilograms of high explosive and travelling at 50 knots, set to run shallow. The torpedo intended for *Australia* missed and vanished. The other struck *Hobart* at 6.45 pm, slamming into her port side aft, just above the wardroom and immediately below Y-turret, but luckily missing the after magazine by a couple of metres. A hit there would have blown the cruiser and all in her to kingdom come.

As it was, the explosion lifted Y-turret clean off its mountings and into the air, to crash back down on the deck again. The ship was plunged into darkness, two of her four propellers were blown off, she took on a slight list to port, and her whole after part was awash. And men died – 13 of them. Seven were officers who had been relaxing in the wardroom or in their cabins directly beneath the explosion. Six sailors were killed, four of them from the crew of Y-turret, who were blown overboard.

Hobart's captain, Harry Showers, another of the RANC original entry class, was on the compass platform within

15 seconds of the hit, ordering action stations and battling to save his ship. Fortunately, there was no fire, electrical power was quickly restored, and one port and one starboard engine were still operating, although, as Showers described it, the entire after section of the ship was 'waving in the breeze'.[24] The captain and his engineer commander, Roger Parker, nursed the cruiser to safety with consummate seamanship:

> With all steering gear destroyed or inoperable, the ship was steered from the Bridge by main engines with steady revs on the starboard forward intact screw, and varying the revs on the damaged port forward screw as necessary to maintain a steady course. With the stern of the ship almost under water, it was necessary to transfer several hundred tons of fuel from the after tanks to forward tanks to restore trim. The stern of the ship was just hanging literally by the starboard side hull plating, as the keel had been blown through and the port side plating and Quarterdeck severed. A steel wire rope was rove round the gunwale to secure the stem. We were able to maintain about 7–8 knots and the weather, fortunately, for the next 24 hours was completely calm. Two American destroyers, which had formed part of the screen when we were torpedoed, stood by us for the trip back to Espiritu Santo, which we successfully made towards midnight on the following day.[25]

It had been a near-run thing. Meiji Tagami and *I-11* got clean away. Luck and good seamanship had saved *Hobart*, but she would be out of the war until December 1944 – a heavy blow to the navy.

PART 4

END GAME

CHAPTER 19

WE'RE GOING INTO TIGER COUNTRY

The debates and arguments over the naval and military strategy for beating Japan raged all the way to the White House, and beyond there to the British, who were concerned the Americans would divert resources from Europe and the Mediterranean.

On the American side, there was continuing friction between the navy and the army. Broadly, Admiral King, and therefore the navy, favoured a north-westerly thrust towards Japan through the central Pacific, bypassing the Philippines, believing it would be less costly in ships, aircraft and men. General MacArthur, though, was adamant that the Philippines must be retaken to honour the promise he had made at outback Terowie in 1942 and so often repeated. Eventually, a compromise was reached: they would do both. A new offensive, named Operation Cartwheel, would be the first move, to begin on 30 June 1943.

Under Cartwheel, MacArthur's early idea of invading the Japanese base at Rabaul was abandoned in favour of virtually encircling it with a ring of airfields and allowing it to wither on the vine. This was one of the best strategic decisions of the Pacific War, bringing about an enormous saving in time, resources and, above all, the lives of thousands of men. At their peak, the Japanese had around 100,000 troops at Rabaul, both army and navy, heavily dug into and concealed by a vast network of caves and tunnels. An invasion by sea would have been long and infinitely bloody.

Cartwheel outlined a two-pronged advance that would neutralise this stronghold. MacArthur would expel the remnants of the Japanese from the New Guinea mainland and occupy western New Britain, the island that had Rabaul at its north. He would also take the Admiralty Islands beyond Rabaul to the north-west, which would give the Allies the magnificent Seeadler Harbour on Manus Island. All this achieved, he would head out beyond the New Guinea 'bird's head' into the Halmahera group of islands, to provide bases for the attack on the Philippines.

Halsey, meanwhile, would advance through the Solomons towards Bougainville. There, he would establish a string of airfields to be used for the bombing of Rabaul. This he did, after a series of fierce and costly battles on both land and sea. By October 1943, a sustained air campaign was under way, an over-whelming three-month onslaught of both land and carrier-based aircraft by night and day to render Rabaul useless as a base for Japanese air and sea power.

The grand sweep and fine detail of Cartwheel are beyond the scope of this book. The bloody victories of the Australian Army's 3rd, 7th and 9th Divisions in New Guinea in 1943 and 1944; the raw savagery of fighting between the Japanese and the US Marines on Bougainville; the growing mastery of the Allies on the sea and in the air: these are the stuff of history. This great span of islands to the north of Australia was the theatre for some of the war's most tremendous battles, driven by the relent-less advance of the Allies and the literally suicidal ferocity of the Japanese defenders willing to die for their Emperor.

In this maelstrom of war, our flagships played their honour-able part.

—

Christmas Day 1943 saw *Australia* and *Shropshire* at sea. There had been a much-appreciated festive celebration a few days before, on 22 December, when a song and dance troupe, the Tivoli

Girls, visited both ships at anchor in Milne Bay, for concerts on the fo'c'sle. They strutted their stuff, in short little skirts, in a 'rousing performance', according to *Shropshire*'s diarist, Stan Nicholls. 'Two months at sea without members of the opposite sex gave the men a much needed boost to their morale and their dreams,' he wrote.[1]

Task Force 74 sailed for the war again at 4 pm on Christmas Eve under Victor Crutchley's command, stronger and more potent than it had ever been, arguably the most powerful Australian naval force to come together so far. There were two groups. Task Group 74.1, led by Crutchley flying his flag in *Australia*, included *Shropshire*, the new pair of Australian Tribal class destroyers *Warramunga* and *Arunta*, and the American destroyers *Ralph Talbot* and *Helm*. Task Group 74.2, with the American Rear Admiral Russell S. Berkey, second-in-command, was formed from the light cruisers USS *Phoenix* and *Nashville*, with the destroyers *Ammen*, *Bush*, *Mullany* and *Bache*.

They headed out in column, *Australia* at the head, on a course slightly west of north that would take them to Cape Gloucester, on the western tip of the island of New Britain. Following behind came an assault force of ships and landing craft full of US Marines, some 12,000 men of the 1st Marine Division who had taken Guadalcanal and who, after long spell of rest and relaxation in Melbourne, were rejoining the Pacific War. Cape Gloucester had a Japanese airfield to be taken, a strip well within striking distance of Rabaul at the other, north-eastern, end of New Britain. The navy would soften up the enemy with a bombardment. That done, the Marines would hit the beach.

The next day was a non-event, as one anonymous poet described it:

'Twas Christmas Day on the *Shropshire*
But the troops were stricken with grief.
They went in expecting roast turkey
But only got bully beef.
And what made it worse for the sailors
As if that were not bad enough.

The cooks had all got their heads down
And there was no Pusser's Duff.[2]

The bombardment began the next day, on time, exactly to plan. On the early morning of 26 December, Admiral Berkey's group of American ships peeled off to their destination, to fire upon landing beaches a little way to the east of Cape Gloucester. *Australia*, *Shropshire*, *Warramunga* and *Arunta* steamed easily into their position off the cape itself, their guns trained ashore. At 6 am, they opened fire in a volcanic eruption of flame and smoke. It was *Shropshire*'s first act of war and, for those of her crew who had survived the loss of *Canberra*, payback at last for their fallen friends.

Now the gun crews would show their mettle, as they would do for the months and years ahead. The main turrets of *Australia* and *Shropshire*, four on each ship, were boxes and mountings of heavy steel armour each weighing 200 tonnes. The gun house, where the gunners laboured, was roughly the size of a modern two-car garage, although with hardly the room. Much of the space there was taken up by the breeches of the two great 8-inch guns themselves, a heavy mechanism of machined steel burnished to a dull, oily gleam. Each gun, known as the BL Mk VIII, was 10.5 metres long, rifled within the barrel to rotate the shell.

To serve these great rifles there was, to the untrained eye, a bewildering array of hydraulic pipes, electrical wiring, switches, valves, dials, levers and wheels, manned by a crew of 14 gunners impossibly jammed into whatever nooks and crannies the designers had left over in the gun house. Some men perched on hard metal seats; others crouched or stood. An officer was in charge of each turret, usually a junior lieutenant known as the Officer of Quarters, a quaintly historic title from the days of wooden ships, muzzle-loading cannon and iron round shot. The Captain of the Turret, generally a petty officer – a gunner's mate – was the senior sailor, supervising the sweating figures who would train the turret or aim, elevate and load each gun. Numbers, these men were called: No. 2 men working the breeches; No. 3s at the ramming gear for the cordite charges; No. 4s at the elevating wheels. Teamwork was critical, honed by endless practice.

Rubber earplugs were provided against the noise, but they were of little use; many men who served in gun turrets for any length of time would end up with damaged hearing, if they were not entirely deaf. Even in cool weather, the gun houses were hot inside, growing ever hotter as the guns kept shooting. The air, if you could call it that, was thick with the fumes of the cordite charges that propelled the shells, and overlain with the sour, heavy smell of hot paint, oil and human sweat. In the tropics, they were ovens. A gun turret was a dangerous and profoundly uncomfortable place, manned by strong, stoic men.

'*Stand by for bombardment!*' There were two types of shell, each of eight inches diameter, 91.4 centimetres long, and weighing 116 kilograms. HE, or high effect, shells – also known as high explosive – detonated on impact. SAPC shells – semi-armour-piercing capped – were designed to penetrate deep into the armoured sides of an enemy ship before bursting. A bombardment of a target on land called for the HE shells, which were readied by more strong men in the shell-handling rooms in the bottom of the ship, and placed into hydraulically powered hoists to lift them to the turrets.

'*All guns! HE shell. Full cordite charge! Load, load, load!*' The mighty breeches would swing open for a hydraulic rammer to slide the shell from the hoist cage into the barrel, pressing its driving band of cupro-nickel tightly onto the rifling. A full charge of cordite, 30 kilograms of it in two silk bags, was packed into the chamber of the gun behind the shell. An electrical connection in the breech was readied to fire the cordite.

'*Breech blocks swing to!*' With the breech closed, the two gunlayers would elevate the guns to the required angle and the trainer would work his hand wheel to keep the turret pointed in the right direction if the ship or the target was moving.

'*Both guns loaded, ready!*' The communications number would report the turret ready to the director control high above the bridge, where the guns would actually be fired. With the gun ready lamps lit, the firing gongs would give their metallic *ting-ting*, and then would come the order.

'*Fire!*' The electrical charge would set the cordite burning, and the enormous pressure of its expanding hot gases sent the shell spinning along the rifling and bursting from the muzzle at a speed of 855 metres per second. Depending on the elevation of the gun and other factors such as wind speed and direction, heat and humidity, it would take about 15 seconds for that shell to travel ten kilometres, with a rushing sound through the air like a steam locomotive express at high speed.

In the gun house, there was a buffeting, stupefying concussion of heat and sound like the opening of the doors to Hell itself, as a blast of high-pressure compressed air blew the barrels clean. Freed of their projectile, the barrels recoiled some 60 centimetres back into the gun house and were lowered again to be reloaded. In a well-drilled ship, this whole process would take just 12 to 15 seconds, to be repeated again and again. A good rate of fire was five or six shells each minute.

This crushing bombardment went on for an hour and 20 minutes, with the two heavy cruisers firing 730 rounds of their 8-inch shells, and the destroyers about 900 from their smaller 4.7-inch guns. To put the finishing touches to this onslaught, as the bombardment was ending, five squadrons of B-24 Liberator bombers dropped 500-pound bombs on a target hill beyond the beaches, followed by another squadron of B-25 Mitchells, which unleashed white phosphorous bombs. The enemy had been taken totally by surprise. The men of the 7th US Marine Regiment were in the landing craft, the LCMs, ready to swarm ashore onto the beaches labelled YELLOW 1 and YELLOW 2, as the official history recorded:

Charging ashore to the sound of their own shouts, the Marines splashed through knee-deep water onto narrow strands of black sand. There was no enemy response – no sign of human opposition – just a dense wall of jungle vegetation. On many stretches of YELLOW 1, the overhanging brush and vines touched the water; there was only a hint of beach. Led by scouts forced to travel machete in one hand, rifle in the other, the assault platoons hacked their way through the tangled mass, won through to the coastal trail, and crossed it into the jungle again. Once they had passed over the thin strip of raised ground back of the beaches, the men encountered the area marked 'damp flat' on their maps. It was, as one disgusted Marine remarked, 'damp up to your neck'.

Under the swamp's waters was a profusion of shell and bomb craters and potholes, places where a misstep could end in painful injury. An extra obstacle to the terrain's natural difficulty were the hundreds of trees knocked down by the air and naval gunfire bombardment. The roots of many of the trees that remained standing were so weakened that it took only a slight jar to send them crashing. The swamp took its own toll of casualties, dead and injured, before the campaign ended.[3]

Job done, at 8.30 that morning Task Force 74 returned to Buna on the New Guinea coast, its ships unharmed, its men exhilarated by their achievement and the relief of a return to harbour without loss. This would be the pattern of their lives for the opening months of 1944 as General MacArthur pressed his advance onwards to the Philippines and – with Halsey in the Solomons chain to the east – completed the reduction of Rabaul. There would be days and nights under way in company, the bombardment of a hostile shore, yet little of the enemy to pose a threat on, above, or below the sea.

That February 1944, *Australia* began another month in refit at Garden Island – leave! – with another update to her radar, new gun barrels to replace those worn by the constant firing, and sturdier tripod masts. Crutchley shifted his flag to *Shropshire* to stay in the fray. In March, she and the destroyers under the command of Emile Dechaineux took part – another bombardment – in the invasion and occupation of Manus in the Admiralty Islands, which, by mid-April, were under Allied control, with some 4000 Japanese soldiers dead at the cost of 300 American lives.

With their unique energy and dazzling feats of logistics, in six months the Americans turned the sleepy Seeadler Harbour at Manus into one of the Pacific's biggest and busiest naval ports.

A 100,000-tonne floating dock capable of taking a battleship
was towed out from California in nine pieces and reassembled.
Wharves and warehouses were laid out around the shores for
some 30 kilometres, with four all-weather airfields and accommodation for 40,000 men, plus a 3000-bed hospital, and not
forgetting the usual American flourishes of the well-stocked PX,
or Post Exchange, mess halls, officers' clubs, football, tennis and
volleyball courts, and guest accommodation for visiting VIPs
reckoned to be on a par with a four-star hotel Stateside. It cost
the American taxpayer a staggering US$238 million, or, in 2015
dollars, about US$3.3 billion. Seeadler would be a grand foun-
dation for the drive to Tokyo. Its mere existence drove the final
nail into the Japanese coffin at Rabaul.

With his imperious gaze fixed firmly on the Philippines,
Douglas MacArthur planned to drive the army, naval and air
forces of his South-West Pacific Command west along the
northern coastline of New Guinea. Cartwheel had been an
overwhelming Allied success in the South-West Pacific, forcing
the Japanese back wherever they were encountered, or leaving
them isolated and largely impotent where they were not. But
the USN – Nimitz in Hawaii and his boss, King, in Washington – remained wedded to their preferred strategy of bypassing
the Philippines and moving upon Japan along the chain of small
islands – the Marshalls, Ponape, Truk and, finally, Guam and
the Marianas – through the central Pacific.

To counter them, MacArthur prepared a shifting series of
plans codenamed Reno, all aimed at carrying him beyond New
Guinea and up through the Molucca Islands of the Netherlands
East Indies, which he would seize as his springboard for the
Philippines. Reno subtly evolved as the turf wars raged in Washington, with MacArthur and his envoys giving ground here and
seizing some there, but the goal remained constant: he would
return.

Buffeted by MacArthur in one ear and Nimitz and the navy
in the other, the Joint Chiefs reached the only possible compromise: they would give both men most of what they wanted. On

12 March 1944, the Chiefs decreed that MacArthur should move north-west across New Guinea towards the Philippines while Nimitz would have his advance on Japan through the islands of the central Pacific. MacArthur had won his battle with Washington. So far. There would be more to come. With elaborate courtesy, he invited Nimitz to visit him in Brisbane, and, offering equally lavish compliments in return, the admiral accepted.

On 25 March, MacArthur and his entourage were waiting as Nimitz's seaplane from Hawaii taxied to a wharf on the Brisbane River. He had pulled out all the stops, with the inevitable suite for his naval guest at Lennon's and a grand banquet in the hotel ballroom that night. For his part, the amiable Nimitz had come laden with gifts: rare orchids for Mrs MacArthur and sweets, toys and some Hawaiian playsuits for six-year-old Arthur. Their talks went well as they divided up their resources and shared their plans, the sailor secretly amused by the soldier's tendency to strike poses and pontificate.

'His courtesy and cordiality towards me and my party throughout my visit was complete and genuine . . .' Nimitz wrote to King. '[T]hen he blew up and made an oration of some length on the impossibility of by-passing the Philippines, his sacred obligations there – the redemption of 17 million people – blood on his soul – deserted by American people etc etc – and then a criticism of "those gentlemen in Washington who, far from the scene, and having never heard the whistle of pellets etc, endeavour to set the strategy of the Pacific War".'[4]

Returning to Pearl, Nimitz pursued his thrust north-west across the Pacific with gathering strength and confidence. The Japanese, for their part, continued to seek their holy grail of the *Kantai Kessen* – the crushing victory at sea – which had so far eluded them. The crucible for this triumph would be the waters off the Mariana Islands, a volcanic archipelago some 2600 kilometres east of the Philippines, where they had substantial land-based aircraft that could support their battleships and carriers.

The Battle of the Philippine Sea, as it became known, began on 19 June, another mighty clash of the two navies that was history's greatest battle between carriers. The Americans deployed no fewer than 15 heavy and light carriers bearing 956 aircraft. The Japanese had nine carriers with 450 aircraft on their decks, plus another 300 at airfields in the Marianas. For two days, they struggled for mastery in the sea and air, with the Americans grimly gaining the upper hand. A legend was born with the reported remark of a fighter pilot at a debriefing in the new USS *Lexington*. 'Why, hell, it was just like an old-time turkey shoot down home,' he said, and the phrase stuck. The Great Marianas Turkey Shoot destroyed some 700 Japanese carrier and land-based aircraft, and their trained crews. Three Japanese fleet carriers were sunk, two of them by submarines: the brand-new *Hiyo* and *Taiho*, and the Pearl Harbor and Coral Sea veteran *Shokaku*. The Americans lost just 123 aircraft and there was some minor damage to the battleship *South Dakota*. The once-dominant Mitsubishi A6M Zero had been bested by a new American fighter, the tougher and faster Grumman F6F Hellcat, which had begun replacing the F4F Wildcat from early 1943. The IJN's air fleet was effectively torn to pieces, never again able to replace either its aircraft or its experienced pilots.

By September, MacArthur – much further to the west – was poised for his great leap towards the shores of the Philippines. New Guinea's northern coast had been effectively secured, from tip to tail. On 15 September, he descended with overwhelming force on the island of Morotai, a speck of volcanic rock and jungle at the northernmost tip of the Moluccas in the Netherlands East Indies, around 500 kilometres north-west of New Guinea.

Australia and *Shropshire* were there for the now traditional bombardment to soften up the defences, but when the invading GIs of the 31st Infantry Division – and, later that day, MacArthur himself – struggled ashore through chest-high surf, the small Japanese garrison had withdrawn inland. There were sporadic skirmishes for the next few weeks, but by early October Morotai was safely in Allied hands.[5]

As they had done at Manus, the Americans rolled out another sprawling air and naval base within weeks. And, at the same time, the redoubtable 1st Marine Division landed on the island of Peleliu, 1500 kilometres east of the Philippines, to protect MacArthur's right flank. Unlike at Morotai, the fighting there was bloody and protracted.

—

The men of *Australia* and *Canberra* performed their roles as cogs in this vast war machine, their progress marked by strange names on unfamiliar charts: Hollandia, Humboldt Bay, Tanahmerah Bay, Wakde, Biak, Morotai. Boredom became an enemy itself, the monotony of seemingly endless days under a broiling sun at sea, with only rare glimpses of the Japanese. Then, suddenly, something would erupt, a bout of frenzied activity.

For several days in June, the ships of Task Force 74 tussled with Japanese aircraft and destroyers near Biak, an island off the north-western tip of New Guinea. *Shropshire* missed it. She had gone to Sydney for leave and the nautical equivalent of a grease and oil change, leaving *Australia* flying Crutchley's flag, with three American cruisers and a flock of destroyers. In the late afternoon of 3 June 1944, they were jumped from the sun by three or four dive bombers, which they fought off, although with minor damage from a near miss to the cruiser *Nashville*. Two days later, Japanese torpedo bombers found them well after midnight and wheeled into an attack, but their torpedoes missed and sped harmlessly past. Then, on 8 June, they brushed with a force of five enemy destroyers, which they picked up by radar shortly before midnight.

Victor Crutchley had 14 destroyers with him at the time, including *Arunta* and *Warramunga*. Working up to full speed, they turned due north to engage in that most thrilling of all naval encounters, a stern chase in the black of night. Crutchley sent eight of the destroyers racing ahead like hounds at a fox, with the slower *Australia* and the other cruisers battling to keep up, but it was a night that ended in sour anticlimax. The Japanese were simply faster, outrunning them behind thick clouds of smoke. The Americans and Japanese exchanged fire at long range, with the Americans scoring several hits and receiving none, but after a couple of hours their quarry got clean away. 'It was a bitter disappointment,' Crutchley wrote.[6]

As well he might, for it was his last meeting with the enemy in the Pacific. On the afternoon of Monday 12 June, Task Force 74 steamed into Seeadler Harbour with *Australia* at the head of the column and flying the red and white flag of the Rear Admiral Commanding the Australian Squadron. The next day, that flag was hauled down for the last time, as Victor Crutchley relinquished his command, returned to Britain and disappeared into history. He had been in the job for his allotted two years, and he left politely well regarded, if not exactly memorable. A few months later, the Americans awarded him the Legion of Merit with the rank of commander, a high decoration for a foreigner. He was knighted in the Order of the Bath in the King's birthday honours of 1946, served for a time as the RN's Flag Officer Gibraltar, and died in 1986, a retired full admiral, at the age of 92.

His replacement was John Collins, who returned to the rank of Commodore and, by now, was feted as an authentic hero and the public face of the navy. So much so that even the *Australian Women's Weekly* was caught up in the excitement, publishing an admiring feature article complete with colour portrait:

COMMODORE (First Class) John Augustine Collins, Companion of the Order of the Bath, Cross of Knight Commander of the Order of Orange Nassau, has made history in the Royal Australian Navy.

He is the first Australian to attain the highest fighting command in the RAN and the first Australian to attain flag rank in the service of his country . . .

I soon knew and liked his characteristic smile, quick-wittedness, and unusual sense of humour. Officers and ratings do not resent the limelight that has fallen on this one man – rather, they like it. Naval men know that Commodore Collins accepts any praise that comes his way on behalf of his team . . .

But that is not the only secret of John Collins' success. Not for personality alone was he the youngest cruiser captain in the Mediterranean. Ask any man in the RAN and he will tell you;

'Collins is a sailor. A real sailor!' To the man at sea, that means something.

He is an individualist – it is noticeable in his every movement, word and action. Wherever he is, John Collins dominates the company – unintentionally, but naturally. His manner is so completely easy that one does not notice this at the time . . .[7]

At Manus, Collins hoisted the symbol of his new rank and command in *Australia*, a red-and-white swallow-tailed pennant, on Tuesday 13 June 1944. His old term mate from the RANC, Harold Farncomb, might have allowed himself a wry smile if he read any of the media adulation, for he shunned publicity and scorned journalists as much as Collins courted them. But, by now, Farncomb himself had moved on. After more than two years in command of *Australia*, in March 1944 he had returned to Britain as captain of one of the new class of escort aircraft carriers being churned out of the dockyards, HMS *Attacker*.[8] He was replaced in *Australia* by none other than Captain Emile Dechaineux, who had been very much a destroyer man until he left *Warramunga* for this, his first cruiser command. Collins's place as captain of *Shropshire* was taken, briefly, by another of his term mates from the RANC, Harry Showers, who in turn handed over to an RN officer, Godfrey Nichols, in September 1944.

At the age of 46, Charles Alfred Godfrey Nichols was just old enough to have seen the final years of the First World War as a midshipman in the battlecruiser HMS *New Zealand*. For much of his career between wars, he had been a navigator in destroyers and cruisers, and, for a short time, in a submarine. In this war, he had captained cruisers in the Mediterranean and the South Atlantic, and, for a while, had been ashore in London as a Deputy Director of Naval Intelligence at the Admiralty. If *Shropshire*'s Australians were surprised to find themselves led by an Englishman at this stage of the war, they soon enough got over it, for Nichols proved to be a more than competent seaman, and a humane and well-liked captain.

These were not the only comings and goings. On a less exalted level, there was a steady stream of arrivals and departures from the Task Force as men were promoted, or sent on leave, or fell ill, or were transferred to other ships upon whatever need or whim drove the personnel managers at Navy Office in Melbourne.

In the ebb and flow of operations, it was not always easy. That May, David Hamer, no longer the teenage snotty of 1941 but a fully fledged lieutenant, spent almost three weeks traipsing around the South-West Pacific vainly trying to catch up with *Australia*. It was almost comic. While a sailor could make do with a single kitbag for his gear, as an officer Hamer had to have working uniforms, action uniforms, and even dress uniforms – khaki ones, blue ones, white ones – that would serve him from the Arctic to the equator as might be required, a vast wardrobe that he crammed into 'one ordinary trunk, one steel trunk, three suitcases and a steel hat box'. He had a travel warrant as far as Port Moresby, but when he got there no one had the faintest idea where *Australia* might be. Pressing onwards, for a fortnight he humped this tremendous collection of luggage in and out of aircraft around much of northern New Guinea, hitching a lift here and there as he could, living largely on US Red Cross doughnuts and coffee. Once, he chased over to Manus Island, with no result, and then back again to the newly captured airfield at Hollandia, where an American GI gave him a lift in a jeep:

> He was quite pleased to have me, for the area between the airfield and the port hadn't been fully cleared of Japanese, so he sat me on top of my luggage in the back of the jeep with a sub-machine gun in my hands. Fortunately we saw no Japs, but when we got to the port – Humboldt Bay – there was no sign of *Australia*. I nearly burst into tears. I managed to get some accommodation in a tent with some US Marines near the beach and tried to decide what to do next. The following morning everything changed, for I saw across the bay the unmistakeable three-funnelled silhouette of *Australia* coming into the harbour. But how was I to get a message to her . . .?[9]

Some fast talking got him a ride on board an American landing craft, and he and his imposing pile of luggage were eventually deposited – filthy dirty and dripping wet – on *Australia*'s quarterdeck, where, as he wrote, the commander 'was eyeing me up and down as if I should be thrown down the garbage chute'.[10]

It was not a cheerful arrival, for the commander was the ferocious Wilfred Hastings Harrington, a haughty disciplinarian disliked the length and breadth of the navy; Hamer, as a cadet at the naval college, had once accidentally whacked him across the head with an oar. Harrington, though, appeared to bear no grudge, and the lieutenant, with real experience behind him as a navigator, gunnery officer and watch-keeper in the destroyer HMAS *Norman* in the Indian Ocean, was no longer easily cowed. He quickly settled into his new ship, with his action station as an Officer of Quarters aft in X-turret and – best of all – laying his head at night on a bunk in a single cabin, an impossibly tiny space but one he could call his own.

—

By the northern autumn of 1944, the Axis partners were losing the war, irrevocably. Italy had long since surrendered and gone across to the Allied side, with Benito Mussolini eking out a grotesque existence as Hitler's puppet in a villa at Lake Garda in Lombardy. The Führer himself had nearly been killed in an assassination attempt by a group of army officers on 20 July, saved only by their briefcase bomb being placed against a heavy table leg that shielded him from the explosion.

In Europe, the Allies were thrusting north through Italy, entering Rome on 5 June. The next day brought the mighty Operation Overlord, the Normandy invasion of Western Europe. Paris was liberated on 25 August. From the north and east, the Red Army was rampaging towards Berlin and the Führerbunker. Germany itself was being bombed by the Americans in the day and by the British at night, and at sea the *Kriegsmarine*'s surviving battleships were bottled up in harbour and the U-boat war was faltering and fading. In 1940, Germany had lost just 24 U-boats; in 1944, 231 were destroyed by Allied action of one sort or another, with the death of nearly 8000 submariners, many of them on their first tour of duty.

The Empire of Japan was in no better straits, being ground down ever more forcefully with each passing month. As Admiral Yamamoto had recognised and warned well before Pearl Harbor, Japan did not have the economic strength to replace its losses in ships, aircraft, weapons and men. After a faulty start with the scandal of constant torpedo failure, USN submarines had begun to exact a heavy toll throughout the Pacific, most notably in the South China Sea, the highway to and from the Japanese home islands and its conquered possessions. In 1944, the Japanese merchant fleet shrank by nearly half, from five million to 2.7 million tonnes, and supplies of food, fuel, medical equipment, weapons and ammunition to Japan's far-flung army divisions were dwindling precariously. The IJN still retained many of its battleships and aircraft carriers, but they were regularly short of fuel and, as we have seen, its air strength had been cut to pieces, beyond salvation, in the Marianas Turkey Shoot.

And so events moved inexorably towards a battle for the Philippines, with the Americans, as the advancing power, holding the advantage of choosing time and place. MacArthur decided to throw his invading legions ashore on the island of Leyte, 600 kilometres to the south-east of the capital, Manila, on the island of Luzon. Leyte Gulf, a wide and deep expanse of water facing east towards the Philippine Sea, was lined by sandy beaches suitable for an amphibious assault, with a coastal highway and flat lands for the construction of airfields. The invading force would be the US Sixth Army, of four infantry divisions, Ranger battalions, artillery and other troops – more than 200,000 men.

To carry and support these soldiers, the USN assembled an armada such as the world had never seen and never would again. There were more than 700 ships, in two fleets.

The 7th Fleet, under the command of Vice Admiral Thomas C. Kincaid, would be the Central Philippines Attack Force, to conduct the invasion itself. Kincaid had six battleships, 18 escort carriers, 11 heavy and light cruisers and 108 destroyers, with more than 420 troopships and amphibious craft. Australia's contribution to the 7th Fleet, under the command of John Collins, consisted of *Australia* and *Shropshire* and the new destroyers *Arunta* and *Warramunga*. The Australian LSIs – landing ships (infantry) – *Westralia*, *Kanimbla* and *Manoora* would help carry the American troops. The little River class frigate HMAS *Gascoyne* was sent along as a coastal survey vessel, with the motor launch HDML 1074.

The 3rd Fleet, under Bull Halsey, boasted another 17 aircraft carriers, six battleships, 16 cruisers and 58 destroyers. His carriers could deploy 1074 aircraft. Halsey would stand off at a distance to the north-east of Leyte Gulf, to cover the invasion. He, too, had a fleet train of oilers and supply ships.

These forces were assembled with increasing urgency. Invasion day – A-Day, as it was called – was set for Friday 20 October 1944.[11]

As the defending power, the Japanese had to prepare for any eventuality, so they drew up four distinct plans, all with the name SHO-GO, meaning Operation Victory. As it became more apparent that first the Philippines and then Leyte Gulf would be the battleground, they adopted SHO-GO-1, devised by the man who had replaced Yamamoto as Commander-in-Chief of the Combined Fleet, Admiral Soemu Toyoda. Still the admirals clung to the doctrine of *Kantai Kessen*, the idea of the annihilating victory, although at this stage of the war they were at least rational enough to realise that this next throw of the dice would probably be their last.

The ground troops in the Philippines, the 14th Army, were commanded by none other than General Tomoyuki Yamashita, the so-called Tiger of Malaya, who had taken the British surrender at Singapore in 1942. On land, the army and navy had between them fewer than 500 aircraft.

Inevitably, the Japanese naval plan was again enormously complex, with no one in overall command on the spot at sea and yet relying on clockwork timing and flexible communication and cooperation between four separate forces. The Northern Mobile Strike Force of Vice Admiral Jisaburo Ozawa had six aircraft carriers, including the *Zuikaku*, the last surviving veteran of Pearl Harbor, with three cruisers and eight destroyers. The Second Strike Force, commanded by Vice Admiral Kiyohide Shima, had three cruisers and seven destroyers. The Central Force – and the most powerful – under Vice Admiral Takeo Kurita, contained five battleships, including the giant 18-inch *Yamato* and *Musashi*, with 12 cruisers and 15 destroyers. And the Southern Force, commanded by Vice Admiral Shoji Nishimura, had two older battleships, *Yamashiro* and *Fuso*, with six cruisers and 12 destroyers.

The Mobile Strike Force was to be the sacrificial goat, its name no more than a grim euphemism, for the ravages of the previous months and years had left the decks of its carriers almost bare of aircraft. Admiral Ozawa had exactly 107 planes, a derisory number even to defend his ships let alone launch an attack on enemy carriers. His sole task was to lurk to the north-east of the Philippines as a decoy to lure the American main force away from Leyte – at which point he expected, with Japanese *Bushido* fatalism, to be utterly destroyed.

That done, it was hoped the way would be clear for the other three Japanese forces to crush the invading Americans. Approaching from the west, Kurita's powerful battleships of the Central Force would make their way to Leyte Gulf through the San Bernardino Strait. Shima's small Second Strike Force would descend from the north-west to join Nishimura coming up from the south-west, and these two would then head for Leyte through the Surigao Strait.

Everything about SHO-GO-1 smacked of desperation. As well as the shortage of aircraft and trained pilots both on land and sea, the ships were low on fuel and ammunition. At the higher levels of command, there was a pervasive pessimism grounded in the belief that a noble death in battle might now be inevitable, although infinitely preferable to a surrender that would dishonour the Emperor. The war would have to be prosecuted to the bitter end.

On the afternoon of Thursday 19 October 1944, the short and pudgy figure of Vice Admiral Takijiro Onishi stepped out of a staff car at Mabalacat Airfield north of Manila, the air base known to the Americans as Clark Field. Onishi was a troubled man, and not merely because he had been bombed by the Americans on the drive north. Newly arrived in the Philippines from Tokyo to command the IJN's 1st Air Fleet, he had been dismayed to find how few aircraft and pilots he had left. Deceived by its own propaganda, Navy Headquarters had led him to believe there would be thousands of fighters and bombers at his disposal. Instead, there were a pitiful few hundred.

Reluctantly, Onishi found himself forced to embrace a solution he had rejected in staff discussions before he left Tokyo: suicide attacks. They were the only option remaining, the only possibility of halting and perhaps turning the American tide. That evening, at the ragged tent that made do as the command centre of the 201st Air Group at Mabalacat, he delicately put the idea to his Operations Chief, Captain Rikihei Inoguchi, and the Air Group leader, Commander Asaichi Tamai. There would have to be a *Tokkotai*, he said with delicate euphemism, a Special Attack Unit. Pressed further, he expanded:

> In my opinion there is only one way of assuring that our meagre strength will be effective to a maximum degree. That is to organise suicide attacks composed of Zero fighters armed with 250-kilogram bombs, with each plane to crash-dive into an enemy carrier . . .[12]

The two officers agreed. Later that night, Tamai called in one of his younger pilots, a naval academy graduate and bomber captain, 23-year-old Lieutenant Yukio Seki, and told him he had been selected for the honour of commanding the first of the *Tokkotai*. He explained what it meant. We cannot know for sure what happened, for there were only the two of them in the room, but Seki is said to have hesitated only briefly, eyes closed, before willingly accepting this sacred duty to the Emperor.

The next morning, Admiral Onishi gave orders for the 23 pilots of the 201st Air Group to parade before him in a courtyard outside their quarters, where he explained their good fortune to be chosen as Samurai knights of the *Bushido* warrior tradition and told them:

> Japan is in grave danger. The salvation of our country is now beyond the powers of the ministers of state, the General Staff, and lowly commanders like myself. Thus, on behalf of your hundred million countrymen, I ask of you this sacrifice, and pray for your success. You are already gods without earthly desire ... you are going to enter on a long sleep ... I shall watch your efforts to the end and report your deeds to the Throne. You may all rest assured on this point ... [13]

There would be four units formed: *Shikishima*, *Yamato*, *Asahi*, and *Yamazakura*, the names taken from a well-known patriotic poem:

> Asked about the soul of Japan,
> I would say
> That it is
> Like wild cherry blossoms
> Glowing in the morning sun. [14]

A miracle was needed. And heroic sacrifice. Every educated Japanese, every young man there that fateful day, knew of the two great typhoons of 1274 and 1281 that had miraculously destroyed the fleets of the Mongol invader, Kublai Khan, and saved *Yamato*, an ancient name for Japan. The Divine Winds, they were called: *Kamikaze*.

—

'We're going into Tiger Country,' Warwick Bracegirdle told his men. *Shropshire*'s gunnery officer, a veteran of the early, violent war years in the Mediterranean, knew better than most the dangers ahead in the Philippines. The bombardment runs they had been doing along the northern coast of New Guinea, exciting at first to the novices, had become humdrum after a while, with little or no interference from the enemy. There had been time for scrambling games of hockey on deck during the dog watches, and Hollywood movies for the crew at night. This new venture would be very different.

On Friday 13 October 1944, Humboldt Bay at Hollandia almost literally seethed with ships. There were 471 vessels all told, of every shape and size from blunt-nosed landing barges to the big cruisers and troopships. One by one, in stages, they weighed anchor and threaded their way out to the open sea, to form a great convoy for a voyage to Leyte of 2000 kilometres and seven days. The date was noted – sailors are a superstitious lot – and there was much grumbling about Black Friday and bad luck, but away they went, at a plodding seven knots, the fastest safe speed for the landing craft. *Australia*, with Collins flying his Commodore's pennant, sailed with *Shropshire*, *Arunta* and *Warramunga* that afternoon, as part of Task Group 77.3, a mixed force of four cruisers and seven destroyers commanded by the American Rear Admiral Russell Berkey in the light cruiser *Phoenix*.

The trip was uneventful, even monotonous, beneath blue skies only occasionally darkened by a sudden tropical downpour, but it was enlivened by a meeting with the rest of the invasion fleet coming in from Manus. By noon of 19 October, they were indeed in Tiger Country, 200 kilometres to the south-east of Leyte Gulf itself. Now it was time for the ships' companies to change from khaki shorts and shirts into the heavy, hot and hated battledress, which they knew they would be wearing for days, perhaps weeks, ahead. There was a heightened awareness of a great venture afoot, producing tautened nerves and private thoughts. As one of *Shropshire*'s diarists, 24-year-old Leading Writer Jim Yeomans of Randwick, recorded: ' "Just-in-case kits" were packed into convenient bags by most of the men, and these contained motley items that had been received from home – condensed milk, barley sugar, processed chocolate, biscuits, raisins etc. Into this kit also went as a rule a wallet, bankbook, photo of his beloved and, in the case of the Casanovas, the much prized "address book".'[15]

That evening all the ships streamed paravanes. It was as well they did for, just before dawn the next morning, *Shropshire* caught one. Bracegirdle was on watch as Principal Control Officer:

'Port lookout bridge, I think we have a mine sir, in the port paravane.'

I said 'very good' and jumped to look into the water over his shoulder. Sure enough, in the phosphorescent wakes caused by our bow wave was a huge, horned Japanese mine, about 500–1000 lbs of explosives lodged in the cover, bobbing about 20 and 30 feet from the port side just below the bridge and near the port 40mm Bofors mounting. It had enough explosive to make a hole in the ship's side as long as a Bondi bus.[16]

It was a sight to chill the blood. A cutter on the towing cable should have severed the mine's mooring wire, allowing the thing itself to float free and away, but in this case it hadn't. Bracegirdle feared, with good reason, that it could be washed or dragged into *Shropshire*'s thinly plated hull at any minute. It would be instant destruction. Almost whispering, he ordered the quartermaster to steer a rigidly straight course, alerted the damage control party on watch below decks, moved the Bofors crew out of harm's way over to the other side of the ship and then, finally, called the captain. To Braces' astonishment, Godfrey Nichols appeared on the bridge in his pyjamas, took a look at the mine, asked what was being done about it, said, 'Guns, that's fine,' and returned to his bunk with instructions to be called again before dawn action stations.

Bracegirdle took it as a remarkable vote of confidence from a captain as cool as the proverbial cucumber, as indeed it was. With the break of dawn, a cable party on the fo'c'sle began, very gingerly, to haul in the paravane wire to cut it. As they did so, the mine gave a lurch – a heart-stopping lurch – and bobbed free, to float astern. The danger had diminished, but it was by no means over. Nichols, as nonchalant as ever, ordered the Chief Yeoman to alert the rest of the fleet and had the mine marked by a smoke float. To everyone's immense relief, the thing was finally detonated by Bofors shells fired from the ship next astern. It had been a breathtaking introduction to Tiger Country.

And now it was A-Day. That dawn at Leyte came fine and clear, with light airs on a calm sea, an orange tropical sun rising upon the two palm-lined invasion beaches – codenamed RED and WHITE – to the north of the bay. At seven o'clock, precisely on time, the battleships *Maryland*, *Mississippi* and *West Virginia*, along with three accompanying destroyers, opened up a mighty bombardment in thunderous array, sending up towering plumes of smoke ashore.

An hour later, with all the choreographed precision of a ballet, the transports began moving into their positions to commence the intricate business of their amphibious invasion. Boats and landing craft slipped into the water in a churn of criss-crossing wakes; signal lamps blinked messages; destroyers and cruisers jockeyed for their places, carefully avoiding the red-and-black shoal warning buoys that had been placed the day before by the Australians of *Gascoyne*. Above, dive bombers from the escort carriers roared low over the beaches.

When the battleships had finished – exactly 30 shells from each of the 28 big guns – it was time for the cruisers, again to the minute, at nine o'clock. *Australia* and *Shropshire*, with *Phoenix* and *Boise*, slipped through the battleship line and opened up with their main armament, followed soon after by *Arunta* and *Warramunga*. Like some symphony in lethal crescendo, a supporting barrage of literally thousands of rockets rained down in a parabola from 11 LCIs – landing craft (infantry) – swarming a kilometre from the beaches.

At first, there was barely any enemy response. The Japanese either went to ground or withdrew to the foothills of the Leyte mountains well beyond the beaches. The landings themselves began unopposed from ten o'clock, the boats driving forward in wave after wave – 16 of them – to discharge their troops ashore. Eventually, the enemy recovered enough to open a sporadic mortar fire from positions concealed in the jungle. It was well directed, and three landing craft were hit off Red Beach, producing the only Allied soldier casualties of A-Day: 49 men killed. As the infantry moved inland, the unloading of supplies began in ever swelling amounts. *Australia* and *Shropshire* continued to fire their big guns on and off through the morning, as requested by the troops ashore.

To everyone's puzzlement, there was almost no response from the Japanese in the air. They had expected the skies to be black with Zeros, with Kates, with Bettys, with Vals. A handful of bombers turned up through the morning without scoring a hit, and one was shot down. A lone bomber suddenly appeared in the afternoon, just after four o'clock, flying boldly through an ineffectual barrage of anti-aircraft shells to loose off its torpedo at the cruiser *Honolulu* about eight kilometres off shore. It blew a hole that stopped the ship dead in the water, killing 60 of her crew. From *Australia*'s bridge, John Collins saw it happen. 'The plane jerked away like a wood pigeon and succeeded in escaping despite intense anti-aircraft fire,' he wrote.[17]

Douglas MacArthur watched the invasion he had unleashed from the bridge of the cruiser *Nashville*, which had brought him up from Manus. The famous gilded cap jammed on his head, the famous corn-cob pipe clenched between his teeth, he gazed imperiously towards the beaches, entirely aware that his personal photographer was snapping shot after shot of his noble profile. After a quiet lunch in his cabin, he appeared on deck that afternoon in a freshly pressed khaki uniform with open-necked shirt, wearing sunglasses, and took a ladder down into a landing barge with the new President of the Philippines, Sergio Osmeña, a group of aides, and four carefully chosen reporters who could be relied upon to provide the required purple prose for America and the Allied world to savour.

The coxswain gunned the engine and the barge wallowed towards Red Beach, where the army was by now firmly established ashore. So too was a movie cameraman. The barge grounded in the shallows, its bow ramp rumbled down, and MacArthur stepped from it into knee-deep water, striding the couple of metres to the sand as the cameras rolled and clicked. In fact, some of the GIs watching on the beach sniggered at the stagey theatricality of it all, but no such disrespect made the newsreels.

There was a hitch. It took an hour for the radio gear to be set up for the general's carefully scripted broadcast to the Philippines people, but eventually it was ready, mounted on a jeep near a clump of palms. After he was introduced by a radio reporter from the American CBS Network, MacArthur took the microphone and delivered a speech that reads, now, as fulsome histrionics:

> People of the Philippines. I have returned. By the grace of Almighty God our forces stand again on Philippine soil – soil consecrated in the blood of our two peoples. We have come, dedicated and committed, to the task of destroying every vestige of enemy control over your daily lives, and of restoring, upon a foundation of indestructible strength, the liberties of your people . . .
>
> Rally to me. Let the indomitable spirit of Bataan and Corregidor lead on. As the lines of battle roll forward to bring you within the zone of operations, rise and strike. Strike at every favorable opportunity. For your homes and hearths, strike! For future generations of your sons and daughters, strike! In the name of your sacred dead, strike!
>
> Let no heart be faint. Let every arm be steeled. The guidance of divine God points the way. Follow in His Name to the Holy Grail of righteous victory![18]

A light drizzle turned to a downpour as MacArthur finished, but nothing could have dampened the moment of his triumph. He had come a long way from Terowie. Landings in this northern sector of Leyte at WHITE and RED beaches had gone well, and in the south, at ORANGE, BLUE, VIOLET and YELLOW beaches, they had been, if anything, more successful. There had been some traffic jams and blockages of supplies, but they were little in the grand scheme of things. The legions were ashore, and they had caught the enemy napping. For all his grandiloquence, for all the posturing that amused his fellow generals and admirals, and in answer to the GIs who called him Dugout Doug, MacArthur could truly say that the Liberation of the Philippines had begun. Destiny had called, and he had answered.

The invasion force settled down for the night.

CHAPTER 20

I HAVE BEEN GIVEN A SPLENDID OPPORTUNITY TO DIE

Australia's luck ran out the next day, a little after dawn. It was Saturday 21 October, Trafalgar Day, celebrated by the navy as the anniversary of Nelson's final great victory over the French and Spanish in 1805. At 6.05 am, a single-engined dive bomber roared low along the flagship's port side and crashed into her foremast. Thirty men were killed instantly or died later, and another 64 were wounded, some seriously.

With the ship at anchor, the night before had been uneventful, save for a few flares and star shells that lit the sky from time to time. As ever, it was hot and humid. Men slept at their action stations, still clad in their heavy battledress, sprawling awkwardly wherever there was a space. David Hamer stretched out on top of X-turret, a hard and unyielding bed, but at least the fresh air was better than the fug in the gun house below. As the dark of night faded to the pale grey of morning across Leyte Gulf, there was the routine pipe of 'Stand to the Dawn', when an enemy air attack might be expected, and *Australia* stirred to life again. The order was given to weigh, the propellers slowly began to churn, and the flagship prepared to take position for another round of bombardment or whatever the day's orders might bring.

Des Shinkfield, a 19-year-old midshipman from Camberwell in Melbourne, had been below in the transmitting station for most of the night. He too decided he needed some fresh air, so he asked permission to go up to the aircraft plot behind the compass platform to relieve another officer there, Lieutenant Fred Boylan. As dawn broke, they picked up three planes on the radar, but the blips disappeared as quickly as they had come, lost in the 'grass', the jumble of light on the screen. Quite possibly bogeys, they thought – the American slang that everyone used for an unidentified but probably hostile aircraft. They reported them to the bridge.

Other eyes saw these planes too, at first as specks that appeared out of the western half-light over Leyte itself. Cliff Hopping, a young signalman from Wollongong, spotted them from his station on the flag deck – two of them, he thought, coming in fast and low over the port side. Jim Luxford, another signalman, saw them as well. The Signal Boatswain, Warrant Officer 'Knocker' White, tried to reassure them. 'Don't worry, they're ours,' he said.

Most men who saw the planes that day identified them as Vals, the Aichi D3A dive bomber favoured by the IJN, but it seems they were more likely Sonias, the Mitsubishi Type 99 Assault Plane flown by the army. They were similar aircraft, with a fixed undercarriage and a long, two-man cockpit, difficult to tell apart. Some counted two planes; others counted three.

Val or Sonia, one of them peeled off and made a run at *Shropshire*, which was lying a little astern of *Australia* on her starboard quarter. She opened up with everything she could get going: the chatter of machine guns, the throaty pom-pom-pom of the Bofors, a barrage of tracer shells pumping and arcing through the morning air. It seems likely the plane was hit at least once, and some in *Shropshire* thought they saw one wheel of the undercarriage dip briefly into the sea as it curved away to the west. Then it turned and came back again, with at least one other aircraft, and headed towards *Australia*. Ordinary Seaman Reg Edmonds, an 18-year-old from Adelaide and a communications number on *Australia*'s starboard pom-pom phones, had almost a front-row seat:

> All of a sudden I heard somebody shout, and looking up I saw the first plane pulling out of his dive with machine-guns blazing

out of the wings. He was so low I saw his bomb released and instinctively ducked. The bomb landed ten feet from the bows and never exploded. By this time all hands were at their guns.

As the second plane came in he strafed us with both machine-gun and cannon and we opened fire. Our gun hit him once and set the plane on fire – this was at 90 degrees starboard. He still came on and by the time he reached 135 degrees starboard the fire had gone out. All this time we were firing into him. He turned over our stern and came straight down for us . . .[1]

At his perch atop X-turret, David Hamer was leaning back against the steel screen around the 20-millimetre Oerlikon guns when he saw the two. 'God, they're Japs,' he shouted. Springing to his feet, he yelled at the Oerlikon crews to open fire, and then dived down the hatch to his cubicle in the gun house, ready in case his big 8-inch guns were needed.

Whether knowingly or not, the second Japanese pilot had chosen the best possible angle for an attack. Training stops had been installed on *Australia*'s 4-inch anti-aircraft guns and on the pom-poms to prevent them aiming too far aft and acci-dentally firing into the ship itself, but, tragically and almost incredibly, it meant they could not reach the plane until it was almost on them. By then, it was too late.

Further forward, on the compass platform, the gunnery officer, Lieutenant Commander Richard Peek, watched aghast as the aircraft screamed in from the port quarter. He called out to Captain Dechaineux. 'Look at that! She's aiming for us,' he said. Just above them, in the air defence position, Able Seaman Phillip Turner, from Hobart, had the most terrifying view of all. He could clearly see the pilot's head and shoulders in the cockpit. Mesmerised, he stood there as the plane scraped the forward funnel with its starboard wing and then crashed into the port leg of the tripod mast, where it broke into pieces.

Most of the aircraft toppled overboard. But its fuel tanks erupted in a hellish ball of orange flame and black smoke, an explosion of such force that it bent and twisted the steel of the upper bridge structure, the director control, the radar lantern.

With a screech of tortured metal, the mast slumped at a drunken angle. A lethal rain of debris and burning gasoline showered onto the bridge itself and, below that, onto B-turret. Death took almost everyone high up in the air defence position quickly and mercifully, including the Air Defence Officer, Lieutenant Commander Harrie Gerrett. Others died in protracted agony. Ian Debenham, a 19-year-old kid from Toorak, promoted to sub lieutenant just three months before, ran screaming down the fore-and-aft bridge alight from head to foot, and had to be physically knocked out before they could carry him for medical treatment below, where he died later of burns and shock.

With a start of horror, Phillip Turner realised he was on fire – his battledress, his flesh and even his beard were burning – but he survived, beating at the flames with his bare hands. By some miracle, he saw a gap in this furnace, hurled himself through it, and plunged upside down onto the compass platform beneath. Staggering to his feet, he found a figure crumpled in the corner. The man was wearing a gold-leafed cap. Turner recognised the navigating officer, Commander John Rayment, also badly burnt. Dazed, in pain from his own wounds, Turner asked if there was anything he could do. 'No, son, get out of it,' Rayment said, in a voice of such even calm that Turner never forgot it.

For Keith Thorne, a 25-year-old from Sydney in the high angle director, this was a third brush with death. As an able seaman, he had been torpedoed in the Atlantic in an armed merchant cruiser, and he had survived the loss of *Canberra* at Savo. Chosen for officer training and now a newly promoted sub lieutenant, he was saved again by a quirk of fate. Thinking the morning was a bit chilly, he had put on a Burberry overcoat, which protected most of his body from the flames. Burnt skin, though, was hanging in blackened shreds from his hands and lower legs, and the pain was excruciating. He wandered in a daze to the sick bay, where they gave him morphine.

When Des Shinkfield opened the door of the plot at the rear of the bridge, he could see only flames and burning bodies, a grisly inferno. The falling wreckage and the rivers of flaming gasoline, or perhaps both, had killed or wounded everybody on the compass platform. Commander Rayment, who had joined *Australia* the day before the war broke out and been with her ever since, died of his wounds not long after he spoke to Turner. Lieutenant Maurice Jones, a Kiwi and the Action Officer of the Watch, was killed when the radar aerial from the 8-inch fore director fell on him. Commodore Collins was badly burnt and was carried below.

Captain Dechaineux was found crouched on the compass platform, with his face and hands burnt and swollen with blisters, and blood seeping from a wound in his stomach the size of a man's fist. Reg Walker, a 21-year-old leading seaman from Launceston, was told to help take him below, carrying him down ladders to the sailors' recreation room in the fo'c'sle, where the doctors were treating an ever increasing tide of the wounded and dying:

> He was in a semi-sitting position, hanging on to part of the bridge, and asking all the time about how severe was the damage. His only concern was not how serious his injuries were; he was concerned about his officers and men.
>
> He tried desperately to move his legs. There was a sigh as he endeavoured to move himself, and I think he was trying to not let everyone know just how much he was suffering at the time. We put him in the rec room with the others. There was no separation between the captain and the others. There were moans and groans and some of them were dreadfully burnt, in the latter stages of dying . . . there were people screaming, swearing, others praying . . .
>
> I remember him saying 'I think I'm going to be ill.' He leaned forward a bit . . . and fluid passed from his wound.[2]

Up on deck, the damage control parties quickly got the upper hand over the fires on the bridge and around B-turret, the fortunate result of months and years of training. In the sick bay, the rec room and the nearby petty officer stokers' mess, the doctors were cutting away burnt and bloodied battledress, staunching wounds, applying bandages, giving morphine to those in pain and coating burns with grease, the common treatment of the time. When they ran out of medical grease, they used engine grease, thought to be better than nothing.

The Surgeon Commander, Jim Flattery, had been a prominent winger for the Sydney University rugby league club before he joined the navy in 1923. He was a big man, and the crew had nick-named him 'Guts' after a famous incident in which he had become stuck in a hatch. Now he was wrestling with the worst emergency of his medical career, a young sailor with only bloodied stumps where his legs had been. It was no use: Able Seaman Richard Parkinson, a 24-year-old from Moonah in Tasmania and one of the crew of the port pom-pom, died that afternoon.

Australia's Anglican chaplain, the Reverend Robert Mawson, moved among the wounded and the dying, giving what comfort he could, and later in the morning *Shropshire* sent over her Catholic Sin Bosun, the widely liked Father John 'Cocky' Roche. Jack Langrell, the canteen assistant, went to the rec room to see what he could do to help:

> In the canteen I had big tins of orange juice which I brought down and gave to the Sick Bay and said 'use this where you can.'
>
> There was one fellow, a lad of about 18, nicely dressed in his clean battledress, and he was dead. I couldn't see anything wrong with him, I said to the Sick Berth Attendant 'What happened to him?'
>
> He said 'Have you ever heard "died of fright?" That's what killed him. There's nothing wrong with him, he died of fright.'
>
> I saw Commodore Collins lying on some lockers outside the Sick Bay. I said to the bloke, 'do you realise the Commodore's out there lying on some boxes?' He said 'We're not worrying about him. We're trying to save the fellers that are dying. He's not dying.'[3]

About two hours after the aircraft hit, Captain Dechaineux, the stalwart warrior who had survived Dunkirk and German E-boats in the English Channel, the quietly spoken artist's son from Tasmania, succumbed to his wounds as he lay among his men in the sick bay. The news of his passing spread through the ship, casting an added pall over this terrible day, for the ship's company had liked and respected him – they had nick-named him 'Chainhooks' – and they lamented his loss. A true gentleman, they said. At the age of 42, he was the fourth of the RAN's cruiser captains to be killed on active service, leaving his wife, Mary, and two children old enough to know only that Daddy would not be coming home. A week later, when news of the deaths was announced in Australia, the poet and war corre-spondent Kenneth Slessor, who had known Dechaineux, wrote a tribute for the *Newcastle Sun* newspaper:

> Australia's Navy is young in history, but old in battle. Its tradi-tions have been bitterly won. Yet the men who have written them in their own blood would not have wished it otherwise.
>
> Emile Dechaineux, who died from wounds received while commanding HMAS *Australia* at the Philippines landing, was a captain who will pass into that naval story. In every way, in every moment of his life, he made his men feel that they, too, were part of a tradition . . .[4]

The commander, Harley Wright, took over the ship. Wright had been at his action station in the after control position, a post located well away from the bridge for just this very good reason, that he could take command if the captain was wounded or killed on the bridge. His most urgent task was to 'fix' the ship, as it was known – to establish exactly where they were – and, seeing David Hamer, he told him to take over as navigator. Hamer had won an Admiralty prize for navigation in 1942, but this was a daunting assignment:

> The trouble was that I had no charts, for all the relevant ones had been destroyed on the bridge. I had some duplicates sent up from below, and then endeavoured to fix the ship. I hadn't been on the bridge at all in Leyte Gulf – we had been at action stations all the time – and couldn't get anything to fit. Eventually I had the brainwave – very belatedly – of checking the accuracy of the gyro repeat I was using, and found it was misaligned by

20 degrees. Everything fitted after that, and I was able to hand the navigator's job over to someone else and go up to the Air Defence Platform, by now cleared of killed and wounded, and set up some command system for the anti-aircraft guns . . .[5]

Like a surfer dumped and battered by a wave, *Australia* picked herself up, breathless and hurt but alive. The death toll was appalling and the list of wounded men clinging to life scarcely less so, but the survivors carried on as best they could, for there was no alternative. There would be time for private grieving for shipmates lost, but that would have to come later.

The damage to the ship herself, though impressive to look at, was relatively superficial. None of her vitals had been damaged, as they might have been had a bomb struck her or a torpedo ripped into her hull. It appeared that her attacker might have been carrying a bomb or perhaps an artillery shell, for there were smears of some yellow chemical around the site of the fire, possibly picric acid, an explosive the Japanese used in their naval shells. But, if so, it had not detonated. *Australia*'s engines and power plants were still in working order; the mess decks and galleys were still liveable; the ship was seaworthy – she could move under her own steam.

That afternoon, the sailmaker, Bob Moore, turned to the grisly task of preparing the dead for a burial at sea, stitching the corpses into shrouds of their hammocks or heavy canvas sail-cloth, weighted at the feet. The service was that evening, the living solemnly crowded onto every vantage point aft, the dead lying in a long line on the quarterdeck as Chaplain Mawson intoned the hallowed words of the naval rite:

Unto Almighty God we commend the soul of our brothers departed, and we commit their bodies to the deep; in sure and certain hope of the Resurrection unto eternal life, through our Lord Jesus Christ; at whose coming in glorious majesty to judge the world, the sea shall give up her dead; and the corruptible bodies of those who sleep in him shall be changed, and made like unto his glorious body; according to the mighty working whereby he is able to subdue all things unto himself . . .

Thirty splashes. A bugler sounded 'The Last Post', and they were gone. In company with the damaged *Honolulu* and escorted by *Warramunga* and an American destroyer, *Australia* slipped away from the battlefield with the farewell signals of her companions to send her on her way.

'Sorry we couldn't down that bastard before he hit your beautiful ship,' said the battleship *West Virginia*.

From Captain John Roberts of the cruiser *Boise*: 'Regret extremely to learn of your casualties. My personal respects to your Commodore and your Captain. Hope your officers and men recover quickly and that *Australia* soon returns to lend us her strong support.'

And from *Shropshire*, their chummy ship: 'We deeply regret your misfortune this morning which deprives us of many friends. The best of luck to you. Hope we meet again soon.'

After the war, many of *Australia*'s veterans and Hermon Gill, the official naval historian, quite understandably believed this to have been the first Kamikaze attack in the Pacific. This seems unlikely. Japanese records are scant at best, but it is generally accepted now that the Kamikaze campaign did not begin until four days later, 25 October. It's probable that the pilot who hit *Australia* simply lost control of his aircraft. The result was the same.

On 27 October, *Australia* was at Manus, where the wounded, including John Collins, were sent ashore to the American naval hospital. That afternoon, they were paraded in divisions on the quarterdeck for a visit by none other than Admiral Sir Guy Royle, an RN officer of mediocre talents who had succeeded Ragnar Colvin as the First Naval Member of the Naval Board in Melbourne. A glittering apparition in white and gold, Royle broke the unwelcome news that they would not be going to Sydney for repairs but to Espiritu Santo in the New Hebrides. That was a disappointing blow to men desperate for home leave, but his next words, crassly insensitive, pierced them to the core:

I don't know whether you realise the significance of the date on which so many of your shipmates were killed and wounded. It was October 21st, Trafalgar Day, and I am sure your shipmates would have been proud to die on the same day as England's greatest naval hero.[6]

Proud to die? There was a rumble of anger from the ranks before him, barely subdued by the officers. David Hamer, who noted the words in his memoirs, thought it 'the most extraordinary speech I have ever heard'. Des Shinkfield thought it was 'bloody stupid'. As indeed it was.

Two days later, their new captain was piped aboard: John Malet Armstrong – Jamie to his friends, 'Black Jack' to his sailors – the officer who, as the ship's commander, had so boldly led the rescue of the crew of the downed RAF Sunderland north of Scotland in 1940. Tall and darkly handsome, he had Scottish lineage he could trace back to a thieving, turbulent family of Border reivers under the Stuart kings. His grandfather, Commander Richard Ramsay RN, had been wounded three times in the Crimean War and had chased slavers off the west coast of Africa. Jamie, now 44, was a man of the same mould, with a buccaneering air about him.

—

The Battle for Leyte Gulf was, in fact, four separate battles, each one an epic clash of naval arms that would have made history on its own. The first round on 24 October, known as the Battle of the Sibuyan Sea, was inconclusive: the Japanese lost the giant battleship *Musashi*, a sister to the *Yamato*, and the Americans lost the light carrier *Princeton*, with 108 men killed. For some heart-stopping hours at Leyte, the Americans came close to a terrible defeat. Exactly as the Japanese had planned, Bull Halsey took the bait. Impetuous and aggressive, he was lured into taking his entire 3rd Fleet chasing after the sacrificial Japanese decoy group, the so-called Mobile Strike Force of near-empty carriers well to the north of Leyte.

It was the biggest mistake of his career. Charging off and away with all his modern battleships and his fast carriers, he left the rest of the American forces in and near the gulf nakedly exposed to enemy attack, protected only by a light air cover and a handful of destroyers. If the Japanese had pressed home that advantage, they might well have won the day, and for a while they were close to doing so. But as had happened so often before, they faltered at the final hurdle and left the field in disarray.

When the Japanese recovered from the initial reverse of the troop landings, they threw themselves into the fray, mustering every aircraft they could scrape together for a furious assault from the skies. With *Australia* and *Warramunga* out of it, only *Shropshire* and the new Tribal-class destroyer *Arunta* were there to fly the Australian flag. Warwick Bracegirdle had been right about Tiger Country. For three long, exhausting days, *Shropshire* was under relentless attack, the men endlessly at action stations, nerves jangling and close to breaking point, the brain aching for relief as one enemy dive bomber or torpedo run was beaten off and replaced by another. It was bad enough for the men working in the close heat below decks; it was far worse for those out in the open, who could see the planes as they came over. The sky never seemed to be clear. Time and again, there would be the 'Air Raid Red' warning and a new wave of bogeys would dive down, jinking through the black puffs of exploding shells, some to drop their bombs or torpedoes, others to be blasted out of the air in a cascade of smoking wreckage.

Yet some men found reserves of mind and body that carried them above and beyond the exhaustion and the fear. Roy Cazaly, a 25-year-old leading seaman from Melbourne, the captain of *Shropshire*'s eight-barrelled port pom-pom, seemed almost to exult in the conflict, as if it were a personal matter between himself and the entire Japanese Navy. Small but wiry and muscular, he was the only son of the legendary St Kilda and South Melbourne ruckman Roy Cazaly senior, and perhaps he had inherited his father's lightning reflexes and cool courage, for he was a maestro of his art. There was no radar control for the pom-poms – it was all done by the naked eye – and Cazaly had a joystick to lay and train the guns on the aircraft coming at them. He was brilliant at it, a deadly shot, and they lost count of his kills. Mackenzie Gregory, by now a two-striped lieutenant, admired him no end:

Cazaly would shoot all down the port side, and we had a tripod main mast . . . just aft of where his gun was and it had a section, a triangle that he could shoot through that triangle through to the starboard side.

The captain would ring the Check Fire bell which meant the guns should stop. You'd hear the port pom pom chattering on and the old man would say, 'Get me Cazaly!' and Cazaly would go up to the bridge and he was a reserve leading seaman. He was only in for the war.

He'd salute the captain and the captain would say, 'Cazaly when I ring the check fire bell, you'll stop!' And Cazaly would say, 'Sir, if I can see them, I'll shoot at them.'

He'd salute and walk off.[7]

The worst attacks came on that morning of 24 October, beginning at around breakfast time. *Shropshire* was moving into position for another bombardment, all at action stations, the hands munching on boiled eggs or, if they were lucky, baked beans and pork, when the alarm sounded. The radar plot reported between 80 and 100 aircraft coming in, and from that moment it never stopped – waves of planes to port, to starboard, ahead, astern, in terrible array. A Zero attacked the ship directly, machine guns yammering, and was driven off by the 4-inch. Bombs dropped on the port beam and dead ahead, the ship shuddering as they exploded in columns of filthy brown water. A nearby LST – landing ship tank – went up in flames, like Guy Fawkes night, everyone said. Down in the transmitting station, one of the operators there, Bandsman Allan 'Chan' Redding from St Kilda in Melbourne, kept a running diary of the action:

11.00 am Latest reports lost 7 fighters in raids this morning, Japs 19. Estimated 120 bombers came over altogether. Have bogeys on screen distance 60 miles closing.
11.05 am 3 groups approaching, 40, 35, and 30 miles. Air Raid Red just received.
11.15 am 7 groups now, one mixing it with our fighters.
11.20 am Smoke floats being dropped all over the Bay. We are proceeding out to sea a little way with tankers to oil, smoke

everywhere, we are also making smoke, and dropping floats. Latest air raid 2 for 18. We have 2 tankers, 3 battleships, several cruisers and numerous destroyers waiting to oil, smoke everywhere, more tankers, we are circling.

12.25 pm Another enemy aircraft shot down. Have been closed up for 8 hours so far and no dinner yet! Lots of enemy aircraft still around.

12.30 pm Our fighters have just intercepted another enemy group 30 miles ahead of us. Temperature 96 degrees [35°C].[8]

Shropshire fuelled from an American tanker that afternoon, wreathed in a choking pall of smoke thrown up as a screen to hide her and the rest of the fleet from the attackers. Then the game changed. In his flagship, the 7th Fleet commander, Vice Admiral Kincaid, was getting reports from carrier planes of a strong enemy fleet steaming towards the Surigao Strait, which would lead them into Leyte Gulf itself. This was Vice Admiral Shoji Nishimura's Southern Force of the old battleships *Yamashiro* and *Fuso*, and the heavy cruiser *Mogami*, with three more cruisers and eight destroyers. Vice Admiral Shima's Second Strike Force of cruisers and destroyers should have been there too, but strict radio silence had left them in the dark, badly delayed, and they would not arrive until it was too late. Kincaid ordered his support force, under Rear Admiral Jesse 'Oley' Oldendorf, to lay a deadly trap, to be sprung that night.

It was a clear night, the seas like dark glass. Oldendorf methodically set out his defence in four layers. The first to meet the Japanese as they came up from the south would be a swarm of swift and powerful torpedo boats, 39 of them: 51 tonnes, 24 metres long and capable of a rip-roaring 41 knots from their three 12-cylinder Packard engines. With a crew of 18, they mounted four 21-inch torpedo tubes on deck and a bristling array of machine guns and, in some cases, rocket launchers.

Next, there were four destroyer divisions, two to hold back and two to thrust down either side of the strait to launch torpedo attacks on whatever had managed to get past the PT boats. *Arunta* was assigned to one of these, DESRON (destroyer squadron) 24.

Then, after the destroyers came two groups of cruisers, one on the eastern flank of the strait and another, including *Shropshire*, lying in wait to the west. Finally, and above all, there were six battleships – *Mississippi, California, Maryland, Pennsylvania, Tennessee* and *West Virginia* – a floating wall of guns and steel equipped with the latest radar, a battle line that spoke of the USN's tremendous powers of recovery: five of them had been bombed at Pearl Harbor, two of them sunk on Battleship Row.

The Battle of Surigao Strait began at 10.36 pm, under a sky lit by a quarter moon, when *PT-131* saw Nishimura's battleships on her radar, steaming steadily northward at the entrance to the strait. For almost four hours, the PT boats attacked like a pack of sea wolves, snarling and snapping in and out of range in a violent profusion of searchlights, torpedo shots, gunfire and smoke screens. For all their dash and vigour, though, they scored not a hit, although they did inform Oldendorf what was coming his way. When they retired, Nishimura plodded on up the strait unmolested for three-quarters of an hour with four destroyers in the lead, followed by his flagship *Yamashiro*, his second battleship *Fuso* a kilometre astern, and then the heavy cruiser *Mogami* a further kilometre in the rear. Some way behind them came another column, the remaining three cruisers and four destroyers.

The moon had set by now, but if Nishimura believed that his way to Leyte Gulf was clear in the calm and dark, there was a rough awakening at 3 am when the destroyer squadrons descended on him in coordinated torpedo attacks. From the eastern side of the strait, at a range of about 9000 metres, five American destroyers fired a spread of torpedoes with devastating effect. Three of the leading Japanese destroyers were hit, one of them blowing up and sinking, and the other two being seriously disabled. And one torpedo struck Nishimura's flagship, forcing her to flood two of her magazines, although it failed to stop her. Worse, more torpedoes slammed into the *Fuso*, which caught fire and sheered out of line, then exploded, rolled over and sank.

Hardly was this over when the second lot of destroyers, among them *Arunta*, attacked from the western side, leaping towards the enemy at 25 knots. At a range of 7000 metres, *Arunta*'s captain, Commander Alf Buchanan, fired his four torpedoes. The destroyer's doctor, Surgeon Lieutenant Shane Watson, recorded the moment on deck:

> I was standing just abaft our tubes on the port side as the torpedoes were fired and saw them all enter the water, saw through glasses two tracks in the correct general direction. We turned into our own smoke and retired at speed. I watched through glasses out astern for hits as we swung in and out of the smoke. When I saw three orange flashes in the distance well spaced and at fair time intervals I could not say if they were the correct striking time for our torpedoes. On the way out I saw another destroyer on our port quarter turn and fire torpedoes and turn into his smoke. We picked up our two destroyers, who had fired five each, and retired.[9]

So far, not an Allied ship had been scratched. But in yet another American destroyer attack, two more Japanese destroyers were finished off, leaving just three ships in the enemy column: the limping flagship *Yamashiro*, the cruiser *Mogami* and the destroyer *Shigure*. It was time for the bigger guns of the Allied cruisers and battleships to take the stage. *Arunta* had turned back for another bite and had to be ordered out of the line of fire. Admiral Oldendorf ordered the battle line to open up at 3.50 am. The Japanese fired back.

Shropshire had been waiting quietly with the other cruisers on the western side of the Strait, virtually marking time, backing and filling at ten knots to keep station, with her radar operators all the while glued to the approaching action. They were ready: Captain Nichols and 'Guns' Bracegirdle on the bridge; the men in the main turrets, and the 8-inch and 4-inch high angle directors; the Chief Gunner's Mate Arthur Cooper and his team below in the transmitting station; Guy Griffiths, the rate officer, who had first met the Japanese as a midshipman when *Repulse* was lost off Malaya in 1941 and now, as a lieutenant, was about to meet them again; Able Seaman Arthur Revell, the B-turret rangetaker; and Leading Seaman John Turner in the radar plot. These men and hundreds more bent to their duty in a calm that was almost eerie as the enemy crept forward, crept closer. It was a rare and awesome thing for a cruiser to be preparing to meet an armoured battleship of more than twice the size and power, an encounter of David and Goliath if ever there was one, and every man jack was aware of it. Chan Redding was still keeping his diary in the transmitting station:

> *3.45 am* A large flash on our starboard bearing – a few star shells around.
>
> *3.46 am* From Destroyer 124 – 'Have one skunk dead in the water, we are going in to present our skunk with 5 fish'.
>
> *3.50 am* Our Battlers are about to open fire – cruisers ordered to stand by to open fire.
>
> *3.51 am* Battlers firing – 2 hits scored.
>
> *3.55 am* Enemy now firing on our force – we have opened fire – 'Broadsides'.
>
> *3.59 am* One of our Battlers has been straddled.
>
> *4.01 am* 'Straddle'.
>
> *4.08 am* 'Commence, Commence, Commence!' 32 broadsides – target was a Battler, she's burning brightly – revenge for HMAS *Canberra*.[10]

The turrets were trained, the gun ready lamps glowed, the firing gongs made their tinny ting-ting noise. Bracegirdle gave the order: 'Shoot!' Shropshire, on a course of 90 degrees, exactly due east towards the enemy, opened fire first with her for'ard 8-inch A- and B-turrets. Blinding spears of orange flame blasted from the gun muzzles as the shells streaked away for their flight of 15,000 metres. This was shooting by radar on a target as yet invisible to the eye, something unthinkable even two years earlier when *Canberra* was lost at Savo. At an almost nonchalant ten knots, *Shropshire* reversed her course in an easy arc back around to 270 degrees to bring X- and Y-turrets to bear and then, for the next 12 minutes, she kept firing broadsides, shuddering and lurching as the great guns went off in unison. In one glorious moment, an explosion in the distance produced a blaze of light, and in its glow Bracegirdle saw the Japanese battleship's towering bridge structure silhouetted like some great black pagoda. He was convinced they had scored a hit. Perhaps so, perhaps not. The other cruisers and battleships were also pouring in their broadsides, also radar directed.

Hunted and wounded, *Yamashiro* fought back. The flashes of orange fire from *Shropshire*'s broadsides made her a distinctive target (the Americans used flashless cordite) and at least four salvoes of *Yamashiro*'s great 14-inch shells soared over the Australian cruiser with that express-train roar. Any one of those shells could have blown her out of the water, but none touched her. In the words of John Turner in the radar plot:

> I think that we all just about 'shit' ourselves when our lovable skipper 'Old Nick' took us straight up the middle with three Yank battlers on our port and three on our starboard sides in the midst of the Japanese over and short falls – each time the Japanese tried to direct their fire on the six Yank battlers.[11]

Shropshire got away 32 broadsides in just over 12 minutes, to much satisfaction all round. Arthur Cooper reckoned that they scored 28 straddles, shells right on target. They had been well tested and had come through. At 4 am, normally the start of the morning watch, *Yamashiro* staggered around to a course west by south, burning like a torch, and into another salvo of torpedoes from another destroyer division. The cruiser *Mogami* slumped to a halt after a shell exploded on her bridge, killing every man there. More torpedoes still: *Yamashiro* took on a list of up to 45 degrees. Her captain gave the order to abandon ship and she sank at about 4.15 am, taking Vice Admiral Nishimura with her. The destroyer *Shigure* managed to flee.

Only then did Shima appear with his Second Strike Force, to perform in a tragicomedy of errors. The 16 torpedos he fired in what he thought might be the general direction of the enemy scored not a hit – two were found aground and unexploded on an island – and, in the confusion, his flagship *Nachi* collided with the crippled *Mogami*. Shima beat a hasty retreat. The tail of the Japanese force was cleaned up and despatched further down the strait in the next few hours, a crushing defeat.

With calm restored and dawn beginning to break, the horrors of the battlefield slowly emerged. The strait was a swill of flotsam, of wreckage from the ships, of bobbing Japanese corpses and living survivors clinging to rafts, clinging to bits of timber, clinging to whatever they could find. Some of the American destroyers slung cargo nets over the side to rescue the men in the water, only to find that they swam away, some of them with fists shaking defiantly and cries of *Banzai!* It was startling, inexplicable, utterly alien.

The official USN history never mentioned it, but there are enough memoirs and reminiscences of those who were there to confirm that some American destroyers deliberately then went astern and ground not a few of those enemy sailors to mincemeat in their propellers. It was a war crime, beyond doubt, but then history is written by the victors. The Americans lost just 38 men killed, in the destroyer *Albert W. Grant*, which had been hit and damaged by several shell hits – most of them friendly fire.

Beyond its immediate strategic importance, the Allied victory at Surigao Strait enters history for two reasons. The first was radar: this battle was a singular triumph of radar detection and radar-controlled gunnery in a great battle at sea. Radar had failed at Savo in 1942, its embryo technology and the mistakes of barely trained operators beaten by the keen eyes of Japanese lookouts and Japanese skill at night-fighting. At Surigao, the march of science had turned the tables for the Allies, to render Oldendorf's force well-nigh invincible. The IJN had no match for it.

But there was more to Surigao. It rang down the final curtain on storied centuries of naval theatre: of the shattering clash of two battle lines, of columns of leviathans – at first wooden, then steel – meeting to struggle for mastery in belching shot and shell, fire and smoke. There was not one aircraft at Surigao, not one carrier in the offing, no submarines. Nishimura advanced in a column and Oldendorf placed his line across it – 'crossing the

T' – classical battleship tactics that would have been familiar to
Blake at Portland and Tromp at Texel, to the Comte de Grasse
and Graves at the Chesapeake, to Nelson and Villeneuve at
Trafalgar, to Togo and Rozhestvensky at Tsushima, to Jellicoe
and Scheer at Jutland. This would never happen again.

—

Meanwhile, further north, things were not going so happily for
the Allies, although they began well enough. Searching aircraft
of Halsey's 3rd Fleet found Admiral Ozawa's decoy force of six
near-empty carriers, the so-called Mobile Strike Force, on the
afternoon of 24 October. Taking the bait and cracking on all
speed, Halsey's carriers were within striking range before dawn
the next day and – one after another – they launched six waves
of fighters, torpedo bombers and dive bombers at the Japanese.

This became the Battle of Cape Engaño, named for a promon-
tory at the northernmost point of the Philippines. It was a crushing
American victory. Halsey and his deputy, Vice Admiral Marc
Mitscher – who took tactical command – had 64 ships and 787
planes at their disposal, including ten carriers and six battleships.
Ozawa had a trifling 17 ships and 29 aircraft. To their credit, the
Japanese did not flinch and they put up a ferocious anti-aircraft
barrage, but there could be only one result. The Mobile Strike
Force was cut to pieces. Four carriers were sunk, including the
veteran *Zuikaku*, plus a light cruiser and two destroyers, before
Ozawa could make his escape on the evening of 25 October.

But it was a hollow win for the Americans. In racing north
so impulsively, Halsey had left the light escort carriers and
destroyers of Admiral Kincaid's 7th Fleet without support if
trouble came. And come it did. At breakfast time on that same
25 October, Admiral Kurita's powerful Central Force – largely
intact after the encounter in the Sibuyan Sea – was spotted by
an American reconnaissance plane, and almost immediately it
began appearing on American radar screens, moving south-east
out of the San Bernardino Strait. And this time the situation was
reversed. Kurita still had four fast battleships, including the great

18-inch-gunned *Yamato*, plus eight cruisers and 11 destroyers. The much weaker American front line, an escort carrier group codenamed 'Taffy 3', of six light carriers and seven destroyers, suddenly found itself surrounded by the heavy splashes of battleship shells. These escort carriers were small, unarmoured ships of 10,000 tonnes full load, carrying no more than 28 aircraft, and capable of a bare 18 knots, flat out. The Americans built 50 of them in just two years, an extraordinary feat, but they were never meant to stand against battleships.

Yet they now faced just this peril, and there was no help to call on from Halsey, whose battleships had gone north with him. Taffy 3's commander, Rear Admiral Clifton 'Ziggy' Sprague, did what any good American would do when the Injuns come over the hill – he got his wagons, his carriers, into a circle. He launched his aircraft to attack, and he radioed appeals for assistance. And then the fickle blessings of the weather landed on his shoulders, as a rain squall concealed him from the enemy. It was now up to his destroyers to do what they could.

This was the Battle of Samar, named for the Philippines island north of Leyte. With extraordinary courage, those destroyers – the tin cans, as the Yanks called them – hurled themselves at the enemy battle line. They fought like demons against overwhelming odds, spitting and snarling with their torpedoes and deck guns, three of them going to the bottom in a blaze of glory. An escort carrier, *Gambier Bay*, was also sunk. In the nick of time, two more escort carrier groups joined in and their aircraft tipped the balance. They sank two Japanese cruisers, one of them *Chokai*, which had led the Japanese charge at Savo.

This unexpected American resolve unnerved and confused Kurita so much that he feared he had run into a much stronger force, probably the fast and powerful carriers of Halsey's 3rd Fleet. He blinked. With no carriers of his own, he turned tail and went back the way he had come. Once again, the IJN had faltered and failed to seize the victory within its grasp. Samar, though, was an expensive win for the Americans, with more than 1000 men killed.

Halsey returned south, still sulking after what he took as a public rebuke from Nimitz in Hawaii, but he arrived too late to do anything. Thus ended the great part of the Battle of Leyte Gulf, an American victory beyond doubt, giving the USN mastery of the seas. The landing on Leyte had been secured, fulfilling MacArthur's promise, although much heavy fighting lay ahead on land in the Philippines. Yet the Japanese had one more weapon to unleash.

—

On that fateful morning of Wednesday 25 October, six Zero fighters of the *Shikishima* squadron of the *Tokkotai* suicide unit, led by Lieutenant Yukio Seki, lined up on the grass field at Mabalacat, each one carrying a 250-kilogram bomb slung below the fuselage. These were the planes the Americans called Zekes.

There was little ceremony as they bumped off down the runway, just friends to wave them farewell. Three more Zekes took off as an escort, commanded by Chief Warrant Officer Hiroyoshi Nishizawa, a leading Japanese fighter ace. They headed south-east, and by 10.30 that morning they had the five remaining small carriers of Taffy 3 in sight below.

The Americans were pulling themselves back together again after their violent encounter with Kurita. Stood down from General Quarters, they were enjoying a coffee if they had no particular task to do. Other men were busy clearing the flight decks, trundling aircraft below into the hangar decks, where they could be serviced, refuelled and rearmed for whatever might appear next. There was a small Combat Air Patrol aloft but it did not spot the approaching enemy.

At 10.49 am, after the six Kamikaze pilots had chosen their targets, Seki banked into a dive, the agreed signal for a general attack. Coming out of the sun, he headed his plane for the *Kalinin Bay*, which had already taken a pounding in the Samar battle, hit by 15 different shells of varying sizes. Two more followed him down, the attack recorded in the carrier's action report:

Destroyer escorts on the starboard bow commenced anti-aircraft fire and three Zekes were sighted over the USS *White*

Plains. One of the Zekes crashed off the starboard bow of this ship. Automatic weapons opened fire on the attacking aircraft. More Zekes began to dive on the formation from astern. The leading one was hit by anti-aircraft from this vessel and was smoking when it made a suicide crash dive on the port side of the flight deck, disintegrating and causing numerous fires which were extinguished in less than five minutes.[12]

Seki's plane gouged a long scar in the wooden flight deck, but his bomb failed to explode. The second Zeke slammed into the port side of the *Kalinin Bay*, demolishing the aft smokestack, and the third – hit by anti-aircraft fire – missed altogether and crashed into the sea. Another of the *Tokkotai* pilots headed for the nearby *Kitkun Bay*, aiming straight at the bridge with his machine guns chattering. He hit the port catwalk, where his bomb exploded, and then he, too, fell into the sea. The fifth Zeke seen aiming for the *White Plains* was blown to pieces by her anti-aircraft fire.

The sixth plane went for the escort carrier *St Lo*, coming in as if it were about to land. At the last minute, the pilot hammered it down into the flight deck near the number 5 wire, where it exploded in a sheet of flaming gasoline before shooting over the bow. At first, the damage seemed only superficial, but there was worse to come, for the Zeke's bomb had plunged below to the hangar, where there were fuel lines out and bombs ready to be loaded, as Captain Frank McKenna reported:

> Within one to one and one-half minutes an explosion occurred on the hangar deck, which puffed smoke and flame through the hole in the deck and, I believe, bulged the flight deck near and aft of the hole. This was followed in a matter of seconds by a much more violent explosion, which rolled back a part of the flight deck bursting through aft of the original hole. The next heavy explosion tore out more of the flight deck and also blew the forward elevator out of its shaft. At this time, which I estimate as still shortly before 1100, I decided that the ship could not be saved. With the smoke and flame, I was even uncertain as to whether the after part still was on the ship, though later I had glimpses of it.[13]

It had been horribly quick. The carrier was rocked by more explosions, seven in all, with some of her crew blown overboard and other men diving to escape the fires. McKenna gave the order to abandon ship, and her people took to rafts or began to swim, more desperately as the carrier took on a heavy list, at first to port and then to starboard. Her Air Officer, Lieutenant Commander Richard Centner, scrambled down a line on the starboard side:

> Just before I went over the side a very great explosion took place. As I swam away from the ship I observed that the ship gradually started to roll to the starboard. All personnel seemed well clear of the ship when another very large explosion occurred. The roll to starboard seemed to be accelerating and the stern began to settle. When she was on her side the stern was almost completely under water. She continued to settle stern down and to roll until she had completed a half-roll. When she was three-fourths under water she was almost vertical. She went under in this attitude leaving no fire on the surface of the water. One large and numerous minor explosions occurred after she sank.[14]

The *St Lo* was the first ship to be sunk by a Kamikaze aircraft. The explosions and fires killed 113 men, and another 30 died later of their wounds.

Watching from above, Warrant Officer Nishizawa saw the damage done and flew back unharmed to Mabalacat, where, exultant, he reported the success of the mission, with the customary exaggeration of the number of ships damaged or sent to the bottom. Equally delighted, Admiral Onishi, the instigator of this murderous new form of warfare, moved swiftly to form new navy Kamikaze units in the Philippines and beyond, invoking the customary calls to honour and sacrifice of the *Bushido* warrior code.

Over time, elaborate rituals were devised to sanctify the insanity, a gross perversion of the Samurai ethic. Before their last take-off, the young pilots would cleanse themselves with a steaming bath, drink a ceremonial cup of sake and compose a traditional Japanese death poem. They would help each other don the white *hachimaki* headband with its red rising sun, a symbol of courage, and the *senninbari*, a talisman belt of 1000 stitches, each sewn by a different woman. The Kamikaze mania spread to the army as well, and by the end of the war some 5000 young men had died for it. The burning spirit of Japanese youth had found a new, exalted way to honour the Emperor and defend the home islands, it was said. Petty Officer First Class Isao Matsuo of the IJN's 701st Air Group wrote this letter home from the Philippines on 28 October 1944:

Dear Parents:

Please congratulate me. I have been given a splendid opportunity to die. This is my last day. The destiny of our homeland hinges on the decisive battle in the seas to the south where I shall fall like a blossom from a radiant cherry tree.

I shall be a shield for His Majesty and die cleanly along with my squadron leader and other friends. I wish that I could be born seven times, each time to smite the enemy.

How I appreciate this chance to die like a man! I am grateful from the depths of my heart to the parents who have reared me with their constant prayers and tender love. And I am grateful as well to my squadron leader and superior officers who have looked after me as if I were their own son and given me such careful training.

Thank you, my parents, for the 23 years during which you have cared for me and inspired me. I hope that my present deed will in some small way repay what you have done for me. Think well of me and know that your Isao died for our country. This is my last wish, and there is nothing else that I desire.

I shall return in spirit and look forward to your visit at the Yasukuni Shrine. Please take good care of yourselves.

How glorious is the Special Attack Corps' Giretsu Unit whose Suisei bombers will attack the enemy. Our goal is to dive against the aircraft carriers of the enemy. Movie cameramen have been here to take our pictures. It is possible that you may see us in newsreels at the theatre. We are 16 warriors manning the bombers. May our death be as sudden and clean as the shattering of crystal. Written at Manila on the eve of our sortie.

Isao.

Soaring into the sky of the southern seas, it is our glorious mission to die as the shields of His Majesty. Cherry blossoms glisten as they open and fall.[15]

CHAPTER 21

ALL GUNS OPENED FIRE BUT HE STILL CAME ON

Beyond the reach of the enemy by now, Espiritu Santo was relief, blessed relief. *Australia* arrived there on 3 November 1944. She was secured to a buoy in the harbour and immediately set upon by the Seabees, the USN's construction engineers of legend. With that unique American combination of energy and know-how, the Seabees hurled themselves into the job of repairing *Australia* for sea and for battle. For the Australians, accustomed to muddle and delay, all the tangled knots of navy and dockyard red tape at home, the speed was dazzling. Within a day, a crane had plucked out the battered tripod foremast and the fore director, and replacements were being welded, the Seabees virtually making up the engineering plans on the back of an envelope as they hustled along.

Even better, Espiritu Santo brought the chance for men to unwind free from fear and exhaustion. True, it was not Sydney or home, but it was perhaps the next best thing. It was there that the American author and former naval officer James A. Michener would set his *Tales of the South Pacific*, to eventually became the Broadway and then Hollywood musical *South Pacific*, with its romantic fantasies of purple volcanic peaks, palm-clad beaches, sloe-eyed island girls and a bustling American naval base teeming with blonde nurses.

The reality was not quite that good. But the Yanks were genuinely welcoming, with their hot dogs and coffee and cold beers and ice cream in unlimited supply at wonderfully cheap prices; there were Hollywood movies aplenty, and tennis courts, and beaches for swimming and sunbathing, which they took to with gusto.

On the rebuilding side of things, *Australia* rang with the sound of hammers and welding. The Seabees rustled up one of the USN's brand-new SG surface radar sets, installed two more radar sets sent up from Sydney, rewired everything and, for good measure, threw in three more Bofors guns and some more Oerlikons. The damaged parts of the bridge were rebuilt. David Hamer reckoned that the same job done in Sydney would have taken months, but by 30 November all was ready, and that day the ship sailed for Manus again.

Shropshire, still in the Philippines, had been having a much tougher time, under almost constant attack from the air, with the Kamikaze menace growing. In just two nerve-racking days in late October, she shot down two bogeys and escaped by the skin of her teeth when one bomber dropped a torpedo that missed her stern by three metres. Another couple of days brought a typhoon, which was at least a change from being bombed, but by 21 November she, too, was back in Manus, her ship's company exhausted but unharmed. They held a thanksgiving church service for their delivery, where, recorded Chaplain Cyril Alcorn, they raised £110 ($7500 today) for the families of men killed in *Australia*.

And there was, at last, the chance to do something about the 'ickies', a painfully itchy prickly heat that showed itself in pinpoint red spots all over your body, mostly in the groin or armpits. This was the bane of naval life at sea in the tropics. Everyone had it, brought on by long hours at action stations in heavy battledress without the chance of a wash or a shower, and probably not helped by nervous stress as well. David Mattiske, a 19-year-old *Shropshire* Ordinary Seaman from Murtoa in the Wimmera wheatbelt in Victoria, reckoned you could never get rid of it:

> In a harbour routine with regular work and meal times it could be controlled by showering often, if necessary several times a day, and changing into clean clothes as often as possible. The itch drove one

mad, the scratching causing more damage. Extreme cases of the heat rash and other skin diseases were painted by the sick bay daily with Gentian Violet. We had one case so bad the sick bay recommended that the only cure was to return to a cool climate. This recommendation was rejected because the man was an expert on the 4-inch gun deck and could not be spared.[1]

A few men came and left. Mac Gregory, who had been Officer of the Watch in *Canberra* on that tumultuous night at Savo, turned up on 8 December with the two stripes of a lieutenant on his epaulettes, after a quiet spell in the old cruiser *Adelaide*. The replacement for the recuperating John Collins arrived a day later: none other than Harold Farncomb, who hoisted his broad pendant in *Australia* as the new Commodore Commanding Australian Squadron and Task Group 74.1.

Farncomb had returned from seven months in his escort carrier, the RN's HMS *Attacker*, which had supported the Normandy landings and later operated in the Mediterranean. He wore, also, the medal of the Distinguished Service Order, bestowed for his earlier time in the Pacific. But the strain was beginning to show, at least to those in the know. He had been in active command at sea since before the start of the war with barely a moment's rest, a burden that might have cracked many men and that should never have been placed upon him by the nabobs of the Naval Board. That they did so was appalling and almost certainly unequalled in its cavalier disregard for his welfare, although Farncomb accepted it without complaint. But a 'flimsy', a report on his conduct made by a British admiral, followed him home with a cool warning:

> This officer suffers from one failing, namely a tendency to fortify himself with liquor prior to the ordeal of facing an important social occasion. I am informed that normally he does not over indulge and this is borne out by the efficient manner in which his ship and her aircraft are handled and commanded.[2]

It was during this stay at Manus that Warwick Bracegirdle, *Shropshire*'s gunnery officer, pulled off the stunt that stunned and

amazed his shipmates and enshrined him in naval legend. With
the tacit approval of Captain Nichols, he vanished with a couple
of cases of Scotch whisky lifted from the wardroom store. He
never quite explained how he did it, but he conjured up a miracle.
Two days later, out of the blue, a tug and a lighter appeared
alongside *Shropshire* bearing not only 13 American Bofors guns
but also vast amounts of ammunition and the Seabee technicians
to install them, which they proceeded to do. Nichols, delighted,
asked no questions. The Oerlikon anti-aircraft guns they got rid
of had a range of 1000 metres. The Bofors could shoot accurately
for 5000, a massive increase in firepower. Nobody bothered to
ask the permission of the Naval Board in Melbourne, on the
very reasonable assumption that it would provoke only another
blizzard of red tape.

Both *Australia* and *Shropshire* were now considerably different
to the ships that had begun the war, and they looked it. Taller
and stronger masts encrusted with radar aerials were the most
visible sign. If nothing else, the war had spurred on advance-
ments in science and technology, and the radar of 1945 had
made a long march on the primitive apparatus that failed with
such disastrous consequences at Savo. It had revolutionised the
search for the enemy on the sea and in the air, and navigation
and gunnery control with it. And it had signalled the end of the
Walrus reconnaissance planes, which went back to the RAAF.
On the bridge, there was TBS, which, with quirks of jargon and
the odd cultural hiccup smoothed over, meant that Australians
and Americans could talk to each other in real time without
the clutter and delay of messages, signal pads, flags and lamps.
The two navies were working as smoothly as one, although the
Australians occasionally groaned beneath the burden of voluminous American operational orders that seemed to cater, in
endless detail, for every eventuality from a battleship fleet action
to a blocked toilet.

Along the decks, the ships' upperworks bristled with the new
anti-aircraft batteries, and within weeks they would dispose
of their torpedoes and depth charges, which were no longer

of much use either. Below, the accommodation was distinctly more cramped than in the palmy, regatta days of peace, when each cruiser had carried a complement of about 650 men. The demands of war had added many more – gunners, radar operators, signalmen, cooks, even doctors – all of whom had to be found a place to sleep, eat and shower. At the outbreak of war, *Australia*'s ship's company had numbered 725 men. By December 1944, she was carrying 1078. And space was tighter still if a Commodore and his retinue were on board.

Some things were unchanged: nurtured by successive waves of engineers, artificers and stokers, the great turbine engines, four in each ship, still sang as sweetly as the day they had first turned. If *Australia* and *Shropshire*, with their three tall funnels, now looked a little old-fashioned alongside the muscular lines of the new, two-funnelled American cruisers, they were still fast and powerful vessels to be reckoned with, and crewed by sailors who proudly and rightly held themselves to be as good as, if not better than, the men of any other navy, friend or foe.

Christmas 1944 came early. On 15 December, the supply ship *Merkur*, a former Burns Philp island freighter, arrived from Australia with bags of mail and, to everyone's pleasant surprise, the makings of a banquet of turkey with stuffing, roast potatoes, plum pudding and brandy sauce, even fresh fruit. That did mean they would not be going home for Christmas, they realised, but at least they could celebrate in style. With nowhere to stow this mountain of food, the cooks turned on the feast two days later, on the 17th.

Well-worn navy tradition had it that the upper and lower decks swapped roles on this one day of the year, and *Shropshire*'s officers served dinner for the men with the inevitable Brace-girdle togged out as Santa Claus in a cotton-wool beard, maroon dressing-gown and seaboots, the ensemble rakishly topped off by a tin helmet. Every man got a bottle of beer – properly chilled, to much approval – and there were carols on the fo'c'sle led by the ship's band, and a conga line of dancers that wound its cheerfully unsteady way from the wardroom to the torpedo space, which had been decorated with palm fronds.

There was, though, an underlying melancholy, a homesick longing for friends and family that no amount of gaiety could erase. *Shropshire* had not been home since June, and *Australia* not since her refit in March. Mail deliveries were still infuriatingly irregular – either a deluge or a drought – which five years of war had not brought the authorities any closer to solving, as Farncomb acidly pointed out in one of his first letters back to Melbourne.

On 26 December, the Task Group sailed again. The two heavy cruisers, plus *Arunta* and *Warramunga*, were back to business, back to the lethal seas and skies of the Philippines.

—

At the turn of the year, both Germany and Japan were fighting a war that could end only in their defeat and the unconditional surrender that Roosevelt and Churchill had laid down a year before at Casablanca. Both nations refused to recognise it. The American check at the Battle of the Bulge in the dense forests of the Ardennes in December 1944 had given Hitler new hope, and, ensconced in his Berlin bunker with Eva Braun, he harangued his aides with fantasies of new wonder weapons that would bring him triumph again. The V2 rockets had begun to rain down on London. But all the while, the Soviet Red Army was rolling towards him.

The Japanese Empire was crumbling, from China in the north, Burma in the west and the Philippines in the east, but its armies – short of food, arms and ammunition – fought on nonetheless with fanatical resolve. The Americans had begun bombing Japan itself in December, first concentrating on aircraft factories and then, in the following months, gradually expanding the campaign to the mass firebombing of Tokyo and other cities. The IJN was now little more than a shell of its once mighty self. At a stretch, it could bring together four battleships, four fleet carriers and around 35 destroyers, a negligible force against the ever expanding American fleets, leaving its admirals ever more reliant on the aircraft and young men of the Kamikaze squadrons.

Allied morale was high. Roosevelt had been elected for his fourth term in November. Britain, drained financially by the cost of the war and emotionally exhausted by the toll on civilians at home and her fighting men abroad, battled along stoutly nonetheless, ever more the junior partner to the Americans. British spirits were strong, and that December London was buoyed by the glittering premiere of Laurence Olivier's film version of Shakespeare's *Henry V*, in Technicolor, defiantly patriotic, with music by William Walton. Churchill's private secretary, Jock Colville, wrote, 'The PM went into ecstasies about it.'

In Australia, John Curtin had been laid low by a coronary occlusion in November 1944, to spend two months in bed in Melbourne looked after by his daughter, Elsie. He was at the Lodge in Canberra for Christmas, by himself, not well enough to get properly back to work until the end of January. The holiday season itself was curiously flat, partly due to a ban on Christmas advertising and even shop-window displays, brought in to discourage what the government and its more flinty bureaucrats feared might be a rush of extravagant spending.

At sea in the Pacific, the USN was savaged not by the enemy but by Typhoon Cobra, which struck 450 kilometres east of the Philippines on 17 December and raged for two days, with winds of up to 120 knots, or 220 kilometres per hour. Halsey had been warned of its presence, but, inexplicably, he sailed his Task Force 38 directly into the eye of the storm. Three destroyers, low on fuel and therefore unusually top heavy, were sunk, and 790 sailors were drowned, a toll as heavy as any exacted by the enemy.[3] The rest of the fleet was badly battered, with 186 carrier aircraft either lost overboard or smashed to pieces. Chester Nimitz – newly promoted to the five-star rank of Fleet Admiral – ordered a formal enquiry, which found that Halsey had 'committed errors of judgement', although not enough of them to warrant punishment or sanction.

—

Douglas MacArthur's next move was towards Luzon, the Philippines' biggest island and home to the capital, Manila. This was still firmly in Japanese hands. Invasion day was set for 9

January 1945 at Lingayen Gulf, in the island's north-west corner, an almost rectangular expanse of water about 30 kilometres wide and 50 kilometres long, fringed by sandy beaches ideal for putting troops ashore.

This would be the biggest amphibious operation yet mounted in the Pacific. After a massive naval bombardment, the US 6th Army would land about 68,000 GIs on S-Day alone, building up to more than 200,000 in the following few days. The planners did not expect Lingayen to be heavily defended on land and nor did they anticipate any significant attempt by the enemy to meet the invasion at sea, although they were prepared for it. Danger would come from the sky, from a possible 800 or so land-based fighters and bombers estimated to be in the Philippines. More, perhaps, could be sent from Formosa or the Netherlands East Indies.

Vice Admiral Kincaid's 7th Fleet would run the naval side of things – yet another armada of transports and the battleships, carriers, cruisers and destroyers to support them: warships by the hundred. As he had done at Leyte, Vice Admiral Jesse Oldendorf would command a significant part of this fleet, the Bombardment and Fire Support Group – Task Group 77.2 – of six battleships, 12 escort carriers, eight cruisers and 46 destroyers, including *Australia*, *Shropshire*, *Arunta* and *Warramunga*. The route to Lingayen would be from an assembly point at Leyte Gulf, then south-west down the Surigao Strait of recent memory, with a turn to the north-west for a more or less direct course through the Sulu Sea along the western perimeter of the Philippines islands, a journey of three days.

First away was a Minesweeping and Hydrographic Group, some 85 ships in all, including the Australian frigate *Gascoyne* and the sloop *Warrego*, which left the gulf on Tuesday 2 January at a dogged ten knots, the usual drudgery of keeping pace with the slow-movers. Oldendorf sailed the Bombardment Group before dawn on Wednesday 3 January, the sun rising on the port quarter to bring on a bright blue day with the odd bank of cumulus cloud and a light breeze that ruffled the water into small white feathers.

The calm was too good to be true, and so it turned out. It was Tiger Country again. At 7.30 am, about ten bogeys appeared, all from different directions, three of them aiming fast and low for *Gascoyne*. Two bombs fell well clear of her starboard quarter, but a third whistled alarmingly across her fo'c'sle and splashed into the sea just a few metres abreast of her bridge, also on the starboard side, although without exploding. If it had gone up, it may well have holed her and sunk her. Four of those aircraft were shot down, but it was by no means the end of the affair. The enemy was gathering.

Soon after 5 pm the next day, about halfway into the trip, a dive bomber flashed into sight at about 15,000 feet, peeled off into an almost vertical dive and crashed into the flight deck of the escort carrier *Ommaney Bay* in a blinding explosion that killed 93 men. The crew abandoned the burning hulk and she had to be sunk by a destroyer. Nerves were fraying, and that evening some of the ships – including *Shropshire* – began firing at a strange light in the sky, which, to wry grins all round, turned out to be the planet Venus.

Friday began quietly enough, again in weather so gloriously calm and clear that it seemed to mock the dangers and the fears. In the Australian ships, as the morning wore on, men munched on a bully-beef sandwich at their action stations, those on deck constantly scanning the skies for the hated enemy – or the flies, as they had begun to call them, the murderous, pestilential flies.

They came shortly after 4 pm, when the convoy was about 140 kilometres west of Subic Bay to the north-west of Manila, and there were waves of them both high and low, as many as 50 or 60 bombers and fighters. The air was filled with the roar of engines, the chatter and bark and crash of gunfire, the mushroom puffs of smoke from the exploding anti-aircraft shells, and the crump of bombs erupting in columns of water. Nothing should have been able to survive such a barrage, but some flies did.

Arunta was struck first. She was out on the destroyer screen when two planes came heading straight for her at 5.30 pm. Commander Buchanan ordered 25 knots and opened fire, which sent one of the aircraft sheering off, but the other – a Zero with a bomb slung beneath it – headed straight for the bridge, growing bigger with every second. Buchanan flung his helm hard over for an emergency turn to starboard and the destroyer answered it handsomely, the plane missing by a couple of metres and plunging into the sea to port. But the bomb blew a hole in her side, killing one able seaman instantly and wounding a petty officer, who died the next day. Her steering gear jammed and it took long into the night to fix it, all the while guarded by a slowly circling American destroyer.

In *Australia*, at the rear of the Bombardment Group, David Hamer, the Air Defence Officer, was calling the action from the air defence position, directly behind and above the compass platform, his voice crackling through the ship's loudspeakers:

> Group of Bogies bearing 265, 50 miles, closing. Friendly fighters bearing 260, closing Bogies. All AA positions stand by to close up . . .
>
> Friendlies have intercepted but some bogies have broken through. Range now only 20 miles. Close up tight! All positions look out bearing red 90. Keep a good lookout on the disengaged side . . .
>
> Zombies Red 80, low on the water . . .
>
> Alarm port, Red 80, low on the water, six aircraft . . .

It was 5.35 pm. *Australia* opened up with everything she had, her 8-inch main armament, the 4-inch high angle, the pom-poms and finally the closer range Oerlikons, in hellish symphony. Three aircraft made it through, three Zeros. The first was hit, bursting into flames and diving vertically into the sea. The second had its tail blown off, sending it smashing across the flight deck of the nearby carrier *Manila Bay*, with 14 killed. David Hamer had his eye on the third Zero:

> This last fellow's coming right for us. He's crossing ahead. Starboard side stand by. Starboard side open fire!
>
> He's turning towards us. Now he's turning right over the top of us. Look out, he's coming in!

John Clarke, a 20-year-old able seaman from Preston in Melbourne, was on the starboard pom-pom as that third plane shot across *Australia*'s bow:

> I turned the gun onto him when he was about 150 yards on our starboard beam. Then he did an amazing thing.
>
> He climbed straight up into the air until he reached about 200 feet, then rolled over onto his back. As he went up he seemed to stop right in the centre of my sights. The red spot on his side vanished as the pom pom hit him.
>
> He rolled over and screamed back at us with wings at right angles to the water. As he came in we poured everything at him. About 100 feet from the ship's side he was a flaming ball with two wings. Then I realised that nothing would stop him and with a great crash and a flash of flaming petrol he hit us.
>
> I was thrown right off the gun to find myself in the cover of the whaler which was stowed abaft our mounting. Then there was the job of getting back to the gun, which was pointing straight up in the air and still firing away by itself. On reaching the gun I turned her off, then the remainder of the crew having returned we set about reloading and filling her up with water to get ready for another attack.[4]

Clarke was lucky. The plane had rocketed past him between the second and third funnels, to crash on top of one of the aircraft cranes and the P2 4-inch mounting, the rearmost 4-inch gun on the port side. Every man in that gun crew was killed. So, too, were eight men at the P1 gun, and still more at the pom-poms and in the ammunition supply parties. A total of 25 men died in just those few terrifying minutes of carnage and the fire that followed, with 30 wounded. More might have been killed but for the daring of Stoker Petty Officer Merv Evans, of Northcote in Melbourne, who struggled to get a hose into the seat of the fire and stopped it spreading to a nearby ready-use ammunition locker. John Clarke, shaken to the marrow but still alive, did what he could for his shipmates at the P2 gun, but it was precious little:

Sailors had died right on the job; one man had his hand still on the interceptors and he had died in the act of closing them. The crew were lying around the gun, some with shells in their hands, and the thing that struck me most was that every man was still at his station.

Along the upper deck we could see more dead and wounded and our gun had not escaped. The captain of the gun had been very badly wounded in the legs and there were one or two shock cases . . . we were nauseated and completely at a loss to know what would next go on. We didn't talk much that night, and we didn't feel like having anything to eat.

We had a short sleep, knowing that next morning was to take us into the mouth of the Gulf . . .5

Strangely, and for all the human loss, the damage to the ship herself was relatively slight. She could carry on, and she did, and so did her men with her, anguished and grieving though they were. On the way to Leyte, Jack Langrell had been chatting with a mate, Henry O'Neill, a 34-year-old leading seaman who'd joined the navy in 1928 and was the gun captain on P2. O'Neills were always nicknamed 'Peggy' in the navy. Both men had been through the fatal attack the year before, and they were tossing up their chances. 'We'll be all right, Peggy,' Jack told him.

That evening, as the sun went down, Jack was one of the working party helping to retrieve the bodies, to carry what was left of them and to lay them out for the sailmaker on the fo'c'sle by the breakwater. He found Peggy with his face blown off.

Other men were also shockingly burnt and maimed. Some were naked or nearly so, their battledress stripped away. They were sewn into their hammocks that night, each one of the 25 sad bundles weighted at the feet to sink it, and the next day they went over the side. There was nothing else to do. Bodies could not be stored in the heat. *Australia* had no chaplain at this time, and the ship was at action stations, in Tiger Country. There was no funeral service for them, no rite of farewell and burial, no fine words, no soaring requiem, no rifle fired, no bugler sounding a plangent 'Last Post' – only a final drop into the cruel sea. 'You might have given a mate a bit of a quiet blessing, but that was it,' Jack said.[6]

The captain carried them and the ship. As the plane attacked, he remained standing on the for'ard end of the bridge, unflinching, while – as the navigator, Commander Jack Mesley, recalled – 'most of the rest of us tried to dig holes in the deck with our bare hands, from a prone position'. Armstrong got the damage reports as they arrived, and it was clear to him, and to Commodore Farncomb, that *Australia* should persevere. What was left of the crane was shoved over the side. The terrible problem would be replacing the gun crews, asking new men to step up to take the places of their dead shipmates. This they did, with some hurried training on the spot.

Though she was in the thick of it, *Shropshire* went unscathed, and the armada swept on through the night for its entry into Lingayen, where it would begin softening up the defences for the invasion proper three days later.

Saturday 6 January brought good weather again, ideal for air attacks. *Shropshire*'s action cooks threw together a breakfast scathingly described as 'one bottle of tomato sauce to four gallons of hot water . . . swimming in this messy concoction were a few thin "streaks" of spaghetti'. Arthur Cooper, the Chief Gunner's Mate, with memories of the Mediterranean, cracked that if that's what the Italian Navy had lived on, 'it's no wonder they turned and ran away'.[7]

By 10.45 am, both *Shropshire* and *Australia* were in their assigned positions to bombard Poro Point, at the eastern mouth of the gulf, and their 8-inch guns opened up.

The flies started to arrive just before noon, beginning a wave of Kamikaze attacks that brought frightening death and destruction for the rest of the daylight hours and into the evening. Again, the skies were rent by the sights and sounds of air combat. The first to be hit was the battleship *New Mexico*, struck by a plane that flew past *Shropshire*'s starboard side at masthead height, had its tail shot off and caught fire. It stayed in the air long enough to crash on the battleship's bridge, killing, among others, her captain and a British observer, Lieutenant General Herbert Lumsden, who was Winston Churchill's personal envoy to MacArthur's headquarters. Another Briton, Admiral Sir Bruce Fraser, although standing nearby, escaped unscratched.

And on it went, in rising fury. Within a few hours, all before sunset, a minesweeper was sunk and another battleship – *California* – along with three destroyers and two cruisers were crashed into and badly damaged, including the heavy cruiser *Louisville*, which lost 41 dead, including a rear admiral.

Then it was *Australia*'s turn again. At 5.34 pm, her lookouts and gunners saw a Val dive bomber out to starboard, coming at them straight out of the lowering sun, across the water at a height of maybe 15 metres. The 4-inch opened up first, but the plane kept coming. John Clarke, still at his pom-pom, got him in the crosshairs of the gun sight and opened fire:

> As he came on, the plane was almost obliterated by the bursting shells pouring out at 1000 a minute. Still he came, but now he was starting to go down in a shallow dive towards the water. For a moment it looked as if he would hit the sea, but he jerked himself up just before his tail unit dropped into the water. Then, about 50 yards from the ship, his port wing dropped off and immediately he swung off course and with a terrible rending crash he hit the upper deck. Had it not been for his wing coming off I would not be telling this story, for he was coming right at the gun and I would have got him right between the eyes. All the way in he had been firing his guns, and one cannon shell passed between our heads and burst in the ready use magazine where we had over 2000 rounds already laid out on the deck for loading. Had it struck them the magazine would have been blown to pieces and all the gun's crew with it.[8]

Another 14 men died, including the whole of the S2 gun crew and most of the men at the S1, with another 26 wounded. And there was an insult added to death and injury in this attack: the Val had been carrying a bomb made from a British 15- or 16-inch naval shell with an impact fuse fitted on its nose, possibly one obtained at the naval base in Singapore. They could tell because they found identification and lettering in English on the remains of the shell's base plate. Yet, again, the damage to the ship was not as bad as it might have been. Although the impact had gouged another hole in the teak decking, the blast of the bomb went upward and the fires were quickly put out. Parts of the pilot's body were found in the blackened debris and were swept unceremoniously over the side.

Luck continued to ride with *Shropshire*. She was attacked by several aircraft during the afternoon, one of them crossing from port to starboard over the bridge and very nearly giving a haircut to Stan Nicholls, a 19-year-old from Woodville in South Australia, the navigator's yeoman. At his action station on the compass platform, Stan was so close he could see the white scarf wrapped around the pilot's forehead. He dived to the deck and found out only later that he'd wet his pants in fear. That aircraft smashed into the sea. Later, at 6.30 that evening, a dive bomber came at them almost vertically, just off the port quarter. Mac Gregory was Officer of the Watch:

> Looking into the sun I saw an aircraft at about 1,000 feet diving straight for the bridge. We cleared the bridge, and flattened out on the deck of the wing of the bridge. There was a tremendous explosion. I believed we were hit by this Kamikaze, as liquid splashed all around me I thought it was petrol and expected it to burst into flames at any moment. I reached out my hand to run it across the splash, and licked my fingers, salt water, not petrol after all.
>
> What a relief, Roy Cazaly had quickly seen this attack, swung his Pom Pom around and onto the target, with a devastating burst of fire, he shot this Japanese aircraft in two, half falling close to our starboard side, where a bomb on board exploded. The bridge is 60 feet above sea level, and the force of the impact and explosion threw a wave of sea water up onto the bridge. The other half of this plane crashed close to our port side, adjacent to the bridge.
>
> I was still in one piece, but it left me shaken but very grateful to the skill of Leading Seaman Roy Cazaly, who was awarded

a Distinguished Service Medal for his efforts. It was indeed, a close run thing, and but for the Captain of the Port Pom Pom, I would not be alive today.[9]

Some men on the upper deck saw a small figure parachute from that aircraft before it came apart, and there were cries to Cazaly to 'shoot the bastard', but he refrained, and seconds later the man slipped from the harness and plummeted into the sea.

There was one more attack on *Shropshire* that evening, and in this she was saved by the nearby *Gascoyne*, who marvellously scored a direct hit with her after 4-inch gun at a long range of about 4000 metres. Debris splattered onto the cruiser's quarter-deck, prompting a cheerful signal from Captain Nichols asking *Gascoyne* to be more careful about where she dropped her rubbish next time. The Australians were looking out for each other.

Afterwards, the Bombardment Group stood out to sea again, for a mercifully quiet night in which, once more, *Australia* disposed of her dead. Now there were only enough people to man one 4-inch gun on either side, but, battered and bruised, she carried on.

The next day, 7 January, was quieter in the gulf, as if the enemy was also regathering, and there were no flies to be bothered with. Both cruisers carried out some routine shore bombardments, retired again for the night and were back early on the morning of 8 January.

Impossible as it seems, *Australia* was hit again. And again once more. The sun was still low in the east, still rising over the land mass of Luzon as she moved into line in Lingayen at the rear of the Bombardment Group. On this fourth day at action stations, the ship's company by now was operating on adrenalin alone, somehow finding the reserves of strength and will to carry on when every nerve and muscle cried out for rest and respite, for a place of safety.

They did not have long to wait for the action to begin again. It was 7.20 am when the first zombie came in on the port quarter, the enemy's preferred position for an attack. They recognised a Dinah, a twin-engined Mitsubishi Ki-46 normally used as an army reconnaissance plane, swooping in with four Wildcats

from the Combat Air Patrol hot on its tail. Ordnance Artificer
Cluny McPherson, a 23-year-old from Glen Iris in Melbourne,
saw it coming:

> All guns opened fire but he still came on. When only 50 feet
> from our port quarter the plane disintegrated under the heavy
> fire from the port pom-pom and short range weapons aft. A large
> piece of the engine hit the ship's side, making a hole three feet
> square in the captain's day cabin and glanced off into the water.
> The gun crews on X-turret and the quarterdeck were drenched
> with high octane petrol, which fortunately did not ignite.[10]

Surprisingly, no one was killed or even scratched. But the damage
control parties were still cleaning up when a second Dinah
appeared, this time amidships on the port beam and barely
skimming the water, its intentions very clear. Every gun that
could be brought to bear poured a heavy fire into it and, at about
ten metres away, the propeller of its starboard engine flew off and
cartwheeled onto the ship, slicing into a Carley float lashed to the
galley bulkhead. The gunfire beat the aircraft down into the sea
but its bomb exploded right at the ship's side, tearing her plates
open into a hole on the waterline of around five metres by four
metres, opening her up to the sea. Fairly quickly, *Australia* took on
a list of some five degrees to port, which was slowly corrected by
shoring up bulkheads and pumping and flooding. Again, no one
was injured, although the impact had been very close to the transmitting station, where it could have wreaked havoc.

Still she carried on. And so did her men. In this new and
terrible form of warfare, it was the people on the upper decks who
were now in the firing line, and they knew it all too well. Once,
it had been the men below who felt themselves to be in the most
danger, from a torpedo fired by some unseen submarine, or shell
fire from an enemy on the surface, and they would joke morbidly
about their slender chances of survival, of getting out. In this
Kamikaze onslaught, though, they were relatively protected, for
the suicide planes did not have the power or the momentum to
penetrate into a ship's vitals. It was their shipmates up top who got

it now, and there was something utterly alien, even obscene, in the thought that a man was willing to kill himself in an effort to kill you. Part of the Kamikaze weaponry was psychological, the sheer terror these planes aroused as you could see them coming straight for you, and it began to tell, pressing even strong men to the edge and more.

The ship's doctors, already occupied with the burnt, wounded and maimed, now had to surmount their own fears and turn to what they called neurotic casualties, sailors broken in mind and spirit but just as certainly victims of war. Curiously, they noted that many of those most severely affected were men also recognised as some of the best, most loyal and competent in the ship. And, more often than not, they were older men, too, with wives and children at home. The symptoms were obvious, distressingly so. These men were pale and grey, often weeping and trembling, with convulsive attacks, vomiting, and sometimes confusion and loss of memory:

> The men felt that their ship was singled out for special attack – a counter-attack on *Australia* in a double sense. Even if an enemy plane were 50 miles away, they were convinced that, among dozens of ships, it was coming straight for their own. After these assaults many exhaustion states were seen: men lost their grip, and cried out that they could stand no more. In such circumstances it was difficult to treat large numbers of serious injuries and mental casualties as well.[11]

'Guts' Flattery, the Surgeon Commander, prescribed injections of morphine to calm them, and later they were given bromides as well, along with a constant and very deliberate assurance that they were not cowards, that their fears were normal and understood. Some responded well and recovered quickly, but there were others who could not.

It was true that some men, a handful, left their posts as lookouts and the like and ran for cover when a plane was coming. In theory, it was desertion in the face of the enemy, but it was also the desperate urge to survive, and it mattered not a jot in the scheme of things. If you were not working a gun, there was no point, none at all, in simply standing nakedly exposed for the sake of it. And other men found in themselves a store of courage that perhaps they never knew they had. David Hamer wrote in his memoirs:

> during the second Dinah attack I was leaning over the side of the ADP, looking at the Bofors gun crew below and hoping that they would shoot it down (for the aircraft always seemed to be coming straight at *you*) . . . many of the crews were undertrained replacements, and one 17yr old I was watching was loading the clips of ammunition into a Bofors. It was certainly his first action, and he had only loaded a Bofors gun once before. The aircraft must have seemed to be coming straight at him, he must have been terribly scared, but he wouldn't look up, just concentrated on loading the gun accurately. It was beautiful.[12]

The rest of that day passed without an attack, and *Australia* limped into position at a cautious 15 knots to carry out her assigned bombardment. Soon, they found that firing her for'ard 8-inch guns out to port was straining nearby bulkheads, so they fired only to starboard. The Japanese had shifted their attention to the invasion convoy coming up from Leyte, a force that included the Australian transports *Kanimbla*, *Manoora* and *Westralia*, and they were jumped at about 7 pm. *Westralia* shot down a Zeke that was aiming for her bridge, sending it crashing into the water astern.

In *Australia*, the fear that they were being singled out was becoming widespread. The enemy seemed hell-bent on destroying the Australian flagship above all, for no other ship had taken four hits at Lingayen. Certainly, the Japanese knew she was there, for she had been threatened several times by the propaganda broadcaster Tokyo Rose, and in some detail, even down to naming the captain. And *Australia*'s distinctive three funnels were easy enough to pick from the air. *Shropshire*, although looking almost identical, had not been hit once. Perhaps it was Commodore Farncomb's red-and-white broad pennant that made the flagship stand out, some people thought, but that was a long bow to draw, for it would have been nigh impossible for a pilot to see it as he flew and jinked at speed through the smoky puffs of anti-aircraft fire.

The invasion began well before dawn the next day – S-Day, 9 January – the troopships and transports and landing craft sweeping into Lingayen under starlit skies with almost choreographed precision. The Americans were well practised now, with the lessons of Guadalcanal and Leyte and the Gilbert Islands and so many more taken and learnt. As the sun rose, a new bombardment began. So, too, did a new Kamikaze attack, with the light cruiser *Columbia* taking her second hit, killing 24 men.

At 9.30 am, the bombardment halted and the landings began, wave after wave of landing craft ploughing in towards the beaches for the rest of the morning. There was little opposition from the enemy on land, and by the afternoon the beach head was secure enough for Douglas MacArthur himself to go ashore from the cruiser *Boise*. His landing craft took him close by *Shropshire*. 'G'day, Doug!' they shouted.

But *Australia* was struck once more. It was early in the afternoon, at 1.11 pm. Four Vals turned up out of the blue. Two were shot down by the Combat Air Patrol, and one aimed for the battleship *Mississippi*, scraping across her fo'c'sle and plunging into the water nearby, where its bomb detonated and took 22 lives. The fourth plane aimed for *Australia* in a long, curving dive. Des Shinkfield was standing on the deck outside the fore director, getting some sun and fresh air, when he saw it coming off the port bow. The Oerlikons on top of B-turret began firing and Des raced back inside to take what little shelter there was:

> I thought there would be a big explosion and I really thought this would be it. I kept my eyes on this aircraft to the very last minute. It came so close that I felt I could have touched the wing with my outstretched arm . . .[13]

Nearby, in the air defence position, David Hamer also saw it. By this time, the young lieutenant had taken enough, more than enough. His blood rose. Impulsively, he jumped up onto the plotting table as the plane headed for him, standing there in the open air. The men who watched him do this said he shook his fist at the oncoming Val, like the Greek god Ajax defying the lightning, although Hamer later had no memory of doing so. The aircraft roared over the top of him, about two metres above his head. One wing scraped the 8-inch director and then clipped one of the tripod legs of the foremast, which sent the plane smashing into the for'ard funnel, which was cut almost in half. Some of the debris went down the remains of the funnel – the pilot's torso was found there a day later – but the rest of the plane went over the side and its bomb did not explode. Hamer, a little embarrassed, climbed back down from his table. No one was hurt, not even scratched.

This was the final attack on *Australia*. She was like a punch-drunk boxer now, battered and bloodied but still on her feet, still at her duty. Her men were at their emotional end, mentally and physically exhausted, wracked by uncertainty, haunted by fear, driven beyond endurance and yet with no choice but to endure, which somehow most of them did. They moved like automatons, unthinking, unquestioning.

Happily, the rest of the afternoon was quiet, with *Australia* able to transfer 12 of her more severely wounded men to *Manoora*, which carried better medical facilities. That evening, at the danger hour, all the ships were told to make smoke to conceal them from the air; a choking blanket lay over Lingayen, and no suicide plane got through.

Then *Australia* was told that she had done enough, that she could go. Her long agony was over. A wave of relief ran through the cruiser. That night, with *Arunta* and some of the damaged American ships, she was ordered out of Lingayen and south in a convoy back to Leyte. She went with the acclaim of her comrades in arms, a spontaneous outpouring of admiration and affection from around the fleet. Admiral Oldendorf signalled personally: 'Your gallant conduct and that of your ship has been an inspiration to all of us.' From the battleship *New Mexico*, the British observer, Admiral Sir Bruce Fraser, sent a long message. 'I feel very proud of the RAN,' he said. 'I thought the *Australia*, which seemed to be singled out for attack, dealt with every situation with great courage and determination, and this fact speaks for itself for, after all the damage she sustained, she carried out her duties until the landings had been completed and the task accomplished.' Fraser knew what he was talking about: he had been in command at the stirring Battle of North Cape off Norway on Boxing Day 1943, where the German battleship *Scharnhorst* was sunk.

Shropshire stayed on at Lingayen, and luck stayed with her. She and the rest of the fleet were roughed up in a storm off the gulf that pounded them with ten-metre waves, but no Kamikaze ever touched her. Yet it had been a costly exercise for the Allied navies in those first two weeks of January, with 24 ships sunk by Kamikazes and another 67 damaged.

Australia arrived at Leyte on Friday 12 January, out of harm's way at last, her men relieved but subdued after their torment and the death of so many of their shipmates. The silence was strange, almost eerie, a return to another world without the deafening scream of aircraft and the crash of gunfire. For a while, men spoke to each other almost in whispers, as if talking too loudly might bring the horrors down upon them again. A temporary patch was put on the cruiser's damaged side, and slowly life began to return to something approaching normal. Spirits soared when they learnt that they would be going home, via Manus. Nobody knew it or even suspected it, but *Australia* had fired the last shots of her war.

It was late January when they saw Sydney again, on a truly lovely Sunday morning of such serenity, such perfect peace, that the war seemed impossibly far away. Despite the official secrecy, word had got around that the flagship was coming home, and there was a flotilla of tooting, honking, whistling small craft and ferries to greet her as she wound her way up harbour, still missing half a funnel, the ship's company manning the rails in fresh white uniforms. For all the men with families interstate, there was 28 days' leave, while the ship herself went to the Cockatoo Island Dockyard for a long refit.

Jamie Armstrong had one more task to perform, perhaps the

most burdensome job to be laid upon any commanding officer. At Lingayen, 44 men had been killed in action, or had died of their wounds, or were – in that chilling, indefinite phrase – missing, presumed killed. The captain wote to the relatives of each one. Alan Lade was a 20-year-old able seaman from Bridport in Tasmania who had joined the navy in October 1942, the month he turned 18. This is the letter, elegant and heartbreaking, that Armstrong wrote to his mother, Sylvia:

HMAS Australia
c/- GPO
JANUARY 28, 1945

Dear Mrs Lade

I wish to convey to you my sincerest sympathy on the loss of your son, who is missing and must be presumed killed in action in Lingayen Gulf in the Philippines.

Your son was at his action station (a four inch gun) about 6pm on January 6th and we were under air attack at the time. The gun was in action and firing at the enemy when it received almost a direct hit. He must have been killed instantly and can have known nothing about it.

A memorial service with full naval honours was held on our return to non-operational waters on Sunday, 14 January.

I realize what a great loss it must be to you and how young he must seem to have taken on a man's responsibilities. He gave his life for his country and the freedom of the world and no man can do more.

Knowing how much the men miss their shipmates I extend to you their deepest sympathy and mine.

Yours very sincerely,
J. Armstrong (Captain).[14]

———

As they went on leave to homes scattered around the country, the men were told not to talk about the Kamikazes, or the damage done, chiefly to avoid any word getting back to the Japanese of how effective their tactics had been. Censorship closed off any account of *Australia*'s return home to Sydney. The newspapers mentioned only that she had arrived at 'an Australian port' for a brief period of repairs. In February, the papers carried photographs of smiling sailors being welcomed to their home towns, with carefully filleted accounts of enemy 'bombing' at Lingayen, but again nothing of the suicide attacks.

There was another reason for the imposed silence, too. Post-traumatic stress disorder was unknown at this time. The official view, the medical consensus, was that the horrors the men had endured were best not talked about, that the past should be put behind them and forgotten so they could get on with their lives. In April, a memorial service for *Australia*'s dead was held at St Andrew's Anglican Cathedral in Sydney, but it was reported in only a few brief paragraphs in the papers. The sacrifice made by ordinary families, now so common, took but a few lines:

> Ordinary Seaman Kelvin John Alderman, of HMAS *Australia*, which took part in the landing on Luzon Island, Philippines, has quite recovered from his wounds and spent the weekend with his parents, Mr. and Mrs. C Alderman, of Goulburn, late of Grafton. Kelvin is the third of the Alderman boys to offer his services to his country. Noel, of HMAS *Perth*, reported missing in the Java Seas, 1942; Stuart, A.I.F., discharged, is a patient at Prince of Wales Hospital, Randwick, having undergone an operation for his injuries received whilst on duty.[15]

A week into his leave at home in Melbourne, a puzzled David Hamer was ordered to present himself at the Naval Board for a meeting with the Second Naval Member, Commodore Harry Showers. It was unheard of, a mere lieutenant being summoned into such exalted company. Dressed in his best uniform, wondering what crime he might have committed, he was offered coffee and closely questioned about *Australia* and the Kamikaze attacks. After ten minutes of this, Showers then ushered him into the presence of the First Naval Member, the very same Admiral Sir Guy Royle who had given such offence at Manus with his remark about the Trafalgar Day dead of Leyte.

After more coffee and talk about the Kamikaze attacks, Hamer – more bewildered than ever – was told to go back to wait in Showers' office, where, as he recalled:

> the Second Naval Member came in and explained everything. I had been recommended for the nation's highest award, he said, and as the Australian Navy had never had a VC ... the First Naval Member didn't want to pass it on without meeting me first. Now he had, everything was satisfactory and I could expect an announcement in a few weeks.[16]

That announcement never came. A week later, Hamer was summoned again by a very embarrassed Showers and told that the Americans were anxious that no award should be made that might highlight the Kamikaze problem. So no VC, unfortunately; the nomination would be withdrawn.

A few weeks later, he was awarded the lesser Distinguished Service Cross, along with four other officers. Harold Farncomb became a Companion of the Bath, Jamie Armstrong got a Distinguished Service Order (one better than the Distinguished Service Cross), and both men were awarded the blue-and-white ribbon of the US Navy Cross, a decoration second only to the Medal of Honor and rarely given to non-Americans.

Those were the days when there were different medals for officers and sailors, no matter the degree of their gallantry. Thirteen of *Australia*'s sailors were given the Distinguished Service Medal, among them John Clarke, the courageous able seaman from the starboard pom-pom, and Stoker Petty Officer Merv Evans, who had so bravely fought the fires after the first attack.

To this day, no member of the RAN has been awarded the Victoria Cross.

CHAPTER 22

O LORD, THOU KNOWEST HOW BUSY WE ARE TODAY

New York! The name itself seemed to sparkle in the sun, promising and inviting. *Australia* passed through the tidal strait of the Narrows and into the bustling expanse of New York Harbor on 18 June 1945, the Australian national flag flying proudly at the main. The crew manned the rails, neat files of them facing outwards along the upper deck, standing at attention but drinking in the spectacle of the Statue of Liberty out to port by the Jersey Shore and the towers of Manhattan rising on the starboard bow. A tug helped nudge them into Pier 26 on the Hudson River in Lower Manhattan, the lines were secured, and Captain Armstrong rang down to finish with engines. *Australia* had been here before, on her journey home from Britain in 1928, but this ship's company had not. They had come a long way from Lingayen Gulf.

The world had come a long way too, although the war on Japan continued in South-East Asia and the Pacific. In Tokyo on 9 June, the Prime Minister, the elderly Admiral Kantarō Suzuki, told the Diet that 'unconditional surrender means that our national structure and our people will be destroyed. Against such boastful talk there is only one measure we must take, to fight to the last.'[1] Suzuki's heart might not have been in it – like his friend Yamamoto, he had opposed the war from the start. Yet nemesis awaited. In Washington, the Joint Chiefs had approved

Operation Downfall, the invasion of the Japanese home islands planned to begin on 1 November if all else failed. On the island of Tinian, a speck of limestone and coral in the Marianas chain of the central Pacific, all else was taking form. The US Army Air Force's innocuously named 509th Composite Group was training to drop the new atomic bomb.

Europe, though, had arrived at war's end. Hitler committed suicide in the ruins of the Berlin Chancellery on 30 April, and his long-term toady at the *Oberkommando der Wehrmacht*, Generaloberst Alfred Jodl, signed the Instrument of Unconditional Surrender in the French cathedral city of Reims on 7 May. In San Francisco, the delegates of 50 countries, with Australia's Herbert 'Doc' Evatt very much to the fore, were readying to sign the charter of the United Nations, which would happen on 26 June. The day after *Australia*'s arrival in America, the victor of Europe, General of the Army Dwight D. Eisenhower, got an ecstatic welcome from four million New Yorkers on a triumphant ticker-tape parade. The city was partying as never before.

Australia's repair job in Sydney had taken nearly four months – longer than predicted, although there was no great surprise in that. Even then, it was not finished, so, with the Cockatoo Island Dockyard needed to service the RN's newly formed British Pacific Fleet, it was decided that *Australia* should be sent to Britain to get the work completed. She sailed from Sydney for Plymouth on 24 May with a sour little cloud of controversy following her across the Pacific. Some officers and sailors who had been in the ship through the bad times had been posted out of her. Men who had stayed with her through the ordeal of the war, who had endured the Kamikaze nightmare of the Philippines Campaign, who had given their all, abruptly found themselves denied what they saw as the reward for their endurance, a pleasure cruise to Britain.

The official excuse was that there was still a war on, and their skills and experience were needed in other ships, but it was a hard blow. When he had to break the news to the ship's company, Armstrong publicly apologised and said he'd had no say in it, which

was true. But worse, and more unfairly still, some of the replacements were men they called 'barrack stanchions', people who had
spent the war far from the sharp end, propping up an office or a
depot ashore, and who had the contacts to wangle a place on the
trip. It was found that one of the new officers had never been to
sea before. The row eventually made the newspapers:

> Officers from base establishments and new recruits replaced
> more than 60 per cent of the regular crew of HMAS *Australia*
> less than 24 hours before she sailed for England recently for
> repairs and refitting . . . One naval officer described the journey
> as a 'base wallahs' cruise'. Officers worked overtime trying to
> pull strings to have themselves drafted aboard the *Australia*.
> Many who rarely saw the sea by virtue of their musterings
> rushed the trip . . .[2]

The percentage was wrong, but the rest of the story was essentially correct. The Navy Minister, Norman Makin, blustered,
'I view with grave concern the licence that certain sections of
the press take in expressing for publication statements that are
either grossly exaggerated or totally untrue,' but he had to admit
that '23 officers and 128 ratings were drafted out of the ship from
a complement of about 1000 men'.[3] Des Shinkfield was one of
those who missed out, saddened to watch her sail from Sydney
without him. The barrack stanchions were coolly treated.

America was a last-minute addition to the trip, supposedly at
the personal invitation of Admiral Ernie King, and Armstrong –
very surprised – got word that he was to go to New York only as
he left the Panama Canal. The Australian Government seized the
opportunity for some flag-waving public relations. For six days,
the Big Apple and the USN responded in kind, with sightseeing
tours, parties and a dance for 300 sailors at the luxury Roosevelt
Hotel just a block from Grand Central Station. That dance did
not begin well. The men rushed the free bar when they arrived,
at first ignoring the flower of American womanhood invited to
dance with them and causing their hostess to ask, in a puzzled way,
if Australians did not like girls. It sorted itself out soon enough.

There was more. The Anzac Club, opened in 1940 by the expatriate New Zealand actress Nola Luxford on West 56th Street, flung wide its doors. There was a press conference on board the ship. 'A FIGHTING SHIP FROM DOWN UNDER ARRIVES HERE,' headlined *The New York Times*, complete with photograph, and the captain was quoted as saying that the Kamikaze plane was 'a great nuisance and a weapon with a great psychological effect', but that it caused little damage.[4] After that, there was a glamorous cocktail party on the quarterdeck for 400 people. Then it was off to the studios of the CBS Radio Network, where Armstrong and David Hamer were guests on the hugely popular *March of Time* newsreel program, giving an extraordinary dramatic performance in which they re-enacted a Kamikaze attack, complete with theatrical sound effects whipped up by the producers.

The Mayor, the flamboyant Fiorello La Guardia, declared 22 June to be Australia Day, and the ship's company, rifles at the slope and led by Hamer, marched from Central Park along 5th Avenue to Rockefeller Plaza, where there was a large model of an aircraft carrier nicknamed 'The Fighting Lady'. An American admiral gave a rousing speech, to which Armstrong responded in kind, before an enthusiastic audience – cheers, applause – which included the visiting New South Wales Premier, Bill McKell. The show finished with two national anthems and the USN ceremony of the Retreat.

The visit was a smashing success, as Armstrong reported to the Navy Board:

> The Ship's Company behaved with great decency and restraint, and I was very proud to hear quite unsolicited testimonials to their good behaviour from all who came in contact with them. We had only one case of drunkenness in the streets and one case of fighting when two of our men resented slurs cast on Britishers by US Soldiers. I think this was quite remarkable as few Australian sailors were permitted to buy their own drinks and were often embarrassed by the excess of liquid hospitality offered.[5]

Tired, and perhaps a little under the weather, they sailed again on 24 June, heading for Plymouth, loaded with American cigarettes, chocolates and other luxuries, and carrying McKell and his wife for the trip across the Atlantic. For some of the old lags, it felt strange, almost incredible, to be steaming placidly across an ocean that had been a U-boat hunting ground only so recently, one of the most fiercely fought theatres of the war, a killing field. The sea graves of countless ships and tens of thousands of sailors, friend and foe, famous and anonymous, lay deep beneath them. It was hard to credit that peace had finally arrived.

Curiously, McKell and Armstrong hit it off on the crossing, so much so that the politician made the naval officer a surprising offer: would he like to become the next Governor of New South Wales? The incumbent, Lord Wakehurst, an English aristocrat, was due to retire, and McKell, a Labor premier, was keen to put an Australian in the job for the first time. Armstrong thought about it and said he was interested – only for McKell to find when he arrived in London that Whitehall and Westminster wouldn't have a bar of the idea. A naval captain was far too insignificant a figure, they thought, especially an Australian one, and, anyway, there were plenty of the right sort of British chaps to choose from.[6]

Fog dogged them on the way across the Atlantic, but it cleared as they entered the English Channel early on the morning of Sunday 1 July and hoisted a paying-off pennant, the slender red and white flag traditionally as long as the ship itself and often longer – an extra foot for every year of service – that signals the end of a commission. *Australia*'s was so long, streaming far astern, that it had to be supported by balloons.

There was a heart-stopping moment as they passed the white pillar of the fabled Eddystone Light in the Channel for the run into Plymouth Sound. Their radar picked it up first, and then the bridge lookouts, who reported aircraft heading towards them, quite a lot. It was puzzling. The heavy thrum of big engines grew louder and then down upon them swooped three flights of Sunderland flying boats in perfect formation, dipping their wings in salute.

They were from the RAAF's 10 Squadron, still stationed at the Mount Batten seaplane base near Plymouth, where they had spent much of the war. Circling low, these great birds that had battled above the Atlantic – and sunk six U-boats – escorted the cruiser all the way into the Sound. Coastal Command had not forgotten *Australia*'s rescue of the crew of Sunderland P9620 in the Atlantic in 1940, the exploit in which Armstrong had gone over the side to help lift the airmen from the water.

By ten o'clock, the cruiser had dropped anchor and the watch on deck was readying for the inevitable invasion of admirals and assorted VIPs, who duly arrived. If anything, the British outdid the American welcome. It was a frantically busy time, sometimes approaching chaos, for the ship had to get rid of all her ammunition and most of her oil while men were being given leave ashore. For the first week and more, the captain found himself swept up in a round of courtesy calls, lunches, cocktail parties, conferences and dinners with still more admirals, port captains, engineer captains, dockyard superintendents and local lord mayors. There was an official visit from the First Lord of the Admiralty, Brendan Bracken, a confidant of Winston Churchill who, in his youth, had done some jackarooing at Echuca in Victoria. Many of these grandees had to be received with all due ceremony, which meant a constant and disruptive turning out of a guard and the band.

As the ship gradually wound down, many of her sailors were sent ashore to be billeted in Plymouth's nineteenth-century Raglan Barracks, which had just been vacated by the Americans. They were paraded before the barracks commander, who gave them a cheerful welcome and, to their huge amusement, announced that he expected from them the highest naval standards of personal cleanliness – they were to have a bath at least once a week, whether they needed it or not.[7]

———

All the while, great events crowded in. Bracken's visit might well have been his last to any ship as First Lord, for, on Thursday

5 July, the British people voted at a general election to cast aside Winston Churchill and the Tories and to entrust their post-war future to Clement Attlee and a Labour government that would deliver sweeping social and economic reform. With so many servicemen and -women still overseas, the votes were not counted until 25 July, but the result was an emphatic, even shocking, rejection of that Promethean figure who had led Britain to victory and inspired the western world. 'It may well be a blessing in disguise,' Clementine Churchill told her husband. 'At the moment it seems quite effectively disguised,' he replied.[8]

Australia too passed a political milestone, with the death of John Curtin, also on 5 July. He had been ill for most of the year, becoming ever weaker in body and mind towards the end, although the seriousness of his condition was kept from the people. Curtin knew that the war was ending with victory certain, but he did not expect to see it and, in his lucid moments, he had begun planning what he expected would be a state funeral. Despite the entreaties of some his friends and ministers, there would be no religion to it, he decreed.

On the night of 4 July, Curtin's official driver and perhaps his closest confidant, Ray Tracey, went to his bedroom at the Lodge to bid him goodnight and found him grey and barely conscious. Mrs Curtin was there, as recounted by his biographer, David Day:

> Elsie had tea with him just before midnight, when he told her 'Go on, Mrs Curtin, it is best that you go off to bed now.' Before taking his nightly sedative he told her 'I'm ready now.' She gave him a final kiss and settled down to wait in the next room. Four hours later she was called back in for the final moments . . .[9]

The body lay in state at King's Hall in Parliament House, where the man who would shortly become Prime Minister, Ben Chifley, wept at the open casket. Curtin was flown to Western Australia with an RAAF escort of six Kittyhawk and six Boomerang fighters, to be buried in the Karrakatta Cemetery in Perth with a final salute from his son, John, an air force sergeant. Politics was a gentler, more generous business then; one of his pall-bearers was the Leader of the Opposition and of the very newly formed Liberal Party, Robert Menzies, who paid a tribute almost unimaginable in our time, describing his opponent as:

> one who sought nothing in politics except the good of all others, as he understood it; who followed his lights with unswerving fidelity; who really believed in justice; who saw politics clearly as a conflict of ideas and not as a sordid battle of personal hostilities and ignoble ambitions.
>
> It was possible, and from my point of view necessary, to attack on political grounds John Curtin's politics or his public administration; it was impossible and unthinkable to attack his probity, his honesty of purpose, the man himself.[10]

John Curtin was just 60 when he died. It seems right to say that he was another victim of the war. On 8 July, *Australia* lowered her colours to half-mast in respect, and ten days later Armstrong and 100 of his officers and men attended a memorial service at Westminster Abbey, a high pageantry of muffled great bells, the sonorous prayers of the Dean of Westminster and the full choral Anglican ritual, which might not have impressed Curtin himself.

But life went on. It was a good time for an Australian sailor to be in Britain, for the shared exertions and sacrifices of the war had engendered a close camaraderie that expressed itself in a warm hospitality from the locals. In Plymouth, the RN organised sightseeing tours, dances, lunches, free cinema tickets, cricket games, and swimming and tennis competitions. And, happily, the base was teeming with Wrens – members of the Women's Royal Naval Service – who were more than happy to welcome their Down Under cousins, almost as much as they, in turn, were happy to be welcomed.

Armstrong allowed his men generous leave, which most of them used to go up to London, where they were invited to stay in private homes or at a billet set aside for them at Gloucester House in Chelsea's Sloane Square. Officers were offered honorary membership of the smarter service clubs around Piccadilly. For some, there was the joy of family reunion. By extraordinary coincidence, Russell Clark, a 22-year-old stoker from Sunshine in Melbourne, ran into his elder brother Lloyd, 24, an air gunner in the RAF's 70 Squadron who had spent nearly three years as a prisoner of war at Stalag Luft VI in Germany after his Wellington bomber was shot down near Benghazi in the Middle East in 1943.

In both Plymouth and London, you could barely walk a block without encountering some hideous bomb site, a deep crater or a pile of fire-blackened rubble where the *Luftwaffe* had done its worst, and civilian food-rationing was more tight than ever, but people were doing their best to put the war behind them. The war on Japan was very distant.

This longing to return to normality produced what came to be called the Victory Cricket Tests, five three-day games played that first post-war summer between a team that was very nearly an England Test side and a scratch group of whichever Australians could be pulled together from servicemen based in Britain, captained by army Warrant Officer Lindsay Hassett. They were never recognised as official Tests but they were the next best thing, played before big and appreciative crowds. To his delight, Armstrong was invited to a day's play in the third match at Lord's, where the grand old man of English cricket, Sir Pelham 'Plum' Warner, entertained him in the Long Room and showed him a set of stumps and bails made of teak from the old battle-cruiser *Australia*. Both men admired a dashing spell of bowling from a promising young Australian, Flying Officer Keith Miller, who just a few months before had been flying Mosquito bombers against the V2 rocket sites in northern Germany.

Not all of it was play. On Monday 16 July, a train carried 360 of the ship's company up to London for a formal march through the streets. It was a stirring affair – led again by David Hamer – that took them along that historic processional route from the Mall, through Admiralty Arch, along The Strand and Fleet Street and past St Paul's Cathedral – still defiantly standing – to Guildhall in the City, where there were tables loaded with free

beer, and a lunch and official welcome from the Lord Mayor. The
Royal Marine band that accompanied them managed 'Waltzing
Matilda' but did not have the music for 'Advance Australia Fair',
Hamer reported.[11] More grandly still, Armstrong, Hamer and
11 other men were called to an investiture at Buckingham Palace
on 20 July, where the King decorated them with their medals for
Lingayen:

> I had some conversation with the King. 'What job did you have,
> Lieutenant?'
> 'Air Defence Officer, Your Majesty.'
> 'Oh,' and he hung the medal on. As I remember, there were
> some reasonable refreshments after the ceremony.[12]

Wheels, though, were moving within wheels. Back home in
Australia, the Naval Board had for a while been wrestling with
ideas for a post-war future for the RAN that, the planners
hoped, would include carriers and a fully fledged Fleet Air Arm
of modern aircraft to fly from them. It was a bold call, but the
war had demonstrated emphatically the dominance of air power
at sea. If there were to be carriers, there would have to be men
with the experience to command them, officers whose war
service had marked them for higher things. In that high British
summer, Jamie Armstrong learnt that he would not be bringing
Australia home. He was ordered to take command of the RN's
HMS *Ruler*, one of the dozens of escort carriers turned out by
the Americans under the Lend-Lease program.

On Monday 6 August, *Australia*'s ship's company paraded in
divisions at the Raglan Barracks. Their departing captain stood
before them for the last time, that tall, erect figure who had led
them through so much and in doing so had earned their respect
and admiration, and, in some cases, perhaps, their devotion.
There were tears in his eyes, glistening beneath the heavy black
eyebrows.

'Goodbye, you pack of bastards,' he said. And he was gone.

—

Shropshire stayed in the fight. She emerged from Lingayen with barely a scratch and not a casualty – although the enemy had tried hard enough – but the ship's company was exhausted from the grinding effort of staying awake and watchful at action stations, under relentless attack for what felt like days on end. The dangers, the fear of sudden, violent death, had haunted men's minds, as they had in *Australia*. At his station high in the air defence position one night, Guy Griffiths noticed one of his young sailors shivering, with his teeth chattering. It was a cool evening, but that was not the reason. 'I don't think I can do this much more,' the boy told him.

It had been a tough day and there were still bogeys about. At not quite 22 years of age and with a lieutenant's second gold stripe still fresh on his uniform, Griffiths was hardly older than this distressed boy, but he had seen a lot of the war by now and he knew what to do:

> I had a yarn with him and told him I couldn't really do without him, because he was my key communications number to all the outlying posts. I said, 'You hang in there, because you're a very important man in the group.' And he did that, bless his heart, and never said another word.[13]

Captain Nichols, too, had helped hold them all together. A mild-mannered, deeply religious man, he offered a short prayer to the crew before they went into Tiger Country, first at Leyte and again at Lingayen: 'O Lord, Thou knowest how busy we are today. If we forget Thee, do not Thou forget us. For Christ's sake, Amen.'

It was a singular choice to be heard on the decks of an Australian man-o'-war. The words had been uttered first by Sir Jacob Astley, the Royalist Major General of Foot at the opening clash of the English Civil War, the Battle of Edgehill, fought in 1642. Nichols had judiciously changed Astley's original first person 'I' to the plural 'we'. If not all the ship's company recognised that, nor the historical significance, they certainly appreciated the sentiment. Nichols had the habit of walking around the ship to nooks and crannies where a captain was rarely if ever seen, simply to offer his thanks and encouragement to the men working there. After the initial surprise, the scrambling to attention and the saluting, he would stay chatting informally and easily, a habit that endeared him to them. David Mattiske, the young man from the Victorian Wimmera, admired him as:

> the most loved and respected officer the entire ship's company had ever known. Efficient, precise, never over-bearing, wise and kind, courageous and cool under fire. As a lookout on the Compass Platform, although only an AB, I saw him close at hand for some hundreds of hours in very testing situations, and never once saw him flustered . . .[14]

On 16 February 1945, *Shropshire* was in Manila Bay at first light, standing off the fortress of Corregidor, which had been surrendered to the Japanese by a starving and exhausted American and Filipino garrison in 1942. Now was the time for redemption. A powerful American task force patrolled the bay while Thunderbolt P-47 fighters and twin-engined Boston bombers strafed and rocketed the beaches and the deep tunnels. *Shropshire* joined the bombardment, firing 48 rounds from her 8-inch guns before returning to what was by now the relative safety of Lingayen. Corregidor was recaptured by the US Army by 1 March, with nearly 7000 Japanese dead and just 50 survivors to be taken prisoner.

At Lingayen, Nichols announced that the ship would be returning to Sydney at last, for a refit, via Seeadler Harbour in Manus. There were no cheers as once there might have been, just a subdued relief. With *Arunta* in company, they passed through the lovely green islands of the China Strait off south-eastern New Guinea on 13 March, the barometer dropping all the while, and the next day they were in the jaws of a hurricane.

With the wind howling in the rigging like some mad beast, one great roller would lift *Shropshire*'s bows almost vertically, it seemed, and then plunge her with a shudder into the deep green of the next one, untold tonnes of sea water foaming and smashing over the fo'c'sle and onto A-turret. On the compass platform, they clung on for dear life, blinded by the spray and driving rain, speculating about how far she could roll with her extra top-weight of new masts and aerials, but unable to do anything but press on. At times, the smaller *Arunta*, out on the port beam, would simply vanish unseen into the troughs, and then miraculously labour out again. Below, it was chaos, for, as they found, no matter how much you stowed and lashed and battened down, something would always break loose and set off a chain reaction on the heaving decks.

Eventually, the storm wore itself out, or they passed through it, and when it was safe to go back up on deck again they discovered that the power of the water had sheared away the blast shield of the for'ard Bofors, with sheets of steel and the heavy bolts holding them simply ripped off.

In calmer waters, the captain broke the news that President Roosevelt had died at his country home and health spa in Warm Springs, Georgia, to be succeeded in the Oval Office by his vice president, Harry Truman.

A couple of days later, they were gliding down the line of the New South Wales coast out to starboard, and they entered Sydney Harbour early on 16 March, a Friday, with the band playing on the quarterdeck, to secure to the No. 2 Naval Buoy off Garden Island. The war news in the papers was largely optimistic, a triumphant sweep onwards against the Germans in Europe and the Japanese in the Pacific, although with an ominous hint of grave developments to come:

Harsh Treatment of Australian P.O.W.s
CANBERRA, Friday.— The discipline imposed on Japanese-held Australian prisoners of war in occupied territories was believed to be brutal, with savage punishment inflicted for trivial breaches.

This is stated in a report tabled in the House of Representatives to-day by the Prime Minister, Mr. Curtin.

In Japan, Formosa, Korea, and Manchuria, the Japanese, in the main, are believed to be observing the provisions of the Prisoners of War Convention in the treatment of prisoners.

The report added that groups of Australian prisoners had now been moved from occupied territories to Japan, Korea and Manchuria. The transfers had been made with complete disregard for their health and safety. It estimated the number of Australian prisoners of war in Japanese hands at 18,718, but added this number was subject to considerable revision:

> The majority of Australian prisoners of war who had worked on the Thailand–Burma railway are believed to have been moved from Siam. Those who remained were probably now mainly held in base camps, where conditions of food and accommodation must be considered reasonably good . . .[15]

For *Shropshire*'s sailors, though, it was time for leave and freedom, time to return to home and family. Clutching their rail-travel vouchers, David Mattiske and half a dozen of his Victorian shipmates headed straight up George Street for the Great Southern, a friendly pub near Sydney's Central Railway Station where they could get a few beers before catching their train south that night. 'Pouring the lovely cold brown stuff down apace,' they lost track of the time and suddenly discovered that the train was about to leave.[16] There was a frantic, boozy dash across Railway Square, dodging trams and the peak-hour traffic, but when they reached the platform the station staff were shouting 'all aboard' and a big crowd blocked their way. Mattiske grabbed a luggage trolley, and they all clambered on top of it and charged helter-skelter down the platform, mowing down the onlookers, as their train began to move. They hurled their bags through open carriage windows, where other sailors caught them, and they jumped on board in the nick of time.

At his home town of Murtoa, Mattiske had three weeks of peace and relaxation to put his life back together, although the place seemed a bit empty with most of his mates away at the war. Like most of his mates, he did not talk much about the war, least of all about the Kamikaze menace. They kept their knowledge to themselves. Sharing it would only worry Mum or the missus.

The refit in the dry dock at Cockatoo Island saw *Shropshire*'s torpedo tubes and depth-charge chutes removed and the now obsolete Oerlikon anti-aircraft guns replaced by 15 new single Bofors, a signal improvement. Back in the water, she went south to Jervis Bay for a work-up to knock her back into some sort of shape and to give the new gunnery officer, Lieutenant Commander Bill Marks, the chance to get his eye in. The popular and much-admired – even notorious – Warwick Bracegirdle had finally left the ship in Sydney to go ashore as a gunnery instructor, and he would not fire another shot in anger in this war. He went with much acclaim from officers and sailors, and was much missed.

The cruiser sailed back to the war on 3 June, and by the middle of the month she was at Seeadler again, where Harold Farncomb came on board to hoist his broad pennant once more. There was one more campaign to fight.

—

In all the history of war, there has been nothing to match the wave of death and violence that swept northward up the Pacific in the first seven months of 1945. The American thrust towards Japan was as unstoppable and indomitable as the Japanese themselves had appeared to be just three years earlier. Employing new weapons, new ships, planes and vehicles, and a strength of numbers unimaginable before the war, the Americans conquered the empire's island strongholds one by one. Farm boys from Texas and Montana and Iowa, slum kids from Pittsburgh and the Bronx, crew-cut graduates from Annapolis and West Point prevailed over the chrysanthemum flower of Japanese manhood brainwashed into a mass suicidal resistance.

After five weeks of the closest combat, the US Marines took the small island of Iwo Jima, 1200 kilometres south of Tokyo, on 26 February, at the cost of 6821 of their own dead and more than 18,000 Japanese. The image of the flag-raising on Mount Suribachi endures as an American icon.

But the fighting was still more bloody in the battle for Okinawa – or the *tetsu no bofu*, the typhoon of steel, as the Japanese called it – which saw 21,000 Americans killed and possibly more than 100,000 of the enemy until final victory there in mid-June. Desperate to defend Okinawa, the IJN made its last roll of the dice in April with Operation *Ten-Go* – Operation Heaven One – sending the leviathan battleship *Yamato* and nine other warships to meet the American fleet. It was a sortie every bit as suicidal as the Kamikaze air attacks, for, even in the event of a victory, the force did not have enough fuel to make it back to Japan. Overwhelming American air power sank *Yamato*, a light cruiser and four destroyers on 7 April, for minimal loss.

On the Japanese home islands, the firebombing of Tokyo began on 10 March, with an experimental attack on the inner suburb of Shitamachi. Before dawn that day, 334 B-29 Superfortress bombers flying at just 500 feet unloaded their lethal cargo on its densely packed wooden and paper buildings, setting the suburb ablaze in a holocaust fanned by 30-knot winds. By the close of the day, around 100,000 people were dead, a million were huddled homeless and 40 square kilometres of Tokyo were a heap of glowing, smoking ash. The killing was so vast that it was said the last waves of American pilots could smell the stench of burning flesh in their cockpits, forcing them to don their oxygen masks. This was just the beginning of the carpet firebombing of Japanese cities.

The Australian services were largely left behind in this onslaught, to the point where questions were being asked about the army's apparent idleness. Yet the island of Borneo and its rich oil wells and supplies of rubber were still in Japanese hands, and strongly so, and the US Joint Chiefs of Staff and Douglas MacArthur were keen to get in there. Operation Oboe was put together in six parts, to successively liberate strategic areas of Borneo, the landings to be carried out entirely by Australian troops. Southern Borneo could then provide a platform for the retaking of Dutch Java.

Oboe was controversial at the time, and it remains so. On the recommendation of General Blamey, the Australian Government was reluctant to get involved in Borneo, believing that an invasion could be costly in both lives and materiel when the

Japanese could just as easily be cut off from their supplies and left to surrender or starve. On 18 May, the Acting Prime Minister, Ben Chifley, wrote to MacArthur to suggest as much. The Generalissimo was horrified. On 20 May, he shot back that any withdrawal of Australian forces 'would disorganise completely not only the immediate campaign but also the strategic plan of the Joint Chiefs of Staff'.[17] Meekly, the government gave in, and Oboe went ahead, although not all of it.

The first leg, Oboe 1, was the capture of the island of Tarakan, off the north-east coast of Borneo, beginning on 1 May. After the usual bombardment from air and sea, the army's 26th Infantry Brigade, part of the 9th Division, landed and fought for seven bitter weeks until the last Japanese positions were taken on 20 June. More than 200 Australians died, including the renowned Lieutenant Tom 'Diver' Derrick of the 2/48th Battalion, one of the Rats of Tobruk, who had won a Distinguished Conduct Medal in North Africa in 1942 and the Victoria Cross in New Guinea in 1943. Many of these Australians were fresh young troops, though they fought with the commitment and courage of veterans, but in battles that were almost entirely futile. Little was achieved. The main objective of repairing the airfield on Tarakan proved extremely difficult in the swamps and bogs, and in the end it was barely used.

The next target was the island of Labuan, a Japanese strong-hold in Brunei Bay in Borneo's north-west, the operation codenamed Oboe 6. The rest of the army's 9th Division was to secure this and the Brunei coast and hinterland, capturing oil fields and rubber plantations, from 10 June. *Shropshire* joined the bombardment for a couple of days in mid-June, although in a relatively minor role, happily untroubled by the enemy. The gunners in the 8-inch turrets did all the hard work, loading and firing shell after shell, with the rest of the crew taking it almost absurdly easy. The aerial terrors of Leyte and Lingayen were now but a horrible memory, for, although the Kamikaze menace was still real and lethal in waters near Japan, it had evap-orated this far south. There were no planes nor pilots left. One of the ship's doctors, Surgeon Lieutenant Commander Clive Statham, of Sydney, wrote that he 'sat relaxed in a deck chair, idly prospecting on the fall of shot . . . other dry idlers sunbaked indelicately clad, swam over the side, slimmed their figures by gymnastics . . .' Statham was amused when he went for a run ashore on Labuan to see that:

> A Japanese, alleged to be the military governor of the island, had just been delivered to 9th Division by a trio of Dyaks. The unfortunate celestial, a very large man, was encompassed in a small wickerwork basket, lashed up like long pig, his hands secured at the small of his back, knees under chin, his whole person having been compressed into the small container by the use of expert violence. The basket, slung on two long poles, was carried by a pair of head-hunters with a savage in line abreast . . .[18]

The diggers had it rather tougher than the sightseeing naval surgeon. Fighting went on in Brunei until war's end, again largely purposeless, to mop up an exhausted enemy who posed no possible threat to Australia nor anyone else, at a cost of more than 200 Australian lives.

Job done at Labuan, *Shropshire* then joined Oboe 2, the last leg of the Oboe operation, an assault on Balikpapan on the south-east coast of Borneo. Balikpapan was a big port, with oil tanks and a refinery, that had been taken by the Japanese in 1942 and was heavily defended. Now the Australians would get it back again, employing overwhelming power. Beginning on Sunday 1 July, this was the last great amphibious invasion of the war and the biggest ever undertaken by the Australian services, with more than 33,000 men to be landed from a fleet of American and Australian transports and landing craft.

Task Group 74.1 was back in business again, with *Shropshire* flying Commodore Farncomb's broad pennant in company with the faithful *Hobart* and *Arunta*, and the brand-new American Fletcher-class destroyers *Hart* and *Metcalf*. They arrived off Balikpapan on 27 June and opened up their bombardment that afternoon, to create as much havoc as possible while the invasion fleet was days away, still trudging slowly towards them and the beaches. Three years of hard-won Allied experience – of error and failure, of improvement and success – had by now brought a clockwork, almost theatrical precision to this last great act. The forces arrayed were tremendous. First the survey vessels and minesweepers went in, to sort out safe passage for the bigger ships and the landing craft – a dangerous business. Then under-water demolition teams would follow, to get rid of any sunken obstacles or booby traps – a still more hazardous operation. All the while, the bombardment continued, unleashing a ferocious fire on whatever the ships, and the aircraft above, could see of Japanese positions – the oil storage tanks, the refinery, railway lines, barracks, anti-aircraft batteries – and reducing the palms of the jungle shore to smashed stumps.

Offshore, in addition to Task Group 74.1, there were two further American cruiser and destroyer groups; the Attack Group itself – including the Australian troop transports *Manoora*, *Westralia* and *Kanimbla* – and, further in the background, three US escort carriers. For five days before the landing, the skies were filled with attacking bombers, both American and RAAF, nearly 200 Liberators, Mitchells and P-38 Lightnings, with Beaufighters and Kittyhawks weaving their way through their midst.

The invasion itself was the aggregation of this might and power. The morning began with two hours of air and sea bombardment, wreathing the shoreline in choking smoke and tongues of flame. As the landing craft began to move in, the small rocket ships hammered the beaches, with only some ragged Japanese artillery and mortar fire replying. The Australian diggers splashed ashore from nine o'clock, 17 waves of them landing without a casualty, to be met by a panorama of ruin and desolation. The enemy had abandoned what was left of their bunkers and dugouts and fled to the hills and the jungle beyond.

Shropshire fired her big guns on and off for eight days, withdrawing only once to refuel and utterly untouched by an enemy that could no longer take to the skies. Ruefully, the men complained that their worst moment was on the night of 2 July, when the ship was ordered to keep shooting from eight o'clock that night until four the next morning, ensuring that nobody got a wink of sleep. In the end, she simply ran out of targets, and by 19 July – her war over – she was back at liberated Manila. Recovered from the injuries he'd received at Leyte, John Collins arrived to take over again from Harold Farncomb, who hauled down his Commodore's broad pennant on 22 July and flew back to Sydney.

Balikpapan was largely subdued by the end of July, with 229 Australians killed in action or dying of their wounds. It was the last Australian campaign of the war and, like the rest of Operation Oboe, entirely pointless, at a needless cost in lives. Not Tarakan, not Labuan, not Balikpapan served any strategic purpose whatsoever, their capture doing nothing to reduce any enemy threat or bring the war to an earlier end. The decisions to embark upon it had all been political, the Australian Government under pressure from the glory-seeking MacArthur and from the Dutch, who wanted to regain their Netherlands East Indies colonies with Australia's help. In a final irony, the Dutch had the barefaced effrontery to protest later 'that the bombardment at Balikpapan was carried out with excessive vigour and the damage was far greater than necessary'.[19]

The true tragedy of Borneo had already played itself out in the months before: the evils of the Sandakan Death Marches. There were three of them, in which Australian prisoners of war were slaughtered in cold blood, or died of disease or starvation. At war's end, of 2390 men who had been imprisoned at Sandakan, only six survived to tell of the horrors they had seen and endured. These were the worst atrocities inflicted on Australians by the Japanese.

—

At noon on 15 August, the voice of the Sun God himself was heard on radio to deliver the *Gyokuon-hoso*, the Jewel Voice Broadcast, in which he conceded Japan's defeat. It was not a live broadcast, but a recording Hirohito had made at his palace the day before. It crackled from the propaganda loudspeakers installed in towns and villages and what was left of Japan's big cities, and it was heard on short wave across the ruins of the Emperor's short-lived and blood-soaked Empire. The millions of his listening subjects were both puzzled and astounded, for Hirohito had never spoken to his people before, and the form of language he used was of such courtly obscurity that many of them had trouble under-standing him. More shocking still, almost incomprehensible, was the thought that Nippon had been beaten.

The speech was a cynical masterpiece of self-serving decep-tion and evasion, a travesty that did not once mention the word surrender and offered no recognition of Japanese guilt, let alone any apology for the war fought in Hirohito's name and over which he had so disastrously presided. With Hiroshima and Nagasaki lying in nuclear ruin, Hirohito could say only:

> . . . Despite the best that has been done by everyone – the gallant
> fighting of our military and naval forces, the diligence and assi-
> duity of our servants of the State and the devoted service of our
> 100 million people – the war situation has developed not neces-
> sarily to Japan's advantage . . .

In the final days, Vice Admiral Takijiro Onishi, the father of the Kamikaze, had pleaded for the war to go on by any means. By now, he was the Vice Chief of the IJN General Staff. On 13 August, he stormed into a late-evening meeting of govern-ment ministers at the Prime Minister's residence in Tokyo, almost apoplectic, eyes brimming with tears. 'If the entire nation commits to accepting the sacrifice of 20 million people, then victory will be ours!' he shouted.[20] An air-raid siren sounded and the ministers turned him away.

Onishi heard the Jewel Broadcast at his home at IJN Head-quarters and realised, finally, that all was lost. That evening, clad in ceremonial robes, he penned a suicide note to be read not as an apology for sending thousands of young pilots to die but for the unfortunate fact that his strategy had not worked:

I wish to express my deep appreciation to the souls of the brave special attackers. They fought and died valiantly with faith in our ultimate victory. In death I wish to atone for my part in the failure to achieve that victory and I apologize to the souls of those dead fliers and their bereaved families.

I wish the young people of Japan to find a moral in my death. To be reckless is only to aid the enemy. You must abide by the spirit of the Emperor's decision with utmost perseverance. Do not forget your rightful pride in being Japanese.

You are the treasure of the nation. With all the fervour of spirit of the special attackers, strive for the welfare of Japan and for peace throughout the world.[21]

Seated on the floor, he withdrew a Samurai sword from its scabbard and plunged it deep into his stomach, drawing the blade sideways in the prescribed ritual for *seppuku* and then stabbing himself in the chest and throat. It did not kill him. Vomiting blood and lying in agony, he was found by a friend, Yoshio Kodama, a powerful figure who would survive the war to become a corrupt and fabulously wealthy businessman, a leader of the Yakuza – the Japanese Mafia – and a founder of the Liberal Democratic political party.

Kodama offered to finish the job in the traditional role of the *Kaishakunin*, the assistant who beheads the dying man, but Onishi refused to let him do it. It took the admiral 15 hours to die. He left a haiku poem:

Refreshed,
I feel like the clear moon
After a storm.[22]

The sword with which he killed himself is now in the Yushukan War Museum at the Yasukuni Shrine in Tokyo, where, to this day, Japanese war criminals are honoured as heroes.

CHAPTER 23

THEIR SACRIFICE WAS NOT IN VAIN

Tokyo Bay. The victorious ships of the Allied navies began arriving in stately procession from Monday 27 August 1945, led by the battleship *Missouri*, the 'Mighty Mo', flying Admiral Halsey's four-starred flag, and, for the RN, HMS *Duke of York*, carrying the Commander-in-Chief of the British Pacific Fleet, Admiral Sir Bruce Fraser. On they came – battleships, cruisers, destroyers – salt-stained and war-worn, dropping anchor in long lines in Sagami Wan, a great sweep of the bay south-west of Tokyo with a view of the snow-capped Mount Fuji. The carriers remained at sea, partly to prepare their aircraft for a mighty fly-past over the surrender ceremonies, but also as a precaution against any 11th-hour suicidal attack by some fanatical enemy commander. The US naval historian Samuel Morison recorded that a blood-red sun set that night directly into Fuji's crater, as if signifying the eclipse of the empire.

News of the Japanese capitulation had begun to spread to the Allies early on the morning of 15 August, several hours before Hirohito's broadcast. *Shropshire* heard it with the rest of Task Group 74.1 in Subic Bay, on a hot day heavy with humidity. There were no wild celebrations, no cheering, no exultant cries of victory; more an unscrewing of the tensions and anxieties of war, with the solemn realisation that they had survived leavened by the memory of shipmates who had not. John Collins signalled the ships under his command:

I wish to congratulate every officer and man of His Majesty's Australian Squadron on his share in our final victory announced by the Prime Minister of Great Britain this morning. I rejoice with you that the Japanese have been forced to surrender.

We have every reason to be proud of the part played by the Royal Australian Navy during six years of war across the seas of the world, and I say again to all hands 'Well Done'. Let us always remember with sad pride our lost ships and their companies and thank God that their sacrifice was not in vain.[1]

In fact, it took a while for the news to sink in. The war had seemed as though it would never end. Now it had. The next day, the ships were festooned with signal flags, church Services of Thanksgiving were held, and the order went out to splice the mainbrace, the traditional navy signal for a party. By happy coincidence, the supply ship *Merkur* had turned up in Subic from Australia at exactly the right time, laden with beer and parcels of goodies for a celebration. *Shropshire*'s ship's company proceeded to get happily drunk, the men cracking coldies in their messes and the officers throwing an evening party on the quarterdeck for 400 guests from nearby Allied ships, the festivities described in the *Porthole* book:

Well decorated with greenery and well illuminated with all kinds of fancy lights, including a kangaroo set up in the mast, *Shropshire* was going really gay. There was magnificent hospitality for everyone – good food and drink galore and goodly company.

The evening went apace and, unrecognised, a couple of lads had dressed up as officers to get in for their share. The first indication that they were not quite at home came in a message from the Flag Lieutenant – to the effect that the Commodore would be greatly displeased if these two young officers continued to wear their caps.

They removed their caps and settled into some hard drinking, no doubt believing that one swallow does not make a summer. All went well until their divisional officer recognised one fellow by the back of his head! The game was up!

A few days later the two braves appeared at the Commander's table. The Commander dealt with them in a way that was as wise as anything Solomon ever did – and nary a shadow of a smile was on his face.

'You had a good time?'

'Yes sir.'

'Well, the mess share is sixteen shilling and eight pence, and you'll pay the Mess treasurer when convenient.'

'Yes sir!'[2]

With *Australia* still far away in Plymouth for her refit, *Shropshire* was assigned to lead the Australian presence in Tokyo Bay. She anchored there on 31 August, with *Hobart* and the destroyers *Bataan* and *Warramunga*, which had come with her from Subic, via Okinawa. In all, there would be nine Australian ships present for the surrender – the destroyers *Napier* and *Nizam* had arrived as a part of the British Fleet, and the corvettes *Ipswich*, *Ballarat* and *Cessnock* were sent as well.

'All hands are in good heart but looking forward to the days when they will be released to their families and are all anxious for detailed news of demobilisation plans,' wrote *Ballarat*'s captain, Commander Neven Read, in his Report of Proceedings.[3] Read had been the first to arrive and, something of a humourist, signalled *Shropshire*, 'If we knew you were coming we would have baked a cake' – a crack received with thin lips and raised eyebrows on the flagship's bridge.

Shropshire anchored a rifle shot away from HMS *King George V*, the British battleship that had hunted the *Bismarck*. The bay held 258 warships, imposing lines of them stretching away into the haze.

From seven in the morning of Sunday 2 September, the good and the great began to arrive on board *Missouri*. The surrender documents would be signed on her quarterdeck, which, on this ship, was not astern but to the starboard side of the No. 2 main turret. The day brought scattered cloud, threatening rain. *Missouri*'s captain, Stuart 'Sunshine' Murray, had taken extraordinary pains to get the protocol right, from correctly piping his guests on board to ensuring that the personal flags of the rivals MacArthur and Nimitz were flown at exactly the same height, to the inch.

At almost the last minute, there was a panic when the surrender documents, flown out from Washington, were found to be too big for the elegant mahogany table the British had sent over from *Duke of York* for the occasion. Murray grabbed the nearest four sailors and charged down to the wardroom himself to get the table there, only to find to his chagrin that it was – of course – bolted to the deck. So they dashed into a sailors' mess, snatched up the nearest table and a coffee-stained green baize cloth to cover it, and got it on deck just in time. Murray's men crowded every vantage point overlooking the ceremony but, taking every precaution, there was a Combat Air Patrol circling above, and *Missouri*'s anti-aircraft batteries and radars were manned and ready.

Nimitz arrived just after eight, MacArthur about 20 minutes later, each man dressed in khaki drill uniform with open-necked shirt and received with due ceremony before disappearing into Halsey's cabin. The Japanese came aboard at nine, mounting a gangway from an American destroyer: first the newly appointed Foreign Minister, Mamoru Shigemitsu, clad in morning suit and top hat and limping stiffly, for he wore an artificial leg after a bomb attack by a Korean nationalist in 1932. He was followed by the Chief of the Army General Staff, General Yoshijiro Umezu, another fanatic who had wanted to carry on the war but had been personally ordered to sign the surrender document by Hirohito. They found themselves confronting a line of brass from the Allied nations that had fought them – the United States, China, Britain, the Soviet Union, Australia, Canada, France, the Netherlands and New Zealand – including the portly and Sam Browne–uniformed General Blamey, who would sign for Australia. There, too, were the gaunt figures of Lieutenant General Jonathan Wainwright, who had surrendered in the Philippines in 1942, and the British Arthur Percival, who had handed over fallen Singapore, both of them newly liberated from their imprisonment in Manchuria.

John Collins, a relatively low-ranking Commodore, stood in the second row, with other Australian Army and RAAF officers. They were fortunate to be there. With condescending hauteur, the British Government had claimed the right to sign the surrender document for the empire; there was no need for the Pacific dominions to sign, said Whitehall, and this had been approved by the US State Department, they claimed. This was entirely untrue. Evatt, the Australian External Affairs Minister, was aware that MacArthur wanted an Australian signature, and told London that Blamey would attend 'in his own right and not as an appendage of Admiral Sir Bruce Fraser'. With that objection, and more from Wellington and Ottawa, the British Dominions Secretary, the egregious Lord Addison, backed off. Come the day, all was sweetness and light again.

After a prayer, the US national anthem and then a pregnant silence, MacArthur and Nimitz emerged, with the general making a short and no doubt carefully scripted speech that was broadcast around the world:

> . . . It is my earnest hope, and indeed the hope of all mankind, that from this solemn occasion a better world shall emerge out of the blood and carnage of the past – a world dedicated to the dignity of man and the fulfilment of his most cherished wish for freedom, tolerance and justice.

The Japanese signed first, and then the Allied delegates. It took 23 minutes. As the ceremony ended, the clouds parted and the sun came through. MacArthur, walking off, clapped an arm around Halsey's shoulder and was heard to say, 'Bill, where in the hell are those airplanes?'[4] On cue, they came, an air fleet of USN carrier aircraft and US Army Air Force B-29 Superfortress bombers, 1200 of them roaring overhead in perfect arrow formations, the sight and sound of victory.

—

Accustomed as they were to conformist obedience to authority, the Japanese people by and large submitted to the rule of their conquerors with humility. Their world had been turned upside down, their cities reduced to ruins, and for months after the surrender many millions remained hungry and homeless, despite the provision of American aid. MacArthur was their overlord, a truth brought home to them with shocking clarity by a widely published photograph of his first meeting with Hirohito, taken at his headquarters on 27 September. The Emperor had come to visit him, the mountain to Mohammed. This was an astounding thing in itself, but more startling still was the sight of the Generalissimo standing stony-faced, in everyday khaki and with hands on hips, beside the submissive figure of their morning-suited Sun God. It was an emphatic display of mastery.

The Australian sailors were not permitted ashore at first, for nobody was quite sure what their reception would be nor what there was for them to do if they did set foot on this blasted, defeated land. Eventually, they were allowed to go, with strict warnings about their behaviour. There was to be no looting and they were not to eat the food; they must not accept invitations from the locals and, if they were accosted, they should form a circle and face outwards. In the event, few of them struck any trouble, beyond the usual cheating taxi-driver wearily familiar to sailors in any foreign port.

Guy Griffiths went to see what was left of the Yokosuka Naval Base south of the Tokyo port of Yokohama, where he came upon a mass of Japanese midget submarines of the sort that had raided Sydney. Out of curiosity, he found his way up to Tokyo and took a tram ride to a terminus and back, struck by the awesome stretches of blackened wasteland wrought by the firebombings. The teenaged midshipman who had escaped the bombing and sinking of *Repulse* off Malaya in 1941, who had gone on to serve in an RN destroyer on the British east coast, who had survived the Kamikazes of the Philippines was now, at the age of 22, a seasoned lieutenant, entitled to wear the Distinguished Service Cross with its blue and white ribbon for – as the citation said – 'gallantry, skill and devotion to duty whilst serving in HMAS *Shropshire* in the successful assault operations in the Lingayen Gulf, Luzon Island'. His had been an extraordinary war.

Eventually, working parties of shipwrights and electricians and the like were sent ashore to help rebuild quarters for the occupation troops, not least of them the Yokohama Yacht Club, which was turned into a British naval canteen. In Tokyo, David Mattiske and some mates wandered along what was left of the famous Ginza, where he bargained with a shopgirl for a kimono.

The victors were making their mark. In the second week of September, a handful of *Shropshire* sailors were told they would be taking part in a formal ceremony to raise the Union Jack at the newly recovered British embassy. Mattiske was one of them. Their Australian khaki uniforms being deemed not posh enough for such a grand affair, the men were ordered over to *King George V* to be issued with white British uniforms, including the voluminous knee-length shorts they scornfully called Bombay Bloomers. No Australian sailor would be caught dead in them. When the great day arrived, these vast garments had all been snappily re-tailored short and tight, in the approved Australian fashion. Greatly displeased by this outrage, the RN petty officers in charge of the show retaliated by lining up the *Shropshire* contingent almost out of sight at the end of the driveway.

The formalities over, the day ended on a happier note with sandwiches and ice-cold Japanese beer turned on in the embassy garden. Mattiske and a few mates set about a little freelance sightseeing, discovered an open door in the rear of the embassy and found themselves in the Ambassador's office. Nothing ventured, nothing gained. Rifling through the desk, Mattiske saw a pile of visiting cards handsomely made of heavy white cardboard, goldlined and embossed with the royal Coat of Arms. As you would, he shoved a fistful of them inside his shirt.

The next morning, back in the ship, a thought occurred. What a tremendous souvenir they would be if he could get Commodore Collins and Captain Nichols to sign them. In flagrant breach of all the rules of naval discipline and hierarchy, taking his career and his liberty in his hands, this lowly able seaman boldly found his way aft and knocked on the Commodore's door:

Commodore Collins looked up from the desk at which he was seated, recognised me from the days when I was one of his lookouts and he was Captain. He seemed amused by the situation and called me to come in. I told him of the Ambassador's cards, showed him what they looked like, and asked for his autograph. He examined the card with interest and, with a chuckle, penned his signature.

Then next door to the Captain's cabin. Captain Nichols was highly amused, was delighted to sign, and said something about a good show and that I had something worth keeping. My friends later were amazed at my audacity in getting these signatures.[5]

Soon enough, boredom set in, and so did the chill of autumn. Sitting at anchor – swinging around the pick, as they called it – was tedious to say the least, and hardly relieved by bouts of painting the ship or scraping the dulled brass work back to its pre-war gleam. A typhoon kept them on the hop for a couple of days, with steam up and the ship ready to slip at the first sign of trouble, but that too expired. Hoping to raise morale, Nichols took the ship south on a short cruise to the port of Wakayama, a place of beaches and ancient temples, where they got to go sightseeing ashore again. There, too, they exchanged visits with a British destroyer, HMS *Whelp*, whose first lieutenant was a certain Prince Philip Mountbatten. Other men drew lots for a trip to the picturesque mountain resort of Nikko, north of Tokyo.

All the while, there was the longing for home. The war had ended. They were serving no useful purpose in Japan, so far as they could see. The youngsters who had signed on only for the war grew ever more discontent, worried for the future and beginning to fear that when they got back – if they ever got back – all the jobs would be taken. Boys who had set aside apprenticeships or university studies for the duration and were now young men wondered what was to become of them in the brave new world they had fought for. There would be not much for Bofors gunners or signalmen or radar operators in civilian life, they thought. Perhaps there would be another Depression, as they had known in the pinched years of their childhood.

And when, oh when, would they get out? The government had set up a points system for discharge, they knew. You got two points for each year of service, two more for every additional month, and, if you had dependants, an additional point per month. And you could be discharged early if your return to civilian life was somehow deemed essential, or on compassionate grounds, whatever they might be. It was confusing, to say the least, and when men asked their officers to explain it, they knew little more.

At last came deliverance from this purgatory, the sublimely welcome pipe for leaving harbour. *Shropshire* sailed for Australia on 18 November, Mount Fuji glimpsed through the mist as they left the bay. On the way home, she was unexpectedly diverted to Wewak in New Guinea, where she picked up nearly 600 soldiers of the army's 6th Division, who had also been wondering when they would be repatriated. On the last day of the month, she tied up at Sydney's Garden Island, home for Christmas.

—

Life in Britain had long since palled for *Australia*'s ship's company. They had been generously welcomed and they were grateful for it, but home called ever more strongly. They celebrated the setting of the Japanese sun on a dark and drizzling evening in Plymouth, with distress rockets soaring into the night sky, searchlights sweeping the sound, and an exuberant gathering on the Hoe, where there was a cheerful bonfire burning at the statue of Francis Drake. A few days later, there was a dance in the gym at the Raglan Barracks, attended by droves of friendly Wrens. Some serious relationships were being formed.

A new captain joined on 20 November: David Harries, who had served in both *Australia* and *Shropshire* before and had spent time during the war as the Australian naval attaché in Washington. A few of the luckier crew members were suddenly posted back home while others were scattered here and there. To his astonishment, David Hamer was sent off to join the Allied Control Commission in occupied Germany, keeping an eye out for Nazis in hiding.

With the war over and any sense of urgency long gone, and to everyone's despair, the ship's refit plodded along at a desultory pace. Faced with the prospect of the dockyard shutting down for Christmas, Harries decided to make do as best he could. It was time to leave. *Australia* was back out in the Sound on 17 December under her own steam, running through a bare minimum of trials while the captain embarked on the obligatory round of farewell calls, lunches, dinners and cocktail parties. Lady Astor, the eccentric wife of the newspaper tycoon Viscount Astor, newly retired as the local Conservative MP, threw a grand farewell for most of the crew and the usual clutch of local admirals and civic worthies. As dizzy as ever, she startled the gathering by publicly announcing that she was planning to divorce her husband to marry the playwright George Bernard Shaw,[6] but it was the quality and quantity of her liquor that got them in:

LADY ASTOR DEPARTS FROM TEETOTAL PRINCIPLES
LONDON, Wednesday. Lady Astor, departing from life-long teetotal principles, yesterday supplied plentiful quantities of Devonshire cider for 400 Australian guests when she entertained the ship's company of HMAS *Australia* at a farewell party at Plymouth before the ship's departure for Australia.

Lady Astor presented the ship's company with a silver tray bearing the inscription, 'Presented to Captain James Greene, master of the sailing ship "Waterloo" by cabin passengers to commemorate the best voyage from London to Sydney in 1852.'

Lady Astor found the tray in a Plymouth antique shop.[7]

At last, the ship was free. With 150 passengers on board, some of them Australian and New Zealand servicemen heading for home, plus a contingent of British Royal Marines, she sailed from Plymouth on 20 December. It was a sad parting for some: 19 of the crew had married English girls, and several dozen more were engaged, and it would be a while before they were together again. For the rest, it was a relief to be away.

They weathered a violent gale off Ushant and spent Christmas at sea passing Tenerife in the Atlantic. Torrential rain met her at

Durban in South Africa in early January 1946, clearing just in time for the ship's sides to be painted before the long leg across the Indian Ocean to Fremantle, where she arrived on 25 January, berthing to the strains of an army band.

For the next few weeks, *Australia* made a slow, triumphal progress around the southern capitals. There was a march through the streets of Perth, and 18,000 people came on board for a look around. Adelaide turned on a tremendous welcome, perhaps because the cruiser had carried home one of the city's famous sons, Lieutenant Commander George Gosse, a reservist who had made a name for himself as a frogman in the hazardous trade of disarming enemy mines under water.[8] In Melbourne, she met up with *Shropshire* and *Bataan* for another march of the men of all three ships, cheered by a crowd of 75,000 people.

Yet her arrival in Sydney, her home port, went almost unnoticed. She slipped in through the Heads on the morning of Saturday 16 February 1946, streaming a long paying-off pennant, and secured to the No. 1 Naval Buoy in Farm Cove. Family and friends of the crew were waiting at the Man o'War Steps for their long-anticipated reunions, but greater Sydney paid no attention. The war was over, long over, and people were getting on with the peace. Warships and homecoming sailors were not news any more, no matter how glorious their record. A few newspapers published a photograph of *Australia* at rest in the harbour, but there was nothing more: no march, and no greetings from the assorted dignitaries who once would have flocked to be entertained on her quarterdeck. Quietly, unobtrusively, her ship's company began to melt away on leave or – for those with their service done – to quit the navy forever, taking with them memories good and haunting, and friendships forged to last a lifetime.

From its small beginnings at the outbreak of the war in 1939, the RAN had expanded at a dazzling rate. At war's end in 1945, there were 337 ships flying the White Ensign, from cruisers to the smallest motor launches. The strength had peaked at 39,650 men (and women, including WRANS and nurses). Of those who wore the uniform, 1852 men had been killed in action, had died of wounds or were missing, presumed dead. They were low figures against the much larger army count, but for a young navy they were a heavy toll, taking some of the best and brightest.

Australia herself was going into reserve. The navy had no use for her in the immediate future, so far as anyone could see. A small crew stayed on to strip her of her ammunition and her stores, to slowly shut down the arteries that had kept her a living thing.

Captain Harries, in his final Report of Proceedings to the Naval Board, noted that she had steamed exactly 250,101.3 nautical miles since her pre-war commissioning – about 463,000 kilometres – or 16 times around the world. She had spent 20,980 hours at sea, or nearly two and a half years, at an average speed of 16.6 knots.

With her vitals cold and still, her masts and flagstaffs bare, *Australia* was taken by tugs to the Dolphins at Athol Bight below Taronga Zoo, a cluster of wooden piles and wharves where old ships were tied up, placed in mothballs, out of the way.

There she would lie with her ghosts, quietly rusting, for two years.

—

Shropshire had the last hurrah. Splendid in a smart new coat of naval grey, brass work aglow, she lay at Princes Pier in Melbourne waiting to take on board the Australian Victory Contingent, the servicemen and women handpicked to march in a great empire parade through London, a soaring coda.

It was Thursday 18 April 1946. That morning, Melbourne gave them a grand goodbye, 155 of them, from each service, three army winners of the Victoria Cross to the fore. Clouds of confetti fluttered down, flags waved, and the cheering followed them along Swanston Street as they swung past the saluting dais at the Town Hall. At the pier that afternoon, friends and family milled around for their farewells, the excitement fizzing.

For a while there, it almost didn't happen. On the very eve of their departure, one of the chosen, Sergeant Albert Curtin, a 27-year-old digger from Bondi, was told that he would not be going. After weeks of practice drill, the deputy commander of the contingent, Brigadier Murray Moten, had decreed that his marching was not up to scratch. He would embarrass them all.

There was uproar. Curtin had enlisted in 1941, leaving his protected occupation as a shearer to be trained as a medical orderly and sent to the army's 2/4th Commando Squadron, his unit through the war. In May 1945, at the Battle of Tarakan Hill in Borneo, he had won the Military Medal 'for gallantry and devotion to duty', risking his life beneath a storm of enemy machine-gun fire to tend to wounded commando mates. Back in civvy street, he had given up his job as a metal polisher to put on his uniform again and make the trip. And now here was some stuck-up blimp saying he was not good enough.

Naturally, the rest of the contingent went on strike. If Bert Curtin couldn't go, they wouldn't either, and they said so very loudly. The row made the newspapers. The brigadier, outnumbered and outgunned, could only back off. Curtin was on board as *Shropshire* pulled away from the pier that evening, her rails lined with khaki and blue, the band playing on the quarterdeck and festoons of coloured paper streamers stretching and snapping as the tugs edged her out into the bay. The ship's for'ard magazine had been emptied of shells and explosives, and filled – along with every other available space – with gifts of food for a Mother Country still ground down by post-war rationing. She had another new captain, Harry Showers, who had commanded *Hobart* when she was torpedoed.

The bold sergeant and his land-lubber comrades might have had second thoughts when filthy weather hit them in the Great Australian Bight, setting the ship rolling and pitching like a mad thing. Again, the rails were crowded with khaki and RAAF blue, this time groaning figures retching from the torments of seasickness, but the storm cleared after a day or two for an easy run to Fremantle and another send-off.

Happily, the rest of the voyage went smoothly, with Cape Town turning on its usual friendly welcome and, later in the

Atlantic, an uproarious Crossing of the Line with the hallowed nautical frolic of King Neptune and his barber and bears. Even the notorious Bay of Biscay behaved itself, and on 30 May a Channel fog parted to reveal the Isle of Wight, where a tug was waiting with a pilot to bring them into Portsmouth, old Pompey itself, as the sailors explained to their passengers. A Royal Marine band on shore played them to their berth at the Pitch House Jetty, 'Waltzing Matilda' echoing across the water.

Eager anticipation gripped them now, an admixture of awe, wonder and sheer exhilaration. They were a select band – 30 from the RAN, including two women; 166 soldiers, ten of them women; and 59 from the RAAF, with seven women – all of them thrilled at the thought that here they were to fly the Australian flag at this unique hour in the history of the empire for which they had fought. Some of *Shropshire*'s old hands who had been to Britain before affected a nonchalant air, but in truth they too were swept up in the euphoria.

The day after their arrival, they took the train from Portsmouth. Arthur Cooper, the Chief Gunner's Mate who had been in *Shropshire* since 1943 and was Warwick Bracegirdle's right-hand man through the Kamikazes of the Philippines and the battle at Surigao, kept a diary:

> At Waterloo Station in London we stretched our legs by a short march to the buses and in a few minutes we were viewing the battle-scarred face of this great city of London. Big Ben boomed out its familiar chimes as we passed the Houses of Parliament and a mental flash of its familiar chimes over the wireless back home brought to mind the fact that this famous clock could at least be called the 'Hub of the Empire.' The drizzle continued as we reached Kensington Gardens but, quickly proceeding to the tents allotted and getting our luggage, we donned dry clothes.
>
> The gardens had been converted into a tent city, the German POWs being employed in this duty. The whole area was covered by row after row of neatly laid out tents and fences and seemed so wonderfully picturesque among the leafy trees of foliage green. Besides the bell tents which were our quarters loomed

large marquees – the NAAFI [Navy, Army and Air Force Insti-
tutes] canteens, mess tents, showers, drying tents, hospitality
tents, post office, telephones – nothing was forgotten . . .

Here we encountered uniforms and men of the fighting
services of countries from all over the world. Signboards at strategic points indicated the locality of various camp groups. The
Canadian, Australian and New Zealand contingents were quar-
tered in close proximity to each other, and soon friendly back
chat was being passed between the camps.[9]

For all the cold hand of austerity, summertime London was en
fête. The Australians were showered with tickets to movies, plays,
concerts and sporting events. There was a glamorous dinner
dance at the Boomerang Club, a wartime home from home at
Australia House in the Strand, where the invited English girls
bought raffle tickets for parcels of Australian food. Lieutenant
General Sir Oliver Leese, an affable figure who had commanded
Australians in the Middle East, had the lot of them down to his
estate in Surrey, where he turned on an old-time country fair,
complete with sideshows, bands and a circus.

And the royals came to visit the Dominion camps in the
gardens, the King in the uniform of an Admiral of the Fleet,
the Queen a cloud of feathers and mauve silk, with Princesses
Elizabeth and Margaret Rose in tow. For some of the Australians, this regal vision was all too much. John Peck, the son of a
navy stoker from Melbourne and now an army lieutenant, had
led a war of epic adventure, beginning when he enlisted in 1939
at the age of 17 by fudging his age up three years. Captured on
Crete in 1941 while still a private, he escaped from the Germans
countless times, fought with the partisans in both Greece and
Yugoslavia, ran an underground escape route for Allied airmen
out of Italy to Switzerland, and was eventually recruited into
the cloak-and-dagger British Special Operations Executive as a
captain, in which role he dashed about behind the lines blowing
up trains and bridges and the like. When he was captured for the
last time in 1944 wearing a German officer's uniform, he dodged
a firing squad by skipping off during an air raid. None of this,

though, had prepared him for his first visit to London nor the terrifying ordeal of answering the Queen's questions about his escapades. Rendered speechless, all he could do was nod at her, he told the papers later.

Ever the showman, Winston Churchill, visited, homburg-hatted, cigar-chomping, beaming cherubically and flashing those V for Victory fingers. The way back to his car was blocked by Australians wanting to pump his hand and be photographed with him. The carnival gaiety moved on. Over the next few days, squads of former Allies began arriving: American and French, Dutch and Norwegian, Belgian and Greek, although the Russians stayed away and so – sadly – did the brave Poles, now at Moscow's bidding. But the show was coming together:

> Practice continued daily and the leafy shades of Kensington Gardens echoed and re-echoed to the sounds of marching feet. Men from Iraq, Luxembourg, China, Fiji, the *Evzones* of Greece, Egyptians – there they were in their thousands. Uniforms gay and gaudy, plain khaki, bare-footed warriors from the wilds of India – all practising and pacing as they pounded those solid roads and walks of dear old England.[10]

This parade would be the last hurrah not only for the war but for the glories of empire itself. Just a year later, 1947, those wild and barefooted Indians would have their independence from the Raj, the subcontinent convulsed by the bloody partition of Hindu India and the new Muslim nation of Pakistan. Other colonies would follow, like tumbling dominoes. In his blood, tears, toil and sweat speech to the Commons in 1940, Churchill had proclaimed he had 'not become the King's First Minister in order to preside over the liquidation of the British Empire', but the world had moved on. The Japanese had left behind a new seething nationalism in colonial peoples, who had seen that their white masters were no longer invincible. When the marchers of the Victory Parade stepped out from Hyde Park at Marble Arch on the morning of Saturday 8 June, it was the beginning of Britain's long retreat from east of Suez, from dominion over palm and pine.

First came a rumbling motorcade of tanks, armoured cars, guns, jeeps and assorted military hardware – such exotica as mobile laundry washing-machine trailers, airfield snow ploughs and a balloon winch with hydrogen cylinders – and the ambulances and fire engines of London, more than 500 vehicles tailing back for six kilometres on a winding route from Regent's Park via Tower Hill, south across the river over London Bridge, back again at Vauxhall and along Millbank to Parliament Square.

There, these machines met the marchers – some 40,000 of them – who had swung 12 abreast through the West End, along bomb-damaged Oxford Street, then down Charing Cross Road and Northumberland Avenue to the Thames Embankment, band after band playing them on. From the shadow of Big Ben, they tramped along Whitehall past the Cenotaph to Trafalgar Square.

Scotland Yard estimated that five million people turned out to cheer them to the echo, and the BBC broadcast the march in the first television pictures seen in Britain after the war. The Australian sailors were led by Lieutenant Commander Richard Peek, who had been on the bridge as *Australia*'s gunnery officer when Emile Dechaineux was killed.

Along the Mall and past Buckingham Palace they went, up Constitution Hill with the summery lawns and trees of Green Park on their right, and onwards to Hyde Park Corner. Above them, in wave after wave, there came Hurricanes and Spitfires, Lancasters and Sunderlands, and the new jet aircraft of the RAF – Meteors and Vampires – the formations led by the legless fighter ace Douglas Bader. A light drizzle turned to London rain as the Australians, weary and footsore, finished the march back to the camp in Kensington Gardens. Then it was over.

—

One *Shropshire* lad did not march. Tom Thurlow, the young signalman who had laid down flags to cover the body of his elder brother Jim when *Canberra* was lost at Savo, had other things in mind. On and off through the war, he had written to Audrey

Simons, the English rose he had met in Oxford in 1943, and she had written back.

On leave in London, he decided to look her up. Back in Oxford again, he found she wasn't married. There was no time to lose, so he proposed and she said yes. 'It's a bloody long way to take a girl,' her father said, but he gave his blessing. That left one more hurdle: the rules said Tom had to get permission from his captain – a worrying moment. But Showers said yes as well, and gave him honeymoon leave 'until half an hour before the ship sails and make sure you're on it'.

The Anglican parish church of Cowley St John was a ten-minute walk from Audrey's home, a Victorian building of mellow grey stone set in a leafy churchyard. They were married there on 22 June 1946, beneath a soaring stained-glass window, Tom in his uniform, Audrey holding a bouquet of roses, as he recalled later.

> Aud's brother Roger was the best man. During wartime England everything was in short supply and all the friends and neighbours donated food for the reception. That meant giving up valuable ration tickets they could ill afford. Clothing was also rationed, but Aud was fortunate enough to borrow a wedding dress and veil, etc. She said the only clothes of her own were underclothes and her shoes. The underclothes were made up from a silk parachute which didn't stand up to testing after repair. It was typical of the English people during the war, to share and help each other whenever possible.
>
> We left late in the day on our honeymoon and went to Devon, where we stayed at Bramley Grange, which was arranged for us by Australia House, London, and was a retreat for snobs and senior service officers. We didn't mix too well so the next day we went back to London and Australia House, and they got us into the Strand Palace Hotel . . .
>
> We thoroughly enjoyed ourselves in London, and each evening went to the Strand Brasserie and had sardines on toast most nights. Sardines were plentiful and we liked them. We explored London and its famous sights. Then came the time to

rejoin the ship and go home. A few of my shipmates and I were friends of an official at Australia House and he got Audrey on top of the list for passage to Australia.[11]

Shropshire sailed from Portsmouth on 1 July, for a leisurely cruise home via the Mediterranean and Suez, back in Sydney by the end of August. Pondering his future, Tom Thurlow decided he'd had enough of the navy and, with his bride on the way out to Melbourne and a new life to be made with her, he applied to be discharged.

There was a snag. In 1940, he had signed on for 12 years, and the navy would not let him go simply because he wanted to. Like so many others who had gone to war, he had to buy his way out – discharge by purchase, in the cold bureaucratic phrase. It cost him £36, taken out of his back pay, an unkind cut for a young man who had given the navy and his country the best years of his youth. But that December, at the age of 23, he was free at last, free to go back to Geelong and the banks of his beloved Barwon River, the sailor home from the sea.

Tom and Audrey Thurlow were happily married for 62 years, raising a family of four children. He was at his happiest in the peace and solitude of a country block he had bought in the bush at Deans Marsh, in the gentle hills of the Pennyroyal Valley where he had holidayed as a kid, and where he would keep fit by cutting wood for his fire and the neighbours'. The memories of the war stayed with him, as they did with all his shipmates from *Canberra*: the horrors of that night off Savo in 1942, the shriek and crash of enemy gunfire, the ship listing and burning, the cries of the wounded, the bodies of the dead. When Tom had come home from leave after the battle, his mother was holding out hope that Jim, listed as missing in action, might still turn up. At the age of 19, Tom had to tell her he'd found the mutilated body of her elder boy, that he would never be back. These were not things he cared to talk about very much.

Audrey died in 2009. Tom lived on a little longer, to die peacefully on a sunny August morning in 2012 at the age of 89. At his funeral, his coffin was draped in the naval White Ensign and it bore his sailor's cap with an HMAS *Canberra* tally band. There was a photograph of Jim, too, for Tom had insisted that this should also be the funeral his brother never had. The date was 9 August. It was 70 years to the day since *Canberra* was sunk.

Exactly a year later, as he had wished, they scattered his ashes in the sea, on a wet and gloomy day at Blanket Bay, a crescent of silver sand and steel-blue waters in the Great Otway National Park. Tom had often talked about the seabirds that would follow the ships. As his remains drifted on the water, a great sea eagle appeared and hovered over them.

CHAPTER 24

THE ROYAL AUSTRALIAN NAVY HAS DONE IT AGAIN

While *Australia* lay asleep in reserve at Athol Bight with only the seagulls for company, *Shropshire* had one last trip in her. In late 1946, with Fearless Frank Farncomb once again hoisting his broad pennant as Commodore, she sailed with the destroyer *Arunta* to join the British Commonwealth Occupation Force in Japan.

If this sounded impressive, in reality it amounted to very little, no more than an exercise in showing the flag, although to what point it is hard to say. There were new young sailors and a clutch of fresh midshipmen to be put through their paces as the ship wandered in a desultory way from Yokohama to Kure to Kobe, with a snowy Christmas in Tokyo Bay and side trips to Hiroshima and Nagasaki, but the chief occupation seemed to be entertainment given and received. In every port, Farncomb embarked on what must have been an exhausting round of official calls, lunches, receptions, cocktail and dinner parties with generals, admirals, provost marshals and diplomats of one stripe or another, none of which can have helped what was becoming his serious problem with alcohol.

There was a landmark for him and for the navy. On 8 January 1947, at the age of 48, he was promoted to the rank of rear admiral. His old rival, John Collins, was promoted the same day, making the two of them the first graduates of the RANC to reach the rank. The RAN had its own home-grown flag officers at last.

Shropshire sailed from Japan the next month, on a leisurely cruise home via Hong Kong and Manila, and on 17 March she was back in Sydney, on the No. 2 Naval Buoy. She would never again move under her own steam. Tired and growing obsolete, she was no longer wanted or needed in a navy trying to chart a new course for itself in the post-war era, and she was sent off to rust in that sad graveyard at Athol Bight, where she stayed until 1954. That July, the government announced that she had been sold as scrap to a British buyer for £102,800 (approximately $3.5 million in 2016).

The news made only a few paragraphs, although a couple of papers reported with some relief that she would not endure the ignominy of meeting her end in a Japanese breaker's yard. In October, *The Sydney Morning Herald* paid her a final farewell:

CRUISER SAILS TO DOOM

By a Staff Correspondent

The 10,000-ton Australian cruiser *Shropshire*, now moored at Cockatoo Island, will sail from Sydney next week on her last voyage – to a ship breakers' yard at Inverkeithing, Scotland.

Only a few of those who see her go will recall the part she played in a major, but little known, wartime naval battle, when a Japanese task force in Leyte Gulf menaced the American invasion of the Philippines.

Shropshire completed her service with the Royal Australian Navy in October last year. It was then decided it would be uneconomic to try to modernise the 25-year-old cruiser, and she was offered for sale.

In July this year she was bought by a British firm for breaking up for scrap. An ocean-going tug has been sent to Sydney to take the veteran in tow for the voyage to Scotland.

It's a sad enough end for a ship with a long record of useful service, and a distinguished war history.[1]

So ten years on, Leyte Gulf, the greatest naval battle in history, was 'little known'. Early on the morning of Saturday 9 October, the Dutch tug *Oostzee* took *Shropshire* under tow for the four-month journey to Britain.

There was not another naval ship in harbour as she left, not one to pay respects. A few ferries and small craft blew their horns or sirens. A couple of hundred people had gathered on shore to watch her labouring through the Heads and out into the Pacific swell, gazing after her as she faded into the far horizon whence she had come.

—

Australia was taken back out of reserve when *Shropshire* paid off in May 1947, essentially to act as a training ship for young officers and sailors. She went into the Captain Cook dry dock at Garden Island to be scraped and painted, and after her stores and ammunition were loaded she once again became the fleet flagship, with Farncomb on board. That July, when they ran her at full speed over a measured nautical mile, they found the old lady could still turn out a spanking 30 knots.

Yet the future was passing her by. Just as *Australia* took to the water again, the Chifley Labor government made the pivotal decision to buy two British aircraft carriers at a bargain price of £3.4 million, and then to press on with building a Fleet Air Arm.

Two carriers of the Majestic class, of 18,000 tonnes full load, were already partly built in Britain and readily available. The first, HMAS *Sydney III*, was commissioned in 1949. The second, HMAS *Melbourne III*, took a lot longer to complete, as she was constantly being updated with each leap forward in naval aircraft technology, with the likes of the new angled flight deck, and modifications to take jet aircraft. To fill the gap, the navy borrowed a similar British carrier, HMS *Vengeance*. *Melbourne*'s budget blew out to more than £8.3 million – an eye-watering figure for the time – and she was not delivered until 1955.

It had been a long hard road to get there. After the war, there was cut-throat competition within the Defence Force, a fierce struggle by admirals, generals and air marshals to seize for their own service as much of the shrinking defence budget as they could get their hands on. They fought like alley cats. It was wasteful and destructive, reaching a high point of absurdity when a retiring Chief of the Air Staff, Air Marshal Sir Donald Hardman, went public to declare that navies and armies were things of the past and largely useless.

'The Air Force in this country, for offence or defence, is the only force worthwhile,' he said, in an interview for *Aircraft* magazine that caused uproar when the newspapers picked it up and put it on their front pages. With the limitless confidence of tunnel vision, Hardman asserted that a few bombers could do the work of a dozen destroyers and that aircraft carriers were of limited value as 'one big bullet below the waterline can sink them'.

Warming to his theme, he proclaimed:

> The Army is the nigger in the woodpile. It costs a tremendous amount of money training people who can't be sent out of Australia except as volunteers, and are of no immediate use in a hot war because they have to be trained all over again.[2]

Hardman then stepped nimbly from the wreckage and returned to the RAF in Britain.

It did no good. Having lost the battle of the carriers, the RAAF then fought for control of the aircraft to be flown from them. To the very public chagrin of the air marshals, the navy won that one too, with the clinching argument that a ship's company was a unique whole, a band of men who must be sailors first and above all. The RAN would train its own pilots and observers, and the technical crews to maintain its aircraft. In 1948, the navy moved into a ramshackle, abandoned RAAF airfield at Nowra on the New South Wales coast south of Sydney, and in May that year it was formally commissioned as a Naval Air Station, HMAS *Albatross*.

It was a great stride in the new direction. Yet it spelt the beginning of the end for the last heavy cruiser. As an admiring feature article in the *Navy* magazine ventured at the time, 'the carrier's silhouette, replacing that of the battle cruiser *Australia* and that of the three-funnelled second *Australia* and *Canberra*, will become to Australians the most familiar symbol of their Navy's strength'.[3]

And so it did. Naval aviation was glamorous, exciting. Bright young officers who once might have gone into the seaman specialties of gunnery or navigation vied to become pilots, with a badge of golden wings to add to the stripes of their rank. The bridge and wardroom of an elderly cruiser offered little attraction. *Sydney* did indeed become a familiar, imposing sight in her namesake city, the biggest ship the navy had ever owned.

But *Australia* trooped on, like some grand dame of the stage and screen reduced to supporting roles. After she was worked up again, her first trip in 1947 was the inevitable visit to Japan, Shanghai and Hong Kong for more diplomatic flag-waving and cocktail partying. For the next few years, she settled into the pleasant, almost languid peacetime routine of spring and summer cruises – to New Zealand; to the February regatta in Hobart; to the Brisbane Show, the Ekka, in August; to Melbourne for the Cup in November; with the occasional exercise in between. It was almost as if the war had not happened.

The Korean War, too, passed her by. When that broke out in 1950, the navy sent its newer ships, first the frigate *Shoalhaven* and the destroyer *Bataan*, and later *Sydney* with her squadrons of Fireflies and Sea Furies, whose pilots frequently flew from a flight deck freshly cleared of ice and snow. There was no call any more for the thunder of *Australia*'s 8-inch guns in a shore bombardment.

She had her moments, though – the occasional flurry of action and drama that recalled her glory days. The ship was cleaning up in Jervis Bay after a refit in late July 1950 when her captain, George Oldham, suddenly got a signal ordering him to drop everything and head immediately for Melbourne. At first, this was not a welcome message, for the ship was in a filthy state after her time in dockyard hands and every man jack had been aloft, or on the upper deck or over the side, chipping away rust and painting. She was at eight hours' notice for steam, which meant it would take a while to get going. Oldham, though, was an experienced hand who had won the Distinguished Service Cross for 'skill, determination and courage' as *Shropshire*'s executive officer at Leyte, and he sailed as soon as he could, at sunset.

The reason became clear on the way south: a medical rescue mission to the Antarctic, no less. The only doctor at the newly established Australian scientific and exploration base on distant Heard Island, Serge Udovikoff, had diagnosed himself with acute appendicitis and had radioed for help. Two merchant ships, the *Perthshire* and the *Port Phillip*, had turned south from the Indian Ocean to reach him, but the cold, the high seas and the winter weather had beaten them back. *Australia* would have to go instead.

Heard Island, which was then and remains Australian territory, may be the most desolate place on the planet. It lies 4000 kilometres to the south-west of Perth at 53 degrees latitude, almost as far south as the notorious Cape Horn, a speck of barren rock and glaciers dominated by the active volcano of Mawson Peak, a mountain higher than Kosciuszko. In winter, whipped by constant gales, it snows almost every day, with temperatures rising to just 0.3 degrees Celsius and a bare six hours of pale daylight. *Australia* was to head there with all possible speed.

At Melbourne's Princes Pier, Oldham took on the arctic clothing and extra winter provisions ordered for the crew, and at a run he set about refuelling and preparing the ship for the hazards of the voyage. Figuring there was every chance of ice and snow encrusting her upper decks and adding weight and possibly instability, he took the precaution of lightening her load topsides by putting ashore most of the boats and odds and sods of equipment such as minesweeping paravanes.

Then, to his astonishment, he learnt that *Australia* had been dubbed 'the Mercy Ship' by the media, and he was suddenly besieged by journalists. Seizing the opportunity for some good publicity – the turf war with the RAAF was still raging – Navy Office sent him two newspaper reporters, two photographers, and a cameraman to film the expedition for the Movietone cinema newsreel. With them came a specialist civilian meteorologist, a couple more scientists, and two additional doctors who would replace Udovikoff at the base. Oldham's official report of this odyssey is a delight to read:

> The news of our intended employment with its attendant flavour of adventure was received throughout the ship with jubilation. An air of excitement prevailed during the brief period at Port Melbourne and men of all branches were to be found voluntarily assisting in the work to be done. Friends and relations of the ship's company had come to Princes Pier to wish us 'Bon Voyage' and the ship sailed at 2230 on 27th July in a holiday atmosphere resembling the departure of an overseas liner.[4]

Oldham himself was rather less jubilant, not at all certain of what he was getting into. The navy rarely ventured so far south, and certainly he had never done so, let alone with a crew heavily salted with young, trainee sailors barely out of the naval depot. It was 5600 kilometres from Melbourne to Heard Island. With wry amusement, he found that the only reference book he could get hold of, the Antarctic Pilot and Admiralty Sailing Directions, was next to useless; it noted with glum detachment that 'the waters surrounding Heard Island are treacherous, owing to the presence of rocks and shoals, while the force of the gales, combined with poor visibility due to fog, mist, rain and snow, make navigation extremely hazardous'. Not much help there.

Hopefully, radar might pick up drifting icebergs if there were any, but, as an extra precaution, he formed his experienced officers, petty officers and leading hands into extra teams of lookouts, to supplement the trainees who 'could barely be relied upon to show the fortitude, alertness and concentration necessary for this unpleasant task'.[5]

With everything that remained on deck lashed down tightly, gun and searchlight sponsons boarded over, extra lifelines rigged and hoses at the ready to pump heated sea water if ice did begin to form, *Australia* headed south into the Antarctic winter. Depending on the weather and the seas, Heard Island was about a week away. *Australia*'s engines, the great Brown-Curtis turbines, were humming as smoothly as ever, but the flaws and infirmities of old age began to show. The steam heating coils that kept the fuel oil from congealing into a useless sludge in the cold were not working – they had barely been used in her entire life – and the commander, Donald Clarke, and his artificers battled to bring them back on line, successfully in the end.

Somehow, news of this defect had reached the media before they sailed – 'dangerously unprepared' was the line in the newspapers – and a day out of Melbourne Oldham was surprised to get a radio-telephone call from an ABC reporter who wanted to know what was happening. He dodged the issue by pretending the reception was too poor to understand the questions. The Minister for the Navy, Josiah Francis, came out to stoutly deny there was a problem.

At least it was warm in the engine and boiler rooms. As *Australia* steamed further south, the cold grew more bitter, the weather more foul and the seas more contrary. By Monday 31 July, she was butting into gales reaching Force 11, winds of more than 100 kilometres per hour tearing at the watch on the bridge, and steep, short seas rising at her in violent, foam-crested waves of ten metres and more. As bad luck would have it, the ship was too long for the troughs between the peaks, which meant a hammering. Oldham brought her down to eight knots as she toiled through this tempest, and flooded the torpedo bulges on her hull to give her more ballast, which steadied things a little.

To relief all round, the cold front passed the next day and the barometer rose, offering gentler weather and the opportunity for 16 knots again. Below decks, though, the living was miserable, and after a few days the high spirits of the departure from Melbourne gave way to a sullen despondency, and even to fear among the younger sailors who had never experienced weather so foul.

As they passed through 40 degrees south latitude – the infamous Roaring Forties – and towards the 50s, the air temperature dropped to below freezing, and the extra electric radiators dotted around seemed to make little difference. With every scuttle and hatch dogged tightly closed and the men forbidden to go on the upper deck, the bulkheads began to sweat a greasy condensation, and blocked scuppers inevitably flooded the mess decks and flats. Ice began to form on the upper decks, on the director tower, on the non-steaming funnel, on the bridge itself, on the guard rails and the faces of the gun turrets.

Things got worse again when the ship's water supply suddenly choked up. This was a crisis, and a dangerous one. On Friday 4 August, with the island still three days away, they discovered that *Australia*'s distilling plants had almost stopped turning sea water into the fresh water needed for drinking, bathing and – critically – feeding the ship's boilers. There were just three days' supplies of feed water left. If that ran out, the boilers would have to be shut down and the ship would be dead in the water, drifting and helpless.

For a while, no one could work out what had gone wrong, which was more worrying still, until one of the civilian scientists on board told the captain that the sea was very likely full of plankton, which could block the system. A couple of whales had been seen nearby that day; they were probably feeding on it. Oldham signalled the Navy Board that he might have to abandon the mission and head for Fremantle, but luck was with them and the next day they moved out of this plankton belt and the distillers began working again. Building up the feed-water supplies for the boilers meant water restrictions for the ship's company, though, and a ban on showering and washing added to the discomfort and discontent below.

Fuel itself was the captain's next concern, a knotty problem he had to weigh against the weather. The weather reports from both Heard Island and the civilian meteorologist on board, Aubrey Gotley, suggested that a cyclone might be building up ahead of them, which could see the ship unable to close the shore. Oldham pressed on at an economical 13 knots, which he judged would give him a margin of safety, if not complete freedom from worry. He wished he had been able to refuel at Fremantle.

The island loomed up early in the forenoon watch of Monday 7 August, both beautiful and forbidding, a dazzling vision of snowy peaks and light-blue glaciers. Their navigation had been impeccable. They found Atlas Cove, on the island's north-western tip, where they would have to put a boat ashore to reach the base, but even as they did so the gale backed to the south-west and strengthened to Force 8, or gusts of up to 70 kilometres per hour, bringing showers of snow, sleet and hail. The waters of the cove itself were lashed with foam and spindrift, no safe place for a ship's boat. Oldham had no choice but to hold off. He took *Australia* around to rest in the lee of the island for the remainder of the day and the night, in the hope that the next day might improve.

And it did. There was no sign of a cyclone. The barometer held steady. Not long before dawn on the Tuesday, the men on the bridge in the morning watch were awestruck by a glorious display of the aurora. They glimpsed a fringe of clear white light beyond the island to the south, which increased to three rays of dazzling white light stabbing into the heavens, with a disc of bright purple glowing at the zenith like some brilliant celestial cartwheel, tinged with vivid green, yellow and orange. It lasted for about five minutes, fading as suddenly as it had come, a rare and beautiful sight.

Perhaps it had been an omen, and a good one. The gales began to ease that morning, back to a stiff but manageable 34 knots or 60 kilometres per hour at six o'clock, and slackening still over the next hour, safe enough to get one of *Australia*'s motor cutters in the water. Taking no chances, the captain put one of his senior seaman officers in charge of the boat, Lieutenant Commander Bill Dovers.

With the two relief doctors on board, Dovers took the cutter into the cove through small flurries of snow but the wind dropped still further until, miraculously, it was dead calm at the shore, with barely a ripple on the water. There was no time to waste. Dr Udovikoff had been carried down to the water's edge, where he was quickly loaded into the cutter – along with the gift of a bottle of French champagne for the captain from the base scientists, and a pair of penguins for the ship – and within half an hour he was on board the cruiser, a slim, bearded figure, pale and weak, to be helped to the sick bay. His feet had barely touched the deck before the cutter was back on board and *Australia* was curving away from the island and its perils, on a nor'east course for Fremantle. 'Sorry I have been a bother,' Udovikoff told his rescuers.

The trip back was uneventful, apart from another bout of foul weather, which led to the accidental escape of the penguins. On the afternoon of Monday 14 August 1950, mission accomplished, *Australia* berthed at Fremantle's North Wharf, to the applause of hundreds of onlookers and the tears of the doctor's wife and four-year-old daughter, who were reunited with him in the sick bay.

The rescue had aroused tremendous popular interest, the journalists on board filing reports each day for their papers. It was a parable for the new post-war Australia, and satisfying to national pride because of it. Serge and Taissa Udovikoff, both in their 30s, had arrived in the country only the year before, on a ship carrying migrants from the post-war chaos of Europe. Variously described as Polish or Ukrainian, they were officially listed as stateless refugees, and Taissa and their child Natalia were still living at the Northam Migrant Camp outside Perth while Serge was at Heard. New Australians they were, and the nation could claim proudly that it had done its bit to welcome them. As ever, there was some minor public carping about the cost of the exercise, but the prevailing mood was expressed well enough in this editorial in the Adelaide *News*:

> The Royal Australian Navy has done it again. In keeping with the best traditions of the silent service, HMAS *Australia* has completed successfully its mercy mission to take off new Australian Dr. Serge Udovikoff from Heard Island.
>
> The desperate plight of Dr. Udovikoff, stricken suddenly with acute appendicitis at his lonely Antarctic outpost, first focused world attention on the rescue drama. Suspense grew as rescue ships turned back from the dangers of storm-swept icy wastes.
>
> Then the Navy stepped in. Within hours of the decision the cruiser was speeding south on a 3,500-mile dash that will cost

about £35,000. New dangers were met and overcome at the island. Now the *Australia* is on the way home, 'mission completed.'

It's a way they have in the Navy.[6]

Behind the scenes, not everything was quite so rosy. *Australia* was seriously undermanned. The Korean War had seen her stripped of qualified officers and senior sailors, especially in the engineering department, and Captain Oldham was concerned about the morale of his ship's company, as he told the Navy Board:

> The shortage of personnel to cope with a large backlog of cleaning and maintenance combined with the necessity to resume training as soon as practicable at full pressure made the goal of a clean ship appear a long way off, and much encouragement was needed to counter an air of despondency which began to show itself particularly in Captains of Tops and other senior ratings . . .
>
> . . . the conduct of the ship's company has been less satisfactory than at any time in the past eight months. The number of minor offences such as slackness, unpunctuality and petty leave-breaking has shown a considerable increase, and there have been two desertions during the month.[7]

This gloomy report reached Francis, the Navy Minister, who demanded an explanation. In November, he got one from John Collins, by now Chief of the Naval Staff and newly promoted to the rank of vice admiral:

> A lot of young men with no sea experience found themselves in bad conditions in heavy weather, cooped up in unavoidably crowded mess decks. These young men, once the novelty of the mission had worn off, began to wonder whether life at sea was all they had imagined. I have no doubt the experience has done them some good, but they would undoubtedly have been happier sunning themselves in northern waters.
>
> I agree that it is regrettable that the modern youngster gets his tail down when things get a bit tough, but he soon gets it up again. I feel we must remember that *Australia* is a training cruiser and is not manned by experienced seamen.[8]

The Heard Island rescue was *Australia*'s last great exploit. In the years left to her, she went about the humdrum tasks of a training ship along the east coast, the grandeur and the glory gone. She kept up appearances as best she could, but maintaining her old skin and bones was an unending, losing struggle. Men chipping away at rust on her decks or bulkheads would sometimes find their tools digging a hole through a thin steel plate.

Occasionally, she would be pressed into service as a vice-regal yacht, to carry a state governor or the Governor General around the Barrier Reef, but she went for many long months without firing a gun. Mostly, she was putting national servicemen – Nashos – through their paces, showing them the rudiments of a sailor's life. National service was brought in during the Korean War in 1951, requiring all 18-year-old males to do 176 days of recruit training, in whatever service they chose, although if you selected the RAN or the RAAF you had to agree to serve overseas if necessary. The navy changed the terms a little, with its recruits doing four months' continuous training, then two weeks each year for four years in the Reserve. Over six years, until the scheme ended in 1957, a total of 6862 young men wore the navy uniform as Nashos. Many of them did their time in the *Aussie*, as they called her.

At the end of 1953, on 6 December, the government announced the inevitable. *Australia*'s days were drawing to a close:

> The cruiser, HMAS *Australia*, once the flagship of the Australian Fleet, is to be scrapped. It will be sold out of service for scrap after it has paid off in the middle of next year.
>
> The Minister for the Navy (Mr. McMahon) said to-day that the ship was worn out after 25 years' arduous service. It had reached a stage at which it would be uneconomical to continue its upkeep.
>
> Although *Australia* could still develop its designed power it was due for extensive structural repairs costing about £200,000. If retained in commission engineering maintenance which would become necessary before the end of next year would cost £15,000 more . . .

Mr. McMahon said: 'The name of the famous ship and the engagements in which it figured will always form a glorious place in Australian history. They were in the highest traditions of naval warfare.'[9]

It was the beginning of the end, an unglamorous end. Unlike her forebear and namesake, the great battlecruiser, she would have no heroic climax, no salutes or music, no wreaths floating on the sea above her last rest. *Australia II* would go quietly. But in the months left to her, there were a few tasks to perform and honours to reap. In March 1954, the navy announced she had won the Gloucester Cup, the award for the most efficient ship in the fleet. That same month, she put to sea from Sydney as part of the naval escort for the liner *Gothic*, which was carrying the Queen and the Duke of Edinburgh for their first royal tour of Australia. At the Barrier Reef, the Queen went on board for an hour and posed for a formal photograph with the entire ship's company.

On 6 May, on passage from Sydney to Queensland, *Australia* opened up with her great guns with the Governor General, Field Marshal Sir William Slim, as a passenger. It was the last time she would fire them. Appropriately, the gunnery officer, the man who gave the order to shoot, was none other than David Hamer, by now a lieutenant commander. She fired five single gun salvoes and then 13 broadsides from A-turret, to use up the last of the 8-inch shells on board. As her final commanding officer, Captain Alan McNicoll, noted in two terse lines, this was very likely the last time that these 8-inch guns were fired in any of the Queen's navies. All but one of her sister ships in the RN had already been broken up. A few days later, she answered an SOS from a Dutch landing craft in trouble off the north Queensland coast and towed it, through heavy weather, to Cairns.

So she made her goodbyes, her curtain calls. Her farewell to Brisbane was not without incident. After a helter-skelter police chase through Fortitude Valley, four of her sailors were arrested at gunpoint in a stolen car. 'A celebration of the cruiser's last trip,' their lawyer told the court. 'They are men with fine records.'

Apparently sympathetic, the magistrate let them down easily with a fine of £20 each.

More than 13,000 people trooped up the gangway when she was opened for a final public visit at the New Farm Wharf, with the police having to lock the gates to manage the crush. On 25 May, there was a crowd of about 200 to see her cast off, with the army's Northern Command band playing the song 'Goodbye' from the operetta *The White Horse Inn*. The haunting 'Maori Farewell' followed her as she edged out into the river flying a red-and-white paying-off pennant 250 metres long, held up by two hydrogen balloons. The ship's company manned the rails. Cars along Kingsford Smith Drive honked their horns as that familiar silhouette glided down towards Moreton Bay and the open sea, on course for Port Phillip Bay.

Her Melbourne goodbyes were similar, with a cocktail party on board at Princes Pier, where she had tied up so often before. When she proceeded to sea again for the last time, on Saturday 29 May 1954, swarms of motor cruisers and yachts followed in her wake, and the corvette *Gladstone* with the Flinders Naval Depot band on board played her out past Portsea and Point Lonsdale.

All the while, there were appeals to save her from the scrap yard, to keep her afloat as a museum, or a training ship for boys, or an old sailors' home. Veterans' associations wrote impassioned pleas to cabinet ministers and the newspapers. They were not going to let her go quietly. Letters to editors poured in:

> Sir – Not only to many sailors, but to many mothers of sailors, does a warship's last voyage mean something.
>
> To me, as a sailor's mother, the last voyage of HMAS *Australia* revives memories of ardent prayers for her safety during the war – prayers that were answered.
>
> At that time I was a WAAF [Women's Auxiliary Air Force] officer serving in General Douglas MacArthur's Central War Room in Brisbane, and on the records there HMAS *Australia* was shown as 'Task Force 44.' Daily, in the course of my secret duties I glanced at the position of Task Force 44 and my heart

would rejoice that she was safe and afloat because my boy was a mid-shipman aboard her.

The gallant cruiser did not carry the name of Australia in vain. Amid all our political and commercial bitterness, Australians should spare a moment of silence for prayer while the gallant vessel still remains intact as a wonderful symbol.

Nancy Gunn. Bossley Park.[10]

Others were less sentimental, as in this dour letter from a retired merchant seaman:

Sir – While blandishments and sentimentality by the shipload are lavished on this inanimate object, HMAS *Australia*, it may be remembered that among her special features that received particular attention in the Press, on her arrival in these waters, were the excellent target that her ample freeboard presented to an enemy and the unusual size and magnificence of the captain's quarters. Give her a stained glass window on Garden Island and break her up: we want the steel to build bigger and better *Australia*s.

A. MacGregor
Chief Engineer, M.N. Retired[11]

On the trip north towards Sydney, as they passed Gabo Island the next day, the ship's company cleared lower deck and gathered on the quarterdeck for a Sunday-morning church service, the last ever. The weather was fine, with only a gentle swell, and 'the ubiquitous albatross kept us company', recorded the chaplain, Graydon Swain, a Methodist. 'Our prayers were thankful prayers because a ship, and so many who sailed in her, had been spared to be "a safeguard unto our most gracious Sovereign . . . and a security for such as pass on the seas upon their lawful occasions".'[12]

A heavy fog shrouded her entry into the harbour on Tuesday 1 June – one of the worst on record, according to the Weather Bureau – and *Australia* had to feel her way to Garden Island by radar. No bands welcomed her, only the grunt of foghorns. She went alongside the cruiser wharf at 10.30 am, the lines snaked ashore and, one last time, Captain McNicoll gave the order 'finished with engines'. That night, the wardroom gave a farewell party on the quarterdeck, almost a wake, beneath a red-and-white awning, with the ship ablaze with lights the same colour. One of the guests was Mary Fogarty, the widow of Lieutenant Commander Francis Fogarty, who had been the first of the ship's company to die, shot down in the Walrus at Dakar in 1940. There were admirals aplenty, several of them former captains of *Australia*, for to command her had always been a reasonably sure path to flag rank. In time, McNicoll would become a vice admiral, with a knighthood, as Chief of the Naval Staff.

The Naval Board sent a final signal:

> On this the last day on which HMAS *Australia* will act as a unit of the Fleet, the Naval Board express their great regret that the active life of this fine old fighting ship has virtually come to an end after 26 years.
>
> The battle honours on her quarter-deck give testimony of her gallant six years of war service, which the people of Australia will remember with pride and gratitude.
>
> There were few officers and men of the Royal Australian Navy during the past two decades who had not the honour of serving in her, and thus it can be truly said that the whole Navy has been imbued with that sense of courage and fortitude which HMAS *Australia*, for so long the flagship, has personified.
>
> It is the wish and hope of all that there will one day be another *Australia* to carry on the proud tradition.[13]

Since her commissioning at Clydebank in 1928 – how long ago it seemed – *Australia* had steamed 1,157,500 kilometres. No ship of the RAN had served for so long, nor travelled so far. She had sailed all the seven seas, north and south, east and west, from the fogs and chill of the Denmark Strait and the North Sea to the furious storms of the Great Southern Ocean and the tropics of the Atlantic, the Pacific and the Indian Oceans.

Two kings and a queen had walked her decks. Countless thousands of men had lived and worked and played aboard her in peace and war, death taking 86 of them. Her ordinary seamen had become chief petty officers, her midshipmen captains and admirals. The living would remember the *Aussie* all their days, mostly fondly, although sometimes not. For most of her life, she had been a happy ship, but not always. Those who fought on her in war, though, were rightly proud of her and their service, and in the capital cities each Anzac Day they would march behind banners bearing her battle honours both inherited and won, their ranks dwindling with the years.

At her best, *Australia* embodied an evolving idea: that of a truly Australian ship commanded and crewed by Australian naval seamen equal to any in the world. It was a notion that had taken faltering steps at first, but her name and her presence carried it forward with increasing confidence. The Australian people who saw her unmistakeable three-funnelled shape in their harbours, in their newspapers, or on the newsreels at the cinema recognised and cherished her as a symbol of nationhood. She was the flagship, their flagship.

So much had changed in her time. When she was commissioned, Britannia ruled the waves. Like their British cousins, *Australia*'s Officers of the Day in harbour were still patrolling their patch in cocked hats and frock coats, telescopes tucked under the arm. There was a vast social and disciplinary gulf between upper and lower deck, officers and sailors – or ratings, as they were then called. Gunnery was god. Aircraft at sea were regarded as vaguely useful for reconnaissance, perhaps, but certainly not as any threat to a well-armed surface vessel. Radar was only the germ of an idea in the mind of a few boffins.

As *Australia*'s career came to an end, the USN was the dominant power at sea, although challenged for that role by the Soviet Navy in the Cold War. The first nuclear-powered submarine, the USS *Nautilus*, was being built and would be commissioned in September 1954. The RAN had embraced air power in its two carriers and was thinking seriously of a submarine force of its own. Australian defence scientists were at the drawing board working on the home-grown Ikara anti-submarine missile for surface ships, and the navy's first purchase of American warships – the DDGs, or guided-missile destroyers *Hobart*, *Perth* and *Brisbane* – was but a few years away.

It was high time for *Australia* to go. In August 1954, stripped and gutted, she was formally decommissioned and returned to Athol Bight. Without fanfare, on Saturday 26 March 1955, another Dutch tug, *Rode Zee*, towed her empty hulk from the harbour on the long journey to Barrow-in-Furness in Lancashire.[14]

She was broken up there a year later, the hammers and oxy-acetylene torches achieving what the Kamikazes never could.

EPILOGUE

A big and cheerfully eager crowd is milling on the wharf at
Fleet Base East, which is the modern name for the Garden
Island Dockyard in Sydney and the complex of navy offices that
climbs up the hill at Potts Point. There are young and old, male
and female, some in best white naval uniforms with medals,
both officers and sailors. Many more are civilians – relatives
and friends or invited guests – all enjoying the sun of a perfect
autumn morning. But for the uniforms, it might be a crowd off
to a carnival race meeting.

A warship towers above them like a great, grey cliff of steel,
and it is her they have come to see. It is Friday 28 November
2014. With all pomp and circumstance, a new HMAS *Canberra*
is to be commissioned into the RAN this day. She will be the
third of the name, after her sad predecessor lost at Savo, and
after *Canberra II*, an Oliver Hazard Perry class guided-missile
frigate, went out of service in 2005.

This ship is strikingly different to either. Enormous, in fact.
At 27,831 tonnes, she and her sister *Adelaide*, which is still being
built, will be the largest ships the navy has owned, by far. The first
Canberra displaced some 10,000 tonnes. The carrier *Melbourne*, fully
loaded, came in at about twice that. *Canberra III* dwarfs them both.

The cruiser *Canberra* was British built, the frigate American.
This third of the name is Spanish, for no more does the RAN

automatically seek out British or American ships to buy off the shelf. *Canberra III* was designed and partly built by the Spanish shipbuilders Navantia, adapted from their delightfully named *Buque de Proyección Estratégica*, or Strategic Projection Ship. After the usual delays, cost overruns and other contractual tangles and disputes, she was finished off by the BAE company at Williamstown in Victoria. All up, she and *Adelaide* will cost around $3.1 billion.

Lamentably, the RAN calls *Canberra* an LHD, which stands for 'landing helicopter dock', about as lumpy and unglamorous a name for a ship as you could think of, surely devised by a committee of bureaucrats. A better term might be the name she was originally designed to carry in her Australian role – an amphibious assault ship – which gives a closer idea of what she can actually do. To the untrained eye, though, she looks like everyone's idea of an aircraft carrier, with a high, slab-sided hull, a long flight deck sloping gradually upward at her bow, and an island superstructure rising on her starboard side. And certainly she is that, for she can carry up to 18 helicopters on deck and in a cavernous complex of hangars and workshops below. The flight deck is 202 metres long.

But there's more. On her four decks, she has space for four big and fast diesel-powered landing craft, up to 110 small trucks or light armoured vehicles, and 12 of the army's Abrams main battle tanks, plus just over 1000 troops. To launch or recover those landing craft, she can lower herself deeper into the sea, or dock down, as it is called, by filling a tank in her stern that can hold 4.2 million litres of water, or the equivalent of almost two Olympic swimming pools. The stern door opens; the landing craft swim in or out.

To protect herself, *Canberra* has a defensive armament of four Typhoon stabilised weapon systems, which is a fancy name for rapid-firing guns all remotely controlled. And she can clip along at a bit over 20 knots. In short, she is equipped to mount a medium-sized invasion by land, sea and air, be that for the purpose of making life swiftly and extremely unpleasant for some unspecified troublemaker or – more likely in these times – for humanitarian assistance missions or disaster relief.

Only in one detail is she less than her predecessors. The first *Canberra* carried a wartime crew of about 1000 men, many of them engaged in the physical labour of scrubbing decks, manhandling shells, loading ammunition and working guns. Automation means this new ship's company will number around 400 men and women, of which about 60 will be army soldiers and three from the RAAF, all of whom live and work in air-conditioned comfort that would have dumbfounded their forebears. The messing spaces for officers and sailors are restaurants, with enticing menus of wide variety. There are recreational areas including two gymnasiums and a couple of internet cafes, and a hospital with two fully equipped operating theatres, recovery wards and an intensive-care unit, with attendant pathology and radiology services, a pharmacy and a dental surgery. All this and more for around $2 billion per ship.

Meanwhile, the people on the dock are growing a little restless, but eventually they are summoned on board to find their way up a wide gangway, then up more steel ladders, and then out onto the enclosed hangar space beneath the flight deck, which is open facing aft to the sun and blue sky. The ship smells of fresh paint and gleams like a new knife. There are long rows of chairs set for an audience of several hundred, with a central aisle for the great and good to march down. And in this audience there are more admirals than you could poke a telescope at, both current and retired, for the navy is family and it likes to invite the relatives for its feast days and high occasions such as this.

There is none more welcome than Rear Admiral Guy Griffiths, who, in his 90s, surely must be the RAN's oldest surviving flag officer and yet looks as spry and trim as a man 30 years younger. What memories he must bring. All the while, he is greeted by men who served with him, they too in their 80s or 90s, who offer a cheerful 'Hello, sir' and get a shipmate's handshake in return. It turns out there are quite a few old *Canberra* and *Shropshire* men here, some who have come all the way from

Western Australia. And there, too, is 'Canteen Jack' Langrell, almost weighed down by the chestful of medals he earned as a fresh-faced kid in *Australia II*.

My host for the day is Paul Moggach, *Canberra*'s Commander Air, which means he is in charge of flying operations and anything else to do with aviation in the ship. A pilot himself, he was the last commanding officer of 817 Squadron, the Sea King helicopters, and is now doing what he regards as his dream job, although today that rather less glamorously means dashing about doing his bit to ensure the ceremony goes off without a hitch.

The VIPs arrive in ascending order: the Fleet Commander, Rear Admiral Stuart Mayer; Vice Admiral Tim Barrett, who is both a seaman officer and an aviator, and Chief of Navy; Vice Admiral Ray Griggs, Deputy Chief of the Defence Force, and his boss, Air Chief Marshal Mark Binskin; the then Prime Minister, Tony Abbott; and finally the Governor General, Peter Cosgrove, himself a former Defence Force chief. The band marches on, to the brass and thump of the 'Royal Australian Navy March', composed and first played in 1913. Cosgrove, with Mayer alongside, inspects the guard.

There are speeches, saying all the right stuff. Chaplains offer prayers and blessings and the 'Naval Hymn' is sung for those in peril on the sea. Remarkably, the show is stolen by the new commanding officer, Captain Jonathan Sadleir, who transferred across from the Royal Canadian Navy in 1997 and retains a twangy Canadian accent. Thanking his ship's company for the demanding job of getting *Canberra* ready for this day, on time, his voice falters and his eyes glisten with tears. It could have been mawkish – and what would Farncomb, Collins or Dechaineux have thought? – but it actually strikes a note of pride and gratitude that goes down well.

Comes the moment. Slowly, smoothly, hand over hand, aware that he has all eyes upon him, a young leading seaman hoists the White Ensign on the staff at the stern. It is the very same flag that was hauled down when the frigate *Canberra II* was decommissioned; someone had kept hold of it for just this day.

And the new ship inherits the pennant number of the old, a big, white L02 painted on her superstructure. *Canberra* is now one of Her Majesty's Australian Ships. Band and guard march off. Ceremony over.

What happens next is intriguing, a glimpse of how far the RAN has come in a century and more. At the for'ard end of the hangar deck, there are tables laid out for a handsome buffet lunch, open for all-comers. What would those old cruiser captains and admirals make of this? In their day, there would have been a select party for the officers and their guests, smoothly served by white-jacketed stewards on some flag-hung quarterdeck, with maybe beer and sandwiches for the sailors – the lower deck – in their messes if they were lucky. At today's affair, gold-braided captains and commanders join the queue for plates and food with young sailors and their husbands, wives or partners. They mingle, the conversation flowing easily, with respect for rank but without deference. These days, a highly qualified sailor in electronics, or communications technology, or some other arcane naval art or science might well be paid more than the captain of his ship.

Truly startling for the ancient mariners, though, would be the sight of women in uniform. Women sporting a leading seaman's killick, the crown and anchors of a petty officer, or the gold braid of a three-ringed commander or four-ringed captain, with perhaps the crossed-swords badge of a Principal Warfare Officer. Today, the officer in charge of the Duty Watch is Lieutenant Rebecca Wilson. It is no longer exceptional in the RAN for a woman to command a major warship. One day, not far off, *Canberra* will have a female commanding officer.

The navy already has its first woman flag officer, Rear Admiral Robyn Walker, who is a medical doctor and administrator, an acknowledged world expert in diving medicine, and a graduate of the Australian Institute of Company Directors. At the time of writing, she is Surgeon General of the Australian Defence Force. In a year or two, another woman rear admiral will command the fleet or, as a vice admiral, will be Chief of Navy, appointed on merit. Nothing more certain.

A civilian perception of the RAN, fed by the media, is that women in uniform are at constant risk of sexual abuse or bullying. Yes, that does happen. But it is almost certainly less common than in other large Australian institutions or corporations where the spotlight does not shine. The service is more socially responsive now, far more so than even ten years ago. One of the guests I meet today is Chief Petty Officer Ray Rosendale, an Indigenous Australian and the navy's adviser on Indigenous Cultural Affairs. A veteran of *Canberra II*, he now mentors a slowly but steadily increasing number of black kids in uniform.

For the traditionalists, though, a small disappointment remains. The RAN has never commissioned another *Australia* and probably never will. Nobody has ever explained why. There was an early push for the second LHD to carry the name, but rumour says this was scuttled by the Defence Minister of the time, the South Australian Liberal senator Robert Hill, who wanted *Adelaide* as a primer for the parish pump. If so, he got it.

Another possibility is that an *Australia III* would be just too risky in these days of hyperactive media scrutiny. One mistake, one accident, one drama – a sex scandal on board, a fatal fire in the engine room, a helicopter dropped over the side, a bunch of sailors drunk and arrested ashore in Singapore or San Diego, a collision in the South China Sea – and you have a public-relations nightmare in the name of the nation. Better not chance it, perhaps they say. If so, that is a shame, the fading of a proud tradition.

As I write these words, I find I really do not want to end the book on this glum note. Casting around my research – piles of the stuff – I find a small but intriguing fact that somehow I had overlooked.

It is this. On that bright Sydney morning in 2014, the sailor who raised the White Ensign at *Canberra III*'s commissioning was named Thurlow. Leading Seaman Communications and Information Systems Stewart Thurlow, to give him his full title, the new handle for what they once called a signalman. My thoughts fly back to Signalmen Tom and Jim Thurlow and that fatal night in *Canberra I* at Savo.

I make more enquiries but it turns out that Stewart is no relation. The coincidence, though, is very satisfying, the symmetry perfect. Somewhere beyond wind and water, the gods approve.

Yours, aye.

WHO'S WHO

Here is a brief cast list of the principal players in this book, to help readers keep track of who they were, where they went and what they did. Their ranks are given here as they appear upon the stage.

Armstrong, Captain John Malet, RAN. Commander in *Australia* at the outbreak of war, and later became her captain from October 1944. Endured the Kamikaze attacks. Variously known as Black Jack, Jock, Jamie.

Bracegirdle, Lieutenant Commander Warwick, RAN. Gunnery officer in *Perth* at the outbreak of war, and in *Shropshire* 1942–45. A popular, much-respected officer.

Collins, Captain John, RAN. Joined the navy in the first year of the RANC, 1913. Captain of cruiser *Sydney* in 1940, sank Italian cruiser *Bartolomeo Colleoni*. In 1942, supervised the retreat from Java. Commissioned *Shropshire* as an Australian warship in April 1943. From 1944, appointed Commodore in Command of the Australian Squadron, in flagship *Australia*. Seriously wounded at the Battle of Leyte Gulf in October 1944. Attended Japanese surrender in Tokyo, 1945.

Colvin, Admiral Sir Ragnar, RN. British naval officer, First Naval Member of the Australian Naval Board 1937–41. Head of the RAN, and the Australian Government's senior naval adviser.

Cooper, Chief Petty Officer Arthur, RAN. Joined the navy in 1927. Chief Gunner's Mate in *Shropshire* from 1942, right-hand man to Bracegirdle. Wrote valuable notes and diaries.

Crace, Rear Admiral John, RN. Australian born but a British naval officer, also known as Jack, appointed Rear Admiral Commanding the Australian Squadron in 1939. Performed well in command of the RAN/USN cruiser and destroyer squadron Task Force 44 at the Battle of the Coral Sea, 1942. Returned to Britain after the battle.

Crutchley, Rear Admiral Victor, RN. Winner of the Victoria Cross in the First World War. Successor to Crace in command of the Australian Squadron. In command of the RAN/USN cruiser and destroyer squadron at the disastrous Battle of Savo, 1942. Returned to the United Kingdom in 1944.

Curtin, John. Australian Labor Party politician. Leader of the federal opposition in 1939. Appointed Prime Minister after the fall of the conservative government in October 1941. Formed a strong working relationship with US General Douglas MacArthur. Died July 1945.

Dechaineux, Captain Emile, RAN. Tasmanian born, joined the navy in 1916. Commanded the British destroyer HMS *Vivacious* at Dunkirk, 1940. Captain of *Australia* from March 1944. Killed at the Battle of Leyte Gulf, 21 October 1944.

Eastick, Able Seaman Harold, RAN. Joined the navy in 1926. Kept a diary in *Australia*.

Elias, Stoker Edward, RAN. Joined the navy in 1926. Convicted of the murder of Stoker John Riley in *Australia* in 1942.

Farncomb, Captain Harold, RAN. Classmate of John Collins at the RANC, 1913. Commanded cruisers *Perth*, *Canberra* and *Australia*. In command of *Australia* at the Battle of the Coral Sea, and at the Battle of Savo. Replaced Collins as Commodore Commanding Australian Squadron in 1944.

Feldt, Lieutenant Commander Eric, RAN. Classmate of Collins and Farncomb, but quit the navy in 1922 to work in colonial New Guinea. Returned in 1939 to establish the Coastwatchers network.

Fletcher, Rear Admiral Frank Jack, USN. In overall Allied command at the Battle of the Coral Sea, where he left Rear Admiral Crace and the Australians to fend for themselves. Also commanded at the Battle of Midway. Commanded the aircraft carriers at the Allied invasion of Guadalcanal in 1942, and left the battle prematurely. Deemed insufficiently aggressive, he was sidelined to the northern Pacific in November 1942.

Getting, Captain Frank, RAN. Naval College classmate of Collins and Farncomb. Killed while captain of *Canberra* at the Battle of Savo, 1942. Unfairly criticised after the battle for not being ready.

Gordon, Stoker Albert, RAN. Joined the navy in 1936. Convicted of the murder of Stoker Riley in *Australia* in 1942.

Gregory, Sub Lieutenant Mackenzie, RAN. Known as Mac, joined the navy as a cadet midshipman in 1936. Was Officer of the Watch in *Canberra* at the outbreak of the Battle of Savo. Later served in *Shropshire* and was present at the Tokyo surrender in 1945.

Griffiths, Lieutenant Guy, RAN. A midshipman in the battlecruiser HMS *Repulse* when she was sunk by the Japanese off Malaya in 1941. Later served in *Shropshire* through the Kamikaze campaign.

Halsey, Admiral William, USN. Also known as 'Bull' Halsey. An able and aggressive American carrier-force and fleet commander throughout the Pacific War.

Hamer, Lieutenant David, RAN. RANC classmate of Guy Griffiths, 1937. Air Defence Officer of *Australia* from May 1944, throughout the Kamikaze attacks. Able and courageous, he wrote an invaluable memoir.

Keats, Supply Assistant Russell, RAN. Quiet, sensitive young musician from Sydney, killed at Savo in 1942.

Langrell, Canteen Assistant Jack. The son of a sailor, served in *Australia* throughout the war, present at all her battles.

Loxton, Midshipman Bruce, RAN. Joined the navy in 1938. Badly wounded on *Canberra*'s bridge at Savo in 1942. In later life, demonstrated conclusively that *Canberra* had been torpedoed by the Americans.

MacArthur, General Douglas. US Army General appointed Supreme Commander, South-West Pacific Area, after his escape from the Philippines to Australia in 1942. Capable and energetic but an almost neurotic self-promoter. Worked well with Prime Minister John Curtin but was jealous and suspicious of US Admiral Chester Nimitz. Occasionally disparaged Australian soldiers in private but never hesitated to take public credit for their achievements.

Mattiske, Able Seaman David, RAN. From the Wimmera in Victoria, a keen young observer on board *Shropshire*.

Menzies, Robert. United Australia Party (i.e. conservative) Prime Minister of Australia at the start of the war. Forced from office by disloyalty in his own party in August 1941. Opposition Leader from 1943.

Mikawa, Vice Admiral Gunichi, IJN. Able commander of the IJN 7th Fleet and victor of the Battle of Savo in 1942.

Muirhead-Gould, Rear Admiral Gerard, RN. Naval Officer in Command of Sydney Harbour 1940–44. Bungled his handling of the Japanese midget-submarine attack in 1942. Critical of the conduct of Frank Getting and *Canberra*'s crew at Savo.

Nichols, Captain Godfrey, RN. British naval officer, captain of *Shropshire* from September 1944. Quietly competent, much admired by his men.

Nimitz, Admiral Chester, USN. Appointed Commander-in-Chief, US Pacific Fleet, immediately after the attack on Pearl Harbor. Quietly spoken but strong willed, arguably the chief architect of victory in the Pacific, one of the war's best admirals on any side.

Onishi, Vice Admiral Takijiro, IJN. Commander of the First Air Fleet in the Philippines in 1944, known as the 'father' of the Kamikaze campaign.

Riley, Stoker John, RAN. Joined the navy in 1939. Murdered in *Australia* in 1942.

Shinkfield, Midshipman Desmond, RAN. Junior officer and keen observer in *Shropshire*.

Stewart, Captain Ross, RN. British naval officer, captain of *Australia* from August 1939 to August 1941.

Thurlow, Signalman Jim, RAN. Sailor from Geelong who joined the navy in 1940. Killed in *Canberra* at Savo in 1942.

Thurlow, Signalman Tom, RAN. Jim's younger brother, who joined the navy the same day as him. Also in *Canberra* at Savo but survived and later served in *Shropshire*.

Turner, Rear Admiral Kelly, USN. Able USN amphibious commander in the Pacific. Clashed furiously with Frank Jack Fletcher at Guadalcanal in 1942.

Yamamoto, Admiral Isoroku, IJN. Commander-in-Chief of the Combined Fleet. Though reluctant to go to war, he planned Pearl Harbor and the early Japanese naval campaigns in the Pacific. Killed in 1943 when his aircraft was ambushed and shot down by USN fighters.

THE LEGAL CAMPAIGN FOR THE RELEASE OF ALBERT RONALD GORDON AND EDWARD JOSEPH ELIAS, FORMER STOKERS ON HMAS *AUSTRALIA*

Here is a summary of the events following the sentencing of Albert Ronald Gordon and Edward Joseph Elias on 18 April 1942, narrated in Chapter 12.

While Albert Ronald Gordon and Edward Joseph Elias languished in jail, a variety of campaigners took up their cause. Elias's widowed mother, Mrs Christine Byrnes, and a family friend, Mrs Sonita Francis, wrote to influential people to gather support for the death sentences to be commuted, enlisting senior figures in the clergy and sympathetic members of state and federal parliaments.

Mrs Francis's involvement raised eyebrows, though. People in the know at the top of the tree thought she was a prostitute and spy. A note from the Director of Naval Intelligence, Commander Rupert 'Cocky' Long, warned the Naval Board about her:

Doris May Francis, alias Sonita Francis, alias Sunny Francis, alias Mrs Rist, nee Perry, was the subject of much suspicion and investigation by Commonwealth authorities ... due to her close and persistent association with naval personnel, particularly young officers. It was believed that under the cloak of immorality she was engaged in espionage on behalf of her employer, successive managers of the Mitsui company, Fukuda and Okada ...[1]

Spy or not, Mrs Francis got a polite if noncommittal reply to a letter she wrote to John Curtin asking for his support. So too did a crusading left-wing cleric, Ernest Burgmann, the Anglican bishop of Goulburn. The new Catholic Archbishop of Sydney, Norman Gilroy, joined the campaign as well.

After the High Court's ruling that the court martial, the verdict and the sentence of death had all been lawful, the Curtin government found itself in a legal tangle. Neither the Prime Minister nor the cabinet – nor the Navy Office – wanted the men to hang, so a way had to be found of changing the death sentence to life imprisonment. At first, it was thought the Governor General, Lord Gowrie, could simply commute the sentence on the advice of his ministers, with the stroke of a pen.

But then they found that he could not. Because everything had been done under British law, the Governor General of Australia had no role in the matter at all. An appeal would have to be made to King George VI.

At about this point, the tangle became a great diplomatic and constitutional knot. To much consternation, the government realised that Australia was not the independent, sovereign nation everyone had imagined. Federal parliament had never got around to ratifying the Statute of Westminster, an act of the British parliament in 1931 that had cut the (white) Dominions free to make their own laws and manage their own affairs as 'autonomous communities within the British Empire, equal in status, in no way subordinate one to another in respect of their domestic or external affairs ...'

Canada, South Africa and what was then the Irish Free State had signed on. But Australia, under successive conservative governments, continued to cling to Mother's apron strings (as did New Zealand). Robert Menzies, when he was Attorney-General, had made two attempts to get the Statute ratified as Australian law in 1937, but the House of Representatives simply was not interested enough to go to a vote; a couple of the states also lodged nitpicking objections, and the bills lapsed.

Herbert Vere 'Doc' Evatt, Labor's Attorney-General and Minister for External Affairs (and a former High Court judge himself) launched into a characteristic frenzy of activity, firing off cables to London left, right and centre, pestering British ministers to do this and that, and to advise George VI to commute the sentence. The British, with rather more on their minds than a distant colonial murder, quite understandably dumped the problem back in Evatt's lap. Australia should approach the King herself.

This was done. Acting on the advice of his Australian ministers, George VI exercised the royal prerogative of clemency, and on 10 August 1942 Canberra was informed by telegram that Gordon and Elias had been spared the noose.

Evatt then set about getting the Statute of Westminster adopted by the Australian parliament, and on 1 October a bill to do that was introduced into the House of Representatives. Predictably, there was much shouting and wringing of hands on the Conservative far right: here was a weakening of the ties with the Mother Country in her hour of need, a bonanza for enemy propaganda and the like. Sensible opposition figures, though, including Menzies, supported the government, and on 9 October the Statute of Westminster Adoption Act was signed into law, made retrospective to 1939 and the start of the war. There is a delicious irony in the fact that it had taken a murder and a pair of convicts to get it done.

But the campaign for Gordon and Elias was not yet over. They were now in Goulburn Jail in southern New South Wales. Mrs Byrnes and the mysterious Sonita Francis kept up their agitation for a retrial, or a shortening of the jail term; in fact, for anything they could get. The original defence counsel, Paymaster Lieutenant Trevor Rapke, had never wavered in his belief that the court martial had been improperly conducted, and he kept on with the case as well. Important people chimed in with letters to Curtin and Evatt, and questions were asked in parliament. Archbishop Gilroy (not yet a cardinal) wrote to the Governor General. Ministers and senior Labor figures had their doubts as well. Even in wartime, there was no great fondness for the navy in the more radical sections of the Labor Party, which regarded the senior officer class as a pack of Pommified stuffed shirts. The pressure built until, in December 1943, the government decided to put the thing to bed once and for all.

Evatt set up what amounted to a royal commission. Mr Justice Allan Maxwell of the New South Wales Supreme Court was given three matters to investigate: whether there were any substantial defects in the proceedings at the court martial; if there were such defects, could they have led to a miscarriage of justice; and was there any case for 'remitting the whole or any portion of the terms of imprisonment'.

Maxwell sat in camera, which was possible under the wartime security regulations and a convenient device to keep any embarrassing or unpleasant matters away from the reptiles of the press and the public gaze. A squad of King's Counsel turned up for the show, two of them representing Gordon and Elias, with Rapke as their junior. When it became apparent that Farncomb's conduct as prosecutor was under scrutiny, he too was provided with a King's Counsel. Maxwell had before him every word spoken at the court martial and the witness statements collected before it – but, again, no hint of the homosexual aspects of the murder.

That changed, as Maxwell would learn in the most extraordinary fashion. By sheer coincidence, Malcolm Stening, the doctor who had first treated Stoker Riley in *Australia*'s sick bay, happened to bump into Maxwell at a private gentlemen's dinner at Sydney's exclusive Australian Club. Riley had personally told Stening that Gordon was a 'poofter', and Stening knew all the ship's gossip. As he put it in his memoirs:

> On sitting down to dinner my place was next to the judge, who confided that on that afternoon he had been sitting 'in camera' on the trial of two sailors who had been sentenced to death

without a scintilla of evidence as to their guilt. His face was a study when my first-hand evidence enlightened him.[2]

Maxwell sat for seven days. He was not able to examine any of the original naval witnesses, for they were all serving at sea, including Farncomb and Commander John Armstrong, who had originally questioned Gordon and Elias on the night of the murder. But he went thoroughly through the transcripts and statements before him, and he delivered his report to Evatt on 1 March 1944.

If he had indeed told Stening at the dinner that there was not a 'scintilla of evidence' of guilt, it certainly wasn't reflected in his finding. 'I am left in no doubt at all as to the guilt of the prisoners,' he said. 'It was inescapable that [they] were the attackers and were jointly concerned in inflicting the wounds on the victim from which he later died.'[3]

Maxwell was critical of the matter that had so upset Rapke: Farncomb's statement to the court martial that he was convinced of the men's guilt. He called it 'a substantial defect', although, he added, not enough to have caused a miscarriage of justice. Elsewhere, he praised Farncomb's handling of the prosecution.

But, again, the allegations of homosexuality were buried. Again, not a word. Clearly, Stening had tipped Maxwell off about them, but – for whatever reason – the judge decided not to go down that alley. Instead, with lofty judicial insouciance, he expressed some puzzlement that there appeared to be no motive for the murder:

> I am constrained to point out that which was relied on very strongly by counsel for the prisoners, namely the absence of any proof of any motive at all. This is obviously a matter to be given full weight. It is true that in principle it is not necessary that the prosecution should, upon evidence, establish a motive; nevertheless it is equally true that one looks for it, and in the present case no motive has at any rate satisfactorily been proved in evidence.
>
> In my view, the matter should be viewed upon the basis that there is therefore no evidence of any motive for any attack or the particular attack in question.[4]

If Maxwell had looked for a motive, as he put it, he hadn't looked very hard. In fact, he fudged it, with a fine judicial hand. But he did take one step forward: there were good, mitigating reasons, he said, for the life sentences to be cut back. Here, he gave great weight to Farncomb's appeal for clemency, with its depiction of the arduous conditions at sea in wartime. Maxwell did not say by how much the jail terms should be shortened, but he made it clear that a life sentence was too long.

The government accepted the report, no doubt relieved that there need be no further upheaval. Evatt eventually pressed Maxwell to suggest what length the sentences should be, and the judge replied that he thought 12 years was appropriate. That, too, was accepted.

As the years rolled on, and with the end of the war, Gordon and Elias were largely forgotten. They had disappeared from the public eye. With various remissions of sentence and amnesties available to all prisoners over the years, their time was shortened again. Gordon was released on 11 September 1950 and Elias a week later. As the naval historian James Goldrick wrote in his thesis:

> HMAS *Penguin* was to forward to the Superintendent of the Emu Plains Prison Farm a serge suit, shirt, tie, collar, braces and hat for issue to the men on their discharge. Apart from the normal allowance made to men on release, they would receive nothing else. A later application by Elias in 1951 for compensation for loss of kit he possessed in 1942 was rejected outright by the Navy.[5]

The question arises: would a trial before judge and jury in this twenty-first century have convicted the two? The answer is yes, almost certainly. The circumstantial evidence was overwhelming, and a trial today would have had access to DNA reports and other modern techniques of forensic science. The homosexuality issue would have been aired at length in cross-examination, adding considerable weight to the prosecution case. A strong motive would have been established.

There might, perhaps, have been a difference if Gordon and Elias had been represented separately. On balance, it seems that Gordon alone wielded the knife and did the killing, with Elias as his accomplice. Counsel for Elias alone might have made much of that, obtaining a lighter sentence for his client.

But that is speculation. Viewing a historical event through a modern prism can be entertaining, but it can give a false picture. Seven decades ago, in wartime, with Australia under the threat of invasion, and with the vastly different social and sexual values of the day, justice was done nonetheless.

ABBREVIATIONS

ABDA command	the joint command of the Americans, British, Dutch and Australians
AIF	Australian Imperial Force
AWM	Australian War Memorial
BEF	British Expeditionary Force
IJN	Imperial Japanese Navy
NLA	National Library of Australia
RAAF	Royal Australian Air Force
RAN	Royal Australian Navy
RANC	Royal Australian Naval College
RANVR	Royal Australian Naval Volunteer Reserve
RN	Royal Navy
TBS	talk between ships (short-range radio)
USN	United States Navy

ACKNOWLEDGEMENTS

Writing this book has been like weaving a tapestry, drawing together the strands of lives and events. Some of those strands were vivid and strong. Others were faint and wispy, almost lost in the haze of many decades past or the fog of war. I could not have found them and gathered them, however imperfectly, without the help of hundreds of people who gave their time and knowledge.

My first and deepest thanks go to the men who went to sea in the three heavy cruisers, in peace or war. The diaries, memoirs, and letters they left behind were priceless; to have access to them was a pleasure and a privilege, an author's dream. Those still with us are now in their nineties – some going strong, others in fading health – but all I spoke to were more than generous with their memories.

They include 'Canteen Jack' Langrell, whose love for Australia was inspiring and humbling, and whose recall of the smallest detail was extraordinary. I must also thank my old friend Lieutenant Gavin Campbell, a survivor of the Burma–Siam Railway. I met Gavin when I was writing my first book about HMAS *Perth* and he appears here again. I was honoured to give the eulogy at his funeral in 2015, but I wish he had been here to read this book. So too Commander Dick Bourke, who put aside the pain of a long illness to speak to me from his sickbed in Sydney and who also died before I had finished writing. My thanks as well to David Mattiske, Des Shinkfield, and to my friend Rear Admiral Guy Griffiths, who, almost uniquely, fought in three wars – the Second World War, Korea and Vietnam – and who embodies the finest qualities of the RAN. Eric Geddes of the RAAF talked to me at length about his lifelong fight for justice after the Battle of Savo. Christine Bullivant of the HMAS Australia Association was wonderful, as were many members of the *Canberra–Shropshire* Association.

Families were unstinting. Diccon Loxton, the son of Commodore Bruce Loxton, gave me full access to his father's voluminous files and a splendid lunch to go with it. Commodore Peter Dechaineux, son of Emile Dechaineux, was equally kind. My gratitude also to Brennan Keats, the younger brother of Russell Keats, most especially for his beautiful memoir, *Quiet Waters*; Stuart Kean, grandson of 'Mustard' Kean; Jeanne Tyack, daughter of Tom Thurlow and niece of Jim; and Peter Taylor, son of Harold Eastick. Barbara and Andrew Hamer, the wife and son of Captain David Hamer, kindly gave permission to quote from his privately published memoir, an absolute gold mine. Alan Parker's midshipman's diary was valuable, too: his family gave me a copy when they discovered he had been my teacher in 5th Class at primary school.

Anyone writing Australian naval history will eventually encounter Mackenzie 'Mac' Gregory, whose blog 'Ahoy – Mac's Web Log' (http://ahoy.tk-jk.net) is another treasure chest of hard fact and priceless anecdote. I first met Mac when I was writing the *Perth* book; I emailed him again as I began this one, only to find he had died the week before. His knowledge and experience were unmatched, and I am indebted to his son Raymond for allowing me to dig into his life's work.

Another friend, Rear Admiral James Goldrick, was as always a mine of information. James is unique: been there, done that. He has commanded warships of the RAN, and the international task force in the Persian Gulf, achievements which illuminate his other life as one of the world's truly eminent naval historians and academics. Blue-water history buffs will understand me when I say he's Australia's mirror to Alfred Thayer Mahan, the great American naval thinker and writer. Whether on grand strategy or what sailors ate for breakfast, no knotty question is too much for James to answer. His superb thesis on the murder in *Australia*, written for his MA at the University of New England, saved me months of work.

The navy cherishes its history and tradition at the RAN Sea Power Centre in Canberra, where David Stevens, John Perryman and Petar Djokovic were quick with help. The Naval Historical Society at Sydney's Garden Island was also terrific, especially patient with my questions on the now extinct art and science of 8-inch gunnery. Thanks also to the archive staff at the Australian War Memorial and the National Library in Canberra. Trove, the Library's searchable online database, is a national treasure; it was shocking to learn while writing this book that its funding has been slashed by an ignorant and uncaring federal government.

The US Navy's History and Heritage Command was another important resource, as was London's Imperial War Museum. Britain's RAF Coastal Command Association rummaged around for me as well.

There are naval friends, both retired and still serving, too numerous to mention here, but I am thankful to them all for their counsel and encouragement. The RAN's senior leadership has always supported me to the hilt. A special shout to the Maritime Commander, Rear Admiral Stuart Mayer; Commodore Lee Goddard; Captain Ivan Ingham; Lieutenant Commander Desmond Woods; and to Commander Paul Moggach ('the last Shark Boss'), who hosted me at the commissioning of HMAS *Canberra III*.

Every effort has been made to trace holders of the copyright to works I have quoted, but many are unknown and beyond reach. If they emerge after publication I will, of course, be pleased to acknowledge them in future editions. I do especially thank the US Naval Institute Press at Annapolis, Maryland, for permission to quote from *The Japanese Navy in World War II*; Tom Thompson of ETT Imprint, Exile Bay, for allowing me to use an extract of Dame Mary Gilmore's 1942 poem 'HMAS *Canberra* and her Men'. David Day, chair of the Australian Society of Authors, happily permitted me to borrow some lines from his landmark biography of John Curtin. And an admiring, respectful thanks to Commander George Hermon Gill – mariner, journalist, naval officer and war historian – whose two-volume official history of the RAN in the Second World War is the sea mark for the rest of us.

Big thanks, too, to the people at Penguin Random House, who have backed me all the way into this, my third book for them (with a fourth to come). Nikki Christer, Alison Urquhart, Kevin O'Brien and Catherine Hill are the publishers and editors that authors hope for but rarely find. Kevin, in particular, saved me time and again from howlers, blooper and literals; any that remain are mine, not his.

Last of all: family. As he did for earlier books, my elder son James Carlton took infinite time and patience to draw the beautiful maps and diagrams. Going beyond the call of duty, his own research turned up a number of errors in what are usually regarded as the definitive maps of several battles.

And my final thanks and love to my wife, Morag Ramsay, who, with endless patience, managed to juggle her media career and the care of our son, Lachlan, while the author was buried for weeks and months at his computer.

NOTES AND REFERENCES

CHAPTER 1: SO I AM TO BE SUNK

1   The light cruisers *Melbourne, Sydney* and *Encounter,* and the destroyers *Warrego, Parramatta* and *Yarra*.

2   Quoted in G. L. McCandie, *Genesis of the Royal Australia Navy,* Government Printer, Sydney, 1949, p. 288.

3   *The Sydney Morning Herald,* 9 April 1924.

4   Ibid., 12 April 1924.

5   A third royal cousin joined in: Tsar Nicholas II of Russia.

6   This is covered in much greater detail in my book *First Victory, 1914,* William Heinemann, Sydney, 2013.

7   Quoted in *First Victory,* p. 31.

8   Arthur Jose, *Official History of Australia in the War 1914–18,* Vol. IX, Australian War Memorial, Canberra, 1941, p. 153.

9   It is likely she is still the only Australian warship to have rounded Cape Horn.

10   Jose, p. 264.

11   The Battle of Jutland can be counted as a narrow British victory. Britain lost more men and ships than Germany, including three battlecruisers, but the German fleet retreated to harbour and never again seriously challenged the Royal Navy for mastery of the North Sea.

12   A public outcry saw them released early, at the end of the year. There is more on Dalmorton Rudd and his brother at www.navy.gov.au/biography/leading-seaman-dalmorton-joseph-owendale-rudd.

13   The future Edward VIII, then Duke of Windsor.

14   *The Sydney Morning Herald,* 1 October 1923.

15   *Adelaide News,* 30 January 1924.

16   *The Sydney Morning Herald*, 4 April 1924.

17   *The Newcastle Morning Herald*, 3 March 1924.

18   *The Daily Herald*, Adelaide, 2 February 1924.

19   *The Australian Worker*, 23 April 1924.

20   The polished timber table from the admiral's cabin is now at Old Parliament House, Canberra.

21   Vice Admiral Sir Frederick Field and Rear Admiral The Hon. Sir Hubert Brand.

22   Captain Henry James Feakes, *White Ensign, Southern Cross*, Ure Smith, Sydney, 1951, p. 214.

23   *The Sydney Morning Herald*, 14 April 1924.

24   Bruce media statement, reported in *The Sydney Morning Herald*, 14 April 1924.

25   *The Sydney Mail*, 16 April 1924.

26   *The Sydney Morning Herald*, 12 April 1924.

27   *Country Life Stock and Station Journal*, 18 April 1924.

CHAPTER 2: THE WAY OF THE COMMONWEALTH IS FORWARD

1   Edwin Brady, *Australia Unlimited*, George Robertson, Melbourne, 1918, p. 511.

2   *Spectator and Methodist Chronicle*, Melbourne, 21 August 1918.

3   Statistics from the Commonwealth Department of Health, www.health.gov.au/internet/main/publishing.nsf/Content/about-pandemic-history#1918.

4   *The Argus*, 22 July 1919.

5   *The Australasian*, 26 July 1919.

6   *Brisbane Courier*, 27 July 1920.

7   The Hon. J. W. Percival MLC to the NSW Under Secretary for Lands, letter, 6 August 1926.

8   In 2015 dollars, about $2.2 billion. Figures from the Australian Bureau of Statistics, Commonwealth Yearbook, 1925.

9   In today's numbers, a five-star admiral.

10   His chief assistant was the brilliant Commander Bertram Ramsay, who, as an admiral in the Second World War, would oversee the evacuation from Dunkirk in 1940 and the naval part of the D-Day invasion in 1944.

11   Viscount Jellicoe, *Report of the Naval Mission to the Commonwealth*, *Vol. 1*, Ch. 5, www.navy.gov.au/sites/default/files/documents/Jellicoe%20of%20Scapa%20Vol%20I_opt.pdf.

12   Ibid.

13   Ibid., p. 15.

14   The Reserve Bank's historical inflation calculator suggests this would be approximately $1.5 billion in 2016 dollars.

15 Jellicoe, p. 24.
16 This line stayed there until the 1960s.
17 *The Bulletin*, 20 January 1920.
18 *The Sydney Morning Herald*, 10 September 1920.
19 Quoted in the *Daily News* (Perth), 3 January 1921.
20 Gill, Series 2, Vol. 1, p. 19.
21 *The Daily Telegraph*, London, 3 January 2002.
22 *The Sydney Morning Herald*, 8 December 1934.
23 Ibid.
24 'William Francis Forbes-Sempill', British National Archives KV 2/871, http://discovery.nationalarchives.gov.uk/details/r/C11050182.
25 The Germans had frequently used Zeppelin airships at sea.
26 Vice Admiral Sir David Beatty, Report to the Admiralty, 24 June 1916.
27 'Notes on the Case of Squadron Leader Rutland, RAF', MI5, British National Archives KV 2/337, www.nationalarchives.gov.uk/documents/nov2000.pdf.
28 Approximately AU$180,000 in 2016.
29 Hansard, House of Commons, 22 January 1942.
30 *The Sydney Morning Herald*, 1 June 1927.

CHAPTER 3: THE TREMENDOUS VALUE OF THE SEAS EAST OF SUEZ

1 With the loss of 1198 lives, 128 of them American, which aroused anti-German outrage in the US.
2 Cloot was Scottish dialect for cloth. Cloot men would upholster a ship's interior where needed.
3 *The Newcastle Sun*, 18 March 1927.
4 *The Glasgow Herald*, 18 March 1927.
5 A senior sailor in charge of policing, usually a chief petty officer. Commonly nicknamed 'the Jaunty'.
6 Sir John Collins, *As Luck Would Have It*, Angus & Robertson, Sydney, 1965, p. 16.
7 F. B. Eldridge, *A History of the Royal Australian Naval College*, Georgian House, Melbourne, 1949, p. 43.
8 Named for Sir John Jervis, Admiral of the Fleet the Earl St Vincent, who beat a French fleet at the Battle of Cape St Vincent in 1787. Pronounced Jarvis.
9 *The Naval Discipline Act 1866*. A British law, it remained in force in Australia.
10 Eldridge, p. 47.
11 Supposedly derived from a nineteenth-century habit of midshipmen wiping their noses on their jacket cuffs. Eventually, 3 buttons were placed there to stop them doing it.

12   Later King George VI and Queen Elizabeth (the Queen Mother).
13   Collins, p. 42.
14   HMAS *Choules*, a landing ship dock, formerly the Royal Navy fleet auxiliary vessel *Largs Bay*.
15   Robert Hyslop, 'Hyde, Sir George Francis (1877–1937)', *Australian Dictionary of Biography*, National Centre of Biography, Australian National University, 1983, http://adb.anu.edu.au/biography/hyde-sir-george-francis-6782.
16   Claude Choules, *The Last of the Last*, Hesperian Press, Perth, 2009.
17   Among them, my father, the sprinter Jimmy Carlton.
18   *The News*, Adelaide, 19 July 1928
19   Ibid.
20   Slang for the Chief Bosun's Mate, a senior sailor.
21   *The Advocate* (Burnie), 22 October 1928.
22   Author conversation with the Kean family, January 2015.

CHAPTER 4: BLIGHTED BY THE WITHERING TOUCH OF POVERTY

1   *The Evening News* (Sydney), 3 September 1930.
2   *The Sydney Morning Herald*, 4 September 1930.
3   *The Evening News* (Sydney), 3 September 1930.
4   *The Newcastle Morning Herald*, 4 September 1930.
5   *The Evening News* (Sydney), 3 September 1930.
6   *The Barrier Miner* (Broken Hill), 22 June 1929.
7   W. S. Ramson (ed.), The Australian National Dictionary, Oxford University Press, Oxford, 1988 (cited on Wikipedia, 'The Susso', https://en.wikipedia.org/wiki/The_Susso).
8   *The Farmer & Settler* (Sydney), 30 July 1930.
9   *The Sydney Morning Herald*, 3 September 1930.
10   Approximately $21 per day in 2015 dollars.
11   Approximately $150 per week in 2015 dollars.
12   Stevens, David, *The Royal Australian Navy: A History*, Oxford University Press, Melbourne, 2001, p. 89.
13   Ibid., p. 90.
14   Plagued by mechanical problems, they were no great loss.
15   Essay No. 1, Economy in Defence, 1930. Quoted in Stevens, p. 85.
16   If today's officer has ever heard of the term, it would not occur to her to use it.
17   Much later, as Admiral Lord Mountevans, he would sit as a Labour peer in the House of Lords.
18   *The Cairns Post*, 22 May 1931.
19   Philip Jay, 'Musings of a Matelot', AWM MSS 1083.

20 The horse actually fell, but recovered and shot to the head of the field.

21 *The News* (Adelaide), 9 November 1932.

22 Ibid.

23 *The Morning Bulletin* (Rockhampton), 10 November 1932.

24 *Mercury* (Hobart), 10 November 1932.

25 *Truth* (Melbourne), 5 November 1932.

26 *Truth* (Sydney), 4 December 1932.

27 *The Sydney Morning Herald*, 24 August 1936.

28 A cable jack is a handspike fitted with a fulcrum and stand. It is used for lifting heavy cables to enable slips to be passed underneath.

29 Jay.

30 *Townsville Daily Bulletin*, 12 February 1937.

31 Rope and tackle used for lowering a boat to the water.

CHAPTER 5: HEARTS OF OAK ARE OUR SHIPS

1 Cartland would claim privately that Kent had fathered her daughter Raine, who would become Princess Diana's stepmother.

2 National Archives of Australia, A6686, p. 2.

3 *Brisbane Courier*, 5 December 1934.

4 First performed on New Year's Eve 1760 at the Theatre Royal, Drury Lane, London.

5 A. W. Grazebrook, 'First to a Flag: The Life of Rear Admiral H. B. Farncomb', an essay in *Reflections on the RAN*, Kangaroo Press, Sydney, 1991.

6 Michael Bloch, *Ribbentrop*, Crown Publishers Inc., New York, 1992, p. 281.

7 Ian Kershaw, *Hitler: Hubris*, Penguin, London, 1998, p. 558.

8 He did, in one of history's little ironies, beating the German Baron Gottfried von Cramm 6–2, 6–4, 6–4.

9 M. A. Payne, *HMAS Australia*, Naval Historical Society, Sydney, 1988, p. 22.

10 Eventually, 740 of them were built. The British called their version the Walrus. A splendidly restored model is on show at the RAAF Museum at Point Cook, Victoria.

11 The strike on Taranto was eventually made, and successfully too, but not until 1940, from the carrier *Illustrious*.

12 Daniela Baratieri, Mark Edele and Giuseppe Finaldi, *Totalitarian Dictatorship*, Routledge, London, 2013, p. 115.

13 As a full admiral and Commander-in-Chief Western Approaches, Horton won the Battle of the Atlantic against the U-boats in the Second World War.

14 Quoted in Payne, p. 32.

15 Ibid.

16   *The Sydney Morning Herald*, 11 December 1936.
17   *Townsville Daily Bulletin*, 12 December 1936.
18   Tota Ishimaru, *Japan Must Fight Britain*, Paternoster, London, 1936.
19   *The Argus*, 19 May 1936.
20   *Daily Express*, 17 November 1936.
21   Australian Government Department of Foreign Affairs and Trade, 'Historical Documents', Vol. 1, 1937–38, www.info.dfat.gov.au/info/historical/HistDocs.
22   Ibid.
23   Hansard, J. A. Lyons, 24 August 1937.
24   Australian Government Department of Foreign Affairs and Trade, 'Historical Documents', Vol. 2, 1939, www.info.dfat.gov.au/info/historical/HistDocs.
25   *The West Australian*, 15 February 1938.
26   Ibid.

CHAPTER 6: AS A RESULT, AUSTRALIA IS ALSO AT WAR

1   Australian Government Department of Foreign Affairs and Trade, 'Historical Documents', Vol. 2, 1939, www.info.dfat.gov.au/info/historical/HistDocs.
2   Ibid.
3   *The Sydney Morning Herald*, 2 September 1939.
4   Robert Menzies, National broadcast, 3 September 1939, http://aso.gov.au/titles/radio/menzies-speech-declaration-war/clip1/
5   Allegedly because returning seamen would guzzle Devon's famous cream teas when they got ashore.
6   Hoe: an Anglo-Saxon word meaning a sloping hill or ridge.
7   Australian Government Department of Foreign Affairs and Trade, 'Historical Documents', Vol. 2, 1939, www.info.dfat.gov.au/info/historical/HistDocs.
8   Ibid.
9   Ibid.
10   Ibid.
11   Ibid.
12   J. C. H. Gill, 'Feldt, Eric Augustas (1899–1968)', *Australian Dictionary of Biography*, http://adb.anu.edu.au/biography/feldt-eric-augustas-10163/text17953.
13   Eric Feldt, *The Coast Watchers*, Oxford University Press, Melbourne, 1946, p. 24.
14   Ibid., p. 25.
15   The ship to which Napoleon Bonaparte surrendered in 1815.
16   Crace Community Association, archive-au.com/page/1231543/2013-01-24/http://www.crace.com.au/news/the-crace-vision.php.

17   It still stands, under heritage protection.

18   *Goulburn Herald*, 26 September 1892.

19   *The Queanbeyan Age*, 18 October 1899.

20   Founded in 1841, the school saw the cream of British admirals pass through its doors before it closed in 1991. The last of note was Admiral John Foster Woodward, who commanded in the Falklands War of 1982.

21   Quoted in Chris Coulthard-Clark, *Action Stations Coral Sea*, Allen & Unwin, Sydney, 1991, p. 7.

CHAPTER 7: PUT YOUR HAND INTO THE HAND OF GOD

1   *The Argus*, 19 December 1939.

2   Winston Churchill, *The Second World War, Vol. I, The Gathering Storm*, Houghton Mifflin, New York, 1948, p. 476.

3   Sir Geoffrey Whiskard to Robert Menzies, letter, Australian Department of Foreign Affairs and Trade, *Documents in Australian Foreign Policy*, Vol. 2, No. 314, 30 October 1939.

4   G. Hermon Gill. *Australia in the War of 1939–1945*, Series 2, Vol. I, RAN 1939–42, Australian War Memorial, 1957, p. 86.

5   Jankers – army and navy slang for a punishment less severe than detention.

6   Edgar Blau, private papers, AWM PR03441.

7   *The Courier-Mail*, Brisbane, 23 December 1939.

8   *The Sydney Morning Herald*, 23 December 1939.

9   *Westralian Worker*, 22 December 1939.

10   From 'God Knows', by Minnie Louise Haskins, a poet and academic at the London School of Economics, 1908.

11   Australian Government Department of Foreign Affairs and Trade, 'Historical Documents', Vol. 2, 1939, No. 129, 30 April 1940, www.info.dfat.gov.au/info/historical/HistDocs

12   Churchill, House of Commons, 13 May 1940, Vol. 360, cc. 1501–25.

13   As a young commander, he had been on Lord Jellicoe's staff during his inspection of Australia in 1919.

14   Winston Churchill, *The Second World War, Vol. II, Their Finest Hour*, Houghton Mifflin & Co., Boston, 1949, p. 87.

15   W.J.R. Gardner, *The Evacuation from Dunkirk, Operation Dynamo*, Routledge, London, 2002, p. 15.

16   Dechaineux, letter, private papers.

17   Ibid.

18   Ibid.

19   Ibid.

20   Hansard, House of Commons, Vol. 361, cc. 787–984, June 1940.

CHAPTER 8: WE SIGHTED SMOKE AND HOISTED BATTLE ENSIGNS

1   Invented just before the war, the technique of degaussing reduced a ship's magnetic field. It was not infallible but it greatly lessened the risk of a ship triggering a magnetic mine.

2   Winston Churchill, *The Second World War, Vol. II, Their Finest Hour*, Houghton Mifflin & Co., Boston, 1949, p. 205.

3   His great-grandfather had been killed at Trafalgar.

4   Churchill, *Vol. II*, p. 205.

5   Quoted in Bruce Taylor, *The End of Glory*, Seaforth Publishing, London, 2012, p. 169.

6   *Daily Mail*, 5 February 2010.

7   Peter Taylor, *A Sailor's Life*, self-published, Perth, 2010, p. 11.

8   HMAS *Australia*, Report of Proceedings, July 1941, Australian War Memorial, 78 44/2, January 1940–December 1941, July 1940.

9   Ibid.

10 Sir John Collins, *As Luck Would Have It*, Angus & Robertson, Sydney, 1965, p. 86.

11 J. Greene and Massignani, A., *The Naval War in the Mediterranean*, Naval Institute Press, Annapolis, Maryland, 2011, p. 86.

12 *The Herald* (Melbourne), 20 July 1940.

13 BBC Radio, 18 June 1940.

14 One of the marines was the writer Evelyn Waugh, a captain.

15 John Williams, *The Guns of Dakar*, Heinemann, London, 1976, p. 25.

16 M. A. Payne, *HMAS Australia*, Naval Historical Society, Sydney, 1988, p. 56.

17 Armstrong, private papers, NLA MS 9675.

18 Mackenzie Gregory, 'Operation Menace', Ahoy – Mac's Weblog, 1984, http://ahoy.tk-jk.net/macslog/OperationMenace.September.html.

19 Ibid.

20 *The Gunnery Pocket Book*, Admiralty Gunnery Branch, London, 1945, B.R. 224/45.

21 Report of Proceedings, September 1940, Australian War Memorial, 78 44/2, January 1940–December 1941.

22 Peter Taylor, *A Sailor's Life*, self-published, Perth, 2010, p. 16.

23 Jack Langrell, conversation with the author, March 2015.

24 Churchill, *Vol. II*, p. 433.

25 John Jordan and Robert Dumas, *French Battleships 1922–1956*, Seaforth, London, 2009, p. 142.

26 *The Examiner* (Launceston), 27 September 1940.

27 Australian Department of Foreign Affairs and Trade, *Documents in Australian Foreign Policy*, Vol. 4, No. 144, July 1940–June 1941, Menzies to Bruce, 29 September 1940.

28 Ibid., No. 152, Churchill to Menzies.

CHAPTER 9: WHAT IRRESPONSIBLE RUBBISH THESE ANTIPODEANS TALK

1   Sunderlands destroyed 26 U-boats during the war – 12 of these sunk by aircraft of the RAAF's 10 and 461 Squadrons.

2   HMAS *Australia*, Report of Proceedings, AWM 78 44/2, January 1940–December 1941, October 1940.

3   Mackenzie Gregory, 'HMAS *Australia* to the Rescue', Ahoy – Mac's Weblog, 1984, http://ahoy.tk-jk.net/macslog/HMASAustraliatothe rescue.html.

4   Peter Taylor, *A Sailor's Life*, self-published, Perth, 2010, p. 23.

5   Sidney Gibbs survived the war, a much decorated Wing Commander.

6   Armstrong, private papers, NLA, ID 1603085.

7   Taylor, p. 28.

8   Ross Stewart, HMAS *Australia*, Report of Proceedings, AWM 78 44/2, January 1940–December 1941, December 1940.

9   Taylor, p. 31.

10 *The Argus*, 6 November 1940.

11 *The Sydney Morning Herald*, 8 November 1940.

12 Paul Hasluck, *The Government and the People, 1939–41*, Australian War Memorial, Canberra, 1952, p. 270.

13 Gill, p. 269.

14 Advisory War Council, Minute No. 48, 2 December 1940, Hasluck, p. 298.

15 Australian Government Department of Foreign Affairs and Trade, No. 212, 1 December 1940.

16 Ibid., 236, 23 December 1940.

17 Mike Carlton, *Cruiser*, William Heinemann, Sydney, 2010, p. 382.

18 Robert Gordon Menzies, *Dark and Hurrying Days*, National Library of Australia, Canberra, 1993, p. 67.

19 Ibid., p. 68.

20 Approximately $875,000,000 in 2014 Australian dollars.

21 For a full account, see Tom Frame and Kevin Baker, *Mutiny*, Allen & Unwin, Sydney, 2000.

22 David Hamer, *Memories of My Life*, self-published, Melbourne, 2002, p. 58.

23 The oldest boy, Rupert Hamer – invariably known as Dick – became a Liberal Premier of Victoria, 1972–81.

24 Hamer, p. 90.

25 Warren A. Bebbington, 'Keats, Horace Stanley (1895–1945)', *Australian Dictionary of Biography*, National Centre of Biography, Australian National University, 1983, http://adb.anu.edu.au/biography/keats-horace-stanley-6906/text11981.

26 Brennan Keats, *Quiet Waters*, Wirripang Publishing, Wollongong, 2008. The reference to 'twenty thousand forces' is unclear, but probably refers to the 2nd AIF being raised for the war.

CHAPTER 10: I THEREFORE DECIDED TO ENGAGE THE ENEMY

1   *The Newcastle Morning Herald*, 13 January 1941.

2   David Hamer, *Memories of My Life*, self-published, Melbourne, 2002, p. 113.

3   Gavin Campbell, conversation with the author, January 2015.

4   Edgar Blau, private papers, AWM PR03441.

5   Ibid.

6   Hamer, p. 111.

7   Harold Farncomb, Report of Proceedings, February 1941, AWM, 78 44/2, January 1940– December 1941.

8   *Australia in the War of 1939–1945*, Series 5 – Medical, AWM, Canberra, Vol. IV, p. 32.

9   Brennan Keats, *Quiet Waters*, Wirripang Publishing, Wollongong, 2008, p. 66.

10 *Admiral Scheer* was sunk in an RAF bombing raid on Kiel on 9 April 1945.

11 And eventually to become HMNZS *Leander*.

12 Farncomb, Report of Proceedings, March 1941, AWM, 78 44/2, January 1940–December 1941.

13 Hamer, p. 117.

14 Quoted in Gill, p. 369.

15 Hamer, p. 115.

16 Gill, p. 370.

17 Keats, p. 56.

18 Alan Parker, Midshipman's Journal, in the possession of the author.

19 Quoted in M. A. Payne, *HMAS Australia*, Naval Historical Society, Sydney, 1988, p. 48.

20 Farncomb, Report of Proceedings, February 1941, AWM.

21 Winston Churchill, *The Second World War, Vol. III, The Grand Alliance*, Houghton Mifflin & Co., Boston, 1950, p. 273.

22 Ibid., p. 265.

23 *The Argus*, 20 June 1941.

24 *The Sydney Morning Herald*, 3 July 1941.

25 Naval Historical Society of Australia, 'Captain Joseph Burnett RAN', https://www.navyhistory.org.au/captain-joseph-burnett-ran/3.

26 *The Dungog Chronicle and Durham and Gloucester Advertiser*, 2 December 1941.

CHAPTER 11: I MAKE IT QUITE CLEAR THAT AUSTRALIA LOOKS TO AMERICA

1   *The Naval Review*, Vol. XXX, No. 3, August 1942. The writer's initials were K. R. B.: almost certainly Lieutenant Commander Kenneth Robertson Buckley.

2   Robert Ian Davies was awarded a posthumous Mention in Despatches. It should have been a Victoria Cross.

3   *Daily News* (Perth), 23 December 1941.

4   Winston Churchill, *The Second World War, Vol. III, The Grand Alliance*, p. 563.

5   *The Herald* (Melbourne), 27 December 1941.

6   *The Sydney Morning Herald*, 30 December 1941.

7   *The Newcastle Sun*, 30 December 1941.

8   Churchill, *The Second World War, Vol. IV, The Hinge of Fate*, Houghton Mifflin & Co., Boston, 1950, p. 7.

9   *Australia in the War of 1939–1945*, Series 1 – Army, Australian War Memorial, Vol. V, 1957, p. 17.

10 *The Advertiser*, 21 March 1942.

11 Ibid.

12 Worth about $7.25 million in 2016 dollars.

13 *The Canberra Times*, 27 March 1942.

14 Douglas MacArthur, *Reminiscences*, The Naval Institute Press, Annapolis, Maryland, 1964, p. 283.

15 Graham Freudenberg, *Churchill and Australia*, Macmillan, Sydney, 2008, p. 396.

16 Also famously known as 'Gob' caps, although the USN never used the term.

17 Pronounced 'Boady'.

18 Hamer, p. 128.

19 Ibid., p. 131.

20 Peter Taylor, *A Sailor's Life*, self-published, Perth, 2010, p. 81.

21 Samuel Eliot Morison, *History of United States Naval Operations in World War II, Vol. 3, The Rising Sun in the Pacific 1931–1942*, University of Illinois Press, Chicago, 2001, p. 266.

22 Chris Coulthard-Clark, *Action Stations Coral Sea*, Allen & Unwin, Sydney, 1991, p. 54.

23 A truly heroic figure who survived not just the Japanese but disease and malnutrition, Vial was commissioned as an RAAF officer. The Americans awarded him their Distinguished Service Cross. He was killed in an air crash in 1943.

24 Morison, p. 389.

CHAPTER 12: TO BE HANGED BY THE NECK TILL THEY BE DEAD

1   They and their crews were eventually found, a week later, by a searching RAAF Catalina. They had got lost and ended up at Rossel Island, at the tip of the Louisiades.

2   Almost impossible to explain, Uckers is a complex form of Ludo.

3   B-deck was a raised platform that carried B-turret, the second of the 8-inch gun turrets, located below and in front of the bridge.

4   This one was secured, upright, to the side of the B-deck platform just forward of the P1 gun, which was the foremost of the 4-inch anti-aircraft guns on the port side of the ship.

5   Elias–Gordon Court Martial, National Archives, NAA B6121, 123V, p. 54.

6   Malcolm's elder brother, Sam Stening, also a doctor, had been in HMAS *Perth* when she was sunk a fortnight before, something that Malcolm did not yet know. Sam became a prisoner of war in Japan and survived the war.

7   Elias–Gordon Court Martial, National Archives, NAA B6121, 123V.

8   Ibid.

9   Jack Langrell, conversation with the author, 19 February 2015.

10 Churchill did not say it, but quipped once that he wished he had.

11 I have provided only an initial for the three other names, for obvious reasons.

12 Elias–Gordon Court Martial, National Archives, NAA B6121, 123V. (The italics are the author's.)

13 Ibid.

14 Peter Taylor, *A Sailor's Life*, self-published, Perth, 2010, p. 86.

15 Roskill would later gain fame as the pre-eminent and official historian of the RN in the Second World War.

16 Modern law would now allow Riley's statements to be given in evidence.

17 Elias–Gordon Court Martial, National Archives, NAA B6121, 123V.

18 Ibid., p. 150.

19 Tom Frame (et al.), *Reflections on the Royal Australian Navy*, Kangaroo Press, Sydney, 1991, p. 196.

20 Ibid., Rapke to Farncomb, letter, 20 April 1942.

21 Chris Coulthard-Clark, *Action Stations Coral Sea*, Allen & Unwin, Sydney, 1991, p. 61.

22 Harold Farncomb to Jack Crace, letter, 20 April 1942, National Archives, NAA B6121, 123V.

23 Ibid.

24   Rapke returned to the Melbourne bar after the war, becoming a
        QC, a distinguished judge of the Victorian County Court, and
        a prominent leader of Australia's Jewish community. In 1964, he
        became the RAN's senior legal officer, the Judge Advocate General,
        with the rank of rear admiral.

CHAPTER 13: PROCEED AT DAYLIGHT WITH YOUR GROUP TO DESTROY ENEMY SHIPS

1   Japanese army operations in the South Pacific area: New Britain
        and Papua campaigns, 1942–43, Australian War Memorial, p. 61
        (website) http://ajrp.awm.gov.au/ajrp/ajrp2.nsf/WebPages/Japanese
        Operations?OpenDocument
2   Ibid., p. 69.
3   Samuel Eliot Morison, *The Rising Sun in the Pacific*, University of
        Illinois Press, Chicago, 2001, p. 46.
4   Fifteen of the aircraft reached China, and one landed in the Soviet
        Union. Eight crewmen were captured by the Japanese in China,
        and three were executed. The rest survived.
5   Many of those cables were not translated and deciphered until
        1946 – rather too late.
6   Jozef Straczek, 'Battle of the Coral Sea', Royal Australian Navy,
        www.navy.gov.au.
7   G. Hermon Gill, *Australia in the War of 1939–1945*, Series 2, Vol. 1,
        RAN 1939–42, Australian War Memorial, 1957, p. 41.
8   To this day, still the oldest man ever to qualify as a USN pilot – a
        record unlikely to be beaten.
9   John B. Black Lundstrom, *Shoe Carrier Admiral: Frank Jack Fletcher
        at Coral Sea, Midway & Guadalcanal*, Naval Institute Press, Annapo-
        lis, Maryland, 2011, p. 29.
10   Quoted in Chris Coulthard-Clark, *Action Stations Coral Sea*, Allen
        & Unwin, Sydney 1991, p. 138.
11   Ibid., p. 205.
12   Coulthard-Clark, p. 95.
13   Jack Langrell, conversation with the author, 4 June 2015.
14   Coulthard-Clark, p. 95.
15   USN term for full speed.
16   Gill, p. 50.
17   *Japanese Army Operations in the South Pacific Area.*

CHAPTER 14: AUSTRALIA CANNOT ESCAPE A BLOW

1   Quoted in Stanley Johnston, *Queen of the Flat Tops*, Jarrolds, London,
        1942, p. 133.

2 Jerry Holden (ed.), 'USS Lexington, Action Report, 15 May 1942', HyperWar Foundation, 8 February 2003, www.ibiblio.org/hyperwar/USN/ships/logs/CV/CV2-Coral.html.

3 Ibid.

4 G. Hermon Gill, *Australia in the War of 1939–1945*, series 2, Vol. 2, RAN 1942–1945, Australian War Memorial, 1968, p. 52.

5 *The Sunday Times* (Western Australia), 10 May 1942.

6 *The Worker* (Brisbane), 7 April 1942.

7 Paul Hasluck, *Australia in the War of 1939–1945*, Series 4 – Civil, Vol. II – The Government and the People, 1942–1945, 1970, p. 225.

8 In 2015, around $678 for the Australian private, $1180 for the American; $3112 for the Australian major, $7370 for the American.

9 Hansard, House of Representatives, 8 May 1942.

10 Ibid.

11 Not until 1946.

12 *The Courier-Mail* (Brisbane), 9 May 1942.

13 Ibid.

14 Gill, p. 53.

15 Quoted in Chris Coulthard-Clark, *Action Stations Coral Sea*, Allen & Unwin, Sydney, 1991, p. 135.

16 He actually duchessed the wrong lot. Convinced the Menzies conservatives would get back to power, he schmoozed them and ignored Curtin and the Labor cabinet.

17 Malcolm Stening, *The Class of '35 at War*, Naval Historical Society of Australia, Sydney, p. 100. The civilising arrival of women officers in modern wardrooms has put paid to the 'wives and sweethearts' toast and a lot – although not all – of the physical hijinks.

18 *The London Gazette*, 28 August 1918.

CHAPTER 15: EACH BEAUTIFUL SHIP FLYING A TREMENDOUS WHITE AUSTRALIAN NAVAL ENSIGN

1 *HMAS Mk III*, Australian War Memorial, 1943, p. 44.

2 Navy slang for an abrupt and speedy posting to a ship.

3 Malcolm Stening, *The Class of '35 at War*, NHSA, 2002, p. 103.

4 These I class submarines, at nearly 7000 tonnes, could carry up to three seaplanes on a hangar deck. They were far and away the biggest submarines ever built until the arrival of US and Russian nuclear boats in the 1960s.

5 Peter Grose, *A Very Rude Awakening*, Allen & Unwin, Sydney, 2007, p. 135.

6 *The Sydney Morning Herald*, 2 June 1942.

7 Grose, p. 153.

8 *The Sydney Morning Herald*, 2 June 1942.

9   Patrick D. Weadon, 'The Battle of Midway', National Security Agency, Central Security Service, 15 January 2009, www.nsa.gov/about/cryptologic_heritage/center_crypt_history/publications/battle_midway.shtml.

10   Tom Thurlow, private papers.

11   HMS *Oxley*, as she became, was lost a week after the outbreak of the Second World War, torpedoed off the coast of Norway by another British submarine, HMS *Triton*. She had been out of position and was mistaken for a U-boat.

12   David Medley, Letters, Ahoy – Mac's Web Log, http://ahoy.tk-jk.net/Letters/DavidMedleyshipmateonCanb.html.

13   Brennan Keats, *Quiet Waters*, Wirripang Publishing, Wollongong, 2008, p. 89.

14   David C. Evans (ed.), *The Japanese Navy in World War II*, Naval Institute Press, Annapolis, Maryland, 1969, p. 221.

15   Grandfather of the Arizona Senator and 2008 republican presidential candidate John S. McCain III.

16   George W. Smith, *The Do or Die Men*, Simon & Schuster, New York, 2003, p. 16.

17   A. A. Vandegrift, *Once a Marine*, Bantam Books, New York, 1964, p. 120.

18   George C. Dyer, *The Amphibians Came to Conquer*, US Navy, 1972, p. 301, www.ibiblio.org/hyperwar/USN/ACTC/

19   Ibid., p. 120.

20   Bruce Loxton, *The Shame of Savo*, Allen & Unwin, Sydney, 1994, p. 71.

21   Merrill B. Twining, *No Bended Knee: The Battle for Guadalcanal*, Presidio Press, Novato, California, 1996, p. 77

22   He was wrong about the Walrus being from the First World War, but to an American eye it probably looked that way.

23   Twining, p. 114.

24   Dyer, p. 294.

25   Quoted in Dyer, p. 317.

CHAPTER 16: FOR SO APPEARS THIS FLEET MAJESTICAL

1   Quoted in *The Amphibians Came to Conquer: The Story of Admiral Richmond Kelly Turner*, George C. Dyer, US Navy Publications, US Government Printing Office, 1972, p. 317.

2   Bruce Loxton, private papers.

3   A. A. Vandegrift , *Once a Marine*, Bantam Books, New York, 1964, p. 19.

4   Charles Nicholls, *HMAS Mk II*, Australian War Memorial, 1943, p. 152.

5   Martin Clemens, *Alone on Guadalcanal*, Naval Institute Press, Annapolis, Maryland, 1998, p. 187.

6   William Shakespeare, *Henry V*, Act III, Prologue.
7   Jones and Idriess, p. 318.
8   Captain Tameichi Hara, *Japanese Destroyer Captain*, Ballantine Books, New York, 1958, p. 104.
9   The Japanese operated on Tokyo time. So their 4.30 am in Rabaul was actually 6.30 am in the Solomons.
10 Thwarted of that prey, *S-38* made up for it the next day by sinking the *Meiyo Maru*, drowning almost all the troops on board.
11 James Griffin, 'Mason, Paul Edward (1901–1972)', *Australian Dictionary of Biography*, National Centre of Biography, Australian National University, 2000, http://adb.anu.edu.au/biography/mason-paul-edward-11081.
12 Eric Geddes, conversation with the author, 2014.
13 Letter to Eric Geddes, US Navy History and Heritage Command, 22 July 2014. Copy with the author.
14 David C. Evans (ed.), *The Japanese Navy in World War II*, Naval Institute Press, Annapolis, Maryland, 1969, p. 230. (I have adjusted the time to Allied or Solomons Island time.)
15 M. A. Payne, *HMAS Canberra*, Naval Historical Society, Sydney, 1973, p. 87.
16 Bruce Loxton, *The Shame of Savo*, Allen & Unwin, Sydney, 1994, p. 98.
17 M. A. Payne, *HMAS Australia*, Naval Historical Society, Sydney, 1988, p. 101.
18 Eugene McClarty, *Pearl Harbor to Tokyo and Beyond*, Southwood Press, Sydney, 2003, p. 29.
19 War Diary, USS *Hunter Liggett*, 8 August 1942, quoted in Dyer, *The Amphibians Came to Conquer*, p. 351.
20 John Lundstrom, *Black Shoe Carrier Admiral, Frank Jack Fletcher at Coral Sea, Midway & Guadalcanal*, Naval Institute Press, Annapolis, Maryland, 2006, p. 435.
21 Vandegrift, p. 128.
22 Ibid., p. 128.
23 Evans, p. 230.
24 Ibid., p. 235.

CHAPTER 17: THE UNSPEAKABLE BLOODINESS MY SHOCKED EYES TOOK IN

1   About 550 metres.
2   Looking a little like a rifle, the blinker tube projected a bright but very carefully directed beam of light for signalling.
3   Bruce Loxton, *The Shame of Savo*, Allen & Unwin, Sydney, 1994, p. xxv.

4 T. M. Jones and Ion L. Idriess, *The Silent Service*, Angus & Robertson, Sydney, 1944, p. 328.

5 Samuel Eliot Morison, *The Two Ocean War*, Naval Institute Press, Annapolis, Maryland, 1963, p. 176.

6 Surgeon Lieutenant Kenneth Morris, personal papers, AWM PR82/086.

7 Stoker Jack Oliver Rozynski, personal papers, AWM PRO1715.

8 M. A. Payne, *HMAS Canberra*, Naval Historical Society, p. 103; Loxton, p. 189.

9 G. Hermon Gill, *Australia in the War of 1939–1945*, Series 2, Vol 2, RAN 1942–1945, Australian War Memoria, Canberra, 1968, p. 151.

10 Ibid.

11 Bruce Loxton, private papers.

12 Ibid.

13 *The Argus*, 21 August 1942.

14 *The Sydney Morning Herald*, 21 August 1942.

15 His career would continue to soar. Regarded as the founder of the RAN's Fleet Air Arm, he became Chairman of the Chiefs of Staff committee and retired as Admiral Sir Victor Smith in 1975, the first graduate of the RANC to reach four-star rank.

16 *The Australian Women's Weekly*, 5 September 1942.

17 Loxton, private papers.

18 Loxton, *The Shame of Savo*, p. xxvi.

19 Ibid., p. 258.

20 Ibid., p. 267.

21 Victor Crutchley to Arthur Hepburn, letter, 21 February 1943, quoted in Shanks, Sandy, *The Bode Testament*, Writers Club Press, Bloomington, Indiana, 2001, p. 506.

22 Winston Churchill, *The Second World War, Vol. IV, The Hinge of Fate*, p. 237.

23 Ibid., p. 460.

CHAPTER 18: YOU HAVE BROUGHT TO AUSTRALIA AN ACCESSION OF NAVAL STRENGTH

1 Quoted in Vic Cassells, *The Capital Ships*, Kangaroo Press, Sydney, 2000, p. 129.

2 Royalty actually had a say. They were, after all, His Majesty's ships. An outraged George V once knocked back a proposal from Winston Churchill to name a battleship after the regicide Oliver Cromwell, and – worried about the navy's love of rhyming slang – he also vetoed HMS *Pitt*.

3 *HMAS Mk II*, Australian War Memorial, 1943, p. 67.

4 *Porthole: A Souvenir of HMAS Shropshire*, various writers, John Sands, Sydney, 1946, p. 12.

5 Australia 9 – England 3, three tries to one.

6   Collins, p. 129.

7   *The Canberra Times*, 8 October 1943.

8   John L. Zimmerman, *Marines in World War II*, *The Guadalcanal Campaign*, USMCR Historical Section, Division of Public Information Headquarters, U.S. Marine Corps, 1949, Appendix A.

9   *The Courier-Mail* (Brisbane), 28 April 1954.

10   Stanley Weintraub, *15 Stars: Eisenhower, MacArthur, Marshall*, Simon & Schuster, New York, 2007, p. 133.

11   Andrew Spaull, 'Dedman, John Johnstone (1896–1973)', *Australian Dictionary of Biography*, National Centre of Biography, Australian National University, 1993, http://adb.anu.edu.au/biography/dedman-john-johnstone-303/text17607.

12   *The Sydney Morning Herald*, 21 September 1943.

13   *The Examiner* (Launceston), 2 August 1943.

14   *Army News* (Darwin), 2 June 1943.

15   *The Sydney Morning Herald*, 3 September 1943.

16   *Adelaide News*, 11 August 1943.

17   Ellen Savage, quoted on 'The Sinking of the Centaur', Australian Government, Department of Veterans' Affairs, http://www.anzacportal.dva.gov.au/history/publications/sinking-centaur/sister-ellen-savage-gm-aans.

18   Only when the official Japanese history was published in 1979 did it become known that *I-177* had sunk the *Centaur*. Nakagawa was tried as a war criminal and sentenced to six years in jail after the war, but that was for another crime in which he machine-gunned British survivors in the Indian Ocean. Nakagawa refused ever to speak about the *Centaur*, and died in 1991.

19   G. Hermon Gill, *Australia in the War of 1939–1945*, Series 2, Vol 2, RAN 1942–1945, Australian War Memorial, 1968, p. 267.

20   Ibid.

21   *HMAS Mk III*, Australian War Memorial.

22   E. B. Potter, *Bull Halsey*, Naval Institute Press, Annapolis, Maryland, 1985, p. 215.

23   Ibid., p. 216.

24   HMAS *Hobart*, report of proceedings, August 1943, AWM 78, 141/1, September 1939–November 1947.

25   R. G. Parker, 'The Torpedoing of HMAS *Hobart* 1942', Naval Historical Society of Australia, www.navyhistory.org.au/the-torpedoing-of-hmas-hobart-1942.

CHAPTER 19: WE'RE GOING INTO TIGER COUNTRY

1   Stanley Nicholls, *HMAS Shropshire*, NHSA, Sydney, 1989, p. 63.

2   *Porthole*, p. 19. Pusser's Duff was a steamed pudding, usually made with suet.

3   *History of US Marine Corps Operations in World War II*, chapter 3, 'Isolation of Rabaul', p. 352, www.ibiblio.org/hyperwar/USMC/II/USMC-II-IV-3.html.

4   E. B. Potter, *Nimitz*, Naval Institute Press, Annapolis, Maryland, 2008, p. 291.

5   Although not entirely. Private Teruo Nakamura fought on, to be captured by the Indonesian Air Force only in December 1974, the last Japanese soldier of the war.

6   G. Hermon Gill, *Australia in the War of 1939–1945*, Series 2, Vol 2, RAN 1942–1945, Australian War Memorial, 1968, p. 435.

7   *Australian Women's Weekly*, 16 September 1944.

8   *Attacker* had an extraordinary career. After a massive conversion in 1957, she became the passenger liner *Fairsky*, carrying European migrants to Australia.

9   David Hamer, *Memories of My Life*, self-published, Melbourne, p. 170.

10   Ibid.

11   Called A-Day to avoid any confusion with D-Day, the Normandy landing.

12   Robert C. Stern, *Fire from the Sky*, Seaforth Publishing, Barnsley, England, 2010, p. 34.

13   Denis and Peggy Warner, *Kamikaze: The Sacred Warriors 1944–45*, Oxford University Press, Melbourne, 1983, p. 75.

14   'Motoori Norinaga: A Scholar-Physician Who Loved Cherry Blossoms', *The East*, Vol. XXVI, No. 1, www.norinagakinenkan.com/norinaga/shiryo/about.html.

15   Nicholls, p. 112.

16   Ibid.

17   Sir John Collins, *As Luck Would Have It*, Angus & Robertson, Sydney, 1965, p. 152.

18   Douglas MacArthur, 'To the people of the Philippines', reproduced by Veterans Community Relations Team MacArthur Forum, Milwaukee, 2013, www.macarthurmilwaukeeforum.com/resources/speech-to-the-people-of-the-phillipines/

CHAPTER 20: I HAVE BEEN GIVEN A SPLENDID OPPORTUNITY TO DIE

1   G. Hermon Gill, *Australia in the War of 1939–1945*, Series 2, Vol 2, RAN 1942–1945. Australian War Memorial, 1968, p. 512.

2   Recording, Dechaineux family private papers.

3   Jack Langrell, interview with the author, June 2015.

4   *The Newcastle Sun*, 28 October 1944.

5   David Hamer, *Memories of My Life*, self-published, Melbourne, p. 179.

6   Ibid., p. 180.

7   Mackenzie Gregory, Australians at War Film Archive, No. 0071, Department of Veterans Affairs, Canberra.

8   Chan Redding, c.o. Arthur Cooper, 'HMAS *Shropshire*', Ahoy – Mac's Web Log, http://www.ahoy.tk-jk.net/GentlemansCordite/Avividaccountofthere-capt.html.

9   Gill, Vol 2, p. 524.

10 Chan Redding, c.o. Arthur Cooper, 'HMAS *Shropshire*', Ahoy – Mac's Weblog, http://www.ahoy.tk-jk.net/GentlemansCordite/Avividaccountofthere-capt.html.

11 Stanley Nicholls, *HMAS Shropshire*, NHSA, 1989, p. 139.

12 Action Report, USS *Kalinin Bay*, CVE-68, 30 October 1944.

13 Action Report, USS *St Lo*, CVE-63, 31 October 1944.

14 Richard Centner, 'Statement', c.o. Chris Centner, The Battle of Samar, www.bosamar.com/pages/centner.

15 'The Last Wills the Special Attack Force Pilots Wrote', Kamikaze, 5 December 2004, www.geocities.jp/kamikazes_site_e/isyo.html.

CHAPTER 21: ALL GUNS OPENED FIRE BUT HE STILL CAME ON

1   David Mattiske, *Fire Across the Pacific*, self-published, Queensland, 2000, Appendix 8.

2   Quoted in *Headmark*, Journal of the Australian Naval Institute, Canberra, Issue 141, September 2011, p. 65.

3   Lieutenant Gerald R. Ford USNR was very nearly washed overboard from the damaged carrier *Monterey*. He lived to become the 38th President of the United States.

4   Interview with Clarke, in Armstrong private papers, NLA, MS 9675 and ID 1603085.

5   Ibid.

6   Jack Langrell, interview with the author, June 2015.

7   Stanley Nicholls, *HMAS Shropshire*, NHSA, 1989, p. 157.

8   Interview with Clark, in Armstrong private papers.

9   Mackenzie Gregory, 'Kamikaze attack', Ahoy – Mac's Web Log, Naval, Maritime, Australian History and more (website) http://ahoy.tk-jk.net/macslog/KamakazeAttack.html.

10 Ibid.

11 *Australian in the War of 1939–45*, Series 5 – Medical, Vol. IV, AWM, Canberra, 1961, p. 161.

12 David Hamer, *Memories of My Life*, self-published, Melbourne, p. 184.

13 Des Shinkfield, *HMAS Australia*, self-published, 2002, p. 161.

14 Armstrong private papers.

15 *The Daily Examiner* (Grafton), 15 February 1945.

16 Hamer, p. 188.

CHAPTER 22: O LORD, THOU KNOWEST HOW BUSY WE ARE TODAY

1   *The New York Times*, 9 June 1945.

2   *The News* (Adelaide), 20 June 1945.

3   *The Advertiser*, 23 June 1945.

4   *The New York Times*, 21 June 1945.

5   'Reports of Proceedings, HMA Ships and Establishments: HMAS *Australia*', AWM78, item 44/5, January 1945–February 1946, Australian War Memorial, https://static.awm.gov.au/images/collection/bundled/RCDIG1073237.pdf.

6   This affair rumbled on for another year. The British Dominion Secretary, a Labour peer, Lord Addison, told McKell that George VI wanted the job to go to the Queen's brother, the Hon. Michael Bowes-Lyon, and, to put the pressure on, this was leaked to the Australian press. McKell refused to accept another Englishman, no matter how blue-blooded, but had to concede defeat on Armstrong and, instead, got the appointment of an Australian Army officer, Lieutenant General John Northcott.

7   David Hamer, *Memories of My Life*, self-published, Melbourne, p. 190.

8   Winston Churchill, *The Second World War, Vol. VI, Triumph and Tragedy*, p. 583.

9   David Day, *Curtin: A Life*, HarperCollins, Sydney, 1999, p. 575.

10 Paul Hasluck, *Australia in the War of 1939–1945, Series 4 – Civil, Vol. II – The Government and the People, 1942–1945*, 1970, p. 590.

11 Hamer, p. 191.

12 Ibid., p. 192.

13 Rear Admiral Guy Griffiths, interview with author, July 2015.

14 David Mattiske, *Fire Across the Pacific*, self-published, Queensland, 2000, p. 112.

15 *The Sydney Morning Herald*, 24 March 1945.

16 Mattiske, p. 198.

17 Australia-Japan Research Project http://ajrp.awm.gov.au/.

18 *Porthole*, various authors, John Sands, Sydney, 1946, p. 44.

19 https://static.awm.gov.au/images/collection/pdf/RCDIG1070720--1-.pdf.

20 Mark Schreiber, 'The Top-Secret Flights That Ended the War', *The Japan Times*, 1 August 2015, www.japantimes.co.jp/news/2015/08/01/national/history/top-secret-flights-ended-war#.VePBo-Louow.

21 C. Peter Chen, 'Takijiro Onishi', Archive.Is, http://archive.is/anZC.

22 John Toland, *The Rising Sun*, Random House, New York, 1970, p. 835.

CHAPTER 23: THEIR SACRIFICE WAS NOT IN VAIN

1 G. Hermon Gill, *Australia in the War of 1939–1945*, Series 2, Vol 2, RAN 1942–1945, AWM, 1968, p. 676.
2 *Porthole*, various authors, John Sands, Sydney, 1946, p. 55.
3 HMAS *Ballarat*, Report of Proceedings, AWM, 78 49/1, December 1942–January 1946.
4 Quoted in John Toland, *The Rising Sun*, Random House, New York, 1970, p. 870.
5 David Mattiske, *Fire Across the Pacific*, self-published, Queensland, p. 126.
6 She did not, but she was infuriated that Astor had demanded she leave the House of Commons.
7 *The Advocate* (Burnie), 13 December 1945.
8 Later awarded the George Cross.
9 Quoted in Stanley Nicholls, *HMAS Shropshire*, NHSA, 1989, p. 266.
10 Ibid., p. 267.
11 Tom Thurlow, private papers.

CHAPTER 24: THE ROYAL AUSTRALIAN NAVY HAS DONE IT AGAIN

1 *The Sydney Morning Herald*, 1 October 1954.
2 *The News* (Adelaide), 16 February 1954.
3 *The Navy*, July 1949.
4 George Oldham, HMAS *Australia*, Report of Proceedings, August 1950, AWM, 78 44/6, May 1947–December 1950.
5 Ibid.
6 *The News* (Adelaide), 10 August 1950.
7 Oldham, Report of Proceedings, August 1950.
8 Collins to Navy Minister, Report of Proceedings, AWM, 78 44/6, May 1947–December 1950, 10 November 1950.
9 *The Newcastle Morning Herald*, 7 December 1953.
10 *The Sydney Morning Herald*, 3 June 1954.
11 Ibid., 11 June 1954.
12 *The Methodist*, 26 June 1954.
13 *The Advertiser*, 1 June 1954.
14 Now in Cumbria.

APPENDIX: THE LEGAL CAMPAIGN FOR THE RELEASE OF ALBERT RONALD GORDON AND EDWARD JOSEPH ELIAS, FORMER STOKERS ON HMAS *AUSTRALIA*

1   Commander Rupert Long to the Naval Board, note, National Archives of Australia, NAA B6121, 123V, p. 18.
2   Malcolm Stening, *The Class of '35 at War*, the Naval Historical Society of Australia, Sydney, 2002.
3   Report of the Maxwell Commission, National Archives of Australia, NAA B6121, 123V, p. 227.
4   Ibid., p. 228.
5   James Goldrick, RADM, 'The *Australia* Court Martial of 1942', Masters Thesis, University of New England, Armidale, 1984.

BIBLIOGRAPHY

BOOKS

Baratieri, Daniela, Mark Edele and Giuseppe Finaldi, *Totalitarian Dictatorship: New Histories*, Routledge, 2013

Barnett, Corelli, *Engage the Enemy More Closely*, Hodder & Stoughton, London, 1991

Bastock, John, *Australia's Ships of War*, Angus & Robertson, Sydney, 1975

Bloch, Michael, *Ribbentrop*, Crown Publishers, New York, 1992

Brady, Edwin, *Australia Unlimited*, George Robertson, Melbourne, 1918

Buell, Thomas B., *Master of Seapower*, Ernest J. King (ed.), Naval Institute Press, Annapolis, Maryland, 2012

Burrell, Sir Henry, *Mermaids Do Exist*, Macmillan, Sydney, 1986

Carlton, Mike, *Cruiser: The Life and Loss of HMAS Perth and Her Crew*, William Heinemann, Sydney, 2010

——*First Victory, 1914: HMAS Sydney's Hunt for the German Raider Emden*, William Heinemann, Sydney, 2013

Cassells, Vic, *The Capital Ships*, Kangaroo Press, Sydney, 2000

Choules, Claude, *The Last of the Last*, Hesperian Press, Perth, 2009

Churchill, Sir Winston, *The Second World War, Vol. I, The Gathering Storm*, Houghton Mifflin, New York, 1948

——*The Second World War, Vol. II, Their Finest Hour*, Houghton Mifflin, & Co., Boston, 1949

——*The Second World War, Vol. III, The Grand Alliance*, Houghton Mifflin & Co., Boston, 1950

——*The Second World War, Vol. IV, The Hinge of Fate*, Houghton Mifflin & Co., Boston, 1950

——*The Second World War, Vol. V, Closing the Ring*, Houghton Mifflin, New York, 1951

——*The Second World War, Vol. VI, Triumph and Tragedy*, Houghton Mifflin, New York, 1953

Clemens, Martin, *Alone on Guadalcanal*, Naval Institute Press, Annapolis, Maryland, 1998

Collins, Sir John, *As Luck Would Have It*, Angus & Robertson, Sydney, 1965

Coulthard-Clark, Chris, *Action Stations Coral Sea*, Allen & Unwin, Sydney, 1991

——*Where Australians Fought*, Allen & Unwin, Sydney, 1998

Day, David, *Curtin: A Life*, Harper Collins, Sydney, 1999

Dull, Paul S., *The Imperial Japanese Navy 1941–1945*, Naval Institute Press, Annapolis, Maryland, 1978

Dyer, George C., *The Amphibians Came to Conquer*, US Navy, 1972

Eldridge, F. B., *A History of the Royal Australian Naval College*, Georgian House, Melbourne, 1949

Evans, David C. (ed.), *The Japanese Navy in World War II*, Naval Institute Press, Annapolis, Maryland, 1969

Feakes, Captain Henry James, *White Ensign, Southern Cross*, Ure Smith, Sydney, 1951

Feldt, Eric, *The Coast Watchers*, Oxford University Press, Melbourne, 1946

Firkins, Peter, *Of Nautilus and Eagles*, Cassell, Sydney, 1975

Frame, Tom, *No Pleasure Cruise: The Story of the Royal Australian Navy*, Allen & Unwin, Sydney, 2004

—— (et al.), *Reflections on the RAN*, Kangaroo Press, Sydney, 1991

—— and Kevin Baker, *Mutiny*, Allen & Unwin, Sydney, 2000

Freudenberg, Graham, *Churchill and Australia*, Macmillan, Sydney, 2008

Gatacre, G. G. O., *Reports of Proceedings*, Nautical Press, Sydney, 1982

Gill, G. Hermon, *Australia in the War of 1939–1945*, Series 2, Vol. 1, RAN 1939–42, Australian War Memorial Canberra, 1957

——*Australia in the War of 1939–1945*, Series 2, Vol, 1. RAN 1942–1945, Australian War Memorial, Canberra, 1968

Grazebrook, A. W., 'First to a Flag: The Life of Rear Admiral H. B. Farncomb', an essay in *Reflections on the RAN*, Kangaroo Press, Sydney, 1991

Greene, J. and Massignani, A., *The Naval War in the Mediterranean*, Naval Institute Press, Annapolis, Maryland, 2011

Grose, Peter, *A Very Rude Awakening*, Allen & Unwin, Sydney, 2007

Hamer, David, *Bombers versus Battleships*, Allen & Unwin, Sydney, 1998

——*Memories of My Life*, self-published, Melbourne, 2002

Hara, Captain Tameichi, *Japanese Destroyer Captain*, Ballantine Books, New York, 1958

Hornfischer, James D., *Neptune's Inferno: The US Navy at Guadalcanal*, Bantam Books, New York, 2012

Ishimaru, Tota, *Japan Must Fight Britain*, Paternoster, London, 1936

Johnston, Dr Mark, *Australia's Home Defence 1939-45*, Department of Veterans' Affairs, Canberra, 2006

Johnston, Stanley, *Queen of the Flat Tops*, Jarrolds, London, 1942

Jones, Ray, *Seagulls, Cruisers and Catapults*, Pelorus Publications, Hobart, 1989

Jones, T. M. and Idriess, Ion L., *The Silent Service*, Angus & Robertson, Sydney, 1944

Jordan, John and Robert Dumas, *French Battleships 1922–1956*, Seaforth, London, 2009

Keats, Brennan, *Quiet Waters*, Wirripang Publishing, Wollongong, 2008

Kershaw, Ian, *Hitler: Hubris*, Penguin, London, 1998

Lavery, Brian, *Churchill's Navy*, Conway Maritime Press, London, 2006

Lewis, Tom, *The Submarine Six*, Avonmore Books, South Australia, 2011

Lind, Lew, *The Royal Australian Navy Year by Year*, Reed Books, Sydney, 2006

Lindsay, Patrick, *The Coastwatchers*, William Heinemann, Sydney, 2010

Loxton, Bruce, *The Shame of Savo*, Allen & Unwin, Sydney, 1994

Lundstrom, John, *Black Shoe Carrier Admiral. Frank Jack Fletcher at Coral Sea, Midway & Guadalcanal*, Naval Institute Press, Annapolis, Maryland, 2006

——*The First South Pacific Campaign 1941–42*, Naval Institute Press, Annapolis, Maryland, 1976

——*The First Team and the Guadalcanal Campaign*, Naval Institute Press, Annapolis, Maryland, 1994

MacArthur, Douglas, *Reminiscences*, Naval Institute Press, Annapolis, Maryland, 1964

Mattiske, David, *Fire Across the Pacific*, self-published, Queensland, 2000

McCandie, G. L., *Genesis of the Royal Australia Navy*, Government Printer, Sydney, 1949

McClarty, Eugene, *Pearl Harbor to Tokyo and Beyond*, Southwood Press, Sydney, 2003

McGuire, Frances, *The Royal Australian Navy*, Oxford University Press, Melbourne, 1947

Menzies, Robert Gordon, *Dark and Hurrying Days*, National Library of Australia, Canberra, 1993

Morison, Samuel Eliot, *The Rising Sun in the Pacific*, University of Illinois Press, Chicago, 2001

——*The Two Ocean War*, Naval Institute Press, Annapolis, Maryland, 1963

Nicholls, Stanley, *HMAS Shropshire*, Naval Historical Society of Australia, 1989

Nicholson, Arthur, *Hostages to Fortune*, Sutton Publishing, Stroud, England, 2005

Payne, M. A., *HMAS Australia*, Naval Historical Society, Sydney, 1988

——*HMAS Canberra*, Naval Historical Society, Sydney, 1973

Pfenningwerth, Ian, *The Australian Cruiser Perth*, Rosenberg Publishing, Sydney, 2007

——*A Man of Intelligence*, Rosenberg Publishing, Sydney, 2006

——*The Royal Australian Navy and MacArthur*, Rosenberg Publishing, Sydney, 2009

Potter, E. B., *Bull Halsey*, Naval Institute Press, Annapolis, Maryland, 1985

——*Nimitz*, Naval Institute Press, Annapolis, Maryland, 2008

Shinkfield, Des, *HMAS Australia*, self-published, 2002

Smith, George W., *The Do or Die Men: The 1st Marine Raider Battalion at Guadalcanal*, Simon & Schuster, New York, 2003

Stanley, Peter, *Invading Australia*, Penguin, Melbourne, 2008

Stening, Malcolm, *The Class of '35 at War*, Naval Historical Society of Australia, Sydney, 2002

Stern, Robert C., *Fire from the Sky*, Seaforth Publishing, Barnsley, England, 2010

Stevens, David, *The Royal Australian Navy: A History*, Oxford University Press, Melbourne, 2001

—— (ed.), *The RAN in World War II*, Allen & Unwin, Sydney, 1996

Taylor, Bruce, *The End of Glory*, Seaforth Publishing, Barnsley, England, 2012

Taylor, Peter, *A Sailor's Life*, self-published, Perth, 2010

Thompson, Peter, *Pacific Fury*, William Heinemann, Sydney, 2008

Thompson, Peter and Robert Macklin, *The Battle of Brisbane*, ABC Books, Sydney, 2000

Toland, John, *The Rising Sun*, Random House, New York, 1970

Twining, Merrill B., *No Bended Knee: The Battle for Guadalcanal*, Presidio Press, Novato, California, 1996

Van der Vat, Dan, *The Pacific Campaign*, Simon & Schuster, New York, 1991

Vandegrift, A. A., *Once a Marine*, Bantam Books, New York, 1964

Warner, Denis and Peggy, *Kamikaze: The Sacred Warriors 1944–45*, Oxford University Press, Melbourne, 1983

Weintraub, Stanley, *15 Stars: Eisenhower, MacArthur, Marshall*, Simon & Schuster, New York, 2007

Williams, John, *The Guns of Dakar*, Heinemann, London, 1976

Williams, John L., *USS Bagley: The Waters Aft*, USS Bagley Association, Laguna Niguel, California, 1992

OFFICIAL HISTORIES AND PUBLICATIONS

Butlin, C. J., Hasluck, Paul, Mellor, P., Schedvin, C. B., *Australia in the War of 1939–1945, Series 1 – Army, Series 2 – Navy, Series 3 – Air, Series 4 – Civil, Series 5 – Medical*, Australian War Memorial, Canberra, 1958–1977

The Evacuation from Dunkirk: Operation Dynamo, Ministry of Defence, London, 1949

The Gunnery Pocket Book, Admiralty Gunnery Branch, London, 1945, B.R. 224/45

HMAS *Hobart*, Report of Proceedings, August 1943

HMAS *Mk I*, Australian War Memorial, Canberra

HMAS *Mk II*, Australian War Memorial, Canberra, 1943

HMAS *Mk III*, Australian War Memorial, Canberra, 1944

HMAS *Mk IV*, Australian War Memorial, Canberra

Jellicoe, Viscount, *Report of the Naval Mission to the Commonwealth*, Government Printer, Melbourne, 1919

Jose, Arthur Wilberforce, *Official History of Australia in the War of 1914–18: Vol. IX – The Royal Australian Navy, 1914–1918*, Australian War Memorial, Canberra, 1941

Manual of Seamanship, HMSO, London, 1940

Morison, Samuel Eliot, *History of United States Naval Operations in World War II*, Vol. 3, University of Illinois Press, Chicago, 2001

Porthole: A Souvenir of HMAS Shropshire, various writers, John Sands, Sydney, 1946

Report of the Maxwell Commission, National Archives of Australia, NAA B6121, 123V

The Royal Navy Officers' Pocket Book, The Admiralty, London, 1944

A Seaman's Pocket Book, The Admiralty, London, 1943

War Diary, *USS Hunter Liggett*

Zimmerman, Major John L., *Marines in World War II, The Guadalcanal Campaign*, USMCR Historical Section, Division of Public Information Headquarters, US Marine Corps 1949

ARTICLES AND THESES

Goldrick, James RADM (ret), 'The *Australia* Court Martial of 1942', Masters Thesis, University of New England, Armidale, 1984

K. R. B., *The Naval Review*, Vol. XXX, No. 3, August 1942

Naval History Magazine, Vol. 6, No. 2, Summer 1992, United States Naval Institute

NEWSPAPERS, JOURNALS AND MAGAZINES

Adelaide News, *The Advocate* (Burnie), *Aircraft*, *The Argus*, *Army News* (Darwin), *The Australasian*, *The Australian Worker*, *The Barrier Miner* (Broken Hill), *Brisbane Courier*, *The Bulletin*, *The Cairns Post*, *The Canberra Times*, *Country Life Stock and Station Journal*, *The Courier-Mail* (Brisbane), *The Daily Examiner* (Grafton), *Daily Express*, *The Daily Herald*, *Daily Mail*, *Daily News* (Perth), *The Evening News* (Sydney), *The Examiner* (Launceston), *The Farmer & Settler* (Sydney), *The Glasgow Herald*, *Goulburn Herald*, *The Herald* (Melbourne), *The Japan Times*, *The London Gazette*, *Mercury* (Hobart), *The Methodist*, *The Morning Bulletin* (Rockhampton), *The Naval Review*, *The Navy*, *The New York Times*, *The Newcastle Morning Herald*, *The Newcastle Sun*, *The News* (Adelaide), *The Queanbeyan Age*, *Spectator and*

Methodist Chronicle, *The Sunday Times* (Western Australia), *The Sydney Mail*, *The Sydney Morning Herald*, *The Times*, *Townsville Daily Bulletin*, *Truth* (Melbourne), *The West Australian*, *Westralian Worker*, *The Worker* (Brisbane)

PRIVATE PAPERS, DIARIES AND ARCHIVES

Armstrong, John, private papers, NLA MS 9675 and ID 1603085
Blau, Edgar, private papers, AWM PR03441
Dechaineux family, private papers
Elias–Gordon Court Martial, National Archives Australia, NAA B6121, 123V
Jay, Philip, 'Musings of a Matelot', AWM MSS 1083
Keats, Russell, private papers
Loxton, Bruce, private papers
Morris, Surgeon Lieutenant Kenneth, private papers, AWM PR82/086
Parker, Alan, Midshipman's Journal, in the possession of the author
Rosynski, Stoker Jack Oliver, private papers, AWM PR01715
Thurlow, Tom, private papers

INTERVIEWS WITH THE AUTHOR

Campbell, Gavin, January 2015
Geddes, Eric, 2014
Griffiths, Guy, Rear Admiral, July 2015
Langrell, Jack, February, March and June 2015

ONLINE SOURCES

Australia-Japan Research Project, http://ajrp.awm.gov.au/
Australian Government Department of Foreign Affairs and Trade, 'Historical Documents', Vol. 1, 1937–38, Vol. 2, 1939, www.info.dfat. gov.au/info/historical/HistDocs
Bebbington, Warren A., 'Keats, Horace Stanley (1895–1945)', *Australian Dictionary of Biography*, National Centre of Biography, Australian National University, 1983, http://adb.anu.edu.au/biography/keats-horace-stanley-6906/text11981
Centner, Richard, 'Statement', c.o. Chris Centner, The Battle of Samar, www.bosamar.com/pages/centner
Chen, C. Peter, 'Takijiro Onishi', Archive.Is, http://archive.is/anZC
Gill, J. C. H., 'Feldt, Eric Augustas (1899–1968)', *Australian Dictionary of Biography*, National Centre of Biography, Australian National University, 1996, http://adb.anu.edu.au/biography/feldt-eric-augustas-10163/text17953
Gregory, Mackenzie, Ahoy – Mac's Web Log, 1984, http://ahoy.tk-jk.net

Griffin, James, 'Mason, Paul Edward (1901–1972)', *Australian Diction-ary of Biography*, National Centre of Biography, Australian National University,2000,http://adb.anu.edu.au/biography/mason-paul-edward-11081/text19725

Holden, Jerry (ed.), 'USS Lexington, Action Report, 15 May 1942', HyperWar Foundation, 8 February 2003, www.ibiblio.org/hyperwar/USN/ships/logs/CV/CV2-Coral.html

'The Last Wills the Special Attack Force Pilots Wrote', Kamikaze (website), 5 December 2004, www.geocities.jp/kamikazes_site_e/isyo.html

'Motoori Norinaga: A Scholar-Physician Who Loved Cherry Blossoms', *The East*, Vol. XXVI, No. 1, www.norinagakinenkan.com/norinaga/shiryo/about.html

Naval Historical Society of Australia, 'Captain Joseph Burnett RAN', https://www.navyhistory.org.au/captain-joseph-burnett-ran/3

Parker, R. G., 'The Torpedoing of HMAS *Hobart* 1942', Naval Historical SocietyofAustralia,www.navyhistory.org.au/the-torpedoing-of-hmas-hobart-1942

Redding, Chan, c.o. Arthur Cooper, 'HMAS *Shropshire*', Ahoy – Mac's Weblog, http://www.ahoy.tk-jk.net/GentlemansCordite/Avivid accountofthere-capt.html

'Reports of Proceedings, HMA Ships and Establishments: HMAS *Australia*', AWM78, item 44/5, January 1945–February 1946, Austra-lian War Memorial, https://static.awm.gov.au/images/collection/bundled/RCDIG1073237.pdf

Savage, Ellen, quoted on 'The Sinking of the Centaur', Australian Govern-ment, Department of Veterans' Affairs, http://www.anzacportal.dva.gov.au/history/publications/sinking-centaur/sister-ellen-savage-gm-aans

Schreiber, Mark, 'The Top-Secret Flights That Ended the War', *The Japan Times*, 1 August 2015, www.japantimes.co.jp/news/2015/08/01/national/history/top-secret-flights-ended-war#.VePB0-Louow

Spaull, Andrew, 'Dedman, John Johnstone (1896–1973)', *Australian Diction-ary of Biography*, National Centre of Biography, Australian National University, 1993, http://adb.anu.edu.au/biography/dedman-john-johnstone-303/text17607

Straczek, Jozef, 'Battle of the Coral Sea', Navy, www.navy.gov.au

Weadon, Patrick D., 'The Battle of Midway', National Security Agency, Central Security Service, 15 January 2009, www.nsa.gov/about/cryptologic_heritage/center_crypt_history/publications/battle_midway.shtml

INDEX

1st AIF 135
2nd AIF 135, 137, 141–143
2nd AIF 2/12th Field Ambulance
410–412
2nd AIF 3rd Division 422
2nd AIF 6th Division 204–206,
222–223, 224, 526
2nd AIF 7th Division 234, 422
2nd AIF 8th Division 234
2nd AIF 9th Division 222, 401, 422,
512
25th Air Flotilla (IJN)
attacks on Allies in Jomard Passage
290–298
Guadalcanal 352, 353–354, 359–360
Operation MO 278–279

A

Abbott, Tony 560
ABDA (Americans, British, Dutch and
Australians) 232, 234, 235
Abyssinian Empire, Italy invades
99–100
Adelaide 528
Adelaide River Stakes 234
Admiral Graf Spee 133–135, 175
Admiral Scheer 134, 135, 187, 213–214,
220, 257
Admiralty Islands 422, 427–428
Advisory War Council 194, 224
Africa Shell 134
Afrikakorps 206, 222, 391
l'Afrique occidentale française 160,
168–169
aircraft navigation 301
Akagi 331
Albert, Otto 50

Alcorn, Chaplain Cyril 472
Alderman, Kelvin John 494
Alderman, Noel 494
Alderman, Stuart 494
Aleutian Islands 329
Alexandria 98, 99, 100, 160
Allen, Darby 64
Allied Control Commission,
Germany 526
Allied Expeditionary Force,
Operation Watchtower 339–345
Allied Naval Expeditionary Force
155–156
Allied shipping 163, 214
Altmark (tanker) 133
American Civil War 124
American East Coast shipping
337–338
Amerika 144
Andes 142
Anglo Australian Squadron 6
Anglo–German Friendship Society
40
Anglo–German Naval Agreement
95–96, 106
Antarctic medical rescue mission
542–549
Anti-Comintern Pact 105
Anzac Club 499
Anzac Cove 101
Anzac Force 243–244, 248, 250, 252,
280 *see also* Task Force 44
Anzac force 117, 135
Aoba 366–367, 376
appeasement 96, 99–100, 103,
106–107, 112
Appleroth, Adolphus 73

Aquitania 142, 208
Arcadia Conference 232
Arctic Ocean 391–392
Arita, Hachiro 104
Armstrong, Commander John Malet
('Jamie,' 'Black Jack')
awards 495, 505
background 126, 455
barrack stanchions to Britain
497–498
HMAS *Australia II*, captain 455
HMAS *Australia II*, executive
officer 172, 175, 185, 186, 242
HMS *Ruler* 505
Lingayen Gulf 483, 493
New York Harbor 496, 498–500
Stoker Riley court martial 264
Stoker Riley murder 259–261
Sunderland P9620 185–186, 501
Victory Cricket Tests 504
Ashley-Brown, Lieutenant Guy 170,
359–360
Ashton, Julian 148
Astley, Sir Jacob 506
Astor, Lady and Viscount 527
Athenia 119–120
Athol Bight 529, 539
Atlantic Ocean Theatre 136–137, 213,
220–221, 500
Atlantis 207, 216
atomic bomb 497, 516
Attlee, Clement 234, 502
Austin, John 230–231
Australia
American troops in 308–309,
403–404
attitudes to British royalty 61
Britain and threat from Japan
33–34, 107–108
Britain claims right to sign
surrender for 522
Combined Operational Intelligence
Centre 280
declares war on Germany 112,
113–114
Duke of Gloucester's tour 87, 88–90
Far Eastern Imperial Fleet
(proposed) 30–31
Great Depression 70–72

Japanese midget submarines in
Sydney Harbour 322–327, 328
Japanese plans to invade 103–104,
108, 275–276
Japanese relations 31–33 *see also*
White Australia Policy
Japanese submarines along east
coast 409–410
Japanese surrender 521–522
nominates MacArthur to command
in Pacific 237
offer of RAN to Britain 119–120
Pacific colonies 31
reaction to abdication of Edward
VIII 102
reaction to George V's death 102
reaction to Operation Menace
178–180
reaction to sinking of *Canberra*
384–385
reserve on Admiralty control over
RAN 119
Singapore conference (1940)
194–195
in South-West Pacific Area 243
Spee's plans to attack 6
Statute of Westminster, failure to
ratify 569–570
threat from Germany 134–135
United States and threat from Japan
233–234
Washington Naval Treaty 11–12,
18, 34
Australia Unlimited (Brady) 21–22
Australian Army 540–541
Australian Broadcasting Commission
72–73, 311–312, 406, 545
Australian Defence Force 540–541
Australian Imperial Forces *see* 1st AIF;
2nd AIF
Australian Labor Party 72, 194, 245,
270, 404–405, 571
Australian National Airways 238
Australian Naval Board 80, 81, 109,
118, 136, 142, 178, 207, 219,
240–241, 243, 269, 285, 454, 505,
554
Australian Navy Office 117, 120–123,
262, 268, 414

Australian Victory Contingent 529–534

Australian War Cabinet 239

Australian Women's Weekly 432–433

Australian Workers' Union 69

Austria 106

automation 559

AWA (Amalgamated Wireless (Australasia) Ltd) 122

B

B-17 Flying Fortresses 297, 315

Backhouse, Admiral Sir Roger 118–119

Bader, Douglas 534

Badoglio, Pietro 99

BAE 558

Baird, Carola 129, 130

Balikpapan 513–515

Ban, Sub Lieutenant Katsuhisa 326

Bank of England 71

Banque de France 169

Bardia 204–206

Barents Sea 167

barrack stanchions 497–498

Barrenjoey Head 207

Barrett, Vice Admiral Tim 560

Bartolomeo Colleoni 164–166

Bataan Death March 235

Bataan Peninsula 235

Batavia 235

Bath, Lieutenant Commander John 262, 267

Batho, Sir Charles 63, 64

Bathurst class corvettes 197–198

Battle of Bismarck Sea 402

Battle of Brisbane 404

Battle of Britain 180

Battle of Calabria 163

Battle of Cape Engaño 464

Battle of Cape Matapan 221

Battle of Cape Spada 164–166

Battle of Coral Sea 300–305 (and map)

Battle of Coronel 7

Battle of Eastern Solomons 390–391

Battle of Edgehill 506

Battle of Espero Convoy 162–166

Battle of Java Sea 234

Battle of Jutland 8–9, 28, 29–30, 40–41, 141

Battle of Leyte Gulf 455–466, 539

Battle of Midway 328–331

Battles of Narvik 143–144, 321

Battle of North Cape 492

Battle of Philippine Sea 429–430

Battle of River Plate 135–136

Battle of Samar 464–465

Battle of Savo 369–378, 388–391 (and map)

Battle of Sibuyan Sea 455

Battle of Stalingrad 391, 415

Battle of Sunda Strait 234–235

Battle of Surigao Strait 459–464 (and map)

Battle of the Atlantic 119–120, 180, 197

Battle of the Bulge 476

Battle of Trafalgar 62, 124 *see also* Trafalgar Day

Battle of Veracruz 281

BBC 110, 200, 534

Bear Island 167

Beasley, Jack 224

Beatty, Sir David 41

Belgium 145

Bell, Augusta 68

Bell, John 355

Bennett, Major General Gordon 234

Bergonzoli, Lieutenant General Annibale 204

Berkey, Rear Admiral Russell S. 423, 441

Betty (Mitsubishi torpedo bombers) 290–296, 352

Bevan, Captain Robert 262, 266

Bevern, Chief Bosun's Mate Bob 381

Biak 431

Binskin, Air Chief Marshal Marc 560

Bismarck 106, 221–222, 520

Blamey, General Thomas 403, 511–512, 521, 522

Blaskett, Harry 213

Blau, Midshipman Edgar 138–139, 209–210, 218, 220, 397

Bletchley Park 146

Bode, Howard D. 244, 296, 322, 325, 326, 327, 365

Battle of Savo 375, 380, 382, 388–389
Panama Canal Zone 389–390
Boer War 270
bogeys *see Kamikaze*
boiler flashback 373
Bolshevik revolution in Russia 23
Boomerang Club 532
Borneo 511–515, 530
Bostock, Air Commodore Bill 194–195
Bougainville 6, 353, 355, 402–403, 422
Bourke, Dick 246, 247, 296
Bourke, Doris 246
Bourke, Patrick ('Paddy') 246
Boylan, Lieutenant Fred 447
Boys, Stoker Ray 373
Bracegirdle, Rear Admiral Sir Leighton 397
Bracegirdle, Lieutenant Commander Warwick ('Braces') 208, 394, 395
    alcohol–weapons trade 413–414, 473–474
    background 397
    Battle of Surigao Strait 460, 461–462
    Christmas Day 1944 475
    gunnery instructor 510
    HMAS *Shropshire*, gunnery officer 440, 441–442, 510
    Leyte Gulf 456
Bracken, Brendan 501
Bradman, Donald 72
Brady, Edwin 21–22
Brain, Captain Lester 90
Braun, Eva 476
Brennan, Christopher 201
Brereton, Major General Lewis H. 230
Bretagne 159, 160
Brett, Lieutenant General George 237, 316–317, 363
Briant, Ella 148–149
Brisbane 64, 87, 90, 241–242, 404, 416, 429, 551–552

Britain
    Anglo–German Naval Agreement 95–96, 106
    Arcadia Conference 232
    Australia and threat from Japan 107–108
    Australia nominates MacArthur to command in Pacific 237
    Australian debt to 71–72
    Australian failure to ratify Statute of Westminster 569–570
    Australian Governors General 500
    British spies for Japan 36–43
    Combined Operational Intelligence Centre 280
    Coronation Review (1937) 133–134
    D-Day invasion of Normandy 155–156
    declares war on Germany 113–114
    Empire 533
    evacuation from Dunkirk 146–148, 150–154
    Far Eastern Imperial Fleet (proposed) 30–31
    First World War 4, 52
    Hoare–Laval Pact 99–100
    Italy declares war on 155, 158
    Japanese plans to attack Empire 103–104
    Japanese relations 33
    Japanese surrender 521–522
    League of Nations 32
    Munich agreement 106–107
    Pacific dominions 522
    Second London Naval Treaty 103
    Singapore conference (1940) 194–195
    support for alliance with Hitler 40
    Washington Naval Treaty 11–12, 34, 62
British 1st Armoured Brigade 222–223
British 7th Armoured Brigade 205–206
British 8th Army 391, 401
British Admiralty 6, 7, 33, 37, 40, 94, 142
    Convoy PQ-17 391–392
    evacuation from Dunkirk 147

Hampshire estates 129–130
Main Fleet to Singapore 109–111
RAN under control of 240–241,
    269–270
British Army 195
British Commonwealth Occupation
    Force, Japan 538
British Embassy, Tokyo 524–525
British Expeditionary Force 146–148,
    150–154
British Foreign Office 37, 196
British Government Code and
    Cypher School 38–39
British Special Operations Executive
    532
Brooke-Popham, Sir Robert 196, 232
Broussignac, Jean Paul 171
Brown, Alf 255, 256, 259, 264
Brown, Archibald 66
Brown, Private Bill 27–28
Brown, Vice Admiral Wilson 249,
    250–251, 280
Bruce, Stanley Melbourne 12–13, 18,
    34, 64, 69, 112, 179–180, 196
Bryant, George 66–69
Bryant, Julia Elizabeth 66–69
Buchanan, Commander Alf 460,
    479–480
Buckingham Palace investiture 505
Buckmaster, Elliott 304, 331
Bulletin magazine 31–32
Buna 279, 336, 402, 427
Bungan Head 327
Bunnett, Petty Officer Colin 178
Burgmann, Ernest 569
burial at sea 453
Burma 234, 406
Burma–Siam Railway 234, 509
Burnett, Captain Joseph 50, 194–195,
    219, 225–228
Butler, Richard ('Rab') 196
Byrnes, Christine 568, 570

C
Cadogan, Sir Alexander 196
cafeteria messing 56, 395, 398–399
Cam Ranh Bay French naval base 180
Campbell, Constance 19
Campbell, Gavin 209

Canada 33, 521–522, 569
Cape Engaño 464
Cape Gloucester 423–427
Cape Horn 543
Cape Otway mined 207
Cape Town 143, 157–158
Cape Wrath 181
capital punishment 269–270,
    569–570
Cargill, Jimmy 324
Carrier Strike Force (IJN)
    Battle of Coral Sea 300–305
    creation 278, 279
    sink Neosho 287–288
    Task Force 17 283, 286, 298
carrier warfare 281, 289, 390–391
    carrier evolutions 300–301
    carrier flight and hangar decks 300
    first carrier battle 305
Cartland, Barbara 88
Casablanca conference 415–416, 476
casualty lists 192, 224
Cazaly, Roy 456–457, 485–486
CBS Radio Network 499
censorship see press censorship
Centaur (hospital ship) 410–412
Centner, Lieutenant Commander
    Richard 468
Central Force (IJN) 438, 464–465
Central Philippines Attack Force 436
ceremony of Colours 88
Chamberlain, Austen 39
Chamberlain, Neville 106–107, 109,
    112, 116, 145
Chambers, Lieutenant Commander
    Thomas 372–373
Champion (tug) 3, 14
Changi Prison 111
Charles II 319, 320
Chatfield, Sir Ernle 47, 48
Chatham Naval Dockyard 319–320,
    395, 397, 398–399
Chifley, Ben 194, 502, 512
Chifley Labor government 540
China 6, 105, 275
    Japanese invasion 108
    Japanese surrender 521–522
    Rape of Nanking 106
China Strait 507–508

Chokai 337, 352–353, 357, 366–368, 370, 376, 377, 378, 465
Choules, Claude 57, 61
Christian Brothers 246
Christmas Day 1944 475
Churchill, Clementine 502
Churchill, Winston 7, 28, 40, 107, 322
  in Admiralty 136, 137, 144
  Australia looks to America 233–234
  Casablanca conference 415–416, 476
  Convoy PQ-17 392
  defence of Singapore 195–196
  Dominion camps 533
  evacuation from Dunkirk 146, 147, 154–155
  evacuation of Crete 222–223
  HMS *Shropshire*, gifts to Australia 392–393
  Hong Kong 232
  invasion of Greece 222, 223
  loses 1945 general election 502
  loss of HMS *Hood* 221–222
  Main Fleet to Singapore 230–231
  Marine Nationale 158–160, 161
  Menzies and 179–180
  Operation Menace, Dakar 169, 175–176, 177
  Pacific Theatre 242–243, 251
  as Prime Minister 145
  Stalin and 392
Ciano, Count Galeazzo 105
cinema 139, 309
Citizen Military Forces 404
City of Rayville 207
Clark, Lloyd and Russell 504
Clark Field, Manila 230
Clarke, Commander (E) Donald 545
Clarke, Flight Lieutenant George 178
Clarke, John 481–482, 484, 495
Clemens, Martin 338, 349
Clement 134
Clyde, Greenock 161–162, 181
Clyde dockyards 4, 36, 45–47
coal lumpers 67
coal-powered ships 10, 57–58
coastwatching network 122–123, 250, 282, 338, 349, 353, 359, 402

Coburg 215–219
Cockatoo Island Dockyard 34–35, 82, 108, 118, 197, 243, 412, 497
Collins, Esther 51
Collins, Vice Admiral John
  background 51, 432–433
  Battle of Cape Spada 164–166
  Commander, Australian Squadron 432, 441
  Duke and Duchess of York, naval liaison officer to 55
  Farncomb and 92–93
  HMAS *Australia II* as training ship 549–550
  HMAS *Australia II*, gunnery officer 49, 55
  HMAS *Shropshire* 398, 401, 515
  HMAS *Sydney II*, captain 109, 162, 163
  HMAS *Sydney II*, executive officer 82
  honours and awards 54–55, 166
  Japanese surrender 518–519, 522
  Leyte Gulf 444, 450, 451, 454
  Mattiske's souvenirs 524–525
  as midshipman 53–54
  RANC 50, 52, 53, 538–539
  Singapore, escapes from 235
  Singapore, posted to 225
  USN 7th Fleet 436–437
Collins, Michael 51
Collins, Rendall 77–78
Colombo 208, 235–236
Colville, Jock 477
Colvin, Admiral Sir Ragnar 118–119, 120, 125, 130, 195, 241
Commonwealth Arbitration Court 69, 71
Commonwealth Defence Act 1903–41 269–270
Communism 105
conscription 404
Conte di Cavour 163, 187
Convoy PQ-17 391–392
Cook, Sir Joseph 47
Cook, Dame Mary 47–48
Cooktown 279
Cooper, Chief Petty Officer Arthur 397, 460, 462, 483, 531–532

Coral Sea 275, 278–281, 283–284 *see also* Battle of Coral Sea
Corregidor 229, 235, 237, 507
corvettes 197–198
Cosgrove, Peter 560
Cotton, Frank 14
Country Party 12, 193, 225
County class cruisers 35–36, 62, 395
Courtis, Wilbur 355
Coward, Noël 88
Crace (Canberra property) 126–127
Crace, Allan 130, 317
Crace, Carola 317
Crace, Christopher 130, 317
Crace, Edward Kendall 127
Crace, John Gregory ('Jack') 127
  in Admiralty 129–130
  background 127–129
  bombed by Americans 296–297, 315–317
  Central War Room 316
  chain of command 243
  Chatham Naval Dockyard 319–320
  Farncomb and 293, 295
  Fletcher's failure to communicate with 290, 297, 306, 314–315
  forms defensive diamond 290
  HMAS *Australia II*, squadron commander 242
  as Rear Admiral Commanding Australian Squadron 130, 240–242
  retirement and farewell dinner 318–319
  Stoker Riley murder 268
  Task Force 17.3 287
  Task Force 44 280–281, 317
  USS *Lexington* 249
Crace, Nicholas 130, 317
Crete
  Battle of Cape Spada 164–166
  evacuation of 222–223, 224, 362
Crimean War 124
Crimes Act 81
Crutchley, Rear Admiral Victor Alexander Charles 144, 339, 341
  background 320–321
  Battle of Savo 381–382, 388–389, 390

Commander, Task Force 44 320, 333–334
Commander, Task Force 74 423
  Guadalcanal 363, 364, 365–366, 368
  honours 432
  reaction to sinking of *Canberra* 387
  relinquishes command 432
  Second-in-Command, Allied Expeditionary Force 344–345
  stern chase 431–432
Cunningham, Admiral Sir Andrew 223, 362
Cunningham, Vice Admiral John 172, 173, 175–177
Cureton, Stan 291
Curtin, Sergeant Albert 529–530
Curtin, Elsie 477
Curtin, John 140–141, 194
  Australia looks to America 233–234
  Battle of Coral Sea 309–312
  Centaur (hospital ship) 411
  Churchill's gift of HMS *Shropshire* 392, 396–397
  death 502–503
  Gordon and Elias 569
  illness 477
  loss of HMAS *Sydney* 228
  MacArthur and 237, 239, 405
  as Prime Minister 225
  radio broadcast 311–312
  reaction to sinking of *Canberra* 384
  re-elected in 1943 404–405
Curtin, John (son) 502
Curtiss floatplanes 252–253
Custance, Rear Admiral Wilfred 119
Cusworth, Fred 333
Czechoslovakia 106, 107

D
Daily Herald (SA) 13–14
Dakar 160–161
  Operation Menace 169–175
Dalgetys Ltd 20
dance crazes 407
d'Argenlieu, Thierry 172
'Darken Ship' pipe 114
Darlan, Amiral de la Flotte François 158

Darling, Lieutenant Commander
Stanley 412
Darwin 104, 234, 237
Davies, Bob 230–231
Davies, Mr and Mrs 188–189, 191
Dawson, Lord 102
Day, David 502
D-Day invasion of Normandy
155–156
DDG warships 555–556
de Chair, Sir Dudley 16
de Gaulle, Charles 168–169, 171,
175–177, 178
de Groot, Captain Francis 72
death sentence 269–270, 569–570
Debenham, Ian 449
Dechaineux, Commander Emile 156,
412, 427
background 148–149
evacuation of Dunkirk 149–154
HMAS *Australia II*, commander
433, 448
HMS *Vivacious* 149–154
killed at Leyte Gulf 450, 451–452
Dechaineux, François and Josephine
148
Dechaineux, Lucien 148–149
Dedman, John 405–406, 407–408
defence
naval defence report post-Great
War 28–31
naval expansion 1934–37 82
naval expansion 1937–39 108–109
of White Australia 32–33
defence budgets 12, 30–31, 34–35
1940–41 197
cost of Far Eastern Imperial Fleet
(proposed) 30
cost of Soldier Settlement Schemes
28
Great Depression 73, 74
post-war interforce competition
540–541
Denmark 143
Derrick, Lieutenant Tom ('Diver')
512
Detmers, Theodor 227
Deutschland 134, 208–209

Devine, Leading Seaman Bill
371–372
Devonport Naval Base 116
Diana (biplane) 90
Dickerson, Petty Officer Edward
77–78
Dinah (Mitsubishi Ki-46) 486–487
Dixon, Lieutenant Commander Bob
289
Dönitz, Karl 187, 220
Donovan, Lieutenant Commander
Jack 175, 253, 254–256
Doolittle, Lieutenant Colonel James
('Jimmy') 277–278
Doolittle Raid 277–278
Doric Star (Blue Star liner) 135
Dover Castle 147
Dovers, Lieutenant Commander Bill
547
Dowling, Bruce 230–231
Downward, Surgeon Commander
Charlie 209, 212, 373–374, 380
D'Oyly Lyon, Admiral Sir George
399
Drake, Sir Francis 116
Dunkerque 159
Dunkirk evacuation 146–148,
150–154
Dunkirk mole 152–154
Dunkirk on fire 150–151
Duntroon 52
the Dutch *see* Holland
Dyer, Bob and Dolly 406–407

E
East Africa 236, 245–246
East Asia Squadron 6–7
Eastern Suburbs, Sydney 328
Eastick, Charles Ambrose 124
Eastick, Harold Lone
Australia diary 124, 161, 168, 170,
174
background 124
Liverpool long leave 188–189, 191
murder of Stoker Riley 261
USS *Chicago* 248
Eastick, John 124
Eastick, Spencer Lone 124
Eastick, Thomas 124

E-boats 156
Eddystone Light 500
Eden, Anthony 119–120, 142
Edmonds, Reg 447–448
Edward VIII 102
Egypt 180
Eisenhower, Dwight D. 497
El Alamein 391, 401
Eleonore Woermann 7
Elias, Leading Stoker Edward Joseph
    court martial 262, 263, 265, 266
    death penalty 266, 269, 271
    legal campaign for release 568–574
    murder of Stoker Riley 255–256,
        258–261, 574
    released on parole 271, 573
    sentence 573
Elizabeth, Princess 141, 532
Elizabeth, Queen Mother 532, 533
Elizabeth II 551
Emden 6, 15, 135, 166
Empress of Britain 142
Empress of Canada 142
Empress of Japan 142
Endrass, Engelbert 187
Enigma ciphering machine capture
    221
Enigma code 146
escort carriers 465, 505
Espero 163
Espiritu Santo see New Hebrides
Ethiopia see Abyssinian Empire, Italy
    invades
Evans, Rear Admiral Edward
    Ratcliffe, RN 75–77
Evans, Stoker Petty Officer Merv
    481, 495
Evatt, Dr Herbert Vere ('Doc') 194,
    269, 271, 497, 522, 570, 571, 573
Evershed Bearing Indicators 173–174

F
Fadden, Arthur 225
Far Eastern Imperial Fleet (proposed)
    29–30, 34
Farncomb, Jean 92, 93
Farncomb, Rear Admiral Harold
    Bruce
    awards 495

background 50, 92–93
Coburg and Ketty Brovig 214–219,
    228
combing the tracks 292–293, 295
Commodore Commanding
    Australian Squadron 473
Duke of Gloucester's passage home
    on Australia 87–88, 90
HMAS Australia II, commander
    473, 489–490
HMAS Australia II, flag captain
    242, 250
HMAS Canberra I 208, 209, 211
HMAS Perth 109, 208–209
HMAS Shropshire 510, 515, 538
HMS Attacker, captain 433, 473
honours 94
Lingayen Gulf 483
Stoker Riley: appeal for clemency
    for Elias & Gordon 267–269,
    573
Stoker Riley: court martial of Elias
    & Gordon 262, 263, 264,
    265–266, 571, 572
Stoker Riley murder 253
Fascism 39–40, 99
fashion 407–409
FBI 42
Feakes, Henry 17
federal election (1943) 404–405
Fegen, Fogarty 187
Feldt, Eric Augustas 50, 121–123, 353,
    402
Felsennest 144–145
Ferdinand coastwatching operation see
    coastwatching network
Fiji Islands 276, 336
Financial Emergency Act 1931 73, 79
First World War 3, 4, 25–29, 36, 57,
    68, 76, 95–96, 246, 320–321
Fitch, Rear Admiral Aubrey 280, 282,
    283, 284, 302, 312–313
FitzRoy, Charles 320
FitzRoy, Henry 320
Flattery, Surgeon Commander 451,
    488
'flat-tops' (carriers) 289
Fletcher, Vice Admiral Frank Jack
    250

Allied Expeditionary Force,
    Operation Watchtower 339,
    342–343, 347, 350
Battle of Coral Sea 302, 303–304,
    305
Battle of Eastern Solomons
    390–391
Battle of Midway 330, 331
Battle of Savo 388, 389, 390
Carrier Strike Force (IJN) 298
Guadalcanal 361–362
Nielsen and 288–289
Task Force 17 280–286, 287
Flinders Naval Depot 11, 58, 73, 86,
    117, 125, 197, 202–203, 244
Florida Island 346, 360, 366
Fogarty, Lieutenant Commander
    Francis 178, 554
Fogarty, Mary 554
Forbes-Sempill see Sempill, William
    Francis Forbes
Forest of Compiègne 155
Foster's Academy, Stubbington 128,
    130
Fox, Torpedoman A. B. 350
France
    Anglo–German Naval Agreement
        96, 106
    armistice with Germany 155, 158
        see also Vichy France
    Dunkirk evacuation 154
    German invasion of 145, 146
    Hoare–Laval Pact 99–100
    Italy declares war on 155, 158
    Japanese surrender 521–522
    Munich agreement 106–107
    Second London Naval Treaty
        103
    Washington Naval Treaty 11
Francis, Josiah 545, 549
Francis, Sonita 568–569, 570
Fraser, Admiral Sir Bruce 484,
    491–492, 518, 522
Freetown, Sierra Leone 157, 160–161,
    169
Fremantle 548
French Indo-China 180
Furutaka 367, 376
Fuso 438, 458–460

G
Gallipoli 101
Game, Sir Philip 72
Garden Island Naval Base
    as Fleet Base East 557
    Garden Island Dockyard 3, 14, 77,
        540
    HMAS Kuttabul (floating barracks)
        326–327, 328
    HMAS Shropshire 401
    Japanese midget submarines in
        Sydney Harbour 324, 326–327
    Naval Prison ('The Corner') 84
Garsia, Captain Rupert 14–15, 413
Gatacre, Galfrey 222
Geddes, Sergeant Eric 354–357
Geelong 332
Geneva Convention 410
Gensoul, Amiral Marcel-Bruno 159
George V
    comments on Australia Unlimited
        22
    as cousin to Kaiser Wilhelm II 4
    death 102
    declares war on Germany 52
    Jubilee 97
    objections to Sir Isaac Isaacs 72
    visits Australia II and Canberra 61,
        62–63
George VI 39, 102, 155, 166
    awards to HMAS Australia II 505
    Christmas Day 1940 address 141
    Churchill's gift of HMS Shropshire
        396, 401
    coronation 107
    Dominion camps 532
    murder of Stoker Riley 252, 569,
        570
    royal prerogative of clemency 570
Georges Leygues 169–170, 171, 177
German surface raiders 206–207
Germany
    Anglo–German Naval Agreement
        95–96, 106
    Anti-Comintern Pact 105
    declares war on United States 231
    Denmark capitulates to 143
    domination of Europe 106
    First World War 4, 52, 155

invades Poland 112–113

invasion of Western Europe 144–146

Molotov–Ribbentrop Pact 106

Norway falls to 143–144

Pacific colonies 6, 31

Pact of Steel 106

reoccupies Rhineland 102–103

Rome–Berlin Axis 105

surrenders 497

Tripartite Pact 180

Gerrett, Lieutenant Commander Harrie 449

Getting, Captain Frank Edmund 50, 334, 335, 369–371, 373, 379, 380, 382, 383, 390

Ghormley, Rear Admiral Robert L. 109–110, 338–343, 361, 362, 388–389, 390

Gibbs, Flight Lieutenant Sidney 182–183, 186

Gill, Hermon 454

Gilmore, Dame Mary 385

Gilroy, Norman 569, 571

Giovanni delle Bande Nere 164–166

Giulio Cesare 163

Glen (Yokosuka E14Y seaplanes) 323–324

Gloire 169–171

Gloster Sparrowhawk 37–38

Gloucester, Prince Henry, Duke of 87–90, 93–94, 97, 101

Gloucester Cup 551

Gneisenau 144, 167

Goebbels, Joseph 105

Goering, Hermann 96, 146

Goldrick, James 573

Gona 336, 402

Gondar 187

Goodeve, Fred 219

Goodwin Sands 150

Goolden, Captain Francis 49, 64

Gordon, Leading Stoker Albert Ronald
court martial 262, 263, 265, 266
death penalty 266, 269, 271
legal campaign for release 568–574
murder of Stoker Riley 255–256, 257, 259–261, 574
released on parole 271, 573
sentence 573

Gordon, Francis 257

Gort, General Lord 146

Gosse, Lieutenant Commander George 528

Gothic (liner) 551

Gotley, Aubrey 546

Gottschalk, Reg 17

Gowrie, Lord 130, 401, 569

Grayndler, Eddie 69

Great Barrier Reef 97

Great Depression 28
in Australia 70–72, 125
murder–suicide 66–69

Great East Asia 180

Great War see First World War

Greater East Asia Co-Prosperity Sphere 276

Greece 222–224

Greenman, Captain William 376–377

Gregory, Jesse 125, 126

Gregory, Mackenzie Jesse ('Mac')
background 125–126
Battle of Savo 369, 370
HMAS Australia 172–173, 185, 186, 245, 335, 374, 473
Leyte Gulf 456–457
Lingayen Gulf 485–486

Griffiths, Rear Admiral Guy 200, 230–231, 245, 397, 460, 506, 523, 559

Griggs, Vice Admiral Ray 560

Grose, Peter 326

Guadalcanal 383
25th Air Flotilla attacks 359–360
Allied Expeditionary Force 337, 338, 346–347, 350, 351
Allied landings 359, 378
IJN attack on 358, 366–368
Japanese attempt to retake 391, 402

Guam 428

guided-missile destroyers 555–556

Gungahlin 127–128, 130

Gunn, Nancy 552–553

Gyllies, Peter 230–231, 245

H

Haakon VII, King of Norway 144

Hagan, Signalman John 254

Halmahera Group of Islands 422

Halsey, Vice Admiral Bill ('Bull')
280, 281, 330, 362, 390, 402, 416,
422, 427, 518
3rd Fleet 437, 464
decision to chase Mobile Strike
Force 455–456
Japanese surrender 522
Typhoon Cobra 477
Hamer, Lieutenant Commander
David 472
Allied Control Commission 526
awards 494–495, 505
background 198–201
Colombo 208
HMAS *Australia II*, attempts to
rejoin 434–435
HMAS *Australia II* gunnery officer
551
HMS *Revenge* 245–246
Leyte Gulf 446, 448, 455
Lingayen Gulf 480, 489, 490–491
march through London 504–505
as Midshipman of Watch 210–211,
217
as Navigator 452–453
New York 499
range plotting 215
salvage party to *Ketty Brovig*
217–218
Handcock, Peter 270
Hara, Rear Admiral Chuichi 302, 303
Harding, Warren 11
Hardman, Air Marshal Sir Donald 541
Harries, Captain David 526–527, 529
Harrington, Wilfred Hastings 435
Harwood, Commodore Henry 135
Hassett, Warrant Officer Lindsay
504
Hawaii 331
Hawkley House, Liss 129–130
Hayakawa, Captain Mikio 368
Heard Island 543, 544, 546–547
'Heart of Oak' (RN anthem) 91
Hellcat (Grumman F6F) 430
Hendon Air Show 98
Henry V 349, 477
Hepburn, Admiral Arthur J.
388–389, 390
Heroic and *Heroine* (tugs) 3, 14

High Court of Australia 269–270, 569
High Seas Fleet 9, 40–41
Hill, Senator Robert 562
Hindenburg 9
Hirohito, Emperor 351–352, 515–516,
521, 523
Hiroshima 516
Hiryu 331
Hitler, Adolf 40, 95, 96, 102–103,
105–107, 134, 144, 155, 206,
223–224, 322
assassination attempts on 435
Battle of the Bulge 476
suicide 497
Hiyo 430
HMAS *Adelaide* 118, 324
HMAS *Adelaide II* 557, 558, 562
HMAS *Albatross* 74, 78, 115, 541
HMAS *Amazon* 94
HMAS *Ambuscade* 94
HMAS *Anzac* 16, 93
HMAS *Armidale* 198
HMAS *Arunta* 412, 423, 424, 431,
437, 441, 476, 538
Balikpapan 513
hurricane in China Strait 507–508
Leyte Gulf 456, 458, 459–460
Lingayen Gulf 478, 491
struck by *Kamikaze* 479–480
HMAS *Australia I*
in 2nd Battlecruiser Squadron 7–8,
9, 53, 60, 114
Battle of Coronel 6–7
ceremonial welcome to Prince of
Wales 11
destruction under Washington
Naval Treaty 12
dismantling 14
in first grand fleet entry into
Sydney Harbour 3–4, 129
mutiny 10
obsolescence 10–11
public protests over scuttling 12–14
scuttling 3, 5, 14–18
specifications 4
HMAS *Australia II*
accommodation 55–56
aircraft catapult fitted 97, 98
building 34–36

cruises 74–75, 78
Duke of Gloucester's passage home
on 87–88, 90–91, 93–94, 101
Evans' farewell party 76–77
fitting out 48–49
as flagship of RAN 59, 60
food ('scran') 138
George V Jubilee 97
George V visits 61, 62–63
Great Depression 74, 76–77
launch 45, 47–48
leave in London 94
Mediterranean Fleet 94–95, 99,
100
naval canteen staff 116–117
patrolling 137–138
recreation in Alexandria 100–101
refit 108–109, 118
returns to Sydney 101
sabotage 83–85
sails from Spithead 64
sea trials 60–61
ship's company 49, 59
ship's organisation 56–57
specifications ix, 35–36
ventilation 138
HMAS *Australia II* in Second World
War
1st Cruiser Squadron 162
under Admiralty orders 157
battle flags 172
Cape Town 143, 157–158
Dakar 160–161
damaged by shells 177
dazzle camouflage 167
escorting 2nd AIF 141–143
as flagship 242
Freetown 157, 160–161, 169
Greenock, Clyde 161–162, 181
Liverpool long leave 188–189
Liverpool: *Luftwaffe* bombing 189,
190–191
officers 126
Operation Menace, Dakar 168,
169–175 (and map)
painted Home Fleet colours 191
propeller replacement 191–192
radio direction-finding 188
repairs 269

rescues Sunderland P9620 181–186
Scapa Flow naval base 167–168
search for *Scheer* 214
Stoker Riley: court martial for
murder 262–269
Stoker Riley: court martial inquiry
571–574
Stoker Riley murder 252–261
Sydney home base 214, 242
target selection 173–174
Walrus 177–178, 250, 251
HMAS *Australia II* in Pacific Theatre
25th Air Flotilla attacks 291–296,
359–360
action stations 295–296
air attacks (1944–45) on x
Allied Expeditionary Force 339
Battle of Eastern Solomons 391
Battle of Savo 381–382, 383, 390
Britain, barrack stanchions
497–498
Cape Gloucester 424–426
fear of *Kamikaze* 489–490
as flagship 334, 431, 432, 433, 441
Guadalcanal 364, 365–366
homecoming 528
Japanese surrender 526
Jomard Passage 286–287, 290–296
Leyte Gulf 443
Lingayen Gulf 478, 480–483,
491–492
Manus Island 432, 454
Milne Bay 422–423
Morotai 430
New Hebrides 471–472
New York Harbor 496, 498–500
night positions 364
Palm Island 414–415
refit 414, 427, 492, 497–498
refit Plymouth Naval Base
500–501, 503–505, 526, 527
sails for home with passengers
527–528
specifications 474–475
struck by Japanese dive bomber
446–454
struck by *Kamikaze* 480–487,
490–491
Task Force 17 285

Task Force 44 280, 283–284, 334
Task Force 74 417
Task Group 17.3 287
Task Group 62.6 339, 341, 344,
    346–347, 348, 350
Task Group 74.1 423
Task Group 77.3 441
USN 7th Fleet 437
under USN orders 285
HMAS *Australia II* post-war
    decommissioned 556
    farewell cruise 551–554
    medical rescue mission to Antarctic
        542–549
    record 554–556
    scrapped 550–551, 556
    Spring and Summer cruises 542
    as training ship 540, 549–550
    as vice-regal yacht 550
HMAS *Australia III* (hypothetical)
    562
HMAS *Ballarat* 520
HMAS *Bataan* 542
HMAS *Bathurst* 197
HMAS *Brisbane* 16, 17, 18
HMAS *Burnie* 235
HMAS *Canberra I*
    accommodation 55–56
    aircraft capability 97
    building 34–36, 47
    cruises 74–75, 78
    fitting out 48–49
    George V visits 61, 62–63
    Great Depression 74
    launch 48
    preparation for war 118
    sabotage 83
    sails from Spithead 64–65
    sea trials 60–61, 64
    ship's company 59
    specifications 35–36
HMAS *Canberra I* in Second World
    War
    under Admiralty orders 157,
        207–208
    alcohol at sea 138–139
    Coburg and *Ketty Brovig* 214–219
    escorting 2nd AIF 141–143
    as flagship 130, 241, 242

food ('scran') 211–212
gunnery 216, 219
laundry 211
midshipmen ('snotties') 209–210,
    211
Plotting Staff 336
recruiting 201, 203
refit 243, 283, 335
search for *Scheer* 214
ship's company 559
training 210
HMAS *Canberra I* in Pacific Theatre
    25th Air Flotilla attacks 359
    Battle of Savo 369–372
    enquiry into loss 386–387
    Guadalcanal 364, 365
    Japanese midget submarines in
        Sydney Harbour 324, 326,
        327–328
    losses and casualties 384–385
    plotting office 371
    radar 335
    sinking of 378–381
    Task Force 44 334
    Task Group 62.6 344, 346, 348,
        350, 354
    torpedoed by USS *Bagley* 372–374,
        375, 376, 381, 387–388
HMAS *Canberra II* 557
HMAS *Canberra III* 557–563
HMAS *Cerberus* 199–201
HMAS *Cessnock* 520
HMAS *Colac* 410
HMAS *Gascoyne* 437, 443, 478, 486
HMAS *Gladstone* 552
HMAS *Harman* 245
HMAS *Hobart* 109
    25th Air Flotilla 291, 294, 296
    Balikpapan 513
    Battle of Eastern Solomons 391
    to Brisbane 307
    as flagship 320
    Guadalcanal 364
    in Second World War 112, 113, 115,
        116, 118, 135, 137, 244
    struck by torpedo 417–418
    Task Force 17 285
    Task Force 44 280, 283–284, 334
    Task Group 17.3 287

Task Group 62.6 344, 346–347, 383
Tokyo Bay 520
HMAS *Ipswich* 520
HMAS *Kanimbla* 117, 324, 334, 437, 489, 514
HMAS *Kuttabul* (floating barracks) 326–327, 328
HMAS *Lolita* 324, 325–326
HMAS *Manoora* 117, 333, 437, 489, 491, 514
HMAS *Marguerite* 14
HMAS *Melbourne* 16, 59
HMAS *Melbourne III* 540, 557
HMAS *Moreton Bay* 117
HMAS *Napier* 197, 520
HMAS *Nepal* 197
HMAS *Nestor* 197, 412
HMAS *Nizam* 197, 520
HMAS *Norman* 197, 435
HMAS *Otway* 74, 334
HMAS *Oxley* 74, 334
HMAS *Parramatta* 228
HMAS *Penguin* 80–81, 573
HMAS *Perth* 109, 118, 137, 208–209, 221, 223, 241, 242
  loss of 234–235
HMAS *Pirie* 198
HMAS *Sabre* 94
HMAS *Saladin* 94
HMAS *Shoalhaven* 542
HMAS *Shropshire* 126, 143, 433
  alcohol–weapons trade 413–414, 473–474
  Australian crew in US 394
  Australian Victory Contingent 529–530
  Balikpapan 513–515
  Battle of Surigao Strait 459, 460–462
  Canberra survivors 397
  Cape Gloucester 424–426
  catches mine in paravanes 441–442
  Churchill gifts to Australia 392–393
  as flagship 427
  George VI visits 401
  homecoming 528
  hurricane in China Strait 507–508
  'ickies' (heat rash) 472–473

Japan 538
Japanese surrender 518–520
Kamikaze 472
Labuan 512
Leyte Gulf 443, 447, 451, 454, 456–458, 539
Lingayen Gulf 478, 483, 485–486, 489, 492, 506–507
Manila Bay 507, 515
Manus Island 510
Milne Bay 422–423
proposed renaming 396–397
refit in Chatham Naval Dockyard 395, 397
refit in Cockatoo Island 509–510
rum ration 398
sails for Sydney 536
sails from Chatham 400
scrapped 539–540
specifications 395–396, 474–475
Task Group 74.1 423
Task Group 77.3 441
tests and trials 400–401
Tokyo Bay 520
USN 7th Fleet 437
HMAS *Stalwart* 92
HMAS *Stuart* 82, 118, 135, 163, 166, 187, 205, 221
HMAS *Swan* 82, 118
HMAS *Sydney I* 6, 15, 58, 135, 166
HMAS *Sydney II* 82, 83–84, 101, 118, 120, 162–166, 225
  loss of 226–228
HMAS *Sydney III* 540, 541–542
HMAS *Tattoo* 74, 78
HMAS *Vampire* 82, 118, 135, 163, 205
HMAS *Vendetta* 82, 118, 135
HMAS *Voyager* 82, 112, 113, 118, 135, 163, 205
HMAS *Warramunga* 412, 423, 424, 431, 433, 437, 441, 454, 476, 478, 520
HMAS *Warrego* 478
HMAS *Waterhen* 82, 118, 135, 223
HMAS *Westralia* 117, 324, 437, 489, 514
HMAS *Yandra* 325
HMAS *Yarra* 82, 118, 235
HMNZS *Achilles* 135, 241, 242, 244

HMNZS *Leander* 142, 214, 217, 218, 220, 244, 262, 267

HMNZS *Philomel* 383

HMS *Achille* 124

HMS *Ajax* 135

HMS *Apollo* 116

HMS *Ark Royal* 159, 171, 172, 173, 385

HMS *Attacker* 433, 473

HMS *Barham* 171, 172, 177

HMS *Bellerephon* 124

HMS *Britannia* 50, 128

HMS *Broke* 76

HMS *Bulldog* 221

HMS *Canada* 53–54

HMS *Centurion* 320

HMS *Collingwood* 141

HMS *Cornwall* 235

HMS *Courageous* 136

HMS *Cumberland* 169–170, 171, 172

HMS *Danae* 15, 129

HMS *Dauntless* 15

HMS *Defender* 223

HMS *Delhi* 15, 17

HMS *Devonshire* 177

HMS *Dorsetshire* 160, 235

HMS *Dragon* 15

HMS *Duke of York* 401, 518, 521

HMS *Eagle* 41, 110, 392

HMS *Eglinton* 149, 156

HMS *Engadine* 40–41

HMS *Excellent* 54

HMS *Exeter* 135

HMS *The Fighting Temeraire* 398

HMS *Fury* 173

HMS *Glasgow* 214

HMS *Glorious* 99, 144

HMS *Gloucester* 164

HMS *Good Hope* 128

HMS *Greyhound* 173, 175

HMS *Havock* 164–166

HMS *Hermes* 38, 160–161, 214, 235–236

HMS *Hood* 11, 15–16, 46, 49, 78, 129, 159, 221–222

HMS *Hyperion* 164–166

HMS *Illustrious* 187–188

HMS *Indefatigable* 9

HMS *Indomitable* 230

HMS *Iron Duke* 49

HMS *Jervis Bay* 187, 213

HMS *King George V* 520, 524

HMS *Lion* 47

HMS *Loch Killin* 412

HMS *Melampus* 62

HMS *Milford* 160

HMS *Nelson* 62

HMS *New Zealand* 9

HMS *Norfolk* 167

HMS *Phaeton* 82

HMS *Powerful* 129

HMS *Prince of Wales* 190, 230, 287

HMS *Queen Elizabeth* 100

HMS *Ramillies* 137

HMS *Renown* 55, 167

HMS *Repulse* 9, 15, 16, 46, 92, 167, 201, 230–231, 287

HMS *Resolution* 159, 171, 172, 177

HMS *Revenge* 57, 245–246

HMS *Rodney* 78, 222

HMS *Royal Oak* 136–137, 225

HMS *Royal Sovereign* 92

HMS *Ruler* 505

HMS *Shropshire see* HMAS *Shropshire*

HMS *Sussex* 94

HMS *The Fighting Temeraire* 398

HMS *Valiant* 100, 159

HMS *Vanoc* 220–221

HMS *Vengeance* 540

HMS *Vernon* 121

HMS *Victorious* 257

HMS *Victory* 62, 398

HMS *Vindictive* 321

HMS *Vivacious* 149–154, 156

HMS *Walker* 221

HMS *Warspite* 143–144, 163, 321

HMS *Warwick* 321

HMS *Whelp* 525

Hoare, Sir Samuel 99–100

Hole, Lieutenant Commander Donald ('Gertie') 215, 218, 219, 370, 371

Holland *see* the Netherlands

Hollandia (Jayapura) 434–435, 441

Holocaust 210

Holt, Harold 310

Holt, Ken 254

homosexuality 257–259, 264, 267, 571–574

Hong Kong 104, 196, 232
Hopping, Cliff 447
Hordern Pavilion 19–20
'*Horst Wessel Lied*' (stormtrooper
    anthem) 105
Horton, Rear Admiral Max 100, 101
Hosho 38
Howden, Harry 64
Hughes, William Morris 28, 31, 32,
    69, 178–179, 233, 245
Hunkin, Chaplain Bill 399
Hutchison, Ernie 217, 220
Hyde, Rear Admiral George Francis
    59–60, 62, 63, 80, 81

I

I class submarines 328
I-11 417–418
I-21 409
I-177 410–412
Ibuki 29
IJN *see* Imperial Japanese Navy
Ikara anti-submarine missile 555
Imperial Conference London (1937)
    107–108
Imperial Defence College 92
Imperial Japanese Navy
    1st Air Fleet 439
    8th Fleet 337, 352
    201st Air Group 439–440
    701st Air Group 469–470
    aviation arm 37–38, 41–44 *see also*
        25th Air Flotilla
    Battle of Eastern Solomons 390–391
    Battle of Midway 329–331
    Battle of Savo 369–372, 373
    Combined Fleet 276–277, 391
    Corregidor 507
    Cruiser Division Six (CRUDIV6)
        353, 355–357
    forces reliant on *Kamikaze* 476
    Fourth Fleet 278
    landings at Lae and Salamaua
        250–251
    midget submarines in Sydney
        Harbour 322–327, 328
    night battle experience 358, 366
    Operation AO 329
    Operation *Ten-Go* 511
    Operations MI and MO 277,
        278–280
    the Philippines battle plans
        437–438
    plans for USN 276–277
    preparation for war 103, 275
    South China Sea 436
    stern chase 431–432
    submarines along east coast of
        Australia 409–410
    Tokyo Express to Guadalcanal 402
Imperial Palace, Tokyo 278
India 104, 533
Indian Ocean Theatre
    Germans 134–135, 137, 192, 203,
        206–207, 213–214
    Japanese 229, 235–236
Indigenous servicemen and women
    562
Industrial Revolution 45–46
Inoguchi, Captain Rikihei 439
Inoue, Vice Admiral Shigeyoshi 278,
    283, 289, 298, 306, 307, 336
International Red Cross 410
Invergordon Mutiny 78
Iowa class battleships 277
Ireland 189
Irish Free State 569
Isaacs, Sir Isaac 72
Ishimaru, Lieutenant Commander
    Tota 103–104
Italian 10th Army 204–206
Italy 142
    Bardia 204–206
    declares war on Britain and France
        155, 158
    invades Abyssinian Empire 99–100
    invades Egypt 180
    Mediterranean battles 162–166,
        187–188, 221
    Pact of Steel 106
    Rome–Berlin Axis 105
    Second London Naval Treaty 103
    surrenders Tobruk 205
    Tripartite Pact 180
    Washington Naval Treaty 11
Iwo Jima 510

J

Japan
  Allied invasion 496–497
  American occupation 522–523
  Anti-Comintern Pact 105
  Australian relations 31–33
  Australian sailors in 523–526
  Battle of Midway 328–329
  British Commonwealth Occupation
    Force 538
  British spies for 36–43
  Doolittle Raid on Tokyo 277–278
  invades China 108
  invades Manchuria 82, 105
  merchant navy losses 436
  Mongol invasion 440
  nationalism in former colonies 533
  neutrality 120
  Pearl Harbor 229–230, 244
  plans for expansion in Pacific
    103–104, 336–337
  plans to invade Australia 103–104,
    108
  post-war militarism 28–29
  as power in Pacific 31
  Rape of Nanking 106
  refusal to surrender 496, 510–511
  Second London Naval Treaty 103
  surrenders 515–516, 520–522
  treatment of prisoners of war 235,
    507–508, 515
  Tripartite Pact 180
  US firebombing 476
  Washington Naval Treaty 11
  White Australia Policy 32–33
Japan Must Fight Britain (Ishimaru)
  103–104
Japanese 14th Army 437
Japanese codes 123
Japanese Naval Air Force 230, 249
Japanese naval communications code
  (JN-25) 279–280, 329, 330
Jay, Philip 77, 86
Jayapura (West Papua) 434–435, 441
Jean Bart 158
Jellicoe, Viscount John 28–31
Jervis Bay, RANC 50, 52, 73, 84,
  114–115
Jodl, Generaloberst Alfred 497
John Brown & Son 4, 36, 45–47

Johnson (Solomon Islands
  Commissioner) 122
Joint Chiefs of Staff Committee 232,
  242–243
Jomard Passage 285, 286–287,
  290–296, 305–307
Jones, Lieutenant Maurice 450
Jorgenson, Ensign John H. 302–303
just-in-case kits 441

K

K-9 326
Kaga 331
Kako 367, 376, 377–378
Kamikaze (Divine Winds)
  damage to Allies at Lingayen Gulf
    492
  first attack 454
  HMAS *Australia II* fear of 489–490
  HMAS *Australia II* struck by
    480–487, 490–491
  IJN reliance on 476
  Leyte Gulf 466–470, 472
  Lingayen Gulf 479–495
  near Japan 512–513
  Onishi proposes suicide attacks
    439–440, 516–517
  opportunity to die 469–470
  psychological effects 488–489, 494
  ritual preparations 468–469
  Tokkotai (Special Attack Unit)
    439–440
  units of 440
Kanno, Petty Officer 1st Class Kenzo
  301
Kantai Kessen 429, 437
Kate (Type 97 torpedo bombers) 298,
  301, 305
Kato, Tomosaburo 38
Kean, Stephen ('Mustard') 57–59, 64,
  73–74, 83
Keats, Horace 201–202, 328
Keats, Russell 201–202, 212–213,
  218–219, 325, 328, 335–336, 369,
  371
Kelly Turner, Rear Admiral
  Richmond
  Allied Expeditionary Force,
    Operation Watchtower
    341–344, 346, 350, 365, 368

background 339
Battle of Savo 380, 383, 388–389
call to arms 347
Fletcher's withdrawal 362–363
Kemp, George 127
Kennedy, Donald 282
Kent, Prince George, Duke of 88, 97
Kerguelen Islands 242
Ketty Brovig 215–219
Kilindini 236
Kincaid, Vice Admiral Thomas C.
436, 458, 464, 478
King, Admiral Ernest J. 337–339,
341, 384, 388–391, 403, 421, 428,
498
Kinugasa 367, 376
Kiouzcois, George Paulos 407–408
Kirkwall 167
knot xviii
Kodama, Yoshio 517
Kokoda 314, 336, 337, 402
Koln 227
Komet 206–207
Konoye, Prince 276–277
Korean War 542, 549, 550
Kormoran 226–228
Koro 341, 343
Kota Bharu 229
K.R. & A.I. (King's Regulations and
Admiralty Instructions) 56–57
Krancke, Theodor 213–214
Kretschmer, Otto 187, 221
Kreuzerkrieg (cruiser warfare) 133
Kriegsmarine 146, 163, 221, 338,
391–392, 435
Kristallnacht 106
Kruder, Ernst-Felix 207
Kublai Khan 440
Kurita, Vice Admiral Takeo 438,
464–465

L

La Guardia, Fiorello 499
Labuan 512–513, 515
Lade, Alan 493
Lae 250–251, 279, 402
land mines 399
landing craft 558

Lane-Pool, Rear Admiral Richard,
RN 83–84
Lane-Pool, Sigrid 83–84
Lang, Premier Jack 71–72
Langrell, Jack
25th Air Flotilla attacks 291–295
background 112, 113, 115, 116
HMAS *Australia* 167, 175, 189, 257,
258
honours 560
Leyte Gulf 451
Lingayen Gulf 482–483
Langrell, Jack, senior 114–115
Langsdorff, Käpitan zur See Hans
133–135
Lark Force 234
Larkins, Surgeon Lieutenant Nicholas
260–261
Latham, John 81
L'Audacieux 174–175
Laval, Pierre 100
Lavarack, Peter 217
law 269–270
Lawson, Harry 23, 24–25
Layton, Sir Geoffrey 225
le Brun Brown, Janet 201
le Roux, Leon 160
League of Nations 31, 32, 99
Leahy, Admiral William 109–110
Leary, Vice Admiral Herbert F. 243,
285, 316–317
Leatham, Vice Admiral Ralph 208,
214, 220
Leese, Lieutenant General Sir Oliver
532
Lend-Lease program 505
Leyte
Allied invasion forces 436–437
Allied landings 443–445
Battle of Leyte Gulf 455–466, 539
Japanese air attacks 456–458
Japanese battle plans 437–438
Leyte Gulf 436, 441
LHD (landing helicopter dock) 558
Liberal Democratic Party (Japan) 517
Limerick (freighter) 410
Lingayen Gulf 477–495, 506–507
Liverpool
Brocklebank Graving Dock 188
Luftwaffe bombing 189–191

Llewellin, Colonel John 111
Lloyd George, David 106
London
  Empire parade through 529,
    531–534
  evacuation of children 113
  HMAS *Australia II* ship's company
    march through 504–505
  Season 96
London Blitz 180, 192, 476, 504
London Chamber of Commerce 39
London Naval Treaty *see* Second
  London Naval Treaty
London Stock Exchange 78
London sub-class cruisers 395
Long, Rupert Basil Michel 120–122,
  123, 568–569
Long Lance torpedo 103, 353
Lord, Phillips 93
Lorraine 160
the Louisiades 252, 275
lower deck 75, 77
Lower Deck Welfare Committee 75,
  79
Loxton, Commodore Bruce L.
  background 246–247
  Battle of Savo 370, 371
  HMAS *Canberra* 334, 348, 359
  homecoming 385–6
  The Shame of Savo 387–388
  wounded 373–374, 380, 383–384
Loxton, Dr Edward Hamilton 246
LSIs (landing ships – infantry) 437
Luftwaffe 96, 143, 145, 391–392
  Dunkirk evacuation 151, 153
  Enigma ciphering machine capture
    221
  Enigma code 146
  evacuation of Crete 223
  London Blitz 180, 192, 476, 504
Lumsden, Lieutenant General
  Herbert 484
Lunga Point 338, 348–350
Lusitania 46
Luxembourg 145
Luxford, Jim 447
Luxford, Nola 499
Luzon 477–478
Lynch, Detective Sergeant Joe 66–67

Lyons, Dame Enid 405
Lyons, Joseph Aloysius 72, 81, 82,
  107–108, 109, 112

M
M-14 324
M-21 325, 327
M-24 325, 326, 327
Mabalacat Airfield, Manila 439–440,
  466
MacArthur, General Douglas
  Australia, sent to 236–237
  Bataan Gang aides 240
  Borneo 511–512, 515
  Brett and 316, 317
  bribe from the Philippines 239
  Centaur (hospital ship) 411
  Clark Field, Manila 230
  Combined Operational Intelligence
    Centre 280, 285, 338
  Curtin and 237, 239, 405
  Halsey 416
  Hirohito 523
  hunger for fame 238–239, 403
  Japanese surrender 521, 522
  Lingayen Gulf 490
  Morotai 430
  Nimitz and 243, 429
  Operation Elkton 416
  Operation Watchtower 339
  the Philippines 421–422, 427,
    428–429, 444–445, 477
  reaction to sinking of *Canberra* 384
  South-West Pacific Area 243
  Supreme Commander Allied Forces
    South-West Pacific 237
MacArthur, Jean 236, 238
McCain Snr, Rear Admiral John S.
  340, 363, 390
McClusky, Lieutenant Commander
  Wade 330
MacDonald, Ramsay 33–34
McInerney, Commander Francis 287
Mackay, Major General Iven 204
McKell, Bill 499, 500
McKenna, Captain Frank 467–468
McKenzie, Foster 255
MacLeod, William 90, 91, 93, 94
McMahon, Billy 550–551

McMahon, Engineer Commander
    Otto Francis 218, 386
McNicoll, Captain Alan 551, 553–554
McPherson, Barbara 200
McPherson, Cluny 487
magnetic mines 157
Majestic class carriers 540
Makin, Norman 270, 396–397, 498
Malaya 195, 229, 231–232, 234, 287,
    339
Malleson, Claud 215–216, 218, 220
Malleson, Sir Wilfrid 215
Manchuria 82, 105, 521
Mansell, Lieutenant Commander
    Francis 262
Mansell, Rhoda 68
Manson, Colonel 411
Manus Island 422, 427–428, 432, 472,
    510
March of Time (newsreel) 499
Marconi 122
Margaret Rose, Princess 532
Mariana Islands 428, 429–430, 436,
    497
Marine Nationale 158–160
Marks, Lieutenant Commander Bill
    510
Marshall, General George 403
Marshall Islands 428
Mary, Princess Royal 48, 64
Mascot aerodrome 39
Mason, Paul 353
Massey, Captain George 61
Matsuo, Petty Officer Isao 469–470
Matsuo, Lieutenant Keiu 327
Mattiske, David 472–473, 507, 509,
    524–525
Mauretania (liner) 142
Mauritius 213
Mawson, Reverend Robert 451, 453
Maxwell, Mr Justice Allan 571–573
Mayer, Rear Admiral Stuart 560
Mayers, Colin 43
measurements xvii
media 543, 545, 548–549, 562 see also
    press censorship
Mediterranean Theatre 82, 162–166,
    187–188, 221, 392
Medley, David 335

Meiyo Maru 352
Melbourne
    Australian Victory Contingent
        529–530
    HMAS Australia II 528, 543–544,
        552
    MacArthur's HQ 240
    riots over unemployment relief fund
        23–26
Melbourne Cup 75, 78, 192–193
Menzies, Robert Gordon 94, 112,
        113–114, 136, 140, 193–194, 233,
        503, 570
    defence of Singapore 195–196
    Greece and Crete 224–225
    loses office 225
    reaction to Operation Menace
        179–180
merchant navy 60, 142, 197
Merkur (supply ship) 475, 519
Mers El Kébir, Algeria 159
Mesley, Lieutenant Commander Jack
        369, 370, 373, 483
Meteor (yacht) 4
MI5 (Military Intelligence) 39, 40,
        41–42
MI6 (Secret Service) 43
midshipmen ('snotties') 53
Midway 277
migrants, post-war 548
Mikawa, Vice Admiral Gunichi
        336–337, 352, 355–357, 358–359,
        374, 376, 377–378
    Guadalcanal 366–368
Millen, Edward 4
Miller, Keith 504
Mills, Charles 198
Milne Bay 337, 422–423
    Fall River air base 354–357
    Japanese attempt to take 401–402
mine laying 206–207
minesweepers 207
Mitchell, R.J. 97, 98
Mitscher, Vice Admiral Marc 464
Mitsubishi 39, 41
Mitsubishi A6M Rei-sen 43–44
Mitsui 569
ML 254 321
Modified Leander Class cruiser 82

Mogami 458–463
Moggach, Commander Air Paul 560
Molotov–Ribbentrop Pact 106
Monash, Sir John 34–35
Montcalm 169–170, 171, 177
Montgomery, General Bernard 391,
    401
Moore, Bob 453
Moore, Samuel 377
Moore Park Golf Course 66
Moran, Commander Bill 236
Morant, Harry ('Breaker') 270
Moresby Attack Group 278, 286, 289,
    307
Moresby Transport Group 278, 286,
    289, 307
Morison, Samuel Eliot 357, 375, 402,
    518
Morotai 430
Morris, Surgeon Lieutenant Ken
    378–379, 380
Mort, Henry 127–128
Mort, Kate 127–128, 130
Morton, Merle 411
Moten, Brigadier Murray 530
Mount Batten seaplane base 501
Mountbatten, Prince Philip 525
Movietone newsreel 543
Muirhead, Robert 49
Muirhead-Gould, Flag Officer in
    Charge Gerard 322–327, 328, 386
Muirhead-Gould, Grace 323
Munich agreement 106–107, 116, 117
Murray, Stuart ('Sunshine') 520–521
Musashi 277, 438, 455
Mussolini, Benito 99, 100, 105, 155,
    166, 206, 435
mustard gas 99, 246

N
N class destroyers 197
Nachi 462–463
Nagano, Admiral Osami 276, 352
Nagasaki 516
Nagumo, Vice Admiral Chuichi 235
Nakagawa, Lieutenant Commander
    410–412
Nanking, Rape of 106
Napoleon Bonaparte 96

national service 550
Nauru 6, 206–207
nautical mile xviii
Naval Air Station, Nowra 541
naval arms races 4, 11–12, 30, 32–33,
    103
naval canteen staff 115–117
naval dockyard police 115
Naval Intelligence 121–123
naval theatre: crossing the T 463–464
naval uniforms 414, 434, 524–525
Navantia 558
Nazi Condor Legion 105
Nazis (National Socialists) 39–40,
    105, 526
Nell (Mitsubishi high-level bombers)
    290–296
Nelson, Lord Horatio 62, 124, 446
Neosho (oiler) 284, 284–286, 288
the Netherlands 145, 146, 152, 511,
    515, 521–522
Netherlands East Indies 234, 235,
    243, 339, 515
neurotic casualties 488–489, 494
New Britain 422, 423–427 *see also*
    Rabaul
New Caledonia 275, 276
New Guard 72
New Guinea 6, 31, 121–123, 243, 249,
    250, 336, 422
    Japanese landings at Buna and
        Gona 336
    Kokoka Track 337
New Hebrides 275, 282, 336
    Espiritu Santo 415, 417, 454,
        471–472
New South Wales coast mined 207
New York Harbor 496
New Zealand 30–31, 33, 243
    German surface raiders 206
    Japanese surrender 521–522
    Singapore conference (1940)
        194–195
    Statute of Westminster 569
    waterside workers in Wellington
        341
New Zealand 2nd Division 222–223
Newcastle and Hunter River SS Co
    Ltd 16

Newcastle Harbour 328
Newland, Senator J. 13
Nicholls, Signal Boatswain Charlie
 254, 348–349
Nicholls, Able Seaman Ray 186
Nicholls, Stan 423, 485
Nichols, Captain Charles Alfred
 Godfrey 433, 442, 460, 474, 486,
 506–507, 524–525
Nielsen, Lieutenant John L. 288–289
Niemeyer, Sir Otto 71
Nimitz, Fleet Admiral Chester W.
 243
 as CinCPac 280–281, 285, 314, 317,
  329, 330, 338, 362, 388, 403,
  428
 Halsey 477
 Japanese surrender 521, 522
 MacArthur 429
Nishimura, Vice Admiral Shoji 438,
 458, 459, 462
Nishizawa, Hiroyoshi 466, 468
Normandy invasion of Western
 Europe 435
North Africa and Western Desert,
 war in 180, 206, 222, 391 see also
 Abyssinian Empire, Italy invades;
 Bardia; Tobruk
North Coast Steam Navigation Coy
 16
North Sea 7, 8
Northcott, Major General John
 194–195
Northern Mobile Strike Force (IJN)
 437–438, 455–456, 464
Norway 143–144, 391
Noumea, French New Caledonia 248,
 338, 342, 361, 383
Nowra 541

O
Obama, President Barack 357
O'Connor, James 24, 25–26
Official Secrets Act 43
Ohmae, Captain Toshikazu 337, 358,
 367
oil tanks, RAN 34
oil-powered ships 59
Okinawa 510–511

Oldendorf, Vice Admiral Jesse B.
 458, 460, 478, 491
Oldham, Captain George 542–549
Oliver Hazard Perry class guided-
 missile frigate 557
Olivier, Laurence 477
Olympic Games 1928 (Amsterdam)
 62
Olympic Games 1936 (Berlin)
 104–105
O'Neill, Henry 482
Onishi, Vice Admiral Takijiro
 438–440, 468, 516–517
Onslow, Richard 160–161
Oostzee (tug) 540
Operation AO (of IJN) 329
Operation Barbarossa 224
Operation Cartwheel 421–422, 428
Operation Catapult 159–161
Operation Downfall 496–497
Operation Dynamo 147
Operation Elkton 416
Operation Ferdinand 122–123, 353
Operation Menace, Dakar 169–175
Operation MI (of IJN) 277, 329
Operation MO (of IJN) 277, 278–280,
 298–299, 307
Operation Oboe 511–515
Operation Overlord 435
Operation Pedestal 392
Operation Reno 428
Operation Sonnenblume 206
Operation Watchtower 338–339
 Allied Expeditionary Force
  339–340
 Australia II conference 344
 Battle of Savo 369–378
 communications 345
 Fletcher withdraws 361–362
 Group Yoke and Group X-Ray
  346–347, 383
 IJN 362–363
 Saratoga conference 342–343
Operation Weserübung 143–144
Orion 206
Ormonde, Able Seaman Jim 253
Oro Bay 413
Orontes (Orient Line) 130
Osborne House, Corio Bay 49–50

Osmeña, Sergio 444
Ostend 320–321
Owen Stanley Ranges 251, 314, 336
Ozawa, Vice Admiral Jisaburo 437–438, 464

P
Pacific Ocean Area 243
Pacific Theatre xiv, 33, 103–104, 206–207, 229, 233, 242–243, 276–277
Pact of Steel 106
Pakistan 533
Palm Island 414–415
Panama Canal Zone 389–390
paravanes 198, 441–442
Parker, Alan 219
Parker, Roger 418
Parkhill, Sir Archdale 84
Parkinson, Richard 451
Parliament House, Canberra 55, 126
pay differentials 308–309
Payne, John 81
peace and disarmament 33–34
Peagam, Flying Officer Reg 282
Pearce, Senator Sir George 12, 79–80, 81
Pearl Harbor 38, 40, 43, 187–188, 229–230, 244, 279, 338
Peck, John 532–533
Peek, Lieutenant Commander Richard 448, 534
Peleliu 431
Pensacola convoy 241–242
Percival, Arthur 521
Perry, Fred 96
Perry, Paymaster Commander Patrick 262
Persée 172
Perth 528
Perthshire (merchant ship) 543
Pétain, Marshal Philippe 155
petrol rationing 193
Peyton, Captain Tom 343
Phar Lap 72, 73
Philip, Duke of Edinburgh 551
the Philippines x, 110, 235, 238–239, 243, 275, 339, 421–422 see also Leyte

Allied invasion 437, 442–445, 477–478, 490
MacArthur and 428–429
Phillips, John 288
Phillips, Lieutenant Commander Ron 256
Phillips, Admiral Sir Tom 230
phosphate trade 206–207
Pikedale Soldier Settlement 26–27
Pinguin 207
Plunkett-Cole, Lieutenant Commander John 370
Plymouth Naval Base 116, 159, 500–501, 503–505, 526, 527
pocket battleships 133–135
Point Lonsdale Lighthouse 397
Point Option 301
poison gas 99, 246
Poland 106, 112–113, 134
Ponape 428
Poro Point 483
Port Moresby 242, 251, 280, 285
  Japanese decide to advance by land 314, 337
  Japanese plans to invade 277
  Japanese postpone plans to invade 307
Port Phillip (merchant ship) 543
Portsmouth Naval Base 61, 63, 94, 116, 159, 531
Portsmouth Naval Dockyard 97
port/starboard xviii
post-traumatic stress disorder 494
Pound, Sir Dudley 137
press censorship 328, 404, 493–494
  see also media
Prien, Günther 136–137, 187, 220
Prinz Eugen 257
prisoners of war 406
  Allied 223
  American 235
  Australian 234
  British 232, 234
  Japanese treatment 235, 507–508, 515
Prisoners of War Convention 508
Provence 159
PT-131 459

public protests over scuttling of
   Australia I 12–14
public rioting in Melbourne over
   unemployment relief fund 23–26
Pulling Regatta, North West Bay 75

Q

Qantas Empire Airways 90, 182
Quarterdeck 75
Queen Elizabeth (liner) 398
Queen Mary (Cunard liner) 142, 208
Quezon, Manuel 239
Quisling, Vidkun 143

R

RAAF *see* Royal Australian Air Force
Rabaul 122
   Allied air raid 352
   Japanese forces 421–422
   Japanese in 234, 249, 250, 251, 278,
      279, 336, 352
   US decision to encircle 421–422
radar 335, 345, 367, 463, 474, 544
Radio 2FC 201
Raglan Barracks 501
Rambi I 214
Ramsay, Vice Admiral Bertram
   147–148, 152, 154, 155–156
Ramsay, Commander Richard 455
RAN *see* Royal Australian Navy
RANC *see* Royal Australian Naval
   College
Rands, Lieutenant Commander
   Walter 101
Rangitane 206
Rankin, Robert ('Oscar') 235
RANVR (Volunteer Reserve) 197,
   263
Rapke, Paymaster Lieutenant Trevor
   262–269, 271, 570–571
rationing 307–308, 405–406,
   408–409
Rats of Tobruk 222
Rayment, Commander John 181, 184,
   262, 267, 284, 290, 448–449, 450
Read, Jack 359
Read, Commander Neven 520
recruiting 197, 307
Red Army 224, 435

Redding, Bandsman Allan ('Chan')
   457–458, 461
Regia Aeronautica 99, 158, 166, 223
Regia Marina 158, 187, 221
Regio Esercito 99
Republic of Vanuatu *see* New Hebrides
Revell, Arthur 460–461
Rhineland, Germany reoccupies
   102–103
Richelieu 158, 160–161, 171, 172
Riefkohl, Fred 364, 365, 377,
   388–389
Riley, Stoker John Joseph 252,
   254–257, 259, 260–261, 264
River Class destroyers 74
riveters 46–47
Roaring Forties 545–546
Roberts, Captain John 454
Robertson, Dahlis 247, 348, 384
Robinson, Private Arthur 27
Robinson, Dolly 397
Robinson, Col. F. W. 397
Roche, Father John ('Cocky') 451
Rocks, The 67
Rode Zee (tug) 556
Rogers, Fred 255
Rome–Berlin Axis 105
Rommel, Erwin 206, 222, 391, 401
Roosevelt, Franklin Delano 80, 146,
   230, 232, 251, 337, 396
   Casablanca conference 415–416,
      476
   death 508
   Joint Chiefs of Staff Committee
      242–243
   MacArthur and 236–237, 239, 241
Rosendale, Chief Petty Officer Ray
   562
Roskill, Commander Stephen 262
Ross, Dr Ian Clunies 192–193
Ross, Commander Trevor 49
Rosyth naval base 7–8
Rowan, Edward James 250
Royal Aeronautical Society 39
Royal Air Force 36, 37, 154
   defence of Singapore 195
   Sunderland P9620 181–186, 501
Royal Australian Air Force 35, 74,
   137, 234

32 Squadron 355
101 Fleet Co-operation Flight 97
817 Squadron 560
Balikpapan 514
Battle of Bismarck Sea 402
defence budget 540–541
Fall River air base, Milne Bay
    354–357
HMAS *Australia II* in Plymouth
    500–501
national service 550
Seagull V 98
Tulagi 282
Royal Australian Naval College *see
    also* Flinders Naval Depot; Jervis
    Bay, RANC
bullying 200, 209–210
establishment 50–52, 92, 199–201
prizes 54–55, 201, 247
syllabus 51–52
Royal Australian Navy *see also*
    Australian Naval Board;
    Australian Navy Office
Australian and British officers
    77–78, 85–86
Australian Squadron 60, 130
Australian Squadron, convoy ZK.5
    242
British flotilla loan 82
casualties 528–529
combat strength 412, 528
defence budget 34–35, 540–541
discharge by purchase 536
discharge points system 526
first grand fleet entry into Sydney
    Harbour 3–4
Fleet Air Arm 36, 41, 505, 540
Great Depression 73–81
Jellicoe's *Report on the Naval Mission
    to the Commonwealth* 28–31
loss of HMS *Waterhen* 223
national service 550
naval aviation 540–542
naval ensign 344
post-war future 505
preparation for war 117–118
protests at pay cuts 78–80
recruiting 83, 244–245
reserve call-up 124

RN training 29, 31
Royal Navy and 7, 60, 285
sabotage 83–84
submarine force 555–556
Tokyo Bay 520
USN and 247–248, 285
Victoria Cross 494–495
women in 244–245
Royal Easter Show 19–20
Royal Mail Steam Packet Company
    51
Royal Marines 78
Royal Naval Air Service 36
Royal Naval Reserve 60
Royal Navy 4
Articles of War 52–53
aviation arm 37
Battles of Narvik 143–144
Convoy PQ-17 391–392
Dover Patrol 76
Far Eastern Fleet in Ceylon
    235–236, 245–246
Grand Fleet in North Sea 7, 8–9,
    53
Home Fleet 162
Main Fleet to Singapore *see*
    Singapore naval base
Mediterranean Fleet 94–95, 98, 99,
    120, 158, 162–166
Mediterranean Fleet losses 223
Mediterranean Force H 159
mutinies 78
officers 53–54
Operation Menace, Dakar 169–175
Pacific Fleet 497, 518
RAN submarines gifted to 74
RAN training by 29, 31
rations 8
rum ration 398
scraps 8-inch gun ships 551
South America Cruiser Squadron
    135
Special Service Squadron 15–17
Washington Naval Treaty ships 35
Royal Navy Torpedo School 121
Royal New Zealand Navy 244
Royal Overseas League 188
Royal Victorian Order 94

Royle, Vice Admiral Sir Guy
240–241, 316–317, 454–455,
494–495
Rozynski, Stoker Jack 379–380
Rudd, Dalmorton 9, 10
Rudd, David 10
Rushcutters Bay gunnery school 117,
197
Russell, Barbara 201
Russia *see* Soviet Union
Rutland, Lieutenant Frederick 40–43
Ryrie, Major General Sir Granville
62–63
Ryujo 391

S

S-38 353
Sadleir, Captain Jonathan 560
St George, Able Seaman Stephen
380–381, 387
St Olaves (tug) 3, 14
Salamaua 250–251
Samar 464–465
Samoa 6, 276, 336
Samwell, Archdeacon Frederick 13
Sandakan Death Marches 515
Savage, Lieutenant Ellen 411
Savo Island 346–347, 358, 364
Battle of Savo 369–378, 388–391
US inquiry into 388–389
Scapa Flow naval base 9, 136–137,
162, 167–168, 400–401
Scharnhorst 144, 492
Schepke, Joachim 220–221
Schepke, Joachim 187
Schleswig-Holstein 206
Scott, Robert Falcon 76
Scrap Iron Flotilla 82, 223
Scullin, James 69–70, 71, 72
scurvy 211–212
Sea Furies 542
Sea King helicopters 560
Seagull III 97
Seagull V 97–98
Second London Naval Treaty 103
Second Strike Force (IJN) 438, 458,
462–463
Second World War 36, 40, 43, 82, 95

Seekriegsleitung (German naval high
command) 134
Seki, Lieutenant Yukio 439, 466–467
Seligman, Commander 313
Selsby, Petty Officer Cook Spencer 323
Sempill, William Francis Forbes
36–40, 103, 229
Senegal *see* Dakar
seppuku 517
Seth Parker (schooner) 93
The Shame of Savo (Loxton) 387–388
Shaw, George Bernard 527
Shedden, Sir Frederick 196
Sheean, Edward 198
Sherman, Frederick ('Ted') 249, 304,
312–313
Shigemitsu, Mamoru 521
Shigure 460, 462
Shima, Vice Admiral Kiyohide 438,
458, 462–463
Shinkfield, Des 446–447, 449, 455,
490, 498
ship-recognition 362–363
Shoho 278, 289, 291
Shokaku 278, 283, 287–288, 298, 307
Battle of Coral Sea 300, 302, 303,
305
Battle of Philippine Sea 430
Showers, Commodore Harry 50,
417–418, 433, 494–495, 530, 535
Shrine of Remembrance, Melbourne
88
Siam–Burma railway 234, 509
signals intelligence network 123
Simon, Sir John 95
Simons, Audrey 400, 534–537
Simons, Harriet 400
Simpson, Wallis 102
Sinclair, Lieutenant Commander
George A. 372–373
Singapore Naval Base 30, 31, 33
Britain requests USN to defend
109–110
conference (1940) to assess 194–195
fall of Singapore 111, 234, 437
Japanese advance on 229
Japanese attitudes to 104
King George VI Graving Dock
opened 110–111

Main Fleet to Singapore 33–34, 48,
      107–108, 109, 230–231
refugees 235
Slessor, Kenneth 452
Slim, Field Marshal Sir William 551
Smith, Lieutenant Joe 301
Smith, Chief Petty Officer Otto 399
Smith, Lieutenant Victor 385
social class and status 50, 75, 561
Soldier Settlement Schemes 22–23,
      26–28
Solomon Islands 122, 275, 277, 336,
      346, 422 *see also* Guadalcanal;
      Lunga Point; Savo Island; Tulagi
   Ironbottom Sound 346, 388
   The Slot 353, 363, 402
Somerville, Vice Admiral James
      159–160
Sonias 447
Soryu 330–331
South Africa 569
South China Sea 436
South Head Port War Signal Station
      325
South Pacific Force 338
South Pacific (musical) 471
South-East Asia 229
Southern Force (IJN) 438, 458, 459
South-West Pacific Area 237, 243,
      285, 316, 414, 428
Soviet Navy 555
Soviet Union
   Anti-Comintern Pact 105
   Bolshevik revolution 23
   German invasion of 224, 231
   Japanese surrender 521–522
   Molotov–Ribbentrop Pact 106
Spain
   civil war 104, 105
   coup d'état 104
Spanish Armada 116
Spanish influenza 23
Spanish–American War (1898) 339
Spee, Maximilian Graf von 6–7
Spencer Gulf mined 207
Spender, Percy 224, 233
spies 36–43
Spirit of Progress 201
Spitfire 97

Sprague, Rear Admiral Clifton
      ('Ziggy') 465
Spruance, Rear Admiral Raymond A.
      330, 331
SS *Kalingo* 409
Stalag Luft VI 504
Stalin, Joseph 224, 392
Stanbury, Able Seaman John 399
Statham, Surgeon Clive 513
Statute of Westminster Adoption Act
      1942 570
Stening, Surgeon Lieutenant Malcolm
      190, 256–257, 260, 319, 323,
      571–572
Stevens, J. Hood 13
Steward, Sir George 25
Stewart, Captain Ross 126, 157–158,
      162, 168, 169, 173, 174, 175, 178
   rescue of Sunderland P9620 181,
      183, 184, 186
stokers 58
Stokes, Lieutenant John 414–415
Storstad 207
Strasbourg 159
Strategic Project Ship 558
strikes and lockouts 69
Stutt, Bill 355, 356, 357, 362–363
Subic Bay 518–520
submarines 34, 555–556
Sugiyama, General Hajime 276
Summer, Joseph ('Mutt') 98
Sunda Strait 226
Sunderlands 182, 501
Supermarine 97–98
supply assistants 202–203
Surigao Strait 458 (and map)
susso (sustenance relief) 70
Suzuki, Admiral Kantar 496
Swain, Graydon 553
Sweden 143
Swordfish 144, 172, 187
Sydney 64, 65, 492, 528, 553–554
Sydney Harbour Bridge 20, 72

T
Tachibana, Itaru 42
Tagami, Lieutenant Commander
      Meiji 417–418
Taiho 430

Tairoa (Shaw Savill steamer) 135
Takagi, Vice Admiral Takeo 278, 283, 286, 287–288, 298, 302, 305
Takasu, Shiro 42
Takeshi, Lieutenant Commander Naito 187–188
Tamai, Commander Asaichi 439
Tanambogo 346, 351, 354, 359
Tangney, Dorothy 405
Tarakan 512, 515, 530
Taranto naval base 187–188
Task Force 11 280–281, 282, 283, 284
Task Force 16 280, 330
Task Force 17 280–286, 288–289, 298, 305
  Battle of Coral Sea 300–301
  Battle of Midway 330
Task Force 44 280–281, 283–284, 317, 320, 328, 333–334, 339, 414, 552–553
Task Force 74 414, 417–418, 423, 431–432
Task Group 17.3 287
  Battle of Coral Sea 305–307
  bombed by Americans 296–297, 317
  Fletcher's failure to communicate with 314–315
  Japanese attack in Jomard Passage 290–296
Task Group 62.6 339, 341
Task Group 74.1 423, 473, 476, 513–515, 518–520
Task Group 74.2 423
Task Group 77.2 478
Task Group 77.3 441
TBS ('talk between ships') 345, 370, 376, 474
teleradio 122
Tennyson-d'Eyncourt, Sir Eustace 35
Tenryu 367, 376
Terowie 236, 238
Thailand 234, 406
Thailand–Burma railway 234, 509
Thomas, Sir Shenton 111
Thorne, Keith 449
Thurlow, Dorothy 331
Thurlow, Jim 331, 332–333, 381, 537

Thurlow, Margaret 331–332
Thurlow, Stewart 562–563
Thurlow, Tom junior 331, 332–333, 381, 397, 399–400, 534–537
Thurlow, Tom senior 331–332
Tinian 497
Tirpitz 106
Tivoli Girls 422–423
Tobruk 204, 205
  Rommel captures 391
  siege 222
  Tobruk Ferry Run 222, 223, 228
Tokyo, US firebombing 476, 511, 523
Tokyo Bay 518–520
Tokyo Rose 489
torpedo boats 458
Townsville 279, 297
Toyoda, Admiral Soemu 437
Toyoda, Captain Teijiro 38, 43
Tracey, Ray 502
trade unions 69, 245
Trafalgar Day 446, 454–455
Treaty cruisers 35–36, 62
Tresco, Elizabeth Bay 83–84, 322
Tribal class destroyers 412, 423
Trincomalee 235–236
Tripartite Pact 180
Tripoli 206
Truman, Harry 508
Truth, Melbourne 81
Tsuzuku, Petty Officer Masao 327
Tulagi 279, 282, 336, 383
  Allied Expeditionary Force 346–347, 350–351, 352
  IJN attack on 358
  Japanese resistance on 351, 352, 354, 359
  Japanese Tulagi Invasion Group 278, 282
  US air raid on 282–283
Turkey 101
Turner, John 461, 462
Turner, Able Seaman Phillip 448, 449
Turner, Rear Admiral Richmond Kelly *see* Kelly Turner
Turner, William 398
Twining, Marine Lieutenant Colonel Merrill ('Bill') 343, 344

U

U-9 95–96
U-29 136
U-30 119–120
U-47 136–137, 220
U-64 144
U-99 221
U-100 220–221
U-110 221
U-559 228
U-boats
  aces 187, 220–221
  American East Coast shipping
    337–338
  in general 163, 182
  losses 435
  Rudeltaktik 187
Udovikoff, Dr Serge 543, 544,
  547–548
Udovikoff, Taissa 548
Umezu, General Yoshijiro 521
unemployment 22–23, 69, 70
unemployment relief fund 23–26
United Australia Party 72, 79–80,
  193, 225, 233
United Nations 497
United States 33
  Arcadia Conference 232
  Australia and threat from Japan
    233–234
  Australia nominates MacArthur to
    command in Pacific 237
  Australian crew of *Shropshire* cross
    394
  Battle of Midway 328–329
  Combined Operational Intelligence
    Centre 280
  Germany declares war on 231
  invasion of Japan 496, 510–511
  isolationism 99, 107
  Japanese espionage in 42
  Japanese surrender 518, 520–522
  League of Nations 32
  Prohibition 64
  Second London Naval Treaty 103
  surrenders to Japan 229
  troops in Australia 240, 241–242
  Washington Naval Treaty 11–12
United States 6th Army 478

United States Army Air Force
  241–242, 277–278, 279, 308–309
  509th Composite Group 497
  Balikpapan 514
  bomb Task Group 17.3 296–297,
    315–317
  turf war with USN 279, 316
United States Marines
  Guadalcanal 339, 340–341, 343,
    351, 359, 360, 378, 383
  Iwo Jima 510
  losses on Guadalcanal 402
  New Britain 423, 426–427
United States Navy 42
  3rd Fleet 437, 455–456, 464
  7th Fleet 414, 436–437, 458,
    464–465, 478
  Asiatic Fleet 110
  'black shoes' vs. 'brown shoes' 281
  Bombardment and Fire Support
    Group 478
  Britain asks to defend Singapore
    109–110
  History and Heritage Command 357
  IJN plans for 276–277
  Pacific Fleet 229, 329
  Pacific Ocean Area 243
  Pensacola convoy 241–242
  the Philippines invasion forces
    436–437, 441
  RAN and 247–248
  Seabees 471–472, 474
  Seeadler Harbour, Manus Island
    427–428
  South China Sea 436
  stern chase 431–432
  Task Force 11 248–249, 250–251
  Task Force 17 250
  turf war with US Army Air Force
    279, 316
United States Sixth Army 436
USN *see* United States Navy
USS *Albert W. Grant* 463
USS *Ammen* 423
USS *Astoria* 250, 252, 347, 364,
  375–377, 382
USS *Bache* 423
USS *Bagley* 317, 360, 364, 369, 374,
  torpedoes HMAS *Canberra*
    372–374, 381, 387–388

USS *Barnett* 383
USS *Bataan* 520, 528
USS *Blue* 364, 366, 367, 380, 381
USS *Boise* 443, 454, 490
USS *Bush* 423
USS *California* 459, 484
USS *Canberra* 396
USS *Chicago* 243–244, 248, 250
  25th Air Flotilla 291, 292, 294, 296
  Battle of Savo 369, 375, 380, 388
  Guadalcanal 364, 365
  Japanese midget submarines in
    Sydney Harbour 323–327
  Task Force 44 280, 283, 334
  Task Group 17.3 287
  Task Group 62.6 345, 346
USS *Columbia* 490
USS *Ellet* 382
USS *Enterprise* 248, 280, 314, 330,
  339, 361–362, 391
USS *Farragut* 287, 297, 317
USS *Flusser* 317
USS *Gambier Bay* 465
USS *George F. Elliott* 360, 366
USS *Hart* 513
USS *Helm* 317, 364, 376, 423
USS *Henley* 317
USS *Honolulu* 444, 454
USS *Hornet* 277–278, 280, 314, 330
USS *Houston* 235
USS *Jarvis* 334, 360
USS *Kalinin Bay* 466–467
USS *Kitkun Bay* 467
USS *Lamson* 244
USS *Lexington*
  abandoned and sunk 312–314
  Battle of Coral Sea 300, 301, 303,
    304
  hit 304–305
  Task Force 11 248–251, 280, 284
  Task Force 17 287, 289, 298
  Tulagi 282
USS *Lexington II* 430
USS *Louisville* 250, 252, 484
USS *Manila Bay* 480
USS *Maryland* 443, 459
USS *McCawley* 347, 348, 350, 365,
  368
USS *Metcalf* 513

USS *Minneapolis* 313
USS *Mississippi* 443, 459, 490
USS *Missouri* 518, 520–522
USS *Mount Vernon* 394
USS *Mugford* 317, 354, 411
USS *Mullany* 423
USS *Nashville* 423, 431, 444–445
USS *Nautilus* 555
USS *New Mexico* 483–484, 491–492
USS *Nicholas* 417
USS *North Carolina* 339, 361
USS *O'Bannon* 417
USS *Ohio* 392
USS *Oklahoma* 244
USS *Ommaney Bay* 479
USS *Patterson* 334, 364, 369, 370,
  374, 376, 380
USS *Pennsylvania* 459
USS *Pensacola* 241
USS *Perkins* 244, 283, 287, 291
USS *Phelps* 313
USS *Phoenix* 423, 441, 443
USS *Pittsburgh* 396
USS *Princeton* 455
USS *Quincy* 347, 349–350, 364, 366,
  375–377, 382
USS *Radford* 417
USS *Ralph Talbot* 334, 364, 366, 367,
  423
USS *St Lo* 467–468
USS *Salt Lake City* 317, 334
USS *San Juan* 346, 350, 364, 382
USS *Saratoga* 248, 287, 339, 361–362
USS *Selfridge* 382, 387
USS *Sims* 285–286, 288
USS *South Dakota* 430
USS *Tennessee* 459
USS *Vincennes* 347, 364, 366,
  375–377, 382, 388
USS *Walke* 287, 291, 307
USS *Wasp* 339, 361–362
USS *West Virginia* 443, 454, 459
USS *Whipple* 283
USS *White Plains* 466–467
USS *Wilson* 364, 376
USS *Yorktown* 250–251, 280, 282, 286,
  298
  Battle of Coral Sea 300–303, 304,
    305

repairs 314
sunk at Battle of Midway 331

V
V and W class destroyers 82
Val (Type 99 dive bombers) 298
Vandegrift, Major General Alexander
    Archer 340–341, 342, 343, 344,
    347, 348, 362, 365, 368
Vanuata, Republic of *see* New
    Hebrides
Versailles Peace Conference 31
Versailles Treaty 96, 102–103, 155
Vichy France 155
    French Atlantic ports 163
    Marine Nationale 158–160
    Noumea, French New Caledonia
        248
    Operation Menace, Dakar 169–175,
        181
Victoria, Queen 4, 320
Victoria Cross 494–495
Victory Cricket Tests 504
Vietnam 180
Villiers, Barbara 320
von Bock, Generaloberst Fedor 145
Von Der Tann 9
von Ribbentrop, Joachim 95
von Rundstedt, Generaloberst Gerd
    145, 146

W
Wainwright, Lieutenant General
    Jonathan 521
Wakehurst, Lord 500
Wales, Edward, Prince of 11, 26–27,
    62, 94, 97, 102
Walker, Commander Frank 374, 380
Walker, Reg 450
Walker, Rear Admiral Robyn 561
Wall Street Crash (1929) 69, 70
Waller, Hec 166, 221, 235
Walsh, Commander John 379, 380,
    386
Walton, William 477
War Council *see* Advisory War
    Council
war crimes 410, 463
War Savings Certificates 406

Warburton-Lee, Captain Bernard
    143
Ward, Eddie 102
wardroom mess dinner 318–319
Warner, Sir Pelham ('Plum') 504
Washington (liner) 394
Washington Naval Treaty (Five
    Power Treaty on Limitation of
    Naval Armaments) 11–12, 18,
    35, 62
Watson, Surgeon Lieutenant Shane
    460
Wavell, Sir Archibald 232
Webb, Commander Charles 413
Wehrmacht 112–113, 224
West Papua *see* Hollandia (Jayapura)
Western Europe, German invasion
    144–146
Westernland 171
Wewak 526
Whale Island, Portsmouth Harbour
    54
Whiskard, Sir Geoffrey 136
White, Warrant Officer 'Knocker'
    447
White Australia Policy 29, 31–33
Whitsunday Islands 315
Wight, Lieutenant Commander Ewan
    369, 370
Wildcats, F4F-3 249
Wilhelm II, Kaiser 4
Williamson, Adolphus Huddlestone,
    RN 53–54
Willis, Jim 200
Willman, Mervyn 356
Wilson, Cliff 228
Wilson, Ensign J. Woodrow 249
Wilson, Lieutenant Rebecca 561
wireless broadcasts 139–140,
    406–407
wireless technology 122
women
    nylon stockings and 408–409
    in parliament 405
    in services 307, 561–562
    sexual abuse or bullying of 562
Women's Auxiliary Air Force 552
Women's Royal Australian Naval
    Service 244–245

Women's Royal Naval Service 503, 528

Wright, Harley 452

Y

Yakuza 517
Yamamoto, Commander Isoroku 38, 276–279, 329–331, 391, 402–403
Yamashiro 438, 458–462
Yamashita, General Tomoyuki 437
Yamato 276, 277, 331, 438, 465, 511
Yamato Shimbun 32–33
Yasukuni Shrine (Tokyo) 517
Yeates, George 373, 380
Yeomans, Jim 441
YE-ZB system 301
Yokohama Yacht Club 524
Yokosuka Naval Base 523
York, Prince George, Duke of 55, 94, 97, 102 *see also* George VI

Young, Sir Mark 232
Yubari 375, 376
Yuhari 367
Yunagi 367, 376
Yushukan War Museum 517

Z

Zammit, Victor 115, 116
Zealandia 226
Zeebrugge raid 9, 320
Zekes 466–470
Zero (Mitsubishi A6M Rei-sen) 43–44, 281, 292, 303, 352, 430, 439, 466
Zuikaku 278, 283, 287, 298, 307
  Battle of Coral Sea 300, 302, 303
  Northern Mobile Strike Force 437–438
sunk at Battle of Cape Engaño 464